Polly Adler in Chicago for the "Battle of the Long Count"
heavyweight boxing championship, September 22, 1927

Madam

The Biography of Polly Adler,
Icon of the Jazz Age

DEBBY APPLEGATE

Doubleday · New York

Copyright © 2021 by Debby Applegate

All rights reserved. Published in the United States by Doubleday,
a division of Penguin Random House LLC, New York, and distributed
in Canada by Penguin Random House Canada Limited, Toronto.

www.doubleday.com

DOUBLEDAY and the portrayal of an anchor with a dolphin are
registered trademarks of Penguin Random House LLC.

Page 555 constitutes an extension of this copyright page.

Text design by Cassandra J. Pappas

Jacket photograph: Polly Adler Collection, Courtesy of Eleanor Vera
Jacket design by John Fontana

Library of Congress Cataloging-in-Publication Data
Names: Applegate, Debby, author.
Title: Madam : the biography of Polly Adler,
icon of the Jazz Age / Debby Applegate.
Description: First edition. | New York : Doubleday,
a division of Penguin Random House LLC, [2021] |
Includes bibliographical references and index.
Identifiers: LCCN 2021037112 (print) | LCCN 2021037113 (ebook) |
ISBN 9780385534758 (hardcover) | ISBN 9780385534765 (ebook)
Subjects: LCSH: Adler, Polly, 1900–1962. | Procuresses—New York
(State)—New York—Biography. | Prostitution—New York (State)—
New York—History—20th century.
Classification: LCC HQ146.N7 A67 2021 (print) | LCC HQ146.N7 (ebook) |
DDC 306.74/2092 [B]—dc23
LC record available at https://lccn.loc.gov/2021037112
LC ebook record available at https://lccn.loc.gov/2021037113

MANUFACTURED IN THE UNITED STATES OF AMERICA

1   3   5   7   9   10   8   6   4   2

First Edition

This book is dedicated to my parents,
Paul "Shan" Applegate and Julie Worrell Applegate

☾

Every town has its celebrated madams, eternal women to be sentimentalized down the years. There is something very attractive to men about a madam. She combines the brains of a businessman, the toughness of a prize fighter, the warmth of a companion, the humor of a tragedian. Myths collect about her, and oddly enough, not voluptuous myths. The stories remembered and repeated about a madam cover every field but the bedroom. Remembering, her old customers picture her as a philanthropist, medical authority, bouncer and poetess of the bodily emotions without being involved with them.

—JOHN STEINBECK, *East of Eden*, 1952

☾

There is in this idea of prostitution, a point of intersection so complex—lust, bitterness, the void of human relations, the frenzy of muscles and the sound of gold—that looking into it makes you dizzy; and you learn so many things!

—GUSTAVE FLAUBERT to LOUISE COLET, 1853

Contents

A Warning

Please be advised that the language in this book may offend some readers. Polly Adler and her contemporaries lived in the golden age of "slanguage," to borrow Walter Winchell's phrase. They spoke in a polyglot patois of show business, sports, gambling, tabloid journalism, and underworld lingo that could be colorful and clever, but also crude, bigoted, sexist, and occasionally obscene. Many of these terms became part of our national vocabulary; others, quite rightly, have fallen out of favor. I have employed the language of Polly Adler's milieu, in both direct quotations and indirect descriptions, as a way to steep the reader in her world, not as an endorsement of that worldview.

Madam

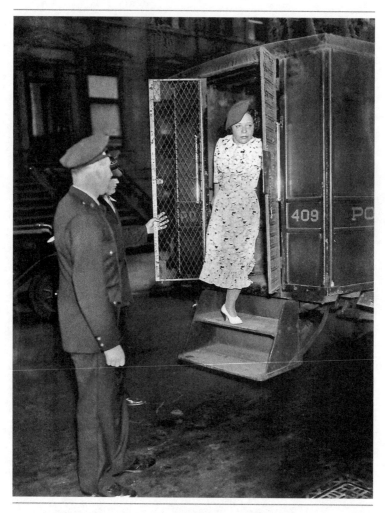

Polly Adler exiting a police patrol wagon after being raided

1

From Nobody to a Legend

The epic slugfest between Jack Dempsey and Jack Sharkey in Yankee Stadium couldn't have come at a better time, as far as Polly Adler was concerned. July and August were always tough months in her business; really, in every branch of Broadway's Billion Dollar Beauty Trust. Action on the Main Stem was slow during the dog days of summer, in this age before air-conditioning. The big money men of Wall Street and midtown decamped to Europe with their wives, or to country homes on Long Island, Westchester, or the Jersey shore. The high-stakes gamblers and racketeers who were Polly's most loyal customers hightailed it to Saratoga Springs for a blissful month at the racetrack. Most speakeasies and nightclubs closed, and the leg-and-fanny revues went on tour, taking with them many of the showgirls who moonlighted in Polly's house of ill repute.

But receipts were down far more than usual in that summer of 1927. Up until now this had been Polly's best year ever. After seven years in the skin trade, she had finally worked her way into the blue-chip clientele who thought nothing of dropping a couple hundred bucks for a roll in the hay and a few rounds of drinks. It wasn't just her house. All that spring Broadway's nightlife was booming as never before, fueled by the soaring stock market and the thriving bootleg liquor industry. The Big Street seemed gripped by a feverish, almost hysterical atmosphere of debauchery, with more shows, more nudity, and more cash changing hands than in any season in memory.

By July, however, the money river mysteriously seemed to dry up. One by one "the after-dark palaces of joy," as *The Morning Telegraph* dubbed them, were closing their unmarked doors for lack of business.

Perhaps it was the spiraling prices in the nightclubs—lately even the top-hat-and-ermine set were starting to grouse about the size of their bar bills. Maybe it was the growing allure of Harlem, which was all the rage among the more daring thrill-seekers. It didn't help that the city was in the grip of a vicious heat wave. Every day 8 million sweating citizens swelled the already-crowded stoops and sidewalks in search of a cool breeze. Every night thousands carried their alarm clocks and pillows to rooftops and fire escapes, hoping for a little relief. Even the hoopla over the historical transatlantic flights of Richard Byrd and Charles Lindbergh, including two tickertape parades up Fifth Avenue, did little to boost revenue. So the return of Jack Dempsey—the biggest entertainment draw in America, bar none—in a major prizefight was like the answer to a heathen's prayer.

Boxing was always a hot topic among Polly's clientele, second only to horse racing. But this matchup between Dempsey, the legendary Manassa Mauler, and the young upstart from Boston had sent the whole city into a frenzy of excitement. Tex Rickard, the impresario of Madison Square Garden who'd set up the bout, was predicting over $1 million in ticket sales. Newspaper coverage of the event was feverish, with more than five hundred reporters and photographers planning to be in attendance, and more than a million words in print before the first bell rang. This was Dempsey's last shot at a comeback, and every high roller who could get his hands on a ticket planned to be there to see it. Everyone in the underworld hospitality industry—the bootleggers, bookmakers, nightclub managers, crap game runners, gold diggers, and prostitutes—was eagerly anticipating the arrival of so many fresh bankrolls eager to be plucked.

Everybody agreed it would be a close fight. The smart money was flocking to the younger, fitter Sharkey, but the sentimental coin was all on the Manassa Mauler. In Polly's social circles—what might charitably be called the Broadway demimonde—Jack Dempsey was the very ideal of a rags-to-riches Horatio Alger hero. "Plus a few things Mr. Alger didn't go in for," Dempsey noted wryly: "beautiful movie and stage stars, a lot of laughs, pressure groups, knocking good guys senseless as a way of life, war, suicide, divorce." He'd clawed his way to the top with a barbaric fighting style and generous helpings of hype. For the last four years, he'd been living the coddled life of a Hollywood celebrity, getting laid, getting drunk, and spending money hand over fist—a combination that had cost him his title in 1926 but burnished his popularity. Now, at the ancient age of thirty-two, he was attempting a feat never seen before: to take back the heavyweight crown.

To be honest, Polly didn't really care who won. "I was never much of a fight fan," she admitted. Nor was she a fan of Dempsey. "I knew him way back and never liked him and still don't." It was common knowledge that his first wife had worked as a prostitute, and rumor was that he had been her pimp—and, Polly noted pointedly, "I cannot deny that I mortally hate pimps." But he was an exception. As a rule, she was fond of boxers. Like prostitution, prizefighting attracted ambitious youths from tough homes, whose only shot at climbing the ladder of success lay in their strong, svelte young bodies.

Like him or not, a good night for Dempsey meant a good night for Polly and her girls. This was the peak of the "One Good Party Era," as one columnist dubbed it, when one well-oiled sucker on a spending spree could cover her overhead for a month or more. In her business, there were always unexpected expenses. She never knew when she'd be raided or shaken down by the cops, or when an overwrought customer might draw the wrong kind of attention, requiring her to shut down and move her operation—each time costing her a bundle of money and putting her at terrible risk. So a wise madam took advantage of every opportunity. And in her experience, nothing made a man want to party like the surging adrenaline of watching two hulking fellows beat each other bloody.

It was Dempsey's former manager, Jack "Doc" Kearns, who'd helped build Polly's reputation as the place for big spenders to celebrate. A fast-talking, wisecracking hustler who favored pastel suits, diamond stickpins, gold-tipped walking sticks, and violet-scented cologne, Doc demanded constant action. He drank voraciously, gambled recklessly, tipped the girls lavishly, had a passion for practical jokes (with a particular fondness for the hotfoot). He routinely bought drinks for everyone in the house, both friends and strangers. When he was in town, Doc was one of Polly's best customers. "He used to tell me that whenever a fighter comes inside a woman, he loses his strength," said Dempsey. "Doc believed that, but you sure couldn't prove it by the way Doc liked to live himself."

Adding to his charm, Kearns usually brought an entourage of newspapermen with him, all eating and drinking on his (or his fighter's) dime. In gratitude, the reporters gave his boxers unlimited ink in their newspapers. Tex Rickard called this "sugaring" the sportswriters. Kearns referred to it as "movement money." Polly's less colorful clients simply called it an "expense account," but the idea was the same. "Like a stripteaser," said Kearns, "I always figured you couldn't get anywhere without exposure."

This was where Polly came in. It was a truth universally acknowledged among the denizens of Broadway that "ninety-five per cent of the sucker money is brought in by a skirt," as one wag put it. That was as true for sports promoters as it was for theatrical producers, factory owners, advertising executives, politicians, or bootleggers. A swell party stocked with easy women was just the thing to convince a fellow to close a contract, make a deal, or pen an enthusiastic column. Like bootleg booze, girls were the grease that made the machinery of the metropolis run smoother.

In that sweltering summer of 1927, Polly Adler was Manhattan's top supplier of party girls. Unlike Jack Kearns, Polly's bacchanalian hospitality earned her no headlines. If anything, her kindness to the ink-stained wretches of the press kept her safely out of them. But it did win her exuberant word-of-mouth at Billy LaHiff's tavern, Dinty Moore's diner, Lindy's delicatessen, the Algonquin Hotel, and the all-male sanctum of the Friars Club—wherever men regaled each other with stories of gorgeous women and epic parties. Her house had become one of the notorious late-night hotspots where a fellow who'd won a long shot at the track or made a killing in the stock market could show off his good fortune.

Unfortunately for the freeloaders in the press box, Kearns and Dempsey parted ways in 1925. But Doc had a new protégé, the welterweight champion Mickey Walker, a scrappy Irish slugger from New Jersey who rivaled Kearns in his appetite for booze and broads. Now, this one she liked. The Toy Bull Dog, as the sportswriters nicknamed young Walker, returned the sentiment. "She was a sharp businesswoman, a financial brain. You had to be somebody to go there, and you had to pay plenty, no matter who you were or how well you knew her," said Mickey. "In my book, she is a real champ."

Doc and Mickey were among Polly's best prospects for raking in some serious dough that week. Right this moment they were on their way back from a raucous romp through Europe. But Doc had telegraphed to say they would be sailing into the port of New York on the day before the big bout. "The Queen Madam," as Mickey called her, was keeping an anxious eye on the telephone, hoping to hear from the boys as soon as they landed. She was counting on the fact that after their weeks abroad, Mickey and his manager would be making the rounds of all the late-night joints, with a mob of thirsty reporters and gossipmongers in tow. Someone was going to get all that business—she just had to make sure she was one of them.

It was exhausting sometimes, always being on high alert like this, waiting for the phone to ring, listening for an ominous knock at the door, and looking over her shoulder for signs of unscrupulous cops, under-cover investigators, blackmailers, and sociopathic customers. When she thought of the thousands of dollars she'd paid out to double-crossing cops and the abuse she took from coked-up racket boys, sometimes it made her blood boil.

But then, that was the secret to her success: her ability to take it on the chin without squawking, then get back up with a smile on her face. To an outsider, "it might seem that I have got Polly Adler confused with Pollyanna," quipped Polly. "I can only say that I am one of those people who just can't help getting a kick out of life—even when it's a kick in the teeth."

Still, enough good weeks, enough big spenders, and she'd leave this racket in a hot minute. Until then, she said—like the good Jewish girl she'd always meant to be—"I would do nothing but work until I had saved enough money to quit the whorehouse and find myself a decent man."

☾

Whore is a word that jars the ear and tastes bitter on the tongue. The English language abounds in more polite, poetic, and precise terms to describe a woman who trades sex for money: *prostitute, sex worker, lady of the evening, working girl, fallen woman, call girl*. Many more are unapologetically rude: *hooker, gash, cunt,* and *piece of hide* were all commonly heard in the dives of New York after the Great War.

Women who made a business of sex in those days often turned up their noses at the term *prostitute*, preferring to call themselves *hustlers, party girls,* or *regulars*. But everyone in the sex trade used the word *whore*. "In those days prostitutes weren't called chippies or tarts or call girls or any other fancy names," remembered the columnist Danton Walker. "They were known, quite properly, by the Biblical name: whores, and their establishments were called whorehouses." It was, after all, one of the world's oldest words, used to describe the world's oldest profession.

No one meeting Pearl Adler on the street would have taken her for a fallen woman, let alone the proprietress of Manhattan's most renowned bordello. "She was homey," remembered the journalist Irving Drutman; "one would have placed her, and how mistakenly, as the ubiquitous mama in a family-run delicatessen." Only twenty-seven years old, give or take, and tiny—barely five feet tall in her highest heels—she had a kewpie doll face and a sweet smile that revealed a girlish little gap between her two front teeth. She dressed conservatively in beautifully tailored clothes, often of her own design. Her hair was fashionably bobbed at the neck, her hands tastefully manicured. No ankle bracelets, heavy makeup, or the jungle-red nail polish associated with women of the night. Her jewelry was a tad showy and she had a well-known weakness for mink coats, but no more so than any ambitious Manhattan gold digger.

It was easy to underestimate her, at least until she opened her mouth. She was blessed with "the voice of a longshoreman" in the words of Oscar Levant—naturally husky and roughened by cigarettes, scotch, and a thousand late nights. It was so deep that telephone callers frequently mistook her for a man, much to her annoyance. "I can still hear her hollering over the phone, 'This is Polly Adler, God damn it. Stop calling me mister,'" remembered one friend with amusement. Thirteen years after fleeing the Jewish Pale of Russia, she still spoke with Yiddish inflections, generously sprinkled with immigrant malapropisms and Broadway slang.

Not everyone liked her, of course. Rival madams didn't care for her upstart ambitions. Some of the Broadway butterflies who worked for her chafed at her ban on drugs and pimps, her insistence that they go to bed with whoever came through the door, and her frequent lectures on social etiquette. Men who were touchy about their own social status often took comfort in belittling her. "I knew Polly Adler," sniped the famously combative writer John O'Hara; "she was a noisy bore, who looked like Mike Romanoff in drag" (a reference to the infamous Russian-born con man–turned–Hollywood restaurateur). She'd been snubbed in public more times than she could possibly remember, even if she had wanted to.

Nonetheless, her fans outnumbered her foes. Slumming intellectuals and Broadway bohemians were tickled by her blunt realism and lightly louche wisecracks. Fellow Jews from the old country found her house *haimish*, a cozy home away from home. Many in the underground gay community—both male and female—found her parlor a retreat where they could relax and be themselves. Everyone, from Park Avenue aristocrats to Lower East Side hooligans, appreciated her ironclad discretion.

"Polly Adler was one of the most fascinating females I ever knew," recalled the playboy songwriter Jimmy Van Heusen. "How the hell do you explain why you like someone? Polly was warm and funny, smart and gutsy and fun to be around. We liked each other and didn't take the time to think about it much."

There were plenty of other madams in Manhattan, but none of them seemed to have the combination of charisma and brains that made Polly one of the "authentic Big Shots" of the town, as one Broadway columnist dubbed her.

Polly was more modest. "I was a creation of the times, of an era whose credo was: 'Anything which is economically right is morally right'—and my story is inseparable from the story of the twenties," she wrote later. "In fact, if I had all of history to choose from, I could hardly have picked a better age in which to be a madam."

She'd opened her first brothel in 1920—a self-styled "house of assignation" in a two-bedroom apartment across from Columbia University—the same year the Eighteenth Amendment to the Constitution, banning the sale or transportation of all intoxicating liquors, became the law of the land. For over a decade, the forces of moral order had been busy shutting down brothels and gambling halls. Now the final piece was in place. "It is here at last!" declared the triumphant Anti-Saloon League. "Now for a new era of clean thinking and clean living!"

Maybe so in Middle America, wherever that was. But in "Gotham and Gomorrah," as that bible of the middle classes, *The Saturday Evening Post*, dubbed New York City, they were having none of it.

By the time Polly was marking her first anniversary in business, Manhattan had become the blazing eastern front of the first great culture war of the twentieth century. In one of the most spectacular examples of the law of unintended consequences in American history, Prohibition gave the world of vice a cachet it had never had before.

"From the parlor of my house I had a backstage, three-way view," remembered Polly with pleasure. "I could look into the underworld, the half-world and the high." Her house became a favorite oasis of the bootleggers and bookmakers who were eager to blow their ill-gotten gains. But Polly had even bigger ambitions, requiring her to master the art of publicity. She cultivated gossip columnists and influential newspapermen, and she frequented the chic nightclubs and late-night rendezvous with a rotating posse of glamour girls.

By 1924, her house had become an after-hours clubhouse for the adventurous Broadway bohemians who gathered at the Algonquin Hotel for lunch; writers, performers, and publicists like Dorothy Parker, Robert Benchley, Donald Ogden Stewart, and the king of the Broadway wisecrackers, George S. Kaufman. Their imprimatur led her to the heavy hitters of Madison Avenue, Park Avenue, and Wall Street.

Executives in the garment industry and the flourishing fields of radio, motion pictures, and advertising employed her girls to woo clients. Wall Street traders passed along stock tips on their way to the bedroom. Racketeers used her parlor as an informal headquarters where they could confer with politicians and judges, away from prying eyes. Gamblers found it a safe haven for high-stakes poker and crap games. Entertainers knew they'd hit the big time when they could afford an evening with her girls. Crooked cops of every rank made her place their home away from home—a decidedly mixed blessing.

There was danger in such notoriety, however. That spring she'd caught the attention of the undercover investigators of the Committee of Fourteen, a coalition of moral reformers committed to stamping out prostitution and sexual deviancy in New York. They'd tracked her to the Kentucky Club, where she was an avid fan of Duke Ellington and his sizzling jazz band. They'd traced her to the Dover Club, where comedian Jimmy Durante had hired one of her occasional call girls to work as a hostess and comic performer. If the Committee decided to stir up the wrong people, she could be in for trouble, no matter how many palms she greased.

Then there was the problem of her parents. With her newfound fortune, Polly had brought her father and two of her brothers to New York from eastern Europe. In June 1927, Moshe Adler filed his naturalization papers to become a citizen, and she planned to bring her mother and three youngest brothers to America in the coming months. Much as Polly longed to see her mother again, she dreaded the prospect of lying to her face. Her father might have understood her career—he was a man of the world—but her mother would be devastated if she learned the truth.

At this point, Polly could have declared victory and retired from the life. In an era when well-paid women made about thirty dollars a week, she was pulling in at least $60,000 a year, well over $900,000 in today's currency. She was heavily invested in the stock market and had saved a fine nest egg—enough to buy into a legitimate business or go back to school. She'd spent enough time around horseplayers and dice-tossers to know the golden rule: the only way to beat the odds was to quit the game when you are winning.

But that wasn't so simple. It was an axiom of the underworld: once in the rackets, always in the rackets. Her career was deeply intertwined with syndicated crime, and the mob didn't look kindly on retirement. As one gangland titan warned her, "Once you're tagged as a madam it's for keeps."

Besides, she wasn't sure she was ready to retire. She was only twenty-seven, but she'd seen enough of human hypocrisy to know that in the square world, she'd be just another nobody, or worse. "As Miss Pearl Adler, the reformed procuress and honest citizen, I was a social outcast," she said tartly. "As Madam Polly, the proprietress of 'New York's most opulent bordello,' society came to me."

The way her luck was running, she just needed to stick it out a little longer, until she had so much money that she'd never have to work again and no one would dare look down on her. Ask any gambler: only a rank sucker would drop the dice when she had a hot hand.

€

The weekend before the fight, the excitement and tension on the Main Stem rose to a feverish pitch. A steady stream of pugs, pimps, degenerate gamblers, and the racketeers who were boxing's biggest fans and, increasingly, its primary investors, began rolling into Manhattan in anticipation of the festivities on July 21. This "Dempsey-Sharkey thing brought the strangest assortment of unique characters into Broadway the Great Alley has ever seen," marveled a reporter from *Variety*, the weekly show business journal. Special trains brought fans from Chicago, Boston, Philadelphia, Baltimore, Washington, and Pittsburgh. They were a tough crowd. When conductors on one "fight special" coming up from Baltimore tried to stop a hundred or so passengers from drinking in one of the cars, a full-scale free-for-all erupted. The fans battered the conductors and crew with such fury that a platoon of police had to storm the train when it got to Philadelphia.

The out-of-towners stampeded into the Roaring Forties, the rough-and-tumble neighborhood between Fifth and Tenth avenues, where every block boasted a dozen speakeasies and a scruffy poolroom. The sidewalks were jammed around Cauliflower Row, at Eighth Avenue and West 49th Street outside Madison Square Garden, where the fight promoters and managers, ticket scalpers, horseplayers, and cauliflower-eared old boxers gossiped and schemed.

They were carrying serious kale and throwing it around with gusto in all the Broadway nightspots. "At one table one night we saw the most notorious gunman in Chicago, surrounded by his henchmen; at another was pointed out to us the leading bootlegger and beer-runner of a midwestern border city, and the mayor of the same city was in his party," marveled the reporter from *Variety*. "There seemed to be no limit to the amount of money the gang had or wanted to spend."

All the bookmakers were seeing heavy action, from the small-time poolroom and cigar-store bookies to the "betting commissioners" down on Broad Street. It was estimated that at least a million dollars changed hands that week. Dempsey was the sentimental favorite, but the younger, fitter Sharkey was heavily favored by the oddsmakers. Even Arnold Rothstein, the Big Street's savviest gambler, was trumpeting the fact that he'd plunged heavily on the Boston gob, betting an astounding $400,000 on Sharkey to win at 8-to-5 odds.

Amid the revelry, there was an ominous undercurrent of anxiety among the Broadway mobsters and their out-of-town guests. Like most madams, Polly prided herself on possessing a sixth sense, an ability to sniff out trouble before it arrived. But no one needed special powers to sense the tempest brewing. New York's volatile underworld had been enjoying a period of relative calm, after two years of violent clashes between gangs vying for control of the city's liquor trade. But a series of unfortunate events was shaking the fragile peace.

On July 9 Jack "Legs" Diamond, one of New York's most notorious strong-arm men, was picked up on a narcotics charge. Nothing unusual in that. But this time it was whispered that the police had been tipped off by Arnold Rothstein, who employed Diamond as a debt collector and bodyguard. Word was that Rothstein was growing irritated by Legs's habit of borrowing large sums of cash and forgetting to repay them. Now Legs was furious and swearing vengeance. Happy as many were to see the hotheaded gunman get a rap on the knuckles, having Legs on the warpath could create a lot of headaches.

But Legs's saga paled when the news came down that same Friday: a federal judge ruled that William Vincent Dwyer would be spending the next two years in the federal penitentiary in Atlanta.

"Big Bill" Dwyer, as he was known to his admirers, was one of Polly's most important patrons. He sported thick black eyeglasses and the plump profile of a well-fed accountant. Over the last seven years, Dwyer had risen from the Irish ghetto of Hell's Kitchen to be crowned the "King of the Bootleggers." Using a potent combination of grease and muscle, he'd built an international smuggling operation and a network of illegal breweries, distilleries, and speakeasies that had grossed an estimated $40 million over the last few years. Along with his partners, Frank Costello and Owney Madden, Dwyer established a powerful cartel, known as the Combine. Together they stabilized the lawless market for bootleg booze in New York and systematically corrupted a huge swath of the Coast Guard, the New York Police Department, and the upper reaches of the judiciary, paying out some $10,000 a day in bribes.

Dwyer was an exuberant host who spent lavishly on "business entertainment" for politicians, judges, and cops. Prostitutes were a critical part of his program of graft and grease, and Polly was the Combine's preferred procurer and party planner. Big Bill was "her benefactor," as a friend delicately phrased it—one with an unlimited bankroll and extraordinary political influence.

So it came as a nasty surprise when Bill was arrested by federal agents. But that was nothing compared to the shock of Dwyer's conviction six months later. He had spent the last year out on bail, filing appeals, but now the verdict was final: he would be spending the next two years in the federal penitentiary in Atlanta. With Dwyer heading off on what he called "a little vacation," Polly was losing both a big chunk of business and a critical source of protection.

Dwyer hadn't even left the city yet, but already rival bootleggers were circling like vultures, looking for cracks in the Combine's monopoly. Polly's house was considered neutral territory by the gangs, where mobster etiquette demanded they set aside any beefs while they were in the house. But if warfare broke out among the tommy-gun tycoons, such courtesies would go by the wayside.

☾

A warm, heavy rain had been falling all week, but on the morning of the fight the showers tapered off, leaving only the echoes of thunder in the distance. But along the Broadway grapevine the rumble of rumor was growing louder.

For several days now, "the gentry who talk from corners of their mouths" had been whispering that the fight was "in the bag" for Dempsey; he was going to knock out Sharkey with a foul punch, some said in the fourth round, others in the fifth. Now, on the morning of the fight the coterie of professional gamblers and big-time bookmakers who orbited around Arnold Rothstein—the "Wise Men of Gotham," in the *New York Sun*'s phrase—who had been touting Sharkey suddenly began hedging their bets, putting down big money at long odds on the ex-champ.

The logic of the wise guys was financial rather than fistic: a Dempsey victory would force a rematch with Sharkey for the heavyweight championship, providing another guaranteed gold mine for everyone in the fight game. And if Dempsey had to win to make the sporting fraternity happy, chances were exceedingly good that he would.

By six p.m. 110,000 expectant fans had converged on Yankee Stadium. Rough pine benches catering to the hoi polloi covered the entire infield. At ringside, hundreds of sportswriters, telegraph operators, and radio announcers took up the first four rows of seats, balancing typewriters over their laps and leaning into their microphones.

The crowd was heavy with celebrities, politicians, high-ranking cops, leading businessmen, and underworld figures. "I suppose you would call it a cosmopolitan assemblage," joked the writer Damon Runyon. "I made a hurried dash down an aisle and fell under the hurrying hoofs of fourteen kings of the world of finance, twenty nine merchant princes, six bootleggers and five ticket speculators, all owners of estates on Long Island and of Rolls-Royce cars." The democratic smell of cigar smoke and sweat wafted on the light breeze over a sea of straw boaters, gray fedoras, and the occasional top hat.

Outside the stadium, spectators perched atop fences, rooftops, and water tanks to peer over the walls. Across the country, a whopping 50 million listeners were gathering around radios in drugstores, barbershops, speakeasies, and pool halls. Back in Manhattan, Polly and her girls finished their primping and then curled up around the radio receiver in her parlor.

At ten o'clock, after a series of preliminary bouts by lesser fighters, the two star pugilists appeared. They strode to the ring through a blinding sea of flashbulbs, as eighty thousand fans rose with a roar, whistling, shouting, and stamping their feet in excitement.

At first the Manassa Mauler seemed almost groggy, with none of his old spark. Sharkey was easily outboxing him, closing the first round with a flurry of slashing blows to the head. By the end of the second round, the once-fierce Dempsey looked ragged and exhausted. By round five, he had deep gashes around his eyes, and his mouth and nose were bleeding, as he kept his head down, batting away at Sharkey's abdomen.

In the sixth round, Dempsey's fists began drifting below the beltline, earning him a warning from the referee against fouling Sharkey. Dempsey ignored him. At the top of the seventh, he drove two sharp blows into Sharkey's gut. Again the referee warned him. Again Dempsey hit low. In outrage, Sharkey turned his head to the referee to complain.

Seizing on his opponent's distraction, Dempsey pounded his famous left hook into the Boston boy's jaw. Blindsided, Sharkey crumpled to the canvas. The referee paused and murmured something to Sharkey, still writhing and clutching his crotch, and then he began to count. When he got to ten, the stadium exploded. The crowd was flinging their hats into the ring, screaming "Foul!" and "Quitter!" while the radio announcers shouted to be heard above the chaos.

It was "an extremely queer, strange, weird, bizarre, and ill-scented finish" to an otherwise splendid event, as the reporter Grantland Rice observed. Even Polly's pals in the press box could not agree on whether "the Battle of the Strange Coincidences," in sportswriter W .O. McGeehan's phrase, had been fixed. But for the gamblers who had guessed right, it was a spectacular night.

As for Polly, the fight went just as she'd hoped. There was nothing to make a man open his wallet and drop his pants like a come-from-behind knockout and a surprise winner.

☾

"No one starts out to be a whore," Polly once observed. She most certainly did not. As a girl in the small Russian village of Yanow, she'd had grand ambitions. An unusually clever and self-possessed child, Pearl Adler was blessed with a passionate desire for an education, in a culture where girls rarely received more than a few years of schooling. Had she been born in America, they'd have dubbed her one of the "New Women," who insisted a girl could be as capable and independent as any boy.

Like the strong-willed daughters in the stories of Sholom Aleichem, she was eager to shake off the confines of village life, to see the world and make something of herself. In Yiddish, she would have said she aspired to be a *mensch*, a person of substance and respect, a Somebody. When twelve-year-old Pearl announced that she wanted to continue her studies in the nearby city of Pinsk, Moshe Adler hired a tutor to help her win one of the few spots reserved for Jews.

But as the old saying went, *Mentsch tracht, Got lakht*—Man plans and God laughs. In 1905, when she was around five years old, the Russian Empire was rocked by an attempted coup against the ruling monarchy. When the revolution failed, Jews became the primary scapegoats. As Pearl grew older and political discontent deepened, the vise of anti-Semitism tightened. Repressive laws and taxes grew heavier, and Jewish neighborhoods lived in fear of being attacked by drunken mobs. In

1913, just as his daughter was readying herself for her entrance exams, Moshe decided he'd had enough. The family was moving to *die Goldine Madina*—the Golden Land of America.

Resettling such a large family required more capital than he had on hand, so they would travel one by one. As the oldest child, Pearl was the first to go, landing on Ellis Island in December 1913. She lived with friends of her father while waiting for the rest to arrive. Six months later Europe was engulfed in war, cutting off all travel from Russia and leaving Pearl stranded among strangers.

She had to make a decision—some would say it was a bad one.

From the perspective of a social worker, Polly's path was a cautionary tale of the evils of dance halls and Coney Island dreams. To the socialists, she was the archetypal victim of an inhumane capitalist system. She embodied the worst fears of the Yanovers, who blamed America for stealing their daughters away from God. For Broadway watchers, she was no different from thousands of high-spirited young women let loose in the city: first a free-wheeling flapper, then a gold digger, and finally a whore. But Polly was determined to buck the naysayers. After seven years in the vice racket, she was not yet in the gutter or the grave.

She was not without regrets. But when pressed, she was unrepentant. "How else could I ever have gotten to a place in life where almost anybody you asked 'Who is Polly Adler' could tell you right off and the kind of business she ran? When could a girl with no education and no social standing have met so many important men—and have them call you by your first name like they did me?"

As the hard-boiled babies of Broadway liked to say, sometimes the wages of sin are a house on Fifth Avenue.

By the time the crowds were pouring out of Yankee Stadium, the house was ready. Champagne was chilling on ice, and the bar groaned with bottles of top-shelf booze. The lights were dimmed in the spacious living room, lending a flattering glow to the girls' cheeks, and the tables were laid out with cigarettes, lighters, ashtrays, playing cards, and dice. The tidy bedrooms were generously stocked with condoms and cotton "pleasure towels," as she called them. A formidable African American maid in a crisp uniform, who went by the snazzy nickname "Showboat,"

prepared to take hats, pour drinks, change sheets, and keep a wary eye out for trouble. A bevy of satin-clad beauties perched on the upholstery, waiting impatiently for the telephone to ring.

It didn't take long. There on the other end of the line was the big fish Polly had been waiting for. Walter Reade, Broadway playboy and theater owner, had hit the jackpot and was looking to celebrate in high style.

Like Doc Kearns and Big Bill Dwyer, Walter Reade was, to quote *Variety*, "a spectacular figure" on the Big Street—exactly the kind of high-profile, hard-partying big spender whom Polly was trying so hard to cultivate. Unlike those two rascals, however, Reade counted as minor Broadway royalty. He was the nephew of Oscar Hammerstein I, the theatrical visionary who had discovered Times Square, and first cousin of lyricist Oscar Hammerstein II, who helped revolutionize musical theater. Up until the Kaiser's War, he had been known as Walter Rosenberg. But *Rosenberg* carried none of the allure of the Hammerstein name, and all the disadvantages of sounding both Jewish and German. So he traded it in for an Anglophile upgrade—dropping the *berg*, translating *rosen* to "red," then tacking on the Old English *e* for an extra touch of class.

Also like Kearns and Dwyer, Reade's tycoon veneer barely concealed his close ties to the half-world of professional gamblers, loan sharks, prostitutes, and political fixers. Although married with two young children, the balding, bespectacled theater owner had a well-deserved reputation as an unrepentant womanizer, a foulmouthed brawler, and an obsessive gambler who at one time was said to keep a roulette wheel in his automobile that could be flipped over to make a craps table. Only six months earlier, in April 1927, Reade had purchased three theaters with an estimated worth of $2.2 million, at Broadway and 45th Street, right in the heart of the Roaring Forties, Manhattan's new Tenderloin District. There was speculation that Reade was acting as a front for a consortium of secret investors, which nowadays was a code word for racketeers.

Whether he possessed good luck or inside dope, it didn't matter to Polly. All she needed to know was that Walter Reade had had the wisdom to bet on Dempsey to win by a knockout in the seventh round, earning a cool $70,000 from his unfortunate bookmaker. Now he was on his way over with a couple carloads of pals to help him spend his winnings.

She directed Reade and his entourage to 115 West 73rd Street, one of the large apartment buildings going up across the Upper West Side, where neighbors were inclined to mind their own business. It wasn't as fancy as her place in midtown, but it was a quick cab ride from Times Square, and it was convenient both for the Broadway butterflies who worked for her and for the racketeers, garment factory owners, and show-biz bigwigs who called the neighborhood home. It was also safer. Down in the speakeasy belt, kidnapping—"the snatch racket," as the rod boys called it—was starting to become a serious inconvenience.

A half dozen of her finest girls were on hand. Gloria Powers, Jean Darling, Eloise Pryor, Frances Marion, Mary Brooks, and Lottie Lee, all white women in their early twenties (although their real names and ages were anyone's guess), were clad in the simple evening dresses and tastefully restrained makeup that she insisted upon. At twenty dollars a trick, men wanted someone who looked like a naughty debutante, Polly insisted, "and not a painted slut." "A lady in the parlor and a whore in the bedroom"—that was her motto.

It was a night that passed into legend—the kind of rip-roaring, no-holds-barred blowout that lucky guests would reminisce about for years to come. There were "corks popping right and left, champagne being sipped out of slippers and other even more exotic receptacles, rose-garlanded dancing girls fighting their way out of pies (at least that's how literary gentlemen of my acquaintance used to tell it)," remembered Polly with pleasure.

The joint was running full tilt when, above the roar, she heard a *thump thump thump* at the front door. Suddenly she was face-to-face with Officer Christopher Confrey and a crew of undercover vice cops. Officer Confrey, a fifteen-year veteran of New York's Finest, had the irksome habit of padding his salary by shaking down prostitutes. It wasn't her first time tangling with him, nor would it be her last.

The pugnacious Walter Reade was savvy enough to know how to take care of these matters. Motioning to Confrey, he offered him a handsome bribe of two thousand dollars to take their business elsewhere. "But the boys weren't having any that night, which meant that seven of the girls and I were hauled out and stuffed into the pie wagon."

Now, this was what got her steamed. She was well known for meeting shakedowns with generosity and good humor. She had squandered a small fortune on tickets to police banquets and fundraisers and had hosted more parties for them, on the house, than she cared to remember. What she resented were the cops who took her bribes, guzzled her booze, and slept with her girls, then hauled her in when they needed to fill their monthly arrest quota, score points with their bosses, or put a bonus in their bank accounts.

"I had been raided before, but this was a four-star, five-alarm, full-dress affair in gorgeous color," remembered Polly. Down the girls went, spilling onto 73rd Street and into the big black patrol wagon. As usual, not one of her "guests" was arrested. But Walter and his pals were not ready for the fun to end. He and his well-oiled revelers clambered into their cars and took off behind the paddy wagon as it made its way to the station house. Polly was fingerprinted and booked under her current alias: Pearl Davidson, age twenty-six.

"However, not even the Bastille could have held us that night," remembered Polly. "Our customers bailed us out almost before we were booked, and when we came out of the station house a great wave of cheers went up from several carloads of gentlemen who were waiting at the curb to escort us back to the house." There they picked up where they left off, lapping up liquor, fondling the girls, and commandeering her kitchen for one of her famous hearty breakfasts.

But while the johns partied on, Polly was already counting her losses for the evening. Once again she had fallen into the clutches of the vice ring, a nearly foolproof system of extortion. One official report neatly summed up their methods: "The stool pigeon or the officer framed the woman, the officer arrested her, the bondsman bailed her out at an exorbitant charge and steered her to an attorney from Lawyers Row, on West 10th Street across from Women's Court. The lawyer gouged her savings and either himself, or through the bondsman, 'fixed' the arresting officer and the District Attorney."

It would cost Polly $200 to $500 per girl to keep them out of jail, split up among the ring. Officer Confrey would get twenty-five dollars per girl to soft-pedal the evidence or skip his appearance in court. John C. Weston, the deputy district attorney for the Women's Court, would get another twenty-five dollars a head to do a poor job prosecuting the case. ("He rode the horse to lose," in the lingo of the racetrack.) If the magistrate was on the take, he too might be paid a fee to dismiss the charge or find in her favor. Everything left over went to the bail bondsmen and the lawyer, and the woman walked free. Those who failed to cough up the cash, or who foolishly insisted on their innocence, were almost certain to be sent off to Bedford or the women's prison. Polly always paid.

The party rolled on until nine in the morning, when Polly and her girls had to return to court to enter their plea. Determined not to miss any of the fun, the drunken revelers once again climbed into their cars and set off in a rowdy parade to the Women's Court in Greenwich Village.

In the dank, gaslit halls of the Jefferson Market Courthouse, Polly and her rambunctious posse picked their way through the throngs of lawyers, pimps, and bail bondsmen shepherding bleary-eyed shoplifters, pickpockets, runaways, and ladies of the evening.

As they made their dramatic entrance into the majestic second-floor courtroom, the clerks, probation officers, and spectators all turned to stare and whisper. There, Polly remembered proudly, "were my girls, tall and beautiful, gliding down the aisle like swans on a mirrored lake, with me bustling along them like Donald Duck." It was going to cost her plenty to spring all of them, but the boost to her reputation was priceless.

The deputy district attorney, John C. Weston, a graying, heavyset man in his mid-fifties, watched the entire scene, "grinning from ear to ear."

"Reduce your prices, Polly," murmured Weston, "and every man here will be your client."

The bustling marketplace in Pearl Adler's hometown of Yanow, Belarus, in the Pale of Russia

2

Man Plans, God Laughs

Pearl Adler never knew quite how old she was. It was a cliché in her business, where age was the invincible enemy, but nonetheless true.

Years later, after all records of her birth had been lost to the ravages of fire and war, Pearl pressed her parents to recall the exact date. Her mother Gittel was sure her firstborn child was delivered on a Sunday two weeks before the Passover holiday, but the year—that Gittel didn't know.

Moshe, her father, was certain that Pearl was a year and a half old when the American president William McKinley was killed by that madman in Buffalo, New York. The assassination had been all the talk when Moshe stepped off the boat in the port of New York, on his first trip to America. Counting backward, Moshe settled on the seventeenth day of the month of Nisan in the year of 5660 by the Jewish calendar, or April 16, 1900, as the *Amerikaners* put it. She was, her father declared, a child of the twentieth century.

"My father," remembered Pearl, "was a tailor, a talkative, temperamental man with big ideas and correspondingly large sense of his own importance." Moshe Adler considered it obvious that he was no mere tailor. Slim and handsome, with deep-set eyes and a thick head of dark hair, Moshe's ambitions always seemed ready to burst the boundaries of their small town in the forests of White Russia. "He must be, I have often thought, a lineal descendant of the Wandering Jew," Polly joked.

Or as one of the Adler cousins put it, "Moshe had a reputation of having *shpilkes*—Yiddish for 'needles under his behind'—a crude way of saying he suffered from wanderlust."

"Though he was gone only a few months, it was long enough for him to become an authority on all things American," remembered Pearl. In Yanow, where fewer than a dozen people had ventured even as far as the nearby city of Pinsk, Moshe Adler was a cosmopolitan, a man of the world, who brought a taste of modernity to their dusty backwater. Over the course of her childhood, her father would travel to the metropolises of Warsaw and Berlin and would return to New York City, making him, Pearl noted archly, "an authority on everything."

After that first trip to America, Moshe basked in the newfound respect of his neighbors who listened to his stories of exotic lands with openmouthed wonder. That was, until he told them about a miraculous contraption that carried the sound of a voice through wires. Why, you could hear a man in Kiev talk just as clearly as if he were standing in front of you.

This was too much for the good people of Yanow to swallow. Who did Reb Adler think they were—ignorant peasants who could be taken in by a traveler's tall tales? Watching his neighbors exchange knowing glances and bemused winks, Moshe's temper rose. He would show these bumpkins. The next day he found an iron pipe and threaded it through the ceiling of their living room up to his second-floor bedroom, then proudly invited the skeptical townspeople to witness his wondrous device. "Alexander Bell had nothing on my pop," joked Pearl.

Whatever the townspeople believed, Moshe was delighted by his new "telephone." He began spending much of his time in bed surrounded by books, bellowing orders downstairs through the pipe. Although barely five feet tall, he possessed a deep, resonant voice that ricocheted through the iron and exited as an unintelligible roar. A simple request for a glass of tea reverberated like cannon fire.

Gittel, a dutiful wife, did her best to "answer the phone" whenever Moshe called. But the booming so petrified the Christian peasant girl who served as their maid-of-all-work that whenever she heard it, remembered Pearl, "she would throw her apron over her head and plunge blindly toward the nearest exit, caroming against chairs and tables and, more often than not, leaving the floor strewn with my little brothers who had to learn early either to dive for safety or be bowled over." The young man who served as Moshe's apprentice in the tailoring business would cower till the bellowing subsided, then dash to the foot of the stairs to beg Moshe to repeat himself. Moshe, outraged by this implied criticism of his invention, would rain curses upon the boy's head, declaring him a fool with wax in his ears, and then blithely resume issuing orders down the telephone.

Pearl was her father's daughter in many ways. She was tiny like her parents, with waves of glossy brown hair and a pale heart-shaped face set off by saucer-sized brown eyes and a cupid's-bow mouth that fell easily into a wide smile, revealing a gap between her front teeth. What set her apart was not her looks but her quickness of mind and spark of personality. She was, as she put it, "an affectionate child, demonstrative and outgoing," and possessed of a self-confidence and a taste for adventure that confounded the expectations of her small town.

Still, it would never have occurred to Pearl, or anyone else, to view this glorified bullhorn as an omen of her future in America, where the telephone would be the instrument of her fortune and fame.

Indeed, no one would have thought much of anything about her future, except to hope she'd make a good marriage, raise a brood of children, and help her husband make a living, just like her own mother. If she were lucky enough to marry a scholar who devoted his days to studying the holy books of the Torah, then perhaps she'd run a small business in the marketplace to support the family.

Pearl adored her mother, but like many keen-eyed eldest daughters, she had no desire to follow in her mother's footsteps. "It seems to me that at a quite early age I began identifying myself with my father—if by identifying is meant preferring a role which would not confine my horizon to the boundaries of Yanow or limit my activities to cooking, sewing, scrubbing and childbearing," she said. "I wanted to get out and see the world and mingle with people and have my say about what went on."

Far easier said than done. Teenage boys often left home to study in the yeshivas or to peddle dry goods in the Russian countryside. But everyone knew the world was full of snares for a young girl. Her like-minded father might give her permission to indulge her desire for adventure, but Gittel was set like a stone against it. In a hidebound town like Yanow, behavior was ruled by the common Yiddish expression "'s past nisht"—

"it's not nice" or "not appropriate"—for a nice Jewish girl to do certain things. A family could be ruined by a girl whose independence cost her her virtue and her virginity. Besides, how would Pearl ever marry without her family there to arrange the match? Better to stay home than risk ending up an old maid.

Even if her parents let her leave Yanow, Pearl faced a formidable barrier of anti-Jewish bureaucracy. To obtain a legal permit to change residence, to work or study elsewhere, cost dearly, between the administrative fees and bribes for the local officials. And where would she go? Jews were forbidden to live in most parts of Russia, except in the rare cases when they could prove to the authorities that they were "useful" Jews in some capacity. It was whispered that some girls were so desperate to go to school in Moscow or St. Petersburg that they agreed to register as "useful" prostitutes so they could get a special passport or "yellow ticket" that allowed them to live in the metropolis.

Worse yet, a girl might actually become a prostitute. Everyone had heard the terrifying tales of men who seduced or kidnapped young girls traveling alone and forced them into sexual slavery, shipping them off to big-city brothels or across the ocean to South America or the Far East.

No, better she should stay home. Not for nothing did the sharp-tongued old ladies of the marketplace mutter the crude warning *Az a meydl falt falt zi shtendik oyfn rukn*—"When a girl falls, she always lands on her back."

☾

Gittel Adler wasn't wrong to worry about her little girl. Whatever the precise day of Pearl's birth, her mother didn't need a fortune-teller to foresee a future filled with dark omens.

Trouble was nothing new for the Jews, of course. In the three thousand or so years since the Lord was said to have made His covenant with the Israelites, God's chosen people have suffered an extraordinary history of persecution. As the old joke goes: "Thou hath chosen us from among the nations—what, O Lord, did you have against us?"

While other ancient ethnic groups vanished from history's stage, the Jews endured even as their enemies passed on. For that reason, anti-Semitism—a term coined to replace the unvarnished German phrase *Judenhass* or "Jew hatred"—is one of the oldest and most persistent of ethnic prejudices. The Bible records its effects hundreds of years before the birth of Christ. But the rise of Christianity gave anti-Semitism new life, as its priests and followers often blamed the Jews for Christ's death and crucifixion. Jews, in turn, learned to fear the Christian church.

Anti-Semitism reached a new peak in the Middle Ages, when Jews were expelled from much of western Europe. Many fled east to the more hospitable lands of Poland, Lithuania, Belarus, and Ukraine. In the 1700s this swath of eastern Europe—home to hundreds of thousands of Jews—was annexed by the Russian Empire. Through the reign of six rulers over the next hundred years, the Jews endured government policies that seesawed between enlightened despotism and fanatical cruelty.

Beginning in 1791, Czarina Catherine the Great issued a series of imperial decrees severely limiting the areas in which Jews were allowed to live. Throughout the Russian Empire, thousands of Jews were driven from their homes and herded into what was dubbed the Pale of Settlement, a narrow band of western Russia that extended from the Baltic to the Black Sea, corresponding roughly to the twenty-first-century nations of Latvia, Lithuania, Ukraine, Belarus, and eastern Poland. A torrent of new restrictions followed, affecting all aspects of life, including which property Jews could own, what kind of work they could do, and where they could travel and go to school. "It was a principle of Russian law that everything was forbidden to Jews unless specifically permitted," as one caustic observer put it.

When the more liberal Czar Alexander II took the crown in 1855, he began relaxing the most oppressive laws restricting Jewish life and encouraging limited assimilation into Russian society. For the first time in decades, optimism stirred in the Pale of Settlement.

It was in this era of comparative peace that Moshe Adler was born in 1875. His family had lived in this corner of Belorussia long before the czars took possession of it. The marshy, timber-rich region known as Polesia was home to scores of villages and towns—each called a *shtetl* in Yiddish—where Jews were a dominant force in the community. Twenty-five miles to the east of Yanow, in the rapidly industrializing city of Pinsk, nearly 80 percent of the population was Jewish by the time of Moshe's birth, making it one of the most Jewish cities in the empire.

Then fate once again turned its face against the Jews. On March 13, 1881, Czar Alexander II was assassinated by a bomb thrown into his carriage in St. Petersburg. When reports spread that a Jewish girl had been part of the plot, once again the Jews served as the bloody scapegoat for the misfortunes of Mother Russia. The first outbreak of anti-Jewish rioting came on at the end of April 1881, in the Ukrainian city of Elizabethgrad. A *pogrom*, they called it, from the Russian word for "devastation." It would not be the last.

By the time Polly was born, the empire regulated every aspect of life for the 5 million Jews of the Pale of Settlement—the "legislative pogroms," as one journalist dubbed them. There were laws drastically limiting where Jews could live, laws prohibiting Jews from making or selling certain goods, running for office, and inheriting or purchasing certain categories of property. The government imposed heavy taxes and fines and placed steep quotas on the number of Jews who could attend school and enter the professions.

It was hard to say which was worse, the day-in-day-out wear of endless red tape, surveillance, and petty humiliation, or the ever-looming worry that the gentiles' general air of contempt could suddenly darken into a storm of thrashings, looting, arson, and rape.

Pinsk was now a raw, bustling factory town, where Jewish entrepreneurs built the first nail and plywood factories in Russia. Until recently, the city's main claim to fame was as a punch line for hackneyed jokes about Jews traveling between Minsk to Pinsk, a form of humor so popular that Sigmund Freud told one in *Jokes and Their Relation to the Unconscious*. Here in Pinsk, the Jews were used to running their own affairs.

Above all, the Pinskers were tough. When a mob of angry peasants and railroad workers stormed the city in 1883, heading directly for the Jewish neighborhoods, a force of Jewish butchers, coachmen, and porters armed with shovels, axes, and whips rose up to drive them back to their fields. Lesson learned: the *pogromers* did not return. (In later years, the legend of the city's fearlessness spawned the common saying that fully one-quarter of the founders of the Israeli government were Pinskers.)

Here there were Jews of every flavor. The city was a hotbed of socialists and trade unionists who dreamed of creating a new Russia through the elevation of the workers. More than a few were unrepentant revolutionaries who preferred to refashion Russia with a stick of dynamite.

Some Pinskers were passionate cultural activists devoted to promoting the revival of a modern Hebrew language. Others argued just as fiercely that Yiddish (the vernacular language of Jewish people in central and eastern Europe) should be the foundation of a new national identity. Atheists shaved their beards and rejected the Torah, insisting that Jews were being held back by ancient superstitions, while a thriving community of ultra-orthodox Hasidic Jews scorned the modern world, seeking only a mystical bond with the Lord.

Still others turned their eyes away from Russia entirely. Many became passionate Zionists, enraptured by the vision of a new Jewish homeland in the land of Israel. And many more began to put their hopes in America—*die Goldine Madina*, the Golden Land—where even paupers had enough to eat, and everyone could curse the czar in peace and freedom.

☾

Outside of Pinsk, down the rough country roads that led to the small shtetl of Yanow, there were few signs that the world was in such an uproar. Yanow was a sleepy community of three thousand souls, surrounded by thick forests, vast swamps, and large estates. In 1900, the likely year of Pearl Adler's birth, the town looked much as it had in 1800. There was no electricity, no sidewalks, no paved streets. A railway line passed by Yanow but did not stop because, it was rumored, the town had not kicked up enough in bribes to earn its own train station.

"At first glance Yanow looked like an all Jewish town," as one townsman recalled. On the street one could see Hasidic men in long black coats and skullcaps and their modest wives wearing wigs or scarves to cover the beauty of their natural hair. There were traditional orthodox Jews sporting beards and short-brimmed cloth caps, and a few freethinkers who wore no beards at all and kept their heads scandalously bare.

In fact, like many towns in the Russian Empire, Yanow was made up of an uneasy mix of ethnicities. Jews represented a little more than half the town's population. The rest were mostly White Russians or Belarusians, along with a smattering of Poles and a rotating cast of Russian bureaucrats and soldiers, with each group practicing its own religion, following its own calendar, wearing its own traditional garb, and speaking its own language. Even the town's name depended on the tongue pronouncing it. The Poles called it Janów Poleski, the Russians pronounced it Ivanovo, and the Jews referred to it as Yanowa, Yanow, or Yanow al-yad Pinsk.

Yanow was reached by four main roads that met in the center of town in a wide-open square, ringed by houses and shops, with a rusty, hand-drawn water well in the middle. On one side of the square rose the grand spires of the Russian Orthodox church. On the other stood the brick church of the Polish Catholics, built on the site where Saint Andrzej of Bobola was brutally murdered by the Cossacks in 1657. Decades later Jewish children of the town, now long grown up, would still describe the shiver of fear they felt whenever they heard the tolling of the church's bells, "with their clanging of *bim-bam, bim-bam.*"

Most of the town's buildings were unpainted wooden affairs with one to three rooms, topped by peaked roofs of straw. The great landmarks of Jewish life were the public bathhouse and the six book-lined synagogues. The Jews lived in the center of town around the market, with their shops, synagogues, and burial grounds tucked in among the tightly packed homes. The gentiles—the *goyim* in Yiddish—lived on the side streets and the edges of town.

Life in Yanow was not easy. "Without exception everyone had to work hard for a living," recalled one townsperson. As in most market towns, Jews were Yanow's storekeepers, tailors, shoemakers, carpenters, blacksmiths, butchers, and teachers. The gentiles controlled the local government and all occupations forbidden to Jews.

The goyim and the *yidn*, as the Jews called themselves, lived side by side but separately, each cocooned in their own cultural traditions and religious rituals. Or as a popular proverb put it, "Live among Jews, do business among Goyim." Some townsfolk spoke of the goyim as a "hard and belligerent people to get along with." For the most part, however, the two communities enjoyed a "mutually contemptuous friendliness."

For *yidn* and goyim alike, the market square was the economic engine of the shtetl. In the summer, the marketplace was dusty and rutted, swarming with flies and stinking of manure. In the winter, thick layers of ice made it treacherous to cross. During the rainy seasons, the square was transformed into a deep pit of black mud that swallowed up shoes, boots, and galoshes. Children remembered times when the mud was so deep it reached to their parents' knees and they had to be carried to school on grown-up shoulders.

At dawn on designated market days, the square would begin to fill up with wagons, pushcarts, and baskets of goods for sale as farmers and peasants from the outlying countryside arrived with their harvests from the forest and farms—grain, fur pelts, hog bristles, sponges, mushrooms, livestock, vegetables, and fruit—to trade with the Jewish merchants.

By midmorning the square would be packed, the air ringing with the braying of women bargaining in Polish, Yiddish, and various dialects of Russian, the melodies of the town's klezmer band or traveling gypsy musicians, and the sounds of livestock. From the open windows of the schools and prayer houses drifted the sounds of children reciting and men arguing noisily over scripture, and the musical cadences of Hasidic prayers.

In the late afternoon the stalls began closing, and the farmers wandered off to the Jewish-run tavern to spend their profits. Then "it was impossible to walk through the street because of all the drunks around filling the street with shouting and wild singing," recalled one Yanower. By daylight, all that would be left were piles of dung and a few sodden peasants sleeping off the vodka and ale, the silence interrupted only by the sound of morning prayers and the clanging chain of the water well.

If the market day was the secular highlight of the week, the Sabbath was the spiritual heart. As sundown approached on Friday, the town beadle would walk through the streets banging on shutters and calling the Jews to put down their tools and close up their shops. The men hurried off to the bathhouse, then to the synagogues for evening prayers, before returning home for the Sabbath meal. "There was a special type of quiet that would prevail on Friday nights outside of town, and you could only hear the sounds of Sabbath melodies being sung from the homes," one townsperson recalled wistfully.

Yet if Yanow could boast all the virtues of small-town life, it also harbored all the vices. The ruling concept of derekh erets—"propriety," or the proper order of society—could be as constricting as it was comforting. For those who didn't fit in, or who longed for something more, it could feel dull, small-minded, self-righteous, and judgmental. Here everyone knew everything about everyone and had for generations.

Underneath the homey air, Yanow was rife with small-town snobbery and internal divisions. The Hasidic Jews looked down on the merely orthodox, the Zionists railed against the socialists, the progressives scorned the traditionalists—and vice versa. Those who showed too much aspiration for their social station were ridiculed for putting on airs. Anyone who showed too much independence from the common wisdom of the community was sure to feel the lash of gossiping tongues.

Social status in the shtetl followed a strict caste system, in which stature was measured by *yiches*, defined in the phrase of one shtetl-dweller as a "lineage of wealth and lineage of learning." At the top of the scale were rabbis and religious scholars, and those whose family possessed a pedigree of exceptional charity, piety, and above all, education. Just below were the *sheyne yidn*, the well-to-do elite, the merchants and small factory owners, who ran the community's institutions. A steep step down were the middle classes, the businesspeople who were not rich but still enjoyed great respect. Next came the *proste*, or ordinary Jews, the skilled artisans who possessed special expertise, like high-end carpenters, furriers, and custom tailors like Moshe Adler. Below them were the less skilled artisans, such as shoemakers and common tailors.

Lower still on the pecking order were the *luftmenschen*—literally translated as "people made of air," who had no steady occupation, special skills, or resources and were forced to "coax a living out of thin air," hustling for a few kopeks by picking up odd jobs or acting as middlemen, buying a little bit of something and then selling it for a small profit. Those in the dirtiest jobs, like water carriers and poor servant girls, stood just above beggars at the bottom of the scale. Some towns even admitted, reluctantly, to harboring a few thieves, forgers, and prostitutes. "Sure we had a brothel. What shtetl and town didn't?" as one shtetl dweller said defensively. "What's the matter, a Jewish girl can't become a prostitute?"

Perhaps most stultifying of all, once the townsfolk put someone "in their place," it was nearly impossible to break free of that identity, to become someone new. In the wry words of one common saying: "God protect us from Gentile hands and from Jewish tongues."

☾

To have a girl as his firstborn child did nothing for Moshe Adler's status in Yanow. With a boy child, there was honor, but a girl? What was a girl but a source of *tsuris*, aggravation and worry? Everyone had heard the well-worn passage from the warnings of the ancient Hebrew scribe Ben Sira:

> A daughter is a secret anxiety to her father, and worry over her robs him of sleep; when she is young, for fear she may not marry, or if married, for fear she may be disliked; while a virgin, for fear she may be seduced and become pregnant in her father's house; or having a husband, for fear she may go astray, or, though married, for fear she may be barren. Keep strict watch over a headstrong daughter, or she may make you a laughingstock to your enemies, a byword in the city and the assembly of the people, and put you to shame in public gatherings.

For good reason were Jewish men accustomed to say as one of their first prayers of the morning: "Blessed be He who did not make me a woman."

But Moshe was different. He and Pearl enjoyed a not-uncommon emotional dynamic, one that shaped the lives of many of history's most accomplished women: a father who was unconventional but self-certain, frustrated in his own ambitions, and eager to channel them into his oldest child, even if she had the misfortune of being a girl. In turn, Pearl had all the attributes of an eldest daughter who was treated like a son: confident, quick-witted, competitive, and determined to prove she was just as capable as any boy. "I have inherited many of my father's traits," she insisted; "his restlessness and quick temper, his adventurous and inquisitive spirit, his stubborn refusal to be satisfied with second best."

Pearl's family line had long shown signs of ambition—a yen for *yiches*—that transcended their status as mere small-town tailors. Family lore tells of how in 1833 Pearl's great-grandfather changed the last names of two of his sons from the humble and starkly descriptive Kravets—from *krawiec*, Polish for "tailor"—to the more heroic name of Adler, adapted from the German word for "noble eagle." No one quite remembered why.

Some relatives said it was because a family member traveling to America had been helped by a German Jew named Adler, and the boys were renamed in his honor. Others had heard that the two sons had fallen gravely ill and their father followed the ancient superstition of changing their names to fool the Angel of Death. More prosaically, and more likely, the names were changed to fool the draft board of the Russian army, which conscripted young Jews based on the number of males in each family. However it came to pass, the name Adler was an act of *chutzpah*, of ambition and audacity, and a promise that Pearl planned to redeem.

The Adlers proudly counted themselves among the *balebatisheh yiden*, the respectable Jews, of Yanow. Moshe was the striving second son out of a brood of twelve. His oldest brother Yishai was the pride of the family. Yishai burned with both the Adler ambition and the reformist fever of the era. He was one of Yanow's first Zionists, campaigning passionately for the creation of a Jewish state and an outspoken advocate of replacing Yiddish with Hebrew as the everyday language of the Jews. He opened one of the region's first progressive Hebrew schools in the nearby shtetl of Gomel. Years later he would become one of the founders of the Israeli city of Tel Aviv.

Moshe inherited none of his older brother's religious or political fervor. But he cut his own kind of figure around town, cultivating the image of a modern man of the world. He was something of a dandy, always impeccably dressed and later sporting a modern Van Dyke, as it was known—a fine, full mustache and small beard—a marked departure from the bushy traditional beard worn by his father and brother.

Long after there were no more Jews in Yanow, Moshe's neighbors remembered his enthusiastic charity and willingness to flout convention. On one memorable occasion, he was trying to collect a large sum of money for a poor family in town, and as a joke, some of the young men promised to contribute to the fund if Moshe dared to make a fool of himself by strolling through the market dressed in what they considered to be the absurd garb of the goyim peasants, "a gentile fur hat and felt shoes." "He accepted their ridiculous offer, and the town turned upside down," remembered his neighbor with amusement.

When he was twenty-two years old, Moshe married Gittel Koval. She was petite, well under five feet tall, but had a regal face, with a small nose, high cheekbones, ivory skin, and lustrous brown hair that she wore uncovered. The youngest of five children, "Gittel was very outgoing," in the words of more than one cousin, and her high spirits made her a favorite among her family.

When Gittel gave birth to their first child, they gave her the Hebrew name of Pearl, meaning "fruit" or "result." A little over a year later the pins in Moshe's bottom began to tingle, and he set off on his first trip to America, leaving his young bride alone to run the house and business. Gittel became, in the word of her cousins, a "real *balaboosta*"—an unusually efficient and hospitable homemaker. "She was the boss of the house."

While Gittel had plenty of reason to complain, there were also distinct advantages to Moshe's absences. Every time he came home, she seemed to become pregnant. In Moshe's eyes, "as in the eyes of the village, a wife's place was either in the kitchen or in childbed," remembered Pearl, and "my subdued self-effacing little mother, alternated uncomplainingly between them."

A year or so after Pearl arrived, Gittel finally gave birth to a boy. After this, babies arrived with punishing regularity. Over the next decade, Gittel bore five boys: Berl, Srol Lieb, Jechial, Szloma, and Szamay, and a second daughter named Slawa. Some ten years later the last of the children arrived, a boy called Baruch. With so many babies coming so quickly, it was a blessing to have a girl child first. Boys might be good for praying, but they were useless when it came to tending toddlers, peeling potatoes, or milking the cow, while her husband traipsed across Europe and the Atlantic Ocean.

"By Yanow standards we were well off," recalled Pearl. She was raised in the bosom of a large, close-knit clan whose warmth eased the daily scramble to make a living. The Adlers lived in a two-story wooden house nestled in a large yard surrounded by a tall wooden fence. Here they kept vegetable and flower gardens, an outhouse, a woodshed, and a barn to shelter their milk cow, horse, and chickens. During the day the living room served as a fitting room for Moshe's customers, and at night it became a bedroom for the apprentice and maid-of-all-work.

Little Pearl grew quickly into a sweet dumpling of a child. Like her mother, she possessed a buoyant personality and natural resourcefulness that made her a favorite among her cousins. Like her father, she bubbled with a curiosity and boldness that set her apart from the general run of girls. She inherited a quick mind and an equally quick temper, and she soon mastered the market woman's talent for colorful curses.

Pearl's first schoolroom was her mother's kitchen. Here she was taught to keep a kosher home, learning to cook, clean, and sew and to say the blessing over the Sabbath candles. In the evening, she might gather with her cousins to play games or to pluck geese and chicken feathers for beds or pillows while telling stories or singing folk songs. Once a week she accompanied her mother to the bathhouse, and on Fridays she helped prepare for the Sabbath. She learned to make homey dishes like chicken soup, *cholent*, a long-simmering pot roast, and chopped liver, a skill that would come in surprisingly handy over the years. From their servant girl, she picked up a bit of Russian.

But as she got older, Pearl began to yearn for lessons beyond the kitchen. "As long, almost, as I can remember I have been driven by a fierce desire to get an education," she wrote years later. Around age five, she had her first exposure to formal schooling, when her oldest brother Berl was taken to the local *cheder* or religious school, where for the next ten years he would study the Torah. For boys, there was no higher calling than studying the word of God. As the old ladies liked to say, "A boy stuffed with learning is worth more than a girl stuffed with banknotes."

By contrast, women were expected to be pious but not learned. As the Jewish American writer Mary Antin recalled with chagrin, if a girl could "sign her name in Russian, do a little figuring, and write a letter in Yiddish to the parents of her betrothed, she was called *wohl gelehrent*— well educated." For a girl, life climaxed with her wedding, and that was not a romantic choice but an economic transaction, requiring parental negotiations, contracts, and a dowry.

Instead, a woman's worth was measured by how well she helped her husband live according to God's law, freeing him from worldly cares so he could study God's word. Men, they "were learners, not earners," as one woman put it. A good wife often handled the family business, making her much more financially savvy than her husband. Instead of Hebrew, which they were discouraged from learning, women often spoke Russian, Polish, or other local dialects and possessed good math and negotiation skills, learned in the marketplace.

The one thing girls did not do was study the laws of God. For in the well-worn words of the ancient Rabbi Eliezer: "He who teaches his daughter Torah is teaching her promiscuity."

☾

Pearl was only three years old when an ill wind began blowing across the Pale of Settlement. In February 1903, the body of a Christian boy was discovered on the outskirts of the city of Kishinev in the Russian province of Bessarabia. A local newspaper accused the Jews of murdering the boy in a plot to use his blood to bake matzo for the Passover holiday, a preposterous lie that whipped up anti-Jewish rage.

On Easter Sunday, a mob led by local priests descended on Kishinev, slaughtering forty-seven Jews, wounding hundreds more, and destroying the Jewish sections of the city. Word of the Kishinev pogrom spread like wildfire, prompting painful soul-searching among the Jewish community. In a city where over one-third of the population were Jews, why had there been no resistance to the pogrom, no fighting back?

That fall the violence came closer to home. On September 11, 1903, at a fair to mark the beheading of John the Baptist in the town of Gomel, where Moshe's brother Yishai lived, a Jewish fishmonger got into a heated argument with a Christian customer, sparking a brawl that resulted in the death of a Russian peasant. Three days later a wild, drunken mob of Russian workmen and peasants returned to the market square determined to take revenge on the town's Jews.

This time the Jews of Gomel were prepared. The *pogromers* were met by armed self-defense units wielding iron bars, revolvers, and knives, organized by the Bund, the Jewish Socialist party, and their rivals in the Po'alei Zion party. This time it "was a fight rather than a pogrom," as Russia's only official Yiddish newspaper described the gruesome scene in Gomel. "Even women fought," marveled a correspondent to *The New York Times*. "Their physical agility and the correctness of their aim was not at all that of a race of cringing peddlers." A new pattern had been set. The Jews would no longer back down so easily.

Unfortunately, this new militancy could do little to protect them from the political instability that was rapidly engulfing Russia. In February 1904, Japan attacked the Russian navy, plunging the empire into war.

In need of soldiers, the Russian army began drafting Jews in massive numbers.

When the army suffered a series of crushing defeats, the government orchestrated a secret campaign of anti-Semitic propaganda, laying the blame on treasonous, revolutionary Jews who had sabotaged Mother Russia on the home front. The government began funneling support to the Black Hundreds, a right-wing vigilante group whose rallying cry was *Bey zhidov!*—"Beat the Jews!" The Black Hundreds helped disseminate thousands of copies of the most insidious of anti-Semitic hoaxes, *The Protocols of the Elders of Zion,* a fictional document claiming to be a secret Jewish plan for global domination. Led by the Black Hundreds, pogroms erupted across the Pale of Settlement.

Local Jewish defense organizations fought back, but with the police and government tacitly backing the vigilantes, they were easily outmatched. Jewish migration from Russia, which had been steadily increasing, suddenly doubled.

Within Yanow, the close-knit Jewish community was splintering from the pressure of these outside forces. Disillusioned young people were turning away from religious orthodoxy to embrace radical politics, secular education, and modern ideas. Young men were shaving their beards and trading their long gabardine coats for the Western suits of the gentile. Young women were refusing to don the traditional wig of the wife or to marry according to their parents' wishes. Some of the bolder young people of the town began attending secret meetings in the forests, circulating underground publications, and organizing surreptitious rebellions against the local authorities.

In Pinsk and other industrial cities, the socialist movement, with its radical vision of a new economic order, was sweeping through the Jewish communities. In Yanow, where there were no large factories, socialism was generally regarded with suspicion. Here Zionism was the great local passion. But Russian officials considered Zionism and socialism equally dangerous and thus declared them equally illegal.

When Pearl was around five years old, the political and social unrest came to a bloody climax. In January 1905 government troops massacred a band of striking workers outside the Winter Palace in St. Petersburg. Fury at the czar's ruthless response sparked a wave of strikes, protests, and pogroms that spread across the empire, climaxing in an attempt to replace the Russian autocracy with a democratically elected parliament.

For a brief moment, the public pressure seemed to work. Terrified by the prospect of a popular uprising, Czar Nicholas II agreed to the creation of a national constitution and a parliament. But by the end of 1905, it was clear the revolution had crumbled. Jews were again made the scapegoat for the failed uprising. Russian authorities arrested Jewish activists and outlawed Jewish organizations of all kinds. Fed by the surge of official anti-Semitism, a new wave of pogroms, more brutal than ever before, tore through the Pale of Settlement.

☾

Pearl was too little to fully understand the hushed conversations and worried expressions of the grown-ups, but the air of anxiety was unmistakable. It could be heard in the fretful way people waited for mail to arrive with the latest news, and in the whispered talk of organizing a self-defense force.

It could be felt in the increasingly tense relations with the goyim of the town. People now shuttered their windows and barred their doors after sunset. Mothers kept their children home during market days, for fear that a squabble over the price of a chicken or a drunken scuffle outside the tavern could quickly escalate into a riot. Always, they kept an ear cocked for the cry of *Mir sholgn yidn*—"They are beating the Jews!"—echoing through the streets as a call for help or a warning to hide.

It could be seen in the increasingly crowded roads as Jews, driven out of their own villages by pogroms or government directives, straggled into Yanow, bearing horrifying tales of being attacked with knives, clubs, and scythes, of old men hacked to death with axes and pregnant women with their bellies slit open, of homes and businesses burned to the ground and people whose hair had turned white overnight from fear.

It could be felt in the tightening vise of new government restrictions and mass arrests on the flimsiest of pretexts. It could be measured in the rising demand for bribes and kickbacks to Russian policemen and bureaucrats, and in the humiliation of watching one's parents grovel and deceive.

"Between the Czar whom you had never seen, and the policemen whom you knew too well, you pictured to yourself a long row of officials of all sorts, all with their palms stretched out to receive your father's money. You knew your father hated them all, but you saw him smile and bend as he filled those greedy palms," as one bitter shtetl girl put it. "I knew how to dodge and cringe and dissemble before I knew the names of the seasons."

As she got older, Pearl grew increasingly restless in this oppressive atmosphere. Anyone with one good eye could see there was nothing for her here. Boys at least had religious school and charitable groups to occupy them, but for girls there was nothing. As late as 1907, remembered one girl from Yanow, "we still did not have kindergartens nor a public school." Instead, parents who could spare a little money hired private tutors to teach their daughters at home, in the few hours that could be stolen from the endless round of chores. "We would be grouped together in groups of four or five girls and studied for one hour a day," remembered one Yanower. But even that was haphazard and temporary.

Between 1907 and 1910, local governments expelled thousands of Jews from their homes throughout the countryside and in larger cities like Kiev, driving the dispossessed into a shrinking number of shtetls. In Yanow, the crowding led to ruinous competition, lowering everyone's standard of living. No matter how clever or hardworking they were, there were simply too many shoemakers, tailors, blacksmiths, and shopkeepers. The once-comfortable town was now filled with beggars and *luftmenschen* who lived always on the edge of hunger.

Then in May 1910 the liberal and socialist factions in the Russian government introduced a proposal to abolish the Pale of Settlement. Enraged, the right-wing and monarchist organizations responded with a new cascade of ferocious anti-Jewish policies.

To many parents, it was increasingly clear that there was little future for their children in Yanow. Those who could scrape up enough money, remembered one girl, began sending "their children to big towns and cities to continue their education, some to become secretaries, some to work in shops, some for a profession, and some for yeshivas, for they saw that in a small town it was not so easy for Jews to get their lives settled."

Pearl was determined to be one of the girls who got out. "By the time I was twelve all my hopes and plans for the future hinged on my winning a scholarship to the Gymnazia at Pinsk," she remembered. In Pinsk, women were teachers, factory workers, charitable reformers, and political organizers of every variety. They could live alone if they chose, and young women and men could socialize freely without chaperones or ruinous gossip. Pinsk's spunky girls would go on to be some of the most famous women in twentieth-century Jewish history, including the best-selling novelist Anzia Yezierska, the political activist Emma Goldman, and Golda Meir, the fourth prime minister of the state of Israel.

"I knew I was starting with a couple of strikes against me since only one scholarship was available to the Jewish children in Yanow and custom decreed it should go to a boy," recalled Pearl. "But I screwed up my courage and sought help from the most learned man in our village, the Rabbi."

Pearl was lucky, but many girls were not so fortunate. When fifteen-year-old Emma Goldman begged her father to let her continue in school instead of marrying the man he'd chosen, he furiously refused, shouting as he threw her French grammar book into the stove, "Girls do not have to learn much! All a Jewish daughter needs to know is how to prepare gefüllte fish, cut noodles fine, and give the man plenty of children." The father-daughter generation gap would become one of the great themes of Jewish American literature, explored by Isaac Bashevis Singer, Sholem Asch, Mary Antin, and Anzia Yezierska, and the subject of the classic Broadway musical *Fiddler on the Roof*.

But Moshe recognized the value of a clever daughter, especially in attracting a good husband. He gave not only his blessing but also the money to pay the rabbi to prepare her for the entrance exam. Every day the rabbi tutored her in the Russian language, Hebrew history, and mathematics.

"What a temptation to say that hard work and persistence paid off, and that as the villagers cheered and the family wept for joy I was handed the scholarship (who's going all the way to Yanow just to make a liar of me?) by Rasputin in person," Pearl wrote years later.

"But the truth is I never did know how I made out, for when prize day came around I had already traveled many miles along a road which did not lead to Pinsk."

☾

What changed Pearl's fate? Perhaps it was the latest round of anti-Semitic decrees, including the expulsion of Jewish students from Russian schools and the tightening of educational restrictions. It could have been the ominous news from Kiev that a Jewish man named Mendel Beilis had been arrested and charged with the ritual murder of a gentile boy, setting off a vicious anti-Semitic backlash in the Russian press. Fear was mounting throughout the Pale as the date of Mendel Beilis's trial approached in late December 1913. No matter what the verdict, it was sure to be a calamity for the Jews.

Then there was the loosening of old ties. After the Gomel pogrom, Moshe's oldest brother Yishai emigrated to Palestine with his family. In 1906 Moshe's beloved father died, and several more of his siblings abandoned Yanow for the far-off city of Chicago. Several members of Gittel's family left around the same time to settle in New York City.

Perhaps it was simply necessity. Moshe's own house was filling up with hungry mouths even as making a living was becoming ever more difficult. The arrival in Yanow of a new, rabidly anti-Semitic chief official added to the pressure. Or it may just have been the restlessness of the Wandering Jew.

Whatever the reason, Moshe came to a decision. "My father, who was always toying with the idea of transplanting the family to America, finally hit upon the plan of sending us over in installments," remembered Pearl. When he heard that a cousin was sailing to the United States, Moshe decided that Pearl would accompany her.

With typical perversity, the Russian government put huge hurdles in the way of Jews who wished to emigrate. Getting permission to leave required waiting many months and paying an exorbitant fee to obtain the proper papers—or an equivalent price in bribes and forgeries to circumvent the process. A steamship ticket to the United States cost approximately forty dollars, and most emigrants paid a steamship agent or travel broker—what we would now call a human smuggler—to shepherd them to the seaport for an extra fee. The brokers planned the route, paid off the soldiers at the border crossings, arranged places to sleep, and handled any necessary bribes along the way. On top of that, all emigrants were required by law to have the equivalent of twenty dollars in hand when they arrived, to ensure that they would not become beggars or thieves. Altogether it was a substantial investment.

At first, Pearl was distraught at the idea of leaving her family to travel alone to America. Her mother was beside herself, weeping and begging Moshe not to send away her little girl. But as Pearl put it, "A husband's word, of course, was law, and my mother's tears, her protests that I was only a baby, cut no ice with father."

To contemporary eyes, it might seem shocking to send a thirteen-year-old girl alone thousands of miles across a hostile continent and a dangerous ocean to live among strangers. Indeed, the U.S. authorities felt much the same. So in that same year of 1913, they mandated that no girl under the age of sixteen and unaccompanied by parents be legally admitted into the country (a rule that was routinely broken).

Most people, however, simply found it impossible to scrape up enough money for an entire family to emigrate at the same time. In most ethnic groups, husbands or young males would go ahead to find work in the United States, then put away money to bring over the rest of his family. But for Jews of this period, who expected women to shoulder worldly responsibilities from an early age, teenage daughters were commonly the first in their families to travel to America, where they would live with friends or relatives while they saved enough money to pay for their family's steamship tickets. In 1913, the year Pearl arrived at Ellis Island, the Hebrew Sheltering and Immigrant Aid Society estimated that 13,588 "unaccompanied Jewish girls" came through the port of New York, out of the 101,330 Jews who immigrated from eastern Europe. Gittel's own thirteen-year-old niece had set off for America only a few months earlier, and she was fine. Pearl's twelve-year-old brother Berl would follow several weeks later, and the rest of the family would not be far behind.

All the same, townsfolk could fill a mother's ears with dire warnings about the dangers of sending a child alone to face conniving steamship agents, brutal police officers, and roughneck sailors. She could have her few possessions stolen by pickpockets, grifters, or unscrupulous ticket brokers along the way. Most terrifying of all were the stories of ruthless kidnappers who snatched girls off the ships and sold them into the brothels of Argentina.

But Pearl enjoyed the remarkable, sometimes foolhardy resilience of a teenager, and "once I grew used to the idea, I was excited and eager to be on my way," she remembered.

On the day of her daughter's departure, Gittel packed an old potato sack with a few belongings, along with four loaves of black bread, four salamis, some garlic, and apples. Pearl bade a tearful goodbye to her four little brothers and finally her beloved mother. Then she and her father set out for the railway station in the next village, where he solemnly hugged her and then turned her over to the travel broker. As soon as she settled into the stiff wooden seats of the third-class compartment of the passenger train, exhaustion overwhelmed her excitement. She fell asleep almost instantly.

When she awoke, she found her cousin huddled on the seat next to her. "She was a pale, sad-eyed woman, with an air of mournful abstraction," remembered Pearl. The two were part of a group of emigrants heading for the German port city of Bremen in the Prussian Empire. Nearly one thousand miles lay between Yanow and Bremen, but the most difficult part of the journey came at the outset, as they crossed the western frontier where Russia bordered Poland and eastern Prussia.

The travel broker dealt with the logistics of the trip, herding them along rough country roads and onto trains, handling the bribes and dealing with officials. Some of their group were traveling with forged or incomplete papers, or leaving the country illegally to avoid the draft, so they had to sneak across the border into Germany to avoid the authorities. When they got to Danzig, they left the train, and the broker led them into a series of murky tunnels where they could slip past the Russian soldiers manning the border.

Emerging in Germany, the travelers boarded another train that took them on to Bremen, where they would be processed by the steamship company. Bremen was one of the busiest and most modern of the debarkation points that funneled immigrants onto ships, and it was run with the efficiency and ruthlessness of a factory assembly line. A bewildering number of officials and bureaucrats conducted innumerable inspections of papers, possessions, and persons. The most dreaded was the final medical inspection, right before setting sail. Terrible stories, many of them true, were told of doctors turning away people with bad eyes or weak lungs and sending them home with nothing.

Young, healthy, and confident, Pearl passed through the bureaucratic gauntlet quickly and without complaint. But her cousin grew increasingly frightened until finally she broke down into tears. "I am afraid," the young woman wailed. "I cannot go to a strange land. We must ask the official for permission to go back. You ask him, Pearl; you're little. He won't be angry with you."

"When I saw it was useless to argue with her, I made my first adult decision," Pearl remembered. "Let my cousin go back; I'd go on! I went over to the emigration officer, turned on the tears, and talked him into giving me a re-entry permit—one only." She brought the permit to her waiting cousin, then declared that she was heading on to America and bade her farewell.

That night Pearl boarded the German steamship SS *Neckar*, setting sail on November 27, 1913. Built in 1900, it was newer, cleaner, and more spacious than many of the steamers that ferried immigrants from Europe to America. Nonetheless, it was designed for efficiency and profit rather than luxury. While the first- and second-class rooms were roomy, even elegant, down in steerage people were packed like pickled herrings with no pretense of privacy or comfort. The third-class accommodations were tucked into the hold at the back of the ship, where the rocking of the waves was most violent. Each dimly lit compartment slept 200 to 400 people on thin mattresses atop narrow wooden bunks, stacked one above the other, three high.

In good weather, the sturdier immigrants could escape to the open air on the crowded third-class deck. But it was December, and the voyage was tempestuous. The cold wind and merciless waves drove the immigrants down into the cabins, where seasickness pinned them miserably to their berths. Occasionally a wave of vomiting would run across the hold, adding to the stench of body odor, garlic, damp clothing, and the few, inadequate toilets. For those who had enough stomach left to eat, meals were served out of huge kettles, ladled into tin dinner pails. Hungry passengers crowded around, pushing and shoving. Blessed with a strong stomach, Pearl felt fine and well fed from her potato sack of provisions.

For many passengers it was a harrowing journey spent in a miserable stupor. But for Pearl, it was a glorious adventure. It was thrilling to be surrounded by the babble of Russian, Polish, Swedish, Italian, Danish, and Hungarian voices. "I would stay up most of the night snacking on salami and singing Russian folk songs—to the annoyance of my ailing shipmates who quite often rewarded my vocalizing with a cussing-out," she remembered. "But when the epidemic of seasickness subsided they made a pet of me, and for the rest of the voyage I had it—as the saying goes—good."

One morning, after nearly two weeks with nothing in sight but the steel-blue ocean, the weather was cold but clear enough that the third-class deck was crammed with passengers taking in the fresh air. Suddenly, recalled Pearl, "everyone rushed to the rail and began screaming and waving. I was certain that we were sinking and stayed where I was, too frightened to move. Then one of the men grabbed me and set me up on his shoulder."

There, towering above her on the horizon, was the copper-green figure of a woman. In one hand she raised a torch in welcome, and in the other she held what looked to be a book.

"'Look!'" the man shouted in Yiddish. "'The American Lady! The Statue of Liberty!'

"And in a moment I was shouting as wildly as the rest of them. We had come to the Golden Land."

Pearl transformed from greenhorn to Coney Island vamp, 1914

3

The Jazz Baby

The hardest part came at the very end. Little Pearl had been a brave girl all through the long, frightening journey from Russia. She'd slipped past German border guards, eluded swindlers, pickpockets, and kidnappers, and weathered a gut-wrenching voyage across the Atlantic Ocean.

But now, as she stood by the ticket window in the majestic oak-timbered waiting room of the Union Railroad Station in Springfield, Massachusetts, she found herself fighting to hold back tears. One after another, the other passengers on the train from New York were greeted by loved ones and then trundled away. Soon the train chugged off, and the waiting room was empty, but still no one came for the pale little girl in the threadbare coat. "I, left alone with my potato sack, discovered that I was tired and hungry and homesick," Pearl recounted later. "All I wanted to do was cry."

The stationmaster came over and looked at the slip of paper pinned to Pearl's coat, with the address of her intended destination. Speaking in German, a language close enough to Yiddish that she could pick out his meaning, he told her not to be scared, that someone would soon come fetch her. He gave her a piece of candy. "Feeling a little better, I settled down to wait, but my morale was completely shattered when it grew dark and the big electric signs flashed on," recalled Pearl. "I had never before seen anything like them, and I was petrified."

It was only one long day after she'd disembarked on December 10,

1913, at the immigrant inspection station on Ellis Island, in the New York harbor. Fear mingled with anticipation as the passengers made their way down the gangplank and into the Great Hall to be processed. This place was dubbed "The Isle of Tears" for good reason. Everyone had heard the anguished whispers that people could be turned away for mysterious reasons, separated from their families, and forced to return to their homelands with nothing.

Swept along by sheer exhilaration, Pearl passed swiftly through the bureaucratic hurdles that stood between her and her new life. She and her possessions were treated to kill any lice that might have stowed away. Doctors checked the health of her lungs, eyes, feet, and spine and examined her for mental defects. Clerks examined her entry papers and peppered her with questions in Yiddish: Who were her parents? Where and when was she born? Were her parents married when she was born? What was her religion? Was she an imbecile? A criminal? An anarchist? A polygamist? A prostitute? To what address was she going? Did she have a job waiting for her? Did she have twenty dollars in her possession to prove that she was not a pauper? If anyone noticed that she looked awfully young for someone who claimed to be seventeen years old, they let the lie pass.

For a lively girl like Pearl, the greatest danger lurked beyond the gates of Ellis Island. The lurid fears of the old folks at home were not as far-fetched as they seemed. Young girls who came to New York without family, money, or the ability to speak English, who had no one to meet them at the immigration station, were often no better than lambs let loose among wolves. The port of New York was infested with men—"white slave traders," as they were then called, or "sex traffickers" in today's language—who lured newly arrived immigrant girls to New York's vice dens or onto ships bound for South American brothels.

But Pearl, for the first time in her life, was kept safe by the vigilant bureaucrats and moral uplifters who made it their mission to steer young girls from the path of evil. A Yiddish-speaking volunteer or immigration agent sent a telegram to the guardian listed on Pearl's paperwork, one Israel Resnick, formerly of Yanow and now a resident of Springfield, Massachusetts. Then the agent put her, with her final address pinned to her coat and her potato sack in hand, on a train to her new home, some four hours to the north. Speaking in Yiddish, the agent explained that she must sit still when it was moving.

"He could have saved his breath," remembered Pearl wryly. "Of course I would sit still. I was too scared to move a muscle." When an obviously American lady sat down beside her, Pearl stared with fascination at her strange clothing. But when the lady smiled and tried to speak to her, Pearl shyly shook her head in wide-eyed silence. She spent the next several hours staring out the window at the unfamiliar winter landscape and listening to the babble of voices around her, trying to make out what they meant.

"Excitement sustained me till I was in the depot," she said, but as the minutes passed into hours, she slipped into despair. Finally, at long last, an older couple appeared and came up to claim her. After a brusque introduction, Israel Resnick tossed her potato sack over his shoulder, then motioned to his wife and the three of them set off for her new home; "I remember looking back and smiling at the station master, who waved good-bye."

☾

Why Moshe had chosen Springfield, Massachusetts, for Pearl's new hometown is a mystery. After all, they had family in New York and Chicago, where there were old, well-established Jewish communities, unlike Springfield. Instead, she was sent to stay with what the Jews called *landsmen*, people who came from the same village or town, whom she did not know at all. Odder still, several weeks after Pearl left Yanow, Moshe sent out the next installment in his plan, buying a steamship ticket for her next-younger brother, Berl. Berl landed in the port of Baltimore only a few weeks after Pearl. But instead of joining his sister, he was sent to stay with Gittel's family in Chicago.

Nonetheless, Springfield had promise. In 1913 it was a booming regional metropolis—"a clean, progressive, thrifty city of 100,000"—an American version of Pinsk, if Pinsk had traded its earnest revolutionary aspirations for Springfield's peculiarly American mix of exuberant optimism, passionate boosterism, and to borrow a phrase from the novelist Sinclair Lewis, "one-hundred percent pep."

Springfielders prided themselves on being up-to-date. They boasted of their go-ahead business atmosphere, efficient public institutions, and peaceful labor relations at a time when many cities were being rocked by strikes and lockouts. They bragged of the city's 150 miles of paved, tree-lined streets, its unusual number of telephones, its motorized fire trucks (the first in the world, they insisted), and a model streetcar system that carried contented workers to the city's 330 factories. Long nicknamed "The City of Homes" for its many ornate Victorian houses, local entrepreneurs had recently rechristened it "The City of Progress."

The first Jews had arrived in the city three decades before, a trickle of immigration that swelled as the troubles in Russia worsened. By the time Pearl arrived, it was the largest Jewish community in western Massachusetts and, they noted proudly, the most prosperous. "In fact there is no city where I have seen as many automobiles owned by Jews as there are in Springfield," observed one astonished car salesman in the *Jewish Advocate*, New England's leading Jewish newspaper.

"The City of Progress" may have suited Moshe's tastes. But for Pearl, Springfield was a city of strangers. Her father had sent her to stay in the care of his friend who had left Yanow in 1907, when Polly was just a little girl. Israel Resnick was listed in the city directory as a Hebrew teacher, but like many newly arrived Jews, he paid his bills by working as a self-employed peddler of dry goods. It took him five years to save enough to bring over his wife and four youngest children, in June 1913, only six months before Pearl arrived. Now they were all sharing an apartment along with his oldest daughter, her husband, and their young toddler. By a stroke of luck, the Resnicks had a daughter the same age as Pearl named Rivke.

It was a short walk from the train station to the Resnicks' cramped apartment near the heart of the city's Jewish community, in what was then called the North End. This densely packed neighborhood of wood-framed two- and three-family houses had once been home to the city's Irish population, until new waves of immigrants began to roll in from Italy and Russia. (In the 1960s, these blocks would be demolished to make way for the Massachusetts Turnpike.) Her new neighbors were a mix of Irish Americans, Russian Jews, and a smattering of Germans, Italians, and French Canadians.

For those who have always been at home in their world, among those who speak their native tongue, eat the same foods, and laugh at the same jokes, it takes a great leap to imagine the excitement, fear, and disorientation of making a new life among strangers. Especially for a girl of thirteen. Decades later Pearl would speak of her years in Springfield with a forced cheer that hints at bitter memories.

Her relationship with the Resnicks was odd, she later recalled. "I was fed and clothed and taken care of. No one struck me or spoke to me harshly. No one was unkind. Instead their attitude toward me was one of complete indifference. All my life I had been an affectionate child, demonstrative and outgoing. Now, surrounded by the unresponsive Resnicks, I had to learn to live within myself."

But her excitement about school swept all this aside. On December 15, 1913, less than a week after she stepped onto the shores of the Golden Land, Pearl entered the high-ceilinged halls of the Chestnut Hill Grammar School. With the Russian immigrant's typical disregard for bureaucratic accuracy, she enrolled in the evening school program for "Illiterate Adults" under the very Americanized name of Annie Adler, age sixteen. She was accompanied by her guardian, Israel Resnick, who listed her as living at his address but signed his name as Max Adler, undoubtedly assuming there'd be fewer questions if he seemed to be a family member.

Again, good fortune—and a phalanx of progressive do-gooders and reform-minded bureaucrats—was looking out for the girl. Only three months before Pearl arrived in Massachusetts, the state legislature passed sweeping new child labor laws. For the first time, the state set limits on what age and under what safety conditions children could be employed and how many hours they could work. Most important to her, the new laws also mandated that every minor up to the age of twenty-one who could not read and write in English must attend day school or a public evening school until they reached a fourth-grade level of mastery, with a stiff twenty-dollar fine for any parent or guardian who violated the law.

To top off her luck, Springfield's school system was among the best in the country, with its innovative kindergartens, evening trade schools, and brand-new high schools of commerce and trade. For the rapidly rising tide of foreigners, the city had a generous system of bustling night schools and, most remarkably, the American International College, devoted solely to educating recent immigrants.

At the Chestnut Street Evening School, Pearl made her first American ally in her teacher, a kind woman she later referred to as Mrs. O'Sullivan. Mrs. O'Sullivan patiently took extra time to help the greenhorn girl as she struggled to master English and the strange ways of her new country. "But perhaps the most valuable thing she taught me was to take a joke," remembered Pearl. "Thanks to Mrs. O'Sullivan, when the other kids laughed at the slips I made, I could laugh with them. Being a woman of heart, she understood that for people who have had little opportunity to acquire the social graces, laughter sometimes can be the saving one."

Polly couldn't have chosen a better place to, in the common Yiddish phrase, *oysgrinen zikh*, "ungreen" herself, or become Americanized. Here in Springfield girls of every kind joined clubs, played sports, acted in plays, competed in contests, and attended concerts, dances, and moving picture shows. For the first time in her life, Pearl was mixing with the goyim and enjoying it. Her earliest friends in the United States were the two Irish American girls who lived next door. They included her in their games, taught her English words, "and never made fun of me."

Of course, there were pockets of prejudice. Even progressives would agree that the influx of immigrants over the previous thirty years had radically challenged this city that still proudly boasted of its Puritan forefathers. But here Jews were only one small group among many, and the city consciously strove to be a melting pot—as long as the final flavor of the stew was one hundred percent American.

That first winter Pearl threw herself into her new life with characteristic gusto. One of her few mementos of that time is a photo of herself and a young friend in theatrical costumes, clearly delighted as they posed in a dramatic tableau. In March 1914, Pearl finished her first term of evening school, bringing home a report card brimming with A's, which Israel Resnick signed without one word of praise or comment.

Her pride turned abruptly to ashes when she realized that her good grades were proof that she had well exceeded the nettlesome requirements of the new child labor laws. Now, declared Mr. Resnick, no more school. She had completed the mandatory term of schooling and mastered the basics of English. It was time for her to go to work.

"Since I was only five months away from a diploma, I pleaded with him to allow me to finish, and in the end he relented," she remembered.

She could continue attending evening school, said Israel Resnick, but she must find a job immediately. Here in America everyone paid their own way.

Under the new laws, minors who wanted to quit school had to apply for a certificate from the school superintendent to prove they had reached an educational level equal to the fourth grade. If they wished to work, their guardians were required to provide proof that the child was at least fourteen years of age, in the form of a birth or baptismal certificate, a legal passport, or if all else failed, a testimonial from a medical doctor—none of which she had. Pearl must write to her father and have him sign a false affidavit declaring her to be sixteen, Resnick insisted.

The day after the paper arrived from her father, Pearl obtained her work certificate and found a job in one of the city's many paper factories, most likely in the massive brick factory of U.S. Envelope on Cypress Street. Springfield was a major producer of paper products, an industry that was heavily dependent on cheap female labor. The "City of Progress" was, quite literally, run on the backs of thousands of impoverished young women.

Girls or women did almost all the work at U.S. Envelope, feeding the machines that folded, gummed, and stacked the finished envelopes, then banding and packing the envelopes in boxes. It was repetitive, unskilled labor, with no chance to learn new skills or move up the ladder. For a five-and-a-half-day week, working from six-thirty in the morning to six at night, Pearl earned three dollars, a low wage even among the paper factories. Most of it went to the Resnicks for room and board, leaving her only pennies to spend on her own needs.

Thus she learned the first lesson of the orphan: a girl without parents to take care of her is a second-class citizen in the world. She was crushed to discover that she had risked her life and sacrificed everything only to find she was doomed to spend her days in a backbreaking struggle for food and shelter.

Her brother's fate was even crueler. A photo taken just before Berl left home shows a beaming boy of thirteen or so, with a strong cleft chin, deep-set eyes, and thick black hair slicked back with a patent leather shine. He was short, like all the Adlers, only five feet two, but sturdy. For reasons known only to himself, Moshe sent his young son to stay with

Gittel's cousin in the Maxwell Street neighborhood of Chicago. But she was struggling herself, with a new baby of her own and no time to look after a motherless teenager, so Berl was left to roam the streets.

The squalid and lawless neighborhood of "Bloody Maxwell"—or "Jew Town" in local lingo—was "the Wickedest District in the World," in the considered opinion of the *Chicago Tribune,* and notorious as a nursery for juvenile delinquents. Boys like Berl learned to steal as soon as they could run, snatching fruit and candy from peddlers and small shopkeepers, or boosting the bottles of cream that milkmen delivered to housewives' doorsteps every morning. By the time he was fourteen, he was fast acquiring the skills of the professional thief—a *yegg* or *gonif* in underworld argot—working his way up from casual larceny to serious burglary. A year or so after arriving in America, the cops collared Berl for theft, and he was sentenced to two terms at the St. Charles School for Delinquent Boys.

"There is not much to remember about those years," Pearl lamented later. She joined the new Carnegie free library and spent what little spare time she had reading or writing to her family. The letters from Yanow were full of tragedies: the ravaging of the village by the Cossacks, the death of her little sister from malnutrition.

Cheerful Gittel Adler, who used to bubble with high spirits, showed the toll of separation in a photo snapped in their yard in Yanow surrounded by her four youngest boys. Pearl, to mark her graduation from grammar school, had a set of photographic postcards taken in a studio on Main Street, posing in a white linen dress borrowed for the special occasion. But there was little joy in her solemn expression, and her eyes seem heavy with sadness. Each mirrored the other's sorrow.

But soon enough they would all be together again in the *Goldine Madina.*

☾

By the summer of 1914, Pearl's luck seemed to be changing. On June 24 the *Jewish Advocate* reported that Russia was loosening its emigration policies to allow Jews to leave the country legally and cheaply, dispensing with the need for extortionate fees, forged passports, underground travel brokers, and bloodsucking bribes. Pearl was overjoyed to receive a letter from her father saying that they would soon be sailing for America.

Her high hopes lasted little more than a month. On August 2, 1914, shocked Springfielders opened the pages of the *Springfield Republican* to find the headlines shouting the terrible tidings: GERMANY AND RUSSIA AT WAR. EUROPE'S ARMAGEDDON HAS BEGUN. All transatlantic steamer service to and from the Continent was suspended. Communication between Russia and the United States was almost entirely cut off, with no one leaving and little mail getting through. The War to End All Wars had officially begun, dashing the family's plans to reunite.

All through that summer and fall of 1914, Pearl spent her days in the dismal din of the paper factory. She returned to her studies when the next semester began in December, this time enrolled as Pearl Adler, age fifteen years and nine months. Her last school day, March 25, 1915, was a mix of pride and sadness. Unlike most of her fellow students—including Rivke Resnick—she would not be going on to the evening high school. The Chestnut Street Evening School would be her last formal schooling for the next forty years.

Now there was nothing to keep her in Springfield except an exhausting, dead-end job. "How I was to go about it I had no idea, but I knew that I must make a life for myself," she later recalled. "Was I to spend all my days like a mole, hidden away from the sun, buried behind the dark walls of a factory?"

There were hints of feelings more painful than boredom and discontent. Family lore has it that one day Pearl was seen walking hand in hand down a neighborhood street with a Christian boy. Working and going to school with the goyim was one thing, but for most shtetl Jews, there were few greater taboos than those banning romance—God forbid marriage—with a gentile. Pearl might have been American enough to mix with the goyim, but the Resnicks were not. Shocked by her apostasy, she was now dead to them. The family even sat shiva, the ritual period of mourning, as if she had gone to the grave. They did not kick her out, but after that, they shunned her.

True or not, the old rumor suits Pearl's own story of how she left the "City of Homes" in the spring of 1915. Moshe had told her that they had a cousin who lived in Brooklyn, New York, and she began to think, why not try her luck there? So one night at the dinner table, as the family sat silently chewing their food, she made up her mind.

"I'm going to New York," she declared abruptly and waited tensely for their reaction.

"Pass the mustard, [Rivke]," said Israel Resnick, stone-faced.

☾

Brownsville, New York, was a long, jolting journey by train, subway, and streetcar, through Manhattan, across the East River to the borough of Brooklyn, past Prospect Park and Crown Heights and Eastern Parkway, almost all the way to the swamps of Canarsie, where the metropolis trailed off into marshy wasteland. It was clear as soon as she stepped off the tracks that the streets of *Brunzvil*, as the Jews called it, would not be paved with gold.

The buildings seemed dropped down helter-skelter along the trash-strewn streets. Wood-framed double- and triple-decker apartment houses and brick tenements, festooned with long lines of drying laundry, were interspersed with empty lots of rubble and weeds. Storefront synagogues were tucked among the small factories, stables, garages, pawnshops, butchers, bathhouses, pool halls, and candy stores. The occasional chicken or milk goat still roamed the empty lots, interrupting gangs of children playing hopscotch and punchball—stickball for boys who couldn't scrounge up a stick. Everywhere there were Jews, leaning out of windows, pushing carts and baby carriages, gossiping on stoops, and yelling at children, all in the homey cadences of Yiddish.

Pearl's surprise deepened as she approached the address she had been given. The Resnicks hadn't been rich, but compared to her cousins, they lived like the czar. No. 366 Powell Street was at the end of a long row of six-story, redbrick tenement houses, each crisscrossed by a steep iron fire escape in the front and pierced in the back by a narrow air shaft that let in a sliver of light. Entering the vestibule, it was too dim to see much, but one couldn't miss the stench emanating from the small shared toilets on the hall landing of each floor, always in danger of overflowing, mingling with the odors of the acrid coal-fired kitchen stoves, the kerosene used to battle bedbugs, and the rotting garbage and horse manure wafting up from the streets.

But whatever trepidation Pearl felt disappeared as soon as she stood at the door of their apartment and explained who she was. Her cousin, Breina Freedman, "really made me feel that I was being welcomed from the heart. Pulling me over the threshold, she gave me a big bear hug, the children kissed me and patted me and fussed over me," delighted by her arrival. The Freedmans might have been poor, she remembered, but "they lived like human beings with warm blood in their veins, not like cold fish."

The Freedmans were her mother's people. The dominant force in the family was Pearl's thirty-six-year-old first cousin Breina, the daughter of Gittel's oldest sister. Breina was a tall woman, unlike the rest of the family, but she shared the high cheekbones and commanding temperament of the Koval women. "She was formidable," recalled her nephew, a "real boss, a *balaboosta*," like her aunt Gittel. Warm and generous, with a peppery temper, over the years she would provide a home for many of Pearl's cousins when they first landed in America.

Breina had left Yanow for New York when Pearl was still little, joining her husband Nathan, a quiet man who had come to the United States several years before and worked as a self-employed carpenter. They settled in the bustling Brooklyn neighborhood of Brownsville, where rents were cheap and one could live among fellow Jews. They shared their small apartment with their five children.

Brownsville was "New York's rawest, remotest, cheapest ghetto," as Alfred Kazin, the neighborhood's most eloquent chronicler, described it. It sprang up in the early years of the twentieth century, developed by Jewish garment factory owners and real estate speculators, who promoted Brownsville as a refuge from the crowded tenements and dangerous streets of Manhattan's Lower East Side.

By the time Pearl arrived in 1915, the neighborhood had long ago lost its reputation as an airy suburb. Almost a hundred thousand Jews were crammed into approximately two square miles, so many that it was fast becoming the largest concentration of Jews in America and was dubbed "the Jerusalem of America." Nearly everyone here were *proste yidn*—common Jews—who worked nine- and ten-hour days in the needle or building trades or, if they were unlucky, as *luftmenschen*, buying a little of this, selling a little of that, out of baskets, pushcarts, or a tray hung around the neck.

Years later many Jews would look back on Brownsville with genuine nostalgia as an American shtetl, the last great home of *Yiddishkeit*, where one could live one's whole life without learning a word of English or mixing with the goyim. The neighborhood would become the subject of some of the twentieth century's finest memoirs, novels, and stories, including Alfred Kazin's *Walker in the City* and Henry Roth's *Call It Sleep*. But as in all shtetl stories, the flavor was bittersweet.

Many of these remembrances dwell lovingly on the Brunsvillers' passion for education and self-improvement, on the immigrant parents who sacrificed, and on the children who sought to redeem their sacrifices by leaving the neighborhood and its poverty behind.

But many more, both in and out of Brownsville, considered it "one huge cesspool of illiteracy and hoodlumism," as one writer put it. By the time Polly arrived, it rivaled the Lower East Side in wretchedness and crime. "Brownsville was tougher," remembered one boy whose mother moved him from the Lower East Side in a futile search for something better. "More guys carried guns and instead of six beatings a day there were about six an hour."

"The way we lived it was a miracle that the whole neighborhood didn't end up in the can for life," mused the boxer Sammy Aaronson. "Everyone in Brownsville who grew up honest did it by mistake." Back in those days, remembered one former resident, "every New York Jew could feel certain about one thing; he was superior to anybody living in Brownsville."

Older Jews in the neighborhood looked on with horror as their children spurned the ancient traditions. They laid the blame on America itself, this godforsaken country where all their children seemed to go money-mad. It was the most common of curses: *A klug tzu Kolumbusn*—"A curse on Columbus" (presumably for discovering America). *Gelt, shekels, mezuma*—whatever they called it back in the old country, here in America, in Anzia Yezierska's phrase, "money takes the place of God."

It was easy enough for the old folks to moan and criticize. In the shtetl, as the editor Harry Golden noted pointedly, "money *wasn't* important, since there was none." But in America, with money anything was possible.

And why not? Why shouldn't money be the common denominator in a place where nearly everyone was a stranger? Money was a universal language that everyone understood, no matter who they were or where they came from. For Jews, who were never entirely free of the yoke of anti-Semitism, money was a particularly powerful tool that helped them to transcend—or at least compensate for—the barriers imposed by bigotry.

"Your money is as good as anybody else's money," observed the reporter Michael Herr, "and it doesn't come fairer than that, or more democratic."

☾

Pearl was thrilled to be among family again. Still, it was not easy to be a boarder. The Freedmans' cramped second-floor apartment offered no chance of privacy, and it was easy to feel like an intruder. Pearl slept on a hard leather couch in one of the main rooms. Washing up was done at the kitchen sink, and baths were taken in a tin tub that doubled for laundry or in one of the public bathhouses. Heat came from coin-fed gas meters, keeping the apartment cold and stuffy in the winter. In the summer, the air steamed and stank so of sweat and kerosene that people slept on the roofs and fire escapes. In all but the worst weather, everyone escaped to the street and the stoop in search of air and space.

As soon as she settled in, Pearl found an entry-level job in a corset factory that paid five dollars a week. Although corset making wasn't much, it was better than the paper mill. Corsets were less seasonal than other forms of fashion, so the work was a little steadier than most, and the workshops were reasonably clean and well ventilated, to protect the delicate fabrics from ash, smoke, and debris. The seamstresses were represented by a strong union, and unlike her dead-end job in the paper factory, here she had at least some chance to move up in skill and pay.

But in other ways, her situation was no different. Out of her five-dollar weekly paycheck, she paid her cousins three dollars for room and board and spent $1.20 for carfare and lunches, leaving less than a dollar to spend on clothes, shoes, toiletries, and other necessities. Pearl rose at six a.m. and worked nine to ten hours bent over the needle, a backbreaking job that required constant close attention amid the deafening din of sewing machines. On weeknights she would mend, wash, and iron her clothes, eat a meager meal, and go to bed. On Sundays, her one day off, she slept late in the afternoon, getting up to eat, wash her hair, and then go to sleep again.

Although she was happier living with her cousins, "I was a mole again, spending the long days working, coming out of the factory into darkness," Pearl lamented. "And I felt strongly that it would always be like this for me unless I got more education."

She enrolled again in night classes. After work, she walked a mile each way to and from school, saving the nickel it cost to ride the trolley so she could afford lunch. But this left her so exhausted, she couldn't help drifting off to sleep in class. After returning to her cousins', "Sometimes I'd be so beat that I'd flop down and go to sleep fully dressed," she recalled. With no time to do homework or anything else, she soon gave up on night school.

So Pearl made the factory floor her new schoolroom. Her closest pal was a plump redhead who went by the very American name of Eva. She was "full of bounce and wisecracks, and rumor had it that she was a bit of a rounder"—a girl who liked to party, as we might say today.

Eva and the other girls introduced Pearl to American teen culture, *Brunsvil* style. The lively girls of the corset factory provided a thorough education in American ways, practicing English by singing ragtime song lyrics, gabbing about clothes and the stories they saw at the nickelodeons, sympathizing over old-fashioned parents and newfangled men.

One day after work Eva told Pearl she had a date lined up with a couple of sports, as she called them, and was looking for an extra girl. Did she want to come along? Pearl wasn't sure. Every girl in Brownsville had heard the lurid warnings about "white slavers" who kidnapped innocent girls from dance halls, drugging their drinks or stabbing them with narcotic-filled needles.

Seeing her hesitation, Eva laid a hand on Pearl's arm. "Listen, kiddo," she said, "I know you're a good girl, and no guy's gonna get fresh with you or give you drinks while I'm around. You tell your folks not to worry." Pearl required no more persuasion.

That night she assembled the best of her shabby wardrobe and tried to muster some glamour. "Technically, I guess, this was my début as a 'painted woman,' for I had daringly dusted my nose with cornstarch and rouged my lips with coloring obtained by soaking red tissue paper in a bowl of water." Then it was off to the Nonpareil Dance Hall.

In 1915 Brooklyn, like the rest of America, was in the grip of a dancing craze. New York City boasted hundreds of dance halls, from glitzy ballrooms featuring full orchestras to makeshift dance "academies" tucked up a flight of stairs, or grubby concert saloons enlivened by a piano player or a four-piece band and liquid refreshments. It was cheap entertainment, with unescorted women paying between five and fifteen cents to enter, available nearly every night of the week till the early hours of the morning.

Here you didn't need to know anyone or be formally introduced— the boys just came up and asked you to dance. Back in the old country, girls were "not supposed to talk to a young man, or take a walk, God forbid," as one girl recalled in amazement, but here? "Who was chaperoned? Not in this country."

Around the edges of the room, knots of kids stood chatting and surveying the crowd, and couples sipped on beer, seltzer, or fancy cocktails. Girls could be spotted smoking cigarettes, sitting on boys' laps, singing to the music, shrieking with laughter, sneaking outside or retreating to a dark corner for a little privacy with the boy of their choice. The most popular spot, as many people observed, was the ladies' restroom, which was always packed with girls gossiping, giggling, and puffing on cigarettes. Brownsville was known as the place to go for ragtime music and cocaine, both of which flourished in the local dance halls. In tougher joints, there was usually a slick stone-faced mug or a time-tattered tart in the washroom or the back corner selling small decks of cocaine or heroin.

Pearl was immediately swept away by the pulsing beat, unpredictable rhythms, and brazen melodic hooks of the ragtime band. The sight of the bodies on the dance floor was unlike anything she'd ever seen. The dancers pressed belly to belly, clinging close, and spinning wildly, arms and legs flailing in time to the syncopated beat—everyone moving exactly as they pleased, paying no heed to the dictates of chaperones or formal dance steps.

Within five minutes of setting foot on the floor, remembered Pearl, "I was convinced that was where I wanted to spend the rest of my life. Before the evening was over, I had mastered the waltz and one-step, the two-step and the cake walk, and had been informed by my partner that I was a 'real cute little trick' and had 'the makin's of a nifty stepper.'"

Pearl began going to the hall every Sunday afternoon, becoming a regular among the mob of ragtime-crazed kids. She spent every spare moment practicing her steps and was soon entering dance contests around Brooklyn, winning prizes of candy, kewpie dolls, loving cups, occasionally even cash. "It was considered very hot stuff to jump into a split in the middle or end of a number, and my favorite partner was known as Jack Split because of his skill in this department," remembered Pearl with pleasure. "Like other teams, we had a small but devoted 'fan club,' an unofficial claque, who did their best to applaud us into the prize money when we appeared at the Halsey Theater on amateur nights."

She quickly discovered that while she didn't have much choice in her home life or work, she enjoyed a dizzying freedom in her leisure time. She could escape the ugliness of the tenement and the factory at moving picture theaters, ice cream parlors and picnics, or simply by putting on her best hat and promenading on Pitkin Avenue with a gaggle of girls until late into the night. For Brooklynites, one resident remembered proudly, "Pitkin was Broadway and Fifth Avenue combined." For less decorous fun, she headed to the public playground at Saratoga and Halsey streets, a glorious riot of dance halls, movie theaters, and a boxing club.

But all these amusements paled when she discovered the nickel paradise of Coney Island. Only a five-cent trolley ride from Brownsville, located on a spit of sand at the far edge of Brooklyn, Coney Island was the "Poor Man's Eden," declared Jimmy Durante, who got his start in show business pounding the piano in the Coney Island beer halls. It was world famous for its crowded shoreline and sensational amusement parks, featuring fantastical architecture and rowdy rides that sent riders topsy-turvy, tumbling them together and tossing hats and skirts into the air. "The men like it because it gives them a chance to hug the girls," as one amusement park worker put it, and "the girls like it because it gives them a chance to get hugged."

Coney's streets bustled with concession stands, sideshows, photo booths, penny arcades, and music halls. On sunny days, the beach teemed with folks picnicking and swimming in long woolen bathing suits that could be rented from the bathhouses that dotted the shore. On balmy evenings, they danced in the open-air pavilions perched on wooden piers above the beach.

There was also a more menacing side to the family fun. "Sodom by the Sea" was what reformers and wisecrackers called Coney Island.

Here a holiday-goer could drink, gamble, get a tattoo, have their palm read, watch a prizefight or a burlesque show as well as have their pockets picked, nose punched, and clothes stolen. On Coney's famous Bowery, a dozen saloons stood on every block, where the waiters doubled as pimps and many entertainers were openly gay, often working in drag. Despite efforts to clean out the streetwalkers, prostitutes of both sexes roamed Surf Avenue and held court in the sawdust-strewn saloons. Tucked among the cafés, beer halls, and cigar store bookmakers were scores of small clapboard brothels or houses of assignation, where prostitutes took their prey and couples could rent rooms, no questions asked.

Pearl adored Coney Island. The pages of her photo album are filled with snapshots and postcard portraits of her and her friends, posing in rented bathing suits or their best finery, snuggling up against some fellow with a look of glee. The problem was, even at only a nickel a throw, the cost of these wondrous pleasures added up.

It didn't take long to discover that flirtatious girls who didn't mind being pawed or kissed by a stranger could usually find a fellow willing to pick up the tab for an evening's fun. Bolder girls, who took a more businesslike attitude, flocked to Coney Island for the season, padding their purses by picking up men. Girls who spent too many summers hanging around those Bowery beer halls or "got in Dutch," to borrow Jimmy Durante's euphemism, were ripe recruits for the waiter pimps.

☾

For good or ill, Brownsville's poverty spurred ambition. This dingy, dangerous neighborhood would later become famous as a breeding ground for boxers, gangsters, socialists, intellectuals, entertainers, and strong-willed Jewish mothers, all determined to find a way up and out of the neighborhood. As Alfred Kazin observed, it was "notoriously a place that measured all success by our skill in getting away from it."

Even the hoodlums thought of Brownsville as a training ground on their way to bigger things. "Like a ballplayer, that's me," boasted Harry "Pittsburgh Phil" Strauss, a suspect in at least thirty contract killings for the infamous Murder, Inc. "I figure I get seasoning doing these jobs here. Somebody from one of the big mobs spots me. Then, up to the big leagues."

Poverty made Pearl's generation of Brunsvillers impatient and mistrustful of putting their faith in someone else's hands. "Everything moved fast," remembered the Brownsville boy–turned–Hollywood agent Swifty Lazar. Everyone was trying to work an angle. "The idea that someone would *want* to work for anyone else was completely foreign; we all dreamed of getting out and being our own boss."

A Brownsville boy with any hope of moving up in the world could follow one of several standard avenues. He could study hard, gain admittance to City College or better, and become a doctor, a lawyer, or other professional. Less scholarly types could work their way up to being a small subcontractor in the garment industry or the building trades, then to a big boss. But for those who lacked the patience or temperament for the slow and steady path, "there were only two ways to make enough money to be able to move uptown and wear spats: become a gangster or an entertainer," as the comedian George Burns observed. "And both of them were considered equally respectable."

For ambitious girls, it was not so simple. A wedding was still the great goal, but in America the traditions of the shtetl were turned upside down. Here husbands were expected to be the breadwinners, and respectable wives did not work outside the home. But marriage in Brownsville was no brass ring. For most women it meant an endless cycle of childbearing, hard-luck housekeeping, and scraping to make ends meet.

Some lucky young women became stenographers, typists, department store clerks, or at the pinnacle of prestige, schoolteachers. ("Typists had more yikhes [*sic*] than shop girls," observed one editor, "it helps them get husbands.") But that required far more education and polish than Pearl possessed.

Had her family been politically inclined, she might have found her friends among the union activists and young socialists of Brownsville's bustling Labor Lyceum. But socialism had no place in the Freedman home. "They had no political consciousness," remembered one Koval cousin; "to use a Yiddish word, they were *balbatish*," concerned above all with respectability and material success. "In the Freedman family the question was 'What were you worth?' Everyone knew what that meant. It didn't mean listening to Beethoven's string quartets."

Nathan Freedman was himself an aspiring boss, that natural-born enemy of all socialists. Pearl had an excellent head for mathematics, and he enlisted her to do bookkeeping for his growing carpentry business. But bookkeeping didn't offer much inspiration; besides, that too required more education.

Instead, claiming the birthright of the American teenager, Pearl threw herself into the pursuit of happiness through popular culture. On this score at least, having no parents was a distinct advantage. Unlike the obedient daughters who were obliged to turn over their pay envelopes to their family, for Pearl, once she paid her room and board, the rest was hers to spend as she pleased.

"I had developed a new craving," she later remembered. "I wanted finery." She and her friends weren't interested in the sensible shoes, tasteful hats, and plain, durable fabrics urged on them by frugal adults. Instead, they took their cues from movies, magazines, the shop windows along Pitkin Avenue, and the glamorous older girls of the dance halls.

Pearl and her friends were paragons of working-girl fashion, sporting impractically high French heels, daring skirts that showed off the ankles, and girlish empire waistlines that dispensed with the hourglass corsets that made it impossible to dance.

Legs were in and breasts were out of style, remembered the full-bosomed Pearl. "In order to make myself as flat in front as possible, I used to bind myself with strips of white cloth—so tightly that sometimes when I was bending over my machine I'd nearly pass out. It was only after the girls at the factory found out about my 'mummy wrappings,' and as a result of much kidding, that I finally unpent myself."

It took some ingenuity to dress as she liked, when even an inexpensive hat cost fifty cents and a cheap store-bought dress cost more than a week's pay. She learned to shop for fabric remnants from the pushcart men on Dumont Avenue, and sewed her skirts, blouses, and underwear by hand. Shoes were the biggest challenge; old clothes could be mended or made over, but leather-bottomed shoes wore out quickly on the pavement and were expensive to replace. While window-shopping on Pitkin Avenue, Pearl became obsessed by what the girls called a "Jap Mink"—or, to give it more dignity, a "Japanese Mink," a cape made of dyed cat fur—featured in one of the windows. "Every day I walked an extra two blocks just to see it," she remembered. "But of course it was a pipe dream—I was doing well to own more than one pair of drawers."

Pearl modeled her new look on Theda Bara, the glamorous star of the 1915 hit movie *A Fool There Was*. Bara's character was named "The

Vampire," for her hypnotic ability to seduce any man, robbing him of his wealth, health, even his life. "The Vamp" was a new kind of female character in American pop culture, the unashamed and unrestrained femme fatale who used sex as a weapon. A *Fool There Was* made Bara the first modern sex symbol of the twentieth century and spawned a national "vamp" craze among both filmmakers and moviegoers.

Like Pearl, Bara was "short, bosomy, and a trifle plump" and, movie studio propaganda notwithstanding, the daughter of a Jewish tailor. In the slang of the day, Pearl styled herself a "baby vamp," a "sport," a "jazz baby," or a "flapper." She copied Bara's exotic getups and heavy makeup, sporting ruby-red lips and black kohl-rimmed eyes and arranging her long dark hair as Bara did, in a figure-eight topknot with small waves of hair framing her face. She practiced Bara's signature sexy look, her chin tilted down, gazing up seductively from under heavy-lidded eyes.

Headstrong, spirited, and unabashed in their pursuit of pleasure, she and her friends adopted styles that had once been associated solely with prostitutes: wearing makeup, smoking cigarettes, taking a drink, going out at night alone, talking to strange men, and giggling over risqué jokes. To the shocked grown-ups who complained, the girls answered defiantly: "I am earning my own living and can do as I please."

The far more pressing problem was that, as cheap as these pleasures were, they were still out of reach for the average working girl's budget. That was where men came in, since men earned twice as much or more, than the average working woman. Without a man paying her way, no factory girl could afford to go to the halls every weekend, enter dance contests, or spend a day at Coney Island.

Back in Yanow, courtship was cheaper. A boy might visit a girl in her parents' parlor or meet at social gatherings, but they didn't go out on the town with the fellow footing the bill for them both. But in a city that glittered with amusements, old-fashioned courting seemed dull and obsolete. Polly picked up a new habit that her friends called "treating," or what might now simply be called "dating." Put bluntly, it was a sort of sexual barter: pleasure exchanged for pleasure—the treat of a day at Coney Island, a little present, an ice cream soda, is exchanged for the charm of feminine company and the potential prospect of some kind of sexual intimacy.

How much a man spent on a girl was considered a critical measure of her popularity. One astonished reporter captured the competitive ethos of two girls at Coney Island comparing their outings.

"What sort of time did you have?" asked the first girl.

"Great," replied the second. "He blew $5 on the blow-out."

"You beat me again. My chump only spent $2.55."

For some young women, it became a game to see how much they could get in exchange for how little they had to give. Coney Island was especially popular because girls paid only the cost of the five-cent subway fare out and back, "and for the rest of it the boys you 'pick up,' 'treat.'" "When the girl is both lucky and clever," observed the progressive reformer Belle Linder Israels, "she frees herself from her self-selected escort before home-going time, and finds a feminine companion in his place for the midnight ride in the trolley." Not every girl was so lucky.

Still, everyone knew a girl had to give *something* if she wanted to attract and keep a fellow. "Don't yeh know there ain't no feller goin' t' spend coin on yeh fer nothing?" explained a more experienced girl to her greenhorn friend. "Yeh gotta be a good Indian, Kid—we all gotta!"

Those young women who treated regularly, especially those who were willing to "go the limit," were dubbed "charity girls." But a charity girl walked a fine line. She might have sex with a boyfriend, or fool around, in pursuit of a night of dancing or a new pair of stockings, and no one would be the wiser. But there were two taboos for which a Brownsville girl would be shunned: openly trading sex for money and becoming pregnant out of wedlock.

"In Brownsville, the women were curious without curtains, and you may be sure that little escaped them," remembered one young Brunsviller. "When a girl strayed and had an illegitimate child: woe to that girl and woe to that family!"

☾

In the early summer of 1915, as Pearl was discovering the heady delights of Coney Island, the German army was advancing into the Pale of Settlement, forcing the Russians to retreat to the east. On August 19, 1915, the German War Office in Berlin announced that the kaiser's forces had rolled through Yanow and would soon take Pinsk. Before they fled, the Cossacks set fire to Yanow, burning everything but the Russian Orthodox church and a dozen or so gentile homes near the edge of town.

That September in Pinsk, the czar's army managed to halt the German advance, but it couldn't push them back farther. The two powers were now trapped in a vicious stalemate within spitting distance of Yanow. In many ways, however, the town fared better than much of the Pale. The Pinsk region was a critical section of the Eastern Front as the primary point of access to the railroad leading from Moscow to Warsaw and points west. With its proximity to the front lines and the railway, the Germans placed their regional command center in Yanow, nicknaming it "Klein Berlin" or "Little Berlin."

All of the town's gentiles fled east into Russia as the Germans approached. After the fire, only a few dozen Jewish families remained, living among the rubble in the cellars of the charred houses, clinging to the hope that the Germans might offer an improvement upon the cursed Russians. The army seized all livestock, farmland, and buildings, forcing the remaining Jews to work in the fields and construct roads, factories, hospitals, and rail lines to support the German war machine. At first there were continual shortages of food, medicine, and other necessities, made worse by the influx of refugees from the surrounding areas, but as the Germans settled in and the Jews rebuilt the town, the presence of the military headquarters ensured stability and prevented pogroms.

News from Yanow was rare, although Pearl continued to exchange letters from her family whenever the mail could get through. Her father wrote that the Germans had confiscated their cow, horse, and sleds and killed their chickens—"a disgrace to a man in my position," he complained.

The troubles in Europe would soon be uppermost in every American mind. Nineteen seventeen brought revolutions of all kinds, setting the Jews of Brownsville abuzz with excitement. In February 1917 a popular uprising toppled the Russian Empire, and in March Russia's new provisional government abolished the Pale of Settlement forever. Later that year Great Britain, after wresting control of Palestine from the Ottoman Empire, issued the Balfour Declaration, a first concrete step toward the establishment of a national homeland for Jews, bringing joy to the Zionists.

On April 6, the United States finally joined the war. Almost overnight New York became the central hub of America's war effort and a major transit point for shipping both men and matériel out to combat. The Brooklyn Navy Yard had already begun building submarines and warships. Now the U.S. government was erecting a massive warehouse complex on the Brooklyn waterfront to store army supplies and ship them to the soldiers in France. When the draft got under way in the summer of 1917, large military camps sprang up in Queens, Brooklyn, and the Bronx.

Pearl lost her job at the corset factory when the U.S. War Industries Board asked the women of America to stop buying corsets so the metal stays used to gird women's waists could instead be put to war production. But she quickly found another, better job in a factory on Blake Avenue making uniforms for soldiers. She was soon promoted from hand stitching to a sewing machine and worked as much overtime as she could get.

Brooklyn was teeming with troops on their way to the front. The presence of so many handsome young men, glamorized by a uniform and the hazy prospect of heroism, or at least a heroic death, was irresistible. The working-class girls of New York went "khaki-mad," to the alarm of social workers, military officials, politicians, and parents. Everywhere soldiers, sailors, and young women were swarming in packs, in parks, drugstores, and dance halls, or just roaming the streets, eyeing one another, flirting, laughing, and picking up one another. It was a scandal, claimed the Women's Committee on National Defense, the "open and disgustingly familiar necking on the part of young people who admitted that they had known each other for only a few hours or minutes."

They weren't just "necking" or "petting," in the parlance of the day. The ever-looming threat of a fiery fate in the trenches of Europe encouraged many young women to "go the limit" who wouldn't have dared in less heady times. In their more romantic moments, the "victory girls," as they were dubbed, saw themselves as patriots, providing aid and comfort to men facing death. The boys in uniform were inclined to agree.

As one soldier summed up the prevailing point of view: "We are fighting for you girls, and you ought to do something for us." Did they ever! Bold, besotted couples could be spotted rutting on benches, on the grass in public parks, in dim halls and alleyways. Rates of premarital sex, sexually transmitted diseases, illegitimate births, elopements, and rash marriages all rose precipitously in 1917.

Pearl, with her heavy makeup, vampish airs, and obvious appetite for fun, might not have been as fast as she looked, but she was no wallflower. From Breina's point of view, now was the time to settle down. The time-honored way to calm a wild-haired girl was to find her a husband. Breina, "who believed in leaving nothing to chance," Pearl noted dryly, had a suitor already in mind, a neighbor boy she called Willie Bernstein.

Pearl was only seventeen, but as she herself observed, back in the old country plenty of girls her age already had children of their own. So the matchmaking began. To carve out a rare hour or two of privacy, Breina's oldest daughter was sent to stay with a friend. The littler cousins were sent off to a carnival for the evening and told not to return before nine o'clock. When Willie arrived, Breina and Nathan greeted the young man in the parlor and then casually retreated to the kitchen, leaving Pearl alone to size up her future husband.

"Willie in person turned out to be quite a letdown—scrawny and pale, with a bad case of acne, and wearing an ill-fitting uniform," remembered Pearl—a disappointment to Breina, who hadn't realized he'd been inducted into the military only three days before. He didn't have much in the way of personality, "and it did not add to his charms that he considered dancing sinful." But he was pleasant enough, and he was interested in her, so they began going steady.

Their courtship was a compromise between the old and new worlds. It wasn't an arranged marriage, but it sure wasn't a trip to Coney Island. They settled into a routine, with Willie spending Wednesday, Saturday, and Sunday evenings at the Freedmans', chastely chatting with Pearl and her cousins.

Willie's deployment to Europe was fast approaching. The night he announced that his troop had received their orders to ship out, Breina "gave me a poke and look which said plainly, 'Close the deal at once,'" recalled Pearl. Willie clearly shared her urgency. As soon as Breina and Nathan stepped off to the kitchen, he grabbed Pearl and pulled her to him, kissing her hard on the lips.

"Well, I knew this was supposed to be my shining moment, but my only thought was that Willie's complexion didn't look any better close up," sniffed Pearl. "When I drew back he must have thought I was offended at his freshness, for he hastened to make clear that his attentions were honorable."

It had all gone according to Breina's plan. All Pearl had to do was say yes. But at the last instant, she could not do it. She gently explained to the bewildered young man that she could not marry him simply because she did not love him. Once Willie got past his disbelief and realized she was really serious, he bade a cool goodbye and abruptly left.

Breina was furious at Pearl's inexplicable behavior. Why lead the boy on, then not close the bargain? Did she want to be a dried-up old maid?

"But how could I explain my feelings to her?" asked Pearl later. "My reason for rejecting Willie wasn't only that I didn't love him. Even more than that, perhaps, it was because I so hated the one thing we had in common—our poverty."

☾

With Willie gone, Pearl threw herself into work, earning a raise and a promotion to a more complex sewing machine. But this satisfaction didn't last long. She was still broke, still uneducated, "still without a place in the sun," she recalled. "I was restless and discontented. I kept thinking that surely life must offer me other alternatives than a factory job and a Willie Bernstein."

It was a perfect time to fall in love. One day in the late autumn of 1917, a new foreman appeared on the shop floor. Frank, she later called him. All the girls were immediately smitten by his sharp clothes, good looks, and arrogant swagger. "Up to that time I had never even thought of making a play for anyone, but this is different, this was love," remembered Pearl.

That morning Pearl "vamped" Frank with every trick she could muster, doing her best to exude hypnotic sexual energy as she pushed the rough khaki fabric through her machine. Finally, Frank casually strolled over and leaned down, as if to check her work.

"Come to my office right after lunch," he said.

"I almost strangled," Pearl remembered. She waited anxiously through the lunch hour, not sure if he was going to flirt with her or fire her. But the moment she stepped into the office and saw the look in his eyes, it was clear she was not going to be canned. He wanted to know if she would go to Coney Island with him that night. It was the end of the season, and he had to pick up some clothes he'd left at one of the summer cottages, before they closed it up for the winter. He could use the company, if she would like to come.

"Would I? My voice has always been low and husky, but it dropped a full two registers on that 'Yes,'" she remembered.

Pearl's good fortune was the talk of the shop for the rest of the afternoon. She floated through her work as the girls dissected the situation, and "when one girl—trying, I guess, to figure out what I had—said, 'Well, you know, Pearl does look kinda like Theda Bara,' my cup was full. I felt like the *femme fatale* of all time."

In coming decades, the stereotype of the Jewish mother would evoke an overanxious, overprotective woman who makes her child neurotic with her worries and expectations. But for children of the shtetl and the ghetto, a vigilant mother could literally make the difference between life and death. Breina "felt sorry for Pearl, not to have her parents. We all did," said Breina's daughter-in-law. She looked out for her cousin, of course, but not with the same sense of obligation as to her own child. Certainly any mother paying close attention would have forbidden her daughter from going to Coney Island that night. It was cold, dark, and disreputable, with every decent attraction closed for winter and only dingy saloons and bawdy houses open for business.

When Pearl stepped off the train that evening, the streets were deserted, and the concession stands and attractions were boarded up. An icy wind blew through her coat as she followed Frank to one of the many rickety wooden houses that rented rooms, no questions asked. She was chilled to the bone by the time they got inside.

She warmed herself while Frank packed a small bag, and they chatted and joked about the people they knew at the factory. When he finished, Pearl stood up to leave.

"What's your hurry?" he asked. "The evening is young."

The room had a phonograph—a hand-cranked record player—and Frank put on a recording of the vaudeville comic Harry Lauder singing funny songs in a Scottish accent. He patted the cushion next to him on the sofa, motioning for her to join him. When she sat down, he suddenly leaned close and began pulling out the long pins that kept her hat fastened to her hair.

"All of a sudden I got scared," as Pearl told it. "I jumped up from the couch and said it was time to go. Instead of answering, he went over to the door and locked it. When I resisted him, he knocked me cold."

Pearl woke up with a bruised jaw and a face swollen from tears. The next morning she skipped work, explaining to Breina that she'd hurt herself falling. For three days she stayed away from the factory, too traumatized even to leave her bed. On the third day, Eva came to see her, and Pearl told her everything.

"She called it rape," remembered Pearl, "and though I winced on hearing this ugly word, still it did reduce what had happened to a size where I could handle it." Stories like Pearl's were as common as cockroaches on the rough streets of Brownsville, and to realize she wasn't alone gave her a measure of perspective and comfort.

But Pearl needed money, and with no other job prospects, she was forced to return to the factory where Frank was waiting. She had been back at work for a month when she realized she was pregnant. "Though my feelings about Frank were the same I would have for a dangerous reptile, only more so, the child inside me was his, and I asked him to marry me," Pearl recalled. "His answer was to kick me out of his office."

There was only one solution, Pearl decided after talking it over with Eva. She must get an abortion.

Abortion was illegal in New York, but so was birth control. Condoms were not legalized until 1918, when the military began to champion them as protection against the epidemic of venereal disease afflicting American soldiers. Women with money and resources could purchase under-the-counter chemical suppositories or rubber devices to block off their cervix, including diaphragms, pessaries, and cervical caps. But poor women had few options other than the withdrawal method and douching with dubious homemade concoctions. The overburdened wives of Brownsville were so eager to control their pregnancies that in 1916 the sex educator and activist Margaret Sanger opened America's first birth control clinic on Amboy Street in the heart of the neighborhood, defying the law and making national headlines. When Sanger was arrested and put on trial in February 1917, Brownsville women were her staunchest supporters.

All in all, it was much easier to get rid of a pregnancy than to prevent one. Women who couldn't find or afford a doctor relied on folk remedies or patent medicines to abort. The more determined ones tried to empty their womb with shoe button hooks, coat hangers, knitting needles, and toxic douches, which frequently led to bleeding, infections, infertility, and death. The lucky ones found a doctor who would do the job with clean hands and tools, although usually without anesthetic.

In Brownsville, where beleaguered wives were known to have as many as ten abortions over the course of a lifetime, it wasn't so hard to find a doctor who would perform the procedure. But the first one Eva took her to wanted $150, an astronomical sum for a girl making no more than ten dollars a week. All Pearl had was the thirty-five dollars that she'd been saving toward her fur cape. Frank, the bum, refused to help.

Eva found another physician who would do it for thirty-five dollars. But when Pearl told him how she'd gotten there, he kindly charged her only twenty-five and told her to use the last of her money to replace her tattered shoes and stockings.

☾

"I tried to put all this nightmare behind me," Pearl wrote afterward. "But though I went through the motions of living, I was changed—I had lost heart, I no longer had hope." Even the news that the Germans had surrendered, and the joyful delirium of Armistice Day, couldn't lift her depression.

Not long after the armistice, Frank began to pursue her again, pestering her for sex and threatening to tell the Freedmans about her pregnancy if she refused. Again her worldly friend Eva offered advice. With the end of the war, the uniform factory would be shutting down production, and she would have to find a new job anyway. Why not move out on her own? She was already paying her cousins room and board. Better to give her money to a stranger and buy her independence. Why stay in Brooklyn at all, when the skyscrapers of Manhattan beckoned only a trolley ride away?

This was no small proposition. Low-skilled garment factory girls simply did not make enough money to live alone and rarely enough even to rent a room in a boardinghouse. What she was planning isn't clear. Why flee her family and her neighborhood instead of just quitting her job and finding other work? How would she find the money to move when she'd just spent every nickel of her savings?

But she and Eva seemed to have a plan. They agreed to meet up in

Manhattan one Sunday evening to look for a place for her to live. That morning Pearl bought some glossy satin fabric from one of the pushcarts on Dumont Avenue and basted up a stylish black dress overlaid with a lace tunic. She ran out of time to finish it properly, but she wore it that night as she rode the cars into Manhattan to meet Eva.

The two girls met up in the lobby of a hotel at 28th and Broadway, the heart of New York's old Tenderloin, where raucous saloons, gambling rooms, and bawdy houses stood side by side with the music publishers of Tin Pan Alley. They were loitering in the lobby, chatting and admiring Pearl's new dress, when a tall, raven-haired young man with a charismatic smile gave them the eye. Eva smiled back, and the bold young man walked over to introduce himself. He was a dress salesman by the name of Harry. "Harry proved to have a very funny line," recalled Pearl, and her friend laughed uproariously at his jokes. Would the ladies like to join him at a cabaret for a drink and a dance? Eva said she had another engagement but suggested that Pearl go.

"Alone?" Pearl asked, her courage faltering.

"Sure," Eva said. "Harry'll be good for what ails you."

Harry Richman turned out to be a grand fellow. Another poor Jew, born even worse off than her, he'd spent the previous six years hopping trains and playing piano in saloons and whorehouses, hoping to break into big-time vaudeville. In the late winter of 1918, at twenty-four years old, he was trying to scratch up some dough by working as a dress salesman while he made the rounds of the cabarets, music publishers, and theatrical agencies.

They strolled up Broadway into the dazzling white lights of Times Square. At the Winter Garden Theater on West 46th Street, he led her up a set of stairs into what turned out to be one of the swellest nightspots in Manhattan. The Bal Tabarin was a swanky new top-hat-and-tails supper club, where the bandleader, a clarinetist named Ted Lewis, was making a sensation playing a crazy new form of ragtime the papers were calling jazz.

Pearl had never been to a cabaret, but Harry's savvy more than made up for her nervousness and naïveté. He seemed to know everyone in the place. "Hat-check girls, waiters, the maître d', some nicely dressed people at one of the tables—they all spoke to Harry and smiled at me," she remembered with fresh wonder.

Harry turned out to be a real cutup, and Pearl quickly began to loosen up and enjoy herself. "Up to that time I had never had anything stronger than soda pop," she remembered, "but when Harry asked me if I would have a highball, not wanting him to know how small-timish I was, I said 'Yes.'"

Harry asked if she danced. In the hot phrase of the day: "I'll say she did!" She regaled him with stories of all the contests and prizes she'd won. "But as we fox-trotted out onto the floor, my knees felt as if they had an extra joint in them and I tripped over Harry's feet," she recalled. She righted herself and continued dancing. Then a wave of dizziness hit her. He saved her from tumbling to the floor, but in the hubbub she caught the heel of her shoe in the hem of her hastily sewn dress. As they struggled to unhook her shoe and keep her upright, the seams gave way, tearing the fabric and shredding the dress.

Quick-thinking Harry grabbed her coat, wrapped her up, and led her down to the sidewalk. Leaning her against a building, he paused to regroup.

"Now then, my little Irene Castle," he asked, "where do you live?"

"When I looked at Harry he seemed to have a twin brother, and his voice came from very far away." He repeated the question.

"Brooklyn," mumbled Pearl.

"Everything happens to me," Harry muttered grimly.

He hailed a cab and asked her for her address. By then Pearl had passed out.

"I later learned he took me to a hotel where he was acquainted with the management, got me a room, and turned me over to the night maid," Pearl explained. "I have a vague recollection of being thrown into a tub of cold water, then blackout again."

When she awoke, sunlight was flooding the room. She pulled herself up and took stock of her situation. On the dresser was her bag with "powder, rouge, union card, and capital of fifteen cents." Next to it was an envelope, with a note from Harry explaining that he hadn't been able to take her home because he had no idea where she lived, but he had left some money in the envelope for the hotel bill.

Perhaps her adventure was intended as a casual pickup, a treat, a little hanky-panky in exchange for a night on the town. Or she might well have meant it to be "a trick," exchanging sex for cash in hopes of raising enough money to move out on her own. It may have been just as innocent as she said it was. Whatever she intended, she ended up in a hotel room with an envelope of dollar bills.

Years later, long after Harry Richman had found fame on Broadway as a song-and-dance man known by his signature tune, "Puttin' on the Ritz," he retold the story of that night in his memoir. "I flirted with her on the street, picked her up, took her dancing, and she somehow managed to lose her pants in the middle of the dance floor," wrote Richman. "We had many a laugh over that for years."

But that was not how her cousin saw it when Pearl finally found her way home, tattered and hungover, her purse a little heavier than it had been the day before. "My mother-in-law came to the top of the staircase and saw Pearl half undressed," said Breina's daughter-in-law of the confrontation. "Breina had a terrible temper. And she had her own daughter who was the same age."

Who could blame Breina? Her sweet small-town cousin had come to seem like a different person in the last three and a half years. She had spurned the husband Breina had arranged and instead spent her nights in dance halls, running with wild girls, dressing like a *nafka*, a hussy, going God knows where with God knows who, and had become moody and secretive. Breina had had enough.

"I had stayed out all night, my dress was in rags, she was not interested in hearing my story. All she wanted was for me to get out—and to get out as of that minute," remembered Pearl. "I did not argue with her. I wrapped my clothing in a newspaper and went."

Standing forlornly in the subway station wondering what misfortune could befall her next, the newspaper tore open, and her meager bundle of stockings, shirtwaists, and underwear scattered over the filthy platform. As she scrambled to pick up her things, "I could not help thinking that at least when I left Yanow I'd had a good stout potato sack in which to carry my possessions. I began to laugh. I couldn't help it," Pearl remembered.

"So far, I had certainly racked up a row of goose eggs in the Golden Land. I had failed in my quest for the education I might have gotten in Pinsk, I had lost my virginity, my reputation and my job. All I had gotten was older."

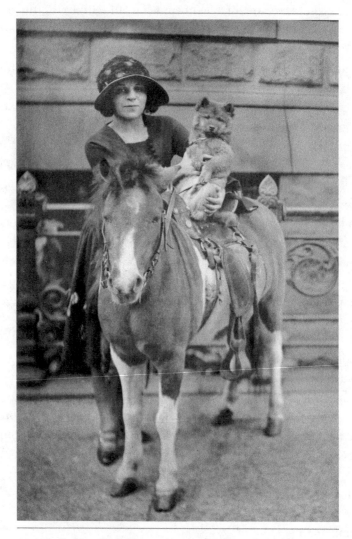

Pearl—now Polly—as a young hustler with Nicko,
her beloved Chow Chow puppy, 1921

4

What's a Nice Girl Like You Doing in a Place Like This?

Why should she stay in Brownsville when for the price of a nickel fare she could change her fate? A plague on Brooklyn. Manhattan was the *Goldine Madine,* and that was where she was heading. All the proof she needed could be seen from the window of the elevated train as it rumbled across the majestic gray bulk of the Brooklyn Bridge or the sleek silver span of the Manhattan Bridge. There, shimmering above the East River, rose the gleaming spires of the Manhattan skyline.

Nothing about Pearl would have seemed special to the other passengers on the subway car, tucked behind their newspapers or drowsing on the rattan benches. With her cheap cloth coat and run-down heels, she could have been mistaken for thousands of young working girls who came to Manhattan every day to seek their fortunes.

But Pearl was determined to find "a place in the sun," as she put it. Not for her a careworn marriage and a passel of children, never a new dress or a dime to call her own. Even if she'd wanted to swallow her pride and return to her cousins, after the bitter fight with Breina, she was no longer so welcome.

In December 1918, Pearl was eighteen years old, more or less. Five years in America had not yet scrubbed the Yiddish accent from her husky voice. In her makeshift bundle, she carried letters from home, photos of her family, and the undershirt and rough woolen shawl she'd worn on the voyage from Yanow. With her wide eyes, dimpled cheeks, and petite proportions, standing barely five feet tall in her stockings, she still had the doll-like features of a young girl.

Pearl alit in Manhattan that December day armed with a grade-school diploma from the Springfield Evening Grammar School, a union card, and forty-nine dollars in cash. For everything else, she'd have to rely on her keen wits and restless ambition.

☾

Her first task was to find a new place to call home—far easier said than done. She began her search in the midst of a severe housing shortage, exacerbated by wartime inflation that had caused rents to skyrocket. With the end of the war, Manhattan was awash with people arriving from somewhere else, all of them looking for a place to rest their heads.

The city was swarming with demobilized soldiers and sailors on their way back from the front, still clad in their uniforms, their discharge pay burning in their pockets. The boys in uniform were nearly rivaled by the civilians pouring in from America's farms, small towns, and provincial cities, lured by the vibrant depictions of Manhattan in national magazines and neighborhood movie houses.

The hotels were bustling with conventioneers, buyers, salesmen, and businessmen of every stripe, eager, after the austerity of war, to bring home the latest styles and the newest innovations the great metropolis had to offer. The most ostentatious newcomers were the freshly minted "war millionaires" who had grown rich supplying the military machine. Bankers, factory owners, industrialists, profiteers, and speculators of every species, hailing from places like Pittsburgh, Chicago, and Kansas City. "All the thieves of the Republic," the sharp-tongued critic H. L. Mencken called them, "all laden with cash, all eager to spend it, all easy marks for the town rogues and panders."

In January 1919 New York was now the most prosperous city in the most prosperous nation on earth. Scores of smokestacks rose along the edges of the island, and the Hudson and East rivers were glutted with barges, and boats of every size, hauling people and goods to and from narrow piers jutting out from the shoreline. There were still as many horses as automobiles in the streets, but Pearl had never seen traffic like this, so crowded and chaotic that the world's first electric traffic signal had just been erected on Fifth Avenue. Crisscrossing the roads were electric streetcars and the elevated railways—the El, as it was universally called—that ran two stories aboveground along Second, Third, Sixth, and Ninth avenues, billowing dirt, rattling windows, and casting inky shadows over the streets below.

Unlike Brownsville, where a Jew could live her whole life without speaking English, Manhattan was a small island of many tribes that daily jostled one another in the city's streets. With the end of hostilities in Europe, immigration into the city had nearly resumed its prewar levels. Italians led the charge, followed by Russian Jews fleeing the Bolshevik revolution. Jews had colonized the Irish strongholds of the Lower East Side and West Harlem, while Italians claimed East Harlem and Greenwich Village. But that too was changing. Above 110th Street, southern refugees from the reign of Jim Crow were moving to the brownstones of Central and West Harlem, fast transforming it from a Jewish enclave into the cultural capital of Black America.

For more affluent arrivals, the heart of New York lay between Madison Square and Central Park. Here were the well-polished jewels of the city: the fashionable shops of Fifth Avenue, the exclusive men's clubs and grand hotels. At the edges of the park loomed the dazzling marble mansions of Millionaire's Row on upper Fifth Avenue, and the ornate Beaux-Arts apartment-hotels of the Upper West Side. West of Fifth Avenue, from Times Square to Columbus Circle, were the theaters and glossy cabarets of Broadway's Great White Way, bathed in the silver light of millions of incandescent bulbs, blinking their dazzling come-ons.

For those of coarser tastes and smaller pocketbooks, the real action lay a few blocks south in the dilapidated row houses of Hell's Kitchen and the old Tenderloin District. Sporting men and scarlet women frolicked in sawdust-strewn saloons, dance halls, gambling houses, and brownstone bordellos, while the streets echoed with the blare of ragtime bands and song-pluggers pounding away on pianos. Then there was Union Square, the great, gritty gathering spot of the masses. Ringing the square were penny arcades, barrooms, vaudeville and burlesque houses, "half and half" theaters that mixed moving picture shows with live acts, and swarms of streetwalkers. Here was the grand headquarters of Tammany Hall, the city's most powerful political organization.

Below Fourteenth Street, in the narrow lanes of Greenwich Village, Italian immigrants and lace-curtain Irish mingled with would-be bohemians and revolutionaries. At the southern tip of the island rose the mighty New York Stock Exchange at Wall and Broad streets, where messenger boys, brokers, and bankers in bowlers and spats thronged the narrow lanes, under a canopy of telegraph and telephone wires.

Polly roamed the frigid sidewalks of the poorer quarters, knocking on the doors of dim tenements and shoddy rooming houses, searching for an inexpensive furnished room. But beds of any kind were in short supply in those hectic days after the war.

She finally finagled something at 323 Second Avenue, a run-down brick row house, just south of Nineteenth Street. She'd landed on the edge of the "Gashouse District," named for the towering gas tanks that lined that stretch of the East River. The stench of gas and chemicals leaking from nearby factories often wafted through the streets, mingling with the smell of manure from the horse market and stables above 24th Street. Besides the odor, the neighborhood's main claims to notoriety were its vicious street gangs and its native son, Charlie Murphy, the powerful political boss who ruled over Tammany Hall and the Democratic Party.

Still, she'd finally found a room of her own. "Did I say room? It was a windowless hallway leading to the basement flat occupied by the janitor and his family," quipped Pearl.

The rent was ten dollars a month, payable in advance. Her landlords were a Hungarian and German couple, and her fellow tenants were a cut above her economically. She was the only single woman among them. To stay there, she'd have to make money like a man.

Pearl's cubbyhole wasn't much more comfortable than the hard leather couch at the Freedmans', but crummy as it was, this makeshift room offered her the first taste of privacy and independence she'd had since she'd come to America.

❦

Now settled on Second Avenue, Pearl lit out to look for a job in the garment factories that lined lower Broadway and Fifth Avenue. A cold wave settled on the city in the first week of January, turning the avenues into frigid, wind-whipped canyons and making every step a misery. During the day, Pearl trolled the streets in her threadbare coat, searching for work. In the evenings, she ate in one of the cheap cafés that dotted the neighborhood, where a decent meal could be had for about a quarter. By the end of the first week, she had turned up nothing. Both her confidence and the leather soles of her shoes were wearing thin.

Then one night, sitting alone in a café, she met a nice man in this roiling sea of strangers. Abe Shornik, as she called him, was nearly her father's age and had immigrated as a child from a Russian shtetl much like Yanow. One night when the place was crowded, they shared a table and struck up a conversation. After that they often ate together. Abe offered a sympathetic ear and took a special interest in the lonely girl.

"I had selected a very tough neighborhood in which to reside," Pearl remembered. The streets around Union Square were teeming with men looking for a good time and women hoping to provide it. In the afternoon, streetwalkers lingered in the lobbies of the better hotels or strolled the sidewalks, trying to catch men's eyes in the reflections of the plate-glass windows. After dark they roamed Fourteenth Street and St. Mark's Place, cruising the quiet preserve of Stuyvesant Park, along with their male counterparts, the self-styled "fairies." The neighborhood contained dozens of spots like the one where she met Abe—tatty tearooms, storefront delicatessens, and cheap eateries that served respectable patrons during the day but became the hangouts of the city's underbelly when decent people were in bed.

Second Avenue below Fourteenth Street was even worse. Known as the "Jewish Rialto," it was home to the Yiddish theaters, cafés, and shops that catered to the Lower East Side's Jews. But after the shops closed and the theaters let out, it became a lawbreaker's paradise, protected by payoffs to the Democratic politicians who had ruled "the old Fourth Ward" for five decades. Even the battle-hardened undercover agents from the Committee of Fourteen, the city's longtime moral watchdogs, were shocked by how openly criminals cavorted along the avenue. "Second Avenue is the underworld's asylum," as one undercover investigator declared with only slight exaggeration. "Guerrillas, pimps, thieves, gunmen and gamblers loiter on every corner and in front of every cigar store, lunch room, pool room and drug stores and ice cream parlors.

Every crime that has to be committed is planned on Second Ave." In the Jewish underworld, there were few higher compliments than to call someone "a big *Second Avenue Man*."

Prostitutes and their protectors were so plentiful that the stretch from Tenth Street to Houston was known as Pimps' Row. Even honest cops dared not interfere with the oily men bedecked in gaudy silk shirts, diamond stickpins, and patent leather boots. Patrolmen "were simply told to keep away and not to interfere," or they'd likely find themselves demoted to walk the beat in some godforsaken corner of Brooklyn or Queens.

By now, Pearl was no greenhorn. Nonetheless she was shocked when Abe pointed out the burlesque dancers, chorus girls, factory workers, and department store clerks who were picking up extra income by peddling their companionship. "I eyed them covertly, embarrassed even to be caught looking at them," she remembered. "I wondered how any woman could sink so low."

Two more weeks passed. Still she found no work. She economized even further, living on stale rolls, spoiled fruit, and bags of peanuts, whatever she could get for a penny or two from the pushcarts. As her pennies dwindled, her anxiety and hunger mounted. She was a *luftmensch* in the cruelest sense of the word: living on air, with no job, no skills, no resources, a soul who "starved to death three times a day." If she didn't find the money for her next month's rent, she'd be out on the street.

She was nearing the point of starvation the next time she ran into Abe on Second Avenue. He asked why he hadn't seen her around lately. "When I explained I couldn't afford it, he not only bought my dinner but stuck a five-dollar bill under my plate. Either his kindness changed my luck, or having eating money in my poke gave me more assurance— the next day I landed a part-time job at the Trio Corset Company."

With that act of generosity—a hot meal, a kind word, a five-dollar bill—Pearl took the next step into her new life.

☾

At ten o'clock sharp on the morning of Tuesday, January 21, 1919—just as Pearl was to begin her new job at the Trio Corset Company—twenty thousand young seamstresses, many dressed for the occasion in their finest holiday clothes, calmly turned off their sewing machines, set down their needles, and walked out of the factories of Manhattan's garment district. Gathered on the pavement below 38th Street, they unfurled handmade banners and began marching en masse down Fourth and Fifth avenues to their union halls. The International Ladies' Garment Workers Union was officially on strike.

Within days, the picket lines had swelled to over thirty-five thousand women, demanding a forty-four-hour workweek, an end to seasonal lay-offs, and a 15 percent raise. Union Square was feverish with protesters, picketers, and pamphleteers. Any hope that the garment strike would be resolved quickly faded as winter melted into spring. For a girl like Pearl, with no family and no savings to fall back on, the long strike was nothing short of a disaster. It was not until April that the factory owners finally surrendered, agreeing to most of the women's demands.

But Pearl's troubles were not over. At the end of April, just as the seamstresses were settling their strike, postal workers discovered some thirty-six packages containing booby-trapped bombs that had been mailed to prominent men across the country, timed to arrive on May Day, the annual celebration of international Labor Day. When news of the bomb scare spread, down on Union Square a howling pack of soldiers and unemployed veterans smashed the doors of the Russian People's House, tossing men down the stairs, setting fire to books, and forcing a frightened huddle of immigrants to sing "The Star-Spangled Banner." Swarming uptown, the mob set upon the offices of the Social-ist Party newspaper, driving hundreds of people into the streets scream-ing, as they beat them with clubs.

The May Day massacres set off a bloody summer of strikes and riots across the country. In Brownsville and the Lower East Side, angry housewives organized rent strikes and bread boycotts. In July, when one hundred scrubwomen at the Mutual Life Insurance building struck for shorter hours, they threatened the scabs with sticks and paving stones. Then when police stormed the building, they turned their weapons on the cops. When the actors' union shut down the Broadway theaters in August, the chorus girls' auxiliary, "the prettiest strikers in history" in the estimation of the *New York World*, paraded down to Wall Street in open cars, swarming the banks and brokerage offices, passing out pamphlets and charming the press. The city's needle trades, from corset makers to furriers, were nearly paralyzed by walkouts.

Frankly, Pearl didn't want to remake America into a workers' paradise—she just wanted her fair share. Even when the ladies' union succeeded in wresting a forty-four-hour week and a raise in pay from the bosses, it didn't really matter. Pearl was at the bottom of the heap any way she looked at it.

"Now, looking back at those months, the only impressions which remain are of unrelieved drabness, of hurry and worry and clawing uncertainty," Pearl remembered later; "my recollections of this period are all of the stench and sourness and dirty-grayness of poverty, of the panicky day-after-day struggling to keep my head above water." How she survived she never really said.

At the end of 1919, after a full year of hunger, anxiety, and loneliness, she made a decision. She went to find Abe Shornik.

☽

It was bitterly cold the first week of January 1920, especially on the Upper West Side of Manhattan, where the wind roared in from the Hudson River. Out of sheer kindness, as Pearl told it, Abe Shornik brought her there to meet a friend of his, the wife of a dress manufacturer with ties to the theater industry, to see if she might offer Pearl a job. Pearl had never ventured this far uptown before, but whatever hesitation she might have had evaporated as she gazed in wonder at the glories of Riverside Drive.

"My visit there was an eye opener," marveled Pearl. To the west of Riverside Drive spread the magnificent expanse of the Hudson. The east side of the avenue boasted some of the grandest apartment buildings in the city, rising like terra-cotta wedding cakes a dozen stories high, guarded by brass-buttoned doormen. Instead of ragged urchins and noisy pushcart peddlers in the streets, she saw chic women swathed in fur, well-fed gentlemen in homburg hats, and gleaming automobiles manned by uniformed chauffeurs.

In January 1920, Riverside Drive was the pinnacle of nouveau riche luxury. "Allrightnik's Row" the Jews called it, using "Yinglish" slang for Jews who'd made good, who'd done all right for themselves (in contrast to the no-goodnik or good-for-nothing bum). Unlike the Upper East Side, where the city's Protestant elite dwelled and Jews and immigrants were distinctly unwelcome, the Upper West Side admitted all comers, regardless of where they were born or what they did for a living. So many newly affluent Jews were moving to the neighborhood, it was known as the "Gilded Ghetto."

Abe brought Pearl to the most beautiful apartment she'd ever seen. While she was getting her bearings, she was introduced to a tall, willowy brunette with wide eyes and a luminous smile who went by the name Garnet Williams. Garnet was an aspiring singer, freshly arrived in the city and looking for a break.

"In the years since that night I have seen many beautiful girls," remembered Pearl, but Garnet had something special. "To me she was both the enchanted princess in the tower and the fairy godmother who made your wishes come true. I don't know how to say it—any more than I know how she did it—she made you feel *good* about yourself."

The two young women struck up an instant friendship. Just after the new year, Garnet invited her new friend to move into the nine-room apartment that she was renting on Riverside Drive. "I thought she was kidding," Pearl remembered with fresh astonishment. But Garnet insisted, explaining that she was expecting her mother and dad to arrive soon. Until then, "I would be doing her a favor to come and stay."

That was just Garnet's way. "She wouldn't be content merely to give you the shirt off her back; she would hand it to you on a gold platter and make you feel you were saving *her* life by taking it." How could Pearl say no?

☾

It was a sweet story the way she told it, but not a very likely one. The details of how Pearl found herself living with a showgirl in a deluxe apartment on Riverside Drive didn't add up. How an unemployed singer and an out-of-work factory worker managed to pay the rent on a nine-room apartment (while also keeping her dingy room on Second Avenue), she never even tried to explain.

There is an ancient question, usually posed as a lecherous joke, that every woman in the sex trades has been asked at least once: "What's a nice girl like you doing in a place like this?"

"Just lucky I guess" was the universal punch line, funny or not.

Like all women in her line of work, Pearl detested the Nice Girl Question. "I figured it just wasn't any of their damn business," she insisted heatedly. But among johns, as the customers were universally known, it was a favorite topic of conversation, especially in the better bordellos. "They considered that her story was one of their privileges and included in the price they had paid for their entertainment," explained one prominent madam with disdain.

It didn't take long for novices to discover that the honest answer—"making money"—was not what the customer hoped to hear. So they learned to answer the Nice Girl Question in a way that would titillate and flatter the johns. Most men preferred a sob story, as long as it didn't ruin the libidinous mood. "They like it best if you say you were ruined by an older man and were innocent," another madam explained to her new recruits. "Make it sad and cling to him as you say it. That, too, is what they come for. You'll find fucking is only part of our service to our guests."

Years later, when Pearl decided to tell her life story for public consumption, she was remarkably candid on an array of shocking subjects. But when asked how she survived the turbulent year of 1919, she turned uncharacteristically cagey. When pressed, she laughed off questions about her early years in the sex trade, especially the question of whether she had ever turned tricks herself. "I had to be a madam, I was never pretty enough to be a hustler," she insisted self-deprecatingly, using a common slang term for a prostitute.

There is a turning point early in the career of nearly every professional prostitute when the potential rewards of whoring appear before her in compelling detail. Suddenly, selling sex seems to offer the answer to all her problems, a quick path to a glamorous new life filled with cash, clothes, and camaraderie. Calling oneself a whore starts to seem like a sign of smarts and a badge of honesty—even honor—in a rotten world. For Pearl, that moment arrived right after the new year in 1920.

When forced finally to describe her underworld education, out of habit she chose a sad, sweet story of hunger, despair, and innocence beguiled, emphasizing "what a bitter, hope quenching, miserable sort of existence it was for a girl of nineteen."

But in her more candid moments, her answer to the Nice Girl Question was short, simple, and unsentimental: "Economics, I suppose, drove me into it. I had no wish to marry a pickle factory foreman, or work for $3 weekly in a Brooklyn corset factory," she said later. "I was tantalized, as many American are, by glimpses of an easier and more gracious life."

She left hints of a very different story. Underworld gossip insisted that she started turning tricks around the age of seventeen. At least one hooligan remembered seeing her at the time of the Armistice, hanging around the notorious Winter Garden Cabaret, at 50th Street and Seventh Avenue, a popular sporting world rendezvous under the famous Winter Garden Theater. Crime buffs would remember it as a favorite hangout of Gyp the Blood, murderer for hire, before he was sent to the electric chair. The Garden Cabaret "was a combination night club and bordello," recalled the Broadway producer Nils Thor Granlund, best known by his initials N.T.G. "They had dancing girls and girls who did song numbers, but they all had to be prostitutes."

In private, Pearl also spoke of a mysterious woman named Ruth who helped initiate her into the life. Committee of Fourteen investigators made note of a "Ruth Ryan," a well-known, high-priced prostitute who worked the cabarets and dance halls along the Gay White Way, padding her income by procuring girls for men staying in the midtown hotels and for weekend parties in the resort towns of Atlantic City and Lakewood, New Jersey—the kind of parties, the investigator noted, where "every girl is a lay."

Whether she was influenced by Abe or Ruth or some other well-meaning friend, Polly was ready to take the next step in her underworld education.

Although she didn't know it then, the baroque apartment buildings and elegant brownstones of Allrightnik's Row were hived with hustlers and gimme girls of every variety, from freelancing roommates who picked up sailors on leave to elaborate harems that catered to the carriage trade. Almost certainly Abe Shornik brought her to some kind of discreet brothel or call flat to introduce her to a madam or landlady, as such women were euphemistically called, who were always looking for fresh young faces.

Abe would have objected to being called a pimp. A pimp, as one longtime denizen of the Tenderloin explained, considered himself "a sort of business agent" for the women in his stable. "He attended to getting bail for her when she was arrested, paid wardmen for protection, arranged with madams to give her employment, rented the furnished room or apartment where he lived with her, drummed up trade for her when he could, did any kind of chore that might help their profits. He beat her up regularly, took every last cent from her he could lay hands on, bought the hop for their nightly jubilees, and cohabited with her."

Instead, Abe had all the marks of a "cadet," or in Yiddish a *zushiker*. The cadet's "occupation is professional seduction," as one vice committee report described it, recruiting women for the sex trade. Madams, pimps, and prostitutes themselves called it "breaking in" or "turning out" a girl. Sometimes cadets "turned out" square girls from scratch, but more often they concentrated on persuading charity girls and occasional trick-turners to become full-time professionals by entering a whorehouse. They were, in the words of one medical journal, "the Devil's pilots of an underworld."

Each step in the turn-out process had only one aim: to break down a woman's straight identity and replace it with a "racket mentality." Or as one plainspoken pimp put it, "Turning out a square broad means literally changing her mind."

The cadet's standard practice was to strike up a friendship with a girl like Pearl, who gave off the scent of poverty and loneliness. He offers advice and a sympathetic ear, earning the girl's trust. As her situation grows more desperate, he buys her dinner and slips her a little money, asking nothing in return. Casually, he begins to reshape her values, introducing her to hustlers, pimps, and party girls who aren't burdened by the straight world's scruples. He points out all the young women who are picking up extra cash on dates, making it seem as if everyone does it. She begins to make friends among the "regulars," as they called themselves, who all seem to dress better, have more fun, and live an easier life.

For a flirtatious, free-spirited girl in need it wasn't hard to conclude that hustling was a harmless way to fill one's purse. How was it so different from going on a date, where she had to "put out" for her evening's entertainment? Or from flirting with a fellow in the hope that he'd pony up for a new pair of stockings or a week's rent? As the hustlers liked to say, 'they were just selling what they'd been giving away before, and what any man would take for free if they could get it.'

Financially, the argument was unassailable. As the regulars pointed out, a reasonably good-looking woman turning several tricks a night, at an average of one to five dollars per customer, could make thirty to fifty dollars a week. "Do you suppose I am going back to earn five or six dollars a week in a factory," demanded one incredulous lady of the evening, "when I can earn that amount any night, and often much more?" Prostitution enjoyed steady demand, required few special skills and very little operating capital, and dealt in an infinitely renewable resource.

Most compelling of all was the rare feeling of power that came from the ability to attract a man and persuade him to hand over his precious cash. For a first-timer, those early tricks can create an exhilarating sense of independence, as she realizes that she can take care of herself with nothing more than her own natural resources, and a kind of euphoria at finally beating the system, at wresting something of her own out of this stingy, screwed-up world. For a young woman who had little else, such jolts of confidence and control could be intoxicating—especially when the alternatives seemed so grim.

The next step is the jump from freelancing to entering a brothel. A busy bordello offered plenty of advantages. A skilled hustler could make three or four times what she would on the street, with far fewer risks. In case of arrest, the madam would cover the bail and pay the right people to get the case dropped or minimized.

But it wasn't for everyone. A woman usually had to live on the premises for a week or more at a time, and she had little control over her work hours or choice of customers. Perhaps worse, waking up in a brothel made it impossible to pretend that she was merely partying to pay a few bills. The "turn out blues," they called it—that sickening feeling when the novice is forced to admit that she has truly become a whore.

In truth, Pearl fit to perfection the profile of the potential prostitute. It wasn't simply that she was poor. After all, there were many more poor women in New York than there were hustlers. "But there is more than one kind of poverty," she later observed. "There is emotional poverty and intellectual poverty and poverty of spirit. As well as material lacks, there can be a lack of love, a lack of education, a lack of hope."

Well, why shouldn't she try it? After all, what had "respectability" done for her since she'd left Russia? Her "respectable" family had kicked her out of her homes in Springfield and Brooklyn, and her "respectable" boss had raped and humiliated her. In her world respectability meant, at best, a meager wage in a chump job, a joyless marriage, and a passel of underfed children.

However she got to Allrightnik's Row that winter, the effect was electrifying. In retrospect, she said later, that glorious apartment on Riverside Drive was "no more luxurious than that of any upper-middle class New York family, but to me it was a revelation of how people—the people in the sun—could live, a miracle of richness and comfort."

"Now at last my nebulous longings came into sharp focus and crystallized, now I saw the goal I must set myself," she declared. "There really was a 'Goldine Madina' and it was right here on Riverside Drive." She just had to find a way to stay there.

☾

Those first few weeks of 1920, Pearl was overwhelmed by her good fortune. She was dazzled by Garnet's spacious apartment, fitted out with steam heat and modern plumbing, and by the rows of elegant shops and restaurants.

But behind these dignified facades dwelled a raffish melting pot of the chic and the shady. "The small town of the Upper West Side," as the bank robber Willie Sutton fondly called it, was where wealthy theatrical producers, garment industry moguls, and vaudeville and motion picture stars rubbed shoulders with "the better class of hoodlums." That March 1920, investigators estimated that at least five hundred apartments on the West Side were devoted to "unlawful purposes," including bookmaking, all-night crap games, marathon poker sessions, safe houses for burglars, and call houses.

Among the cognoscenti, the Upper West Side was known as the district of loose women, some five thousand of them by official estimates. It stretched from Columbus Circle, where men had their choice of no fewer than eight high-end bordellos just on the block between West 58th and 59th streets, all the way up to 135th Street in Harlem, where mixed-race bawdy houses and anything-goes buffet flats were the local specialty. In between were an untold number of "love nests," as the tabloid press dubbed them, where shapely chorines entertained their boyfriends, and millionaires stashed their mistresses, spawning a well-worn joke: "Are you married or do you live on 72nd Street?" Here was where hotel clerks would overlook a conspicuous lack of luggage or wedding ring, where women in makeshift studios offered "private dance lessons" to lonely men, and models and showgirls scraped up a living by shedding their clothes in shabby shared hall rooms while waiting to be discovered.

Garnet's apartment was a favorite gathering spot for the stay-up-lates who were just finishing work around midnight and looking to let off a little steam. Like Garnet, most of them were trying to claw their way to stardom. This was the heyday of live entertainment, and Manhattan was its bawdy, boisterous capital. It was home to more than fifty legitimate theaters, hundreds of smaller venues, and every imaginable kind of performer, including acrobats, magicians, animal acts, comedians, singers, jugglers, female impersonators, sideshow freaks, serious actors, and hoofers of every variety, from tap dancers to cooch dancers.

Pearl knew nothing about show business—she'd never seen a play or any show more elaborate than the live song-and-dance acts that performed between movie reels—but she was thrilled by her roommate's friends. They bubbled with jokes, wisecracks, and outrageous behavior. They knew all the hot dance steps and popular songs, and their speech crackled with the latest slang and naughty double entendres. Fellows were *sports*, *pals*, *gees*, and *mugs*; women were *frails*, *twists*, *tomatoes*, *dames*, and *Janes*. Most of them swore like stevedores, and even the primmest freely tossed around the curse du jour: "Nuts!" or "Nertz!" in Brooklynese.

And how they dressed! The boys were as vain as the girls, preening in their "jazz suits," with their ultrawide lapels and pinched waists set off by candy-striped shirts, and their hair slicked back with brilliantine until it shone like patent leather. The girls wore their necklines low, their hemlines short, and their dresses daringly tight. Tossing off the constraints of corsets and garter belts, they rolled down their sheer silk stockings to show off bare thighs and dimpled knees. They powdered their faces, rouged their cheeks and lips, and tinted their eyelashes with mascara made from coal and petroleum jelly. Shedding the long curls, puffs, and pompadours that were so fashionable before the war, they cropped their hair into short, soft bobs that swished around their ears when they danced—styles that only scarlet women, radical bohemians, and lesbians had once dared to wear.

To be sure, these were not people her cousins would have approved of—they were *sheygetzim* and *nafkeh*, hoodlums and hussies, by Breina's standards, no-goodniks one and all. They thumbed their noses at the stuffed shirts who looked down on theater people as only one step removed from the gutter. They were shockingly casual toward matters of the flesh, smoking cigarettes or cheap cigars and guzzling liquor with gusto. There were girls who wore trousers, and boys with freshly plucked eyebrows, sporting flashy red ties and lavender cologne, and there was no predicting who would pair off at parties. Most of them seemed to have no more schooling than she did—many hailed from Russian shtetls just like hers—but they oozed charisma and personality. To Pearl, they were glamour incarnate.

Garnet's pals happily befriended the wide-eyed girl. "They liked me, I think, because being so naïve I made a good straight man," she remembered. "I was constantly being called on to watch (and, of course, applaud)." Best of all was when Garnet sang, accompanying herself on the guitar: "My favorite number was 'Moonshine Valley,' and I pestered her for it constantly." They christened her with an American nickname— Polly—a new name to match her new life.

☾

Thus, Pearl made her debut in the intoxicating world of Broadway. Nowadays the term *Broadway* is associated almost exclusively with the theater district around Times Square. But early in the twentieth century, Broadway was New York's avenue of pleasure, of sporting life, of excitement, sensation, and fun. It took its name from the long crooked avenue that angled from the southern to the northern tip of Manhattan. It was the first street in New York to be fitted with gaslights, then with electric lights. This attracted hotels, restaurants, theaters, saloons, cabarets, and dance halls. Most cities of any size had a "White Light District," as they were called, but Manhattan's was the gaudiest of them all.

Yet Broadway was more than a street, as its admirers often observed: it was a state of mind. It was devoted equally to pleasure and profit— especially the profits that came from peddling pleasure—and took its manners and morals from the shadowy worlds of theater and gambling. Here the devil-may-care defiance of bohemia met the unfettered commerce of capitalism, where all desires could be fulfilled if the bankroll was big enough.

The brazen Broadway ethos ran like rivulets throughout the canyons of Manhattan. It coursed through the old Madison Square Garden at 26th Street and Madison Avenue, the mecca of gamblers, bookies, loan sharks, sportsmen, suckers, and circuses, and through the glittering department stores of Herald Square, where Broadway's fashions were marketed to the masses. It blossomed in the Harlem nightspots, where African American entertainers were introducing the hot new sounds coming out of Charleston, New Orleans, and Chicago. It flowed west to the Hudson River piers, on Luxury Liner Row, where massive passenger ships arrived from Europe. Broadway's bedroom community was the Upper West Side, only a short hop by taxi, subway, or the Sixth Avenue El.

Pearl didn't know it then, but it was her great luck to arrive during Broadway's last golden age, before Hollywood usurped it as America's prime mythmaker. Untold numbers of playwrights, novelists, filmmakers, newspaper reporters, publicists, cartoonists, and songwriters took the gritty, glittering avenue as their muse, spinning stories of would-be Cinderellas and Horatio Alger heroes come to seek their fortune. Wordsmiths and wise guys made a sport of inventing nicknames for Broadway's giddy combination of hotheaded ambition and cold-eyed profit taking, of starry-eyed hopes and blighted dreams: the Big Street, the Main Stem, the Hardened Artery, Rue de Revelry, Larceny Lane, Grifters Gulch, Sucker Street.

The glamour had a shadowy side. No profession besides prostitution was so stigmatized as show business. Decent people, with good homes, happy families, and solid educations, simply did not become entertainers, any more than they became pickpockets or pimps. It attracted those who seethed with restless ambition but couldn't or wouldn't follow the slow and steady path. Turning occasional tricks and peddling drugs were common ways for performers to eke out extra income in a precarious profession. Musicians, vaudevillians, prostitutes, professional gamblers, strongarm men, and drug dealers—all lived a vagabond lifestyle, working late hours in sketchy places for low pay, that fostered a unique camaraderie and an easy come, easy go broad-mindedness.

The Big Street was an oasis of tolerance for outsiders and rebels. They spoke in the accents of Dublin, Liverpool, Sicily, and Pinsk, of Pittsburgh, Peoria, and a thousand tiny tank towns. But Broadway had a special appeal for Russian Jews, who were shut out of the more established professions. "If you want to spot the Broadwayite in embryo, a good idea is to take a spin down through the Lower East Side some Sunday afternoon," observed the columnist Mel Heimer. Jews were surging into the theater, songwriting, and fashion industries, and the rising fields of motion pictures, publicity, and popular journalism. As one early expert noted, "it is not an exaggerated statement to declare that seventy-five percent of the amusement output in this country is in the control of Hebrews." They were also deeply involved in Broadway's darker arts—especially gambling, loan sharking, fencing of stolen goods, drug dealing, and prostitution.

Pearl—now known as Polly to all but her close friends—quickly discovered that Broadway was as welcoming to women as it was to Jews. "Broadway's Billion Dollar Beauty Trust," as one publicist dubbed it, was the great economic engine of the Whizzy White Way. Warm female flesh and the titillating air of sexual possibility encouraged men to spend more freely, whether they were gambling, drinking, or buying tickets. Without Broadway butterflies, as the press dubbed them, the wine, women, and song racket would collapse like a two-legged stool.

Broadway was one of the very few places in America where a single woman had a shot at earning a decent living. A game, reasonably good-looking girl could pick up plenty of cabbage, in the slang of the day. The musical revues, cabarets, and vaudeville and burlesque shows employed thousands of women in varying stages of undress. A young woman who was exceptionally dewy could model for the magazine illustrators who kept their studios on West 67th Street. The less talented worked as dime-a-dance girls in the closed dance halls, where men paid ten cents for every turn around the floor, or in the garment showrooms on Seventh Avenue, modeling the latest styles for out-of-town buyers with roaming hands as they "felt the fabric" or "examined the fit" of the dresses.

☾

That spring Garnet got her big break. She was cast in a musical revue called *Cinderella on Broadway*, produced by the legendary Shubert brothers and scheduled to open in July at the Winter Garden Theater.

Musical revues were the hot ticket in 1920 and a prime pillar of the Broadway Beauty Trust. Essentially extravagant variety shows strung along a slight story line, revues featured a mix of comic skits, dance numbers, popular songs, and the most critical ingredient: scantily clad showgirls. "Girls of every type and setting," sighed one appreciative critic, "girls of every charm and grace—just girls, girls, girls; bevies and bevies of wondrous, beautiful girls." Florenz Ziegfeld and his famous *Ziegfeld Follies* were the gold standard, a clear cut above the Shubert brothers in music, sets, and costumes. The Shuberts compensated by sexing up their leg shows, as they were nicknamed, with more nudity and risqué humor.

But Garnet quickly discovered that the reality of being in a big show was not the bowl of cherries that the magazines and movies made out. Rehearsals—and thus paychecks—wouldn't start till May at the earliest. The Shubert brothers were notorious cheapskates, paying their chorus girls the bare union minimum of thirty dollars a week and refusing to cough up for the extra rehearsals and performances they often demanded. Lee and his brother J.J. were also notorious lechers, even by the standards of Broadway. "Mr. Lee was discreet; Mr. J.J. was coarse and didn't give a damn," one of their press agents recalled, "but they both believed in mixing sex and business."

"What they did to those girls wasn't fair," the choreographer Agnes de Mille recalled hotly. "If you didn't sleep with them you didn't get the part. The Shuberts ran a brothel: let them sue me." Hungry chorus girls learned to tolerate the brothers' wandering hands, casually fondling their breasts and pinching their bottoms in rehearsals, and pressing them up against the wall in the hallways. Favored girls were summoned to their offices to have sex with the brothers on their lunch breaks or after matinees. ("They'd give the girls ten dollars each," remembered the lyricist Irving Caesar, "and the girls made them happy.") Complaining would only get a girl fired and, quite possibly, raped.

The Shuberts were hardly alone in their predatory predilections. Forty-Second Street, the main theatrical thoroughfare, was lousy with men proffering stardom in exchange for sex. "The Christian producers were out for Jewish girls, and the Jewish producers wanted the *shicksas*," noted the actress Barbara Barondess. "They didn't feel guilty this way." (Barondess's strategy for fending off passes was to wear sanitary napkins and pretend to have her menstrual period every time she showed up for an audition.) Women who lasted were those who didn't make too much of a fuss about the sex-for-opportunity equation.

As for Garnet, she'd finally set her dainty foot on the first rung of the ladder to stardom. What did it matter how she got there as long as she continued to climb?

Then one day Garnet appeared in the apartment wearing a beautiful Chinese robe, unlike anything Polly had seen before, made of soft black satin with wide sleeves and a red dragon embroidered on it. As she was admiring it, Garnet mentioned that it was what she liked to wear whenever she went on a "hop party." When Polly looked confused, her friend held up her sleeve so Polly could smell its pungent aroma.

"What kind of perfume is that?" she asked.

"Not perfume, honey, hop," Garnet said. When Polly still seemed puzzled, she added, "Opium—don't you know?"

At first, Polly was sure she was kidding, but then how could anyone joke about taking drugs? Everyone had heard wild tales of sinister Chinatown opium dens. And anyone who'd lingered on the street corners of Brownsville had heard tough-talking kids bragging about snuffing cocaine and seen the strung-out junkies who hung around the pool halls and cigar stores.

To Polly's surprise, Garnet explained in enthusiastic detail, describing the elaborate layout used to smoke opium; the long flutelike pipe, the small alcohol-lit lamp, and the *yen-hok*, a long needle shaped like a crochet hook that was used to form the sticky black pills of opium. Still, Polly refused to believe her. "She knew how gullible I was and how the others always were stringing me along, so I tried to tell myself this was just another gag."

But Garnet wasn't joking. "Smoking hop," or "kicking the gong around," as it was known colloquially, was the preferred pastime of many of Polly's new friends. Hopheads or pipies, as they were often called, considered themselves a cut above the users of heroin or morphine. "You'd be surprised: wealthy people smoked opium, millionaires, rich people," one former junkie explained. Even after the federal government cracked down on its importation, hop remained the high of choice for showbiz folk, call girls, prosperous criminals, and rich bohemians.

For denizens of the night, especially prostitutes, dope was a professional tool, a way to jazz up their energy, to loosen them up for a night's work, and to unwind or forget afterward. "Most girls in this business use it," as one hustler-turned-junkie explained. "You have to be cheerful and lively when you go on dates. Men are paying you, and they expect to be entertained." When the party was over, dope helped distract the mind from "stark reality." "Sometimes your very soul revolts against those awful male hands," she added wistfully.

Now that she'd confessed, Garnet no longer tried to hide her habit from Polly. Opium, with its elaborate equipment and rituals, was a sociable drug, and she began hosting hop parties almost every night. These gatherings literally reeked of the forbidden. Garnet would cover the floors with cushions or mattresses and stuff fabric under the cracks in the door to the hall, taping the windows and doors or covering them with blankets to keep the strong stench of smoke from seeping out. Partygoers sat cross-legged or lay on their hips, turned to face the lamp and the tray of paraphernalia. A "chef" formed the tarlike opium into small pellets, then placed them in a long pipe that would be passed around until everyone had their fill. Novices often fell into cold sweats and vomited before being overtaken by a gentle euphoria. More experienced smokers chatted, snacked on hard candies or fruit, and listened to music, sometimes shedding their clothes to be more comfortable, or slipping off to have intense, languid sex. Much of the time they simply gazed into space, mesmerized by "pipe dreams," eventually falling into a deep sleep.

Garnet pressed her roommate to join in the fun, but Polly wanted nothing to do with the pipe and thought she shouldn't either. The more Polly resisted, the more snappish and short-tempered her friend became. But when Polly talked of moving out, Garnet begged her to stay, and she relented. "It was a nerve-wracking, even dangerous situation," remembered Polly, "but I thought surely when her mother got there the parties would have to stop."

When Garnet's family finally did arrive, she was shocked to find that her "dad" was not much older than Garnet. When Polly asked about the age difference, Garnet broke into laughter, then explained that he was her mother's gigolo. Polly had no idea what a gigolo was but assumed it meant he was some sort of exotic performer. "When I learned the meaning of the word it was quite a letdown," she recalled. Perhaps he was a gigolo, ever on the lookout for women to support him in a life of leisure. In light of later events, *pimp* might've been the better word.

Either way, it wasn't a good sign.

☾

The hop parties did not stop with the arrival of Garnet's mother. Instead, they shifted to the apartment of one of Garnet's smoking pals, a young woman named Edna Kirkwood. "There was no reason I had to go, but I tagged along," Polly admitted. "I would not smoke opium, but I was dazzled by the parties."

Edna Kirkwood was in her twenties (her birth date depended on who was asking), Chicago-born, with wavy auburn hair, small gray eyes, and a winning smile. She was not as beautiful or talented as Garnet, but she had "a finish, an authority," that Garnet lacked. She must have had something, because Edna had hit the gold digger's jackpot. Officially she was a stenographer—someone who could type and take dictation by shorthand, a job made obsolete by computers. In actuality, as Polly explained, Edna was "the mistress of a well-known Wall Street man."

Like stenography, the role of a mistress is an occupation that has fallen on hard times. Back in those days it was often observed with a leering wink that the one job usually led to the other. As the wisecrackers liked to say: "When the struggling stenographer stops struggling, she often discovers she doesn't have to be a stenographer."

That wasn't entirely a joke. At a time when divorce was frowned upon, and single women had few good options for supporting themselves, it was surprisingly common for men who could afford the luxury to take a mistress. The era "was abounding with millionaires who kept their sweethearts in love nests that dotted Manhattan all the way from Murray Hill to Riverside Drive," remembered the keen-eyed, sharp-tongued screenwriter Anita Loos. A pretty playmate waiting uptown was safer and more convenient than a casual pickup. For men riding high, whether on Wall Street, Riverside Drive, or Second Avenue, an expensive mistress was a potent status symbol. "As soon as they were affluent enough, they usually bought themselves one or two show girls," remembered Willie Sutton of the high-class hoodlums. "Once a man had acquired a blonde or two, he was considered to have reached the big time."

Hunting for well-heeled sugar daddies was big business among the Broadway demimonde—not for nothing was the avenue dubbed Gold Diggers Gulch. A successful mistress honed the natural resources of the Broadway butterfly—the slim figure, the pretty face, the flamboyant sex appeal—to an art. She had to cultivate the ability to listen, to anticipate a man's needs, to offer the thrill of novelty and the comfort of monogamy, to provide all the pleasures of a relationship and none of the burdens. It wasn't as easy as it looked. The boredom and jealousy, the family holidays spent alone, and the often-vast difference in age all created temptations that could easily spoil a lucrative relationship.

Perhaps the biggest challenge was bringing the affair to an economically advantageous ending. The key, counseled wise women, was subtly persuading one's swain to skip the sentimental folderol, the flowers and chocolates and trinkets, and to give gifts of hard assets. Real estate or stocks and bonds were best, but furs and jewelry were welcome too—anything that could be sold or pawned for cash in an emergency. (Art deco bracelets studded with diamonds, rubies, and sapphires were particular favorites among the gold diggers of the 1920s, who laughingly called them their "service stripes.") Mistresses who didn't look to the future found themselves on the skids as they aged, slipping from man to man, each a little less secure than the last, until they were turning tricks like a common whore.

Polly didn't name Edna's "well-known Wall Street man," but he was most likely a thirty-three-year-old financier named Leonard Kennedy. Unlike most of the men she'd met so far, Kennedy was what the sociologists would call a White Anglo-Saxon Protestant, with impeccable WASP credentials. A descendant of the *Mayflower* pilgrims, an alumnus of Andover and Yale University, he'd begun his career as a bond salesman and now earned $100,000 a year as the vice president of a small steel company. He was in the process of opening his own engineering consulting firm. Kennedy was one of a new generation of ambitious *arrivistes* on Wall Street, brilliant and well educated, from respectable but not wealthy families. They were cynical about money yet zealously determined to acquire as much of it as they could, as fast as possible, and were none too scrupulous about how they did it. Leonard liked to quip, said his fellow Yalies, that "he is a theoretical anarchist, but that he usually votes Republican."

When Polly met him, Leonard and his close friend, the investment banker Clarence Dillon, were in the midst of masterminding a colossally corrupt scheme to take over the management of Goodyear Tire and Rubber Company, an international conglomerate that was teetering on the verge of bankruptcy. When the deal went through, Leonard (who, by no coincidence, ran his consulting company with only a single stenographer to aid him, according to *The New York Times*) made an astronomical amount of money—nearly $1 million for twenty-five months of work—with the secret proviso that he kick back 45 percent of his profits to a shell corporation owned by Clarence Dillon's wife. In the unregulated world of 1920s Wall Street, such secret self-dealing was not illegal, but it was undeniably unethical, as confirmed by government investigators and by the judge who later overturned most of its provisions. Nonetheless, Leonard walked away with little more than a scolding, taking his windfall with him.

This was serious dough, and Leonard was happily dropping a generous chunk of it on Edna. He set her up in a magnificent duplex apartment on West 86th Street with a full staff of servants and closets bursting with elegant dresses and furs. He provided her with a car and chauffeur and an allowance of $2,000 a month (approximately $27,000 in current dollars).

Leonard was never going to marry Edna—he had a wife tucked away in the affluent suburb of Rye, New York, who would soon give birth to a daughter—but by way of compensation, he put away a hundred thousand dollars in a trust, to be given to her when the affair ended. It was a sensible investment at a time when newspapers and men's clubs were full of anxious stories of wealthy husbands blackmailed by unscrupulous lovers. An unhappy former mistress was a dangerous creature—especially if she happened to be the stenographer who had helped set up his shady shell company.

The mere idea of such sums was incredible to Polly. "Naturally enough, the thought occurred to me that I couldn't make two thousand dollars in a factory if I worked overtime for five years. And as for a hundred thousand—well, I just didn't believe there was that much money in the world."

Edna's hop parties attracted a more cosmopolitan crowd, who made Garnet's friends look like pikers. Draped on the enormous white fur rug where Edna held court lounged some of the biggest names in theater, motion pictures, and Tin Pan Alley. They were "first-nighters" in the slang of the day who attended the openings of all the big shows and patronized the chic cafés, and spent weekends on the rolling estates of Long Island and New Jersey.

Polly was still green enough that she had to be told who most of these big names were, but even she recognized the movie stars. She was shocked to see the young comedienne Mabel Normand, one of Hollywood's biggest stars, lying on her hip in Edna's apartment, her famously milky skin and coquettish eyes looking wan and wasted. Normand's drug use was one of the worst-kept secrets in showbiz; her cocaine habit alone was said to cost as much as $2,000 a month. But she was hardly the only one. The early motion picture business was rife with high-living, hard-partying, bed-hopping drug users. Many of the actresses who ran in Normand's crowd—long-forgotten sparklers like Olive Thomas, Alma Rubens, Barbara La Marr, and Constance and Norma Talmadge—were enthusiastic dopers.

Polly became a fixture at Edna's parties. Edna took a liking to the girl, and in return, Polly remembered, "I followed her around like a puppy dog." Edna gave her a crash course in high style, suggesting a more flattering hairdo and subtler makeup, showing her how to use lipstick to give herself a fashionable bee-stung pout. She spiffed up her table manners, "wising me up on various points of etiquette." Although Polly never acquired a taste for the pipe, Edna's friends took up the naïve but enthusiastic girl as an amusing mascot. They nicknamed her "Hop Toy"—smoker's slang for the tiny pills of opium and the petite containers used to store them—"because I was so small and because I was always hopping up and down in my eagerness not to miss anything."

Polly was happy to serve as an audience and straight man for these hams and hoydens. One of the most famous of her new friends told her she had eyes like Nazimova's, referring to the raven-haired, Russian Jewish movie star who'd made a career playing exotic seductresses, and offered to arrange for a screen test for her. Polly, who'd already picked up the Broadway habit of world-weary wisecracks, replied with the clear-eyed, self-deprecating humor that would come to be her trademark: "I said (calling my shots better than I had any idea) that probably the only pictures I'd ever pose for would be taken for the Rogue's Gallery."

Edna's air of refinement only made her drug addiction all the more baffling. "When not taking drugs," Polly recalled, "she was kind and discerning and fastidious—a woman who bore no resemblance whatsoever to the crazy slut that was herself hopped up." If she hadn't seen with her own eyes what dope could do, Polly mused, "I might have sought this escape during the frantic, hectic years to come." Instead, she developed a lifelong loathing for drugs.

One evening at Edna's in that spring of 1920, she met a young man from Cincinnati named Ernie Levin. Ernie was everything a girl could hope for—handsome, a good family, a college graduate—and most important, he shared her distaste for drugs. The two of them began to duck out of the parties and go for long drives through the city. Soon they were seeing each other whenever he came to New York.

Finally, he confessed that he was in love with her. Polly was thrilled. "Here is a nice Jewish boy, educated and all, the kind of man my parents would approve of me marrying," she remembered thinking. She began dropping hints about marriage.

Two months or so after they began their affair, Ernie called to say he had big news and wanted to see her right away. This was it, Polly was sure, as she prepared breathlessly for his proposal. But when he arrived, a triumphant Ernie announced that he had just become engaged to a lovely girl from his hometown. He wanted Polly to be the first to know.

It was yet another hard lesson in heartbreak. "I realized how foolish, how unrealistic, I had been. I wasn't pretty, I wasn't well educated"—and in her current situation, she could never qualify as the girl next door. It was devastating, but in a very different way than with Frank. "I may fall in love again," Polly told herself bitterly, "but so help me the next man I get starry-eyed over is going to have to lay his cards on the table before I'll pick up my hand."

Meanwhile Garnet was spiraling out of control. When opium became harder to get, she turned to other drugs, slipping into the vicious cycle of the nighthawk: a snort of cocaine to pep up, a shot of heroin or morphine to calm down, another hit to sleep. She lost weight and became "very hard to handle—sullen and nasty, sometimes violent." At the theater, she began showing up late and missing rehearsals, but when anyone tried to talk to her about it, she erupted in fury. By this point, the beautiful girl no longer cared. All she wanted was dope.

"There was nothing I could do," Polly lamented. "Just talking never got anyone off the junk, and I had neither the authority nor the knowledge to take stronger measures."

Finally, she recalled primly, when Garnet began "to display Lesbian tendencies toward me, I knew I had to get out of there."

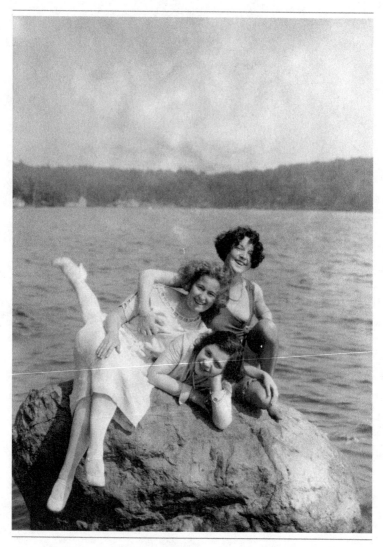

Polly, her business partner Edna Kirkwood, and a friend in Lake Hopatcong, New Jersey, playground of the vaudeville and burlesque crowd, 1923

5

Liquor and Lust

Nick Montana was the first to spot Polly's leadership potential. She was only twenty years old and hadn't been in the game very long, but he saw something promising in the bright, bubbly girl that set her apart from the average tart.

In turn, it would have been easy for Polly to mistake Nichola Montana for just another two-bit punk. The city was thick with aspiring wise guys like Nick, who all shared the same hard-luck story. Born in a tiny mountain village in southern Italy, where jobs and food were scarce, he'd immigrated to New York at the age of two and spent a hardscrabble childhood on the streets before dropping out of school to become a sneak thief and a gambler—the standard entry-level jobs of the underworld. He'd worked for a while as a "betting commissioner," a fancy title for a bookmaker's runner, picking up and paying off bets, and strong-arming deadbeat bettors. Like many scrappy ghetto boys, he took a brief turn as a boxer before deciding to find a less bruising way to make a living.

His best asset was a face that made a girl look twice: full lips, curly black hair, and wide, heavy-lidded eyes fringed with long, lush lashes— bedroom eyes, as the true confession magazines used to call them. A face like that made pimping a natural option. But young Nick could see that the world's oldest profession was changing, and he had bigger ambitions.

In the five years since Polly first stepped foot in America, the wine, women, and song racket had been radically disrupted by political pressures, new technologies, real estate opportunities, and greed—the usual New York story.

Back in 1913, the city was teeming with opportunities to buy sex. Men looking for fun needed only to stroll through one of the city's many sporting districts, downtown along "the Rialto" of Fourteenth Street, on Allen Street in the Lower East Side, or in the gaudy Lower West Side entertainment districts, known colloquially as "the Tenderloin." Street-walkers brazenly solicited passersby at all hours, and sporting women haunted the drinking spots, theaters, and cheap hotels. Bordellos oper-ated openly in the tenements and brownstones and brazenly advertised their wares in gentlemen's guidebooks.

Alarmed by the rising tide of sin, the Committee of Fourteen, a pro-gressive coalition of good-government reformers, medical advocates, and religious and social service organizations, had been campaigning for years to clean up the morals and health of the city. Their most perni-cious enemies were "The Devil's Siamese Twins": "liquor and lust," "the saloon and the brothel."

By the time Polly returned to New York City in 1915, their efforts had begun reaping rich rewards. The reformers pressed through laws outlawing narcotics, prizefighting, and bookmaking and successfully fought to keep the ban on birth control and Sunday baseball games. They exposed the ties between corrupt city officials, police protection of prostitution, and the alcohol and brewing interests. They struck a death blow to the red-light districts, passing new vagrancy laws that made it illegal to offer sex or "lewd acts" for money and instituting mandatory testing for venereal disease among convicted prostitutes.

The entry of the United States into World War I boosted their efforts when it was discovered that thousands of young soldiers were suffer-ing from syphilis and gonorrhea. In response, the federal government outlawed prostitution within a ten-mile radius of any military encamp-ment and banned the sale of alcohol to soldiers. By the summer of 1917, Tenderloin Districts in all major cities with barracks or posts were being shut down for good.

Then the forces of purity and progress rode the patriotic fervor of the war to their greatest victory yet. On January 16, 1919, the United States ratified the Eighteenth Amendment to the Constitution, prohibiting the production, transport, and sale of intoxicating liquor. This was followed by the so-called Volstead Act, granting federal and state governments powers to enforce the ban. At the stroke of midnight exactly one year after the amendment's passage, the Noble Experiment of Prohibition, as it came to be known, would commence.

New York City would be the primary testing ground of the new law. "The failure or success of Prohibition as far as the world is concerned is its failure or success in New York," as even the Anti-Saloon League conceded. Broadway would be the epicenter of the battle. As the federal enforcements agents liked to say: "Beat Broadway, and mop up the rest of the country at leisure."

In early January 1920, as the drop-dead date approached, the mood on Broadway grew gloomy and anxious. At the notorious Tokio Cabaret on 45th Street, a worried waiter frankly summed up the problem for a Committee of Fourteen undercover investigator; as he put it, "the Tokio couldn't exist without Booze and Cunts." Many places had stocked up on legal liquor before January 16—at the Tokio they had already switched to serving it in white china coffee cups and jacked the price up to a dollar a drink—but supplies couldn't last forever.

Nonetheless, Broadway had no intention of giving up the title of wettest spot in America without a fight. Within a week, illegal speakeasies began springing up like mushrooms across the city, in basements and backrooms, in respectable brownstones, dim tenements, and side-street hideaways. The early drinking spots were often little more than small apartments stocked with some wooden tables and chairs, a piano or phonograph, maybe a few cheap rugs or framed lithographs of undraped women. "All you need is two bottles and a room and you have a speakeasy," as one politician pointed out. By February 1920, according to one count, the 10,343 licensed saloons and barrooms of 1919 had been replaced by more than fifteen thousand speakeasies.

To the surprise of both the woeful Wets and idealistic Drys, the Noble Experiment of Prohibition was not going as planned. Of course, any philosophical vice peddler or Broadway oddsmaker, had they been consulted, would have called Prohibition a long shot at best. The vice trades had survived the crusades of self-appointed sin chasers for centuries. There would always be a black market for forbidden pleasures; adding liquor to the list of contraband only enlarged and energized it.

Outlawing liquor created a financial windfall for the criminal classes.

Young fellows who had been knocking over stores, pimping, picking pockets, passing counterfeit bills, or running small scams were flocking to the lucrative business of quenching the city's illicit thirst. Bootlegging gangs, loosely organized around ethnic lines—dominated by the Irish, Jews, and Italians—sprang up across the city, setting up secret stills, robbing warehouses where industrial alcohol was stored, cutting it and delivering it to speakeasies, and retailing it to eager customers.

"With surreptitious drinking," noted *Variety*, the hometown paper of the Broadway regulars, "surreptitious romancing was a natural short and quick step." As with liquor, the market for sex had not disappeared along with the sporting districts—it had merely scattered and gone underground. Clandestine call houses were springing up as fast as speakeasies. That winter investigators counted some five hundred of them just on the West Side, and in the whole city "approximately 200,000 women in the regular army of vice."

Nor had closing the brothels and saloons put an end to political corruption. In March 1920, just as Polly was learning the tricks of her new trade, sixteen police officers were accused of running a "vice ring" that had blackmailed over five hundred prostitutes. The police commissioner, Richard Enright, was an old-school cop who generally cast a tolerant eye over the foibles of his officers. But the press and the Sunday school set had latched onto the story and were whipping up public anger. To quell the scandal, Commissioner Enright ordered a cleanup of the wicked West Side, creating "a great exodus of disorderly women," in *The New York Times*'s words. In their wake, they left hundreds of unexpectedly empty apartments, an army of frustrated customers, and a temporarily chastened vice squad, who were lying low until the tempest blew over.

Nick Montana saw opportunity in this new era of clean living. But while most of the city's young rowdies were throwing themselves into the booze business, Nick was drawn to the softer, if less prestigious, "woman racket."

For Nick, these disruptions presented a sterling business opportunity. Madams needed two things that were increasingly hard to come by in this new landscape: a steady supply of girls and a pool of cash in case of emergencies. Moving the brothels from brownstones to apartment buildings was good for evading cops and blackmailers but made it harder to recruit new girls and connect with customers. The reduced scale of operations meant more madams were small-timers, so were less likely to own their building or possess the savings to make bail after a raid.

When Polly met Nick, he was creating a thriving new business as a "booker"—not to be confused with bookmakers who handle sports betting, but a sort of talent agent who supplied disorderly houses with fresh faces. He developed a network of madams seeking experienced working girls and recruited a roster of hustlers whom he rotated through various call houses around the city. The girls stayed a week or two in each house and then moved on to the next one when their novelty waned. In return, Nick collected a small fee or a percentage of the girl's earnings, sometimes from the girl, sometimes from the madam who ran the house, sometimes both. In case of police raids, he provided cash to put up bail and pay off the police and magistrates. As his bankroll grew, he began backing a string of small whorehouses in apartments around Manhattan.

Years later the newspapers would describe Nicholas Montana as a "big-time pimp," a *puttaniere*, in the words of his countrymen. But he balked at that. Nick envisioned himself as the Henry Ford of the sex trade, turning the cadet's role into something resembling a modern assembly line.

That spring, as Polly was anxiously casting about for a new situation, Nick proposed to set her up in her own apartment on the Upper West Side. A house of assignation, she would later call it, "a trysting place for his mistress." But from the start, it had all the earmarks of a modest call flat, with Polly living there and bringing in girls to quietly turn tricks. Nothing fancy, a couple bedrooms, a living room and kitchen. But if done right even a small joint like that could haul in the dough. If she got into trouble with the law, Nick would handle it. All she had to do was run the place.

"I jumped at his offer," she remembered.

In June 1920 she once again packed up her belongings. "I had progressed from a potato sack to a battered old theatrical trunk," a gift from Garnet's mother, and had filled out her wardrobe with hand-me-downs from Garnet and Edna, including her "pride and joy," a bird of paradise, an extravagant hair ornament made of rare bird feathers that was then the height of jazz baby chic. Till the very end of her life, she would treasure it as a memento of her arrival on Allrightnik's Row.

"It was a thrill to have a place of my own, but my thoughts were tempered with sadness," remembered Polly. On June 24 *Cinderella on Broadway* received a gala opening at the Winter Garden Theater, wowing audiences with a grand finale featuring "a human roulette wheel" draped with half-naked chorus girls—"to be sure, more Broadway than Cinderella" observed the critic for *The New York Times*.

Garnet had long ago been fired.

€

With Nick's backing, Polly rented a furnished two-bedroom apartment at 620 West 115th Street, in the Upper West Side neighborhood of Morningside Heights, at the southern edge of Harlem. The Arleigh, as the building was called, was one of dozens of large elevator apartment buildings that had begun replacing the old-fashioned row houses before the war.

Once an Irish enclave, this corner of Harlem had recently begun attracting the *ernst yidn*, the earnest Jews of the rising middle class, who were fleeing the poverty and crime of the Lower East Side. Columbia University, then an all-male school, was directly across the street from her apartment, and Barnard College for women was just around the corner, lending a scholarly air to the neighborhood. Her neighbors were doctors, professors, club women, and other bookish types who would never suspect a professional floozy among their neighbors, especially a pert, apple-cheeked girl who was easily mistaken for a Barnard student.

Luckily, not all those Harlem-bound strivers were so earnest. Just south of Polly's new nest, at West 110th Street and Broadway, was a rowdy clutch of gin mills and dance halls fondly known as Little Coney Island. One block north, West 116th was fast becoming notorious as the uptown outpost of the Second Avenue underworld. It boasted dozens of poolrooms, call flats, gambling joints, and speakeasies, and many of the city's busiest moving picture houses and vaudeville theaters, as well as Grupp's boxing gym, an Irish stronghold where Jack Dempsey began his rise to fame. The New Vienna Restaurant, over on 116th Street and Lenox Avenue, was a popular hangout for professional gamblers, fight promot-

Polish passport of Pearl's father, Moshe Adler

Pearl's hometown of Yanow, Belarus, in the Pale of Russia,
during the muddy season, 1916

Pearl's mother, Gittel, and
younger brothers in Yanow, 1914

Pearl in a borrowed dress
for her grammar school
graduation, 1914

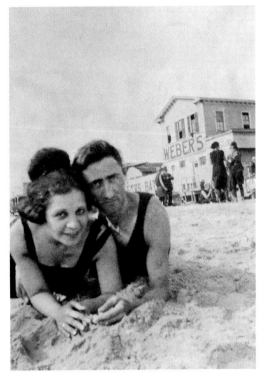

Pearl as a teenager enjoying the pleasures and perils of Coney Island, 1915

Mystery Enters Dope Case

SEIZED in a narcotic raid on 8th ave. apartment, Miss Garnet Williams (left), who said she once played Cinderella on Broadway, was bailed yesterday by fashionably dressed woman who refused to divulge identity in West Side court.

—Story on page 25.

(NEWS photo)

Polly's best friend, Garnet Williams, in the *New York Daily News* after her arrest for possession of heroin, August 28, 1925

The Jefferson Market Women's Court in Greenwich Village, where Polly spent many unhappy hours awaiting trial

Arnold Rothstein—"The Brain"—gambler, grifter, and banker to the underworld

"Smiling George" McManus, the professional gambler who spread Polly's reputation among the high-rolling dice players, and the accused murderer of Rothstein

Lindy's delicatessen, where the underworld ate cheesecake with the "tinsel aristocracy" of Broadway, Tin Pan Alley, and the Friars Club

William "Big Bill" Dwyer—
"King of the Bootleggers"—
an important early patron
of Polly's services

View of the Harding
Hotel—a notorious nest
of hoodlums—and Polly's
main brothel from
1924 to 1934, 201 West
54th Street, the brick
building to the right

Police lineup of key members of the Broadway mob: Eddie Diamond, Jack "Legs" Diamond, Thomas "Fatty" Walsh, and Salvatore Lucania aka "Charlie Lucky" aka "Lucky Luciano," 1927

Polly's brother Benny Adler after his release from Sing Sing Prison, 1925

Texas Guinan—
"Queen of the Night Clubs"—
whose chorus girls occasionally
moonlighted in "Polly's Follies"

The madcap boys of the Club Durant—Jimmy Durante, Eddie Jackson,
and Lou Clayton

ers, dope peddlers, arsonists, confidence men, and a squadron of pimps who rotated their girls through the West Side call houses.

For the discreet hustler, it was an ideal setup, close to the action but surprisingly safe from prying eyes. In these vast buildings, it was nearly impossible for cops to know which apartment a woman was in unless they had inside information. The more welcoming apartment houses, where the superintendent or owner was in on the racket, often had multiple call flats in the same building.

It may be that Nick used Polly's apartment as his personal house of assignation, a place to meet his girlfriend or lend to pals, as she later claimed. But however they began, within weeks of moving in, Nick asked her to turn it into a small call flat where she hosted women for hire. "His request didn't shock me—far from it," said Polly; in the last six months, "I had met plenty of girls who made no bones about their being available for a fee." She'd seen the way the town's fat cats flung around their dough in the local joy joints. "Why shouldn't some of it be flung my way?" she figured.

With Nick's help, she soon had three girls coming to her apartment several nights a week to service the men whom Polly recruited from the nearby speakeasies, delis, and dance halls. Soon she was pulling in a hundred bucks or more every week—four times the average white male worker's salary.

"It was in this informal, almost casual, fashion that I began my career as a madam," she admitted later. "I told myself I didn't invent sex, nobody had to come to my place who didn't want to, the girls were never novices—I insisted on that—and came in with eyes wide open."

In truth, morality hardly figured into her calculations. "It paid my rent," she said flatly. Later she would defend this choice as sensible, even inevitable, hardly a choice at all given her circumstances. "I am not apologizing for my decision," she declared frostily. "My feeling is that by the time there are such choices to be made, your life already has made the decision for you."

☾

On August 25, 1920, after years of intense debate over the role of women in public affairs, the Nineteenth Amendment to the U.S. Constitution took effect, guaranteeing women the right to vote. Polly paid no attention to this momentous event. As she put it, "I was too busy running a house to spare a thought to running the country."

For the last two decades, progressive crusaders had labored mightily to bring an end to the traditional "double standard" between the sexes, that ancient belief that it was perfectly reasonable for a man to pursue his personal pleasures however he saw fit, while making a pariah of any woman who veered even slightly from the path of chastity. Instead the reformers argued for what they called "the single standard" of morality requiring all men to practice the same virtuous habits as their wives and daughters.

So it came as a tremendous shock to discover that the young girls of America had a very different plan for demolishing the double standard. As one critic quipped, they advocated "the single standard of drinking." Eager to see what all the excitement was about, respectable wives and daughters who would never have set foot in an old-fashioned saloon began flocking to the new speakeasies, discovering the pleasure of getting plastered in public.

It wasn't just the tippling. To the bewilderment of the high-minded suffragists who had campaigned so courageously for political equality, these newly liberated young women were using their hard-won freedom to adopt the habits of hussies and fallen women.

For women of easy virtue—for women generally—the speakeasy upturned the rules of feminine propriety. Five years earlier only show-girls and ladies of the evening bobbed their hair, bared their calves, and smoked cigarettes. Now debutantes were frequenting dives that would give a sailor pause, wriggling like cooch dancers to the barbaric blare of jazz, and laughing at jokes that made gentlemen blush. Virginity was fast falling out of fashion among Polly's generation as the rate of out-of-wedlock sex soared after 1900, jumping from approximately 13 to 51 percent over the decade.

Girls like this would once have been called *harlots, floozies, bums,* or *tarts* and would've been treated as such. Now they called themselves *flappers*—English slang for a prostitute or a brazen young girl, a word that had been sanitized and adopted by the American garment industry to describe the teenagers who were increasingly setting the fashion for readymade clothing.

That year the rising tide of adventurous young women drawn to Man-

hattan's freedom was becoming a deluge. The whole "flapper manifestation of 1921," as the *Times's* style reporter, Helen Bullitt Lowry, dubbed
it: "career girls" eager for experience, would-be bohemians practicing
vague theories of free love, jazz babies in search of thrills.

All these young charmers, eager for someone to buy them a good
time, were great for business along Gaiety Gulch. But for those who were
used to the easy distinction between good and bad women—between
"show girls" and "nice girls"—it was more than a little bewildering.
"You could tell the Broadway girl to cut it out," as one café proprietor
complained; "and so you could keep the dancing in your place within
certain bounds. But I ask you how can I send the head waiter up to
an innocent-looking little girl, whose mother lives on East Seventieth
Street, and tell her to cut that sort of dancing?"

Even New York's police commissioner felt the need to instruct his
confused officers, who were accustomed to harassing bold women who
dared stroll the streets alone after dark. The NYPD's new training man-
ual spelled it out plainly: "Do not attempt to judge a woman by her manner of dress. Just because she has blond hair, has her face powdered, and
walks jauntily, she is not necessarily a prostitute. Many innocent girls
possess such an appearance without knowing the suspicions it arouses."

Plenty of naysayers predicted that the rise of the flapper would put
Polly and her colleagues out of business. Why would a man pay for sex
when the city seemed to be teeming with amateurs eager to jump into
bed for free? According to the prudes and pessimists, prostitution was a
dying industry, like a buggy whip factory in the age of the automobile.
But old-timers—the same ones who considered the Eighteenth Amendment a sucker's bet—saw the odds differently. No one ever went broke
betting on the desires of men.

In the early careers of most madams, it is easy to marvel at the magnificent wisdom of combining business with pleasure, especially the
pleasure of a burgeoning bank account. Russian Jewish immigrants
had a saying: America *Gonif!*—America the Thief! Sometimes they
uttered it with wonder at the topsy-turvy ways of the New World, akin
to the phrase "Only in America!" Only in America could a girl with
no education, no dowry, and no family connections—with nothing but
chutzpah and smarts—catapult from starvation to affluence overnight.
Sometimes it was a cry of grief and bitterness: America *Gonif*—America,

the thief who steals children from the hand of God and the bosom of the family. Only in America could a girl become rich selling her body and seem to pay no price.

In a world of saps and suckers, Polly had been smart enough to land on Easy Street. By her calculations, the long-term prospects of the flesh racket were not her worry. She wasn't going to make whoring her life's work; "like everyone I've ever heard of who has gone into this business—be she madam or prostitute—I regarded it as just a temporary expedient, a means to an end." She just needed to stay in business long enough to build up financial reserves. "I'd quit when I had enough capital to finance a legitimate enterprise," she insisted.

At the rate she was hustling, that should be only a matter of months.

☾

Polly's new prosperity couldn't have come soon enough for her family.

In the seven years since Polly last laid eyes on her brother Berl—or Ben or Benny as he was now known—he had become a hard-eyed, battle-scarred young man with a long rap sheet acquired on the streets of Chicago. While she was haunting Brooklyn dance halls, Ben was picked up for theft and did two terms at the St. Charles School for Delinquent Boys. Several months after being released, he was arrested again and sent to the Illinois State Reformatory in Pontiac for another yearlong stretch. This time he lasted less than a year on the outside before being sent back for sticking up some poor moke for eight bucks.

Just as Ben was due to be released, on December 2, 1919, a warrant arrived from the Immigration Service declaring him an undesirable alien and ordering his immediate deportation from the United States pending a final hearing. At the hearing, the desperate teenager pleaded with the investigator, "I don't want to be sent back to Russia." It was not mercy but a legal technicality that saved him, when the Immigration Service discovered that the combined length of his prison sentences was a little too short to meet the precise requirement of the law. In February 1920 Benny Adler walked out of the Pontiac County Jail and hightailed it to New York City.

Across the ocean, conditions were worsening for her family. Gittel, Moshe, and their five sons had survived a Cossack invasion and the German occupation. When the war ended, Yanow came under control of the newly formed Polish Republic. Unfortunately, the Poles rivaled the Russians in anti-Jewish sentiment and resumed the harassment and pogroms. The situation grew more dire when Poland began battling the newly formed Soviet Russia for control over Belarus. In April 1919 the Polish army rounded up and slaughtered the Jewish leaders of Pinsk, a crime so bold and cruel that it sparked an international outcry and a panicked exodus of Jews fleeing their new occupiers.

Polly was well aware of the trouble at home; the Pinsk massacre was splashed across the headlines of nearly every newspaper in New York. Although she no longer spoke to her cousins in Brooklyn, she still wrote regularly to her family and sent them money whenever she could spare a few dollars. Now in the spring of 1920, she began sending them unheard-of sums. "I accounted for the money orders, which I now sent monthly, by saying I had a job managing a corset factory." A little lie, well justified to spare them pain.

That spring the border skirmishes between Poland and Russia erupted into all-out warfare, with Yanow once again on the front line. With bloodshed looming and his pockets full of dollars from his newly rich daughter in America, it was only natural that the needles in Moshe's bottom began to tingle once more. Adding to the urgency, the Yiddish newspapers were filled with uneasy rumors that the U.S. government was planning to radically restrict the number of immigrants allowed to enter the country from Russia. Moshe decided it was time to leave.

In May the Russians retook Pinsk and began surging westward through the former Pale of Settlement. As their tanks rolled through the villages, they sent out dragnets, kidnapping Jewish males and forcing them into the Red Army to serve as cannon fodder. Polly's brother, Srul Lieb, was in terrible danger, as was Moshe. By June, the Soviet forces were close enough for them to hear the rumble of artillery. Finally, the decision was made: Moshe would leave first, followed by Srul Lieb. For the time being, Gittel would stay behind along with the four youngest boys.

Moshe's impending arrival in America created a cascade of conflicting emotions in Polly. For all her defiance, guilt and fear simmered just below the surface, she recalled. "I used to have terrible nightmares in which my father would chase me down the streets yelling, 'Kirva! Bliad!'" Whore! Bum!

Her shame was spiked with long-festering anger. "I must admit that many times in my thoughts I had blamed my father, thinking that things wouldn't have happened as they did if I'd had a home and parents to turn to," Polly confessed; "I'd vowed if I ever got the chance I'd humiliate him with the knowledge of what had befallen me, his daughter, whom he'd shoved out into the world at the age of thirteen."

On July 17, 1920, Polly's father arrived in the port of New York, a slim, elegantly dressed man, clad in a three-piece suit with an immaculate white celluloid collar. He sported a lush head of dark hair, a small goatee, and a magnificent handlebar mustache, a style more fashionable in Europe than in New York.

Polly's worry was not wasted. As soon as Moshe arrived in Brooklyn, Breina filled his ears with stories of her wild behavior, her unaccountable rejection of poor Willie Bernstein, and their final blowup. But instead of disapproval or disgust, Moshe was stricken with remorse. It was his own fault, he told Breina. He'd been a fool to send his children across the ocean all alone.

As for Polly, now that her father was finally here, her resentment, her hunger to see him suffer as she had, began melting away. "I saw how cruel and useless it would be," she said later. "So instead of making father feel bad, I did my best to make him feel even better. I told him that I was engaged to a nice Jewish boy, a Rabbi's son (In cases like this why not make it good? It costs no more)." Moshe would have to wait to meet her "fiancé," she explained, since he was a traveling salesman, out on the road selling dresses. Later she told him that she broke off the engagement.

As long as Moshe stayed tucked away in Brooklyn, she was safe from discovery. Nonetheless, her father's presence added an irksome swath of subterfuge to an already risky enterprise. But what choice did she have? On September 9, 1920, her younger brother Srul Lieb landed in New York, a handsome young man who took after her father in looks, with a sweet smile, an unruly cowlick, and an expressive crinkle around the eyes. Here in America, he declared, he would be known as Irving.

He'd left just in time. Two weeks later, as the Jews of Yanow prepared for the fall harvest festival of Sukkoth, pro-Polish forces tore through the countryside around the town, raping, plundering, and slaughtering nearly one thousand souls.

❨

With her cheerful personality, quick wit, and distinctive baritone voice, Polly quickly began to cut a fine figure among the West Side's scarlet sisterhood. She was warmly welcomed into the sorority of good-time girls and crooked janes who slept till noon and greeted the day with the proverbial "whore's breakfast": "a cocktail, a cigarette and the *Morning Telegraph,*" the holy writ of the city's horseplayers and stage folk.

But Easy Street wasn't as easy as the name promised. "Men, bootleg hooch, men, speakeasies, men, jazz trombones, men, insinuating saxophones," as one madam described it—it was an exhausting routine that required unforeseen discipline. When Polly wasn't entertaining johns, she made the rounds of all the spots where a man might look for a good time, building a network of "go-betweens"—waiters, bartenders, chauffeurs, poolroom attendants, cabdrivers, busboys, and elevator operators—who were happy to send men her way for a small commission.

Hotels were especially ripe hunting grounds. In second-rate establishments, the bellhop or elevator operator might, for a small gratuity, dig up a hustler and bring her to a guest's room. In better hotels, he'd more likely hand the guest a card with his name on it and direct him to a nearby call flat, adding the madam's commission to the guest's gratuity on the bill. The richest pickings were the grand midtown hotels—the Waldorf Astoria, the Biltmore, and the Hotel Astor—where the managers were happy to overlook the flirtatious young women lounging in their lobbies as long as they were discreet, well dressed, and tipped generously. "We've personally seen a dozen pick-ups in as many minutes in the Astor corridors," reported *Broadway Brevities,* the Main Stem's annal of scandal.

"The Mecca of the demimondaine" was the glamorous Biltmore Hotel, next to Grand Central Station, a favorite of upscale Tammany politicians and Ivy League boys who rendezvoused under the famous Biltmore clock. The Biltmore's foyer—"Lover's Corner" they called it—was renowned for its "little ladies of leisure," always appearing in pairs. "That gives the sucker his pick of two babes instead of one," as one expert explained, and helped fend off nosy house detectives. "Two dames sitting together have always got the alibi that they just dropped in to wait for a friend."

In the evenings, Polly might drop into one of the West Side dance halls that catered to young bachelors out on the town. These overheated chumps were easy pickings although pikers in the pocketbook. But the halls were brimming with discontented dime-a-dance girls, weary of furtive passes, clumsy gropings, and sore feet, who might consider moonlighting for her.

The biggest spenders appeared around midnight, after the theaters let out. They could be found frolicking in the dwindling number of old-fashioned cabarets scattered around Columbus Circle that catered to the sporting crowd—the kept women, wild society girls, high-rolling gamblers, Wall Street speculators, and "tired businessmen," in the phrase of the day, belatedly sowing their wild oats. *Young and handsome* generally meant broke, so clever cuties focused on the would-be Romeos with thinning hair, expanding waistlines, and expensive suits. The ones who were just stewed enough to unfurl their bankroll but not so much that they'd already spent it.

Polly might stop in for a nightcap at one of the Harlem joints that welcomed both Black and white patrons, like Baron Wilkins's black-and-tan cabaret, a favorite after-work resort of the West Side hustlers. Or she'd end a hard night's work at one of the many all-night Jewish delicatessens. Most were modest mom-and-pop storefronts that served Jewish comfort food. But on Broadway, especially up in Harlem, something about the all-night delis "seems to draw an unwelcome element of people, weak in mind, loose in morals, dangerous to the community," lamented *The New York Age*, the newspaper of record for Harlem's African American community.

Anyone looking for Polly was likely to run into her at Reuben's at Broadway and 73rd Street, or Pomerantz's between 119th and 120th on Lenox Avenue, where the night owls lingered over a bowl of matzoh ball soup or coffee cake, going over the day's profits and losses and picking up the latest scuttlebutt. She struck up a friendship with Arnold Reuben, famous for his namesake corned beef sandwich, and rival deli owners George Pomerantz and Connie Immerman, whose deli on 131st Street sold foul cut-rate booze, far more profitable than even the best sandwich.

It was no longer a mystery to Polly why drug use was so ubiquitous in her new profession. Cocaine and heroin were pouring into the city at unheard-of rates, although no one was quite sure of the source. Wise guys laid the blame on Prohibition; with liquor hard to get, the demand for other kinds of kicks skyrocketed, and with so many chumps drinking rotgut hooch, ferocious hangovers had become a local epidemic. "You can take only so many hangovers without hitting the bottle when you first wake up," one vice cop explained. "And for some of them, even whiskey won't be strong enough."

Polly had to overlook the fact that for many of her best customers, a party wasn't complete without a bump of something strong. Many of her new compatriots, especially the pimps, ran a lively side hustle peddling dope. Jewish gangs dominated the cocaine and heroin trade outside Chinatown—in this field, the Brownsville boys were first in class. So she developed an eagle eye for the symptoms of junkies and snowbirds, the needle marks and nodding of the heroin users, the jaundiced complexion of the hop head, the nose stripped bare of hair from snorting cocaine, the twitchy muscles and chalky skin of the ether addict.

Polly hadn't seen much of Garnet lately, but occasionally she caught up with Garnet's mother Helen, who never ceased complaining about her leech of a boyfriend and drug-addled daughter. One morning, early in the summer of 1920, Polly awoke to the insistent ringing of the house phone. Helen was on the line nearly incoherent, sobbing and begging Polly to hurry over to the rooms where she and Garnet were living.

She arrived to find Helen frantic and Garnet high as a kite. Helen's boyfriend had vanished, along with her savings, leaving them penniless, with a stack of unpaid bills and the rent overdue. Garnet moved in with her drug dealer, while her mother, desperate for cash, came to work at Polly's house.

Soon even Garnet's dealer lost patience with her nasty mood swings, and she was back on the street. Helen helped her find a cheap furnished room and gave her money for food and rent and a small, daily ration of dope. Polly was mystified by Helen's behavior until one night, in a voice choked with guilt, Helen let the story tumble out.

The trouble began when Helen caught her then boyfriend, Hal, sexually abusing her young daughter. "I should have left Hal right then and there, but instead I took it out on my own flesh and blood," said Helen in anguish. She kicked Garnet out of the house the next day. The girl was only twelve years old, but she looked older and could sing a little, so she found work in a rough Chicago dive as a "table singer," a euphemism for an entertainer who mixed with the customers, sang for tips, sold drinks, and occasionally turned tricks.

Garnet was eighteen years old when Helen finally realized her terrible mistake. By then, she wanted nothing to do with her mother; "it was not until she became an addict that she let me come and visit her," said Helen. "By that time she had become so degraded that what I had done to her no longer seemed so bad."

If Polly was shocked by Helen's tale, it didn't last long. Such stories of abuse would become a sickeningly familiar refrain. Early experiences of incest and sexual assault were as common as colds in the flesh trade. Indeed, there was hardly a woman on Broadway who could claim to have escaped unscathed.

Tears streaming down her cheeks, Helen paused and reached for Polly's hand. "Let me bring her here, Pearl. I know you hate drug addicts, but please, please make an exception in her case," she pleaded. "Let her come and stay until I've saved enough to take us back to Ohio."

A coked-up dope fiend was a dangerous item in a whorehouse, but Polly had not yet been hardened by experience. She reluctantly gave in to Helen's pleas. "And that was how a mother and daughter came to be working side by side in my house. It was also how I became aware that in some people sexual gratification is obtained in dark and terrible ways," she recalled grimly. To her surprise—and profit—she discovered "there were men who would pay double and triple for the kick of having a mother and daughter in bed with them."

Polly was fast shedding the last of her square taboos and prejudices about sex, but in matters of personal finance, she remained stubbornly middle class. She was adamant that Helen squirrel away some of that hard-earned cash. Green as she was, even Polly could see that a woman her age needed an exit plan. Ten years, at the outside, was all most hustlers could count on. By their late twenties most had aged out of the big money, losing their looks and often their health. For those who stayed in the life it was a steep, steady decline, from call flats, to two-dollar houses, to streetwalking. Smart cookies got out while the getting was good.

It was a great relief, although a financial loss, when Helen finally decided to return to Ohio. Garnet stayed on, turning tricks while Polly continued nagging her to take the cure. Finally one day she just disappeared.

Four months after her stillborn debut as a Broadway Cinderella, Garnet finally got her write-up in *Variety*, the bible of the showbiz mob. One Garnet Cortes, later corrected to Garna Lee—"reported to have been in musical comedy"—was arrested in Cincinnati along with two young men, ex-convicts, and charged with driving a stolen automobile from New York to Ohio. After she was acquitted in December 1920, she dropped out of sight for a while.

The last time Polly saw Garnet was in late August 1925. She'd been arrested for possession of heroin along with Peter Alessio, a drug dealer and circus sideshow grifter who billed himself as the "champion tattooed man in the world"—a rare and freakish phenomenon in those days. She was held for $100 bail, a substantial sum that she did not possess—leaving her to spend a painful night in jail, suffering the pangs of withdrawal from dope.

As she was being arraigned the next morning in the West Side court, in walked "a fashionably dressed young woman who refused to give her name," in the *Daily News*'s phrase, who handed over $100 cash for her release, leaving her tattooed companion to rot in jail while he awaited his court date. Polly was always cagey whenever the law came up, so she never admitted to bailing out Garnet, although she did describe the horror of seeing her friend in such a state. Her friend was so haggard and filthy, said Polly, that "the only thing I recognized about her was her beautiful smile." Polly took her back to her apartment, bathed her, fed her, and gave her a bed for the night.

"Again, I begged her to take the cure, offering to pay the hospital bills, and she promised to begin the following week." Polly handed her enough cash to pay her hotel bill and tide her over for the weekend— a fateful mistake. Garnet promptly disappeared and failed to show up when her case was called to court on September 5, forfeiting the money Polly had put up for bail.

She resurfaced one evening several weeks later when the money was spent. Again Garnet offered an addict's assurances, swearing she would check herself into a sanitarium on Amsterdam Avenue that Polly knew of. Again Polly gave her a hundred dollars and sent her on her way. But this time, she secretly followed behind. There, leaning against a lamppost was an old woman, waiting with a small packet of drugs. Just as the money was about to change hands, Polly yanked her away, roaring curses at the crone, who took off as fast as her heels could carry her.

Enough already! Polly was through. Garnet couldn't even look her in the eye. When Polly let go of her arm, the girl slunk off into the darkness.

Several years later Polly ran into a mutual friend, a songwriter named Leon Flatow, who told her that Garnet was living down in Chinatown with a Chinese man—a racial taboo breached by only the most hardened drug addicts.

A few months later Garnet Williams was dead. "I was glad to know she was out of her misery," said Polly flatly. Whenever the melody of "Moonshine Valley" floated in the air, her thoughts returned to her friend as she was that first day on Allrightnik's Row, "so shining and debonair. She weighed only fifty pounds when she died."

☾

December 7, 1920, was a Tuesday, hardly the busiest night in a hookshop. Polly and one of her girls—Florence Lang, age twenty-one—were lounging in her living room at the Arleigh when they heard a knock. Polly opened the door to find two policemen, who brusquely shouldered their way into the apartment. One grabbed hold of her to keep her from running off. The other ransacked the place, searching for money and drugs and perhaps a few souvenirs to take home to mama.

The officers hustled the two frightened girls down the stairs and tossed them into the Black Maria, the drafty black patrol wagon that hauled unlucky souls to the local station house to be booked. "I had not yet learned to cover my face with my arms, and all the people of the neighborhood were gathered outside, pointing at me and gaping," remembered Polly. "Just so had I gaped in the restaurant that time when Abe point out the prostitutes."

This was the next phase in the madam's career: when she suddenly realizes the hidden perils of life on Easy Street. At the station house, she was booked, photographed, and fingerprinted under the name "Pearl Howard," of 620 West 115th Street, and charged with being an incorrigible person. (In an era when government record-keeping was still in its infancy, it was perfectly common to get away with giving false names to the police, at least until they got wise.)

She was allowed a phone call to Nick, who arranged for a bondsman to bail her out and a lawyer to defend her in court. Then it was back into the paddy wagon, jostling among the drunks, as they made their way to the Jefferson Market Courthouse in Greenwich Village. The former Women's Court is now a public library and still stands at the corner of Sixth Avenue and West Tenth Street, a redbrick neo-Gothic pile ennobled by stained-glass windows and a turreted clock tower. This improbably fanciful monument to womanhood gone astray had once served as a marketplace for grocers, butchers, and tradesmen. Now instead of bargain-hunting housewives, its dingy halls were thronged with bedraggled ladies of the evening, waiting their turn before the magistrates.

Polly was pushed into a small holding cell with other accused shoplifters, pickpockets, addicts, and lushes, the hardened old hands and the naïve first-timers crying quietly in shame and fear. Fortunate women had pimps or pals come bail them out directly. The unlucky stayed till morning, when they were marched up to the second-floor courtrooms, past a gauntlet of leering spectators, to be arraigned, tried, and sentenced. Polly and Florence were among the lucky ones. Their trial was set for December 15.

Nine days later the two young women returned to face the formidable figure of Magistrate Jean Hortense Norris. A classic suffragette with a Tammany twist, Magistrate Norris helped turn out the newly enfranchised female voters for the Democratic Party ticket. In 1919, as her reward, she became the first woman ever appointed to the bench in New York City.

But anyone expecting Magistrate Norris to show special sympathy for the softer sex was severely disappointed. She was notoriously harsh on female offenders, handing out stiff sentences accompanied by humiliating lectures. Around the courthouse she was known for her haughty airs, peering imperiously through pince-nez glasses perched low on her nose, with an exaggerated patrician accent that masked her working-class Brooklyn-Irish upbringing. As the *Evening Post's* crime reporter, Milton MacKaye, quipped, "More than one humble streetwalker incarcerated in the workhouse for one hundred days, was warmed and comforted by the knowledge she had been sentenced by a lady."

Despite her righteous reputation, Magistrate Norris was not above doing the occasional favor for her Tammany friends. For well-connected or well-heeled defendants she could be persuaded to dismiss a case for lack of convincing evidence. Then again, evidence gathering was not a strong suit of most patrolmen. Nick Montana must have pulled a few strings, because to Polly's great relief, the charges against her were dismissed.

She had avoided prison, but the experience was a kick in the gut. The police now had her photo and fingerprints on file and knew where she lived. Worse still was the shame. Even if her family did not yet know her secret, her neighbors certainly did.

A year before, Polly was sure that life was making her decisions for her. This time she was determined to choose her own fate: "As I saw it, it came down to this: Did I want to leave my apartment on Riverside Drive and go back to a hole on Second Avenue?"

Her decision was instant and obvious. "So far as I was concerned the Golden Land was still Riverside Drive and I was determined to stay there," she declared. "I regarded it as just a temporary expedient, a means to an end. I'd quit when I had enough capital to finance a legitimate enterprise."

&

New Year's Eve is a gloomy night in a whorehouse, as a rule, running only half a nose ahead of that sentimental favorite, Christmas Day. Time was the great enemy of the professional femme fatale, so it was hard to find pleasure in the passing of another year. Adding insult to injury, even the most neglectful of men generally feel compelled to greet the new year beside their wives or sweethearts, so the girls didn't even have the distraction of brisk business.

For Polly, about to mark her one-year anniversary as a madam, this was her first experience with that annual undertow of regret. Her arrest in December had brought home the perils of the primrose path and had made her more recognizable to the police. Having her father and brothers here, whatever comfort that brought, had only increased the danger of discovery.

But this year it wasn't only the sporting women who felt a chill on that last day of the year. No one on Broadway had high expectations for the first officially dry New Year's Eve. The lights of Times Square were as brilliant as ever, but the Avenue was losing some of its luster. The glamorous lobster palaces and baroque barrooms that had drawn the silk-stocking crowd found they couldn't pay their bills without booze to cover their costs. One by one they were being replaced by movie theaters, delicatessens, and chop suey restaurants selling cheap Americanized Chinese food. This New Year's Eve promised as much fun as a church picnic, lamented nostalgic Broadwayfarers.

At noon on December 31, 1920, it looked as if the naysayers were right. A squadron of 291 special agents and a brace of plainclothes policemen were stationed up and down the Big Street, and three uniformed cops patrolled every major block, dampening the mood.

But something strange was brewing. By midafternoon, patrolmen were picking up men from the sidewalks, so soused they could no longer walk. By dusk, the crowds around Times Square were "probably the largest in the history of the city," in the estimate of *The New York Times*, most of them bulging with hip flasks. In all the hotel ballrooms, restaurants, and cabarets, waiters, bellboys, and checkroom attendants were peddling pints of gin to those who didn't already have their own stash. By midnight, pie-eyed patrons were openly swigging from bottles, flasks, and false-bottomed canes.

Ferret-eyed policemen and federal agents were everywhere, but that only seemed to add to the naughty delight. Whenever a lawman was spotted, a cry would go up and the booze rushed back to its hiding place. "Flasks shot into their holsters. Suitcases snapped. Canes were deftly rearticulated," reported the *Times*. False alarm! "Portable, individual cellars reopened all over the place again and the joy of being illegal became more intense than before."

This was "an entirely new kind of celebration," noted the newspapers, carried on with an unashamed abandon unseen even in the wildest days of the Tenderloin. The chilly streets were thronged with people going from party to party. Broadway rang with the blare of jazz bands, and laughing couples kept breaking into dance steps over the wail of the saxophones or spontaneously linking arms and singing. In theaters, bottles of whiskey were passed over the footlights to the actors and orchestras, and more than a few vaudevillians stepped into the audience to claim a nip. One impetuous young man leaped onstage and carried one of the chorus girls off to a party.

It wasn't just Times Square. Manic, uninhibited revelry echoed everywhere, from the Bronx to Greenwich Village: "Wherever there was a restaurant open, there was a miniature Broadway." Tourists filled every hotel room in the city, traveling from as far as a thousand miles away, because they believed that Manhattan "would be the centre [sic] of the wildest celebration," remarked the *Times*. "Probably they guess right."

At three a.m. many of the poshest resorts were still roaring, with cockeyed partyers wandering the halls, inviting strangers to dance or treating them to drinks, and passing out in the powder rooms. In one of Manhattan's most exclusive hotels, the entire dining room played the old kissing game of "post office," stumbling from table to table collecting kisses.

But it was the way the fairer sex was throwing themselves into the debauchery that provided the biggest jolt of the evening. "Never before had women taken so active a part in the annual spree," reported the *Times* with surprise on New Year's Day. "There are eyewitness reports of numerous women in evening dress carried out in a stupor—sometimes by several waiters if the condition of the men of their tables did not qualify them to act as bearers."

The next morning, as an army of white-coated street cleaners swept up the night's debris and revelers awoke to blistering headaches, it was clear that Broadway was going toe to toe with the Anti-Saloon League, and at least for the moment, it was holding its own.

€

Polly was only two weeks into the new year when she crossed paths with that scourge of the working girl, Detective Andrew J. McLaughlin.

Detective McLaughlin was a bum—that was the opinion of every hustler who ever had the misfortune to make his acquaintance. His partner, William Haake, was no Sunday school saint, but McLaughlin took the prize. Even among the vice squad, those masters of the double cross, he was considered a bad egg and a mean drunk, always spewing nasty wisecracks. He often worked alone, a suspicious eccentricity in a department that prized solidarity above all. Behind his back, they called him the Lone Wolf.

He was handsome, no one would deny that, a "classic Celtic type," as the *Herald Tribune* put it, with a thick head of hair and a matinee idol profile. Rumor had it that he was "the special friend" of two or three wealthy women who thought it amusing to entertain a cop at their parties—not a gigolo exactly, more of a novelty item. But few cops were more despised by the whores, pimps, and madams of the West Side.

Like most of the "pussy posse," or "body snatchers," as the vice cops were nicknamed, McLaughlin was a heavy gambler and a boozehound. He could be found most nights in the tougher speakeasies of the West Side, drinking on the house and flirting with the hookers and hostesses. But McLaughlin stood apart for his unchecked greed and unnecessary cruelty. When he raided a cathouse, it wasn't enough to arrest the women and take their money. He had to humiliate them, too, screaming obscenities, busting up their rooms, and roughing them up—and the johns, too, if they gave him any guff.

One Sunday, a couple of weeks into the new year, the Lone Wolf and his sometime sidekick, Bill Haake, were out hunting floozies. A cold wave was blowing into the city in sixty-mile-an-hour gales, driving all but the heartiest souls inside for warmth. It was a tough break for the streetwalkers but a boon for call girls like Polly, who catered to the lazy johns who preferred to phone up for a girl instead of venturing out for their fun.

That didn't help poor Daisy Mills, a young woman meeting Polly's description who listed her address as 323 Second Avenue, where Polly still kept her first rented room. The officers arrested Daisy along with two other young women, roommates who lived uptown and offered the aliases Anna Ferrone and Alice Le Beau. Once again it was back in the paddy wagon to the Women's Court where—despite their advanced ages of twenty-two, twenty-three, and twenty-six—all three were charged with being "Incorrigible Girls" under Chapter 436 of the Laws of 1903.

"As vile as a vice cop" was one of the nursery rhymes of the underworld, for good reason. Officially, agents of the Special Service Division were tasked with ridding the city of prostitutes, professional gamblers, and illegal drinking establishments. They worked undercover in plain street clothes instead of the brass-buttoned uniform of the New York City Police Department.

Unofficially, the vice squad ran a shakedown operation that hauled in millions of dollars in bribes annually. It was a plush position for those who weren't prudish. The stream of graft from vice was so steady and so lucrative that it required excellent political connections and a kickback of several thousand dollars to wrangle a spot on one of the plainclothes squads spread throughout the city.

The vice cops weren't the only ones with their palms outstretched. It was an open secret that the police department ran on a cash-and-carry basis. Rookie cops had to buy their blue woolen uniforms and caps, their nightsticks, service revolvers, and bullets, all out of their own pockets. So it was perfectly natural to assume they had to buy the job itself—and in exchange they deserved a chance to earn back their investment. It was the rare bull who wouldn't accept a small gratuity in exchange for ripping up a ticket or overlooking a minor violation. That was one of the perks of the job.

"The System"—that's what they called it. Even honest cops were expected to do favors for the aldermen, political operatives, and district leaders who helped get them their jobs, and to kick back a portion of their loot. Overly fastidious officers who refused to work within the System found themselves transferred to "Siberia," pounding a cold, lonely beat out in Canarsie or Queens.

Frankly, professional lawbreakers appreciated the System—without crooked cops, no underground operation could survive for long. For the black-market entrepreneurs who supplied the city's forbidden delights— the drug dealers, bookmakers, bootleg booze purveyors, and vendors of young flesh—regular payoffs to avoid arrest were just the price of doing business. In the jaundiced opinion of Polly's pals, the biggest difference between the cops and the robbers was that the coppers had the better racket.

Polly was prepared to pay for the privilege of avoiding prison— that was how the System worked. But she was quickly discovering that this wasn't merely an illicit licensing fee. McLaughlin and Haake had trapped her in a classic shakedown racket. But this one was backed by the law. Criminals bribed the uniformed cops, cynics liked to say, and plainclothesmen blackmailed the criminals.

Her first clue was the sudden appearance of a bail bondsman as she was being booked, one of a dozen or so bondsmen and criminal attorneys headquartered across the street from the courthouse on West Tenth Street, in a set of ramshackle redbrick houses known as Lawyers' Row or the West Tenth Street Bar. Not only did the bondsman offer to put up bail to release her from jail, but if she used the lawyer he recommended, he could guarantee the charges would "go out the window," dismissed for lack of evidence or by acquittal. All for a substantial fee, of course, from $200 to $500, or more if they could get it.

To ensure the victim's cooperation, the lawyer would take possession of her bank book, then personally accompany her to the bank and force her to drain her account. Of that sum, twenty-five dollars or so would go to the arresting officer, who would then fail to show up in court, or make a mess of his testimony, contradicting himself or forgetting details, forcing the magistrate to declare insufficient evidence and let the prisoner go. If the magistrate were so inclined, he—or she—would also get a cut. The rest would go to the bondsman and the attorney.

If Polly refused, she could count on time behind bars.

As far as she could tell, she had only two choices: go to jail or go broke. She could have squawked to the authorities or the newspapers, of course. But she'd memorized the first commandment of the racket world back in Brownsville: "Thou Shalt Not Squeal." No exceptions, not even for a cop. "Ratting on a cop is just as serious a crime as ratting on your best friend," as the murderer Danny Ahearn noted; "your own friends don't trust you when you squeal on a cop." Besides, Ahearn added sagely, "you ain't going to benefit in squealing on the cop, because he always has an alibi, and there's nobody around when he's beating you up."

Polly had barely begun to replenish her coffers since her last pinch. But whatever she had in her bank book, it must have been enough. Twenty-four hours later, she and her flossy compatriots were standing in front of the pride of East Harlem, the Honorable Francis X. Mancuso, a Tammany district leader who'd recently become the first Italian American elevated to the bench. By no coincidence at all, Polly and her incorrigible associates were acquitted.

Two raids in the span of one month—if the blackmailing badge wearers didn't know her face before, they did now. McLaughlin and the other body snatchers made a habit of targeting the same women again and again, keeping tabs on them until they'd had time to rebuild their bankroll, then starting the cycle all over. There was little she could do except change apartments and keep a low profile.

She was never entirely sure exactly how many times she was raided in the course of her career; there were so many pinches that they all ran together in her memory. Nevertheless, she insisted, "it was these early raids which made me wise and cautious," developing in her a sixth sense for danger that would serve her well.

The undercover vice cops were hard to spot without uniforms, so Polly trained herself to look first at their feet; their thick-soled black shoes designed for pounding the pavement always gave them away. One clever madam commissioned a friend to take photos of vice squad officers, "both at work and at play," which she kept in the top drawer of her dresser. (The negatives she stowed in a safety deposit vault.) Other madams paid stool pigeons to point out the new plainclothesmen. Some even paid the stools to bring rookies up to their houses to arrange for regular preventative payoffs.

Right now, however, Polly was broke. That was the real kicker. Every time they emptied her bank account, it just meant that she had to stay in the game that much longer.

☾

She found new digs at 303 West 92nd Street, a five-story walk-up at the corner of West End Avenue, where the management was happy to mind their own business for a price. It was a ripe spot for a bawdy house. The Naval Training Station was a few blocks to the west, so when the fleet was in, the streets were jammed with sailors ready to spend. With four legitimate theaters just up the block, it was a major stop on the "Subway Circuit," the network of stages sprinkled liberally throughout Manhattan, Brooklyn, and the Bronx, that offered a mix of live acts and moving pictures. The blocks between 92nd and 96th on both sides of Broadway were littered with small speakeasies and call flats.

It was an article of faith held by both urban reformers and the underworld that Jewish women made the best madams. This belief was backed up by statistics. In the first decades of the twentieth century, when Jews were approximately 20 percent of New York's population, they owned an estimated 50 percent of the city's brothels. And for good reason.

A successful madam needed to possess the efficiency of an office administrator, the discernment of a talent agent, and the social skills of a den mother. The shtetl tradition of the *balaboosta*—the cheerful, efficient wife who ran both the home and the family business while her husband studied the Torah—developed in many Jewish women the rare combination of practical financial sense and homey hospitality required to run a successful house. This was certainly true of Polly. She was clever, quick on the uptake, had a good head for math, and enjoyed the excellent example of her mother, a *balaboosta* in the classic tradition.

The key to running a high-performing call house lay in managing the telephone. Men who met Polly in her rounds, or were referred by one of her regulars, could call the apartment to request a date. Over the phone Polly screened new customers to ensure they weren't a cop or a madman, a skill that could be honed only with experience. The best madams had an instinct for picking the right girl for the job, which was the key to customer satisfaction, generous tips, and repeat business.

"I have a terrific memory, and that came in handy," she noted, for keeping track of her clients' preferences and proclivities. All the same, close record-keeping was critical. She maintained two ledgers. The first listed the women "on call," with a photo—clothes optional—phone number, and brief description of her measurements, hair color, tempera-ment, and talents. The second detailed in secret code her customers' information, including sexual preferences, payment history, personal quirks, and office telephone numbers or an address where they could be safely contacted. These customer ledgers were invaluable when she was forced to change apartments. A few hours calling old clients, a batch of carefully worded new address cards, and she'd be back in business.

On busy nights, juggling girls, johns, and bedrooms, as well as phone messages and checks, was a hectic, full-time task. "Since my objective was to make my stake as quickly as possible, I took care of my phone twenty-four hours a day, and never said no to anyone who was out to spend, regardless of the hour," said Polly. "I began to find out how much work and thought got into the preparation of an evening's pleasure."

There were other challenges. It wasn't cheap to make the scene, greasing palms and tipping heavily at every turn. Running a house required an endless round of daily payoffs. She had to tip the elevator man who discreetly ferried the customers to her door, as well as the taxi drivers and headwaiters who steered well-heeled johns her way, and dole out bribes to the building superintendents. Just keeping clean sheets and towels on hand cost plenty, and her phone bills were enormous.

Above all, the successful madam needed to be able to save money, a rare habit on Broadway. She had to have cash on hand for emergencies; a sudden eviction after the neighbors complained or, conversely, an unexpected rise in rent after the landlord got wise, or bail for girls who were nabbed while out on a call.

☾

Polly's reprieve from the law was short-lived. This time, though, her brother Ben bore the brunt of it. Ben had settled into a furnished room at 216 West 56th Street, an area known as Automobile Row for the dozens of garages and automobile showrooms that ran up Broadway through the West 50s. Tucked among the garages were some of the city's rowdiest speakeasies and clip joints, and scores of seedy boardinghouses. Cops considered it one of the toughest beats in the city; it was, as one patrolman put it, a "favorite hunting ground for sneak thieves, burglars, and other types of house breakers."

Around there a scrappy kid who wasn't too picky could find plenty of work. He could bust heads in strikes, collect debts for bookmakers, and drive—or hijack—trucks for the bootleggers who delivered illegal alcohol to the city's speakeasies. Officially, Ben held himself out as an unemployed auto mechanic, but the only thing he seemed to have any real knack for was burglary. So like his sister, he took stock of his options and decided to follow what he knew best. He became a professional thief, a *gonif* who usually worked as a "second-story man," breaking in through windows on upper floors.

That winter Ben fell in with a nineteen-year-old ex-con named Meyer Goldberg. He had been casing a house where the owners were out of town and wanted Ben's help in breaking in. They made their move on March 28, 1921, taking the commuter train from Manhattan to a small suburban house on the outskirts of Queens. They found an easy entry and rich pickings, nearly $8,000 worth of jewelry, linens, and clothing, far too much loot to haul home on the trolley. So they pocketed the jewelry, neatly bundled up the rest, and left it in the foyer while they returned to Manhattan in search of a vehicle.

That was a miscalculation. Later that night the owner of the house, one Frances J. Hobbs, returned unexpectedly and was shocked to discover the door ajar, her home ransacked, and a tidy pile of her belongings in the hall. The police sent two armed detectives, who hid for hours in the frigid darkness of Mrs. Hobbs's front hall. The next evening Ben and Meyer returned in a large touring car. As the boys gingerly pushed open the front door, the detectives leaped out with guns blazing. Ben took off running, zigzagging through alleys and yards until he was out of sight. Goldberg and the driver, one Louis Longobardo, age twenty-three, weren't so speedy.

It was "one of the boldest attempts at burglary that has occurred in this city in a long time," reported the *Brooklyn Eagle* breathlessly. The police quickly released Longobardo as a mere driver for hire. (Chauffeurs always had good alibis, as one mobster noted enviously: "He was hired. He don't know what was going on.") But young Goldberg was a different matter.

New York police interrogations were notorious for their savagery. "There's a lot more law in the end of a night stick than in all the legal books," as the cops liked to say. The "third degree" they called it—wielding nightsticks, blackjacks, and rubber hoses to coerce suspects into confession or at least silent repentance. Police brutality was considered the natural by-product of the culture of graft; knowing that criminals could bribe their way to freedom, even decent officers often felt they had no choice but to take justice into their own hands. With or without the blackjack, Meyer Goldberg spilled his guts within hours of being nabbed.

It was the habit of the professional thief to pick up the daily papers to see if his capers had made the headlines. "In theory it was to make sure we hadn't left any clues behind," said Willie Sutton. "The truth was that we always got a great kick out of reading our press notices." Poor Benny never even made it to the newsstand. He was hiding in his shabby hall room on West 56th Street when the police took him into custody later that day. A quick search of his digs turned up a stash of gold jewelry, cuff links, and stickpins, and a suitcase of silk underwear.

How much Moshe knew about all this is unclear. "His father is somewhere in Manhattan, but the police have been unable to locate him," reported the *Brooklyn Eagle*. "Adler says he does not know where he is." But Polly came through. Using the name "Pearl Koval" (her mother's maiden name), she was listed as his next of kin and scraped up enough money to hire a defense lawyer. But his bail was set at $25,000—well beyond Polly's means. So Ben sat in the dank hell of the Tombs, the infamous city jail, for nearly three months awaiting trial.

Putting the lie to the old cliché of honor among thieves, when Goldberg and Adler finally faced the judge, each blamed the other for their predicament. But it did them no good. After Goldberg was sentenced to fifteen years, Ben pleaded guilty to grand larceny in the first degree. On July 11, 1921, the judge sentenced him to five to ten years in the maximum-security prison in Ossining, New York, known by the lyrical nickname of Sing Sing.

This was the big time. Only thirty-five miles north of Manhattan on the banks of the Hudson River, Sing Sing was a sprawling stone fortress with looming observation towers and a six-story cellblock that housed many of history's most infamous criminals as well as America's first electric chair, known to the boys as "Old Sparky."

Ben was lucky, so to speak. Only three months earlier the prison had hired a progressive new warden, Lewis E. Lawes, who had done away with many of the prison's more inhumane practices, banning the most barbaric forms of punishment, the ball and chain, the bully club, and the cat-o'-nine-tails whip. Still, no one would mistake this "government boarding house" for a home. Ben's cell was so small, so coffin-like, a good-size man had to turn sideways to enter the door. A narrow iron bed folded up against the jagged stone wall, illuminated by the glare of a single bare bulb whose dim light flickered ominously every time the switch was flipped on Old Sparky.

If prison was a scarlet badge in the outer world, in the underworld few bona fides were more respected than a stint in Sing Sing. Over the next five years, Ben shared quarters with some of the city's most ambitious young outlaws.

The real boss of the prison, as far as the inmates went, was a twenty-five-year-old gang leader from Hell's Kitchen named Owney Madden, who was serving out a ten-to-twenty-year sentence for murder. "Owney runs Sing Sing," as one cop put it flatly. Under Madden's reign, prisoners enjoyed open gambling, regular boxing matches and baseball games, and a thriving black-market economy. The influence of Madden, along with his second-in-command, a charismatic burglar named Bill Duffy, extended past the prison walls and lasted long after they returned to the outside. As the country's premier "college for crooks," it was only fitting that Sing Sing also boasted the most powerful alumni network.

(

As if matters could get any worse, on July 29, 1921, two weeks after Ben's sentencing, a crew of vice cops from the Third Division raided an apartment at the corner of Riverside Drive and West 74th Street, taking into custody a twenty-year-old white woman who gave her name as "Pearl Davis," Polly's best-known alias, along with one Irene Warner. Irene's price was listed in the police records as twenty dollars a trick, a sign, at least, that Polly was climbing the ladder of whoredom with remarkable speed.

Once again, the long ride downtown in the paddy wagon, the tussle with the clerk, the mug shots and fingerprints, the humiliations of the holding pen, the shakedown by the bondsmen. This time she faced Magistrate Jesse Silbermann, a dark, slim man, with deep circles under his eyes that gave him a cadaverous look. Magistrate Silbermann had been appointed when the mayor decided he wanted, in his own words "a Hebrew from the Bronx" on the bench, as a reward for his service to Tammany Hall. He also enjoyed close ties to the West Tenth Street attorneys and bondsmen at the center of the vice ring.

There was also a brand-new palm to grease. It was clear to the powers behind the vice ring that their racket would run a lot smoother if they had a patsy in the position of prosecutor at the Women's Court. (As one prominent gangster liked to say, "Give me the D.A. and the other guys can have the cops, the politicians and couple of judges.") In April 1921 they found their man: John C. Weston.

In a break with tradition, John Weston was no Tammany big shot. He wasn't even a practicing lawyer. When he was offered the job, he was working as a process server in the Manhattan district attorney's office, and before that he'd been a truant officer and a jewelry salesman. But that was Weston's advantage; unlike most of the "higher-ups" in the Hall, he had no agenda or ambitions of his own, so he was a bargain to bribe.

All he had to do was be lousy at his job. With a crooked cop on the "Perjury Perch"—if he showed up at all—and a crooked magistrate nodding sleepily on the bench, Weston would merely "not ask any more questions than were absolutely necessary for his own protection," as he later put it, and the magistrate would throw the case out of court. For his troubles, he would pocket twenty-five dollars a head.

Now, with Weston in place as the new acting assistant district attorney, the vice ring became a sleek, efficient machine, producing profits for everyone but the hapless women who tumbled out of the paddy wagon every night.

As always, Polly was discharged, this time with a warning and probation of six months. Four days later, on August 5, her fifteen-year-old brother Jachiel arrived at Ellis Island. In America, he declared, he would reinvent himself as Albert.

Even if Moshe did not yet know about Polly's career, there was no keeping Ben's incarceration from him. Perhaps Gittel had been right to stay in Yanow. Here in America, their son had become a thief, and their daughter—well, who knew exactly how she made her living?

As for Polly, until the end of her life she was sure her family blamed her for Ben's fate. But like her brother, the judge's warnings fell on deaf ears. What choice did she have? She was no more employable in the square world than she was a year ago, but her expenses had quadrupled, between lawyers, bail bondsmen, her father and brothers, and of course, her mother and three youngest brothers still stuck in Yanow.

America *Gonif*, indeed.

☾

Now, declared Polly, "I began to do things in a more businesslike way." In a hurry to make her fortune, she stayed open twenty-four hours a day. With more dough, she picked up more class. No more bargain-counter shirtwaists for her, no more of the gaudy finery of Fourteenth Street. Photos from that year show her dressed fashionably but conservatively, her hair in a soft bob, her nails manicured but uncolored by paint, and her face showing no trace of rouge or mascara—a striking retreat from the defiantly rouged cheeks and kohl-lined eyes of her Coney Island days. The only hint of her demanding nightlife was the dark circles under her eyes. Her chic dresses and dainty pumps were accessorized by her new roommate, a purebred Chow Chow dog—an expensive status symbol of the early 1920s—named Nicko.

Finally Polly hit upon a plan to get out. After discussing it with her friend Edna Kirkwood, still living the gilded life of the mistress with plenty of time and money on her hands, it was decided. They would open a clothing boutique around the corner from Polly's apartment.

Like helming a whorehouse, running a dress shop was a proven path to success for immigrant Jewish women. Many of Manhattan's most glamorous designers began as Lower East Side seamstresses, including Hattie Carnegie, Sallie Milgram, and Madam Frances Clyne, who dressed all the big stars both on- and offstage. Even the famous comedienne Fanny Brice ran a dressmaking business on the side, whipping up fashionable knockoffs for the theatrical crowd.

"It was our dream that this shop would be the first of a country-wide chain," claimed Polly. She hoped to be like Ida Rosenthal, a fellow immigrant from Belarus, whose lingerie shop was fast growing into what would become known as Maidenform Bras, or Lane Bryant, who would turn a tiny storefront into a $5 million-a-year maternity wear business.

On what would this national empire be built? The flimsiest of foundations: lingerie.

It made sense. Lingerie was one of Polly's few areas of expertise besides the flesh trade. It was an essential tool of both the mistress and the high-class call girl. Many madams peddled lingerie and peek-a-boo evening gowns to the women who worked in their houses, often buying them back when a girl moved on, then reselling them to the next one to arrive.

As usual, Polly had an instinct for the zeitgeist. By the summer of 1922, the flapper revolution had shaken off its early associations with working-class hussies, free love bohemians, and upper-class rebels to become a national phenomenon. Small boutiques and beauty salons were springing up all over the city, in side-street brownstones and former hotel saloons, catering to the vanity of these frivolous, free-spending flappers, including, as *The New York Times* noted, "an amazing number of lingerie shops."

For the first time outside a bordello or a stage, the female form was being exposed to the open air. Necklines plunged, and sleeves disappeared. Hemlines bobbed up and down, but never again would skirts sweep the top of high-buttoned boots, which were, in any event, being replaced by graceful high-heeled pumps. Sheer stockings, made of silk and rayon, were a shocking new development that added zest to a coquettish ankle. Stiff corsets were replaced by slim garter belts and round elastic garters that allowed fast girls to roll down their stockings and show off their daintily dimpled knees. Pantaloons and petticoats gave way to delicate panties, supple brassieres, and soft, clinging teddies and "step-ins" made of rayon, batiste, or silk, trimmed with lace and ribbon. No spicy Broadway comedy or glossy Hollywood film was complete without a scene of pretty young actresses in their "scanties," cut to show off pert breasts and slim hips.

By July 1922, Polly had banked $6,000 (over $93,000 in current figures). Along with Edna's investment, their new enterprise earned a rating of 10,000 from the credit rating company Dun & Bradstreet, she remembered proudly. They took over the lease of a former jewelry store at 2487 Broadway between 92nd and 93rd streets, just around the corner from her apartment, and announced their new "high class lingerie and hosiery shop" in the pages of *Women's Wear Daily*. She would design the merchandise and handle manufacturing, while Eddy would keep the account books. (In later accounts, Polly called her Neddie.)

As the grand opening approached, their excitement mounted. On July 13 they spent the day downtown in the garment district before returning with their purchases to the Beaconsfield, an elegant building at 587 Riverside Drive. (Whose apartment this was, she never mentioned.) Wilted from the heat, the two women showered to cool off and then, clad only in their scanties, collapsed onto the bed. They left the front door ajar to catch the cool air from the Hudson River, as Polly told it, "but something else blew in besides the breeze—namely, two cops who came marching straight into the bedroom."

There, once again, stood the scum of the vice squad, William G. Haake and Andrew J. McLaughlin.

"What's the big idea?" Polly demanded in fury.

"Whadaya think?" said one of the cops. "Climb into your glad rags, girls. You're coming to the station for a little visit."

"So now I began to realize what it meant to be a marked woman," remembered Polly with anger. Adding insult to injury, they were booked under their real names. The whole thing was a frame-up, Polly insisted. Guilty or not, gossip traveled fast on the Broadway grapevine, and it wouldn't have been hard for the cops to figure out that she and Eddy were sitting on a sizable chunk of cash.

Polly and Eddy were bailed out at a cost of $500 each by Samuel Felix, a crooked bondsman who insisted they hire his colleague, Alexander Lange, one of the most notorious of the West Tenth Street shysters, and were scheduled to face Magistrate Jean Norris.

This time, however, Polly was outraged enough that she decided to take her complaints directly to their boss, Inspector James Bolan, the head of the plainclothes vice squad and the so-called "Czar" of Manhattan's nightlife district, running up the West Side from Hell's Kitchen to Harlem. Compared to his predecessors, who treated the district like a bottomless cash register, Inspector Bolan's personal conduct bordered on saintly. He drank, discreetly, and he was sympathetic to the plight of the gamblers, but he harbored "an almost rabid hatred" of prostitution, as the *Herald Tribune* editor Stanley Walker put it.

By the standards of his profession, Bolan was, as one newspaper reported, "so straight he bends backward." But no lawman could rise to the rank of deputy inspector without the backing of a powerful "rabbi," in the lingo of the bluecoats—a political patron and protector. And Bolan had one of the city's most powerful rabbis: Jimmy J. Hines, boss of the Monongahela Democratic Club of West Harlem.

She showed up at Bolan's office with receipts and paperwork to prove that they were about to open a store, and he listened sympathetically. Maybe she convinced Bolan that she was going straight, or perhaps she went over the heads of McLaughlin and Haake and paid off Bolan directly. Maybe she invoked the names of underworld friends with close connections to the higher-ups in Tammany Hall. One way or another, on July 20, the case was dismissed.

"The incident momentarily took the edge of my enthusiasm for honest enterprise, but I cheered up when I saw our sign lettered in gilt on the window," said Polly. "I used to nearly burst with pride when I overheard people at Pomerantz's restaurant remarking on our beautiful window display," she remembered with pleasure. "Pomerantz admired me, being so young and trying to conduct a business and would sit with me whenever I came in, giving me pointers on how to run my shop."

She and Eddy hoped to draw their clientele from the well-heeled Broadway entertainers who lived along that stretch of the Upper West Side, the showgirls, actresses, and blue-chip mistresses who set the cutting edge of New York fashion. Their strategy seemed to be working, at first. One of their best customers was the vaudeville-singer-turned-opera-star Rosa Ponselle, the spendthrift daughter of a penny-ante Italian bootlegger whose Riverside Drive penthouse was a monument to nouveau riche living.

But Polly quickly discovered that legitimate business was not all it was cracked up to be. Competition in the garment industry was far more cutthroat than in the vice trade. The hours were grueling, from nine in the morning till midnight, and their profit margins were thin. After expenses, each partner drew a modest weekly salary of forty dollars, about what a top call girl could earn in two hours of "partying."

"On top of everything else, our clientele seemed to consist largely of shoplifters," remembered Polly ruefully. "Boosting," as it was known in the underworld, was booming along with the boutiques, especially among women. For some it was a titillating hobby, an afternoon pastime. For others it was a living. Prostitutes often became boosters as they got older, and it was a common occupation among gangsters' girlfriends. There were organized shoplifting rings that offered to steal specific items on commission, while others lifted in-demand items and fenced them door-to-door at cut-rate prices, a particularly popular way to shop among the call house crowd.

Polly wasn't judgmental. She counted plenty of shoplifters among her friends. But it was one more strike against the legitimate life.

Yet for all her complaints, Polly was living well enough. Snapshots show her and her pretty friends lounging at the beach and riding horseback in Central Park—a hot new hobby among the Broadway butterflies, who adored the daring, aristocratic look of the tweed riding breeches. Polly and Edna frolicked at Lake Hopatcong, a New Jersey summer resort popular with vaudevillians, burlesque performers, and the heavy-plunging gambling crowd. She may have gone straight, but she certainly hadn't gone square: in one photo she is tangled in a pile of girls, with one brazen young lady baring her nipple and clutching Edna's more ladylike breast with her free hand.

Of course, Polly may well have been running a discreet call flat, using the shop as a front to fool her family and throw the vice squad off her scent. Millinery boutiques, dressmakers, and department stores had long been hotbeds of clandestine prostitution and unabashed gold digging. It was well known, as one hustler noted, that "a call girl who has legitimate employment in the daytime is rarely bothered by the police at night."

Whether the Polly-Eddy Shop was a legitimate business or a front—or a little bit of both—it took only six months for them both to get their fill of the square life. As a small shop owner struggling to cover her weekly expenses, she was no better off than the masses of impoverished seamstresses and tailors she'd tried to leave behind. In December 1922 they quietly advertised the store for sale but got no takers.

Edna was out by the end of July. Polly kept the store open a little longer as a cover while booking dates for her girls or, as she put it, "doing a little on a side [*sic*] to keep up expenses." By autumn, the Polly-Eddy Shop was no more.

In the end, Polly's desire for respectability paled next to her longing to live the good life, American style. But her foray into lingerie was not entirely wasted. Once she was back in business, she built a profitable sideline selling dainty underthings to the girls who worked for her.

❦

Polly was tired of being a chump. After working her tail off for one year as a legitimate entrepreneur, she had less than she'd started with. Her total assets amounted to her furniture, her dog Nicko, and $800 in the bank.

Polly put out word on the gray-market grapevine that she was looking for an opportunity to make some fast cash. She soon happened to run into two friends—"at least I thought they were friends"—a couple of card sharps named Mike Fogarty and Red Clemens, who made their living by luring unwitting victims into crooked card games.

Card hustlers like Mike and Red were as thick as flies in the pool halls, horse parlors, and speakeasies of Manhattan. Adventurous souls looking for action merely had to stroll the stretch of Broadway between 47th and 49th streets, where a half-dozen or so "tip-off men," in the words of one Broadway observer, "stand in front of certain chop houses to whisper the hotel room numbers of the nightly dice and poker games."

After some chitchat, Mike and Red casually mentioned that they were looking for an outside partner for a simple con job. They had a wealthy mark lined up for a rigged game of poker, but they needed an extra player to pull off the scam. Any chance she would pose as a friend who was joining the game? They'd set her up with a thousand bucks cash to play with. Then during the game one of them would sit behind the sucker and subtly tip her off to the cards in his hand so she could bet accordingly. After she won, they would split the final pot three ways. It was a sure thing, with no risk to her.

She didn't need to be asked twice. They ran through a quick rehearsal, then the mark arrived, a gullible-looking geezer wearing a patch over one eye. Following the prearranged secret signals, she won hand after hand, just as they'd planned. It was exhilarating, she said, as "the sucker kept waving more dough in my face, my eyes got bigger and bigger, and in my mind I was already spending my third of the take."

The stakes mounted until the table was stacked with bills. "Mr. Sap kept on raising me," said Polly, steadily increasing the size of the bets and the size of the pot, until suddenly, to her surprise, "I had nothing left to call with." If she couldn't call, or match the amount of his bet, she would be forced to forfeit the pot, losing all her partners' money.

She and Mike stepped away from the game to confer. He and Red were out of cash, he whispered, but if she could kick in some dough, they'd sweep the whole pot as planned and then hightail it out of there. Polly was all in, she declared, then excused herself to zip around the corner to her savings bank at 98th and Broadway.

The bank teller, who knew Polly, smelled a rat when she asked him to withdraw seven of her eight hundred dollars so she could make a quick killing. The teller tried to dissuade her, but she was too excited to listen. "I jutted around the corner and back to the game, shoved my dough into the center of the table, and called the hand."

The tide turned with sickening speed. One losing hand, then another and another, and suddenly the game was over. She was cleaned out. Before she could gather her wits, Mr. Sap, Mike, and Red had all vanished, along with most of her savings.

She'd been the victim of a classic double cross, an old-school confidence game known as "Playing the Tip." Mr. Sap had been secretly working with Red and Mike, and Polly was the true mark. As in almost all successful con games, they'd trapped her by appealing to her own greed and dishonesty, her willingness to pick someone else's pocket in the pursuit of easy money. Polly, feeling cynical after her failed foray into the square world, had been the perfect pigeon. That she was a woman, without her own mob of miscreants to back her up, made it even easier. What was she going to do, holler to the cops that she'd been swindled by her own scam?

Quick study though she was, Polly hadn't yet developed good "grift sense," that ineffable ability to see all the angles in any situation. But even if she'd been more savvy, she could never entirely avoid "the villain's paradox," as the criminologists call it. Working outside the law, she had no choice but to do business with fellow lawbreakers, who were, by nature and by necessity, untrustworthy. For that reason, there was no commodity on the black market as rare—and as valuable—as trust. Even Arnold Rothstein, the most protected man on Broadway and a double-crosser from the cradle, couldn't avoid the villain's paradox. "The hardest thing in the world is to find an honest partner in a skin game," as Rothstein often complained.

In hindsight, Polly was philosophical. Nonetheless, she still felt the sting five years later, when she spied Mike Fogarty walking down 47th Street. Putting her raspy baritone to good use, she commenced cussing out "the cheap louse."

"Aw, now Polly," he said with a grin, "you're not going to beef about that after all these years!"

"Of course not," Polly said sharply, then recited the first commandment of the grifter: "You have to have larceny in your heart before you can be taken." Better that she learned that critical lesson while she was young and had so little to lose.

This was a critical turning point in her education. Citizens of the half world made a moral distinction between the vice vendor and the *gonif*. The vice dealer sells goods and services that mainstream society wants but disapproves of. But a thief was just a thief, whether he was a silver-tongued confidence man, a slippery-fingered safe-cracker, or a sociopathic skull-cracker. Whatever people said about Polly in the years to come, and they would say plenty, no one would ever call her a thief.

If Polly had any hesitation about leaving the legitimate world behind, it evaporated along with her bankroll. As the summer of 1923 drew to a close, she recalled, "I made up my mind to go back in the whorehouse business and this time not to quit until I was really heeled."

First she had to get back on her feet. That required two things: start-up money and an entrée to the Big Spenders. There was one place to go for both: Arnold Rothstein.

Polly in her first fur coat strolling the boardwalk of Atlantic City, 1924

6

Thumbs Up with the Mob

Renee Carroll never forgot the first time she met Arnold Rothstein. She was still new to the Big Street then, before she shot to fame as Broadway's favorite hatcheck girl.

It was two a.m., and she was sitting in a smoke-filled night-club with Texas Guinan, the most celebrated of the Broadway hostesses, along with a girlfriend and her gangster beau, when a dapper older man approached their table. He had dark, hooded eyes, raven-black hair, a night owl's pallor, and a dazzling row of perfect ivory teeth. He was accompanied by a pair of tough-looking mugs, their hands thrust ominously into the pockets of their skintight suitcoats.

"Hello, Arnold!" Tex greeted him. "Betcha three to two it rains before eleven this morning."

"You're a sucker for wet weather, Tex," Rothstein smirked. "Aren't you even Boy Scout enough to know that rain before seven means clear before eleven? It's all over now."

"Is it a bet?"

"Don't be silly; I'm busy."

Rothstein studied the pretty flapper with the bare legs and ginger-colored hair seated with Tex. Renee was only in her late teens but had long since ditched her family, her birth name, and her orthodox rabbi father. Suddenly he opened his Chesterfield overcoat and pulled a fat roll of bills out of his front pants pocket. He peeled off a greenback and casually tossed it in front of Renee.

"Could you go for one of these?" he asked with a cool smile.

A one-thousand-dollar bill lay on the table. Everyone stared at it silently. "For a minute I felt like the proverbial drowning person whose life goes flashing past in a few seconds," Renee later wrote.

> I remembered working at Roseland at a few cents a dance—and how many dances would make a thousand bucks, and how many dresses I could buy—and pounding that damned typewriter at thirteen bucks per with a fresh boss trying to make it fifteen if—and running away from home and living only a couple of blocks away from my folks for more than a year and never seeing them—and that hostess job in a Greenwich Village club—and walking the streets with a bun in my pocket to be saved for dinner.

Rothstein spoke again. "Tell me when you're ready to leave."

An opportunity was one thing, but this was an order. "Something went molten inside me," remembered the peppery redhead. Summoning her best impression of a hard-boiled dame, she gave the presumptuous stranger what she hoped was a crushing sneer.

Rothstein paused, expressionless, for a moment, then picked up the money, kissed it, and tucked it back into his pocket. Turning to leave, he stopped and once again pulled out his bankroll, peeling off another bill. He leaned over and thrust a crumpled one-dollar bill deep down the front of her evening dress.

"Just to show you I'm a good sport, buy yourself some diamonds—Woolworth's."

He turned and strode out the door, followed by his two goons.

"I don't know today why he did it," Renee mused, although those who knew him better might've had their theories. Longtime habitués of the Booze Belt knew that Rothstein kept a sharp eye out for new girls on the circuit, always on the lookout for fresh faces with fresh appeal for the big spenders. Thinking about the incident later, Renee joked, "I couldn't quite make up my mind whether I was a success on Broadway or a failure in life." Of course, the two were not mutually exclusive.

Polly was more cryptic about how she met Arnold Rothstein, saying only that he was "a man whom I was one day to know well."

They may have first crossed paths on Second Avenue, where he'd gotten his start hanging around the Tammany-run gambling rooms where the old-timers still called him Arnie. Or she might have encountered him up on the Upper West Side in Pomerantz's or Reuben's delis, at least until that autumn of 1923, when he switched his headquarters to a tiny storefront delicatessen at 49th Street and Broadway named Lindy's (made famous as Mindy's in the stories of Damon Runyon, the O. Henry of the blackjack-and-brass-knuckle set). Here he was known as A.R., in homage to corporate tycoons like J. P. Morgan.

A.R. could be found most evenings in a rear booth, back to the wall, flanked by his current strong-arm, Fatty Walsh, a heavyset Irish fellow with a winning smile, or Sidney Stajer, a pudgy little hophead who was the nearest thing Rothstein had to a close friend. Here he held court, conferring with "clients" who sidled up to his table, talking furtively out of the sides of their mouths, and taking calls from the telephone behind the cashier's desk. Old man Lindy wasn't happy about it, but as one waiter explained, "What can he do? An important man like Mr. Rothstein, you do not offend."

On Broadway everyone who was Someone had at least a speaking acquaintance with Arnold Rothstein. People pointed him out to their companions at speakeasies, prizefights, and racetracks, whispering behind their hands while smiling and bowing to his face. Sportsmen followed his wagers with an eagle eye, knowing his reputation as a sure-thing bettor. The gamblers, politicians, and illegitimate entrepreneurs who counted on him for loans and favors knew him as the Big Bankroll, the Big Jew Uptown, or the Brain.

"Arnold stood halfway between the upper and the underworlds," in the words of his long-suffering wife. The newspapers called him a gambler, but that barely brushed the surface. Had he been Sicilian, they'd have called him "Godfather," but in the Jewish netherworld, he was merely an unorthodox businessman. He owned an insurance company and held major investments in Manhattan real estate. He also served as a fence for stolen goods, and provided bail bonds for the criminal classes and the Tammany political machine.

His most valuable service was as a moneylender or, less politely, a loan shark: "He lent money to thieves, blackmailers, dope peddlers, bookmakers, burglars—anyone from whom he thought he could get back his money with interest." As one reporter put it, he was "the short term commercial banker for half the underworld of the United States."

A.R. won national notoriety in 1920 when he was accused of paying eight members of the Chicago White Sox to lose the 1919 World Series. "It was then that the words 'King' and 'Brains of the Underworld,' began to be whispered," remembered Rothstein's wife Caroline. Since then, he'd appeared regularly in the headlines, first accused of bribing the police to protect his high-dollar crap games, then of shooting a cop who had the temerity to raid one of them. That summer he'd been charged with being the mastermind behind a major stock fraud operation and was implicated in a shady "breach of promise" lawsuit brought by a jilted Broadway beauty against her wealthy sugar daddy.

Above all, Rothstein was the city's most famous "fixer," connecting people and resources in times of opportunity and need. He served as the main conduit between the city's law-benders and the politicians who controlled the city's judges, district attorneys, and police force. He passed along bribes, made introductions, and arranged mutual favors, all while taking a cut of the action. He put together deals, facilitated mergers and partnerships, and had a deep pool of his own funds to lend or invest, to start or sustain an enterprise. "In a way he was an investment banker, except that most of his dealings lacked the wispy air-brush of legality," as one friend in the press put it.

Fixing was an art that required a keen knowledge of human nature and a nose for power. A fixer had to know what his targets wanted. Was it women, social status, liquid funds, inside tips, or the opportunity to bet on a sure thing? Did they want straight cash for a service, or should it be couched as an exchange of favors, or a gift with no strings attached but the unspoken possibility of future friendly relations? Was it something sought without shame, or was it a secret, a source of guilt or fear?

That's where Polly came in. Behind Rothstein's icy exterior, he was known for his fine appreciation of female flesh, both professionally and personally. His wife Caroline was a former *shicksa* showgirl who was seen only on special occasions. He also kept a string of blond mistresses hidden in apartments around the city and was known, as one reporter observed, as "one of the best customers of several of the city's more lavish call flats."

Beyond his personal predilection for blondes, Rothstein was a keen believer in the power of the skirt, especially a high-class tomato who oozed both sex appeal and status. Women were one of the most reliable tools in the arsenal of the fixer, the grifter, and the professional gambler. They were, as one crime reporter explained, the "butterfly bait, who are used in practically every known racket."

Much of Rothstein's early success came from paying pretty young women as "steerers" to bring fresh suckers to his gambling houses, roving games, and fraudulent stock brokerages. He paid comely chorines from the *Ziegfeld Follies* and other girlie revues to rope in their wealthy beaux and stage door admirers. As a fence, he had a warm appreciation for female jewel thieves, who worked in teams in restaurants and hotels; women made excellent "inside men" and decoys for burglary gangs, befriending and setting up victims. As a fixer, willing women could be tossed in as bonuses, or mood softeners, as a form of collegial bonding or subtle blackmail. Adding a pretty girl and a case of whiskey could make a crude bribe seem more like a friendly gesture or a glamorous perk. Rumor had it that Rothstein was also involved in the illegal drug trade and cultivated "opium vampires" like Garnet to work as mules, dealers, and lures for new customers.

Most important for Polly's purposes, Rothstein lent money to madams when they needed bail or cash to get back on their feet after a raid, and he had the connections to help spread the word that she was back in business.

A.R. had a long-standing appreciation of the sex trade. He'd built his real estate empire in part by subleasing apartments to ladies of the evening at premium prices and was rumored to have major investments in whorehouses. Besides the hefty profit margins, bordellos were an endless well of lucrative secrets and opportunities for extortion.

Prostitution and blackmail were sisters under the skin, thriving whenever the gap between public obligations and private privileges, between law and desire, grows too wide. In a city of promiscuous businessmen, unscrupulous lawyers, and flirtatious flappers, where sexual mores were changing faster than public morals, blackmail was a booming business. As one crime reporter pointed out, there was more money to be made "hijacking reputations than was ever dreamed of in the hijacking of rum or narcotics." It was whispered that Rothstein backed blackmail gangs that employed sophisticated versions of the old badger game to extract large checks from indiscreet husbands and wealthy heirs.

That fall of 1923, Polly had had her fill of failure at life, to borrow Renee Carroll's phrase. Now she possessed only one goal: to be a success on Broadway. "I had always told my girls: If you have to be a prostitute, be a good one," remembered Polly. "Well, the same applied to me. If I had to be a madam, I'd be a good madam."

This time, she declared, "I was determined to be the best goddam madam in all America."

☾

In the summer of 1923, the national economy finally shook off the last of the postwar recession, ushering in an era of unprecedented prosperity. "It was becoming increasingly fashionable to make money any way you could—except by working for it," Polly remembered. "It wasn't only angle-shooters and corner-cutters and big-city sharpies who were on the 'get-rich-quick' kick."

Down on Wall Street, the stock market entered a spectacular bull market of surging corporate profits and steadily rising stock prices. Up in Albany, the New York state capital, Governor Al Smith repealed the Mullan-Gage Act that had authorized the state's enforcement of Prohibition, paving the way for explosive growth in the illegal liquor trade. The city was awash in newly minted fortunes, eager to be squandered in Broadway's famous fleshpots.

Nobody was raking in the chips like the crowd of bootleggers, grifters, and gamblers who orbited around Arnold Rothstein. Polly had encountered many of them already when they were just the local hoodlums.

Some were primarily bookmakers and game runners like Mike Best, known as "the Baron of Yorkville," the Upper East Side German and Hungarian neighborhood brimming with after-hours joints known as "goulash houses." Or the Boston Brothers—otherwise known as Sam and Meyer Solomon—former pickpockets and purse-snatchers who'd worked their way up from Second Avenue to a big-time bookmaking operation that catered to Wall Street speculators. Meyer's wife, Bessie London, was known in one undercover investigator's estimation as "the cleverest booster gun-mol in the world" (underworld argot for a female shoplifter and pickpocket). Sam's wife, Tillie Gold, was Bessie's pickpocketing pupil and a good friend of Polly's.

Others had been thieves, drug dealers, and strong-arms for hire before Rothstein took them under his wing. The Brain cared nothing for the traditional ethnic partisanship and neighborhood clannishness that marked so many men of the underworld. The dollar, Rothstein liked to say, "had only one nationality, one religion—profit." He favored those with a "modern mercenary spirit," as one scholar described it, who took a more businesslike approach to crime. The ones who showed a talent for strategic thinking and organizational management along with a ruthless capacity for violence.

In 1920 when the Eighteenth Amendment became law, Rothstein began backing the most promising of his pupils in the burgeoning new business of bootleg booze, providing cash, connections, strategic advice, and political protection. "It took a man like Arnold Rothstein to see the potential of bootlegging on a major scale," claimed his young protégé Meyer Lansky. They modeled their operations on Rothstein's gambling syndicates, pooling resources and collaborating across gang lines for their mutual benefit. Soon anyone who wanted to have anything to do with the hooch trade in New York had to confer first with the "Napoleon of Manhattan's gangdom," as one lawyer dubbed him.

In the last three years, A.R.'s acolytes had become New York's "hoodlum aristocracy." Polly certainly didn't know all the ins and outs of their business, nor did she want to. But proof of their success was visible in their sleek limousines, bulky bodyguards, sapphire rings, and flashy custom-tailored suits, carefully cut to accommodate their shoulder holsters without ruining the line of their jackets. It could be seen in the deference they received from the swells who gratefully bought their liquor and bowed to them in the speakeasies.

Polly came to know Rothstein's criminal cabinet intimately. "My clientele consisted mostly of gangsters and hoodlums," she remembered, "some of whom were to become the big shots of the day."

The comedian Milton Berle, who knew the cast of players well, maintained that a Lower East Side gang leader named Irving Wexler was Polly's first important booster in those early days. Irving was better known by his alias: Waxey Gordon, a tribute to his slick-fingered skill as a young pickpocket. A brusque, thickset man with heavy jowls, slightly bulging eyes, and a longtime opium habit, Waxey was well into his criminal career when Prohibition began. He led a vicious gang of pimps, pickpockets, strong-arm *schlammers*, and dope peddlers from Second Avenue who dominated the cocaine trade between New York and Philadelphia.

Waxey ran with a fiercely loyal crew, all Lower East Side Jews, all heavy gamblers and confirmed hopheads. Among Polly's favorites were Charlie "Chink" Sherman, "a nice guy but a toughie," in her words, who was rumored to be a big opium trader, and "Benevolent Charlie" Kandel, "know to me as Charlie Manny, who was Waxie Gordon's partner in the pick-pocket days." Benevolent Charlie now worked as a collector for Rothstein and ran speakeasies and gambling joints.

It was no surprise that Polly should hit it off with the Jews, who, through Rothstein's influence, now dominated bootlegging in New York. But it was an Irishman who became her most important early "benefactor," as one of her well-informed friends put it, although she kept that a closely guarded secret to the end of her life. William Vincent "Big Bill" Dwyer was a jovial fellow with a disarming smile and expressive blue eyes behind horn-rimmed glasses. Rothstein had helped finance Dwyer as he expanded his operation from stealing industrial alcohol from government warehouses into international smuggling. Big Bill had, in one gangland lawyer's description, "an easy way about him and a fine sense of humor." He was a glad-hander, a natural connector who loved the theater and parties and preferred grease to violence.

Dwyer had recently joined forces with another of Rothstein's protégés, Francesco Castiglia, a native of Calabria, Italy, and a child of East Harlem, who now went by the Irish moniker of Frankie Costello. (It never hurt to have an Irish name when conversing with cops.) Frank Costello, his longtime lawyer liked to claim, was "the real Jay Gatsby, with two differences. His guttural rasp could never have formed the words 'old sport.' And he never would have wasted a minute staring across a bay just to spot a 'broad' named Daisy."

In 1920 Frank and his partner, Salvatore Lucania, began buying booze wholesale from Waxey Gordon to retail to Manhattan's upper crust. By the beginning of 1923, Costello was powerful and ruthless enough that Big Bill decided it was smarter to join forces than to compete with him.

Polly first met Salvatore Lucania before he became known as "Charlie Lucky" or "Lucky Luciano," the name that the gentlemen of the press preferred. Charlie had the looks to be a pimp: wavy brown hair, the olive complexion, slightly pockmarked, of his native Sicily, and dark, deep-set eyes that could light up or turn black in a flash. "I knew him before he became the kingpin of the rackets, but success didn't change him," Polly said later; "I never found him to be other than gentlemanly."

Charlie Lucky was at the center of a network of thieves and strongmen who shook down storekeepers, robbed warehouses, and ran crap games, although drug dealing was his primary occupation in those early days. Like all Rothstein's star students, he had a feral intelligence and a natural charisma coupled with a capacity for cold-blooded brutality.

Still, that wasn't how Polly remembered him. "He was always quiet, clean-talking and considerate of the girls and maids," she insisted. On one of his visits, Lucky made a crack about how gloomy the superintendent fixing the sink looked. "What's this guy doing in a house of joy? He looks ready to croak!" When Polly told him the super was suffering from leukemia, Charlie was so embarrassed he gave the sick man $300.

Guided by Rothstein, Costello and Luciano built a glowing reputation as society bootleggers, providing hooch to a high-hat clientele that included not only the finest speakeasies and Broadway celebrities but also scions of the Social Register who bought in bulk to stock their Long Island estates and Upper East Side apartments. He'd invested his profits in a string of drugstores, where trusted customers could buy a pint of gin or a tin of cocaine.

On fur or jewel heists, Charlie Lucky liked to work with an eclectic crew that included Legs Diamond, a skinny, hotheaded Irishman who also worked as a bodyguard and strongman for Rothstein, and Arthur Flegenheimer, aka Dutch Schultz, a wild-eyed Jew from the Bronx whose mild exterior concealed a sociopathic temper. For more complex operations, Lucky preferred to collaborate with Frank Costello and two Lower East Siders, the diminutive but fierce Maier Suchowljansky, better known as Meyer Lansky, and his partner Benjamin Siegel, nicknamed "Bugsy" for his habit of sudden homicidal outbursts.

"We was the best team that ever got put together," Charlie Lucky later bragged. "We knew our jobs better than any other guys on the street. We was like the Four Horsemen of Notre Dame—except what would two Jewish guys be doin' at Notre Dame?"

Polly was especially fond of Meyer Lansky. The "one name I will not use, that is Lansky," she declared when she was contemplating writing a memoir. "I like the guy, don't want the spotlight on him." They were about the same age and hailed from the same corner of Belarus, and they shared a hungry intelligence and a craving to be recognized by the legitimate world. Rothstein initially hired Lansky to specialize in transportation and enforcement—i.e., beating, maiming, and killing—but the kid's real talent was for numbers.

That fall of 1923, the Costello-Dwyer "Combine," as it became known on the street, was joined by Owney Madden, who had returned to civilian life after a long stretch upriver. He had narrow blue eyes and a sharp angled face, and spoke in the accents of Liverpool and Hell's Kitchen, where he enjoyed a reputation as one of the most vicious of the city's Irish gang leaders. "He was small, thin and softly-spoken, but very, very tough," as one boxer described Madden. His term as the unofficial mayor of Sing Sing had given him access to a vast army of ex-cons. Madden formed a handpicked crew of killers and spent much of 1923 muscling in on Costello and Dwyer's operations. Recognizing a natural-born leader when they saw one, they decided to take Madden on as a partner.

By the end of 1923, the Combine controlled the liquor trade on much of the West Side and most of midtown Manhattan. The Internal Revenue Service claimed that Dwyer personally owed about $800,000 in taxes on his 1923 income; in 1924 it estimated his unpaid tax bill at $1.2 million.

❦

The bullet boys may have made their bones as bootleggers, but it was as gamblers that Polly got to know them best. Arnold Rothstein's informal syndicate of lawbreakers ran private high-stakes poker games and secret floating crap games, immortalized in the smash Broadway musical *Guys and Dolls*. To elude cops and stickup men, the games shifted every night through empty garages, hotels, warehouses, and the backrooms of speakeasies in Yorkville, the Upper West Side, and the White Light District.

Although commercial betting was strictly illegal, New York was the mecca of gambling in the United States. This was the Big Apple, as the horse jockeys called it, where the action was always high. The "gambling fraternity," as the newspaper columnists liked to call it, ran the gamut of the social world, from old Plymouth Rock stock, Wall Street barons, and newly minted shtetl-born moguls—who owned their own horse stables and dropped tens of thousands of dollars in a single evening—to white-haired widows who saved their pennies to play the daily numbers lottery and ne'er-do-wells loafing in pool halls, studying the scratch sheets, and borrowing a few bucks to lay the day's wagers.

But no place was more devoted to gambling in all its forms than Hardened Artery. "Nine out of every ten guys along Broadway are betting men; they were when they came to the Main Stem, and if they weren't, they soon were converted," the columnist Mel Heimer noted. "They will bet on everything and anything—on the respective speed of two raindrops skidding down a restaurant window, on the poker hands involved in automobile license-plate numbers, on which horse will finish last in a given race, on whether the next batter will walk or strike out."

Polly's reputation blossomed in the fall of 1923 when she was taken up by the Broadway oddsmaker George McManus. At nearly six feet two inches tall, McManus was a brawny, barrel-chested fellow, with a lantern jaw and a wide crooked grin that lit up when he was in good spirits. He was the youngest son of a retired police lieutenant who had been a powerful player in the NYPD during the heyday of the System. Three of his brothers joined the force, before retiring to join George in his bookmaking operations.

"Smiling George," as boys in the press dubbed him, was a partner with Rothstein and Dwyer in a number of lucrative gambling schemes. Both Big Bill and Smiling George were extroverted Irishmen—Dwyer from Hell's Kitchen, McManus from Harlem—who relished the limelight and the role of lavish host. They also shared that most valued of traits in a madam's estimation: a total disregard for the value of money. McManus was beloved by waiters, entertainers, and gold diggers up and down the Avenue for dropping twenty-dollar tips without blinking an eye, while Bill was famous for never allowing anyone to pick up a check, no matter how steep the bill.

Dwyer, in particular, enjoyed a sterling reputation among lawmen, politicians, and fellow lawbreakers. He was admired for his square deals, prompt payments, and openhanded generosity—in direct contrast to the ice-veined Rothstein, who was notorious for cutting every corner, for squeezing every dime, and worse yet, for being what the gamblers called "slow pay" while personally dunning debtors for even the pettiest of loans.

That fall McManus and Dwyer, along with Owney Madden's brother Marty, were running the hottest regular crap game in New York, with action running as high as $700,000 some nights. The games attracted high rollers from every corner of the country—oilmen, industrialists, stock market speculators, all looking to blow off steam after a feverish night of shooting the ivory cubes. The games didn't start till nearly midnight and often ran till four or five in the morning. When the last die was tossed, the players finished off the night at Polly's.

There was nothing like craps to stoke the appetite for a playmate, Polly soon discovered. Compared with the quiet concentration of cards, where women were considered a nuisance, craps was a glorious circus, noisy, fast, and surging with adrenaline at each roll of the dice. Here women were considered good luck and were often asked to kiss or blow on the dice. Players could multiply their winnings in minutes, as much as 900 percent in just two rolls—an aphrodisiac if ever there was one.

Winners looking to celebrate their good fortune had to worry about muggings and kidnappings, so providing a place that was safe, secret, and always open into the wee hours quickly made her joint the preferred after-hours clubhouse of the late-night dice throwers. Nobody threw around the folding green like a bootlegger on a hot streak. "Money meant nothing to these fellows," she remembered with pleasure; "they sometimes spent five hundred or more in an evening. Whoever won the crap game paid the bill."

They were the ones who set her up as a full-service speakeasy. "It had not occurred to me to sell drinks until one of the bunch remarked that I was a sap to let them buy their booze from a bootlegger and cart it up to my apartment. Why didn't I get smart and sell them drinks at a buck a throw? I took his advice, and, in his own words, cut myself in for a nice piece of change."

She encouraged the johns to buy drinks for the girls, padding the bills further. Of course, a tipsy girl was an uninhibited playmate, but a drunken whore was of no use to anyone. So to keep the girls from getting blitzed, she employed an old trick of barkeeps and brothels, serving the girls cold tea brewed to match the golden color of rye and whiskey. On a good night, her bar bills dwarfed her profits on the bedrooms.

Polly's decision to make herself indispensable to Rothstein's pals was paying off in spades. McManus and Dwyer were two of the most popular men on Broadway, and with their seal of approval, her house quickly gained a reputation among underworldlings as, in her words, "a sort of combination club and speakeasy with a harem conveniently handy." Or a "sort of ladies auxiliary of the legion of the damned," to borrow a phrase from her friend Dorothy Parker.

In a world of villains, she became known as someone a villain could trust. She was not exactly an equal—no "frail" ever was—but she was the rare twist who had real brains, sharp instincts, and moxie. She shared their American sensibility and aspirations, and she spoke their language, literally; Yiddish was the lingua franca of the Jewish underworld and was especially convenient for confounding nosy Irish cops. She was a good sport, with a keen, self-deprecating sense of humor, who could parry their wisecracks and brush off their roughhousing, crude comments, and practical jokes with a smile. Tiny as she was, with her deep voice— even huskier after three years of late nights, unfiltered cigarettes, and bootleg whiskey—she exuded a fierce bantam toughness.

When trouble came, as it inevitably did, she followed the code of silence as completely as the most hard-bitten hustler. "They liked the way that I did business," she remembered with pride, "never squawking when I had to take one on the chin."

She was, to quote the Brownsville brute Pretty Amberg, "thumbs up with the mob." Later, when she was contemplating writing her life story, she made a list of all the mobsters she could not mention in print, and it included almost every major racketeer of the era. "I knew them all," she admitted ruefully. "Most of them died with their boots on. One of the gang was a character called Sammie the Schnook, but why they called him Schnook I don't know. He was smarter than they were—he's still alive."

☾

Finally, Polly was making the kind of money she'd always dreamed of. But the gangsters came at a high price. "They were a wild bunch all right," she mused. Like most of the male half of Broadway, they all adored practical jokes and pranks, the more elaborate the better. "They liked a joke all right—when it was on someone else," especially George McManus. "The kids with him played the jokes and he would get a hell of a kick out of it at my expense."

Polly could tolerate the pranks, the chiseling, and the small cons, although she didn't like them. Unpaid loans and bad checks—stiffs— were regular thorns. "I have enough stiffs to paper my garage," she groused while going through a box of old papers years later. She was freshly annoyed by one dated October 22, 1923. "It was given to me by one of the McManus gang telling me that he was president of the bank. I was gullible enough to believe that," she remembered. "It probably was the bastard's way to teach me not to believe everything told to me."

But it was the ever-looming threat of violence that really wore on her nerves. The brass-knuckle boys might be dressing better, but they remained notoriously hot-tempered and unpredictable, especially when they were on a losing streak or a drunken, coked-up spree. It was an ongoing challenge to keep the overpriced alcohol flowing while making sure that no one died of accidental lead poisoning. To prevent friendly arguments from turning fatal, she requested that the boys check their guns at the door, along with their felt fedoras and bulky overcoats. "I usually hid them in the stove," she remembered, "figuring it wasn't likely anyone would get a yen to bake a cake."

While that cut down on random gunplay, it didn't do much to improve their manners. George McManus, in particular, was a dangerous wild card. "McManus was always quiet, and a gentleman when sober," said Polly. But when he was liquored up, his mood could suddenly turn savage, and his jokes became cruel and dangerous.

Nonetheless, it was a price she was willing to pay. The gamblers and bootleggers were spending like mad, and her reputation was spreading fast. She bought herself some swell clothes and showy jewelry, and began saving up for a mink coat. A full-length mink was the sine qua non of the fashionable flapper, just as monogrammed silk shirts and spotless white spats marked the new status of the bootlegger. "I talked about it so much that when a guy was trying to make a point at craps, he'd holler, 'Come on, little Joe! This is for Polly's mink coat,'" she recalled. "They told me it brought them luck."

Business was so brisk that she soon had the cash in hand and headed down to the fur district, on Seventh Avenue between 26th and 32nd streets, to place her order. The coat was so long it brushed her shoe tops, with extravagant sleeves, each one a full yard of fur, accented with little mink tails trailing off the cuffs.

The night she brought it home, the fellows passed it around while she chuckled gamely, playing the good sport and watching nervously for fear they would spill cigar ashes or drinks on the precious mink before she could safely stow it away. Later that evening, when she'd returned from a chore in the kitchen, one of the gang called out, "Put your coat on, Polly. We'd like to see it again."

But when she opened the closet, it had disappeared. When the boys swore they had no idea where it was, Polly began to panic. The fellows made a show of helping her search, clowning around as they bustled about the apartment.

Suddenly, one of them cried out, "You little dope, why did you put it out on the fire escape?" The boys roared with laughter.

"I laughed loudest and longest of all—with relief," remembered Polly.

But not every joke was so funny. Between answering the phones, keeping an eye on the bedrooms, and serving drinks—"whiskey for the guys, tea in highball glasses for the girls"—it was inevitable that there would be screwups. One night McManus picked up a glass, took a deep gulp, and began gagging and sputtering. "I knew what had happened even before he swiveled around and hurled the glass against the wall, splattering tea far and wide," remembered Polly. "Of course he knew he had got the drink meant for his girl of the evening, and at the rate he was paying, each drink cost more than several pounds of tea."

Everyone in the room froze, awaiting his response.

"Okay, Polly," McManus said evenly, "so you got to make a living. . . . Well, fix me another drink."

But McManus "couldn't stand being played for a sucker," Polly remembered. "He had to get even." The next evening he doctored a tray of drinks with Mickey Finns, as they were known, some sort of mild poison or emetic, usually a horse laxative mixed with crushed ice that induced vomiting or diarrhea. Several of the johns spent the rest of the night vomiting in the alley, and the girls were so sick they couldn't work for three days. It would have been worse if he had used chloral hydrate, better known as knockout drops, which were commonly employed in clip joints to rob unsuspecting customers.

It was a devil's bargain, courting them as customers. Nonetheless, the racket boys possessed a lot of charm for the ladies of the evening. Unlike square johns, who would snub her girls out in public, the rod boys would take them out for joyrides in their sleek sedans and treat them to expensive evenings in the speakeasies.

Yet even among sociopaths and murderers, Polly couldn't escape the humiliating tyranny of respectability. "It was an odd thing," she later noted with uncharacteristic delicacy, that despite their enthusiasm for her girls, "racketeers frowned on men of their calling who got serious with a prostitute." In the underworld, women were second-class citizens, without exception, and prostitutes were even lower in caste.

One night Polly was surprised to come upon one of the regulars—a hard guy she called Dave—standing out in the hallway chatting with Celia, one of her new girls. The next night Dave took Celia on an actual date, and soon he was hanging around the house without the usual posse. Eventually, Dave informed Polly that they were in love, but it was a secret, and made her promise to keep Celia away from the rest of the gang when they came calling. He even offered to make up any money they lost by keeping his sweetheart safe.

Touched by this rare gallantry, Polly agreed. Then one night McManus and his crew stopped by without warning. She shoved the poor girl into a closet, but they could tell something wasn't kosher. Suddenly, McManus strode to the closet and flung open the door. "When they saw Celia crouching there, they dragged her out and mishandled her"—almost certainly she was raped—"and I got pushed around for lying to them."

Dave was enraged when he heard what had happened, but there wasn't much he could do to retaliate. "The hell with those bastards," he swore. "I'm going to marry her and take her out of the damn business." To Polly's surprise, he did. Later she'd see them sometimes in Hot Springs, the gangsters' retreat in Arkansas, where they seemed genuinely happy. But even then, she noted acidly, "a lot of the so-called respectable women who were married to racketeers tried to humiliate Celia whenever they could."

Polly had plenty of friends with muscle, but no one was going to go toe to toe with George McManus and his crew just out of chivalry. Maybe they would do it for a gangster's wife or daughter, but not for a couple of tarts. She hated it, but as she put it, "there was nothing I could do about it. I had chosen running a house as my profession and whatever the customers did, I had to take it and keep smiling."

(

After the horrific incident with Celia and Dave, a fresh start was in order. Like most of her colleagues in this age of clandestine vice, Polly changed apartments at a head-spinning rate. "Nothing unusual for me to move in and out of the same place in the same month, providing the landlord knew and he always knew enough to double my rent," she recalled. "I was like horse shit all over New York."

Polly kept her 92nd Street apartment but moved her main operations to the Abbotsford Apartments at 411 West End Avenue at 80th Street. This stretch of the Upper West Side was home to prosperous garment manufacturers, real estate investors, and financiers. With this crowd, Polly noted, "there would be no rods to stash away, no being pushed around."

Her new quarters boasted ten large rooms and a reputation as a safe building for vice entrepreneurs; most of the apartments were controlled by a real estate company that sublet them to madams, "dance instructors," professional gamblers, and those willing to pay exorbitant rents for the privilege of privacy. Her reputation for quality service spread quickly. As a symbol of her upward mobility, she learned how to drive and bought a Buick Master Six coupe.

But she hadn't counted on the cutthroat competition. West End Avenue, with its elegant, anonymous apartment buildings, was home to scores of the city's high-end call flats and lavish love nests. The exact number of madams was impossible to estimate, but standouts included Peggy Wild—known to her intimates as Margaret Ventimiglia—a tough old Italian broad from East Harlem who ran houses on Long Island and in Saratoga and Brooklyn before moving to the Upper West Side, where she was a favorite of the rough-and-tumble bootleggers. For special cases there was "Doctor" Anna Swift, a severe-looking redhead who advertised herself as a physiotherapist but whose Danish Institute at 8 West 70th Street was actually an exotic "House of All Nations." The Institute offered a roster of German, Swedish, Scottish, French, and Italian masseuses in nursing uniforms, who administered "the off-beat pleasures sought by a sophisticated and twisted clientele. Whips, cat-o'-nine-tails and a whole torture chamber," as Polly described it. "A place for the sexual connoisseur, expensive but exclusive," as the newspaper photographer and onetime customer Weegee put it. "Where bank and social references were required."

But Polly's most powerful rivals were the legendary Sadie the Chink and Jenny the Factory. (No one seemed entirely sure of their legal names, although they were said to be Sadie Schimil and Jenny Morris.) Sadie was a stout salt-and-pepper brunette of middling height with narrow, slanted eyes; "an awful looking creature," in the words of her longtime nemesis, the private investigator Abe Shoenfeld. Jenny was a tall, buxom, blue-eyed blonde whose nickname, "the Factory," was attributed to her hard-nosed work ethic, although among the girls she was known as "Jennie with the big mouth." They were both married to well-known criminal characters but had long ago outstripped their husbands in infamy.

Sadie and Jenny were Second Avenue aristocrats with deep ties to the Jewish underworld and the vice ring. After two decades in business, they had followed the exodus to the Upper West Side, where they opened a chain of cathouses. They emphasized quantity over quality, but a girl knew she would be well taken care of if she were arrested. "It is not a cinch to stay with between 25 and 30 men a day," a prostitute named Shirley Singer told one Committee of Fourteen investigator, but "Sadie and Jennie are just as good as the Bank of England and are known for it."

The established madams of the lush Upper West Side were none too pleased to find this young upstart cutting into their lucrative market. They quickly retaliated, spreading rumors and pulling dangerous pranks to drive away customers and force her out of the neighborhood. They peppered the police commissioner's office with anonymous complaints and then, for a dramatic flourish, sent hearses to her apartment on busy nights so that just when the action was ramping up, said Polly, "a couple of lugubrious characters would appear at the door with the announcement that they had come for the body."

Her new setup didn't last long. "I probably remained here long enough to use the bathroom," she remembered with irritation. "For a few months there I was hopping around like a flea." She had a pal on the police force who tipped her off whenever a complaint was filed, but that only bought her time to pull up stakes and switch to a new apartment.

"It wasn't good business to lead a nomad's life just when I'd gotten my address fixed in peoples' minds, and I saw I'd have to take steps to correct the situation," said Polly. "So I arrayed myself in my mink, threw a saddle on the Buick," and set off for battle. First stop was Riverside Drive to call on "Madam X."

A uniformed maid answered the door and ushered her in. "I had to admit it was a pretty good layout, furniture expensive, comfortable and conservative," said Polly. Madam X was an older woman, in Polly's description, "gray-blonde, chunky, hard-eyed, with an incisive manner," the spit and image of Jenny the Factory. She welcomed Polly graciously, offering tea or sherry.

Polly began to lay out the case for a truce. Manhattan had more than enough men for everyone to make a good living, she said, and in the long run no one benefited from riling up the authorities. Instead of trying to cut her throat, perhaps the good madam ought to imitate her methods and get out and flash some coin if she wanted to attract the high rollers. "You have to spend money," insisted Polly, "if you want to make it."

Madam Y and Madam Z received her in the same grand manner. One loftily offered to lend Polly the use of her Cadillac limousine whenever she desired it. The other introduced Polly to her husband with a distinct air of superiority, as if she were silently saying, "This is something I've got that you haven't," remembered Polly. "But the only thing I wanted from them was to be let alone."

Whatever she said, it worked. No more hearses, no more pranks. But for all her diplomacy and hard work, the payoff was disappointing. She quickly discovered that the "quiet solid-citizen type of businessman" was too well behaved. When he was done with his fun, he wanted to go home to his wife and get a good night's sleep, instead of staying all night, buying drinks, and paying the girls to drink with him.

"The gamblers helped popularize my name, but they played a little too rough," remembered Polly. "The businessmen had better manners but not big enough bankrolls to get me to the top."

☾

Polly decided it was time to expand and upgrade her operations. She kept her apartments uptown as discreet spots for her girls to make dates, or as hideaways in case of trouble. But her main base of operations would now be in midtown Manhattan.

From the outside, Polly's new headquarters didn't look like a step up. No. 201 West 54th Street was an undistinguished brick box, with twenty-one apartments and an entryway so modest that it was easily missed. But her new house possessed that most transcendent virtue: location, location, location.

Heading east on 54th Street toward Fifth Avenue were some of the best addresses in the country, including the prestigious men's clubs, posh department stores, and grand mansions of the old Knickerbocker fortunes and the industrial robber barons. But west of Fifth, the morals declined precipitously. It was, to borrow a phrase from Raymond Chandler, "a nice neighborhood to have bad habits in."

She was now in the heart of the Great White Way, the sixteen blocks of Broadway stretching from Times Square at 42nd Street to Columbus Circle at 59th that were, in one reporter's phrase, "the capital of the underworld, of the half world, and of all the catch-as-catch-can industries of sport and entertainment."

In this last moment before Hollywood commandeered the role, the Roaring Forties and the Feverish Fifties were America's dream factory, a neighborhood entirely devoted to the business of creating and fulfilling desires. This stretch of Broadway was a chaotic patchwork of garish billboards, advertisements, and thousands of white incandescent bulbs that gave a silver shimmer to the air after dusk. Over forty legitimate theaters clustered along the side streets on the southern end of the square. The Palace, the beloved mecca of vaudeville, stood at 47th Street, across the street from the Columbia Theater, the self-proclaimed "Palace of Clean

Burlesque." Gaudy motion picture houses lined the upper end of the Square, jostling alongside the music publishers of Tin Pan Alley and dozens of poolrooms, horse-betting parlors, and backroom clubs.

It was also the capital of bootlegging in America, the nerve center of a national network of liquor producers, distributors, and financiers, as well as the single largest market for their wares. With their ill-gotten gains Rothstein and his coterie were snapping up hotels, office buildings, and townhouses throughout midtown, especially Times Square.

Polly's new building stood on an infamous block in the Fifties where the mob had made major investments in real estate. It was almost certainly mob-owned, as was its next-door neighbor, the Harding Hotel, a notorious nest of hoodlums, gamblers, and hungry young women of questionable morals and dubious talents. Her building's best-known resident was the scandal-scarred beauty Evelyn Nesbit, whose husband, the mad millionaire Henry K. Thaw, had in 1906 murdered the society architect Stanford White in a fit of jealousy; Nesbit had lately been hosting "ether parties" in the building in a misbegotten effort to wean herself from a nasty cocaine and morphine habit.

Big Bill Dwyer kept a hideaway on the next block, and Arnold Rothstein owned the Congress Apartments across the street. At Eighth Avenue—on a stretch of sidewalk fondly known as Cauliflower Alley— was Stillman's boxing gym, where fight fans could watch Jack Dempsey train when he wasn't making the rounds of the Broadway nightspots. West of that was a long row of run-down garages hived with dingy speakeasies and floating crap games.

Like Polly, the mobsters' social aspirations had expanded along with their bankrolls. Where hoodlums and hustlers had once remained cloistered in their ghetto social clubs and Tenderloin saloons, now they wanted to bask in the shining spotlight of Broadway.

"These trigger-happy slobs were vainer than any woman I ever met. As soon as one of them assault-and-battered his way into a bankroll, he would preen himself like a king's mistress," remembered the aspiring impresario Billy Rose. Following Rothstein's example, they cultivated the look of prosperous businessmen, swanning around in monogrammed silk shirts and underwear, white spats, and flashy custom-tailored suits.

"Togged out in his new duds, the gangster was no longer satisfied to pitch pennies in a garage or talk shop in the vat room at the brewery. All dressed up, he needed a place to glow," explained Rose. "And the only place where he was welcome was Broadway."

Flush with cash, the racket boys began taking over the small cafés and speakeasies, turning them into intimate cabarets and supper clubs, or "nightclubs," as they came to be called, adding small dance floors, raucous jazz bands, and racy floor shows featuring young, scantily clad chorus girls. Arnold Rothstein led the way as usual, muscling himself into nearly every successful nightspot in the Whoopie District. "It took plenty of money to set up a joint, with its garish fixtures, its illegal cellar, and its entertainment, and only the gangsters and professional gamblers had enough ready cash to invest in such swank places," remembered the producer Nils T. Granlund. "In the end, they virtually took over the industry, lock, stock and whisky barrel."

The phrase "Broadway mob" had long referred to the regulars, the rounders who made the scene in the theaters, joy joints, and watering holes. But as Rothstein's crew of socially ambitious hoodlums moved in, the title settled on them. The new nightlife was patterned after the boys' tastes—hot jazz, young girls, late hours, and plenty of booze. Decadent but aspirational, it was a status thing for the mobsters, like keeping a mistress or owning a Cadillac.

"A gangster who owned a piece of a famous nightclub was a special fellow," remembered Billy Rose. "When the Capone boys from Chicago or the Purple Mob from Detroit came to New York, he could entertain them in his own saloon. Instead of being merely a hijacker, he was a host." Economically, nightclubs were usually sidelines for the mob, but they were central to their social lives and critical to their new social status. Without the glamour of the clubs, they'd just be crooks, no matter how big their bankrolls.

Of course, busting heads and hijacking trucks didn't always prepare a fellow for the art of gracious hospitality. "Four of my employers, owners for whom I produced shows, were killed," remembered Granlund ruefully. "One of the girls in one of my shows was shot and another was with a gangster when he was bumped off." Billy Rose decided to get out of the business the night Waxey Gordon came in with some business associates. When a harmless lush made a wisecrack that left Waxey unamused, the portly former pickpocket jumped up and drove his knee into the drunk's stomach, then proceeded to give him "the boots." "This consists of driving the heel into a man's face and head and then kicking him in other tender parts of the anatomy. I watched Waxey kick this man's face until there was practically no face left. Then I went into the kitchen and bawled like a baby," Rose remembered. "Next day I unloaded my interest in the club."

Money and fame were the gods of the Great White Way. In that spirit, Polly planned to run her establishment according to the old Yiddish maxim *Gelt geht zu gelt*—"money goes to money." If she wanted to attract the biggest spenders, she was going to have to spend in kind. "I've never liked anything cheap," she sniffed, "including cheap people."

Nonetheless, as more than one observer noted, "on Broadway, money runs a poor second always in importance to fame and glory." If Polly was going to distinguish herself from the other Manhattan madams, she would need a touch of celebrity, just enough to excite the natives but not so much as to stir up the unwelcome attention of the authorities. "And since it would help business, I myself wanted to be tagged as a character," she insisted. "I wanted my name to be a byword and the expression 'going to Polly's' as a euphemism for the world's most popular indoor sport." This kind of branding, as the advertising men over on Madison Avenue called it, was critical to success in the black market, where conventional advertising was impossible and reputation and personal trust had to serve in place of legally binding contracts.

"Whatever I do," Polly once boasted to an inquisitive reporter, "I like to do well, and to win. Any venture I undertook would be absolutely first-rate, first-class." She decided to take her cue from the most successful brand in Broadway history, insisting that she would not be content until she was known far and wide as "the Ziegfeld" of prostitution, in Dutch Schultz's apt phrase.

First, Polly set the stage. Her new apartment was spacious enough for four girls to live in, with a large living room ideal for entertaining. "I had been impressed by Madam X's establishment and I felt like splurging, so I engaged an interior decorator," she remembered. They kitted out the joint in gaudy whorehouse style, designed to conjure aristocratic fantasies of exotic harems. The bedrooms were furnished in French baroque reproductions, "which is sort of traditional for a house," Polly observed. The barroom was Egyptian-themed, a popular craze since the recent discovery of King Tut's tomb, and she set up a Chinese-themed room for gambling, evoking visions of oriental concubines and the current fad for mah-jongg. The walls and surfaces were scattered with racy lithographs—barroom nudes in local lingo—and knickknacks of tastefully undraped goddesses, nymphs, and satyrs.

Next, she hired a cook, a housekeeper, and a personal maid. Most of the white-run brothels outside Harlem generally deferred to the cultural taboos against welcoming African Americans as paying customers or as working girls, but they relied heavily on African American maids and cooks, in addition to the elevator operators, superintendents, and deliverymen who served as steerers, lookouts, and stool pigeons. Women of the demimonde, who were usually only one scant step up from the scullery or the gutter, preferred to hire dark-skinned maids for fear of being mistaken for servants themselves. This pairing was a staple of early talking pictures, in which a clear-eyed, wisecracking Black maid played a comic foil to the social-climbing blond chippie—or in more serious pictures, a confidante and ally—as a symbol both of the gold digger's humble origins and of her new social status.

A good maid was critical to the smooth functioning of a disorderly house. It was nearly impossible to run a substantial operation without a trustworthy second-in-command, someone who could handle the door and the phone, who knew the customers by name, and who could keep an eye on fractious girls and wayward johns, as well as serve drinks, collect payments, and clean the rooms between sessions. Disgruntled or poorly chosen maids were dangerous: they could set a house up to be raided, robbed, or blackmailed, they could skim profits, play favorites among the girls, or shake down the madam.

Indeed, working as a maid in a brothel was among the more lucrative jobs a Black woman could have in those years. Besides being paid a premium to offset the risks of working outside the law, they earned fat tips from happy customers, and girls often paid them extra to do personal chores or bribed them to hide contraband or overlook breaches of house rules. Conversely, if a girl were too uppity or rude, a well-connected maid could cause plenty of trouble for her, steering the best customers to her rivals or ruining her reputation with other hookshops.

Most important to Polly's Ziegfeld ambitions, of course, was hiring top talent. In those years, Times Square offered the single largest pool of beautiful and willing women in the United States. Feminine flesh was available for every price point and taste: "sex plays" for the high-brows of the legitimate stage, glossy musical revues, burlesque shows where chorines tossed aside their G-strings, "flashing her knish," nightclubs where bespangled chorus girls mingled with the lusty audience, and clip joints full of bar girls, some of whom worked as badger game operators, pickpockets, or hookers.

There were hundreds of entertainment agencies, theatrical producers, dancing schools, photographers' studios, and beauticians that catered to would-be stars and professional beauties. At West 52nd and Seventh, John Powers had just opened the country's first modeling agency, at a time when models usually doubled as manufacturers' mistresses or escorts for out-of-town buyers and well-heeled customers. The epicenter of the Broadway Beauty Trust was 42nd Street, a legendary stretch of female pulchritude and flexible morals, boasting a dozen or so theaters, anchored by Ziegfeld's New Amsterdam Theater.

It was all made to order for Polly's purposes. Longtime Broadway watchers swore they'd never seen such a bumper crop of fresh faces as that season of 1923–24. When Ziegfeld put out a call for one hundred chorus girls for the new 1924 edition of the *Follies*, over seventeen hundred applicants showed up, clad in evening gowns, bathing suits, fur coats, and dance costumes, jamming the sidewalks outside the theaters until the police shooed them away. But even the lucky few who landed jobs quickly discovered how hard it was to live on a showgirl's salary. Many picked up extra money moonlighting as entertainers or hostesses in Times Square speakeasies, where they were paid to flirt, dance, and jack up the bills of the customers. When they got sick of making thirty bucks a week for guzzling rotgut gin in smoke-filled rooms and being manhandled by liquored-up customers, Polly's pitch started to look pretty good.

They were all fair game, as far as Polly was concerned. She began recruiting girls in beauty parlors, and drugstores, haunting the powder rooms of speakeasies, nightclubs, and all-night cafés. She appealed to the clothes-mad girls, the women burning with thwarted ambition, the dissipated partyers, and the fresh young things who were just learning the wicked ways of men.

Later Polly would insist that "when a girl came to my house she was no wide-eyed innocent. She was a full-fledged whore committed to the game." That was practical; after all, a girl needed some experience to be interesting in bed. But it was also a matter of principle: "I never wished to have it on my conscience that I had inducted a girl into the life."

But that doesn't entirely square with other accounts. "Miss Adler hastens to assure you that she never started any girl on the way to sin," scoffed one woman who worked for Polly. "Well, she's right there. I was sinful to begin with. Still, I'm not too sure that if a customer—I mean a heavy paying 'John'—had promised Polly a grand for a bit of virtue, she'd have turned him down. I truly don't think Polly had *that* kind of scruples. She was frankly out for the buck (plural) and she tried her level best to please everyone."

"Polly would proposition any good-looking girl she met, no matter where," the songwriter Jimmy Van Heusen recalled. "She'd ask, 'Wouldn't you like to make two hundred dollars in about half an hour without any effort?' As a result, she had dozens of legitimate girls who never were anywhere near her place available via telephone for some well-paid dates with well-heeled swingers. Many a girl turned a trick or two every week or so for years and no one knew about it. Polly was a discreet dame."

To Polly's mind, she was just offering them an opportunity. And if hunger made them say yes, well, it wasn't a knock on her for offering a girl a way to eat and put a decent dress on her back or send some money home to her mother.

As her reputation rose, she began beating Ziegfeld at his own game, hiring his showgirls to moonlight after the curtain dropped. She considered anyone who worked onstage or modeled in the magazines a good catch. "I was a better commodity than some broad off the street," explained one of her moonlighting chorus girls. "Polly could just say to a well-heeled prospect, 'I'll fix you up with Ann X. She's that stunning brunette in the ____ show. You know the one I mean. She makes all the other girls look like drips.' . . . It gave the whole deal a kind of prestige value. I wasn't always available, but that made me more sought after." Johns reveled in the feeling they possessed a prize other men wanted at a bargain price. In the nightclubs, a chump could easily drop several hundred bucks trying to bed a ritzy dame like that.

Soon, in addition to the four professional prostitutes living in, "each night from five to ten show girls would drop by," remembered Polly, "including some of Ziegfeld's and Earl Carroll's kids. They were always sure of picking up the price of a Madam Frances gown." "Polly's Follies," they called her lineup.

The Ziegfeld beauties were her most prestigious hires, of course. But the girls from *Earl Carroll's Vanities* were easier to recruit. Earl Carroll, a scoundrel among scoundrels, preferred to hire "Dumb Doras," as they were known in the theater, firm-fleshed girls in their early teens with little to no experience onstage. "Most were working class girls with guttersnipe cadences," one intimate said bluntly.

Union scale for Dumb Doras was a pitiful $12.50 a week, making them ripe prospects for Polly's proposition, especially since *Vanities* girls were already required to entertain potential investors at wild nightly parties where the producer "dispensed drinks and cocaine" to rich rounders and Broadway big shots, as one guest put it. Carroll's girls "were jaded," remembered the reporter Lester Cohen, despite the fact that they "were young—very young, some of them—and pretty. But they had that tired-of-it-all quality. Perhaps, if you went to a party every night, after the show, sometimes twice on matinee days, you too would seem jaded."

☾

Becoming chummy with Arnold Rothstein's circle gave Polly new stature with New York's finest. Still, she couldn't keep off the police blotters entirely; everyone had to take a pinch sometimes. She became a well-known face around the West 47th Street precinct house, two blocks west of Times Square, the busiest police station and night court in the city. "Polly frequently showed up to bail out her girls here, who had been arrested in the mid-town hotels," remembered one police reporter. "Polly carried cash or a shoebox filled with thousands in jewelry to post with the bondsman so her fillies would not have to spend the night in jail with the common prostitutes."

At least she was in good company. The West 47th Street station hosted more big-name murderers, gamblers, and disorderly show folk than any jail in the country. The night court was often packed with chic slummers in evening clothes who considered it cheap theater, stopping in after a night on the town to snigger and gawk at the floozies, hoodlums, and cockeyed drunks. Several years later Polly's writer friends Mark Hellinger and Charles Beahan would turn this scene into the basis of the 1932 film *Night Court*.

Polly didn't mind the occasional collar. What drove her nuts was having her bank account emptied by the shysters who ran the vice ring. Far better to pay off the boys in blue than to pay the parasites of the West Tenth Street Bar. So she began aggressively courting the vice cops. She became adept at "hundred-dollar handshakes," as she put it, three times the sum they would make if they turned her over to the bondsmen. "I'd cup a C-note in my palm and go around shaking hands, and the cops would take themselves off, all smiles, to pinch some other madam who hadn't developed the gentle art of handshaking to such a fine pitch."

Unfortunately, she soon found herself too popular for her own good. "As a matter of fact, my apartment became a hangout for the police themselves," remembered Polly. Being nearly untouchable did not bring out their best behavior. "Sometimes the law-enforcers gave me more trouble than my rowdiest clients, but there was nothing I could do about it except to hang on to my temper and keep telling myself every business has its drawbacks."

That winter of 1923–24, Rothstein's protégés moved to consolidate their control over New York's competitive liquor market, absorbing or smashing smaller operations and building strategic alliances with outfits in other cities. When visiting gang leaders came to New York to discuss business, the Broadway mobsters wooed their guests with VIP service in the jazz clubs and lavish after-hours parties stocked with friendly flappers. The "bootlegging fraternity," noted *The New York Times*, did a lot more entertaining "than one might suppose at first glance."

The gaudier nightclubs were great for showing off to visiting dignitaries, but for more delicate negotiations—and less inhibited parties—the mob preferred someplace out of public view. A well-equipped bordello like Polly's was more relaxing than a public watering hole; here you were treated like a king, and no one was going to stick their nose in your business or make you feel like you didn't belong.

The turncoat mafioso Joseph Valachi, then a young punk in an East Harlem smash-and-grab gang, remembered how the mob loved going to Sadie the Chink's Harlem hookshop after a big job. "She always had five or six girls in the house, and it was safe there because Sadie was paying off the cops," recalled Valachi with pleasure. "Boy, when one of the girls said, 'Gee, I've heard about you,' it made you feel like a real knockaround guy." ("They were the only girls I saw because I didn't care to settle down," Valachi added primly. "It was no time to start falling in love and worrying about a family.")

But those reliable dames of the old school, like Peggy Wild, Sadie the Chink, and Jenny the Factory, didn't gratify the yen for class that the boys were starting to feel. They were too crude, too rank with the stench of Second Avenue and Little Italy. Polly, by contrast, was young, hip, and funny, always quick with a clever quip or the latest gossip. Her new bordello, with its exotic decor and erotic trappings, was designed to impress the social-climbing ghetto boys and their distinguished guests. Silk sheets, top-shelf liquor, gorgeous girls—with no prying eyes. There was prestige in patronizing Polly's: her sky-high prices and exclusivity were proof that a man had connections and plenty of dough to burn.

Most critically, she gained a reputation for ironclad discretion. "She was the only madam in the whole city I could trust," claimed Lucky Luciano. "If you told her or one of her girls somethin', you knew it wouldn't go no further."

The Broadway mob introduced her to the rising crème of the criminal classes. Her circle of lawbreakers now included the Brooklyn booze baron Frankie Yale and his junior associates: Gandolfo Civito, better known as Frankie Marlow, an incongruously boyish-looking tough, and the handsome but shrewd Giuseppe Doto, who was so vain about his looks that he nicknamed himself "Joe Adonis."

Then there were the farther-flung gang leaders, most of them Jewish, who worked closely with Dwyer's Combine, most notably Boo-Boo Hoff, who ran the Philadelphia underworld with an iron hand; Longy Zwillman from the wild west of northern New Jersey; the Solomon brothers of Boston; the Cleveland Syndicate; Detroit's Purple Gang; and Chicago's Outfit, run by another of Frankie Yale's Brooklyn-born protégés, the moon-faced Al Capone.

It wasn't exactly the high-class clientele she was aiming for, but she was getting close.

Polly showing off the trophy she won at the LaVida Café
dancing contest, February 27, 1925

7

The Double Standard

olly was entering the next phase of her underworld education. That winter of 1923–24 she settled into the rhythms of Times Square. Monday was the hot day at the Palace, when talent bookers, music publishers, and fellow vaudevillians caught the new acts on that week's bill; she could usually count on a few song pluggers or promoters to drop in with promising performers they were wooing with their expense accounts. Friday was fight night at Madison Square Garden and the local boxing clubs, when the wise guys and Tammany boys blew off steam. Sunday afternoon was for nursing hangovers and spending time with the wife and kiddies. Sunday night was wash night, when the bookies settled accounts, and since the theaters were dark for the Christian sabbath, it was a good time to catch the show folk at play.

"The routine of life in my house varied only if some customer on a binge took it over for a nonstop party," remembered Polly. The workday often started at three o'clock, when the stock exchange closed and exuberant brokers dropped by to celebrate the day's victories. It generally ended well after the other late-night joints closed, so she could pick up the professional insomniacs looking for a nightcap or a drunken screw before bed. After the last man stumbled out the door, the girls usually went out for some air, stopping in at an all-night deli or some second-story gin mill that never closed, where they could relax with their own kind, or sneak off to meet their boyfriend-pimps.

They'd reconvene for breakfast before turning in. Over eggs and bacon or hotcakes, they'd talk shop, comparing the quirks and kinks of last night's johns. "Sometimes the episodes reported seemed to us very funny," said Polly, "and we all laughed long and loud—perhaps because the tension of the night was over, and it was a relief to let go." But just as often, the stories were "anything but amusing, and then the girls would yawn and look at their plates, sympathetic but not really wanting to hear and be reminded of humiliating or painful experiences which they themselves had gone through."

Top hustlers considered themselves actresses on an intimate stage, whose task was to persuade the customer that she was wild with desire for him. Nonetheless it was emotionally exhausting to maintain an air of happy nymphomania night after night and never appear bored, disgusted, or mercenary. The job was harder still when it involved humiliation or physical abuse. Working in a house was safer than freelancing, but everyone had stories of johns who suddenly turned violent, bestowing bruises, black eyes, broken bones, or worse.

Of course, pregnancy was a perennial risk. Polly learned which doctors and drugstores would provide under-the-counter diaphragms or other pessary-style birth control devices, along with the complimentary condoms. And if those failed, she needed to know where a woman could obtain a safe abortion or give birth without letting anyone know. Like many sporting women, she had a soft spot for orphans and gave generously to Jewish orphanages.

Even in a scrupulously clean house, sexually transmitted diseases were a constant enemy. Polly learned to identify the pustules and rashes of syphilis and gonorrhea, to spot the small scar on a girl's abdomen from a case of "Broadway appendicitis," as they called pelvic inflammatory disease. Most prostitutes picked up one or the other early in their careers, often without realizing it until they developed dangerous complications, leaving them more vulnerable to the pain-killing relief of morphine and heroin. Many of them dreaded going to the doctor's office, so she arranged for a physician to come by the house once a week to examine the girls and give them a Wassermann test, as it was known, checking for signs of syphilis in their blood.

Far cheerier were the regular visits of Wally Wallace, the house beautician and one of the small army of traveling salesmen who made the rounds of the bordellos, peddling lingerie, cheap evening gowns, and costume jewelry. Nothing brightened a slow afternoon like a gossipy makeover from Wally. "I used to think he was the only real friend the girls had," Polly mused. "Other girls in the same business were, after all, competitors. Men were clients. I was strictly business—I had to be. It was only with Wally that they could let down their hair."

Always, though, they kept an ear cocked for the "shrill metallic urgency" of the business phone, to borrow F. Scott Fitzgerald's phrase. It frayed the nerves sometimes, but the evenings when the telephone sat silent were worse.

Polly cast herself as a strict but fair den mother, squelching petty squabbles and jealous catfights, insisting that her girls were as peaceable as, say, any flock of young chorines sharing a dressing room. But at least one former inmate mocked this Pollyannaish portrait. "I know plenty of girls who worked for Polly and didn't live together like sisters," she sneered. "I've seen enough scratching, clawing and back-biting in Miss Adler's private rooms to swear that sweetness and light were not the order of the day. If the cherished customer did a fast turnabout and tried his luck on a blonde instead of his regular brunette, the brunette was likely to kick up a fuss."

Johns were simpler to master, in many ways. Polly was learning to notice the subtle signs of what pleased a customer, what cooled him off, what flattered him. Men sought out prostitutes for more than sexual relief, she soon realized. They came to assuage loneliness or massage their egos, for relaxation, male camaraderie, or compensation for life's disappointments, for the taste of power or for the relief of letting down their public defenses with someone who wouldn't judge them. Was a fellow looking for an actress to convince him he was a red-hot Romeo, or did he get off on the knowledge that a woman was submitting to him against her own desires? Did he want novelty or familiarity? Did he want his wildest fantasies indulged, or a sympathetic ear?

She was developing a natural aptitude for the delicate psychology of upselling, for persuading customers to spend more money than they'd intended, to tip well, and to come back for more. "Men like flattery," she concluded. "They're vain and egotistical. Women can hold them if they just pretend."

Fellows from all walks of life patronized prostitutes, she was discovering, hidden behind a facade of conventional morality. Her generation, born around the turn of the twentieth century, was the last to grow up with the old red-light districts, common even in small towns, where prostitution was regarded as a settled, if shameful, fact of life, and where boys could gawk in guilty pleasure at the painted women and listen to the vulgar boasts of the older boys. It was still commonplace for young men to lose their virginity with prostitutes, a formative experience that helped shape their sexual tastes.

The rise of the fun-loving flapper was supposed to have changed all that. Yet for all the talk of a revolution in manners and morals, even a casual observer could see that in sexual matters men's attitudes hadn't evolved much at all, except to complain that the women were encroaching on their privileges. True, the ancient and honorable idea that a woman should marry for financial security and social stature was increasingly distasteful to men and women alike. Yet even the most broad-minded men had little appetite for a wife who worked outside the home or, worse yet, earned as much money as he did, let alone one who enjoyed her own extramarital affairs.

Self-styled sophisticates devoured the arguments of sexologists like Sigmund Freud and Havelock Ellis, and the iconoclastic essays of H. L. Mencken and George Jean Nathan. They rose in standing ovation for notorious "sex plays" like *Rain*, based on a story by W. Somerset Maugham, and Eugene O'Neill's *Anna Christie*, and they railed loudly against puritanical taboos and Victorian inhibitions. Nonetheless, most men found it impossible to shake the belief that there were "good women" and "bad women"—one to be worshipped, not touched, the other to be touched, not worshipped, as Polly's pal Mark Hellinger liked to say. Dr. Freud called it the "Madonna-whore complex" : "Where such men love they have no desire and where they desire they cannot love." Or in layman's terms, "You married the first and you 'laid' as many of the second as you could get by hook or crook."

In an age when skewering hypocrisy and liberating the libido were national pastimes, few men seemed to have any interest in deflating the hypocrisies of the double standard. Men on the Main Stem shared a peculiar code of silence that transcended political, economic, and ethnic lines. From convicted killers to captains of industry, they held it as an article of faith that a gentleman never swore, told dirty jokes, or discussed sexual matters in front of a woman. Lying to a woman, however, was considered as natural and uncontroversial as breathing. No one looked askance at a wandering husband out on the town with a woman other than his wife, but "if he was screwing around, he had better have another guy in his company with the broad to make it look all right," warned the Broadway barkeep Toots Shor.

It was hardly surprising, then, that so many men saw visiting a sporting house as a reasonable pastime. "Going to a hooker was not looked down upon then," as one john remembered, unless it became too much of a habit. "It was before the pill; girls weren't giving it away." The idea that a man would be so vain about his own sex appeal that he'd find it insulting to "have to" pay for intercourse would have struck most of them as queerly feminine. Polly's customers considered sexual access to pretty women one of the grand prizes of the good life; whether won through honorable overtures, heartless seduction, or cash on the barrelhead hardly mattered.

Indeed, visiting a respectable bagnio was considered by many to be just good common sense. Some husbands insisted that it was a kindness to their wives to seek sexual relief elsewhere. They couldn't relax or enjoy themselves thinking that they were forcing their wives or sweethearts to do something contrary to a "good" woman's nature. Besides, why coerce a reluctant wife when they could go to a whorehouse and be treated like a king?

There were other advantages. Polly's girls seemed less likely to pass along a "social disease," cause a scene, or ruin the fun with their own needs and desires. A john paid for many things, but most of all he paid for the freedom to walk away as soon as he pulled up his pants. As they saw it, a fellow had to shell out one way or another, whether it was a twenty-dollar bill, dinner and a movie, or a house with a white picket fence, so a smart guy limited his exposure.

Perhaps most significantly, johns ran virtually no risk of arrest or public disgrace. It was not illegal to solicit or pay for sex; only the prostitute committed a crime by offering to perform lewd acts for money. Customers caught in flagrante delicto were allowed to leave the scene of the crime as their partners were hustled off in handcuffs. Police reporters rarely wrote of brothel raids and never printed customers' names. Even gossip columnists and tabloid editors who happily hinted at extramarital affairs, homosexuality, and stray pregnancies rarely breathed a word about dalliances with ladies of the evening.

The double standard was codified even in court procedure. The Women's Court had less stringent rules of evidence for prostitution than for other crimes. When a pimp was arrested, he usually received a jury trial and could be convicted only if the arresting officer's testimony was corroborated by other witnesses. For prostitutes, all the court required was the testimony of the arresting officer, even if the woman's evidence contradicted it.

It was a situation ripe for exploitation on both sides. For men, a steady rise in sexual blackmail was the price of the persistence of the double standard in the midst of so much sexual plenty.

Yet it was a funny thing—as expensive and potentially ruinous as the double standard was, the men who were most vulnerable to its paradoxes showed no interest in abandoning it. That winter the Committee of Fourteen, backed by a small coalition of social purity advocates and women's rights activists, was pushing a bill in the New York state legislature making it illegal to pay for as well as to receive money for sex. Instead of trying to dry up the city's supply of sex workers, they proposed to discourage demand by arresting and jailing the customers. The skeptical press dubbed it "the Customers Amendment."

Polly hated the jump raids, the double-crossing cops, and the System that sucked her dry while affording even the basest of men profit and pleasure. But from a purely financial point of view, the Customers Amendment would be a disaster for her. Even if her customers escaped going to jail, there was nothing like a trip to night court in a stinking paddy wagon, surrounded by floozies and drunks, to put a damper on an otherwise delightful evening.

Just when it looked as if the single standard of sexuality might finally triumph, at least in the courts, the pillars of the community weighed in. When the amendment was proposed to lawmakers up in Albany, it met with fierce opposition from Police Commissioner Richard Enright and his inspectors, the Association of the Bar of the City of New York, the leaders of the Society for the Prevention of Crime, and a singularly united front of Republican and Democratic legislators, magistrates, judges, and lawyers.

The police inspectors insisted hotly that this absurd proposal must have come "from the prostitutes or their lawyers." The attorneys of the bar association protested that defining prostitution as "receiving" sex for money "is an etymological impropriety which can only deform legal phraseology." The incredulous reformers sputtered that under the proposed law, "any girl of any character could have you brought to Court, any one of us," with an accusation of soliciting sex for hire, and "if the Magistrate believed her against us, to jail we would go." The very idea was outlandish.

The Customers Amendment never made it out of committee. As for Polly, she had felt the lash of the double standard too many times not to loathe it. But if she couldn't change it, the least she could do was make it pay.

⟨

Polly's plan to conquer Broadway was exceeding expectations. "Already my girls were known to be the best-looking, best-dressed and best—well, best all-around in New York," she boasted. Boosted by the endorsements of Arnold Rothstein's mob, Polly was raking in the dough. But she had higher ambitions: "What I really was shooting for was the patronage of the upper brackets of society, of theater people and artists and writers (the successful ones)."

As with all black-market wares, Polly's challenge was how to let her target customers know how to find her. The solution was once again provided by Rothstein and his growing portfolio of gilded speakeasies. With plenty of cash rolling in and a reliable house staff, "I was able to take a night off now and then to attend night-club openings. When I'd walk in, surrounded by my loveliest girls, it was always a show-stopper," recalled Polly. "Although the tabs were never less than five hundred, I felt our evenings were a good investment. The clubs were a display window for the girls."

Her purse was crammed with "membership" cards for dozens of joy joints, but she rarely needed them. Surly, thick-necked bouncers peering through peepholes swung open their heavy icebox doors with a warm welcome whenever they spied the diminutive madam and her flock of flossy femmes. The most lucrative were the plush closed-door clubs owned by Owney Madden, the once and future mayor of Sing Sing, along with his managing partners, the affable ex-con Billy

Duffy and a burly former safecracker named George "Big Frenchy" DeMange.

In November 1923 Madden and a bevy of silent investors, including Arnold Rothstein and Harlem's powerful political boss, Jimmy Hines, opened the Silver Slipper in a basement in upper Times Square. On opening night, a dozen of the town's toughest mugs strode in and claimed a front-row table.

"How much did this joint cost to open?" the ringleader barked at the headwaiter.

"About $18,000," he replied nervously.

"Bring $18,000 worth of champagne."

According to local lore, the Silver Slipper took in a total of $60,000 that night, tax free, at a time when the average per capita income for a family of four was a little over $2,000. It soon became the favorite nocturnal rendezvous of the Tammany Hall and Madison Square Garden crowds, and was later immortalized as the Golden Slipper in Damon Runyon's Broadway tales. Many of Polly's best clients came from that "upholstered sewer," as it was fondly known. But she didn't hit the jackpot till she met the mob at the legendary Club Durant.

The Club Durant looked like any of the dozens of closed-door joints in the Feverish Fifties. "Members" had to pass muster with a pasty-faced bouncer, then climb a rickety stairway to a narrow room that had, as one customer described it, "the appearance and the odor of a damp cave." The tiny dance floor was barely big enough for a piano, a four-piece jazz band, and a ring of battered tables and chairs. The sole window facing 58th Street was painted green and covered by heavy black drapery, as were the walls. Liquor was hidden beneath a trapdoor under the coat check room, and customers' guns were checked in the ice chest, as a courtesy to more peaceable guests.

The club was fronted by Jimmy Durante, a roughneck ragtime piano player distinguished by his enormous nose and a raspy, braying voice that came straight from the sidewalks of New York. The managing partner, Lou Clayton, was a swarthy, squint-eyed soft-shoe dancer and, like most men of their ilk, a compulsive gambler and dedicated dice player with a tendency to welch on his debts.

Everyone adored the exuberant, kindhearted Jimmy, but Lou was another matter. As Polly's friend, the writer Gene Fowler, put it, "you either loved and admired him, or feared and disliked him, with no in-between feelings about it." Polly knew exactly how she felt. "He was a crude bastard," she said plainly. "Very few people liked Clayton, he was not as brave as he was pretentious." ("I question his honesty, because he borrowed $100 cash from me," she elaborated; not only did he welch on the debt, he had the chutzpah to be angry when she reminded him of it years later.)

Lou Clayton was a close pal of Polly's prime patron, George McManus. That winter McManus began a habit of stopping by the club with a crew of high rollers after the crap games wound down, seldom leaving without dropping $400 to $800. Then Rothstein started using the club's backroom for his floating crap games. "That made us," remembered Durante with pleasure. "The dice-throwers spread the news. They told everybody to come and get a load of this hot outfit. And did they come!"

Club Durant was, in Polly's estimation, "perhaps the most screwball establishment of all time." Clayton and Durante, joined by a sweet-voiced saloon singer named Eddie Jackson, formed a raucous song-and-dance trio, seasoned in the trenches of small-time vaudeville and Coney Island sawdust joints. It was street-savvy slapstick, an irreverent insiders' burlesque of Broadway—"the haunt of flaming youth, set to music."

"Let me put it this way," remembered the comedian George Burns, "their act made the Marx Brothers look sophisticated. Basically it consisted of throwing insults, lamps, telephones, dishes, whatever they could pick up, at each other, the people who worked for them and the customers. Jimmy's big finish was ripping apart his pianna piece by piece and throwing it at the band. The more things they threw at the customers, the more popular they got."

It was the intimate, spontaneous interaction of the audience that put the place over the top. All the regulars got a big welcome from the boys, with a snatch of song or a joke; if they were entertainers, they might be drawn onto the floor for an impromptu performance. Customers, lit to the gills, heckled the boys in return, throwing cash ("foot money" they called it) or other handy items as they rampaged through the room. Or in Jimmy's immortal catchphrase, muttered with mock indignation: "Ev'rybody wants ta get into de act!"

"The underworld and the upperworld discovered Clayton, Jackson and Durante at the same time," remembered the comedian Eddie

Cantor. They quickly caught the attention of the twilight workers and midnight boulevardiers. First came the sportswriters, theater critics, and late-shift reporters who chronicled Gotham's nightlife. Sime Silverman, the powerful editor of *Variety*, stopped in nearly every evening and brought his showbiz pals. The syndicated columnist Damon Runyon did the same, bringing along the rest of the sporting fraternity.

"We drew the cream of the theatre and Broadway, as well as the bottom layers," remembered Durante proudly. Once the culture mavens discovered the club, the Upper West Side playboys, and proverbial "tired businessmen" followed, then the Park Avenue crowd, too high to go home after the swankier clubs closed, and the hard-partying Wall Streeters who stopped in for an eye-opener on their way to work.

Here, finally, were the trendsetters and tastemakers who would make Polly's name famous. It was, of course, a thrill to sit cheek by jowl with the big stars of the stage, stopping in after work to see what all the fuss was about, fabulous figures like Al Jolson, Eddie Cantor, Sophie Tucker, and the theatrical impresario George M. Cohan. But Polly was hunting for more profligate partyers, the check grabbers and boozehounds, the ones who hated to go to bed, especially alone.

She hit pay dirt when she befriended the flamboyant boxing manager Jack "Doc" Kearns, who had turned Jack Dempsey into an international celebrity. Doc was easy to spot with his flashy suits, diamond stickpins, and lusty entourage of gamblers, hangers-on, and sportswriters, living it up on his dime. One of Broadway's most spectacular spenders, he had a special soft spot for fiery redheads.

She made another conquest in Paul Whiteman, the rotund celebrity bandleader with the toothbrush mustache, who was packing in the crowds at the Palais Royal, the toniest supper club in New York, with his gently jazzed-up dance tunes. His impromptu performances at the Club Durant were the stuff of uproarious legend, especially the memorable night when he struck a pose for the roving spotlight, only to find his plus-sized trousers tumbling down around his ankles. Like Jack Kearns, he was always surrounded by a thirsty posse of musicians, publicists, and Tin Pan Alley flacks.

In her short career Polly had already met her share of police reporters, who hung around the precinct houses and night courts. But someone would have had to point out the highbrow journalists in the audience whose irreverent columns were must-read for the city's sophisticates. George S. Kaufman and Robert Benchley, drama critics for *The New York Times* and *Life* magazine, respectively, the brilliant Nunnally Johnson of the *Brooklyn Eagle*, the humorist Donald Ogden Stewart, the aspiring playwright Charlie MacArthur, and Gilbert Seldes, critic for *Vanity Fair*, all were dazzled by the anarchic, up-from-the-gutter humor. Bob Benchley was a particular favorite of the trio. "I'll never forget the first write-up he gave us," remembered Durante. "The three of us tried to understand what he wrote, the words were so long we put an ad in *Variety* and asked if it was a rag or a boost and he came and explained what it meant."

Polly had more in common with Walter Winchell, a scrappy young columnist and ad hustler for *The Vaudeville News*, and his darkly handsome friend Mark Hellinger, newly arrived on the city desk of the New York *Daily News*. The duo made the rounds every evening, wandering through speakeasies, theater dressing rooms, and less savory resorts, collecting gossip about chorines, rumrunners, entertainers, and Wall Street plungers. As the night wound down, they could usually be found chain-smoking in a dark corner of the Club Durant, Mark tossing back ersatz brandy, Walter scribbling on scraps of paper.

They didn't have much to spend—a newspaperman considered himself wealthy if he could afford to pay both his landlord and his bootlegger—but they were fast becoming known as the chief chatterboxes of the Speakeasy Belt. Besides, their poverty of pocketbook was more than made up for by the world-class playboys who frequented the club, like the wealthy department store heirs John Wanamaker, Bernard Gimbel, and Buzzy Warburton, the automaker Walter Chrysler, and the financier Otto Kahn.

How exactly these men found their way to Polly's establishment was never clear, for good reason. Those sorts of stories—no matter how often they were retold over drinks to gales of laughter—were rarely written down. If Polly later declined to detail her doings that winter, only some of that was due to her famous discretion. That season was a blur of red-faced sugar daddies, glassy-eyed girls, and flashing greenbacks; of smoke-heavy rooms echoing with eddies of laughter, the click of dice, and the blare of saxophones; of tumbling into bed at first light and awakening to a throbbing, nerve-shattering hangover at noon.

☾

"You take for granted the world you live in—at least I think most people do," Polly mused later in life. "Certainly *I* didn't know there was anything unusual about the times, any more than I realized that conditions then were peculiarly well suited to promoting a career like mine."

By 1923, New Yorkers of all ages "had discovered that young liquor will take the place of young blood, and with a whoop the orgy began," remembered F. Scott Fitzgerald. "A whole race going hedonistic, deciding on pleasure." To the surprise of nearly everyone, Prohibition had the perverse effect of transforming the sleazy underworld of vice into a cutting-edge counterculture. "Slumming" had long been the hobby of sporting men, raffish intellectuals, and wealthy young rakes who had so much money and social stature that they could afford to flout conventional morality. Now anyone who wanted a glass of beer was forced to consort with criminals.

This inspired a delicious joie de vivre, at once noble and naughty, as Polly's customer Donald Ogden Stewart remembered nostalgically; it "made you feel that even in a teacup you were defying that damned Puritanical law, and consummating a rebellious act of independence and self-affirmation against the power of the reformers and their spies."

The feeble efforts at enforcement only added to the growing conviction that the claims of law and order were, in reality, an absurd practical joke. Everyone who spent time in the cafés of the bright light district had witnessed drunken cops and federal agents guzzling booze without paying their bills, brawling with customers, then dipping into the cash register for a little bonus on top of their regular bribe. They'd seen judges and magistrates spend their evenings shooting dice and bending their elbows in speakeasies, then appear in court the next day to sit in judgment on the scoundrels and soiled doves who'd provided the party the night before.

Even the rare success stories added little to the dignity of the law. New York's most famous "hooch hounds," U.S. Treasury agents Isador Einstein and Moe Smith, "mixed vaudeville with Volstead," as *Collier's* magazine put it, making dramatic arrests by creating elaborate characters for themselves, using colorful costumes, wigs, accents, and props to trick barkeeps and bootleggers into selling them contraband booze.

Their escapades had a slapstick quality that turned the brass-knuckle boys into comic bumblers.

The pair's zany ingenuity was perfect fodder for the papers, who gleefully chronicled their exploits. Izzy and Moe, as they were universally known, returned the favor, planning their raids to suit the convenience of the press. Broadway welcomed the roly-poly rum sleuths as kindred spirits, despite their regrettable occupation. They were regular visitors to the Main Stem, both on and off duty, and Polly came to know them well, especially Moe, who had a taste for the sporting life.

There was no better example of the topsy-turvy effect of the Eighteenth Amendment than how the word *party* had changed, noted *The New York Times*. Among the demimonde, "good time, party, fun," had long been code words for selling sex, as one vice cop explained. Now those phrases seemed to be on everyone's lips.

Cocktail parties were Manhattan's new favorite indoor sport, styled in the long and merry tradition of private all-male stag parties, smokers, or beefsteak dinners, where rowdy men guzzled liquor, gambled, told dirty jokes, sang off-color songs, and enjoyed feminine entertainment. Tales of wild Broadway bacchanals were fast becoming one of its main exports in movies, magazines, and gossip columns. "The 'party,'" observed the critic Malcolm Cowley, "had in fact become one of the most popular American institutions."

No one appreciated Polly's talents as a party planner more than the sophisticated tricksters known colloquially as the Algonquin Round Table. In the new "Cult of the Party," as the critic Gilbert Seldes dubbed it, they were the high priests. The clique's nickname came from the Algonquin Hotel on West 44th Street, where they met nearly every day for long, laughter-filled lunches, trading quips, plotting practical jokes, nipping from flasks, and inspiring envy in less lively diners. In the evenings they frolicked in dimly lit speakeasies, occupied prime seats at theatrical premieres, and zipped around the city in taxicabs like a perpetual rolling cocktail party.

Their lives all circulated around the theater, as critics, occasional publicists or performers, and aspiring playwrights. But they were a distinct cut above the vaudevillians, chorus girls, and police reporters of Polly's acquaintance. Most of them were college educated, with degrees from Harvard, Yale, and Columbia, and possessed of the sort of table manners, fine grammar, and commanding vocabulary that were in short supply in her set.

They took the brash Broadway wisecrack, spiffed up its grammar, tossed in a few fifty-cent words, and turned it into fodder for glossy magazines and the legitimate stage. Ridicule, not reverence, was the motto of Round Tablers' revolution, and stiletto-sharp sarcasm, acidic irony, and Dadaesque absurdity were their weapons of choice. To those who hadn't felt the lash of their wit or the scorn of their criticism, their artfully comic essays, plays, and verses, their irreverent antics and public pursuit of fun were the essence of metropolitan sophistication. "The people they could not and would not stand were the bores, hypocrites, sentimentalists and the socially pretentious," explained Edna Ferber, the best-selling novelist and a founding member of the gang.

Insisting that they preferred an honest roughneck to a well-bred phony, they reveled in eloquent Irish bartenders and up-from-Second-Avenue Jewish comics, and they bought drinks for girls who hadn't made it past the eighth grade but whose limpid eyes and flirtatious lines implied knowledge far beyond their years. They frequented shadowy speakeasies in Harlem and Greenwich Village, where gay life flourished and Blacks and whites mingled. Their late-night adventures fed the city's gossipmongers—and drummed up business for the proprietors of their favored spots.

To Polly's surprise and pleasure, these pen pushers would become some of her biggest fans. Once she got to know them, it was obvious why they kept coming back: the Broadway literati were, to use a new phrase of the era, sex-obsessed. Next to drinking, their favorite pastime was sexual adventuring, legitimated by the theories of Sigmund Freud and fueled by an endless stream of gin, rye, and whiskey.

One of the first to avail himself of Polly's services was George S. Kaufman, the lead theater critic for *The New York Times*, who was beginning a meteoric career as a playwright and director of hit comedies. He was a lean, austere fellow with a slightly melancholy air, a bushy pompadour, and piercing eyes set behind rimless glasses. Notorious for his brusque manner and devastating wisecracks, Kaufman was considered eccentric even in this madcap crowd; he was a germaphobe who hated to be touched and didn't swear or tell smutty stories.

George's charming wife, Bea, was one of the high-modernist, hard-partying set who worked and played at the publishing offices of Horace Liveright on 58th Street. The Kaufmans' sex life was a matter of frequent and surprisingly well-documented gossip. It was said, on good authority, that after Bea Kaufman suffered a devastating miscarriage early in the 1920s, George lost all sexual desire for her. Not long after that, he found his way to Polly's.

"He did not want to be seen at her 'house,' where he had a charge account," remembered his friend Hudson Strode. Instead, George arranged for one of Polly's girls to wait under a streetlamp on Central Park West. At the appointed time, the playwright would stroll up to her, make a little small talk, then invite her back to a pied-à-terre he kept on West 73rd Street. After they finished, he ushered the girl out with an empty promise to meet again. No money passed between them; instead Polly presented him with a bill at the end of every month.

Despite his shy start, Kaufman would become one of Broadway's legendary lotharios, a "male nymphomaniac," in his friend Max Gordon's phrase. As his success skyrocketed, he took up the popular sport of hunting starlets, petite blondes preferred. "Kaufman was a man who could never satisfy himself in work or in sex," explained one collaborator. "Frequently he employed one as a substitute for the other. It is of no small importance that he was compulsive in both."

Polly welcomed Kaufman's patronage, but his secrecy did nothing for her reputation. That changed when she met his fellow founding Algonquinite Robert Benchley. Bob Benchley—Sweet Old Bob, or SOB, as he sometimes introduced himself—was George Kaufman's antipode. A Harvard man of old Yankee Protestant stock, Benchley radiated warmth. He had a genial, oval face and beaming blue eyes that creased behind a wide, toothy smile, and his bellowing laugh was famous among first-night theater audiences. He was married to the wife of his youth, who was tucked away with their two young sons in the quiet suburb of Scarsdale.

Like Kaufman, Benchley made his living being funny, as the charmingly flippant theater critic for *Life* magazine and a humorous essayist with several brisk selling books to his name. In contrast to Kaufman, who specialized in the artful putdown and the lightning-quick wisecrack, Bench's humor, while occasionally ribald, was gentle, self-deprecating, and usually had the effect of making everyone around him feel funnier than they actually were. His myriad friends extolled his kindness and his utter lack of snobbishness.

When Prohibition began, Benchley was a lifelong teetotaler. Two years into the Great Parch, he decided to join the rest of the Round Tablers happily pickling themselves in bootleg gin. With the zeal of a convert, he developed the kind of bottomless thirst treasured by all liquor peddlers, with an "ability to drink all day and into the evening with not a hint of inebriation," as one friend marveled.

In September 1923 Bench crossed over to the other side of the footlights when Irving Berlin hired him to deliver a comic monologue in Berlin's *Music Box Revue*. His parody of the pompous small-town orator in the mode of Sinclair Lewis's George Babbitt was an instant hit. *Variety*—never easy to please—declared it "a classic of sophisticated nonsense."

His transformation from critic to star was even more fateful than that first cocktail two years before. That winter, for the first time, he was rolling in dough, making $500 a week, big money for a writer. He went on a yearlong spree, spending every dime and then some on bootleggers, speakeasies, and skirts. Surrounded backstage by pretty showgirls— wearing more talcum powder than clothing, as the reviewer for *The Wall Street Journal* observed with approval—he soon acquired a nineteen-year-old blond girlfriend in the chorus.

By the time Polly met him, Bob was the quintessential Broadway flaneur, who seemed to know by name the proprietors and door tenders in every joint from Greenwich Village to Harlem. "There was an unholy joy," said Donald Ogden Stewart, "in going down some steps to a dingy door, sliding back a panel and saying 'I'm a friend of Bob Benchley's— can I come in?'" The answer was always yes for a friend of Bench.

Pals who made the rounds with him were amazed by his fearless taste for rough closed-door clubs with hard-eyed hostesses and iron-fisted bouncers. When one fainthearted companion was doused with a Mickey Finn after offending the thin-skinned proprietor by not sharing Benchley's enthusiasm for his dive, Bob returned to give the thug a scorching scolding. "I don't think many of us would have had the nerve to do that," remembered his admiring friend.

"Polly's was used by a variety of people for a variety of reasons, but

Benchley liked it because it never closed," according to a biographer who interviewed many of his friends. "He could never go to bed—it was as simple as that. He had to stay up later than anyone else."

"No matter where I am, if there are more than four people assembled in party formation, I must always be the last to leave," joked Benchley. "I may not be having a very good time; in fact, I may wish that I had never come at all. But I can't seem to bring myself to say, 'Well, I guess I'll be toddling along.'"

Benchley and his fine friends were charmed by Polly's untutored intelligence, warmth, and good humor. She cultivated a sly, self-deprecating wit, liberally sprinkled with comic malapropisms. And she expertly deployed the knowing wink, the subtle double entendre—what the novelist Frederic Wakeman called "just that right, shrill touch of vulgarity that makes a man feel at ease and comfortably wicked."

"She spoke pure New Yorkese," remembered the journalist Irving Drutman, a mélange of Yiddish inflection, Broadway timing, and burlesque innuendo. When she escorted a client to the exit, she always said (in a slight accent), "Denk you. It's all-vays a business doing pleasure mit you!" chuckled Walter Winchell.

In turn, Polly adored Benchley. "Of all the friends I made during my years as a madam, I think his was the friendship I valued most," she wrote later. "Bob lighted up my life like the sun, and sunny was the word for his whole nature."

The fact that Robert Benchley was fast becoming one of her steadiest and highest-profile customers was soon an open secret among the fast Broadway crowd. "Let's all go up to Pawly's"—uttered in his Yankee accent—became his rallying cry. He was often accompanied by a crew of boon companions; that spring he was spending most of his playtime with fellow humorists Dorothy Parker and his occasional roommate, Donald Ogden Stewart.

Don Stewart, who had already tasted the pleasures of prostitutes in his travels, was an eager convert to Polly's cause. He was in his early thirties, with thinning blond hair, wire-rimmed glasses, and a wide, playful grin that earned him the nickname "Duck Lip." Don, maintained his friend F. Scott Fitzgerald, "could turn a Sunday School picnic into a public holiday." Like Benchley, his irrepressible intelligence and irreverent humor earned him a place of stature at an Ivy League school and early fame as a social satirist. As with Bob, his last two books of "crazy humor," as the critics dubbed it, had been best sellers.

Dorothy Parker was a slim, pocket-handkerchief-size woman, no taller than Polly, with a wispy bob and hazel-green button eyes, fringed by long, upturned lashes. She had a husband, although that wouldn't last much longer. She was the embodiment of the literary flapper; flippant, flirtatious, and risqué, peppering her conversation with witty wisecracks and clever put-downs. "She was always ready to do anything, to take part in any party," recalled Don Stewart; "she was ready for fun at any time when it came up, and it came up an awful lot in those days." Even in that liberated crowd, she was one of the few women who went toe to toe with the boys in writing, drinking, and screwing.

When Polly met Dorothy, she was gaining national fame for her elegantly wrought, bleakly ironic verses and short stories. Flapper verse, the critics sniffed. She offered a fresh and caustic take on the modern-day battle of the sexes, shaped by her suspicion that the sexual revolution wasn't the great gift to women it was cracked up to be.

Dorothy and the other women in the Algonquin circle seemed to take the company of Polly and her professional seductresses in stride. But then, it would have been gauche to disapprove. "The 1920s had their moral principles," as Malcolm Cowley noted, "one of which was not to pass judgments on other people, especially if they were creative artists."

They would drop by Polly's in the afternoon, after a long lunch in the Rose Room at the Algonquin, or after they'd stumbled out of a joint that had the gall to close at three a.m., when they couldn't bear to go home yet. Dorothy and Polly would drink and chat while, in Don Stewart's words, "I went upstairs to lay some lucky girl." They amused themselves by compiling a list of books for Polly to fill her empty cases, including classics, current literature, and signed editions of her new friends' books.

Sharing a bachelor apartment with Don made for a poor night's rest, and not a very private one, so Bench began using Polly's as a hideaway. "Benchley was a regular at Polly Adler's not to partake of the available young ladies," the critic Harold Stern insisted, "but simply because it was the one place in town which he could visit at any hour knowing he would always have a room and a typewriter at his disposal." When pressed by a deadline, he'd often work at Polly's until the piece was finished. He claimed that he wrote some of his best essays that way.

Unlike most men of Polly's acquaintance, Benchley made no bones about being her friend and patron, and he treated her girls with an endearing and authentic gentlemanliness that was rare in a brothel. Yet for all his catting around, Benchley never considered divorcing his wife, and he didn't care to be asked about it. "A man had his wife, whatever their relationship might be, and that was that," he told James Thurber, his friend and fellow humorist. "The rest was his own business."

Polly had never spent time with people like this before. "I didn't even know the meaning of many of the words I was now hearing (and using!)," she recalled. "But I knew that my use and misuse of the new words I was picking up amused my customers, and many of them respected me for my eagerness to learn."

Certainly, this was the first time Polly welcomed legitimate women to the house as drinking customers. Perhaps it meant little to Dorothy; after all, the nighteries were littered with scarlet women for sale. But for Polly, it was extraordinary to be befriended by a woman of such stature, a writer, no less.

They were a world away from the usual bums and floozies, two-bit hustlers and bald-faced hypocrites. They were "legitimate," but they weren't squares or suckers. They used their brains instead of their backs to make their mark on the world, and they didn't seem to give a damn about the judgment of others.

☾

While the glamorous habitués of the nightclub circuit helped spread Polly's name, her bread and butter lay in the less heady corporate trade: the conventioneers, out-of-town buyers, and account executives. Around Times Square there was regular slang for the various forms of suckers who opened their wallets in the presence of a vivacious young woman: the tired businessman (so hackneyed a phrase that it was shortened to TBM), the visiting fireman, the OTB (out-of-town buyer), or most picturesquely, the big butter-and-egg man, a phrase made famous by nightclub hostess Texas Guinan, after a wealthy dairy owner was so overwhelmed by excitement that he picked up the tab for every customer in the club.

Polly's new neighborhood was swarming with traveling men. In the decade since the Grand Central railroad terminal opened, midtown Manhattan had become an international hub of transportation, industry, and finance, as well as the single biggest consumer market in the country. Here was where the nation's movers and shakers came to mingle with investors, vendors, and customers, to make contacts, pursue deals, and keep abreast of trends. Retailers and department stores across the country sent tens of thousands of buyers every season to Manhattan to make the rounds of the mercantile houses and factories. The midtown hotels played host to hundreds of meetings every year, welcoming professional associations, mutual aid societies, lodges, and trade groups, all eager to mix business and pleasure away from the prying eyes of home.

Two weeks into the new year the city was buzzing with the announcement that Madison Square Garden had been chosen as the site of the 1924 Democratic Presidential Convention, to be held in the last week of June. Optimistic organizers estimated it would bring some two hundred thousand visitors from across the country, each of whom would go home testifying to the wonders of the Big Apple. Any national convention was good for the city's gold diggers, but for Polly, who was trying to expand her reputation among the city's pleasure purveyors and power brokers, this one promised to be the mother lode.

The convention was the brainchild of the Honorable Charles F. Murphy, the Grand Sachem of Tammany Hall, Manhattan's mighty Democratic Party organization. Boss Murphy had long nursed the dream of putting a Tammany man in the White House. That January 1924, as the Republican administration in Washington, D.C., was engulfed by a series of bribery scandals, Murphy decided that now was his chance.

Murphy's anointed candidate was New York governor Alfred E. Smith. At first glance Al Smith, as he was universally known, seemed an unlikely choice for the nation's highest office. Born and bred on the Lower East Side when it was an Irish bastion, he evoked an old-fashioned Bowery Boy, with his raspy accent and black cigar tucked into a mouth full of gold teeth, and an old-fashioned brown derby perched on his head. He never finished high school, famously boasting that he'd earned his education working at the Fulton Fish Market.

But Boss Murphy envisioned Al Smith as the standard-bearer of a "New Tammany," a cleaner and more virtuous urban political machine. He had carefully cultivated the exuberant young politician, insulating

Smith from dodgy enterprises and dirty deals and encouraging him to build a reputation as a progressive reformer and champion of working people. "Murphy always made it a point to keep Al honest," as Franklin Delano Roosevelt observed, always keeping his eye on the big prize.

In 1918 Al Smith became the first Irish American Catholic to be elected governor in the United States, and he was reelected four years later in the largest landslide in New York history. If all went as Murphy intended, this summer Governor Smith would become the Democratic nominee for president of the United States.

Wise old Charlie Murphy's plan was nearly perfect, except for the one thing he didn't anticipate: the sudden attack of acute indigestion that took his life on April 25, two months shy of his crowning victory.

"No sooner was he buried than the Dark Ages descended over Tammany's domain," wrote one devoted member of the Hall. "This veil of darkness has never lifted."

☾

It was common to speak of Tammany Hall as a monolithic powerhouse—in common parlance, a "political machine"—but that was misleading. Like the Broadway mob, Tammany Hall was less a unified organization than a confederation of territorial competitors, all jockeying for power. Manhattan was divided into twenty-three official assembly districts, divvied up among thirty-five Democratic political clubs, each with its own clubhouse and leader. The local political clubs functioned much like street corner gangs: a crew of like-minded fellows from the neighborhood who gathered to gossip, shoot dice, play cards, and further their own interests, warding off competitors and building alliances to extend their influence.

In fact, Tammany had a long, unsavory relationship with the local gangs. Gangsters often served as bagmen, who ran secret errands and picked up bribes, and as muscle to settle scores. On election day, politicians paid them to stuff ballots, drive rival voters away from the polls, or intimidate them into voting "the right ticket." In exchange, the thugs got the privilege of shaking down brothels and the lesser gambling joints. If arrested, they could depend on the district leader to pass the word to a magistrate or prosecutor to get them off. Tammany had an equally long and unsavory relationship to vice. Many early district leaders were themselves entertainment entrepreneurs, running saloons, sponsoring prizefights, and taking a cut of the profits from dance halls, gambling houses, and brothels, in exchange for protection from the law.

Polly had no affinity with Al Smith and his good-government supporters who were seeking to rebrand the Hall. Instead, she gravitated to the dubious characters who orbited around Jimmy Hines, the longtime district leader in West Harlem who was the sworn enemy of the late Charlie Murphy and his clean "New Tammany." The son of an old-school Irish district leader, Hines carried unparalleled influence in both the police department and the underworld. He was the ultimate "man higher up," in the parlance of the street. "Hines lacked both principles and scruples," claimed one longtime Tammany watcher. "He was an opportunist, pure and simple." Under his protection, Harlem became a safe zone for the city's vices, where illegal lotteries, hop joints, brothels, and speakeasies flourished unmolested.

Intelligent, soft-spoken, and ruthless, Hines counted George McManus, Bill Dwyer, and Owney Madden as close friends, and he was deeply entwined with Arnold Rothstein. The Big Bankroll loaned Hines money, tipped him off to sure things, occasionally paid off his gambling debts, and did innumerable shady favors for his pals. In turn, Hines helped Rothstein's associates when they were jammed up with the law, or turned the cops on A.R.'s rivals, and occasionally "cooled off" the chumps he'd double-crossed. "I was his father confessor," Hines told a friend—"and he needed one."

It was eminently fitting, as more than one wise guy noted, that the Democrats were meeting in Madison Square Garden, home of the Ringling Brothers' three-ring circus and the bloody sport of boxing. The Democratic convention of 1924 promised to feature an epic clash between city and country, cosmopolitans and small towners, New York City and the rest of America.

The two leading contenders stood on opposite sides of the cultural divide. Al Smith was "city born, city bred, 'city broke,' city-minded, and city hearted," as the editor William Allen White put it. He was Catholic of immigrant stock, a defender of Wall Street, and an avowed opponent of Prohibition. His chief rival, former Treasury secretary William Gibbs McAdoo, was a Georgia-born Protestant and a white-shoe lawyer who backed Prohibition and welcomed the support of the newly energized Ku Klux Klan.

By May, national publications were reporting on "a swirl of conspiracies" surrounding the convention. Suspicions of the big-city sharpies ran high in the hinterlands, with the greatest distrust reserved for what the outlanders scornfully called "Tammany hospitality." Rumor had it that the "Smith-Tammany-Wall Street" cabal was opening "convention barrooms" to take advantage of weak-willed delegates.

They weren't so wrong at that. Tammany planned to pull out every stop to secure the nomination, showcasing New York's famous nightlife. Free-flowing booze and free-thinking women were time-honored tools of political persuasion, but especially in the current climate of scarcity. The Broadway mob was eager to be of service and not just with the libations. All those rallies, all that vote-buying would cost plenty—and nobody put cash in the political coffers like gamblers and bootleggers when allowed to run unencumbered by the law.

All of Broadway was turning out in full force for Al Smith. The Main Stemmers favored Smith because, as *Variety* said frankly, "he is liberal and he is wet." The governor cemented his popularity in 1920 when he signed the Walker Bill repealing the ban against prizefighting, then topped that in 1923 by repealing the Mullan-Gage Act, effectively ending all state-level enforcement of Prohibition.

Variety's Sime Silverman urged Broadway showmen to run "under cover" campaigns for Smith, spreading the message to unwitting audiences. Taking the idea of under cover persuasion to an extreme, Anita Loos recalled that some politically minded "flappers patronized a beauty parlor where a lady barber used to shave certain hirsute areas into the shape of either a heart or a derby hat," in honor of their idol in Albany.

Everyone on the Avenue was planning to be in town for the big show, despite the summer heat. Broadwayites were polishing acts, priming orchestras, and stocking up on liquor, even in places that would normally be winding down for the steamy summer season. Flo Ziegfeld was rehearsing a new *Follies* to open on the first night of the convention. Rum Row was jammed with ships, as importers stepped up deliveries, stockpiling inventory in anticipation of thousands of thirsty delegates. Gambling operations were operating at full tilt as Tammany built up its war chest. Pickpockets were brushing up their sleight-of-hand, and grifters were polishing their pitches, anticipating the stampede of fresh suckers from the provinces.

On May 1, 1924, the El Fey Club opened on the second floor of an empty townhouse at 105 West 45th Street, with Arnold Rothstein and Owney Madden rumored to be among the silent investors. Like the Club Durant, it was a narrow shoebox of a room, featuring a tiny dance floor and a small jazz combo. The liquor supply was kept in the barbershop next door and passed to the bartender through a hole in the wall covered by a loose brick.

What set the joint apart was its flamboyant mistress of ceremonies, the brassy, blond silent film actress Texas Guinan. Tex rivaled Jimmy Durante in her ability to create an atmosphere of explosive, liquor-fueled madness and naughty camaraderie. But unlike the scruffy stag atmosphere of the Club Durant, El Fey's secret was sex appeal, specifically a chorus of lively young girls clad in little more than a string of beads and a wisp of chiffon. Most of them doubled in the mainstage musical revues. But unlike the *Follies*, here at El Fey the audience was close enough to touch as the girls roamed the audience between floor shows, flirting, shimmying, sitting on laps, and tossing back overpriced cocktails.

Armed with confetti, balloons, noisemakers, and tin whistles, the audience was part of the show. Even the waiters got into the act, singing and shouting wisecracks at Texas and the customers. "It was a bacchanalian feast, a Roman orgy, a politician's clambake, all rolled into one," the show's producer, Nils T. Granlund, remembered with satisfaction.

El Fey hit the Roaring Forties like a volcanic eruption. "When Texas waved an arm coated with diamond bracelets, gave that wise grin of hers and cried, 'Hello, sucker!' the public ate it up and hollered for more," remembered Polly. Pleasure seekers vied for the privilege of having Tex empty their wallets as she heckled them from the floor. Her exorbitant cover charges and drink prices made the rickety room, bad booze, and hungry teenage girls in flimsy costumes feel like deluxe debauchery. Very quickly the club started drawing a more upscale mix of Club Durant's customers: bootleg barons, local literati, Wall Street speculators, and Park Avenue swells, as well as Ivy League collegians, visiting

European royalty, powerful politicians, and big butter-and-egg men from the provinces.

"Tex was a hep girl all right, and wasn't above exchanging cracks with me now and then," Polly remembered fondly. Polly and her parade of "prostipretties," as Walter Winchell dubbed them, became part of the nightly spectacle, spreading her reputation far beyond the boundaries of Broadway. Texas insisted that her girls were not allowed to leave the premises with male customers, but if they did a little moonlighting for Polly on their own time, she wasn't one to judge. "There was no difference between her business and mine, Tex said once, except that she could have her name up in lights," remembered Polly. Texas got them all het up, and Polly provided a place to cool down.

A couple weeks later, on May 19, Polly got another big boost to her trade when vaudeville's Marx Brothers—Groucho, Chico, Harpo, and the now-forgotten Zeppo—burst upon Broadway with *I'll Say She Is*, an anarchic parody of the popular Cinderella revues. They drew from the same fast-talking, wisecracking tradition as Clayton, Jackson, and Durante—raw, antic lunacy with a hint of violence, accompanied by a nonstop patter of dexterous wordplay, absurd malapropisms, nonsensical braggadocio, and irreverent in-jokes. The Marx brothers and the Round Tablers formed an instant mutual admiration society, as fellow laugh-getters and manic playmates.

"All the Marx Brothers were the same: They were lechers," recalled Chico's daughter, each with his own flavor. It was family lore that Polly became especially fond of Harpo, the silent clown, with his curly blond wig, oversize overcoat, and battered hat. Chico, the oldest and wildest brother, was also a familiar face. "Chico was the kind of man that would chase us into the dressing rooms," remembered the actress Bobbe Brox. (His nickname, pronounced *Chick-o*, was short for Chicken Chaser.) Groucho, the youngest, she didn't know as well, although he always spoke fondly of losing his virginity in a Montreal whorehouse, despite picking up a case of the clap.

Vaudevillians, when they were in the chips, were always good for Polly's business, especially the comedians. Polly's pals included a full roster of forgotten funnymen, including Milton Berle, Lou Holtz, George Jessel, and Benny Rubin among many others. Almost all of them had been raised dirt-poor in Jewish ghettos and had used humor as their ticket out, the way gangsters used their fists and Polly used sex. They'd spent their youths in the "early vaudeville circuits which were the slums of entertainment," in Ben Hecht's description, and developed their attitudes about sex on the road, where casual affairs and one-night stands were common antidotes to loneliness, and cathouses were the most welcoming resort for a performer in a strange town.

Their headquarters was the Friars Club on West 48th Street, a haven for show people, songwriters, newspapermen, and press agents, all devoted to the Broadway arts of gambling, practical joke tellings, and sidesplitting one-upmanship. As a perk of membership, the "Monastery" kept a full floor of guest rooms for errant husbands on the run from their wives.

She seemed to know them all, and they, in turn, churned out a thousand Polly Adler jokes, establishing her name as a byword for the bedroom, just as she'd hoped.

☾

The city was as hot as a Turkish bath and in a state of high tension when the delegates began arriving for the Democratic convention, along with more than a thousand newspaper reporters. Tammany planned to pack the galleries of Madison Square Garden with Smith supporters, who would noisily attempt to "turn the convention into a Smith glorification meeting." Down on Wall Street, the Boston brothers and other bookmakers who handled election betting kept shifting the candidates' odds, betokening a tough fight for the hometown favorite.

Their hunch proved correct. The convention kicked off with a ten-hour debate over whether to include a plank denouncing the recently revived Ku Klux Klan that was so violent police had to intervene several times to keep the fistfights from sparking a riot. The pro-Klan forces won by a single vote.

Al Smith's name would be placed into nomination by former New York state senator Franklin D. Roosevelt. Roosevelt was an odd choice for this honor. He was considered something of a lightweight by more experienced politicians, nor was he among the governor's inner circle. "Franklin just isn't the kind of man you can take into the pissroom and talk intimately with," as Al put it bluntly.

Smith had been taken aback when his close adviser, Joseph Proskauer, first suggested Franklin for the role. "For God's sake, why?" he protested.

"Because you're a Bowery mick," Proskauer replied, "and he's a Protestant patrician and he'd take some of the curse off of you."

Smith was forced to agree. FDR was a bona fide Dutch aristocrat raised on a Hudson River estate, a Harvard man, and a lifelong Democrat, with a history of standing against the excesses of Tammany Hall. His greatest asset was his famous last name, which he shared with his fifth cousin, the late, beloved Republican president of the United States, Theodore Roosevelt.

The only hitch was that since 1921, Roosevelt had been unable to walk, crippled by what is now thought to be Guillain-Barré syndrome, an autoimmune disease. The convention would be his first official public appearance since his illness.

On the morning of June 26, the Garden was packed to the rafters with nearly seventeen thousand people. Around noon, FDR began slowly making his way across the dais, leaning on crutches and clutching the arm of his sixteen-year-old son Jimmy. When Franklin arrived at center stage, he triumphantly cast aside his crutches, gripped the lectern, and tossed back his handsome head with a wide, radiant grin, then launched into his nominating speech. When he uttered the famous line declaring Al Smith "the 'Happy Warrior' of the political battlefield" and came to his big finish, the Garden erupted into bedlam. It was well over an hour before Roosevelt was finally able to quiet the crowd.

Still, the convention remained deadlocked, ballot after ballot. By June 29 the real action had moved from the Garden to the smoke-filled hotel suites, where delegates dickered late into the night. Meanwhile the Tammany boys used every trick they knew to sway the delegates. "Vanloads of liquor, brought from a nearby storage warehouse were deposited, ten cases in a lot, in the hotel-room headquarters of every State delegation," one journalist reported. "Some of my best men have been hopelessly drunk ever since they landed in New York," railed William McAdoo.

When it became clear that the convention would drag on past all expectations, the out-of-town delegates began pinching their pennies. It was a boon for the hot dog and pretzel vendors and the ladies of the lobby, but a calamity for the empty restaurants, theaters, and supper clubs.

After the ninety-ninth ballot, both Smith and McAdoo admitted defeat. On July 9 the exhausted Democrats nominated John W. Davis of West Virginia, an anticlimactic end to a spectacular debacle. It was the longest and ugliest nominating convention in American history and a disaster both for the Democratic Party and for Manhattan's hospitality industry. Tammany's rowdy, unsportsmanlike enthusiasm for its native son had backfired, turning opposition into bitter animosity toward the New Yorkers and confirming the worst suspicions about the wicked metropolis.

There were a few winners. After his bravura performance, Franklin Roosevelt was being hailed as a rising star in the party. The convention was also a bonanza for Manhattan's scarlet women, according to the disapproving reports of the Committee of Fourteen, especially for the lovely ladies of the *Ziegfeld Follies*, Texas Guinan's El Fey, and Polly's Follies.

⟨

So far, Polly was enjoying a banner year. But, she recalled, "I was still not getting the play I wanted from the socialites and theatrical crowd." So as the convention sputtered to an end, she decided to head north for the annual horse racing season in Saratoga Springs, New York. Everyone who was anyone was decamping to the spa that August, so "I thought this might be my chance to make a bid for their patronage."

Eleven months of the year, Saratoga Springs was a sleepy village, 180 miles up the Hudson from Manhattan, famous for its medicinal mineral waters. But every August it was transformed into "the wickedest city in America," in *The New York Times*'s phrase, where plutocrats and politicians happily rubbed elbows with tinhorn gamblers, jockeys, trainers, bookies, con artists, ladies of the evening, and the racketeers who ran the town's illegal casinos and nightclubs.

Thoroughbred horse racing was in a golden age. Sentimentalists rhapsodized about racing as the noble Sport of Kings, but that was bunk. "Horses are to win bets with," as the bookies liked to say. Money was the real appeal of racing. "At the racetrack it is red-hot, alive, pulsating, and constantly changing hands," as Paul Gallico of the *Daily News* wrote.

"Everyone is talking money, handling money, feeling money, making or losing money."

Many of Polly's heaviest spenders were hopeless "horse degenerates," to use their affectionate insult, who collectively threw away millions of dollars gambling on the nags. Saratoga was on the "Bootleg Trail" that ran from Canada through Albany to points south and had recently become a popular watering hole for horse-mad rumrunners. Led, as usual, by Arnold Rothstein, they began investing in local gambling houses. Rothstein owned the Brook Club, the town's premier casino, paying the local police and politicians 25 percent of the house's winnings in exchange for protection from the law. That summer of 1924 A.R. brought up Meyer Lansky and Charlie Lucky to oversee operations and mingle with the high rollers, recruiting them for high-stakes games back in Manhattan. Occasional rumors that the club's roulette wheels were fixed and the dice loaded did little to dampen business. All the same, it wouldn't hurt to have Polly and her girls on hand to keep the customers distracted.

Saratoga was a perfect place to discreetly make the acquaintance of the blue-blooded playboys she'd seen carousing in the clubs, the profligate young scions of the Vanderbilt, Astor, and Whitney families and nouveau riche captains of industry. Risqué women were considered a key spice of the spa. Prostitutes and mistresses mingled with well-born wives at the track and while promenading on Union Avenue past the jewelry stores, car dealerships, and bauble-filled boutiques where a lucky man could blow his winnings on some lucky girl.

Polly came up ahead of opening day and arranged to rent a house near the track, on a street lined with well-kept Victorian homes. Following local custom, she made a generous payoff to the proper authorities and then sent for ten of her finest girls. She reserved a regular table at the track's venerable white clapboard clubhouse, and on opening day, just before post time, she ostentatiously paraded her harem through the grandstand. "The girls were gorgeous and exquisitely dressed," Polly recalled, "and the men made a circle around us as soon as we were seated."

By her second night in business, the house was filled with paying customers, including a certified celebrity, federal agent Moe Smith, the less popular half of the famous booze-busting duo of Izzy and Moe. The two usually spent August in Saratoga, taking in the races and raiding speaks, often disguised in the distinctive garb of the bookmakers and touts: green caps, loudly patterned suits, flashy yellow shoes, and field glasses.

That morning Izzy and Moe scored a coup when they pinched the bookmakers' favorite gathering spot, the Grand Union Hotel. That evening, in the mood to celebrate, Moe found his way to Polly's. A heavy gambler and unrepentant deadbeat, Moe was not her favorite customer. Twenty years later she was still fuming over an unpaid loan she'd made to "the fat slob," in her words: "eight hundred in notes which will never be paid, stocks in my father's name, which he forged his name to cash."

That night the house was running full tilt when Polly discovered that police were swarming the yard and the chief of police was at the front door.

"Who owns this place?" he barked.

"Why, I have no idea," she dissembled.

"Well, I have," he replied. "We're taking you to the station house."

"Get your hats and coats, girls," she called up the stairs with a sigh. "We're going for a little drive."

Just then the cops discovered Moe huddled behind the dining room door. The sheepish Prohibition agent stepped out from his hiding place to have an urgent chat with the police chief. Whatever he said, remembered Polly, "it saved me a trip to the Jug." (But it didn't change her opinion of the portly professional snoop. "Thanks to Moe for interceding," she conceded. "None-the-less, Moe is a bastard, dishonest, he owes money to everyone in New York including eight hundred to me, which I don't ever expect to get back. No wonder the cocky bum don't have any friends.")

Temporarily placated, the chief told her that she could stay open for a week to recoup her investment, but after that she had to leave town. The embarrassing story of Moe's arrest raced through the Broadway-on-holiday grapevine and back to Manhattan, where it was gleefully reported in the pages of *Variety*.

But trouble returned later that week when one of her new customers, a naïve local, was shocked by the size of his bill at the end of the evening.

"Look," Polly told him, "my prices are the same for everyone. If you don't like them, stay away."

"I'm an upright, tax-paying citizen of this town," the john hollered.

"If you're so upright, what are you doing here?" she shot back.

"This is going to cost you plenty!" he shouted in fury, as he threw down his money and stormed out.

"The little skunk went right from my house to the police and reported that he had been robbed of sixteen hundred dollars," raged Polly. The next morning the chief summoned her to his office. Instead of backing down, she informed him she'd been bilked and, in her words, "gave as character references the men who controlled the biggest gambling houses in Saratoga. They knew I operated on the square."

It was the right card to play. Not only did he dismiss the complaint, he invited her to stay through the end of the racing season.

Saratoga that summer, crowed the *Daily News*, was "gayer and wilder than New York's Broadway ever thought of being." It seemed as if all of Times Square had trekked upstate. The hotels and rooming houses teemed with wealthy wastrels, moneylenders, card sharps and monte men who ran quiet games out of their rooms, and an army of lithesome ladies, all hoping to make a killing.

In the evenings, Polly was a guest of the house at the casinos, where her elegantly gowned girls enlivened the roulette wheels and crap tables. Innuendo-laden jokes abounded, and someone was always sure to ask with a jovial leer, "How is your Rancocas stable today?" After all, explained Polly with pride, the thoroughbreds of Rancocas were the leading moneymakers on the turf, and "my 'fillies' were the best in our business."

"Saratoga was heaven for my girls," remembered Polly. "They all went jock-crazy." Jockeys were diminutive high-class athletes, heroes of the turf who risked their lives every time they rode. The stable owners looked unkindly on their jockeys carousing before a race—no rider could afford the slow reflexes and extra bloat of a night on the town—but something in the Saratoga waters unleashed the wild side of the usually disciplined jocks. A secret after-hours joint like Polly's was hard to resist.

The stable owners were powerful enough to close her down if they discovered their key men getting cockeyed every night. She was especially concerned for a jockey named Lawrence Light, one of the leading riders in Colonel Edward R. Bradley's famous stable, who was besotted with a beautiful girl named Lila.

Polly tried to reason with him. "Kid," she said, "you're at the peak of your career, you've a chance to be the top jockey of the season, but these nightly drinking bouts are going to ruin you. And Lila's not helping you any either. Get smart and leave her alone."

"The hell I will," he barked. "I'm taking her out of your joint tonight."

"Have it your way." Polly shrugged. "Just don't come back again, either of you."

"Not long after, Bradley suspended him and I heard that he developed into an habitual drunkard," remembered Polly. Some years later she ran into Lila coming home one night from the bicycle races at Madison Square Garden. "I noticed a grotesque-looking creature in a black ill-fitting dress, white stockings, heavy make-up and a mop of red hair flying all over Eighth Avenue."

As Polly drew closer, she suddenly realized who it was. "I was so shocked all I could think of to say was, 'Lila, have your teeth fixed.' She put her hand over her mouth and scuttled away while I just stood there stupidly. When I snapped out of my trance and started to run after her, she had disappeared into the night."

After Lila's departure, the girls in the house became so ungovernable that Polly finally sent them back to New York and turned the house into a regular speakeasy; it was just as profitable, with fewer headaches.

Financially, the month upstate was a wash for Polly. "At the end of the season (as the gamblers say) I 'won'—that is, I broke even," as she put it, after a few too many unlucky turns at the craps tables. "But in my biggest gamble I had succeeded. At last I'd made contact with the clientele I'd been shooting for, my address book was crammed with new names, and I knew Saratoga would pay off for me in New York."

☾

One year after her move to West 54th Street, Polly had transformed herself into a Somebody in the Broadway firmament. She was now known for running a deluxe hideaway where a man could have his fun any way he liked it, without fear of being blackmailed, rolled, or swindled. At Polly's you spent plenty, but you got what you paid for and left with your wallet and reputation intact.

Now, when she walked into the nightclubs trailed by her bevy of beauties, she recalled, "there was a whole file of Polly Adler jokes which the emcees would haul out and dust off when we made our center-door fancy entrances, so along with goggling at the girls, the customers would be giggling at quips about me. . . . I'd make a column or two; the latest Polly Adler gag would start the rounds, and no matter where we happened to go, some of the club patrons would follow after us and end the evening at the house."

Her cultivation of the rising young reporters Mark Hellinger and Walter Winchell had paid off handsomely. Their enthusiastic patronage offered a lascivious version of the *Good Housekeeping* seal of approval. Winchell's frisky gossip columns in *The Vaudeville News* had come to the attention of the *Daily Graphic*, a new tabloid competitor to the New York *Daily News*. In September 1924 the publisher hired Winchell to bring his peeping-tom talents to its pages.

To celebrate Walter's promotion, the rowdy members of the Friars Club planned one of the first of a long tradition of "roasts," to be held in Winchell's honor. The young columnist was drumming up attendance when he ran into Joe Frisco, a beloved comedian on the nightclub circuit, famous for his comic stutter, his eccentric shuffling dance style, and his hopeless addiction to the horses.

Winchell urged Frisco to attend the dinner, despite the fact that Joe's wife, Loretta, considered the columnist a mortal enemy. Joe begged off, insisting that Loretta would never let him go to anything in Winchell's honor.

Then don't tell Loretta you're going to the dinner, Winchell insisted. "Oh, tell her you're going to Polly Adler's house."

"Good idea," Joe said with enthusiasm.

"Joe," said Walter gently, "that's a whorehouse."

"I know," replied Joe with a grin. "If I would ditch Winchell for P-P-Polly, Loretta would be so p-p-pleased, she'd open a ch-ch-charge account for me there."

Variety reported that seventy-five of Winchell's new pals came to his "send-off feed." No fewer than twenty-two of these Broadway hams offered toasts, including the Main Stem's favorite public servant, State Senator Jimmy Walker, who gave not one but two well oiled speeches. *Variety* did not mention where they went after the party broke up at two-thirty a.m., but Polly's place was an odds-on favorite.

"As a result of all this publicity (plus a good word-of-mouth from satisfied customers), business got better and better," Polly recalled. "Once, perhaps because of my having to go it alone almost from scratch, I had yearned for love and affection, and I had been willing to go considerably more than halfway to respond to it. But now business came first and personal relationships were second by a country mile."

This was brought home to her one day when she ran into her old beau, Ernie Levin, on the street, four years after he'd told her he was marrying another girl. He'd just put his wife on a train back to Cincinnati, he told Polly, then asked if she wanted to have dinner with him at the Pelham Heath Inn, a roadhouse outside Manhattan that was a popular trysting place for clandestine couples.

Over dinner Ernie asked what she was doing nowadays, and when she told him she was running a house, he didn't blink. In fact, he suggested that they pick up where they had left off. But Polly was no longer a naïve romantic, and Ernie, well, he was no longer the prize she remembered.

"He called me daily for some time, and I must admit I was tempted to go out with him just to sabotage his marriage and make him as miserable as he had made me," she remembered. But she had no time for revenge or for anything else but work. Even on her rare nights off, she spent much of the evening checking in with the maids by phone, and she often had to make a hasty exit to deal with a rogue customer or a visiting cop.

"Although it was part of being 'the notorious Polly Adler' always to keep up a smiling front, always to be the devil-may-care party woman, I never forgot that I was in business," Polly wrote. "I was only 24 and, like other women, I wanted a home and husband, but that part of my life would have to wait. I would do nothing but work until I had saved enough money to quit the whorehouse and find myself a decent man."

Times Square — "the heart of the Great White Way" — in its glamorous heyday, 1925

8

The Party Girl Racket

N ew Year's, 1925, the national gravy train really was beginning to roll," Polly remembered with pleasure. "Everybody had an angle, everybody was raking in the chips, there was no excuse not to have money—and along with everybody else, I was right in there, my front feet planted firmly in the trough."

The White Light District now boasted more than 2,500 speakeasies and 200 nightclubs, up from 300 saloons before Prohibition, all vying to offer the youngest girls, bawdiest songs, and hottest dance bands. Inspired by the success of the El Fey, bootleggers were snapping up townhouses in the East Fifties, turning them into "high class honky-tonks," as *Variety* dubbed them, where sozzled patrons in evening dress and glittering jewels arrived by limousine, flashing bankrolls the size of a man's fist. Starstruck hoodlums were investing in musical revues—"angels," the theatrical producers called them—to gratify the ambitions of their girlfriends, or to scout potential playmates in the chorus. A fair number took up the new fad of golf—a surprising turn for guys who considered a trip to the Belmont racetrack in Queens to be a day in the country.

Scores of small stock-selling shops had popped up in hotel lobbies and small storefronts, accompanied by the jittery chatter of the ticker-tape reader spitting out long ribbons of paper scrawled with current stock prices. Nearly everyone Polly knew was trying to scrape up enough cash to buy a few shares of Ford Motor Company, AT&T, or DuPont. Even cash-poor customers could get into the game by buying "on margin," borrowing the price of the stock from the brokerage, then paying off the loan when the stock went up in value. It was akin to the bookmaker's practice of loaning a broke customer money to make a wager; if the sucker won, he'd pay back the loan and pocket the rest. If he lost, well, that wasn't the bookie's problem, was it? At least the New York Stock Exchange wouldn't send a goon to break a fellow's leg.

Polly's place, with its gaudy trimmings and customer-is-always-right policies, appealed to the swashbuckling new breed of brokers born of the bull market. Their quick, often untraceable profits fueled their playboy antics. If they were crooks, so much the better; it was conventional wisdom among cops and cabaret owners that no one threw around the kale like an embezzler or a swindler on a spree. She began playing the market heavily, trading on inside information from the garrulous drunks and generous johns who passed along stock tips in gratitude for the night's debaucheries.

On January 17, 1925, after nearly four years in Sing Sing, her brother Ben returned to freedom. He had spent nearly one-third of his twenty-four years behind bars, and it showed. Even after he was back in Manhattan, freshly barbered, in a new suit, with a hot meal and a stiff drink in his belly, fellow jailbirds would have recognized his prison pallor and the dead-eyed squint that cloaked all emotion.

Whatever lesson the New York State corrections system intended to teach, it was lost on Moshe Adler's two oldest children. Even if Ben had wanted to go straight, the odds were against him. An ex-con found it nearly impossible to get a square job, a union card, or even a license to drive a taxicab. He was hounded by cops, shaken down by parole officers, and if he turned for help to a friendly politician, he'd likely find himself busting heads on election day or worse. Ask any old-timer: "Once a convict, always a crook."

As for Polly, most of the family was under the impression that she was a successful clothes designer. What their father thought was unclear. Polly had a number of stock-trading accounts and owned at least one building, 176 Second Avenue, registered under Moshe's name and requiring his signature, so he might have had his suspicions. Their Brooklyn cousins occasionally wondered how Moshe Adler managed to live so well for a mere tailor; he never seemed to work much yet was always togged out in bespoke suits, with pockets full of money. Perhaps a man who had survived pogroms, revolutions, and a world war, who had outlasted Polish anti-Semites, Russian Cossacks, and German occupiers, was disinclined to honor the legal niceties of the goyim.

"To have money and to have fun—these were the great goals of life," remembered Polly. That spring the Charleston, a wild windmill of a dance introduced to Broadway by way of Harlem, was all the rage, sparking a vogue for dance contests. To the end of her days, she kept a silver loving cup inscribed "February 17, 1925 LaVida Café Dancing Contest—won by Pearl Adler and George Stack." The diminutive George Stack was a leading horse jockey, with a couple of Kentucky Derby races to his credit. "We did not win on our merits, the judges were friends of ours," remembered Polly with pleasure: the combative dialect comedian Benny Rubin and Sidney Lanfield, a piano player who later became a Hollywood director. "The fix was in—and how! The LaVida Café was loaded with bookmakers and all their votes went for their favorite jockey."

By March 1925, Polly was flush enough to take a real vacation, following the racket boys to their favorite winter resort, Hot Springs, Arkansas (later the birthplace of Bill Clinton, the forty-second president of the United States). Like Saratoga, Hot Springs was known for its natural thermal pools and enthusiastic embrace of every form of vice invented by mankind. The town was a mecca for gamblers, grifters, and gangsters looking to relax among their own kind, and a favorite hideaway for lamsters and rogue politicians. Rival lawbreakers considered it neutral territory, putting aside their beefs while soaking in the baths, playing the ponies, or betting on cockfights and bare-knuckle boxing matches. During high season, prostitutes treated the resort as a busman's holiday, working out of the hotel lobbies or in one of the many bordellos.

Starting an annual tradition, she checked into the elegant Arlington Hotel, conveniently located across from the venerable Southern Club, where she could indulge her weakness for roulette and chuck-a-luck. She took in the thermal baths and played the tourist at the Happy Hollow theme park, a frontier ghost town, riding horseback, playing miniature golf, and posing for photos in a perfectly turned-out riding habit and golf togs.

☾

Back in New York, Polly was fast developing a reputation for throwing "lavish parties, justly famous in the underworld," as one reporter put it. In an age devoted to "the cult of the party" and the quest for new thrills, Polly's decision to become a professional hostess—an entrepreneur of fun in the nation's capital of fun—was prescient.

Midtown Manhattan was the center of a flourishing "party girl racket" that catered to the expense account men who relied on easy women to grease the wheels of commerce. Sales departments, publicists, and account executives—any man who depended on customers or clients for his livelihood—were expected to have a "stud book"—colloquially, a "little black book"—with phone numbers of girls who were "good sports." After an evening of drinking with potential clients, someone would inevitably suggest, "What about some women?" remembered the adman-turn-novelist Sherwood Anderson.

But there were not nearly enough amateur nymphomaniacs to accommodate all the would-be lotharios. So a few phone calls later, they'd find themselves partying in someone's apartment, with the money exchanged so discreetly, or on credit, that many of the guests might not realize the girls were getting paid.

Some firms went so far as to keep party girls on their payroll, often moonlighting models. Others worked through agencies like Lillian Bradley's, who specialized in nude dancers for parties—the "stag racket," *Variety* dubbed it. As an extra treat, some also rented out film projectors and pornographic 16-millimeter films—blue movies or stag films—still something of a novelty, and highly illegal.

"The gift of a woman," to borrow a phrase, had a radically democratizing effect, reducing sinner and supplicant to their lowest common traits as they bonded over contraband pleasures. Rebelling against the rules and indulging in forbidden delights together—and getting away with it—can create an instant camaraderie and a delicious feeling of secret power. The power of "shared transgression," the psychologists call it. As one auto industry salesman said bluntly, "You get a bunch of guys in a room who don't know each other, you get drunk and look at naked women and the next day you're great friends."

Sometimes that bond was laced with something more sinister. "This is the fastest way that I know of to have an intimate relationship established with a buyer," as one president of a large international company explained. "The point, is that I know the buyer has spent the night with a prostitute that I have provided. In the second place, in most cases the buyers are married, with families. It sort of gives me a slight edge; well, we will not call it exactly blackmail, but it is a subconscious edge over the buyer. It is a weapon that I hold."

Polly was now the hostess of choice for the Broadway mob. Big Bill Dwyer, in particular, enjoyed playing the expansive Broadway host, building power as much through schmoozing and hospitality as by strong-arm tactics. As his prime procurer, Polly became an important cog in the Broadway mob's machine.

Politicians, with their oversize vanity, were considered prime suckers for the kind of extravagant perks that burnished the persuasive power of cold cash. Magistrates, judges, and high-level officials who might be reluctant to take money from a no-good gangster were happy to indulge in glamorous soirees, well stocked with sexually available women. A night of expensive carousing fostered warm feelings of friendly obligation, turning what might otherwise seem like crude bribes or shakedowns into mere "favors between friends." Sharing prostitutes was also considered a reliable way to vet potential partners in corruption; any stiff who would turn up his nose at a free roll in the hay was not a fellow you could trust.

But such fellows were rare. It was an article of faith on the Avenue that no one loved a high-end brothel like a public servant. "I have found through personal observation and through authoritative contacts," observed Martin Mooney, crime reporter for the *New York Tribune*, that politicians "are very frequently among the better customers. I would apply the superlative to them were I not informed by those who should know that the super-racketeers themselves are the very best clients of the elaborate establishments where the big-time easy virtue reigns."

Then there was the question of blackmail. If friendly persuasion didn't work, women were a useful way to strong-arm recalcitrant politicos. Polly insisted that she never blackmailed her customers. If she did, the victims left no record. Nonetheless, access to secret information was a fundamental currency of the underworld, one she possessed in abundance. Even trustworthy madams routinely collected compromising information on johns, as a way to ensure that recalcitrant debtors paid up or to enforce agreements and insure bribes. Given her close relationship with the Combine, it is almost certain that she occasionally served as a back-channel source for information gleaned from the pillow talk of politicians, lawmen, and underworld rivals.

For prestigious occasions, the racket boys turned to showgirls, night-club hoofers, and lightweight party girls who were paid fifty dollars a night to make the guests feel welcome. But Polly's professionals were better suited for earthier events. One reporter recalled a deluxe party the Broadway mob threw in honor of some emissaries from the Purple Gang. They'd invited an array of top beauties from the stage and night-clubs. But it quickly became clear that the visitors from Detroit did not understand the fine distinctions among ladies who were paid for their company.

As the situation grew more dicey, at least for the girls, Lucky Luciano took charge. "Listen, fellas, these gals are show gals," he announced. "They work for a living." Ever the good host, Charlie Lucky then put in a call to Polly, who sent over a brigade of her top talent. "Why, they're better-looking than the show broads!" exclaimed one of the bosses.

The incident might have been forgotten except for one particularly fastidious guest, who kept trailing behind the girls when they were not otherwise occupied. Whenever one of them set down her empty cock-tail glass, the gunman picked it up and hurled it against the fireplace, presumably in the interests of good hygiene. "Now, that's a pip!" roared another partygoer in amazement. "How can a broad spread more germs on a drinking glass than in bed?"

⟨

No industry exploited the power of the expense account with more zest than the bawdy souls of Tin Pan Alley. Of all the prize patrons Polly met from the Club Durant, perhaps the most valuable to her trade—rivaling even Bob Benchley—was the celebrity bandleader Paul Whiteman, the so-called "King of Jazz" and the towering ringleader of the Tin Pan Alley tunesters.

As usual, Polly's timing was excellent. Nineteen twenty-five would be remembered as the heyday of the music industry and the year jazz conquered Tin Pan Alley. Live music had never been in such demand. Sheet music and phonograph records were strong sellers, and hotel ball-rooms and nightclubs were putting in the first radio hookups, piping out dance tunes to an eager public. Music publishers were proliferating around the upper end of Times Square, where passersby were treated to the clatter of rehearsal pianos from the open windows in warm weather. Every afternoon the sidewalks around West 47th Street were clogged with tuxedo-clad musicians toting instruments, making the rounds of the talent booking agencies, gossiping and smoking cigarettes while waiting to hear who was hiring that day.

Popular music had changed since Polly was a dance-mad teenager, when ragtime was the signature sound of flaming youth. Ragtime's jaunty, syncopated marches had given way to the richer sounds of the jazz band, in which each instrument contributed a unique voice and melody line, often improvised on the spot, adding swinging rhythms and the bent notes of the blues.

It was a perfect soundtrack for the new sexual revolution—irreverent, propulsive, and uncannily expressive, melding the yearning of the saxophone, the melancholy of the clarinet, the throb of drums, and the raucous joy of the instruments jousting and intertwining. Jazz appealed, in the words of one early music critic, to "the lowest part of our anatomy."

That was no coincidence. Among the demimonde, *jazz* was a synonym for *sex*, used with the same flavor and grammatical abandon as the word *fuck*. The shocked Committee of Fourteen investigators peppered their reports with its variations: "She asked if I wanted to do a little jazzing"; "I used to stop up there for a piece of jazz"; "You don't expect to jazz me in here do you?"

Born out of ragtime, jazz came of age before the First World War in the red-light districts of New Orleans and San Francisco. It was nurtured in bordellos and honky-tonk barrel houses, the cheap dives that featured fast women and barrels of beer. Madams often hired piano players to whip up the party atmosphere in the bordellos. The dance halls and saloons that catered to prostitutes and sporting men featured small ragtime bands that became known for their attention-grabbing improvisation, bold rhythms, and the palpable sparks that flew between the musicians and the audience. These orgiastic flights of improvisation and tricks of rhythm and beat were referred to as "jazzing" the tune.

The celebrity bandleader Paul Whiteman fell in love with ragtime music the first time he heard it spilling out of the brothels of "the Lowers," Denver's red-light district, when he was a teenager picking up extra cash driving a taxi, delivering fares to the cathouses. His early exposure to the pretty whores of the Lowers left him, in his words, "woman shy" but girl crazy and with a passion for sporting house music.

All the same, he was shocked the first time he saw the term *jazz band*, he remembered, "because jazz still meant something entirely sexual in those days." He became an instant convert to the genre and soon became one of its most passionate proselytizers. He took the spontaneous improvisations and swinging rhythms of the small combos and put them down on paper, tidying them up and giving them all a smoother, more orchestral sound. He specialized in brisk foxtrots with "a businessman's bounce," in Rudy Vallee's sneering phrase: not libidinous, but peppy, toe-tapping, and emotionally evocative.

It was Whiteman who convinced the music peddlers of Tin Pan Alley to treat jazz as something more than a naughty novelty. Yet while he was, in the phrase of the day, "making an honest woman out of jazz" ("I never questioned her honesty," he protested. "I simply thought she needed a new dress"), he spent his off hours the old-fashioned way: in Polly's sporting house.

When Polly met him, Paul was "the big and boisterous ringmaster" of a rowdy, money-minting circus, whose elegantly attired musicians became wild men after hours. He weighed around three hundred pounds and was a man of large, if limited appetites. "Really there's only two things a guy wants," Whiteman liked to say. "He wants to get drunk and he wants to get fucked."

Polly met Paul not long after the publicity machine noisily crowned him the "Jazz King of America" (a slap in the face to the Black musicians who gave birth to the style and remained its finest interpreters). Whiteman disavowed the title—"the sultan of symphonic syncopation" would have been more accurate, *Variety* suggested—but he happily reigned as the undisputed emperor of Tin Pan Alley.

In 1924 Paul Whiteman announced to the press that he planned to hold the first ever jazz "concert." "The advice of my friends (and some enemies) was 'Don't do it,'" he remembered. "Who wants to hear whorehouse music on a concert stage?" Ignoring the critics, he asked his friend George Gershwin, a former song plugger with a handful of hits to his name, to compose the first ever "jazz concerto."

On the snowy afternoon of February 12, 1924, Whiteman's orchestra made its formal debut at the Aeolian Concert Hall at West 43rd Street. The hall was packed with a motley audience of vaudevillians, Tin Pan Alleyites, highbrow composers and critics, stars of the symphony and opera, flappers, and wise guys. As planned, the climax came when George Gershwin sat down at the piano to play the pièce de résistance, entitled *Rhapsody in Blue*.

Rhapsody in Blue wasn't jazz exactly, but it caught its irreverent, soulful energy and joyous freedom. It was, as Gershwin described it, "a sort of musical kaleidoscope of America—of our vast melting pot, our unduplicated national pep, of our blues, our metropolitan madness." With this event, "jazz at last stepped forth from the barrooms, bordellos and cabarets into the chambers of the musically elect," as the columnist Ben Gross put it. After this jazz became "Art with a capital A."

The concert established Whiteman as a superstar and George Gershwin as a budding genius whose reputation would grow to mythic proportions, especially among his proud fellow Jews. In years to come, Polly's relatives—who knew almost nothing about her private or professional life—would brag that their cousin knew the great Gershwin.

The portly bandleader was enjoying his extraordinary success to the hilt, as Niven Busch noted in *The New Yorker*, throwing away enormous sums on clothes, apartments, bootleg liquor, "and above all, for parties." With Whiteman's patronage, Polly quickly became the favorite hostess of the song pluggers, music publishers, aspiring hit writers, and renegade jazzers of Harlem and Times Square.

Like all of Polly's best customers, Whiteman hated to be alone. He was usually surrounded by a gaggle of musicians, promoters, and music industry bigwigs, including Abel Green, *Variety's* influential music critic; Jack Robbins, a hard-charging song-plugger-turned-music-publisher who shared Whiteman's taste for African American music; and Phil Kornheiser, the general professional manager of Leo Feist, a top firm on the Alley, and one of Whiteman's earliest backers.

All of them were masters of the art of "payola"—the pay-to-play system of song plugging in which publishers paid bandleaders, singers, theatrical producers, and later radio programmers to feature their songs. It was an accepted, if much lamented, fact that "the publisher with the largest bank account was the one whose songs got the most performances."

Much of that payola went directly into Polly's coffers. "Polly Adler regularly billed the music publishers for 'entertainment' when the lonesome boys came to town," recalled Abel Green. She was the grease that made the backroom deals, the cut-ins, and payoffs go down a little smoother. Jack Robbins regularly led a merry band of tunesters to her parlor on his nightly rounds with his expense account pad in hand, hosting extravagant parties for favored artists, publicists, and critics. Her fan Phil Kornheiser had one of the most capacious expense accounts in the music business and spent many happy evenings paying the "due-bill at a fancy house."

☾

Paul Whiteman's jazzed-up foxtrots paid the bills, but when it came to her own musical tastes, Polly preferred the unbridled bands of the gangster-run sawdust joints and Harlem black-and-tans.

One of her favorite spots to blow off steam was the Hollywood Cabaret, a basement joint just off Times Square at 49th and Broadway, fronted by a toughie named Leo Bernstein, whom she'd known since she was a teenager hanging around the Winter Garden Café. The club became something greater than just another moldy basement joint when Bernstein hired a new house band, a five-piece combo called the Washingtonians, led by a young African American pianist who went by the name Duke Ellington.

Edward Kennedy Ellington was barely twenty-five years old, but he possessed a quiet charisma and natural elegance. Like Whiteman, he sported sharply tailored suits and a trim pencil mustache, and he was driven by enormous ambition and a vast appetite for life's pleasures— scotch and seduction foremost.

At first Ellington's band played ragtime crowd-pleasers, Tin Pan Alley ballads, and jazzed-up dance tunes in the sweet manner of Whiteman's orchestra. But that year they began incorporating the looser, more fluid influences of New Orleans, the gutbucket growls of Chicago, and improvisational solo turns. "Hot jazz," they called it, and the Broadway cognoscenti went wild for it.

The Committee of Fourteen kept a close eye on the club, as did the feds. Occasionally, when business was slack, or he was tipped off to an imminent raid, remembered the Washingtonians' drummer Sonny Greer, Leo Bernstein would come in and say, "You all take your horns home, we're going to have an accident down there tonight." After one unfortunate touch of arson in February 1925, the Hollywood was rechristened the Club Kentucky (although everyone called it the Kentucky Club), same owners, same spot, new name.

The joint was the size of a shoebox, with a handkerchief-size dance floor and ceilings so low that the drummer had to stoop to keep from hitting his head. The audience sat so close to the musicians, they could feel the spray of spit and smell the valve oil from the horns. A handful of gimlet-eyed hostesses—some of whom moonlighted for Polly—worked the room. But when the band was roaring, there was no hotter spot in the city, although, as Sonny Greer recalled, "if a revenue agent came around the doorman stepped on a foot buzzer and the place turned into a church."

The Washingtonians became a favorite of the Broadway mob, who preferred their torrid rhythms and indigo moods to Whiteman's "businessman's bounce." In fact, Paul Whiteman and his outfit became some of Ellington's most ardent fans. "He would come down to the Kentucky, bringing his own home brew with him ('much better'n your stuff'). He'd plunk a century note on the piano ('just a note of appreciation') sit down and grin all night with pleasure," remembered Greer. Whiteman himself admitted that he "couldn't steal even two bars of Duke's amazing music." The club was one of the few downtown niteries that welcomed Black musicians and entertainers as customers. The feisty young white musicians who hung out at Jimmy Plunkitt's speakeasy on West 53rd Street began stopping in after their own gigs ended. "They were 'ofays,' but 'ofays' who were friends not enemies," remembered one music critic, using Harlem slang for white folks (*foe* in pig Latin). Sometimes there were as many as forty or fifty hard-partying "name musicians" in the house, letting loose an impromptu jam session—a rare case of Black and white musicians playing together.

"We usually didn't get through till 7 or 8 in the morning but it was beautiful. So many things happened. All kinds of people mixed there," remembered Greer. "People like Texas Guinan and Polly Adler came in," along with the town's leading hard guys. "A big bookmaker like Meyer Boston would come in late and the first thing he'd do was change $20 into half dollars. Then he'd throw the whole thing at the feet of whoever was singing or playing or dancing."

Polly liked Sonny and Duke, and they returned the sentiment. "She was a petite, gregarious lady, with great charm, whom everybody loved," recalled Ellington, "and she got along great with all the mob guys." She started hiring the two of them for her after-hours parties. At least once or twice a month on a Sunday morning, after the club closed, Sonny and Duke, along with guitarist Freddie Guy, would pop up to Polly's West 54th Street flat to entertain the big spenders. "We'd show around five o'clock," remembered Greer. "Polly would see we got breakfast, and we'd work until around nine in the morning. It was nothing to leave with fifty or sixty dollars in tips."

Like most bandleaders of the era, Ellington was an unapologetic womanizer. His sleek good looks and suave manners were irresistible to female fans, from Park Avenue debutantes to Polly's pretties. Although she generally served a white clientele, her girls sometimes slept with the Black performers who passed through the establishment, both on the clock and off. "One of the girls took such a liking to Duke, she started seeing him on the side," remembered Sonny.

Like Whiteman, Ellington had grander visions for jazz. (He'd always hated that vulgar word, arguing that "we ought to call what we were doing 'Negro music.'") Duke hadn't yet snatched the crown from Whiteman's brow, but he was catching up fast. By the summer of 1926, newspapers were proclaiming him "the Paul Whiteman of Colored Orchestras."

☾

"When you get your education from people, instead of books, what you learn about is pretty much determined by what interests them," observed Polly. The primary interests of her high-spirited customers were sports and politics, which were, as far as she could tell, pretty much the same thing.

The newspaper columnists declared this the "Golden Age of Sports," "with the accent on the gold," as Grantland Rice quipped. Baseball and boxing were the special passions of the city, and she came to know both intimately. "One wealthy American League club owner used to bring his whole team up to my house whenever they beat the Yankees (which was not often enough for me to learn much about baseball), and my ignorance of how the game was played used to give the boys a lot of laughs," she remembered. "It got to be a standard gag that if one of them had stolen a base in the game that day, I would buy him a drink on the house—because I once had said it must take a lot of nerve to steal anything before a whole stadium full of people."

But it was boxing that would play a defining role in Polly's professional life. New York was the national capital of the fistic arts, boasting more than two dozen arenas and scores of neighborhood fight clubs. Major bouts attracted tens of thousands of fans, and the betting action was so high that some bookies specialized solely in boxing wagers. The newspapers devoted oceans of ink to it, assigning their best reporters to cover its ballyhoo, even listing the daily odds for upcoming matches.

It was conventional wisdom that a politician might turn up his nose at liquor, gambling, or women, but they all had a passion for boxing. District leaders were the main promoters of the sport when it was banned, and now that it was once again legal Tammany kept an iron grip on the State Boxing Commission.

But the politicians were facing a new challenge to their hold on the sport. Many of Polly's customers, flush with bootleg cash, were moving heavily into the fight racket, buying up prizefighters just as they acquired nightclubs, racehorses, armored limousines, and blond mistresses. By the end of the decade, mobsters would own the fight game outright.

"Prizefighting and Prohibition gangsters gravitated toward one another like H_2 to O," observed the *Daily News* columnist Paul Gallico. Should a fellow find himself in the clutches of the law, or in the spotlight of the press, or meeting some classy dame, it was handy to be introduced as a boxing promoter. A night in the public scrum of a big match—along with a carefully saved ticket stub—was an ideal alibi against inquisitive cops. Off-duty fighters could double as bouncers, chauffeurs, bodyguards, and general *schlammers*—wherever a pair of meaty fists and a talent for absorbing pain were helpful. It also happened to be one of the easiest sports to fix. The sportswriter Grantland Rice estimated that over a third of all matchups were fixed in those years. More cynical colleagues might have doubled that.

Owning a piece of a boxer was also a great political asset. Madison Square Garden was one of the few places where politicians and criminals could fraternize freely. And nothing delighted a politician or a potential partner like free front-row tickets to a big bout, or a hot tip on a fixed fight. "There is so much money in it that politicians cannot bear to see the pies cut without getting a slice," wisecracked Gallico.

To be honest, Polly admitted privately, she was "not much of a fight fan," but she got along famously with the pugs who frequented her house in the company of their gangster patrons. She became their favorite hostess for postfight frolics. "The big get-togethers of the gangs are at prize fights," as one mobster explained, and a major matchup counted as an "underworld gala, speaking strictly from a society news viewpoint."

On May 5, 1925, the venerable Madison Square Garden—the last one actually located on Madison Square—welcomed an audience of ten thousand to its final bout. Tex Rickard, the self-appointed czar of boxing, was breaking ground on a brand-new temple of fighting arts twenty-five blocks north, just a few blocks from Polly's apartment.

That summer, even before the new Garden opened, Polly got a crash course in the "Sweet Science" when two of boxing's most fabled figures began making her house their home away from home.

Jack "Doc" Kearns arrived in the Big Apple in May, with a new protégé. Lean and wiry, with cold, powder-blue eyes and a sly smile, Doc looked like "a larcenous leprechaun," in one reporter's fanciful phrase.

"When I tell you that Jack Kearns was a charlatan, a rogue, a con man, a promoter and an artist, I say it all with affection and no apology," remembered Teddy Hayes, Doc's longtime wingman and trainer. "Personally," said Kearns, "I prefer to be called a manipulator."

Polly had met Kearns some years earlier, after he'd turned Jack Dempsey into the heavyweight champion of the world and an international celebrity. By 1925, the historic partnership between Kearns and Dempsey had run its course. That spring Kearns, in need of a new meal ticket, signed on to manage Mickey Walker, the current welterweight champion who hailed from the wilds of northern New Jersey. At five foot seven, he was no Dempsey; too bad, since fans preferred the big men. But he was Irish—a throwback to the days before hungry young Jews, Italians, and Poles invaded the game—and boyishly handsome, with a freckled snub nose and a million-dollar smile. Most important, he loved to brawl, ferociously and dramatically, guaranteeing the fans a spectacular show.

In need of funds to train his new pugilist, Doc Kearns made a beeline to Big Bill Dwyer's crew at the Silver Slipper, who were happy to put up cold cash in exchange for a hefty piece of the kid's winnings. They also offered Mickey a chance to pick up some dough working for Dwyer's operation on the Jersey shore, where a retrofitted submarine chaser delivered cargos of smuggled whiskey to be trucked to points west. As a hometown hero, Mickey made a perfect "ice man," delivering Dwyer's payoffs to the local bigwigs, accompanied by a well-armed "chauffeur."

Then Kearns brought on Teddy Hayes, né Weinberg, to supervise Mickey's training. Teddy liked to describe himself as Dempsey's trainer, but he was—as more than one reporter scoffed—more chauffeur, bagman, and fixer. "If anybody loved life more than Kearns or me, it was Teddy Hayes," Mickey remembered fondly. Teddy didn't drink—a valuable habit in that sodden set—but he was second to none in skirt-chasing and love of the limelight.

Young Mickey was dazzled by his charismatic new manager. "Around Kearns every night was New Year's Eve," he said with admiration. When Doc first brought Mickey to Polly's, the youngster was agog at finding himself in "the plushiest whorehouse in town," as he put it. "It was large, beautifully furnished—and men came there for uninterrupted drinking and gambling as well as sex. Polly supplied the food, drinks, cards and girls and, more important, privacy. She didn't care what a person's tastes in entertainment were, as long as he could pay for them."

She never forgot that night either. "I remember the first time I met Micky [sic], a fresh good looking young man," Polly told a friend. "Jack brought him to my place, for all I know the first time with a dame." But the kid's naïveté quickly wore on her patience. "Don't know why, but Micky kept following me around, to be blunt, he wanted to screw me. I begged Jack to keep the kid away from me. I'm not the screwing type. Jack became indignant."

"You should be honored," he insisted. "That kid is the champ."

"Fine," she snapped back. "He's your champ. You sleep with him."

But it was hard to stay mad at the friendly fighter with the infectious grin. "I got to be very fond of him," Polly said. And he felt the same way about the woman he called "Queen Madam."

Mickey was preparing to challenge the current middleweight champion, Harry "the Pittsburgh Windmill" Greb, on July 2, 1925, in one of the most hotly anticipated events of the season. At thirty-one, Greb was an old man in the fight game, but like Mickey, he was a born brawler, with a reputation as one of the dirtiest boxers in the business. "Prize-fighting ain't the noblest of arts, and I ain't its noblest artist," he declared proudly.

Unlike Mickey, Harry Greb needed no special introduction to Polly. Most boxers occasionally patronized prostitutes—pimps were well known as pugilism's most devoted fanbase—but Greb was nearly as famous for his whoremongering as he was for his record in the ring.

"The primrose path was where he did his heavy roadwork," remembered the sportswriter Jim Fair, who spent many hours tagging along on Greb's nocturnal adventures. "On the eve of a fight his manager knew where to find him—bouncing up and down the stairs in the red-light district, a hussy under each arm and a brace bringing up the rear, while the madame put in a frantic call for fresh stuff." Not for nothing did Jim Fair come to call Polly one of his closest and oldest friends.

☾

But the biggest influence on Polly's fate that summer was Jimmy Walker, the favorite son of Tin Pan Alley, Madison Square Garden, and Tammany Hall.

All that spring there was much talk about replacing the current mayor of New York, a stolid Tammany man named John Hylan who had fallen out of favor with Governor Smith and many of the district leaders. Broadway had just the man in mind to replace him.

Like Harlem's Jimmy Hines, James J. Walker, the state senator from Greenwich Village, was raised in the bonny Irish bosom of Tammany. But instead of going into the family business, he spent his youth haunting the vaudeville houses and music halls of Union Square and Tin Pan Alley, trying his hand as a pianist, gag writer, and lyricist. He wrote one hit, the sentimental ballad "Will You Love Me in December the Way You Do in May?" When he found himself unable to repeat the trick, he turned his ambitions to the political stage.

Broadwayfarers of all stripes hailed State Senator Walker as one of their own. He was beloved for repealing the blue laws that forbade baseball games and motion pictures on Sunday, for his outspoken opposition to Prohibition, and for killing the recent "Clean Books Bill" in the statehouse. ("I have never yet heard of a girl being ruined by a book" was his winning argument.) But his crowning legislative achievement was the 1920 Walker Bill, lifting the ban on prizefighting and establishing the New York State Boxing Commission to regulate fighters, promoters, and referees. When he was not in Albany, he ran a criminal law practice that won him many influential friends in Gotham's netherworld.

"Walker was a charmer and a rascal," remembered Teddy Hayes. "Considering how much time he spent at fights, racetracks, ballparks and theaters, he was an authentic political genius." In the speakeasies, the sleek silhouette of "Beau James," as his friend Gene Fowler dubbed him—with his wasp-waisted suits, spotless spats, and brightly hued socks and pocket square, all in varying shades of the same color—cut a sharp contrast to the other district leaders, with their baggy suits and white socks bunched up above their bulky brogans. He had the nimble energy and debonair manner of "a cabaret dancer or a gigolo of the Montmartre," as one reporter put it, with a knowing smile and eyes that twinkled conspiratorially. "He looks, in brief, to be slightly wicked."

In a rare exception to her famous discretion, Polly bragged openly and often of her friendship with the songsmith-turned-state-senator. It was no mystery how they met. "He was a ladies' man, and he was a bottle man," as the columnist Harry Golden put it. Although married, he was regularly spotted carousing with chorus girls in the better dives of the Hardened Artery. It was an open secret that he was carrying on an affair with Yvonne "Vonnie" Shelton, a trim little hoofer from Ziegfeld's chorus line.

"The boom for Walker originated on Broadway, not in Tammany Hall," remembered Gene Fowler. The Combine provided early, influential backing. When the cocky senator approached Bill Dwyer and Owney Madden for a campaign contribution of $25,000, a hefty sum even by today's standards, Dwyer didn't blink. "Let's walk in with Walker," he urged the rest of the mob. Like all good fundraisers, they twisted the arms of their colleagues to drum up support. "Puddit in the paper that you like Jimmy and that people should vote for him," Owney Madden ordered a surprised Walter Winchell. He was happy to oblige.

It was no small task, however, to convince the party leadership to unseat their own man and install another candidate. In a sign of how closely bound Jimmy Walker was to the sporting crowd, the publicity stunt that put him over the top came from the wily brain of his friend Jimmie Johnston, one of the fight game's canniest promoters.

On July 3, the afternoon of the title fight between Mickey Walker and Harry Greb, Jimmie Johnston led a raucous "Win with Walker" pep rally designed to simultaneously boost ticket sales for the big bout and put public pressure on Tammany Hall. Led by Irving Berlin and George S. Cohan, some fifteen hundred rowdy Broadwayites, wearing campaign buttons printed with that dual-purpose motto, paraded to the Tammany headquarters on Fourteenth Street, where they demanded to see the Grand Sachem, George Olvany, to petition him to dump the current mayor and replace him on the ballot with "our Jimmy." The boss said he would take it under advisement.

Several hours later the revelers joined sixty thousand spectators in Yankee Stadium to watch the Toy Bulldog and the Human Windmill beat each other senseless. That fight would go down as one of the most savage championship battles of the century. Harry and Mickey went fifteen brutal rounds, the legal limit. Mickey was barely standing when the final bell rang, his face smeared with blood, his left eye swollen after a gouging by Greb's thumb. It was a close call, but the judges gave the decision to Greb, who, it was soon discovered, had bet his entire purse on himself to win, tripling his bonanza.

But the biggest victor that day was Jimmy Walker. "It was Johnston's 'Win with Walker' parade that got me the nomination," Jimmy would later insist. But the would-be mayor still had to convince the leader of the party, Governor Al Smith. The governor was eager to put his own man in City Hall, and he liked Jimmy personally, but he worried about the senator's womanizing. All the stars on Broadway couldn't convince Al Smith that a man so sincerely indifferent to the demands of the double standard wouldn't end up tarring Tammany's already grimy reputation just as Smith was angling for another shot at the White House.

Over the Fourth of July, the governor voiced his doubts to some of his fellow party leaders. "If Walker could keep out of the Broadway limelight—which he can't—and if he would rid himself of that certain party he has been going around with—which he won't—and go back to Mrs. Walker," Smith mused, "then things might be different."

The next week Jimmy Walker went missing from all his regular haunts. When he was spotted in public, it was only in the most respectable of venues, with the matronly Mrs. Walker by his side. Political observers were astonished by Jimmy's late-life conversion.

But in fine Broadway fashion, it was a performance for the suckers. Instead of rediscovering the virtues of hearth and home, Walker had spent the long summer nights hiding in a penthouse apartment on West 58th Street, arranged for him by a wealthy drinking buddy named Arthur "Grassy" Grashoff, who enjoyed close ties to the Canadian rumrunners. Grassy also provided a discreet butler, a well-stocked bar, and the kind of intimate entertainment Jimmy preferred. "Jim might do as he pleased," Grashoff promised, "on the condition that he make whoopee in the penthouse instead of at Broadway clubs." The penthouse was borrowed from "a luxury-loving dowager who was on a holiday abroad," according to Gene Fowler—and if the dowager happened to be Polly Adler, no one would have been surprised.

At the end of one month in his "Chanel Number Five dungeon," as one pal dubbed it, Al Smith summoned Walker to ask him how he'd managed to turn such a dramatic new leaf. "We all grow up sometime," Jimmy responded solemnly.

The next day the Tammany executive committee met to decide Mayor Hylan's fate. By the time the meeting adjourned, it was official: Tammany Hall was throwing its full weight behind James J. Walker. The only wrinkle left was Vonnie Shelton. After a few reasonable words and, almost certainly, a generous cash gift, Miss Shelton boarded a boat to Cuba and didn't reappear until after the votes were counted.

☾

That summer of 1925, the supple blue notes of the trumpet replaced the wailing saxophone as the siren song of the decade, deposed by the electrifying Louis Armstrong, who was wowing audiences every night at the Roseland Ballroom. Around the corner at the newly rechristened Club Kentucky, Duke Ellington's band featured the charismatic cornetist Bubber Miley, whose gutbucket growls and distinctive wah-wah sound drew a regular crowd of het-up Broadwayfarers.

Paul Whiteman's answer to Armstrong and Miley was Henry "Hot Lips" Busse. "Hot Lips," remembered Polly, "was Paul Whiteman's fair boy," his highest-paid player, right-hand man, and sometime stooge. Busse, in turn, worshipped his boss. He ordered his suits from the same tailor and bought the same model of sports car, even grew a wispy mustache to match his boss's toothbrush bristles. Although he stood half a foot shorter than Whiteman, he could match him drink for drink.

They were both devoted fans of Polly's Follies. Square women often made them feel shy and insecure; the roly-poly trumpeter spoke with a heavy German accent—at a time when Germans were deeply unpopular—and Whiteman, despite his self-deprecating jokes, was excruciatingly sensitive about his obesity. Polly's girls, all fine actresses in their own sphere, could make any man feel like Rudolph Valentino.

Whiteman's orchestra was in town much of that summer, recording, rehearsing, and living the high life. On Monday, August 17, 1925, Busse was drinking at the Hotsy Totsy Club, a sawdust joint at 50th Street and Seventh Avenue popular with the wise mob. The Hotsy Totsy was Legs Diamond's entry into the crowded field of Times Square nightclubs. The feisty Irishman had come up in the world of late, becoming one of Rothstein's most trusted drug couriers, and he was eager to make a splash on Broadway.

His fellow outlaws looked on Legs's new stature with a wary eye. He was a hellion and a heavy drinker—always dangerous in their line of work—and possessed a well-deserved reputation as a double-crosser. "He's a real son of a bitch. Nobody likes him except dames," said one Broadway cop who knew him well. "Guys like Bill Dwyer and Bill Duffey [sic] and Big Frenchy aren't trigger-happy punks. Leave them alone, they'll leave you alone. But that lousy little Diamond is real mean. I think he gets a kick out of killing."

The Hotsy Totsy had an especially shady reputation. Lucky Luciano warned his crew to stay out of the joint, citing rumors that Legs made a habit of inviting rival gunmen for a conciliatory drink in the club's backroom, where, should the conversation go awry, he could discreetly put a bullet in their head, then hoist the limp corpse off the premises like a common drunk. It was said that Legs occasionally blackmailed unsuspecting customers who dallied with the club's hard-boiled hostesses. But among civilians, Legs's sinister reputation only added to the club's crude glamour.

That August night Busse was already well soused, Polly remembered, when he "met one of my girls in the Hotsy Totsy Club." Eleanor Lyman was a dancer in the *Ziegfeld Follies* who was moonlighting for Polly.

Whether Henry knew this fact was hazy—as was everything else that night—but Eleanor's charms cut through the fog of cheap booze. When the bouncers finally shooed them out of the club at ten o'clock the next morning, Eleanor and Henry headed to City Hall, trailed by a "host of other quaffing couples," cracked the reporter for *Variety*, where they borrowed a ring and "committed matrimony."

News of the whirlwind elopement spread quickly. The next day, "when Whiteman was convinced it wasn't one of Busse's characteristic pranks," explained *Variety*, he threw an impromptu reception at Ziegfeld's theater in honor of the emboozled couple.

But the imperial bandleader had no intention of losing his favorite sidekick to a wife—even worse, to a tart. A few days later, recalled Polly, "Paul came to me and offered $10,000 to Elenore [*sic*] if she would annul the marriage." This did not go over well with Henry. "To spite Paul, Buzzy [*sic*] told Paul he can go to Hell, he loved Elenore."

"The marriage didn't last long," Polly conceded. But under New York State law, it lasted just long enough for Busse to owe a hefty alimony settlement of $200 a month. When he protested that he'd been blind drunk, Eleanor offered to settle for fifty grand cash. Whether it was a case of bruised feminine feelings or one of Legs's shakedown schemes was hard to say.

For two years the couple jousted over money—the trumpeter narrowly avoided a stretch in "the 'alimony club' in jail." Finally in April 1927, he and Whiteman hired a private investigator to trail his ex-wife to the Belvedere Hotel, where she was caught "sharing a room with a legally unauthorized male," thus voiding the alimony agreement. "It cost Buzzy a pretty penny to catch Elenore with a guy in bed," concluded Polly.

Whiteman got his own comeuppance for that summer's revels. Ten days after the Hotsy Totsy romance, *Variety* reported with a wink that the portly bandleader had been diagnosed with "blood poisoning"— a well-known euphemism for syphilis. Just another Broadway ending.

⟨

The only blemish on this happy scene was the appointment, in February 1925, of Emory R. Buckner as the new U.S. attorney for the Southern District of New York. A white-shoe corporate lawyer, Buckner had no interest in ingratiating himself with the press or politicians, or in reforming the morals of his fellow citizens, or even in lining his own pockets. He announced that he planned to crack down on the "men higher up," the major smugglers who ran Rum Row and the high-profile nightclubs of midtown Manhattan. To do the job, he brought in his own team of scrupulously clean investigators and attorneys—dubbed "Buckner's Boy Scouts."

Defying the skeptics, on September 23, 1925, Buckner sent two precisely coordinated teams of federal and local officers into the Knickerbocker and Longacre buildings in the heart of Times Square—the headquarters of Waxey Gordon's vast smuggling operation—while another crew swarmed the sidewalks, cutting off all exits. The agents seized maps, charts, passwords, and radio codes and rounded up a score of men. But Waxey was not among them. Tipped off to the raid, he was in the middle of the Atlantic Ocean on a luxury liner headed to Europe.

Three days later, one of Buckner's key informers was found dead in an abandoned limousine in Yorkville. A few weeks later Waxey Gordon made a leisurely return to New York, where he surrendered to the authorities. He could afford to be sanguine. At the end of January, Buckner's lead witness was found with a bullet through his head in the hotel room where the feds had been hiding him before the trial. A case of suicide, insisted the detectives of the West 47th Street station. With no more witnesses, the prosecution was forced to drop the case, and the slick former pickpocket slipped from Buckner's grasp.

☾

Mickey Walker also had something to prove to the skeptics. Retreating back to the welterweight division, Mickey was scheduled to defend his title against Dave Shade on September 25. According to rumor, three nights before the fight Frankie Marlow met Arnold Rothstein in Lindy's where, speaking out of the corner of his mouth to foil the nosy lipreaders, he informed the gambler that the referee and two judges were going to give the decision to Mickey. A.R. immediately began working the phones, laying bets with bookmakers around the country.

The fight was a wild, reckless brawl. Again, Mickey took the worst of it, until the fifteenth round when he suddenly perked up. When the final bell rang, the crowd was clearly in Dave Shade's favor. But the judges saw it differently, and Mickey retained the world welterweight championship "by the gossamer thread," as one sportswriter put it.

Walker's victory enriched Rothstein by $60,000 and Kearns and Mickey by $100,000. After that Mickey and Doc hit the town roaring. "Together we painted the whole town," remembered Kearns. "And we did it with a likely string of fillies."

One memorable evening they ventured out with some $20,000 in cash between them. "*Not unusual*," noted Polly drolly. Breaking Kearns's long-standing rule, Mickey insisted that *this* time he would take custody of their bankroll. After all the joints closed at six a.m., the two decided to end the night at Polly's. "I refused to admit the two play-boys," she remembered. Thoroughly smashed, Doc insisted that Mickey hand over the bankroll, which he did, but they began squabbling when Doc refused to give the fighter two bucks for cab fare.

Polly eased them out of the apartment, but they continued their quarrel on the sidewalk and finally "sat down to settle this friendly drunken argument." Teddy Hayes, who "knew the boys were loaded with dough," was frantically looking for them all over town. Finally he headed to Polly's, where, sometime after sunrise, he found them propped up against the fire hydrant in front of her building, slumbering peacefully, with Doc still clutching the twenty grand.

By the end of January 1926, Mark Hellinger, the *Daily News*'s genial Broadway scribe, put a gentle word of warning in his column. "We see a lot of this fellow, Walker—and we ponder on how it's possible for him to play the nightclubs regularly and still remain a champion," Hellinger mused pointedly. But the boys paid no heed.

Polly didn't approve of wasting talent, but she wasn't one to scold when she was the prime beneficiary. "The largest amount of money I ever blew in one spree was at Polly's," remembered Mickey. "When I was rolling high, I wouldn't let anyone pick up a tab, except maybe Kearns. It made me feel important to grab the check in the company of big shots. In those days, if it got around that a guy blew fifty thousand in a floating crap game, the next day he could get credit almost anywhere.

"Anyway, Doc and I went up to Polly's one evening and found the place full of brokers, politicians, Broadway characters and big-time mobsters. I was pretty well loaded with a package I had picked up at Guinan's. When I saw all these money men, I decided I was going to be the biggest shot of them all. I insisted on picking up the tab for everybody for the whole night's entertainment. They took me up on it pretty quick. Kearns didn't stop me. Polly didn't care. The 'entertainment' lasted two nights and a day. It ended only when Polly's girls complained they needed some sleep. The bill came to about twenty thousand dollars. I paid it without batting an eye."

☾

For the first time in memory, politics was supplanting showbiz and sports as the hot topic on the Rialto. The battle between Mayor Hylan and Jimmy Walker was one of the bitterest primary elections in New York City history. Hylan was in the awkward position of running against both his own party apparatus and the zeitgeist of the city. The overmatched incumbent tried to wield Walker's Broadway ties against him, hurling claims that he was a puppet of the underworld, a mere front for "Arnold Rothstein, the big gambler," who was "the real dictator" of Tammany Hall. If Walker won, Hylan warned, he would turn the city into a haven for gamblers and thieves.

Down on Wall Street the Boston brothers were offering 10-to-1 odds on Walker, and even at those odds, no one was putting money down on the incumbent. *The New York Times* reported rumors that a crew of gangsters named "Jack Diamond," "Frenchy," and "Dutch"—easily recognizable to insiders as Legs Diamond, Big Frenchy DeMange, and an up-and-coming sociopath known as Dutch Schultz—were planning to invade the polling places of the seventeenth assembly district to ensure Walker's chances. In response, Commissioner Enright announced that he was doubling the number of cops at the voting places and calling up the police reserve. But the precautions were unnecessary. Walker won handily.

Broadway's bet paid off handsomely. "Our Jimmy" won by a landslide in the general election, handing Tammany Hall its biggest victory in over two decades.

With City Hall in the bag, Polly's pals in the sporting world turned their attention to the grand opening of the new Madison Square Garden, Manhattan's glorious "temple of pugilism" reborn on West 50th Street. The pessimists who'd warned that Walker's victory would turn New York into a modern-day Sodom and Gomorrah weren't entirely wrong. In the wake of the election out-of-town grifters, gamblers, and hustlers of every stripe were flooding "into the city in seeming belief that New York is to be a 'wide-open' town," *The New York Times* reported, just in time for opening day at the Garden.

On December 3 the festivities were just getting under way when, in a repeat of the Waxey Gordon debacle, a team of federal agents, U.S. marshals, and policemen descended on the Times Square offices of the Combine, and the Lexington Avenue operations center where Frank Costello coordinated liquor shipments. Costello and Dwyer were hauled in, along with some two dozen others, and booked on charges of violating the Volstead Act. Buckner's office crowed that it was "the greatest round-up in the history of Prohibition."

Of all the bootleg barons, Big Bill Dwyer had come closest to grabbing the brass ring. Among underworld players and itchy-palmed law enforcers, the Dwyer name was a magic password that guaranteed good pay, a square deal, and protection from the vagaries of the law. Bill was considered a gentleman by the cops, coast guards, federal agents, and politicians who attended his parties and accepted his bribes. The broad-minded boys of the press hailed him as a prominent sportsman, race-track owner, and theatrical angel—the ultimate Broadway Big Shot.

It was this stellar reputation that brought down Emory Buckner's wrath. "The investigation started through having the name of Bill Dwyer thrown in our teeth in almost every case that came up," Buckner told reporters, whenever the small fry demanded to know why the feds didn't arrest the guy who was making all the money.

Dwyer and his men were quickly bailed out, but prudence demanded that he forgo the grand climax of the Madison Square Garden festivities on December 15, when Mayor-elect Walker and seventeen thousand people, many in black tie and evening gowns, turned out to watch the debut of professional hockey in New York City, courtesy of the team's new owner, William Vincent Dwyer.

☾

Broadway was in a giddy mood that holiday season, and so was Polly. "The year 1926 saw Prohibition gangsters, racketeers and bootleggers enjoying just about their palmiest days," she recalled, and they were throwing money around like confetti. Best of all, she was in love.

Bandleaders were the sex symbols of the day, Polly remembered rue-fully, and "right in style—I fell for one." She met Jimmy Carr over the Christmas holidays when he tumbled in with a crew of partyers after the late-night joints had closed. He passed out in one of the girls' rooms, too liquor-logged to move. So she had his pals haul him into her room while she bedded down on the living room sofa.

Polly roused him around noon the next day. She offered him the standard hangover treatment in those woebegone days before aspirin was widely available—a cup of black coffee and a dose of Eno's salts—then sent him on his way with a friendly warning "not to get so stinko again."

When her private phone rang that evening, she was surprised to hear the hangdog musician asking her to dinner. "I had thought he was the type who went for strictly ornamental females," remembered Polly.

Jimmy Carr was the bandleader at the Silver Slipper, "perhaps the most genuinely Broadwayese of all the Main Stem's establishments," as one columnist dubbed it. The gaudy silver-and-black-striped wallpaper gave the club an air of glamour that eluded most of its competitors, although that civilized veneer could evaporate instantly. Polly was a val-ued customer at the Slipper; Madden and the boys considered it good business to have a madam at hand for customers who were pining for more than a hostess.

Jimmy was a thin, bespectacled fellow who bore a slight resemblance to Eddie "Banjo Eyes" Cantor. He wasn't classically handsome, but he had a sweet face and a charming swagger. When Polly met him, he was a rising star on the Bistro Beat. He was managed by Bernie Foyer, a pugnacious booking agent perpetually chewing on a fat black cigar, who'd recently beaten charges of embezzlement. Foyer recast the band as a comic musical vaudeville act, billing Carr as an "M.D."—"Doctor of Melody"—a sort of cut-rate version of Jimmy Durante's madcap non-sense. They played Dixieland jazz, antic novelty numbers, and peppy foxtrots for dancing. Jimmy was no Paul Whiteman—but he had show-manship that "was made to order for the café dance floor," where flashy improvisation, hot licks, and screwball touches delighted the inebriated, intimate audiences, wrote *Variety*'s Abel Green approvingly.

The Silver Slipper floor show leaned heavily on blue humor and lightly clad ladies and featured future screen stars like George Raft, a friend of Madden's who stopped in to perform his whirlwind Charleston for throw money; fifteen-year-old Ruby Keeler, a sweet kid with saucer eyes who specialized in the black bottom, a current dance craze; and the hard-boiled hoofer Ruby Stevens, not long before she became Barbara Stanwyck.

The idea of competing for anyone's favor against the Silver Slipper's "Beauty Brigade" was laughable to Polly. "Maybe he was looking for novelty," she speculated. "I don't know, but whatever he was looking for he must have found it in me." After that first dinner, they saw each other every night for weeks.

Most nights, after Carr packed up his baton and her last customers stumbled home, they'd meet up at one of the Avenue's dusk-to-dawn joints where the nighthawks hung out after a hard day's hustle. A favorite rendezvous was the Dover Club, on 51st Street, the new home of Jimmy Durante, Lou Clayton, and Eddie Jackson after the feds shut down the Club Durant. Waxey Gordon was rumored to be one of its silent backers.

"The Dover was no angel's paradise," *Variety* conceded. It was perched over a garage, where the odor of gasoline mingled with the smell of cigarettes and Chinese food. The only decorations, swathes of rose-colored fabric draped over the bare brick walls, were riddled with bullet holes where the bouncer had used it for after-hours target practice. The bartender sold cocaine and kept watch over the icebox, where the customers' guns were stashed. A small mattress was tucked into the broom closet, for hitting the pipe during lulls in the action.

The top attraction at the Dover, besides Clayton, Jackson, and Durante, was "Mademoiselle Fifi," a buxom burlesque dancer who provided a comic foil for the boys' antics. Fifi was one of the regular hostesses in the Broadway mob's roster, performing and hustling customers in their various midtown clubs while also freelancing as a call girl and exotic dancer at stag parties. She occasionally worked for Polly, taking her pickups to one of the madam's West Side apartments. Fifi's biggest booster was Sime Silverman, who got a kick out of her fabulous figure, fake French accent, and Dumb Dora act. He dropped a solid chunk of change on her most nights and made her a recurring feature in the pages of *Variety*.

Jimmy Carr was, in Broadway terms, "a right guy." "He was generous and gay and easygoing and considerate," remembered Polly. "He was the first to reach for the check and the first to laugh at the joke." Most important, he didn't seem to mind that she was in the sex trade.

But Jimmy was also a heavy drinker who never knew when the party was over. Everybody called him a prince, remembered Polly bitterly, "and on Broadway a prince is a soft touch." The kind of charmingly profligate, everybody's-pal, drinks-on-the-house character whom she adored as a customer alarmed her in a boyfriend. Then there was his opium habit.

Between the two, "both his health and his bank account took an awful beating, and many a golden opportunity went by because he wasn't in shape to grab it," Polly remembered. "I tried to point out to him that he was jeopardizing his whole future—and for what, except back-slapping from a bunch of free loaders?—but it was a waste of breath."

"Who wants to live forever?" he'd always reply.

☾

Taking a cue from her friends in the sporting world, Polly now began courting the city's newspapermen more aggressively, instituting an open-door policy for nearly anyone with a press pass. Friendly scribes stopped by to blow off steam, cadge free drinks, and pick up the latest rumors. In return, they tipped her off to police raids, nosy newspaper inquiries, and assorted ill winds, and kept her name out of the papers in times of trouble.

It was a natural fit. Journalists—like entertainers—were considered slightly disreputable by the better classes, a bohemian status that most reporters wore proudly. "Don't tell my mother I'm a newspaperman," they joked. "She thinks I play piano in a whore-house." Most cub reporters began their careers on the police beat, hanging around the courts and chronicling the underbelly of nightlife.

Spending so much time around attractive young women engaged in one of the world's most reviled professions was, as one journalist put it, a good way to learn how "to peel away preconceptions and evaluate without prejudice." Many a young reporter found himself infatuated with a pretty prostitute, enjoying heroic visions of rescuing her from a life of shame, only to discover she had no interest in abandoning her lucrative lifestyle to live on the paltry salary of a newspaperman.

These brothel educations bred a complex combination of cynicism and sentimentality and an abiding distaste for bourgeois hypocrisies. Polly came to count many of the town's top newspapermen as close friends, especially the nighthawks: the crime reporters, sports columnists, theater reviewers, and Broadway columnists. The editor Gene Fowler, "an irreverent, hard-living, lusty newspaperman from the Nothing Sacred School of Reporting," became a particular favorite. Like his pal Paul Whiteman, Fowler's tastes were shaped by spending his tender years around the red-light district of Denver, Colorado, where he had an after-school job delivering groceries to the hookshops. "My first real loves were the madams of the Denver underworld," he told the columnist Lucius Beebe—those frumpy older women with cash stuffed in their stockings, who understood the hidden hypocrisies and secret desires of men, who took life as it came and did not pass judgment.

Polly forged an especially close bond with the ever-growing corps of syndicated gossip columnists, who sprang up in the wake of the twin bards of Broadway. Mark Hellinger and Walter Winchell were now mustreads for the smart set. Most insiders preferred Hellinger, who never let anyone pick up a check and who conducted his column with the same playful generosity. But it was the sharp-elbowed Winchell who made the bigger splash. "One day he was a nobody," remembered one Broadway ticket broker, "and the next time you looked, everybody was reading his column and around Broadway you had to decide whether to fear him or favor him."

Walter Winchell was hardly the first gossip columnist to cover New York's "tinsel aristocracy." But he brought something electrifying and new to the age-old art of rumormongering, with his rat-a-tat style and unabashed prurience. His success inspired an army of professional eavesdroppers and urban chroniclers, whose syndicated columns spread the small-town gossip of Times Square to the hinterlands. "Jazz journalism," the pundits dubbed it.

Even the Broadway intelligentsia got in on the act late in 1925, when one of the Algonquin Round Tablers, Harold Ross, started an upscale magazine to capitalize on the new fascination with Manhattan's "metropolitan personalities." The New Yorker took the tabloid cast of characters—politicos, entertainers, mobsters, athletes, cops, firstnighters, and women-about-town—and punched them up with an arch, ironic tone, and "a behind-the-scenes atmosphere," in Ross's words, designed to appeal to well-heeled literary slummers. Its unofficial motto: "Not edited for the old lady in Dubuque."

By the end of its first year, *The New Yorker* had become the darling of New York's smart circles. Robert Benchley, Dorothy Parker, and Donald Ogden Stewart were frequent contributors, with Benchley taking the role of theater reviewer and media critic. Following Benchley's lead, Polly's house became a regular rendezvous for many of the hard-partying staff members, including the managing editor Ralph Ingersoll, the novelist Philip Wylie, who ran the art department, the writers James Thurber and Wolcott Gibbs, and Peter Arno, a recent Yale graduate whose sly cartoons of flappers, sugar daddies, and Park Avenue dowagers became a signature of the magazine. Harold Ross, the founder and editor in chief, was one of the few who failed to fall for Polly's charms. Peter Arno once brought Ross to her bordello, remembered Wolcott Gibbs incredulously, but the eccentric editor brought along a stack of manuscripts "and just read them," while the fun eddied around him.

The press covered the gangster takeover of midtown nightlife with special ardor. Editors loved underworld characters not only because they sold papers but also because, as Florabel Muir pointed out, "it was almost impossible to libel them." Winchell in particular "made it a policy to seek out gamblers, hoods, bookmakers, and whore house madams," noted one critic, but even glossy, highbrow publications cultivated ties with the criminal classes. It was a "status symbol to establish good relations with mob bosses," Winchell's assistant explained.

Winchell and Hellinger regularly popped into Polly's place on their late-night prowls. In a field crowded with playboys Winchell, in particular, distinguished himself by his rapaciousness and vulgarity. Walter was, in the words of one colleague, "a sexual athlete, a stud, a man for all female seasons." As he made his rounds, he kept up a coarse commentary, in his high-pitched, mile-a-minute patter, about women's bodies, appetites, and proclivities, even the way they smelled. Friends liked to joke that he would die of a terminal orgasm.

Brazen as Winchell's womanizing was, his fellow dirt slingers dared not breathe a word of it in print. "Those who live in tin houses shouldn't throw can openers" was one of Walter's favorite mottoes. The uninitiated read this as a righteous protest against hypocrisy. Insiders recognized it for what it was: a cold-blooded threat.

☾

As Polly fell more in love, she became ambitious for her Jimmy. Just look at the new darling of the Booze Belt, the marcelled marvel Harry Richman: when she met Harry in 1919, he was a traveling salesman peddling cheap dresses and a whorehouse piano player. Since then he'd hit the big time as the star attraction in his own nightclub, playing the Palace, dating movie stars, and palling around with magistrates, judges, and the top brass of the underworld. The amount of money he was throwing away on dolls—much of it at Polly's house—was fantastic even by Broadway standards. If that mug could get rich, why not her Jimmy?

Everyone on Tin Pan Alley had some new scheme, some fresh angle in those years. Among Polly's regulars, Paul Whiteman and his drinking buddies, Jack Robbins and Abel Green, were starting a new publishing company to sell "symphonically syncopated" sheet music, spreading the gospel of jazz to America's middle classes.

The irrepressible Jack Robbins was pushing another big idea that year. Silent films were usually accompanied by live musicians. Why not create theme songs for silent movies, as a way to boost sales of sheet music and records? His first experiment was the sentimental ballad "Charmaine," written for the most anticipated film of the season, a remake of the hit war play of 1924–25, What Price Glory? "Charmaine" was Robbins's "#1 Plug" that year, as the song pluggers liked to say, and he was spending a fortune paying bandleaders and singers to feature it in their acts.

Polly decided to start putting her contacts to good use. After all, Phil Kornheiser, as the song picker for the biggest publishing firm on the Alley, could make or break careers, as could Abel Green at Variety. And Jack Robbins loved nothing more than turning unknown talents into stars.

She had her eye on the rising opportunities in radio. Showbiz folk generally looked down on radio as the bastard child of Broadway and Madison Avenue. But in 1926 the airwaves came into their own with the formation of the first national network of radio stations, the National Broadcasting Company, better known as NBC. Some of her Madison Avenue johns were beginning to experiment with the concept of regular, advertiser-sponsored programs and were looking for entertainers willing to buck the Broadway prejudice against the new technology. Paul Whiteman, a decided snob about the new medium, deigned to receive $5,500 to appear for a single performance on *The Eveready Hour*.

So she did what she did best. "I gave parties for big wheels in the advertising business, hoping to land [Jimmy] a sponsored radio show," said Polly. "But invariably he would get pie-eyed and insult the very guys who could do him good." That was no way to woo Jack Robbins, a hot-tempered character who threw around the term *son of a bitch* as if it were *please* and *thank you*. Jack couldn't stand incompetence or carelessness and never hesitated to let any sloppy son of a bitch know it. Abel Green, whose enthusiastic reviews had boosted Carr's profile, began dropping subtly snide comments in the pages of *Variety*.

Each time Polly would be furious and hurt and accuse him of ingratitude. Jimmy snapped back, telling her to mind her own business. "For several days after such quarrels we'd try to get along without each other," she recalled, "but always he'd come back or I'd break down and call him."

At the end of May, Jimmy's band decamped for a two-month gig in Atlantic City. With its famous boardwalk and free-flowing booze, the city blossomed every summer with jazz clubs, bawdy houses, and cabarets. The distance must have been a tonic; when she visited him that July, the two lovers looked positively radiant when the camera caught them in a holiday snapshot.

☾

Back on Broadway, Big Bill Dwyer's trial began on July 7, 1926. The sweltering courtroom was packed with hard guys and reporters, as Emory Buckner's prosecutors laid out their case. They argued that the Combine had imported $40 million worth of liquor between October 1923 and June 1926, under the paid protection of the Coast Guard and the NYPD. Their evidence was detailed and damning and their elaborate descriptions of the Combine's modern methods and bureaucratic structure made the term *organized crime* a byword in the press. "You know," Dwyer told Buckner as they waited for the jury to return, "while you were speaking I thought to myself, I really *should* be convicted."

On July 27, Dwyer was found guilty of one count of "conspiracy to violate the National Prohibition law," a relatively minor charge, but the judge angrily sentenced him to the maximum punishment of two years in prison.

"Somehow the magic of Bill Dwyer's name evaporated," observed the *Brooklyn Eagle* with genuine puzzlement. The contrast with the fates of Waxey Gordon and Frank Costello was stark. Waxey's witnesses were summarily executed, destroying the prosecution's case. Frank Costello's trial was hardly mentioned in the press and ended in a hung jury amid rumors that one of the jurors had been bought. The mob banked the lessons: Keep a low profile. Put a buffer between the top man and the dirty work. Fix the jury. Kill the witnesses.

☾

Having her prime patron and protector out of action had palpable consequences for Polly. Late one night that summer, she picked up the phone to find Lou Clayton on the line. Clayton had recently offended the local ladies of the evening when he was arrested for "using caveman tactics," in *Variety*'s delicate phrase, on a tipsy prostitute named Agnes Cunningham (a "two-dollar whore," in her sister's intemperate phrase, earning her a smack in the eye from Agnes) who'd had the temerity to call him a "Jew bastard" to his face. (Luckily, Clayton noted, three judges and an assistant district attorney happened to be in the club that evening, who could serve as his character witnesses.)

All the same, Polly was delighted to hear Lou say that he was bringing up seven or eight VIPs from the Dover Club. Business was slow that evening, so the girls were thrilled at the prospect of a free-spending party of big shots.

But when she opened the door, her heart dropped. There stood Clayton, accompanied by a blue-ribbon panel of the town's toughest gunmen and gamblers, including George McManus, Mike Best, and Eddie Diamond, Legs's less renowned brother. They were all high, none more than McManus. When McManus was sober, he had his charms—

nobody enjoyed throwing big bills around more than Smiling George—but under the influence, he could be dangerously unpredictable.

"Hello, George, it's nice to see you again," she chirped nervously, as he pushed his way into the apartment.

"Who the hell are you?" he snarled, staring glassy-eyed at her from under his low-slung fedora. "I never saw you before in my life."

"Quit your kidding," she replied with false cheer. "I'm Polly."

"Oh, you're Polly are you?" He jerked out his gun and waved it at her. "If you're Polly, prove it. Go look out the window."

Polly froze instinctively. If she did, she'd have her back turned to him—not a smart move. Suddenly he laughed. "Okay, okay. I was just gonna give you a little scare."

"Georgie, remember when I first started running a house, you used to check your gun with me? How about letting me take care of it now?"

He paused, then thrust the pistol at her and turned to join his friends. Polly shoved the gun into the bathroom hamper, then scurried back to the living room just in time to hear one of them, an Irish bruiser from Hell's Kitchen named Chick Mace, asking one of the girls, "Why do you work for this Jew bastard?"

"Because I like her and she's fair to us," the girl responded.

Chick did not care for this answer. In a flash he whipped off his belt and began lashing her with the buckled end. Polly dashed across the room and grabbed Chick's arm. He tossed her off as if she were a rag doll, but she bounced up and tried again to pull him away. This time he slammed her into the wall with such force that he knocked her senseless. Then he turned his belt back on the sobbing girl. "I ran around the room begging everyone to make him stop," Polly remembered, "but they laughed at me."

"Leave her alone!" Polly shrieked at Chick. "She hasn't done anything to you! I'm the one that's wrong. I deserve the beating for letting you bums up here!"

"That's okay with me," he barked. "Since you deserve it, you'll get it." Now the belt crashed down on her back, ripping through her dress and cutting into the flesh.

Clayton, who had been watching wide-eyed, finally began shouting, "What's the matter with you guys? Have you all turned sadists?"

Two of the gorillas began heading his way, pulling off their own belts as they went. Clayton scampered out the front door. Suddenly a shot rang out, shattering the French doors leading to the bedroom where Mike Best was getting laid. The boys crowded into the room to see if he had been hit. "Jeez, Mike," one of them yelped. "I'm sorry. You okay?" (To hell with Mike's girl, Polly noted bitterly. "She didn't matter, dead or alive.")

Amid the chaos, Polly hustled the girls out of the apartment in various states of dress, sending them to a friend's apartment across the street to hide out until she sent word. But the fun wasn't over yet. With no women in sight, McManus barked at Polly to call up a twist he'd screwed at her place sometime back. She was no longer on her call list, Polly explained, since she'd gone to Hollywood and made it big.

"Then get others," he growled, shoving her. "Get lots of them."

"I can't—not at this time of night."

"Okay then, Polly," he sneered, "we'll all sleep with you" (surely a euphemism).

"Over my dead body," she replied defiantly.

"Okay," said one of them, "if that's the way you want it, that's easy." He seized her by the throat, guffawing as she thrashed around, trying to pry his hands from her windpipe. Finally he loosened his grip and she slumped to the floor.

"She's not dead yet," cried one of them as Polly gasped for breath.

"You dirty, yellow rats," she rasped, "you wouldn't have done this to me before, when I was a green kid, because you'd have been scared I'd call the cops. But you can do it now because you know I won't squeal on you. You know what you are, you dirty sons of bitches?"

A fist crashed into the side of her head. Down she went for the last time. With no more fun to be had here, the boys rummaged through the apartment, pocketing $750 from Polly's stash. As they were heading out, one gagster unscrewed a lightbulb and tossed it onto the sidewalk, where it exploded like a pistol shot. "Apparently this killed them, for they exited laughing merrily," she noted dryly.

Polly was laid up for a while, bruised and swollen, her back raw from the whipping. Several of her friends lit into Lou Clayton for bringing McManus there in that state. Feebly, Lou explained that he had seen the boys were feeling temperamental and hadn't wanted them shooting up the Dover Club.

Sobered up, the murderous bums were not without remorse. They returned all the money by messenger, and whenever any of them ran into her, "they would practically break their necks to avoid meeting my eye." Finally, one night when he could avoid her no longer, George McManus apologized and offered the mobsters' olive branch: a hefty wad of cash. "It gave me some satisfaction to tell him what he could do with it," Polly wrote later. "But what made me feel sicker than anything was the knowledge that there was no way in which I could retaliate."

After the ruckus with Clayton and McManus, Polly decided to take a break from 201 West 54th and moved her main operations to a luxe penthouse at West 58th and Sixth Avenue, a block from Central Park. It was cold comfort.

❧

Polly should have been satisfied. She was now, as one columnist described her, one of "the authentic Big Shots" of Manhattan. Between her investments and savings, she had more than enough money to retire. She was in love with a man who loved her in return. But no matter how high-hat her clientele, no matter how impressive her bank books, it wasn't enough to buy her respect, even from murderers, thieves, and dope peddlers.

At the end of the summer, Bernie Foyer booked Jimmy Carr's orchestra into a high-profile gig at the Castillian Royal, a mob-backed roadhouse in the Bronx, popular with Broadwayites looking for a bucolic outing with all the amenities of Times Square. On September 1 the Castillian Royal threw a rollicking party to celebrate the fall season. All the regular rounders were there. Texas Guinan and her chorus cuties drove up and stopped the show with their new black bottom dance routine. At the climax of the evening, Jimmy played an impromptu wedding march in honor of two newlyweds in the audience, a vaudeville dancer and a songwriter. Everyone in the house hopped up to dance behind the couple, conga-style. Sime Silverman gave Jimmy's act an ecstatic review, heralding great things for the bandleader.

As Jimmy's reputation rose, his romance with Polly had become the source of much unflattering chatter. Not-so-innocent bystanders might be excused for presuming that her flashily dressed, hophead, jazz hound boyfriend was a gigolo or a pimp. Polly was proud of her flossy beau, and besides, gossip was the lifeblood of the Big Street, no shame in that. But she had no idea how much needling Jimmy was getting or how crude the jokes were, until Jimmy's agent decided to inform her.

Bernie Foyer had been on the lam much of the summer dodging grand larceny charges, but now that he was back on the scene, he didn't like what he was hearing about his meal ticket. Jimmy didn't seem to care, however, so Bernie laid into Polly. "Night after night when he was on the bandstand some wise guy with a snootful would dance by and call out, 'Not bad, [Jimmy], ol' boy, not bad!'" Bernie told her accusingly. "'You're dragging down heavy jack waving a stick here, and now we're on our way to your whorehouse to spend some more.'" Even Walter Winchell took a swipe, asking Jimmy bluntly why he was going around with a "broken down old whore and an ugly one at that" when he could have some of the most beautiful dames on Broadway?

"If he lost his temper and started a fight it would hurt us both and accomplish nothing," figured Polly. So Jimmy just took it. "But he never said a word about it to me."

Polly swore that Jimmy never accepted money from her. "If he needed quick cash," she said, "he would borrow it from Arnold Rothstein or some other Broadway usurer." But the idea that people thought he was her pimp steamed her beyond reason. When she confronted him about it, he angrily fired Bernie as his manager, but that didn't stem the snide comments. Jimmy may have fired his agent, *Billboard* reported with a wink, but rumor had it that he "has discovered a place where money grows and will use a wad of it soon to open a nightclub in the theatrical district."

At the end of September, the roadhouses closed for the season, and Jimmy's band returned to Manhattan. Early one morning at the Dover Club, he and Polly were once again hashing out the subject of their relationship, when Lou Clayton and Jimmy Durante signaled their band to strike up a wedding march. As the customers peered around looking for the newlyweds, a waiter strode over to Polly and Jimmy with a big wedding cake and set it down on their table with a flourish. Good-naturedly going along with the gag, they waved and bowed and then led the customers in a grand wedding march around the club. Generous Jimmy bought champagne for the house, and everybody cheered and toasted the "happy couple."

After the audience settled back to their tables, Jimmy turned and asked, "How about it, Polly? Shall we get married?"

"Oh, sure," replied Polly caustically.

"No, I mean it," Jimmy said earnestly. There was a justice of the peace in Connecticut who regularly married impulsive Broadway couples. "We could drive up to Greenwich this morning. What do you say?"

"Stop talking like a fool," she snapped. "You can't marry a madam. Think what people would say."

"To hell with people!"

"You know what they're saying now. How would you like hearing remarks about your wife, Madam [Carr], and her whorehouse?"

"Then get out of the business."

"That wouldn't stop the cracks. Even if I got rid of the house, you'd still be labeled as the pimp orchestra leader who married a madam for her money. So, don't let's have any more of this silly talk. You've got to think of your future."

"To hell with my future!"

Suddenly Polly was engulfed with anger. "To hell with this! To hell with that! That's been your attitude as long as I've known you. Even if I weren't a madam I'd think twice before marrying you. What future would there be for me, married to a guy who doesn't give a damn about anything but kicking the gong around and having enough liquor to carry him from payday to payday?"

The argument continued until the waiters finally swept them out at daybreak. On the sidewalk, people eddied around them, rushing off to the day's work. Jimmy pulled Polly into a final embrace. "I love you," he said, "but I guess that's not enough for you."

Then he let go and walked off into the sunlight.

"So far, our romance had followed the classic Hollywood pattern of boy-meets-girl, boy-loses-girl," remembered Polly sadly. "The difference was that I stayed lost." Perhaps, in Groucho Marx's famous phrase, it was a case of not wanting to belong to any club that would have her as a member. Or maybe she was just being realistic.

By the beginning of November, Jimmy had reunited with Bernie Foyer. Bernie got what he undoubtedly wanted, a meal ticket unfettered by the stench of the whorehouse or, worse, a strong-minded wife. Polly heard from well-meaning friends that Jimmy was running around with one woman after another. "I missed him terribly and many times it took all my will power to keep from calling him," she remembered sadly.

Several weeks after their final parting, Jack Robbins's big Hollywood experiment hit the jackpot when the film *What Price Glory?* became a box office sensation, making his song "Charmaine" a huge hit. A sweet and schmaltzy waltz, it was an incongruous choice for the famously profane story of two American soldiers on the Western Front, competing for the affection of Charmaine, a French harlot, before heading into battle.

Each time Polly heard its final, yearning verse felt like a knife in her heart:

I wonder if I keep on praying,
Will our dreams be the same?
I wonder if you ever think of me too?
I'm waiting, my Charmaine, for you.

At night when Jimmy's orchestra was scheduled to broadcast from the Moulin Rouge, she'd leave the girls to fend for themselves and shut herself up in her bedroom to listen where no one could see her. When the band swung into the familiar strains of "Charmaine," said Polly, "I'd bawl like a lovesick schoolgirl."

Polly standing proudly with her Buick Master Six coupe, July 1927

9

The Underworld Complex

After seven years of Prohibition, "the restlessness of New York in 1927 approached hysteria. The parties were bigger," remembered F. Scott Fitzgerald; "the pace was faster—the catering to dissipation set an example to Paris; the shows were broader, the buildings were higher, the morals were looser and the liquor was cheaper."

Many old-timers reckoned New Year's Eve 1927 as the wildest and wettest in memory. As a courtesy to his fellow revelers, Mayor Walker suspended the new municipal curfew requiring all licensed entertainment venues to close at three a.m. ("I can stay out after midnight and do," Walker explained virtuously, "but there are some people who don't know the time when an entertainment ceases and orgy begins.")

On New Year's Day, while Broadway nursed its hangover, Alfred E. Smith was sworn in for his fourth term as governor of New York. A Tammany man ruled the city and the state and, if Al Smith had his way, would soon occupy the White House. But underneath the veneer of unity, tensions were growing between Governor Smith and Mayor Walker.

Anxious to avoid even a whiff of scandal, Smith was determined to clean up the worst of New York's excesses before he made his second bid for the Democratic presidential nomination. Meanwhile Jimmy Walker, emboldened by his extraordinary popularity with the voters, blithely thumbed his nose at the critics and naysayers.

It was clear that the "Jazz Mayor," as the newspapers dubbed him, possessed the vices as well as the virtues of the Great White Way. "He was glib, vain, prodigal, luxury-loving, and amazingly indifferent to the rules of common honesty," wrote the crime reporter Milton MacKaye. "He played all night and slept half the day, he drank too much and steamed out at health resorts, he praised his Church and ignored its commandments, he bought diamond bracelets at fifteen thousand dollars a crack and would not pay his bills. Yet the city loved him."

New Yorkers thrilled to his quick-witted wisecracks and joie de vivre. Reporters loved him for his colorful quotes and utter indifference to the demands of the double standard, and they protected him, never mentioning his nocturnal adventures, his showgirl companions, or his lackadaisical approach to governing.

But some folks were paying attention. Within months of Walker's inauguration, the Roman Catholic archbishop of New York, Patrick Joseph Cardinal Hayes, was so alarmed by the mayor's behavior that he tried to discipline his high-profile parishioner, sending him a stern message that he was bringing shame on his wife and the church. Walker sent a scorching reply through the archbishop's emissary: "You go back and tell the Cardinal to take care of his two altar boys and I'll take care of myself."

The biggest flashpoint between Governor Smith and Mayor Walker was, as ever, the police department. Smith won the first round of that battle, putting in his pick for police commissioner, the squeaky-clean George McLaughlin. But Commissioner McLaughlin proved himself a tad too upright for Tammany's taste. In March 1927 he made the fatal mistake of raiding the political clubhouse of a powerful Brooklyn alderman, then compounded the insult by charging him with the crime of bookmaking.

"Some folk declared that if I were elected Mayor, this would be a wide open town," Mayor Walker joked that March. "Today not a few of you think the lid has been shut down too tight." Well, that was about to change.

Two weeks after the Brooklyn raid, Commissioner McLaughlin was out. One week later he was joined in retirement by his fellow killjoy, U.S. attorney Emory Buckner. Buckner turned the office over to Charles H. Tuttle, who immediately announced that he had no intention of playing the moral reformer.

The mayor won the next round, installing as police commissioner Joseph A. Warren, a mild-mannered—some would say weak-willed—attorney who also happened to be Jimmy's childhood friend and one-time law associate. Commissioner Warren immediately put an end to the gambling and nightclub raids, brought back the old vice squads, and reinstated every rascal McLaughlin had demoted. The town was officially wide open for business.

℄

The new three a.m. curfew wasn't especially effective in settling down the late-night sinners, but it was a boon for unlicensed hideaways like Polly's. Feeling flush and eager to class up her clientele, she opened a new home base on the Upper East Side. Nightlife was blossoming east of Fifth Avenue, driven there in part by a rash of robberies and jewel thefts around Times Square. On top of that, a recent wave of stickups by coked-up gunmen on West 54th was making her neighborhood a little too hot for her liking.

The Hoffman Arms, at 640 Madison Avenue and East 59th Street, had a slightly seedy reputation, but it was perfectly located for Polly's purposes. To the north was upper Park Avenue, home to more millionaires than anywhere on earth. A forest of skyscrapers bristling with law firms, advertising agencies, corporate headquarters, banks, and brokerages rose just to the south. Luxury hotels and upper-bracket men's clubs dotted the blocks all around. It was especially convenient to Reuben's all-night delicatessen, where the tables were always jammed at four a.m. with rowdy college kids, drunken nightclubbers, and hustlers scanning the crowd for one last trick or chatting with their pimps over corned beef sandwiches. (The predawn scene at Reuben's would inspire Cole Porter's scandalous 1930 ballad, "Love for Sale.")

The building's only disadvantage was its paper-thin walls and old wooden floors that creaked with every step. Polly wasn't the only madam to do business there, but to avoid trouble, she laid down extra-thick carpeting and wrapped the ringer of the phone in cotton to muffle the sound.

The debut of her new quarters was timed to coincide with a major fight at Madison Square Garden, always a lucrative night for her girls. The day of the bout, the cook, maids, and girls readied themselves, then gathered around the radio to listen to the fight and await the tide of high rollers. Hour after hour they sat, long after the fight ended, yet not once did the phone ring. Around five in the morning, they finally gave up hope and went to bed.

The next afternoon she ran into a friend at Reuben's. "Polly, where in hell were you last night?" he growled. "Waxey Gordon made a killing at the fights and was all set to throw a champagne party at your place. We tried to get you a dozen times but couldn't raise a soul. You missed out on a thousand or more."

Polly was even more chagrined when she discovered that most of her fellow tenants were offices that emptied after work hours, so her worries were for nothing. "So we took the cotton out of the telephone and let it ring its fool head off," she remembered, "which, to my relief, it did with hardly a letup."

But her most important improvement was hiring a new maid— "Polly's famous maid," as one friend described her—an African American woman who was known by the splashy nickname "Showboat." Keen-witted, with a commanding presence, Showboat soon became, in Polly's words, "my champion and protector, my confidante and my comforter, and, in my absence, a trustworthy assistant manager." She was also an excellent press agent. "Oh, you'll like my little madam! You'll be right at home with her," she would assure new visitors.

Showboat was especially fond of Bob Benchley, Polly remembered: "She would not let any of the other maids serve him." Bench felt the same way about her. "The Waldorf just isn't in it with you when it comes to service, Polly," Benchley liked to say after an overnight visit. Showboat "never fails to have my suit pressed and my shirt and socks and drawers laundered. What a valet! By golly, she even has a light hand with a razor. And then that terrific smile at breakfast—why, it lights up a room like the sun!"

☾

"I still had a thing or two to learn about my new aristocratic clientele," Polly remembered with a chuckle—"for one thing to know them when I saw them."

Late one night not long after she'd moved to the East Side, she opened her door to find two young men clad in top hats and tailcoats who introduced themselves nervously. She'd heard their names before, but only in the society columns of Cholly Knickerbocker—hardly her typical customer. Guessing this was either a practical joke or undercover cops, she shooed the girls out the back way and then let them in.

"What can I do for you, gentlemen?" she asked, with nerves tingling.

They laughed self-consciously as they peered into the empty apartment and explained that Jim Moriarty, the owner of the Marlborough House, a deluxe speakeasy just up the block, had told them they'd find some girls here. "Aren't you Polly Adler?" they asked uncertainly.

"I'm Miss Pearl Davis," she replied firmly. "I must ask you to leave." The disappointed boys wandered out, while she congratulated herself for listening to her sixth sense.

She decided to check up on their story and stopped in at the Marlborough House, in a once-grand mansion at 109 East 61st Street. "I'd been told that you had to be in Who's Who to get in," said Polly, so she was appropriately awed when she was ushered into a beautifully furnished private office to meet the owner. Jim Moriarty was a distinguished-looking Irishman with graying red hair, whose family had been in the saloon business long before the Great Thirst. The two hit it off instantly, and after some chitchat, Polly mentioned the young phonies who had thrown around his name.

They were no phonies, he responded with amusement. Those boys were bona fide blue bloods.

"Give me a gun, let me shoot myself! How could I be such a schnook!" Polly exclaimed. "Just think—me, Polly Adler—giving bum's rush to the Blue Book. I'll never live it down!"

The East Side was swarming with young college boys, the avuncular barkeep explained. The Marlborough House catered to the collegians with the approval of their parents, who knew his establishment was strictly upper class. He'd heard of her clean reputation and was hoping he could send her some of his more callow customers.

Happy to help, she gave Moriarty a special code to use when contacting her, and she soon became a regular stop on the Ivy League whoopee trail. To keep from reprising her mistake, she added the black-bound volumes of the Social Register, the annual listing of America's upper caste, to her growing collection of books.

But even the authentic blue bloods weren't all they were cracked up to be. The Park Avenuers were shockingly cheap by Broadway standards and often demanded a discount for bringing along their high-toned friends. It must have come as a surprise to find herself stiffed by Roger Wolfe Kahn, the fabulously rich teenage son of Otto Kahn, one of the city's leading financiers and cultural patrons. Roger Kahn sank $250,000 of his father's money into opening a posh nightclub that lasted only six months and had recently returned from Europe with fifty new bespoke suits, but all she got was a rubber check.

Many proprietors didn't care for the patronage of the college set. They had a rambunctious reputation, especially in whorehouses. "The only time I found them a little unruly was during football season," recalled Polly affectionately. "I grew very fond of these boys, who nicknamed me 'Polly-Pal.'" Along with cocktails and condoms, she dispensed the sort of intimate advice and basic medical knowledge they'd never find at home or school.

For all the talk of a sexual revolution, she discovered that many fathers still presumed their sons would lose their virginity to a professional. One of her customers told his two Yale-bound sons explicitly: "Now don't get yourselves mixed up with any floozies! Not that I want to keep you from having fun, but play it safe—go to Polly's.

"Don't worry about the expense," he insisted. "Just charge it to me."

The next time the boys brought along a half dozen of their classmates, putting it all on their father's tab.

"Chips off the old block," chuckled their old man when she presented the bill. "It's okay this time, Polly, but tell the boys next time they call on you that I don't intend to pay for the sex life of the whole damn Yale University!"

By her account, she kept the boys to strict rules, limiting them to two drinks apiece and forbidding what she called "off-color conversation or the practice of unnatural sex by any of my girls." But at least one inmate who worked in the house during her Café Society years mocked the prim picture she painted. "Polly may have steered the scions of the elite from the dangers of 'perverse' love—as she says—but she'd have to do it all over again to prove it to me," the woman told a reporter for *Suppressed* magazine.

"John X, a 'veddy' prominent boy in the Yale-Harvard-Princeton set, was one of my young customers. For a fresh kid, he was mighty fresh.

Also, his demands on a girl's time and effort were fantastic. Apparently, he'd spent all his time boning up on Krafft-Ebbing. He was a real case history if ever I saw one.

"I have never met the senior member of the clan," she added. "I hope he is not quite as degenerate as his son."

☾

"I was now in a position to eliminate many undesirables, and more and more restricted my clientele to the upper brackets of the social, financial, literary and theatrical worlds," recalled Polly. Her friends in the Algonquin set had become the darlings of the adventurous Park Avenue crowd who were eager to escape the stuffy gentility of their own class for the after-dark thrills they read about in *The New Yorker, Vanity Fair,* and the daily papers. The "underworld complex," Damon Runyon dubbed it, with a tip of his hat to Sigmund Freud. They brought their posh friends to Polly's, vastly expanding her roster of deep-pocketed johns.

It was, almost certainly, through Bob Benchley and Don Stewart that Polly snagged the crème de la crème of high society. When she met John Hay "Jock" Whitney, he was a freshly minted Yale graduate who had recently inherited $20 million from his father, a mere pittance compared to the fortune he would receive on his mother's death. Despite his mind-boggling wealth and *Mayflower* ancestry, "Jock was an unsnobbish person," Stewart explained, who had little use for the stuffed shirts of his own class. Along with his cousins Sonny Whitney, Cornelius Vanderbilt Whitney, and Alfred G. Vanderbilt, Jock led the life of a bohemian aristocrat and celebrity playboy. Although fifteen years younger than Benchley, he and Bob became best friends and constant companions in their nocturnal prowls. Polly's parlor became a favorite oasis for Jock, and she came to consider him a genuine friend.

By now the preferred hangouts of the Round Tablers had shifted from the Algonquin Hotel to the intimate basement *boîtes* tucked into the aging brownstones of West 49th Street (later demolished to make way for Rockefeller Center). Their preferred watering hole was Tony's, a smoke-choked basement with little to distinguish it from the city's fifty-five other Italian-run red sauce joints called Tony's. The Committee of Fourteen investigator described it as an "ordinary speak patronized largely by theatrical people and some prostitutes." The proprietor, Papa

Tony, as Polly called him, had an abiding fondness for theater people and literary types. His popularity could be chalked up to the fact that "Tony had the biggest cuff in New York," letting favored customers run long tabs between jobs. Or it could be, as one regular remembered, that he dealt not only in liquor but in cocaine and heroin for trusted friends.

When they were feeling more flush—or when someone else was picking up the tab—they'd head across the street to the higher-toned Puncheon Club, which after a change of address and title became known to history as the "21" Club. It was owned by the genial cousins Jack Kriendler and Charlie Berns, who, like Tony Soma, Jim Moriarty, and Polly, fancied the idea of hosting an underground salon for artists and intellectuals. Women were allowed inside only if escorted by an approved gentleman, which was a boon to Polly's business. "'21' and Polly had enjoyed an informal business relationship," explained the club's greeter, Jerry Berns. "She bought her whiskey from us, and if one of our patrons was seeking temporary companionship we gave him Polly's phone number."

With the cheap exchange rate fueling a new vogue for European vacations, travelers were returning with tales of the fleshpots of Paris, where they could see live sex shows, all-nude revues, lesbian orgies, and cross-dressing streetwalkers, or visit the many *maisons de tolerance*. For those eager to recreate these thrills at home, Polly's house became a place where the fashionable, the wealthy, the criminal, and the bohemian mingled in lavish style.

She offered pleasure untrammeled by the demands of respectability or by bourgeois notions of good taste, where one could cross social barriers without losing caste. For the slummers of the top-hat-and-ermine crowd, patronizing Polly's was titillating proof of their own democratic instincts, their superiority to middle-class morality, and their liberation from inhibition.

For newcomers to Gotham's bacchanalia, an introduction from Polly provided access to the closed-door clubs and clandestine hideaways where they could find narcotics and the companionship of men and women of all races and sexual proclivities. For white curiosity-seekers, Polly's served as a gateway to the mysteries of Harlem. Under Tammany chieftain Jimmy Hines, the neighborhood now rivaled Times Square as a playground for the city's scoundrels and displaced Greenwich Village as a center of sexual experimentation. It was "anything goes" above West 110th Street as long as Hines got his cut: rapacious landlords, bootleggers, extortion, drug dealing, brothels for every taste, and entertainment that ranged from the debauched to the divine.

As the district grew rougher, the Jewish and Irish residents decamped to the burgeoning suburbs of Queens and the Bronx. In their place came African Americans fleeing the Jim Crow South and immigrants from the Caribbean who, like so many newcomers to the city, were too poor to have much choice in the matter. By 1925 Harlem was being hailed as the "Mecca of the New Negro" and was attracting "the most enterprising, ambitious and adventurous of the race," as *The New York Times* put it. It didn't matter to Jimmy Hines—Irish, Jewish, Italian, Black, or Puerto Rican, he welcomed them all as long as they voted a straight Tammany ticket.

Hines gave an even warmer welcome to the racket boys, to the dismay of the locals. By 1926, a score of white-owned cabarets and jazz joints had opened north of 125th Street, many of them with ties to the Broadway mob—and to Polly. The most expensive and renowned were Owney Madden's Cotton Club, where Duke Ellington's orchestra was now the house band, and Connie's Inn, run by her rascally old associates the Immerman brothers, both showcasing top Black entertainers for white sophisticates and slummers.

Polly's customers were among the first to discover the nocturnal delights of "the Great Black Way," led, as usual by Bob Benchley, a self-avowed "Negrophile." Benchley's crowd favored the "black-and-tans" that catered to both Black and white customers, like Small's Paradise, an all-night cabaret famous for its singing waiters and Sunday-morning breakfast dances; and the Nest on West 133rd, where some of the best jazz musicians in the country gathered for late-night jam sessions. The Nest was especially popular with cops. "There wasn't a night in the week when you didn't see one of the officers from the 135th Street Police station there, eating dinner, having a few drinks, and picking up some cash if he needed it," remembered pianist Luis Russell.

Polly's plush patrons would often rent a car for the evening to make the rounds of the hotspots. To keep the party going after the splashy resorts closed at three a.m., they'd head to the smaller hideaways where entertainment included drag performers, ribald singers, and lithesome hostesses who used their nether regions to scoop up their tips. Or they'd stop in at an impromptu rent party, where jazz musicians jammed and sold bathtub gin to make rent. Or they'd put in a call to Money, "a small, thin hunchback with an extremely agreeable face," who was a popular guide to the hidden corners of Harlem.

"Money really cleaned up steering white customers on what they called 'slumming tours,' which usually ended up at a dive run by a girl called Sewing Machine Bertha," remembered Polly. "There they would be shown lewd pictures as a preview to the performance of the same tableaux by live actors, white and colored. Money also supplied reefers and cocaine and morphine so that the 'upper clawsses' could have themselves a real low-down time."

To her surprise, women also began turning up as guests. "At first it was only those who were so rich or so famous or so intellectual or so uninhibited they could go anywhere," recalled Polly. They were actresses, writers, and bohemians of the Broadway variety, like Dorothy Parker and the bold young women of the *New Yorker* staff, who had spent enough time among barroom hustlers to no longer be shocked by the idea of sex for hire—and who would've been embarrassed to admit it if they were. Some of them were lesbians, drawn to the freedom of Manhattan, who found Polly's house a rare oasis where conventional sexual prejudices didn't apply and they could relax and be themselves— and where they might, as often as not, find fellow lesbians among the inmates of the house.

Even square women were coming to the city with expectations that would have been unthinkable even five years before. Percy Elkes, the seasoned proprietor of the Deauville Club, was shocked by the society girls who now frequented his joint. "They come in here with nothin' on, hardly, their wool cut short, their dresses up to—," Elkes fussed to a reporter from *Variety*. "They act like they're hustlin' for Polly Adler."

"This kid that just left—"

"Jail-bait?"

"No. A year over. She'd be willing to give you the works right here."

Never one to let the competition get the best of her, Polly began loading her call list with well-bred but less well-heeled girls, who couldn't afford the nightlife they craved, or who wanted to pick up the price of a fur coat or simply pay the rent.

In his later days as a saloon keeper, Jack Dempsey repeated a story he'd heard about the time a young Katharine Hepburn visited Polly's house in the company of Dorothy Parker, Bob Benchley, and the poet H. Phelps Putnam. It was the summer of 1928, and the twenty-one-year-old redhead was struggling to break onto the Broadway stage. Hepburn was shocked when Benchley suggested they head to "Pawly's" for a nightcap. Ensconced in Polly's parlor with an orange blossom, she started to relax, but she became dismayed as first Benchley, then Putnam, disappeared in the direction of the bedrooms, and finally Parker excused herself to watch "an exhibition."

When it was just the two of them in the parlor, as Dempsey told it, Polly seized the opportunity to make her standard pitch to the aspiring ingenue. "Dorothy tells me you want to be an actress. That's fine but it's a hard life," said Polly sympathetically. "There will be many times when you are hungry and broke and walking the streets wondering where your next meal is coming from. Don't worry. Just come to Polly's. I can always use a gal like you, although you're a special type. Would you consider wearing a nurse's uniform?"

☾

Yet when it came to public appearances, Polly was scrupulous about making sure that her own notoriety would not compromise another woman's reputation or expose her secrets. A young jazz singer named Fran Warren, who'd met Polly through mutual friends, remembered catching sight of the diminutive madam on Fifth Avenue one afternoon. "I called out to her, and she immediately ran in the other direction. Later that evening she called me at my hotel and said, 'Don't you ever acknowledge me in public.' She said if somebody spotted me talking to her, it might ruin my career."

Polly never named publicly any of the legitimate women who passed through her call house. Certain actresses were dogged for years by rumors that they had turned tricks in New York while waiting for their lucky break, including Joan Crawford, Lucille Ball, and Jeanette Mac-Donald, to name only a few. Polly never responded to that sort of ugly gossipmongering. But her cousins, who knew very little about her professional life, remembered Polly bringing the sweet-faced dancer Ruby Keeler and the brassy comedienne Martha Raye out to Brooklyn for supper, referring to them as "her girls." ("Such pretty friends Pearl has!" was the refrain.) And privately, Polly told trustworthy friends that the well-known performers Dorothy Lamour and Libby Holman had gone on dates for her.

Libby Holman was one of the earliest of her upscale recruits, a curvy, olive-skinned brunette with long legs and bee-stung lips. She radiated a "rotten ripe" sexiness, as one friend put it, with wide gray eyes that gave her an enigmatic air that was "so appealing to susceptible masculinity," as Fred Pasley wrote in the *Daily News*.

She was the daughter of a lawyer, who'd graduated from college in Ohio and had come to the Big Apple in the fall of 1924 with the ambition of furthering her education. She enrolled at Columbia University (some sources said the law school, others said the journalism school) and found a place to stay in an all-female dormitory at a branch of the YWCA, with a strict eleven p.m. curfew.

Libby came to Polly's sometime that winter, when her savings had dwindled to nothing and she needed eating money. When she explained that she was a student at Columbia, Polly arranged for her to take an after-school shift, remaining on call until her curfew. "Every afternoon she would arrive after her classes, carrying her schoolbooks, wearing the short skirts, oxfords and beret that were the thing among coeds, and settle down to work," remembered Polly. Libby "was pleasant, smiling, and matter-of-fact about her method of earning a living, and no matter what amount of money was offered her after her deadline of eleven o'clock, her answer was always 'No.'"

As a femme fatale type who could talk about books and hold her liquor, Libby was taken up by Polly's friends from *The New Yorker*, and she was a favorite of the young Princeton crowd. "She was the delight of my patrons for some time, especially one literary gentleman of whom I was very fond. He never failed to ask about her, always with a slow grin spreading across his big good-natured face, until at last he had to shake his head and laugh out loud."

"How's the schoolgirl?" he'd ask.

It didn't take long for Libby to abandon both the YWCA and formal education and instead set her sights on the stage. That year the sultry-voiced siren was finally catching the attention of the Rialto as a torch singer or, as Walter Winchell dubbed her, "a swelegant syncopator." The new curfew and the proliferation of secret, after-hours speakeasies led to a vogue for "confidential singers" who wouldn't draw the noise complaints of a jazz band. These honey-toned crooners, bawdy balladeers, and moody torch singers became Tin Pan Alley's light-skinned take on African American blues singers.

Libby's breakout hit was "Moanin' Low," a hustler's ode to her pimp, in the style of her idol, Bessie Smith. But the biggest name among the swagger set that season was Helen Morgan, a tousle-haired brunette with heavily fringed eyes and ivory skin who crooned ballads of longing and betrayal while sitting atop an upright piano, swinging her shapely legs, and twisting a black silk handkerchief. Something about her quavering soprano, "half-sobbing, half-singing," as Polly put it, touched the battle-scarred souls of the twilight world.

Prostitutes enjoyed a well-earned reputation for sentimentality (song pluggers liked to test lachrymose ballads in hookshops; if the ladies of the house cried, they knew they had a hit). Polly's girls were no exception. They all adored the gay cabaret crooner Tommy Lyman, whose signature tune was "My Melancholy Baby." Whenever he sang, "the girls would seize the opportunity to shed a few tears, and often I could hardly hear the singer owing to the chorus of muffled sobs around me. But then who am I to talk? If anyone sang 'Charmaine' I'd get misty-eyed myself."

Polly became friends with Helen Morgan when she headlined the 54th Street Club, a top-dollar joint just down the block from Polly's apartment. With her tremulous voice and delicate looks, she was a natural bookend to her more raucous neighbor, Texas Guinan. "You went to Guinan's for horseplay," remembered the crime reporter Paul Sann. "You went to Morgan's for blues-in-the-night, washed down with illicit happy juice."

"Sometimes after leaving the House of Morgan, the spenders found their way up the street to the House of Polly," she remembered with satisfaction. "The comedian, Joe Frisco, always got a yak from his audiences when he commented, 'At Polly Adler's p-p-place it's the m-m-man who pays, but at Helen M-m-morgan's everybody p-p-pays!'"

☾

Finally, Polly had gained the stature and clientele she'd yearned for. But notoriety was a double-edged knife. In the fall of 1926, the Committee of

Fourteen hired a new director, an ambitious young reformer with a nose for publicity named George Worthington. Frankly, the anti-prostitution movement wasn't grabbing the limelight as it had during those heady days of the "white slavery scare" before the war. And the Committee's crusade to criminalize johns seemed to be of no interest to anyone. So Director Worthington decided to launch a high-profile campaign against the jazz palaces of Times Square and Harlem.

It didn't take long for Polly Adler to come to Worthington's attention. But between her peripatetic habits and their own naïveté, the investigators were having a hard time finding her. On May 10, 1927, one of them barged into the Kentucky Club and proceeded to quiz everyone in the joint, "if Polly Adler is interested in this place and if she is here at present," he wrote in his report. Every one of them was a fountain of ignorance, except for her old friend Leo Bernstein. "I know a woman named Polly Adler who is a notorious madam and I wouldn't allow a woman of that caliber to hang out in my premises, if that's the woman you have reference to," Bernstein replied indignantly. "Otherwise I don't know where she is located and I haven't seen her for years." If she hadn't already heard they were on her trail, word of this ham-fisted sleuthing would've reached her faster than Western Union.

The Committee lost track of Polly until December 1927, when investigators traced her to a former bouncer at Connie's Inn, a sometime pimp who helped her recruit new girls for her call list. They finally hit pay dirt when they inadvertently connected her to "Mademoiselle Fifi," who'd spent several seasons playing the Dumb Dora straight woman in Clayton, Jackson, and Durante's nightclub act, while doubling as "a hostess prostitute," a stag party "snake dancer," and a procurer who "o.k.s men to 'call houses' and stages 'circuses.'"

Fifi's reputation as a beautiful dimwit with flexible morals was no hoax. True, she did step out with men, she told the investigator, but she took exception to the idea that she was a mere prostitute, explaining virtuously that she'd recently turned down an offer "by a woman who has about six different apartments in the city where she has girls and the best clientele of men call on her. She said that there was a chance for me to make $200 a day, but I wouldn't take that chance as I had to pay at least $1,500 a month for protection alone, while the madam pays $5,000 a month protection. She is well known in the city and I'll tell you her name; maybe you know her too," Fifi concluded. "Her name is Polly Adler.

"Would you like to go up there?" asked Fifi. "I'll take you up and I am sure you will enjoy it." Be warned, however, that he should expect to spend $100 to $150 for the whole evening.

"It sounds expensive," replied the investigator dubiously, thinking no doubt of his already strained expense account. But big game requires big guns, so the following evening the tuxedo-clad investigator found himself in a cab with the pretty snake dancer, resplendent in a white satin evening dress and freshly marcelled hair, heading up to 310 West 93rd Street, between West End and Riverside Drive.

In the lobby, Fifi resumed her role of impromptu tour guide, asking the elevator attendant to let "Polly Stewart or Seward" know they were here, explaining helpfully, "You see Polly changed her name from Polly Adler to this." Polly, who would surely have throttled Mademoiselle Fifi with her own asp had she heard this, had the good fortune to be out. The investigator begged off from further adventures that evening, but the next day Director Worthington pressed him for more action, scrawling emphatic instructions: "Locate Polly Adler Positively."

The Committee of Fourteen succeeded in shutting down a dozen or so call flats over the winter, but Polly remained elusive. They connected her to a prostitute named Peggy Murray, who used Polly's apartments to turn tricks, and they tracked her to Sam Weller's all-night shoe store in Times Square, where show folk and prostitutes could pick up a new pair of pumps along with cocaine, heroin, or morphine. But still no dice. Apparently no one thought to ask her friends on the vice squad.

❦

The unwelcome attention of the Committee of Fourteen was a sign that Polly's notoriety was spreading beyond her control. This was brought home to her early in the morning of July 21, 1927, after the matchup between Jack Dempsey and Jack Sharkey in Yankee Stadium, when Walter Reade's epic bacchanal was crashed by a brace of vice cops. Still, her luck was holding; the apartment was loaded with newspapermen when the cops arrived but not one word of the raid appeared in print.

She wasn't the only one whose nerves were stretched thin that summer. On July 9, Legs Diamond was picked up on a narcotics charge. Arnold Rothstein bailed him out, as usual, and Legs avoided going to trial, but Legs was convinced that Arnold had framed him in retaliation for some unpaid debts. The long-simmering tension between the gambler and the gunsel was now boiling into a dangerous feud.

On July 16, 1927, Bill Dwyer finally exhausted his legal appeals and reluctantly departed for a two-year stretch in the federal penitentiary in Atlanta. With Dwyer gone, Frank Costello and Owney Madden assumed leadership of the Combine. Costello took over the role of political fixer, Madden was the public face of the organization, and Meyer Lansky and Bugsy Siegel served as their primary enforcers.

Dwyer's fall created a powerful temptation for ambitious upstarts looking to muscle in on the Combine's once ironclad monopolies. Waxey Gordon's gang began skirmishing with Madden and Lansky over the lucrative midtown market. The hotheaded Irish boyos, like Legs Diamond and Vannie Higgins, the bootleg boss of Bay Ridge, were furious at being usurped by Madden and Costello, taking particular umbrage at the idea of an Italian as top boss.

Meanwhile an up-and-comer emerged in the Bronx, a twenty-five-year-old German Jew named Arthur Flegenheimer, known on the street as Dutch Schultz. Since he left prison in the early 1920s, he had been kicking around with Rothstein's crowd, working as a driver for Arnold and a bodyguard for Big Bill, and pulling heist jobs with Legs and Charlie Lucky. Over the last year, he and his partner, Joe Noe, had seized control of the booze market in the Bronx, and by 1927 they were one of the Combine's biggest customers.

Like all Rothstein's most successful students, Schultz combined a knack for organizational management with a sadistic temper. "The Dutchman was an arrogant egomaniac," as Willie Sutton put it. "Utterly fearless and ruthless, he had one great fault. He refused to trust anyone at all."

By 1928, Dutch and Joe Noe were pushing into upper Manhattan, forcing speakeasies to buy their ether-spiked beer as far south as 135th Street. They were muscling in on Connie's Inn and the Immerman brothers' booze and numbers rackets, apparently with the blessing of Jimmy Hines. While Waxey wasn't pleased with Dutch's incursions into Harlem, it was Legs who objected most vociferously. He was considering Dutch's ambitions a direct challenge to his own efforts to fashion himself into the next Owney Madden.

These shifting alliances and festering grudges didn't make Polly's job easier. As it was, she had to keep a close eye on the boys if she didn't want to get clipped. "In those days I was an easy touch for any sob story," she remembered, recounting the time in April 1927 when Sidney Stajer, one of Rothstein's most trusted drug couriers—his "stooge," to use her word—asked to borrow a thousand dollars. "Sidney owed Charlie Sherman, better known as Chink Sherman, a nice guy but a toughie. Sidney must have said I know a sap that will loan me money. I remember quite well when Chink and Sidney called." Better to owe Polly than a man who'd barely evaded a murder rap several months before.

When Rothstein heard that she'd loaned Stajer that much money, he called on her with a friendly warning. "You are a kid, Polly, don't be a soft touch for the leeches on Broadway," the gambler said. "I'll pay you the 1000 you loaned Sidney, but don't loan him anymore."

"Did I listen to a smart man who was trying to teach me the ways of Broadway? Like hell I did," remembered Polly with exasperation. "Of course, Sap Polly didn't listen to Arnold. Now the three guys are dead— How in the hell will I collect?"

☾

Trustworthy or not, the easy money boys knew how to throw a grand party. In September she made a whirlwind trip to Chicago to attend what many fans considered the last great prizefight of the decade. Jack Dempsey, fresh from his comeback victory over Jack Sharkey in July, was challenging the Shakespeare-quoting heavyweight Gene Tunney to regain his championship title in Soldier Field on September 22, 1927.

Alphonse "Scarface" Capone had come up in the world since his early days as a bouncer in Frankie Yale's Coney Island saloon. Over the last few years, he'd parlayed his interest in a handful of Chicago brothels into a multimillion-dollar criminal operation. In 1926 he catapulted to national notoriety as he battled rival Irish gangs for control of the city's rackets, terrorizing his foes with a gruesome new weapon, the Thompson submachine gun. Capone's "Outfit," as it was known, was now a crucial hub in the movement of liquor among Canada, the eastern rum-running operations, and the midwestern distilleries and breweries.

New York's racketeers and their friends in the Fourth Estate congratulated themselves on their discretion compared to their western colleagues, but Capone's ambitions worried them. Big Al reveled in the limelight, and between his bloody street battles and his personal appearances in the press, he was drawing unwelcome attention to the bootlegging industry.

Like a lot of women of the night, Polly rather enjoyed "Bighearted Al," as he liked to be called; "I make a habit of judging people only in their relationship to me and such times as I happened to run into Al he was always very pleasant." Frank Costello introduced Polly to Capone early in the 1920s, and she had often entertained the Chicago boys when they were in town on business.

Increasingly, the business at hand was assassination. Or as *The New York Times* called it, the "intercity murder trade." As competition for the New York markets became more violent, the Broadway mob and its syndicate partners began importing hit men from out of town to seize the element of surprise. It was a sort of mutual exchange program for killers that evolved into the murder-for-hire outfit that the tabloids dubbed "Murder, Inc."

Polly remembered distinctly the night Lucky Luciano brought Capone's trusted hit man, "Machine Gun Jack" McGurn, and some of the boys to the house. She recalled with gratitude Lucky's restraining hand when McGurn and Bugsy Siegel, as a practical joke, decided to rearrange the furniture. They'd carried the sofa into the kitchen and were in the process of hauling the stove into the living room, "when they noticed Charlie Lucky looking at them—not saying anything, just looking. In two seconds flat the furniture was back in place and there was no more horseplay for the balance of the evening."

"I'll not forget the fight in Chicago, that was really something," Polly later wrote. Every sports fan who could hitch a ride was heading to Soldier Field for the fight, and wagering was reported to be the heaviest anyone had seen in years. "I bet a Big Five on Dempsey to win," she remembered. "I followed the smart money."

Capone, who counted himself Jack Dempsey's most ardent fan, had offered to fix the rematch in the former champ's favor. Jack graciously refused. Nonetheless, the gangland czar intended to make this the social event of the season, snapping up one hundred top-price seats and inviting every major mobster in the country to fill them. "I remember thinking in 1927 that I was more afraid of who sat at ringside than of who was waiting for me inside the ring," Dempsey confessed.

The Dempsey-Tunney rematch would go down as one of the most controversial bouts in boxing history. In round seven, Dempsey let loose a cascade of punches that sent Tunney tumbling to the mat. But instead of retreating to a neutral corner while the referee counted to ten, as the rules required, Dempsey stood there looming over his opponent, delaying the referee's count and giving Tunney several seconds to catch his breath before popping up just as the ref reached nine. When Tunney won, depriving the once-great Dempsey of his last chance to be champ, those crucial seconds—"the Long Count," it was dubbed— became a national scandal and the wellspring of a million barroom arguments.

"Funny how I remembered the Dempsey Tunney fight, perhaps it's because I got a big lump on my head attending the fight," mused Polly. "When hot shot Dempsey put Tunney to sleep on that historical long count I screamed my head off, you would think I bet a million.

"Then when Tunney kicked the hell out of Dempsey, which made him a winner, I was still screaming, this time for Tunney. Who in the hell cared who won as long as there was a winner. Suddenly I felt something on my noodle, probably a rock. The guy in back said, Hey lady, you must be Nuts—your man is Dempsey."

Well, concluded Polly, "for my money the guy was welcome to Dempsey, I knew him way back and never liked him and still don't."

The real fun came after the fight was over, in her opinion. "Al Capone ran a party for one solid week at the Metropole hotel, all the big politicians from everywhere attended the party, Judges, Mobsters, yours truly included," Polly recalled with pleasure. "Capone was a grand host." Senators, congressmen, show people, journalists, society sportsmen, and gorgeous women all downed top-shelf liquor and danced to the city's scalding-hot jazz bands. Capone himself took up the conductor's baton to direct a swinging rendition of *Rhapsody in Blue*.

Her trip ended in a triumphant reunion with her father's family, including her elusive brother Benny. To commemorate the occasion, she joined her brothers in a family portrait, with Polly looking every inch the grande dame in her diamond sparklers and fashionable fox stole.

☾

Over the years, Polly accumulated so many harrowing stories of suicide and drug addiction that they all ran together in the telling. But Mae Duffy stood out from the others. She'd been a friend of Garnet's, turned on to heroin by her ex-boyfriend, a notorious lowlife known as Tommy "the Bull" Pennochio. Three years later Mae turned up on Polly's doorstep, pale and pathetic, claiming that she was finally clean and asking for a job.

An experienced redhead was always an asset, and Polly was a sucker for self-improvement, so she said yes. But she quickly came to regret it. Mae struck up a friendship with one of her girls, a young Ziegfeld beauty—Marcia, Polly called her—who was turning tricks to support her blind mother; a rare case, Polly insisted, where that sweet claim was actually true. Nothing good could come of that friendship, she was sure.

Her uneasy feeling was confirmed when Marcia failed to show up for work one evening after the theater, and Mae, saying she was stepping out for a soda, abruptly disappeared. The duo finally turned up three nights later. "Mae was charged to the gills while Marcia looked as if she'd been at the bottle the entire time," Polly remembered.

Marcia was out, Polly decided on the spot. Her conscience couldn't abide her becoming hooked on heroin. She urged Marcia to try to get her precious *Follies* job back if she'd lost it while AWOL, then sent her off with a stern warning to stay away from the skin trade and anyone connected with it. She then turned her attention to the glassy-eyed ringleader.

"They were chasing us and chasing us," Mae exclaimed. "We tried to get away, but they chased us."

"Who chased you?"

"They did. They kept asking where you lived and we wouldn't tell. We saved you, we saved you, we saved you—"

There was a knock at the door. Polly grabbed Mae's shoulders and shook her hard. "Who chased you? Who asked you? Tell me!"

"Cops," she giggled, with an addled grin.

Suddenly half a dozen plainclothesmen tumbled into the apartment, all business for a change. This was an end-of-the-month quota raid, so they spurned her bribe; their payoff would come from the shady bail

Polly's dearest friends and favorite customers, Robert Benchley
and Wallace Beery, on the set of China Seas, 1935

Sonny Greer (far left), Duke Ellington (far right), and the Washingtonians
just before they met Polly at the Kentucky Club, 1923

Welterweight boxing champion Mickey Walker and his manager Jack "Doc" Kearns helped popularize Polly in the sporting world

Libby Holman worked for Polly in the mid-1920s before finding fame as a torch singer and Café Society playgirl

Torch singer Helen Morgan perched on a piano in the Simplon Club
just after the repeal of Prohibition, December 1933

Polly and her bandleader
boyfriend Jimmy Carr, 1926

"Showboat"—
"Polly's famous maid"—
in Coney Island, July 20, 1931

Polly with her
brothers, Irving,
Albert, and Ben,
after the Dempsey v.
Tunney heavyweight
boxing championship
in Chicago,
September 1927

Polly's pal and partner
on the vice squad
Irwin O'Leary
(courtesy of Bonnie Jean O'Leary)

Polly's nemesis on
the vice squad, the
double-crossing
plainclothesman
James J. Quinlivan,
1931

"Sting of the Law"—"We ain't got no information, yet,
but Joe's still in there, pumping the other one!"
Broadway Brevities, October 12, 1933

Hot Chocolates, a jazz revue written by Andy Razaf, Fats Waller, and Harry Brooks
and financed by Dutch Schultz, at Connie's Inn in Harlem, 1929

Judge Samuel Seabury and his chief counsel, Isidor J. Kresel,
relentlessly pursued Polly while investigating corruption in
the police department and City Hall, 1930

Police circular offering a reward for information about
the missing judge, Joseph F. Crater, 1930

Corpse of Vivian Gordon—Broadway butterfly and
blackmailer—found in the Bronx, February 26, 1931

New York City Police Department wanted poster for
Dutch Schultz on charges of federal tax evasion, 1934

bondsmen. They arrested seven girls, two maids, and Polly, took them to the station, and booked them.

After she posted bond, they returned to the apartment. As they stepped through the door, Mae burst out, "Thank God, thank God, the cops didn't find what I hid." Then she fumbled behind the bar and pulled out a white paper packet.

Polly grabbed it from her hands and ripped it open. As the telltale white powder scattered across the carpet, she became enraged. "Do you know what you could have done to me?" she roared. "I could have taken a serious rap for being in possession of narcotics! Who would have believed you brought it in? Who would have believed I didn't know it was here?"

Mae, still wearing her coat but suddenly sobered, threw herself onto the sofa, crying hysterically.

"Get out of my house," Polly shouted.

"But where will I go? Where can I go?" Sobbing, Mae fell to her knees and buried her face in Polly's skirt.

Polly was suddenly flooded with memories of Garnet, and all the old feelings of sorrow and helplessness came rushing back. "All right. You can stay, but you're taking the cure. Right here, right now."

"Make me take it," Mae cried, her voice rising. "Oh, you don't know how I hate the monkey on my back. I'll do what you say, Polly, honest to god I will."

They started then and there, embarking on what addicts called the "Cold Turkey" cure, a sudden cessation with no weaning off the drug. Polly gave her a laxative, and Mae made herself comfortable in Polly's bedroom. "Better clear the sharp things out of here," she joked weakly.

As the hours passed without her regular shot, Mae's body went into withdrawal. She became racked with cramps, diarrhea, fevers, and chills, her skin puckering and turning blue like the flesh of a plucked turkey. As the pain sharpened, she grew incoherent, sobbing and shrieking like a madwoman. When she began banging her head against the floor and walls, Polly became frightened and left to look for help.

She didn't have to go far. As usual, there was a party of cops out in the living room, hanging about, drinking, and taking their ease. Officer Irwin O'Leary offered to lend a hand. He was a couple of years older than Polly, Brooklyn born and Irish bred, with a narrow face and kind

eyes. He'd spent several years in the narcotics bureau, before transfer-
ring to the more lucrative work of shaking down speakeasies and framing prostitutes, so he knew what to expect from a desperate drug addict.

When they entered the bedroom, Mae lunged. Irwin caught her in
his arms and let her pound on him until she was spent, then gently laid
her down on the mattress and covered her with a blanket. By now the
girl was incontinent and sweating from every pore. Irwin carried her to
and from the bathroom to clean her, restrained her when she was hurt-
ing herself, and helped Polly shove cardboard between her teeth to keep
her from mashing her lips to a pulp.

By the end of the fourth day, Mae was quieter, barely moving except
to drink a little water when Irwin offered it. On the morning of the fifth
day, Polly awoke in the chair next to the bed, sunlight pouring in from
the window, to find Mae awake, looking pale and feeble but in her right
mind. "Thanks, Polly" she whispered.

"If you knew what you've just been through, you would never touch
drugs again as long as you live," Polly told her as she helped her bathe
and dress.

"I know. I'm cured. I can feel the difference. I don't know how to
thank you."

Polly reached over and placed a piece of white paper folded like a
small packet of drugs on the night table. "I believe you and I'm leaving
this beside you to prove it."

"Quit kidding me. I'm off the stuff forever." Mae smiled wanly.
"Could I have a drink of water? My throat is so dry."

"Sure." Polly stepped out then tiptoed back to peer through the crack
in the door as Mae's trembling hand crept slowly across the tabletop to
the folded paper. She charged back into the room, grabbed the paper,
and slapped her across the face.

"I was only kidding," Mae cried. "I knew all the time you were watching. I wouldn't have taken it for anything in the world!"

Polly was devastated. "I had been a fool to waste time on a junky,"
she concluded bitterly.

But out of this nightmare, Polly and Irwin forged a genuine friendship. "He was as discreet as he was kind," she remembered, a good listener in a world of fast talkers. "I can pay him no higher compliment
than to say that when we were together, I forgot he was a cop." He had

a wife and children out in Brooklyn, but he was also "a playboy and was chronically short of money," a convenient combination for her purposes.

Madams often kept a pet policeman who served as a secret informant and occasional strong arm, used to intimidate would-be blackmailers, deadbeat customers, or rival madams. Sometimes they were lovers, sometimes they were partners in crime, and quite often they were essentially exalted pimps. Some were full participants in running the house, recruiting customers and providing protection, while the madam ran the day-to-day operation—a "he-madam" in whorehouse lingo.

Polly and Irwin became something of an item, attending parties and dances together. They were close enough that her new apartment at West 69th Street and Columbus Avenue was leased under his name. She opened a bank account in Irwin's name. Then she got wise, starting a series of shared stock brokerage accounts to avoid the paper trail of a bank, which required a named depositor. With Polly's help, he was making more money than he'd ever dreamed.

☾

But Irwin O'Leary was an exception. Far more common, in Polly's experience, "were the boys who believed in playing it both ways, and who wouldn't have turned a hair if their own mother happened to be the one caught in the middle."

Under Commissioner Warren, the police were growing greedier and their demands more perverse. Fellatio, as the Committee of Fourteen noted in its annual report, was now standard practice among the city's prostitutes, and lesbianism was increasingly common as Manhattan's reputation for sexual freedom flowered. Together they created a new vogue among the jaded vice cops for "circuses"—a group of women performing oral sex on each other—and its more orderly variant, the "daisy chain." More than one beleaguered madam was asked to organize a circus for a party of cops, only to end the evening in the back of a paddy wagon as soon as the boys finished their fun.

Early in the morning of May 24, 1928, Polly got a call "from a cop whose palm I'd oiled so often it was a wonder the phone didn't slip right out of his hand." He was, almost certainly, Detective William O'Connor who, along with his partner, James J. Quinlivan, ranked among the foulest of the current crop of vice hunters.

They ran with a pack of crooked cops headquartered in Harlem, where, under the indulgent eye of Jimmy Hines, they ran roughshod over the locals. Bill O'Connor's favorite phrase was "bring them to their senses"—meaning "raid them until they pay up." But Bill played second banana to his partner, a beefy sixteen-year veteran of the force who had a reputation as one of the most volatile and violent of the plainclothesmen. Jim Quinlivan, it was said, took in $3,000 the first day he was assigned to the vice squad, and banked some $80,000 in his first year on the job, beyond whatever he blew on craps and horses. He and O'Connor collected "protection money" from some 150 speakeasies, taking in $7,500 monthly, on top of the $150 a week they picked up from various Upper West Side madams.

Detective Quinlivan also owned his own speakeasy, which he kept well supplied with booze confiscated from raids on rival establishments. A compulsive gambler, he bet heavily with George McManus and occasionally ran illegal games. The madams despised him, and he intimidated even John Weston, the weaselly special prosecutor in the Women's Court. When called to testify in court, Quinlivan and O'Connor frequently showed up roaring drunk, and they were loose-lipped loudmouths when liquored up. "I was mortally afraid of him," confessed Weston. "I was fearful that he would expose my bribe-taking."

"One of the boys at headquarters is being promoted to lieutenancy, and we want to throw a shindig at your house tonight," O'Connor told Polly over the phone. "No outsiders, understand?"

"I understand," said Polly warily.

"Jenny the Factory or Sadie the Chink would be tickled to death if we'd chosen their place, but since you got the nod we know you'll see to it everything's Park Avenue style. Nothing but the best, see? Tom is a swell guy, and he's going to be boss in the location you're operating from, so if you're smart you'll turn yourself inside out to give us boys an evening."

How many guests? Polly asked, silently "wishing to God they'd go to Jenny's or Sadie's."

"Ten of us," he replied. "See you at eight."

At eight p.m. the vipers slithered in—fifteen strong instead of ten—already plastered. "One particularly drunk and obnoxious slop yanked me over in a corner and in a portentous manner announced that his name was Johnny," she recalled. Resisting the urge to ask if he'd been named after a toilet, Polly merely said it was an easy name to remember.

"Yeah, well, you ain't going to get a chance to forget it. I've just been transferred to the Fourth Division and now it looks like I'm going to achieve my life's ambition."

"More power to you," she replied. "What is this ambition?"

"Why what do you think? To raid Polly Adler's, that's what's my ambition."

"Oh, go on, Johnny," she said with forced humor. "I'm not *that* bad. Don't you like me?"

"That's got nothin' to do with it," he sneered. "The thing is you're newspaper copy, sister. When Adler's is raided, that's headlines, see? And my boss goes for headlines, and he goes to bat for the boys that grab 'em off for him. So when I'm lookin' at you, Polly, I'm lookin' at a promotion."

Polly stood by glumly as the party descended into debauchery. Smiling through gritted teeth, she watched them smash up the knickknacks and scar the carpets with their cigarettes and cigar butts while manhandling the girls and guzzling champagne—all on her dime.

Around midnight one of the maids called her to the phone. Her cousin was on the line with shattering news: her mother and three brothers were here in New York. Their arrival couldn't have been a complete surprise, but it struck Polly like a blow when she heard her mother's voice for the first time in fifteen years. "The shock of my family's unexpected arrival made me feel dizzy and sick at my stomach and, standing there by the phone, I began to sob," she remembered.

After she calmed herself, she told the maids that she was heading to Brooklyn and asked them to take over.

"Where the hell do you think you're going?" one of the bulls barked when they saw her pulling on her hat and coat.

"Listen, boys," Polly said, "my family has just come here from Russia. I haven't seen my mother in fifteen years."

"So what?" they shouted. "You get that goddamned coat off and give us some fun!"

To defy them would only bring more raids, more complaints, and more hopscotching from apartment to apartment. And of course, it would cost a cartload of cash to soothe their wounded sensibilities.

"Just let me make one call," she said, slipping off her coat with resignation.

The party finally wound down around six a.m. Polly showered and prepared to face her mother. In the long taxi ride to Brooklyn, her excitement was shot through with dread: "I knew that from now on I would have to lie like hell to cover up."

When she got to her cousin's house, Gittel and Polly clung to each other with joyful tears. The family spent the morning recounting their journey and the news from Yanow, while Polly tried to hide her exhaustion, relieved that they didn't ask too many questions.

Her brother Szloma, age fifteen, had been only a baby when she left, and she had never met the two younger boys, Szamaj, thirteen, and Baruch, nine. After a nap, Polly led her brothers to Pitkin Avenue to buy them new clothes. "Now we look just like Americans!" they kept exclaiming.

Polly spent the next few days in Brooklyn helping them settle into an apartment, footing the bill for all of it. Gittel took her daughter's largesse in stride, she remembered wryly. "Is not America the Golden Land?"

☾

It was a miserable summer. Whenever she wasn't working, she was in Brooklyn with her family. "I began to dread these visits more and more," she wrote later. "I always had to be on my guard, had to monitor every word and thought." Instead, she lavished her family with presents and money as a way to show her feelings.

Her career, however, was flourishing. Jimmy Walker's administration had been a boon to Polly's business, with even the mayor himself beating a path to her door. She was assembling a formidable roster of political contacts. That summer her friends in Tammany Hall were busily preparing for the Democratic convention, to be held in Houston on June 26–28, 1928. This time around Al Smith was almost certain to become the party's nominee for the presidency.

On June 10, under pressure to keep the city clean until after the election, Police Commissioner Joseph Warren ordered his officers to sweep the bright light district. They picked up suspicious characters off the street and busted into underworld haunts, hustling them by the dozen into paddy wagons. Anyone without a good alibi was held for forty-eight hours for questioning. "Broadway gangsters are on their toes this week," reported *The Morning Telegraph*.

But Polly, distracted and strained by her secrets, was not. On Friday, June 15, she was spending the Sabbath with her parents when she called to check in with the maid at her Madison Avenue apartment. To her surprise, a man answered. She demanded to know who he was.

"It's the police. Is this Polly?"

"Who are you?"

"It's Johnny, that name you ain't gonna forget—remember?"

"You shouldn't give me a scare like that, Johnny, I thought you were some cop I didn't know," she responded with relief.

"Today I *am* some cop you don't know. I'm here on business. But it might so happen I could change my mind if you get here fast."

Polly quickly made up an excuse to her family, promising she'd be back in a few days, then hailed a cab and sped into Manhattan. When she arrived, she found three of her girls sitting in the living room with a couple of bulls.

"Here she is, boys," Johnny announced with a smirk. "The Queen herself. It's a good thing you didn't horse around getting here. Without you, the pinch wouldn't be glamorous."

"What a kidder you are," she said with a weak laugh.

"Who's kidding?"

Polly began to burn. "You've been sitting here for hours. You've seen no crime committed, and there have been no men around."

"So what?" Johnny shot back. "We'll pull a John Doe out of our little hats."

He walked over to the bar and poured himself a drink. "Your Highness," he said, bowing, "how would you like your ride? In a patrol wagon? Or in our car?"

She was hauled to the station house and booked under the name Polly Adler—a rare and dangerous indignity—along with the three girls. Three days later Magistrate Stanley Renaud dismissed the case for lack of evidence, after she paid a hefty bribe to her lawyer, Emmanuel Bush, which he distributed in appropriate shares to Magistrate Renaud, the arresting officers, and John Weston.

She seethed with fury at the double cross. "But I wasn't a squealer and I just had to take it."

☾

As the Democratic convention approached, the tension between Jimmy Walker and Al Smith was growing more pronounced. The governor's fears had been well founded. Flouting every rule of political life, Walker had fallen in love with a twenty-three-year-old English actress named Betty Compton—an "extremely attractive little tart" in Franklin Roosevelt's considered opinion—who convinced the mayor to leave his wife and move into a hotel. Now the mayor could be easily spotted squiring Miss Compton around town.

Governor Smith pleaded with the City Hall reporters "to give the Mayor the benefit of all doubts," and so far they had. As one newspaperman explained, only partly in jest, they "did not wish to penalize the man for his lack of hypocrisy, when all around him there were public figures who posed in piety and righteousness but cavorted behind the doors of their secret harems."

Nonetheless, Smith worried about the virulent anti-Catholic, anti-immigrant, and anti-urban prejudices that had sunk his candidacy in 1924. So to buff up his appeal to Middle America, he turned once again to Tammany's "favorite Protestant," Franklin D. Roosevelt, to give the nominating speech at the convention. Just as he had four years before, FDR wowed the audience with his extraordinary charm and eloquence, and his obvious affection for Al Smith. As hoped, Smith won the nomination over the objections of the party's Dry wing.

Now that Smith was stepping down as governor, he needed the right candidate to replace himself in Albany, to ensure a strong turnout in his home state in November. Again, Roosevelt appeared to be the ideal choice. True, he still could not walk without crutches, but he had the name recognition and reputation to pull in voters of all stripes.

Franklin had already made it clear that he wasn't interested in running for governor as long as he was unable to walk, fearing that voters would never elect a cripple. Instead, he was throwing himself into physical rehabilitation in Warm Springs, Georgia, determined to regain the use of his legs before reentering the political arena.

Undeterred, Al asked Ed Flynn, the canny boss of the Democratic Party in the Bronx and "a very personal and intimate" friend of Roosevelt, to make another heartfelt appeal. Franklin was clearly tempted by

Flynn's entreaties, but he had two objections. The first was physical: he needed to continue working on his legs if he were to have any chance of improvement. The second was financial: he'd personally sunk a lot of money into the rehab facility in Warm Springs, and he couldn't abandon the enterprise.

To address the second challenge, Flynn offered the services and pocketbook of John J. Raskob, the fabulously wealthy chairman of the Democratic National Committee, who provided the cash to recoup Roosevelt's investment in Warm Springs.

As for the first, more intractable problem, of Franklin's paralysis, Flynn suggested that Roosevelt begin working with Jack Dempsey's former trainer and Polly's loyal customer, Teddy Hayes.

Ed Flynn was introduced to Teddy Hayes by Jimmy Walker. The savvy Bronx boss could see Teddy's potential: after years as second-in-command to that wily genius Jack Kearns, he had developed the skills, connections, and temperament of a first-rate political bagman and go-between. "Teddy can get in more places than Houdini can get out of and is welcome everywhere he goes," the sportswriter Ring Lardner noted. "His chief enjoyment in life seems to come from doing things for people and the only time he gets mean is when you try to pay a check."

What Hayes did for Roosevelt is unclear. "I couldn't help FDR regain the use of his legs," Teddy said later. "No one could." But the two men struck up a warm relationship. "He liked to talk about Dempsey's big fights," Hayes remembered, "and he would press me, wanting to know if any of them were fixed." The chair-bound candidate had, in the words of journalist Frank Scully, "a hankering for the idiom of Broadway" and was always eager to hear the latest gossip from the Main Stem.

Over the years, Polly would come to count some of the most powerful men in America among her customers precisely because she kept their secrets. But near the end of her life, when her health was beginning to suffer and her mind was dwelling on the past, she made a shocking confession to her young friend Max Gershunoff: Franklin Delano Roosevelt had been one of her clients.

It is impossible to confirm Polly's claim, but it certainly wasn't unlikely. It was well known that Roosevelt loved an old-fashioned stag party, and for his birthday every year he threw a men-only bash with all the trimmings. He would go on to host many a rip-roaring smoker in the

White House. And despite his illness, Roosevelt was perfectly capable of enjoying an orgasm. The eminently respectable newspaper publisher Dorothy Schiff later recounted a conversation with Roosevelt's physician about whether "the President was still potent."

"Don't forget, only his legs are paralyzed," explained the doctor.

"How does he do it?" she asked with some naïveté.

"The French way," the doctor replied—that is, through fellatio, a specialty that was rarely practiced among women who were not prostitutes in those days.

As for moral objections, Roosevelt was known to enjoy the company of women who were not his wife, and he indulged in at least one extramarital sexual affair, with Eleanor Roosevelt's social secretary. Nor need he fear public exposure. Conveniently, the Democratic campaign headquarters happened to be in the Biltmore Hotel, where so many pretty young hustlers roamed the lobby that it was known as the "Mecca of the Demimondaine."

If it was true that FDR occasionally enjoyed the services of Polly's call girls, the skirt-chasing Teddy Hayes was an ideal go-between to make the arrangements. Whatever else he did for the governor, Teddy was an excellent ambassador to the Madison Square Garden–Tammany Hall crowd, who remained suspicious of the hobbled Hudson Valley aristocrat. Harlem's Jimmy Hines became an early convert to Roosevelt's cause, as did Jim Farley, the powerful head of the State Boxing Commission, which was, by all accounts, "a branch of the Democratic State Committee," as the reporter Alva Johnson quipped in *The New Yorker*. Hayes even arranged for Jack Dempsey's campaign endorsement.

Wherever the fight crowd went, the Broadway mob soon followed. If Teddy did, indeed, serve as a procurer for Roosevelt's unusual sexual needs, he may also have functioned as a back channel to the mob. It was common practice among sophisticated racketeers and political bosses to use prostitutes as a way to gain leverage and gather compromising material on politicians who could be useful to them.

Long after it became clear that Roosevelt would never again be able to walk, he kept Teddy on as a masseur and Broadway informant. A few years later Teddy would leave boxing entirely to enjoy a long and lucrative career as Ed Flynn's political factotum and right-hand man.

☾

On June 17, 1928, a gorgeous Sunday afternoon, an attractive brunette in a pink dress maneuvered a gray sedan up Broadway through the swarm of shoppers at Herald Square. Sitting next to her as she drove was a well-dressed, heavyset older man. They were idling at the intersection at West 36th Street, when a man stepped out of a nearby automobile, strode to the sedan, and pumped six bullets into the passenger seat. As the killer took off running, the lady in pink calmly slid out of the car and disappeared into the startled crowd.

Over the last eight years, murder had become a daily staple of the news, and in typical circumstances the killing of Edwin Jerge, a low-level dope dealer from out of town, would never have made the front pages. But this one, only steps away from Macy's famous department store, in one of the most crowded corners of the city on a Sunday afternoon, shocked even tabloid-hardened New Yorkers.

Two weeks later Al Capone's old mentor, Frankie Yale, was killed on the street in Brooklyn, when gunmen riddled his armor-plated Lincoln with sawed-off shotguns and machine guns. Jerge had been a junkie and a nobody, but Yale was a true-blue big shot who controlled much of the booze that moved through Brooklyn on its way to Manhattan and points west, in addition to his other nefarious rackets.

When no leads turned up in either case, the newspapers made them a cause célèbre, noting that police had failed to solve at least seventeen gangland murders over the past twelve months. After this, the morgues began filling up fast. "The next three months will be the most violent in the history of New York gangs," reported one insider in mid-September. "I cannot go into details, but the boys are going to shoot it out for beer and dough."

At ten-thirty p.m. on October 5, just as Times Square was beginning to jump, two thugs casually walked up to a slim man smoking a cigarette in front of the Harding Hotel and emptied their guns into his gut. In the chaos, the gunmen disappeared into the crowd. Cops from the West 47th Street station swarmed the neighborhood but to no avail. The victim, Tony Marlow, lived in Polly's building at 201 West 54th and had close ties to Dutch Schultz's gang, whose battle with Legs Diamond for control of the beer trade in upper Manhattan was heating to a boil.

Tony Marlow's murder put the already nervous netherworld on edge. Polly's 54th Street building was hot as hell, with undercover cops keeping constant surveillance on the block and placing wiretaps all over the Harding Hotel. It was impossible to ignore the swirl of rumors and the spiking tensions, or her own fears of getting caught in the crossfire. Between the unsolved murders and the bright spotlight of the presidential race, business was all jammed up for everyone.

At seven o'clock on the morning of October 16, Joe Noe, Dutch Schultz's best friend, was gunned down in front of the 54th Street Club (recently renamed the Chateau Madrid), a half block from Polly's apartment. As Noe fell, a row of guns appeared in the upper windows of the club and sent a hail of bullets into the blue Cadillac driven by Noe's assailants as they sped away. Police found the sedan an hour later, with the body of one of Legs Diamond's gunmen dead in the back seat. Several weeks later Noe died from his wounds. Two murders in ten days, right on Polly's doorstep.

No one was quite sure what the beef was. The cops speculated that it was retaliation for Tony Marlow's shooting. Others blamed it on the feud between Dutch Schultz and Legs Diamond. Bearing out that theory, Dutch, unhinged by the death of his friend, went on a rampage of revenge. But Legs showed no signs of backing down.

Owney Madden was frantically trying to keep the peace. Big Bill Dwyer had just finagled an early release from prison, and in the past he could have settled the dispute. But his word no longer carried the same authority.

Madden might have turned instead to Arnold Rothstein to mediate, as he had the year before when he was feuding with Waxey Gordon. But Rothstein had changed in the last year or so. Everyone was noticing it. "Suddenly, he began to act strange and I suspected maybe he was taking dope," said Maxie Hirsch, a horse trainer who'd worked closely with Rothstein for years. "He started to look like a man suffering from some terrible sickness."

Uncharacteristically for the Big Bankroll, he seemed to be having money problems. Speculation was that the uproar over the Jerge killing and the subsequent shakeup in the narcotics squad had disrupted the lucrative flow of profits from his drug trade. That summer he'd lost heavily on the horses at Belmont but had dragged his feet for months in paying off some $130,000 in markers. A.R. had always been "slow pay," as the boys from Lindy's liked to say, but now he was starting to get a reputation as a welcher.

Over the years, A.R. had made a thousand enemies with his clever tricks, angle cutting, and arrogance, but very few had dared to act on their anger. His invincibility rested on his vast bankroll and powerful political connections; those who crossed him would find their credit cut off and the law nipping at their heels. But after eight flush years of Prohibition, many of his protégés had lapped him in both money and political influence. The master gambler had violated the cardinal rule of the fixer: never make yourself obsolete by allowing your connections to develop their own relationships.

Rothstein's customary good luck seemed to be souring, but that did nothing to cool his frantic betting. "The gambling fever that was always part of Arnie's make-up appears to have gone to his brain," said Meyer Lansky. "It was like a disease and he was now in its last stages. He gambled wildly—even bet half a million dollars on the 1928 presidential election."

Then there was the infamous poker game. Up and down the Main Stem, everyone had heard about George McManus's game, hosted at the Congress Apartments across from Polly's apartment on West 54th, and attended by some of the scene's most notorious gamblers and confidence men. It ran from September 8 to 10, and by the end of three days, Rothstein was the big loser, signing IOUs to the winners for well over $300,000.

The problem was, as Jimmy Meehan, McManus's game runner, put it: "He was not a good loser." As they were getting ready to leave, Rothstein impulsively tore up the papers on which he had written the markers, insisting that they could trust him to pay up even without written records. Those who had forked over cash to pay their own losses were not happy. Their restlessness turned to concern when Rothstein began broadcasting his suspicion that the game had been crooked.

Lindy's was swirling with speculation and disapproval. Not one of these players would hesitate to cheat his own mother, that was a given, but being out-cheated was no excuse to renege on one's debts. As host of the game, it was George McManus's obligation to make sure the players honored their losses, by whatever means necessary. When a week went by and Rothstein still had not made good, the winners began hounding him. Personally, George did not appreciate this smear on his reputation as an honorable gamester.

McManus pressed Jimmy Hines to reason with Arnold, but Rothstein continued to stall. Finally he declared that he had no plans to pay the ill-gotten $340,000. "I'm not going to give them a cent, and that goes for the gamblers and the gorillas," A.R. said defiantly. "I can be found at Lindy's if they're looking for me." Meanwhile McManus was drinking heavily and muttering ominously about his old pal.

By early October, the savvy scribes at *The Morning Telegraph* were predicting that the end was near for the Brain. Rumors circulated openly that a Chicago gang had been hired to collect or, failing that, to rub him out. When detectives picked up word that his death had been fixed for November 3, they set up a patrol outside Lindy's. But when nothing happened, the cops stood down.

Rothstein's troubles were soon overshadowed by the upcoming presidential election. New York City was in a fever of excitement for its favorite son. In anticipation of Al Smith's big day, *The New York Times* erected the first twenty-four-hour newsfeed, a five-foot-tall strip of flashing lightbulbs that wrapped around the paper's headquarters—the zipper, they called it—that would spell out the election results to the crowds in Times Square.

A.R.'s reprieve from the spotlight didn't last long. At 10:47 p.m. on November 4, he was discovered slumped near the service entrance of the Park Central Hotel on Seventh Avenue, bleeding from a .38 caliber slug to his groin. Within minutes, Lindy's was buzzing, and the sidewalk outside the hotel was swarming with grifters and gunmen come to see the fallen gambler with their own eyes.

The news raced through the Broadway grapevine at top speed, all the way up to the Westchester roadhouse where Jimmy Walker and his mistress, Betty Compton, were dancing to the strains of Vince Lopez's orchestra. A little after midnight a man hurried up to the mayor and whispered something in his ear. With rare urgency, the perennially tardy mayor stood up, threw some cash down on the table, and began hustling Betty to the door. The bandleader leaned over to ask what was wrong.

"Rothstein has just been shot, Vince," Walker said grimly. "And that means trouble from here on in."

❲

By the time election day arrived on November 6, prospects were not looking good for the Happy Warrior. Down on Wall Street, the bookmakers were offering 20-to-1 odds in favor of Al's Republican opponent, Herbert Hoover. Nonetheless the mob was doing its best to help. A fresh-faced lawyer and ardent member of the Young Republican Club, Thomas E. Dewey, was serving as a poll watcher at the 110th Street polling station. He was shocked to see unregistered voters being ushered in to cast ballots, right under the noses of the cops.

"The Dutch Schultz mob had people there for the Democrats and there were gangsters with guns that you could see sticking through their clothes at each of the polling places in the school. When some obviously unfit voter would come in, they'd raise such a hullabaloo that everybody was intimidated, and the public did nothing, nor did the police," Dewey remembered in outrage. "Some of my friends got beaten up in that election."

Broadway was lit up like a carnival by the time the polls closed. Times Square was jammed shoulder to shoulder with the biggest election day crowd ever recorded as voters came out to celebrate Al Smith's imminent victory. Thousands of New Yorkers were collectively stunned when the bad news flashed across the New York Times zipper: "HERBERT HOOVER DEFEATS AL SMITH." The devastated crowd melted away, and by midnight the square was deserted, with no one left but a few sodden drunks.

Lying in his hospital bed several blocks from Broadway, Arnold Rothstein's luck finally ran out. As the voters were heading to the polls, the Big Bankroll drew his last breath. Had he lived one more day, he'd have collected well over a half a million dollars betting against the Happy Warrior, plus $200,000 for his wager on the new governor-elect, Franklin Delano Roosevelt.

"He was only forty-six when I saw him last," remembered Meyer Lansky, "but he looked like an old man, as if some great disaster had torn his life to pieces."

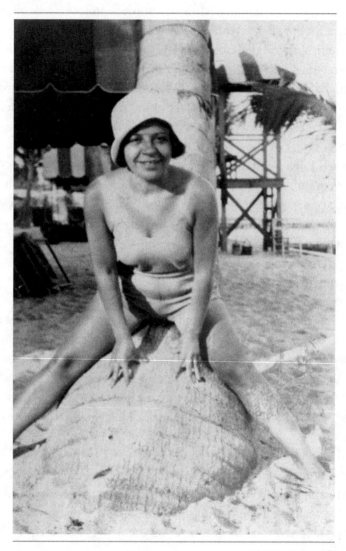

Polly in Miami Beach, Florida—the winter playground
of the Broadway mob

10

The Jewish Jezebel

Rothstein alive had been an unsavory article, Rothstein dead was a calamity," declared the prominent politico and man-about-town Ernest Cuneo. "The trail of blood left by the dying Rothstein led straight to the paths of corruption within the city machine."

Every wise guy and jaded wench on Broadway had a theory of what happened the night of November 4, 1928. Some suggested that the killer was a disgruntled relative of a Harlem politician with close ties to the police. Others insisted the culprit was a former policeman, acting for a combination of district leaders, who had tried to force Rothstein to pay up on a promised kickback. Still others believed it was the Chicago agent of a narcotics gang trying to move in on his trade. Some suggested that Dutch Schultz might have assassinated the gambler in retaliation for the killing of Joey Noe by Rothstein's aide-de-camp Legs Diamond. Others saw the hot hand of Legs Diamond himself, who had been feuding with his former mentor. And, of course, Arnold was known to dabble in the dangerous art of blackmail, in which killing the blackmailer often seemed like a victim's wisest course of action.

One thing everyone agreed on: this wasn't a professional job. "If it had been a professional hit, he wouldn't have been able to walk down the hall and get help," one reporter observed. "It is not customary for underworld slayers to stand by and watch a target stroll off with only one bullet as ballast." The odd position of the wound—awkwardly angled through his groin—and the single bullet pointed to a crime of passion, a warning, or a drunken accident.

Very quickly the primary focus turned to George McManus and the now-notorious three-day high-stakes poker game, in which Rothstein had allegedly been fleeced of some $300,000 that he refused to pay. The evidence against McManus was damning.

There was the fact that less than half an hour before Rothstein was shot, the cashier at Lindy's handed him a phone message from McManus summoning the gambler to George's suite at the Park Central Hotel. In McManus's hastily abandoned hotel room, detectives discovered two half-empty whiskey bottles, several dirty glasses, a wool overcoat with the name George McManus embroidered in the lining, and a chatty chambermaid who was quite sure that shortly before the shooting, she'd seen George in room 349 drinking with a tipsy blond woman on his lap. A revolver, minus one bullet, was found on the sidewalk below the window of George's room. Then there was the incontrovertible fact that George McManus had vanished.

Oddly, the NYPD did not seem to share the public's interest in the missing bookmaker. From the moment Rothstein was discovered bleeding outside the Park Central Hotel, there was a comical *Keystone Kops* quality to the police investigation. By the time Arnold died on November 6, still refusing to name his assailant, the newspapers were already tallying up the errors, omissions, and oddities in the behavior of the police, as well as the contradictions and nearly nonsensical statements coming from police headquarters and the district attorney's office.

To be fair, no one was especially surprised by the sluggish pace of the police investigation. The McManuses were an old and admired NYPD family dating back to the glory days of the System, and several of George's brothers were still on the force. If the bluecoats were less than efficient in their pursuit of him, well, chalk it up to professional courtesy.

All the signs taken together suggested that an inebriated George McManus shot Rothstein because the gambler had refused, once again, to pay his IOUs. Skeptics of this theory cited the inarguable fact that dead men do not pay their debts, noting that it was far more likely that Rothstein was killed because he had trimmed some poor sap, not the other way around. Still, the suspicion had the ring of truth. Everyone on the Avenue knew that McManus could be a nasty drunk with a quick trigger finger. All the same, no one wanted to see Smiling George and his "fantastic floating crap game" locked behind bars.

Nor were the daily papers in any hurry to see justice done. Arnold Rothstein's rubout was mother's milk to the city's circulation-hungry newspapers. Every publication in New York, from the trashy *Evening Graphic* to the buttoned-up *New York Times*, leaped on the story and planned to ride it to the bitter end.

（

The news of Rothstein's murder threw Polly into a panic. She wasn't alone. "The entire street was on edge," *Variety* reported. A large swath of Manhattan, from the Lower East Side to Harlem, had good reason to feel jittery. There was hardly a soul on Broadway who hadn't had dealings with the Big Bankroll.

But Polly was unaccountably nervous. Later she explained away her anxiety, saying that one of her girls had told the cops about the night when a drunken McManus had shot up the French doors in her apartment. She was merely worried, as she put it, that she'd be called to testify that George had a violent temper when drinking. But if that was her fear, then most of the West Side barkeeps should have been quaking in their boots.

A more likely explanation is that on the day of the murder, Polly provided feminine diversion for George McManus in the shape of one Ruth Keyes, a petite twenty-three-year-old "freelance model"—a common euphemism for a part-time prostitute. Like nearly everyone involved, Keyes had trouble keeping the details of that fateful day straight, but all of them suggest that Polly had sent the young model on an afternoon date with McManus.

"Hard boiled and highly-lacquered," as the papers described her, Ruth Keyes was married to a train brakeman back in Chicago, but at the time of the killing she was staying down the hall from McManus at the pricey Park Central Hotel. In the version that made it to press, Ruth met George in the hallway of the hotel, where he introduced himself as "Jack." After a bit of chat, she accepted his invitation to come to his room for a drink. She spent the afternoon with him, drinking whiskey, listening to music, and making whoopie, a fact confirmed by the chambermaid, who walked in to find the pretty blonde perched on the gambler's ample lap.

George was charming company, Ruth remembered. "He did solo dances and sang," she told a newspaper reporter. "'I'm good at parlor tricks too,' he said. He started throwing cubes of ice into the air and catching them in his glass." "How do you like my girlfriend?" McManus boasted to his less voluble companion, a dour fellow by the name of Chick (likely Chick Mace, the Hell's Kitchen thug who went on an anti-Semitic rampage in Polly's apartment back in 1926).

"While I was there," Ruth remembered, "there were only two phone calls and both were for me." (An odd thing, to receive calls in a stranger's room, unless they were from Polly.) When it seemed like the party might break up, McManus, in the spendthrift style that made him so popular on the Main Stem, began peeling off fifty-dollar bills from his hefty bankroll to persuade her to stay. If Mrs. Keyes weren't a professional party girl, clearly she was wasting her talents.

In her initial telling, Ruth left McManus around six p.m., tired and drunk but promising to return later with another girl to round out the party. By way of a rest, she headed up to Small's Paradise, a rowdy Harlem nightclub that didn't get hopping until midnight. But when pressed further, she admitted that—perhaps persuaded by those fifty-dollar bills—she'd kept drinking with McManus and a couple of his chums until a little after ten p.m., when she tottered back to her room. When she knocked on his door (with another girl or alone, depending on the telling) sometime after eleven p.m., no one answered and the door was locked, so she went to bed. In yet another version, she said she called his room at one-thirty a.m. but got no answer.

Around four a.m. she was awakened by several plainclothes policemen, led by one Joe Daley, a well-known detective around both Broadway and police headquarters. They questioned her for a while and then told her to "beat it" out of town. Early the next morning, whether at the behest of the cops or Polly or her own common sense, Ruth bolted back to Chicago, leaving no forwarding address and with no plans to return.

☾

Under normal circumstances, Rothstein's killing would have roiled the waters for a few months and then joined the long list of unsolved murders. But even in death, A.R. had cards to play. To the surprise and dismay of nearly everyone, it turned out that he had maintained extensive financial records, some fifty-six thousand pieces of paper filling two steel filing cabinets (minus the files that disappeared in the tumult).

The panic in the halls of power was palpable. "If these papers are ever made public, there are going to be a lot of suicides in high places," warned Rothstein's lawyer as he turned them over to the district attorney.

Under pressure from all sides, Mayor Walker issued an ultimatum to the hapless police commissioner, Joseph Warren: solve Rothstein's murder in the next four days or resign. Off the record, many city officials were a bit mystified by all the fuss to find the gunman. As one unnamed higher-up grumbled, "We are doing all we can, but why we should care who killed a man like Arnold Rothstein I don't know."

As the hours ticked away, it suddenly occurred to someone in police headquarters that perhaps the mysterious Ruth Keyes might come in handy after all. Commissioner Warren sent officers out to beat the bushes for her, and on November 19—the last day of Walker's ultimatum—they located her in Chicago and escorted her back to New York for questioning.

The investigators emerged from her interrogation triumphant. Mrs. Keyes, they announced, had identified George McManus as the man she'd been drinking with in room 349, and had pointed to a photo of Legs Diamond as one of his companions.

George McManus was a popular man in the White Light District, an upstanding citizen who tipped lavishly, ran a clean game by local standards, and paid his debts. The most lovable man in the world, as Lou Clayton put it, when he wasn't on the sauce. Legs Diamond, on the other hand, was regarded by nearly everyone as a dangerous pest and congenital double-crosser. No one was saying it aloud, but Legs would make a very convenient fall guy.

Almost as soon as the cops began crowing, word came from headquarters, swift and severe: Legs Diamond was no longer a suspect. No further explanation was offered. "It was just one of those things," as the sporting world cynics liked to say.

☾

After three weeks of constant ridicule in the press and anxious rumor-mongering in the speakeasies and political clubs—three weeks in which Jimmy Hines pulled every string he possessed—on November 26 McManus announced that he was ready to leave the Bronx safe house where he'd been hiding, courtesy of Dutch Schultz. Down on Centre Street, in the gloomy citadel of the police headquarters, the mood was giddy with relief. The pressure was off the bluecoats. Now it would be District Attorney Joab Banton's turn to take the heat for slow-walking or, worse yet, solving the case.

Freshly barbered and brimming with good cheer, George got a warm welcome in the courtroom where he was arraigned the next day, shaking hands with a clutch of plainclothesmen. And no introduction was necessary when McManus got to the Tombs, where the commissioner of corrections was a good friend of his brother James. In all the congratulatory hubbub, no one noticed that when booking the suspect, the police failed to either fingerprint or photograph him.

From the moment George was arrested, said Polly, "I was on tenterhooks, fearing I might have to be a witness." Undoubtedly, this had something to do with the reappearance of the elusive Ruth Keyes. On the day McManus announced his surrender, Keyes spoke at length to Banton's aides. As soon as Keyes finished testifying, officers hustled her to the train station and bought her a one-way ticket back to Chicago. (It wasn't their fault, they protested, that she ditched the train when it reached 125th Street and "at last reports was having a great time seeing New York.")

After listening to Keyes's account, the district attorney announced that he was filing an affidavit for the arrest of one "Jane Doe" on a charge of first-degree murder, along with her alleged accomplices, "John Doe" and "Richard Roe." "I can't discuss her now," Banton told the reporters, but "she is very important."

The press, which considered no story truly sensational without a sex angle, was ecstatic at the appearance of this "mystery woman." But it took only a few days for the beleaguered district attorney to begin backtracking. Progress had been made, he told the *Daily News*: "We know who they are and where to lay our hands on them." But something or someone must have intervened because later that very same day, Banton explained to the *Brooklyn Union* that there was no Jane Doe after all. He'd simply been acting under an abundance of caution. When he had filed the affidavit, "he had not had any particular woman in mind but, he explained, should it have been found that McManus was shielding a woman operative she might have been immediately arrested and placed in a cell on the strength of the affidavit."

Two days later the district attorney shifted again. Now he claimed that the previously nonexistent Jane Doe, originally thought to be an accomplice in the murder, was "merely an accessory after the fact," reported the *Brooklyn Standard Union*. "She is reputed to be important in the case only as having aided the escape and concealment of those suspected of direct connection with the shooting." That same day, in a final comical note, the Associated Press reported that Banton had meant to say that Jane Doe was really a man.

After that, the mysterious Jane was never mentioned again. All official records of the investigation were long ago destroyed, so it is impossible to know exactly whom or what Banton suspected. But if Polly was, indeed, Jane Doe she must have been relieved, if not exactly reassured, by the district attorney's erratic performance.

With McManus in custody, it was time for Joseph Warren, Walker's unfortunate police commissioner, to take up his role as designated scapegoat. Humiliated, Warren handed in his resignation. Eight months later he abruptly, suspiciously, and conveniently passed away in a sanatorium at the tender age of forty-seven.

As the city's new top crime fighter, the mayor chose the natty, mustachioed Grover A. Whalen, a department store manager who had no previous police experience but enjoyed close ties to Tammany Hall. The new commissioner's first task was to restore the battered morale of his officers, whose feelings had been badly bruised by the aspersions of the press.

As one of his first acts, he abolished the "confidential" or "shoofly" squad," used by previous commissioners to ferret out graft in the force, and reinstated the old "strongarm squads," the boys of the blackjack and the rubber hose. On New Year's Eve, Commissioner Whalen officially wiped clean the records of every cop on the force, dismissing all but the most egregious disciplinary complaints. To ensure that they stayed clean, he relaxed all sorts of irksome rules, such as those that forbade the searching of dead bodies before medical examiners arrived.

To celebrate the new regime, Detective James J. Quinlivan, the terror of the Harlem vice squad, threw an epic Christmas party for the boys in blue, with a distinguished guest list that included some of the top brass of the department. The pièce de résistance was a brace of beauties, courtesy of Polly Adler, who enlivened the party with a little nude dancing.

They might be panicking about Rothstein's demise down in police headquarters, the district attorney's office, and City Hall, but for the vice squad, business was booming.

☾

That winter of 1928–29, the city seemed to be in a dipsomaniacal fever, chattering about nothing but hangovers, the soaring stock market, and where to get the next drink. "Many people who were not alcoholics were lit up four days out of seven, and frayed nerves were strewn everywhere," remembered F. Scott Fitzgerald.

Wall Street was in a frenzy, despite scattered warnings that the market was overheating. Polly and her pal Detective Irwin O'Leary were plunging heavily, drawing on insider tips from her high-flying customers. They shared several brokerage accounts, which Polly used to pad Irwin's salary without alerting his wife or the tax authorities. They got caught up in the Broadway craze for Anaconda Copper, a Rockefeller-owned mining company, and infamous "pump and dump" scheme in which a hidden pool of investors aggressively drove up the price of the stock, then sold their shares, taking huge profits but decimating their value, at which point they bought them back at a discount. It was tough for the suckers, but for insiders it was like spinning gold from thin air.

Under Commissioner Whalen, the metropolis was running wide open. In May 1929 she took the oath of allegiance to become an American citizen, listing her address as 57 West 58th Street. Polly now had at least half a dozen assignation apartments, in addition to her main house, as well as some six hundred of Manhattan's finest scarlet women listed in her call books.

Out in Hollywood, the rise of the talkies had created a huge demand for both Broadway talent and Wall Street financing, which meant plenty of professional parties. *Luftmenschen* who'd been picking up nickels around Broadway for years were coming back from California with money to burn. Over the last year, the flow of financiers, filmmakers, music publishers, performers, and publicists making the three-day train ride between Los Angeles and Manhattan had ballooned.

It became de rigueur to stop in to see Polly's famous harem anytime a visitor arrived from the Coast. The novelist Richard Condon remembered how, upon starting a job as a young film publicist in Manhattan, he learned that one of his first tasks was providing willing women to entertain Hollywood dignitaries. He was new to "the flesh field," he recalled, "so I asked a friend on the Vice Squad to introduce me to Miss Polly Adler, wherever she might be, and having made an appointment, I called on her at two fifteen p.m. wearing a bowler hat and gloves. I gave her a business card over a round dining room table and we discussed credit terms."

"What are you buying here, fahgossakes," Polly asked with amusement, "leather skins or something?" It was the beginning of both a lucrative corporate account and a lifelong friendship.

She became especially close to the famously misanthropic actor Wallace Beery, one of the film colony's least popular and most successful stars. The craggy-faced actor took an instant liking to Polly when they first met in the mineral baths at Hot Springs. When he suggested he come visit her in New York, she finally confessed, with trepidation, "I run a whorehouse." He didn't blink, she remembered with pleasure. "So what?" he shot back. "You can run fifty of them. To me you are a very nice person." Wally went on to spend hundreds of evenings hanging around her apartment, drinking beer, listening to the radio, snacking on sandwiches or Polly's famous pot roast, while joking and gossiping with the ladies about the foibles of their customers.

Her relationship with the sweet but improvident Irwin O'Leary was also paying generous dividends. They opened a speakeasy together, stocked courtesy of Dutch Schultz and any bottles Irwin picked up in the course of his official duties. These kind of speakeasy-brothel combinations practically minted money.

Despite her prosperity, however, "my luck seemed to have changed,"

Polly recalled. "Nothing went smoothly. There were constant small annoyances." A broken water main flooded her building on Madison Avenue, forcing her to move. Her private apartment was robbed by two employees whom she'd thought of as friends. An auto thief ring stole her car; she got it back, but the incident put her name in the newspaper.

Her biggest headache was, as ever, the NYPD. Under Grover Whalen, the vice squad grew more arrogant and aggressive. Inspired by the roaring success of Detective Quinlivan's Christmas orgy, her girls were in heavy demand for bluecoat bacchanals that winter. Polly soon decided that it would be far easier—and safer—to forgo her cut of the proceeds and let the girls collect their fee directly from the cops. Unfortunately, she hadn't taken into account "the apparently inbred capacity for the double-cross that is characteristic of the vice cops," as the reporter for the *Daily News* put it. After a few of these performances, the bulls began recognizing the girls on the street, then following them to their apartments and shaking them down under threat of arrest. After this she refused to provide any more girls for the vice squad.

"An additional headache at this time was that two of my girls were the mistresses of cops," remembered Polly, "and if either found things at the house not to her liking, a word to her lover would shutter my place and land me in the pokey."

☾

Arnold Rothstein's death marked a critical shift in power within the "Unholy Alliance" of politics and crime. With Al Smith out of office, Jimmy Walker was now the de facto leader of Tammany Hall. As for the newly elected governor, Mayor Walker shared the general Tammany line that Frank Roosevelt was a lightweight and a snob. "To my sidewalks-of-New-York mind," Jimmy said later, Franklin always seemed "to be 'looking down his nose,' or engaged in a slumming expedition." The governor clearly possessed great charm, but "when he tried to exercise his charm upon me in those days, I mistook it to mean that he was patronizing me."

In January 1929, Walker began ousting Al Smith's allies from key city posts to make way for his own men, or what one observer called, "the worst element in Tammany Hall." That spring Jimmy Hines—with Walker's help—led a coup against Smith's choice for Tammany's Grand

Sachem, George Olvaney, and in his place installed John Francis Curry, an old-school district leader who cared far less about policy than patronage. Jimmy Hines now had "his" men in all the big-city jobs. Walker was the front man of the show, but Hines, with his army of voters and gangland backers, was the closest it had to a real boss.

Rolling in their ill-gotten gains, the racket boys were no longer simply supplicants and skull crackers. Now they were the patrons whose war chests kept the political operation turning. When Arnold Rothstein began his career, "the politicians still controlled the criminals," as one crime reporter put it. "He had taught the underworld that it could create private armies that operated for the underworld's benefit, not that of politicians. True, politicians got value from these gangs, but it was no longer their right. They had to pay an increasingly heavy price."

As the bond between the politicos and the tommy-gun tycoons tightened, Polly's role as hostess, social arbiter, and party-favor provider put her ever closer to the center of power. One reporter described, with genuine awe, the rumors of Polly's rare status, how she was "a guest of honor, so to speak, at a dinner given by a Brooklyn society, where she sat enthroned at the speakers table surrounded by city officials and political big-wigs, the only female present." Naturally, she hosted the afterparty at "the Adler *maison de joie* with girls galore to entertain those gentlemen who accepted an invitation to join the Jewish Jezebel in a 'lil' drinkie."

Mayor Walker remained her most honored guest, the one whose name she dropped whenever she got guff from some rookie cop or—as he later admitted—the special prosecutor at the Women's Court. Perhaps more surprising were her deep political connections in the fast-rising Bronx. Ed Flynn, as Roosevelt's secretary of state and the uncontested leader of the city's fastest-growing borough, was beginning to rival Manhattan's fractious Tammany Hall in influence. Among the racketeers, Dutch Schultz, "the bad boy of the Bronx," as the tabloids dubbed him, was speedily building an organization that would give Waxey Gordon's vast enterprises a run for their money. Of the two, Ed Flynn was far more mysterious.

Unfortunately, none of her political pals seemed able to save her from the vermin of the vice squad. In April 1929 she was double-crossed yet again by two old foes from the Broadway squad, Leigh Halpern and Daniel Sullivan. A little after three a.m. on April 28, 1929, they barreled into her apartment at 150 East 52nd Street, brushing past the maid. They stopped to greet Polly in the parlor, then busted into the bedrooms, where they found two young ladies, Bobby Johnson and Lucille Manger, in flagrante delicto with two johns. All four women were arrested, along with the building's elevator operator. Once again they had the nerve to book her under the name Polly Adler. This time, however, she wasn't rolling over.

In a sign of how much power had shifted from the immigrant ghettos of lower Manhattan to the burgeoning boroughs, and how closely she was allied with the party of Ed Flynn and Dutch Schultz, now when Polly wanted to make her wrath known, she appealed to her friends in the Bronx. The powerful Democratic boss and notoriously corrupt Bronx County clerk, J. F. Geraghty, intervened directly to have the case dismissed.

John C. Weston, the Women's Court's mild-mannered special prosecutor, received his usual twenty-five-dollar payoff from her bail bondsmen for this case, but he also got enough political blowback to become genuinely frightened of Polly's influence. Two months later Weston resigned. It was for his health, he told the mystified director of the Committee of Fourteen. The real reason, he later confessed, was fear.

☾

Arnold Rothstein's death also upended the underworld economy. Without his backing, a thousand illicit schemes died on the vine, and without his bail bonds, scores of hardworking criminals languished in jail. The unrelenting news coverage had a chilling effect on the Broadway rackets, "wising up the suckers," in the grifters' lament.

A.R.'s departure scrambled the underworld pecking order. With his old ally gone, Waxey Gordon looked less than invincible, and after some nasty skirmishes with Meyer Lansky and Bugsy Siegel, he decided to transfer his operations to the pastoral climes of northern New Jersey. Frank Costello took command of Rothstein's national gambling syndicate and assumed his role as Gotham's prime political fixer, while Lucky Luciano became the key liaison between the Italian Unione Siciliana and the Irish and Jewish gangs. Owney Madden picked up a number of Rothstein's Times Square assets, including the Harding Hotel.

Legs Diamond made no secret of his longing to take over Rothstein's international drug-smuggling operation. "I think I can pull it off," he boasted. "I think I can get control of the whole drug empire in America, if not next year then soon." Lending credence to those who blamed him for Rothstein's murder, Legs went on a killing spree that winter, rubbing out A.R.'s former strongmen one by one.

Most important for Polly was the transformation of Arthur Flegen-heimer, a midlevel manager in a Bronx beer gang, into the fearsome Dutch Schultz. At first glance, no one would have picked him out as a big shot. He was unassuming in looks, with a sallow, fleshy face and a twisted nose, narrow eyes, and an abrupt, jittery manner. Unlike the pistol peacocks of the Broadway mob, he didn't gamble or throw around money; he wore the rumpled wardrobe of a frugal small business owner, scorning their expensive silk shirts, handmade shoes, and $200 suits.

Dutch's closely knit organization was run with unusual care, efficiency, and cruelty. The Schultz gang gladly did their own killing, unlike Costello and Lucky, who preferred to rely on Meyer Lansky and Bugsy Siegel for wet work. The Broadway crowd was leery of this aggressive newcomer, for good reason. "No one liked Dutch Schultz," one criminal colleague observed. "He was a vicious, pathologically suspicious killer who kept his people in line through sheer terror." Through a combination of ruthless violence and sober management, Schultz had taken over bootlegging in the Bronx and was now skirmishing with Legs Diamond for control of northern Manhattan, Harlem, and the Upper West Side.

As Schultz became more socially ambitious, Polly's provided a natural stopping place, where her friendship and resources could burnish an arriviste's reputation. It didn't hurt that Dutch was, as Meyer Berger noted in *The New York Times*, a "pushover for blondes," who was besotted by the Broadway beauties who were Polly's specialty. Arthur took a shine to the stouthearted, keen-witted little madam; as one reporter recalled, the "almost brotherly affection that Dutch showed to Polly" spawned rumors that they were a romantic item.

That spring of 1929 Schultz was trying on the glamorous role of nightclub owner and theatrical angel. He was now the proud owner of the Chateau Madrid, just down the block from Polly's headquarters on

West 54th. And he was backing a musical revue called *Hot Chocolates*, written by two of Harlem's top songwriters, Andy Razaf and Fats Waller, who was an old friend of Polly's from the Kentucky Club.

As opening night approached, Dutch, in his new role as producer, informed Razaf that the show needed a comic bit, "something with a little 'colored girl' singing how tough it was to be black," as Razaf remembered it. When Andy bridled at the suggestion, Schultz pulled out a revolver and waved it in the composer's face. "You'll write it," he sneered, "or you'll never write anything again."

Unwilling to sacrifice either their necks or their artistic integrity, Razaf and Waller composed the haunting and slyly satirical song "(What Did I Do to Be So) Black and Blue." The evening they debuted the number, Razaf was dismayed to see Schultz lurking in the back of the theater as the curtain rose on the singer Edith Wilson, her lush brown skin glowing against an all-white set. The audience giggled as she launched into the first verse lamenting the prejudice that some light-toned Blacks held against darker-skinned compatriots.

The Dutchman was grinning, Razaf noted warily, but when the audience fell silent as the impact of the lyrics hit them, his smile disappeared. Razaf remembered thinking that his life was literally in the hands of the audience—that if they didn't clap, Dutch might well kill him on the spot. He waited tensely as Edith Wilson built up to the final lines:

> How will it end? Ain't got a friend,
> My only sin is in my skin,
> What did I do to be so black and blue?

When the audience surged to their feet in a standing ovation, he felt a sudden congratulatory slap on his back, then Dutch slipped into the darkness.

The kicker came a week or so later, when the Dutchman summoned Razaf to Polly's bordello on West 54th Street. The bootlegger personally ushered Andy into the parlor and then gestured at the three lightly clad young women in attendance.

"Take all night," Schultz barked. "It's on me. A little bonus."

Like all the top mob musicians, Andy Razaf was well acquainted with Polly and her girls, and no fool, he immediately recognized one of them as Dutch's personal favorite. It had to be a setup, he figured, a payback for trying to outwit the boss. He remained chaste as a church mouse that night.

In addition to dabbling in showbiz, Dutch was cultivating a new passion for politics. He struck up a close relationship with Jimmy Hines, using the Monongahela Club as his uptown office. In return for his protection, Schultz commanded Hines's private army on election days, intimidating voters, stuffing ballot boxes wherever needed, and filling the district leader's pockets with thousands of dollars to grease the voters.

None of this sat well with Legs Diamond, who regarded the arrogant Dutchman as a prime obstacle to his own ambitions. Their feud took a sharp turn early on the morning of July 13, 1929, at the Hotsy Totsy Club, when Legs and his roughneck companion got into a drunken argument with one of the customers. As shots rang out, the crowd dove for the exits while the resourceful proprietor, Hymie Cohen, motioned to the band to play louder to muffle the gunfire. When the band finished playing, two men lay bleeding to death in the empty barroom.

Diamond went into hiding, per usual, and the incident might have been forgotten as just another deadly nightclub brawl. But then the eyewitnesses started disappearing: Hymie Cohen, the cashier, the bartender, the hatcheck girl, several bystanders, and even Legs's current girlfriend—one by one, all vanished. Seven months later Legs resurfaced from hiding. But with no more witnesses, the case fell apart and he walked free.

Polly was a regular at the Hotsy Totsy and knew all the players, including the unfortunate proprietor. "Little Hymie, he was a nice little guy," she mused. "Hymie was shot or got lost, anyway, he was never heard from again. Legs' showgirl sweetheart watched the shooting episode, she too, went by the way of all flesh." Polly was sanguine in retrospect but was well aware it could have been her caught in the crossfire.

"The Hotsy Totsy murders finished Diamond on Broadway. Such a cheap killing in a man's own joint, no matter who did it, was looked on as horribly sloppy work, fit only for the provinces or the Brooklyn waterfront, and the boys marked him for lousy," according to the crime reporter Joel Sayre. "It got so that a self-respecting racketeer wouldn't be seen passing him the time of day."

All this unchecked competition was bad for everyone's business. In the first six months of 1929, New York witnessed 160 murders. That was nothing compared to the carnage in Chicago that February, when Al Capone shocked the nation by mowing down a rival Irish gang in what would become known as the St. Valentine's Day Massacre. But it was enough to raise public ire and cut into everyone's profit margins.

(

In August 1929 Jimmy Walker, "the dapper little Lord Mayor of Gotham," was coasting on personal charm and the fantastic prosperity of Wall Street as he headed into his reelection campaign. That summer stock prices rose nearly 25 percent, doubling levels seen only three years before. Anyone who wasn't getting rich had only themselves to blame.

In the face of Mayor Walker's popularity and the city's economic strength, the Republican candidate to replace him, U.S. congressman Fiorello La Guardia, and the Socialist candidate, Norman Thomas, had little choice but to make corruption their signature issue, placing Rothstein's unsolved murder and his murky ties to Tammany at the center of their campaigns. The fact that George McManus had still not come to trial eight months after his arrest became a rallying cry for Walker's foes. Congressman La Guardia hit especially hard at Rothstein's ties to Magistrate Albert H. Vitale, a Tammany appointee who was leading Walker's reelection campaign in the Italian communities. Rothstein's financial records showed plainly that Magistrate Vitale had borrowed heavily from the gambler before his death.

The Tammany-backed district attorney, Joab Banton, was under heavy pressure from all sides: from the press to put McManus on trial immediately to squash the impression that the Walker administration had something to hide, and from terrified Tammany insiders who were adamant that he postpone the trial until after the election so McManus could walk free without Mayor Walker paying a price at the ballot box. Finally Banton announced that he would bring McManus to court immediately after the election.

Between the upcoming trial and the treacherous final days of the mayoral campaign, it occurred to Polly that now would be a terrific time to take a trip abroad. She made hasty plans for a three-month tour of

Montreal, Quebec, and Niagara Falls, lasting through the holidays and into the new year—plenty of time for the fever of the election and the vagaries of the justice system to play themselves out.

She could afford a long vacation. All summer long she and Irwin O'Leary had been plowing their profits into the stock market and had been richly rewarded. True, stock prices had tumbled since Labor Day—and they'd taken something of a bath on that Anaconda Copper investment—but she'd never seen Wall Street fail to bounce back even higher.

So Polly was unprepared for the news when she stepped off the train in Montreal. On October 24—"Black Thursday," they would call it—a sudden wave of selling orders overwhelmed the New York Stock Exchange, sending stock values tumbling across the board. "I spent the days in a brokerage office, bent over a hot ticker unable to believe my eyes," she wrote later.

Over the weekend the panic seemed to subside, but when the exchange opened on Monday, it was clear that Wall Street was in free fall. She hurried back to New York, where she found her apartment littered with telegrams from her broker, demanding she pay her margin calls. Nearly everything she had, all her savings, were tied up in stocks, and now they were worse than worthless.

> Too numb even to take off my hat and coat, I sat there in that empty apartment for hours, trying to get a fix on the situation. After working and planning for all these years, one turn of the wheel and I was staring straight at double-O—goose eggs again. And now, I thought grimly, I have the family to take care of.

Despite the months of mudslinging, Walker won reelection by a landslide. With the help of Dutch Schultz's gang, Harlem's Jimmy Hines also clocked a major victory at the polls, installing political allies in neighboring districts who extended his influence down the West Side and up to the Bronx. Hines's candidate, the respectable but ineffectual Thomas A. Crain, was elected district attorney. It was the first good news anyone had in that grim month.

Joab Banton's last, unpleasant task as the lame duck DA was to bring

Arnold Rothstein's accused killer to justice. On November 22 opening arguments began in the prosecution of George A. McManus. The reporters who crammed the courtroom treated it as a gangland comedy, as one Broadway character after another took the stand to piously proclaim George's innocence. The foulmouthed Boston brothers, the round little hophead Sid Stajer, the keen-witted "Titanic" Thompson, and the sleazy "Nigger Nate" Raymond described the fantastic sums of money bet on the single turn of a card, muttering out of the sides of their mouths in the distinctive Broadway patois that would soon become the lingua franca of thousands of pulp novels and gangster movies.

For Polly, it was torturous. The assistant district attorney threatened to call sixty unnamed people to testify, including his star witness, Ruth Keyes, whom he was keeping in hiding. The boys at the press table groaned in disappointment when the mysterious freelance model went on the lam just before she was to take the stand.

But justice and Jimmy Hines were merciful. The prosecutor announced that he would not go to the expense of hauling in Mrs. Keyes to testify. She had nothing to add to the case, he explained, except to confirm that McManus had been drinking, and the defense had already conceded that fact.

In the end, Polly worried for nothing. The wheels of justice had been thoroughly gummed up. The district attorney made no pretense of being engaged in the case, turning it over to his purposely inept assistants to prosecute. They offered no fingerprints, no apparent owner for the murder weapon, no motive for the killing, and no evidence that either McManus or Rothstein had been in room 349 at the time of the shooting or even that they'd seen each other that evening. The few witnesses they had secured—the cashier at Lindy's who'd reported McManus's message, the chambermaid at the Park Central who saw McManus in room 349 at 10:20 p.m.—recanted their claims on the stand.

The district attorney's whitewash was so thorough that McManus's lawyer saw no need to call a single witness in the gambler's defense. But just in case there was any doubt of the outcome, the judge instructed the jury to acquit the defendant, which they dutifully did.

Clutching his errant overcoat, McManus bounded down the courthouse steps grinning like an overjoyed jack-o'-lantern at the crowd of congratulatory cops and well-wishers, beaming for the newspaper photographers, and wishing them all a very merry Christmas.

((

With relief, Polly now turned her full attention back to her precarious financial state.

Broadway felt the effects of the stock market crash immediately. Many of her best clients were among the biggest casualties, like the comedian Lou Holtz, who'd been worth more than a million dollars before Black Thursday. Six months later his holdings amounted to exactly $732. Over a third of the theaters went dark, many of them turned into off-track horse betting joints or radio studios, and at least twenty-five thousand stage actors were out of work. Vaudeville, already ailing, was on its deathbed, and without Wall Street plungers to pick up the tab, high-end nightclubs were an endangered species. The pawnshops were jammed with Broadway butterflies hocking jewelry and fur coats.

Yet Polly was surprised to find that, even as suicides, bankruptcies, and bank failures mounted, her business was booming. "I had more customers than I could take care of," she recalled incredulously. Champagne was selling like soda pop, and she was making a fortune on beer, charging a buck for a twelve-cent glass of shaken-up suds. Some fellows who'd been only casual johns were returning night after night for expensive debauchery. Some steady customers lost all interest in sex and came solely to blot out their troubles at the bar. "A whore house is the only place I can cry without being ashamed," as one regular explained.

Many of the men seemed irreparably shattered, like the customer who just kept muttering over and over, "I used to control Wall Street. Now I don't know how I'm going to pay next month's rent." One gentleman, or so she'd always thought, arrived at the house and requested a particular girl, "and then proceeded to practice the most vile, cruel, and inhuman acts until the girl was a physical wreck," Polly recalled with a shudder. "The following morning the man went to his office and shot himself."

The big bootleggers had generally resisted the siren song of Wall Street—"Those stock market guys are crooked," Al Capone famously complained—so they were relatively unscathed by the collapse of Wall

Street. But even they were feeling the pinch in those early days of the Depression. The big dice games had dwindled, the booze market had too many suppliers and too much supply, and the bottom fell out of the protection racket as thousands of legitimate businesses went belly up. The only growth sectors in the twilight economy were loan sharking and the nickel-and-dime betting of illegal lotteries, colloquially known as "policy" or "playing the numbers."

As the overall pie of profits shrank, competition grew more cutthroat, literally. Kidnappings were on the rise, as hard-up hoodlums scrounged for new ways to scare up cash. By the summer of 1930, the underworld had become an armed camp, as hand grenades, machine guns, and homemade bombs became standard equipment in the quest for market share.

Despite her losses in the market, Polly was flush enough to take her annual winter vacation, following the Broadway mob to Miami, Florida, to see a much-touted prizefight between Jack Sharkey and Phil Scott. Among the Broadway mob, Miami Beach was the next big thing, a wide-open town with girls, gambling, and sunshine. The city had long been a transit point for liquor imported from the Caribbean, so when the Florida real estate boom collapsed, and the Crash blasted what was left of the local economy, the bootleggers saw opportunity. Al Capone kicked off the trend, buying a waterfront villa in Miami Beach. Now the Lansky-Luciano-Costello syndicate was investing heavily in the city, buying up politicians, building casinos, horse tracks, and even a grey-hound racing track. Miami was giving Hot Springs a run for its money as the winter playground of the underworldlings.

Polly checked into the elegant Hotel Deauville on Collins Avenue, run by her old friend Benevolent Charlie Manny, where the comely young female "swim instructors" were one of the hotel's most attractive amenities. The matchup between Sharkey and Scott was a bust, but the trip gave her an opportunity see where her girls worked during their winter sabbaticals, including Gertie Walsh's opulent Victorian bordello on Flagler Street, Madam Sherry's Moorish Castle on Biscayne Boulevard, and the mysterious Madam Collette's.

The only blemish on the holiday was an unfortunate raid at the Hotel Deauville after the fight, while Polly's friends were enjoying a high-spade game run by Lucky Luciano, "a swarthy young chap with an ugly scar from his left ear to his collar," as the *Daily News* described him, flashing "a roll of money that resembled a cabbage head." The local police swept up nineteen vacationing "Times Square gamblers" and a little over $130,000 in cash. The next day the sheepish lawmen politely released the suspects and handed back their bankrolls.

☾

Polly returned home to a gathering storm. The troubles began with the magistrates who sat on the city's lowest courts—the ambitious Tammany hacks who were the bread and butter of Polly's political customers. Magistrates were nominated by district leaders and personally appointed by the mayor, so claims of corruption snaked up the political food chain with alarming speed.

The magistrates' racket was especially ripe for graft, since that was where the vast majority of criminal cases were resolved. The opportunities for bribery were so rich that lawyers who aspired to the bench were expected to pay a cool twenty grand to their district leader for the privilege of the appointment. Higher-court robes cost more. Rothstein had long specialized in loaning money to would-be magistrates who didn't have that kind of cash handy, often at discounted rates, inspiring other well-heeled racketeers to follow suit.

The first hints of scandal came in mid-August 1929, when Magistrate Andrew Macrery was reportedly beaten to death during a meeting with Andrew Keating, one of Jimmy Hines's cabal of district leaders. Word was that he'd refused to fork over the $10,000 he still owed Keating for his gown. The accusation that Macrery had paid a politician for his seat on the bench, not to mention that he might have been killed for it, came as shocking news to the average New Yorker. But in those last heady months of the boom, the story didn't gain much traction.

Then in September 1929, Magistrate Albert Vitale's ties to Arnold Rothstein became a centerpiece of the mayoral campaign. In October, County Court Judge Francis X. Mancuso, the pride of Italian Harlem, was forced to resign over financial shenanigans and was indicted for perjury. If voters noticed the growing stench in the courts, they didn't blame Mayor Walker, who handily won reelection that November. Even the farcical prosecution of George McManus was met with a cynical shrug.

So it might have gone on, had Albert Vitale learned his lesson. On December 7, 1929, the magistrate was the guest of honor at a banquet in the Bronx when seven masked gunmen descended on the hall, robbing the guests of money and jewelry, and seizing a policeman's service revolver. Even this wouldn't have caused much stir, except for the fact that within three hours Vitale had arranged for every dollar, every bauble, even the pistol, to be returned to his political club.

The newspapers eagerly descended on the story, especially when it was discovered that the guest list included not only police officers and prominent politicos but also a half-dozen racketeers, including Ciro Terranova, the powerful gang leader of East Harlem. Hammered by the press and the bar association, Vitale finally admitted that he had accepted a $20,000 loan from Rothstein, and that in his four years on the bench he had banked some $165,000 in unexplained income.

☾

On top of the suspicious death of Magistrate Macrery and the almost comical failure to solve Rothstein's murder, Vitale's underworld dinner gave Tammany's opponents a new foothold. In January 1930 the *New York Evening Post* launched a series of exposés into corruption in the magistrates' courts, whipping up public outrage and prompting the Republican-led state legislature to call for an official investigation.

Now it was Governor Roosevelt's turn to walk the political tightrope that had nearly strangled Al Smith. If FDR didn't protect the Tammany leaders, they would turn on him at the polls, torpedoing his reelection in November. But if he appeared to be whitewashing judicial corruption, it could sink his shot at the White House.

Perhaps sensing the ill winds, in May the dapper Grover Whalen resigned as police commissioner. In his place, Mayor Walker appointed Edward P. Mulrooney, a thirty-year veteran of the department who was seasoned enough to neither neglect nor kowtow to Tammany's district leaders.

Next up in what the *Daily News* called "the big parade of New York judges to the bar of criminal judgment" was Magistrate George Ewald, who had been appointed only five months earlier to replace the disgraced Albert Vitale. On July 7 the attorney general indicted him on federal stock fraud charges. He also turned up evidence that Ewald had given $12,000 to Martin J. Healy, the leader of the Cayuga Club in the nineteenth congressional district, in exchange for his seat on the bench. After much outcry, a grand jury was appointed to investigate the purchase of judgeships.

Up in Albany, Governor Roosevelt was deftly resisting the growing clamor for a citywide investigation into corruption among the judiciary. But all efforts to silence the brewing scandal were blown to bits when Judge Joseph Force Crater did not return for the fall session of the supreme court of New York.

The forty-one-year-old Joseph Crater was instantly recognizable by his unusual height and his round, fleshy head, perched on an oddly narrow neck. He'd climbed his way up as a clubhouse lawyer in Martin Healy's Cayuga Club and was a close friend of George Ewald. For the last six years, he'd worked in the law firm of one of Roosevelt's closest allies, U.S. senator Robert Wagner, serving as the senator's personal secretary, or as some would say, his bagman.

Early in 1930, Crater learned of an upcoming vacancy on the New York State supreme court and began pressing Healy, Ewald, and especially Senator Wagner, his most powerful mentor, to lobby for him with the governor. His persuasion worked, and on April 8, Roosevelt appointed him to the bench.

But that summer, Crater became increasingly agitated as the judicial scandals engulfed his political patrons. On August 6, the same day Mayor Walker suspended Healy from his lucrative position as deputy commissioner of the Plant and Structures Department, the judge withdrew more than $20,000 from his various bank accounts, ate a hearty dinner with a seventeen-year-old chorus girl named Sally Lou Ritz, then hailed a taxi on West 45th and vanished into the night.

The danger was now drawing uncomfortably near to the governor's mansion. Judge Crater's career was closely entwined with Senator Wagner. By no coincidence, the senator and the judge had conferred privately about the Healy scandal only one week before Crater vanished. If the governor didn't get ahead of this simmering scandal, it might well sink some of his staunchest allies.

When Crater did not appear for the opening session of the courts on August 25, the facts could no longer be hidden from the public. That very same day Governor Roosevelt reluctantly named the eminent Judge

Samuel Seabury to lead a broad investigation into corruption in the city's magistrates' courts.

News of Crater's disappearance broke on September 3 with the force of a hurricane. The manhunt for the vanished judge blanketed the headlines as reporters raked the city for information.

It quickly came out that the married judge was an extravagant womanizer and a big spender in Broadway's most mobbed-up nightclubs. He was a regular at Texas Guinan's current enterprise, the Club Abbey, a notorious all-night joint in the basement of the Harding Hotel, next to Polly's 54th Street apartment building. (The Club Abbey would return to the headlines five months later when Dutch Schultz tried to kill rival gunman Chink Sherman on the club's crowded dance floor.) A passel of showgirls, nightclub hostesses, and a longtime mistress turned up to talk about their friendships with him, and a strong scent of blackmail hung in the air. Crater had also borrowed money from Rothstein and, it was reported, had been deeply upset by his death. It was all catnip to the tabloids.

Had the judge been kidnapped, or was he being extorted by one of his many illicit ladies? Had he blown town to escape the ignoble fate of his fellow lawgivers? Or had he made the same mistake as Magistrate Macrery and paid the same price? All the theories were perfectly probable, and all were equally sordid.

The tabloids were rooting for a villainess. "Sex is the direct reason for nine-tenths of missing persons," insisted the *Evening Graphic*. Crater's closest colleagues from the bench and bar said plainly that they assumed he'd been murdered. Decades later the highly respected Judge Jonah Goldstein recalled "the well-founded rumor in inner circles" that, like Macrery, "Crater had made a commitment as to how much he would pay for the nomination. Unable to deliver it, those that had made the arrangement with him then delivered the vacancy through his death."

☾

Roosevelt's newly appointed chief investigator, Judge Samuel Seabury, announced that he would turn his attention first to the Women's Court, where the odor was strongest.

From the beginning, Seabury proved to be a more formidable foe than the usual sin chasers. He assembled a team of nine brilliant, idealistic young attorneys and a corps of trusted stenographers who all committed to ironclad secrecy. At the same time, he cannily used the press to his own advantage, recruiting reporters to help track down recalcitrant witnesses in exchange for off-the-record information and occasional scoops.

Within the month, disgraceful stories about the magistrates' courts had proliferated to the point that even seasoned political reporters were lamenting the difficulty of keeping track of all the accusations. While the newspapers were going mad over the unsavory Judge Crater, Judge Seabury's team was methodically gathering witnesses from the flotsam and jetsam of the magistrates' courts, subpoenaing stool pigeons, clerks, cops, magistrates, and scores of angry women. In a shocking move, he subpoenaed the bank records of every single magistrate in Manhattan and Brooklyn.

At the end of September, after weeks of interrogation behind closed doors, Seabury began public hearings. "Personally, I had nothing to fear from Judge Seabury," Polly maintained. "This time the heat was on the law-givers and law-enforcers, not the lawbreakers." Nonetheless, as the tales began tumbling out, her friends took to kidding her. "You'll be getting a little *billet doux* from Judge Seabury any day now, Poll," they joked. "He'll be wanting you to whisper to him about all your friends in court." Polly laughed—a madam always laughed at her customers' jokes—but she found nothing funny about it.

Polly lay low, keeping a nervous eye on the newspapers and whatever information her underworld allies could glean from their moles in the County Courthouse. Seabury's lawyers were leakproof, but Detective Jim Quinlivan had an ally in the outer office who kept him apprised of the subpoenas being issued. Quinlivan wielded this information to warn or intimidate potential witnesses. When Seabury began subpoenaing the vice squad's professional stool pigeons, by definition the most unreliable of criminal conspirators, the vice cop cabal decided that the surest solution was to pay them to skip town until the whole thing blew over.

It didn't take long for the first blow to fall. On October 14 two of Polly's old nemeses, Detectives Leigh Halpern and Daniel Sullivan, were picked up on charges of committing perjury. Two showgirls, with long memories and deep grudges, accused the officers of paying two stool pigeons, Harry Gibson and Monty Booth, to frame them as prostitutes, then lying about the incident in court.

Polly knew the bums all too well. Twice Halpern and Sullivan had double-crossed her, taking a hefty bribe, then arresting her under her own name and demanding yet another payoff for her acquittal. And she was intimately familiar with Harry "the Greek" Gibson, a stool pigeon, procurer, and sometime stage manager of *Earl Carroll's Vanities*, who often steered fresh showgirls to Polly's stable. But investigators didn't connect Polly to these miscreants until yet another young woman came forward to describe how Harry Gibson had lured her to a party with the promise that important men who could help her career would be there, only to discover that she'd been brought to Polly Adler's notorious whorehouse.

Polly made her big debut in the press on October 22, when *The Brooklyn Citizen* reported that process servers were seeking "a woman said to be 'Polly Adler,' the manager of 'call houses,'" and listed two of her addresses. The next day her story was picked up by the tabloids, as more outraged women came forward to describe their experiences with the vice squad's "nefarious frame-up and shake-down ring."

Now the floodgates were open, as attention turned to the sex-drenched scandals of the Women's Court. More than two dozen plain-clothes policemen had already been accused, with more names to come. Nonetheless, Tammany seemed invincible. In November the Democratic slate won with an astounding 91.1 percent of all eligible voters. Franklin Roosevelt was reelected governor by such a wide margin that he was now considered a national front-runner in the upcoming presidential race.

Polly did not share Tammany Hall's equanimity. By the time Halpern and Sullivan and their two stool pigeons were released on bail, she was in a constant state of high alert. On November 17, just as she was finishing dinner, one of the maids called her to the phone. Before she had time to say hello, she heard a man growl, "Hurry, Polly, get out of your house. They're on their way to serve you with a subpoena."

"Who is this?"

"Never mind who it is. Get out fast!"

Polly tossed some clothes into a bag, raced out to the street, and hailed a taxi. As the cab pulled away, a car screeched to a halt in front of her building, disgorging four husky process servers—a surprisingly muscular crew to hand a piece of paper to a 116-pound, five-foot female, she noted.

She checked into a hotel and spent a restless night pacing the floor and chain-smoking as she awaited news. The next morning she picked up the papers to discover that she'd become a national story, with her name splashed across all the syndicated sheets in the country:

Here is Polly Adler, "queen of the vice-ring," as she is tagged in the headlines. Polly is a small, vivacious and energetic Russian woman who has been gossiping with lawyers for the appellate division inquiry into the lower courts. Polly, dealer in girls, has been arrested many times. The word is out that she told the Appellate Division all about a prominent New York and Washington politician who always squared things for her when she got in trouble. The graft inquisitors wanted to hear more, but Polly had departed.

True or not—and she defiantly maintained it was not—loose talk like that could put her in cement shoes. Word came immediately from her police informants: get lost and stay lost until she got the green light to return.

Polly headed across the Hudson River and checked into the Robert Treat Hotel, the finest stopping place in the bustling city of Newark, New Jersey. She had entertained many high officials from the Garden State, and could count on the courtesy of her old friend Waxey Gordon and his young colleague Longy Zwillman, who together controlled organized crime in northern New Jersey.

Nonetheless, her long-sought notoriety was now fueling her paranoia as the newspapers speculated on her whereabouts. "I didn't know where to get a drink, and I was afraid to talk to anyone for fear I'd be recognized," she remembered. Her only visitor was a stool pigeon sent by her friends on the force, bringing news of the latest developments.

Public hearings on corruption in the Women's Court opened on November 24. To the surprise of everyone, Seabury's first witness was none other than John C. Weston, the longtime special prosecutor at Jefferson Market, who had freed Polly more times than even he could remember. For weeks, Weston had been secretly spilling his guts. Now, in front of a packed courtroom, he began laying out the workings of the vice ring, sparing none of the odious details.

The doleful prosecutor confessed that in his eight years serving under District Attorney Joab Banton, he'd been paid approximately $20,000 to free some nine hundred women, working closely with the nefarious bail bondsman of Lawyers' Row. He named all the main players and co-conspirators, including most of the Women's Court magistrates. He made a point of singling out two of the most piggish of the Harlem vice cops, Jim Quinlivan and Bill O'Connor, for the depths of their corruption and their violent, drunken outbursts. He spoke of the leading madams, including Sadie the Chink, Jenny the Factory, and, in his most detailed example, Polly Adler. He claimed he'd seen Polly in court at least eleven times—twice under her own name—and each time had been bribed by her lawyer, Emanuel Busch, to let her go.

Newspapers across the country were electrified by Weston's bombshells, yet oddly, none of the hometown papers even whispered Polly's name. Apparently, Polly's longtime goodwill campaign among the gentlemen of the press was paying off.

Weston's performance was topped the next day by another surprise witness, one "Chile" Mapocha Acuna, a thirty-one-year-old professional stool pigeon who had been employed by no fewer than twenty-eight vice squad detectives to help shake down scores of women, many of them patently innocent. His descriptions of the methods for entrapping them were so disgraceful and luridly detailed that Judge Seabury ordered all ladies to leave the courtroom while he was on the stand.

"Acuna's charges shook the entire Department to its foundations," remembered the future police commissioner Lewis Valentine, "and he occupied the center of the stage for weeks." Afraid for Acuna's safety, Seabury assigned around-the-clock bodyguards to him and his family.

After this, a steady stream of witnesses appeared to elaborate on the workings of the vice ring. Lowell Limpus of the *Daily News* ran a long series of interviews with Acuna, which made prominent mention of "the Notorious Polly Adler." But as long as Polly stayed out of New York State, she could not be subpoenaed or, as she pointed out, arrested and extradited, since she was wanted only as a witness.

What worried Polly most were the rumors that, her stout denials to the contrary, she was in dialogue with Judge Seabury's team. When, on December 1, reporters hinted that Seabury's second-in-command Isidor Kresel had secretly met with Polly in Atlantic City over the weekend, she took it as a signal that New Jersey was too close for comfort. She decided to head west when she read that her old boyfriend Jimmy Carr and his band were playing a long engagement in Pittsburgh. She and Jimmy had long ago patched up any hard feelings, and it would be a relief to see a real friend she could trust.

☾

Meanwhile Judge Seabury's team, led by the brilliant bulldog Isidor Kresel, were plowing steadily through witnesses in private, while also holding public hearings. Their first targets were Magistrate Jesse Silbermann of the Women's Court, who'd freed Polly many times, and her old adversaries, Bill O'Connor and James Quinlivan. Shrewdly, the probers led with the most sympathetic angle, focusing on the "frame-ups" of presumably innocent women, presenting testimony from the nurses, boardinghouse keepers, and hostesses who'd had the bad luck to be caught in the vice ring's indiscriminate net.

As predicted, the newspapers and their readers were aflame with disgust and outrage. Pressing the advantage, Seabury's team announced that they were subpoenaing the bank records and brokerage accounts of every plainclothesman in Brooklyn and Manhattan and were prepared to review "truckloads" of vice squad expense vouchers if necessary. Every one of the twenty-four magistrates in Manhattan and the Bronx was scheduled for questioning, along with scores of cops, bondsmen, lawyers, court clerks, and district leaders. One by one they withered under the force of Seabury's unrelenting interrogations.

To the astonishment of the underworld, for the first time in recent memory, it was the politicians and police who were taking the heat. "While the whole nation was living high off the hog, John Q. Public didn't give a damn how the Tammany boys were getting theirs," Polly observed acidly. But as unemployment rose into double digits and tax revenues tumbled, the hijinks of the Hall and its merry band of thieves weren't so amusing. "For years the cops had been framing girls, or beating up girls, and in general grafting on girls," as one reporter cracked. "Now the idea was irritating, possibly because the cops had steady jobs."

When Seabury turned the spotlight to the vice squad, Polly decided it was time to head south to the more tolerant climes of Miami, where she spent her days by the pool, smoking cigarettes, devouring the New York newspapers, and stoking her anxieties as the coverage became more feverish. She was corresponding regularly with Irwin O'Leary back in New York, who kept her abreast of the inside gossip, including the worrisome news that investigators had heard tales of their relationship and were now questioning Irwin about her—especially her current whereabouts.

Polly's longing to be a celebrity in the great metropolis was finally coming to pass. Reporters who had been barred from printing her name out of good manners and the prudery of their editors now leaped on her as an ideal protagonist in this lurid tabloid drama. "I was twice as exciting because I was missing," she noted dryly. A mysterious madam was a welcome respite from the sordid parade of moneygrubbing middle-aged bureaucrats, and they showered her with some of their most purple prose.

Meanwhile the bully boys were finally getting their comeuppance. Next up were Robert E. Morris and James T. Brady, longtime partners from the Broadway plainclothes squad. "Morris often had been at the receiving end of shakedowns at my house, and it did my heart good to see him finally getting his lumps," remembered Polly. Her contempt for Jim Brady, "the dirty prick," was even greater. Before Seabury spoiled the scene, they'd each been sleeping with rival madams—Lillian Rose and June Reed—and it burned her up every time she recalled how June Reed had sent Brady to harass her.

When she later reminded him of the episode, he chortled nastily, insisting, "You know Polly that I never accepted a cent from whores."

"What a laugh," she remembered sourly. "I remember quite well that I gave those two lice $1,000 outside the courtroom to help me get dismissed from a charge those bastards framed."

Seabury demanded to know how the pair had managed to accumulate more than $70,000 in various bank accounts before moving the cash to the anonymity of safe deposit boxes—"little tin boxes" was the refrain—on an annual salary of less than $4,000. When presented with bank records to jog his remarkably poor memory, Brady recalled that he'd been holding that $14,000 for a friend on the police force, who had, unfortunately, passed away a few months earlier. Morris, when asked to explain how he happened to have deposited $50,000 in two bank accounts, testified that most of it had been a gift from his uncle George, who'd handed him forty $1,000 bills because he was his uncle's "favorite nephew." Sadly, Uncle George had also met an early demise and was unavailable to confirm this tale.

"The death rate for relatives of the vice squad is high," snickered the *Brooklyn Eagle*. The mortal toll only mounted when Isidor Kresel began quizzing Jim Quinlivan and Bill O'Connor about their suspiciously large cash reserves. O'Connor explained that his uncle John had gifted him with a tidy sum, not long before he too met his maker. Quinlivan departed slightly from the script, claiming that he'd won $9,300 from a hot tip on a horse and had handed all his winnings to his mother, who promptly went to her grave, bequeathing it back to him. "Not even an expert like Kresel can quiz a horse," the *Eagle* noted archly.

It was as if, wrote Polly, "the Marx Brothers were writing their dialogue." The squirming postures and "sputtering mouths of red faced policemen who are trying to act righteous and be defiant at the same time," in the *Eagle*'s phrase, added some rare comic relief to the scurrilous proceedings. It would be one of the last lighthearted moments she'd enjoy for some time to come.

The first criminal trials to come out of the vice squad inquiry began in February 1931. The star witness in the perjury trial of Leigh Halpern was Georgia Gray, a showgirl in *Earl Carroll's Vanities*. She was living with Harry Gibson, the missing stool pigeon, before he fled, and she testified on February 19 that Halpern and Sullivan had frequently come by their apartment to confer with Gibson. It took less than a day for the jury to acquit the unrepentant former lawmen, despite the compelling evidence offered by Acuna and several women who'd been framed by him.

Disillusioned by Halpern's extraordinary acquittal, and now terrified for their safety, the other victims who'd agreed to testify against policemen decided to make themselves scarce. "What's the use?" lamented one woman. "You can't beat this lousy game. I'm leaving town."

As for Georgia Gray, when she told the district attorney's office she was worried for her life, the DA promptly clapped her into jail, holding her as a material witness for the upcoming trial of Dan Sullivan. So far, she was the only one behind bars.

Polly on holiday with one of her working girls

11

The Female Al Capone

In the early morning of February 26, 1931, a shapely redhead in a black velvet dress, about forty years old, was discovered with a piece of rope wrapped around her neck, strangled to death, on the side of the highway running through Van Cortlandt Park in the Bronx.

By the time the newspapers had the story, the victim had been identified as Vivian Gordon, a prominent figure in the murky shadows of Broadway. The police decorously described her as "a woman of many acquaintances." One of her fellow gold diggers was more blunt: "Vivian Gordon is the toughest, most desperate blackmailer, extortionist and shakedown artist in this man's town."

It quickly came out that the murdered woman had been tattling to Samuel Seabury and his anti-corruption inquisitors. On February 7 she wrote to Judge Seabury volunteering to testify against Detective Andrew J. McLaughlin—a particularly noxious member of the vice squad with whom Polly had tangled early in her career. Vivian accused Detective McLaughlin of conspiring with her ex-husband to frame her in March 1923, so he could seize custody of their daughter. After McLaughlin's arrest, Gordon was convicted of prostitution and spent two years in the Bedford Reformatory for Women. Now she was taking her revenge.

On February 20 Gordon appeared at Seabury's offices in the Centre Street courthouse to spill her story to Irving Ben Cooper, the fiery racket-busting lawyer who was leading the vice squad inquiry. Besides her complaint against Detective McLaughlin she offered scuttlebutt on a long list of big shots, including Mayor Walker. Cooper wanted evidence to back up her accusations. He was in luck. Blackmailers like Vivian worked their trade by collecting compromising letters, photos, ticket stubs, and the like. She made an appointment to return the following week with corroborating documents.

Gordon's plan to wreak vengeance on the man who put her behind bars might have worked, had she not given in to the impulse to send a letter to McLaughlin boasting that she was about to take him down. Five nights after her meeting with Irving Ben Cooper, she left her Manhattan apartment a little before midnight and never returned.

Searching her suite, the police found seven leather-bound, highly detailed diaries and address books, containing some three hundred names and phone numbers—including nearly every major gangland figure in New York, a score of dirty vice cops, some exceedingly prominent businessmen, and Polly Adler. By the next morning every paper in the city had the story and were already speculating about precisely what was in those diaries. The obvious conclusion to everyone but the NYPD was that Vivian Gordon had been killed to keep her mouth shut.

Of all the ugly accusations and entanglements arising over the course of her long criminal career, it was odd that the murder of a fading Broadway butterfly was the one that seemed to alarm Polly most. She was not fully truthful about many things, naturally; it was professional habit. But this subject of Vivian Gordon was the one with which she struggled the most when she was composing her life story.

Polly's breezy confidence and razor-sharp memory faltered when asked about Vivian, remembered her friend Virginia Faulkner, and she seemed palpably nervous, far more than when speaking of her friendships with still-dangerous mobsters like Frank Costello and Meyer Lansky. Polly's various versions of her relationship with Gordon were riddled with contradictions and gaps. At first she spoke openly of her friendship with "Viv," but in later tellings she denied knowing her entirely. In the end, she settled on the genteel phrase "our acquaintance was of the slightest."

But the Broadway rumor mill said otherwise. It quickly became clear from Gordon's personal diaries and other underworld sources that the dead woman had once been one of Polly's top-dollar call girls, before striking out on her own and parlaying her little black book into a lucrative blackmail enterprise.

Down in Miami Beach, Polly was still lying low, sunbathing, chain-smoking, and keeping a close eye on the New York papers, searching for signs that the Seabury Investigation would soon burn itself out. So it was a sickening jolt to pick up the New York *Daily News* of February 28 and see the headline—"BLACKMAIL, RUM, DRUGS"—splashed across the page in inch-high letters, with her name in the very first sentence of the story:

> Straight into the love factory of the notorious Polly Adler, and from there into the haunts of the Jack Diamond and Vannie Higgins drug and liquor mobsters, went yesterday's trail of the slayers of Vivian Gordon. The red-haired beauty, who used the affections of men as a wedge to pry loose their bank rolls, was revealed as one of the 600 lovely girls on Polly Adler's "call list."

Each new newspaper account was more dreadful than the last:

> That Vivian Gordon was murdered to seal her lips became still more apparent when it was learned that death awaits another woman of scarlet should she return to New York from her hiding place in Havana. She is the notorious Polly Adler, czarina for years of the unofficial red light apartments in the city.

While the tabloids were thrilled at Polly's sensational return to the headlines, the forces of law and order were surprisingly nonplussed. When reporters asked them about Polly's connection to the case, both Police Commissioner Edward Mulrooney and the district attorney for the Bronx, Charles B. McLaughlin (no relation to the deplorable detective), immediately dismissed her from the list of suspects.

In fact, they didn't want to talk to her at all, they insisted. When the chief of police in Miami wired the DA and police commissioner to inform them he currently had Polly Adler under surveillance, and offered to detain her if they wanted to send someone down to question her, they politely but inexplicably declined.

But Polly received no such deference from the Fourth Estate. The crime reporters who knew her well were keeping mum, but that didn't make her untouchable. Gotham's top tabloid, the *Daily News*, assigned crackerjack female reporters Grace Robinson and Doris Fleeson to cover the story. Gene McHugh, the legendary night editor of the *Daily News* whose underworld intimacies were unrivaled, counted Polly as a friend, but they did not, so whatever they discovered on their own hook was fair game.

And they dug up plenty. Grace Robinson buddied up to an out-of-work chorus girl who'd worked for Polly and possessed inside dope, while Doris Fleeson worked her connections among Big Bill Dwyer's old gang.

In a milieu where female friendships were fleeting and conditional, Viv and Polly were well-seasoned comrades and occasional competitors. "When Vivian found herself broke she often worked for Madame Polly herself," Robinson reported. "The dead gal constantly boasted to others of her rich boyfriends, said she didn't have to go to Adler's and just worked to keep her mind occupied." Gordon often brought her own men to Polly's assignation apartments, paying Polly a cut of her fee.

"Polly treated her more as an equal than an employee," wrote Robinson. "She was a kind of high lieutenant in the Adler organization." Although thoroughly hard-boiled, Vivian had a surprising literary bent and wrote poetry, which the newspapers gleefully published:

> *I'm a lady of the evening*
> *With a morning glory's beauty.*
> *The payment for my raiment*
> *I get in devious ways.*
> *When some big and wealthy brute*
> *Wants to love me 'cause I'm cute,*
> *I admit that I submit*
> *Because it pays.*
>
> *I'm a lady of the evening*
> *Just like Cleopatra was.*
> *The Queen of Sheba also played my game.*
> *Though by inches I am dying,*

There's not any use in crying.
I stay and play 'cause I'm that way,
A moth that loves the flame.

But the titian-haired hussy also had a reputation as a troublemaker. Her sense of honor was not very high, to say the least. At some point, Vivian decided to start her own call house in direct competition with Polly, turning to Arnold Rothstein and several politicians for start-up money, protection, and contacts. But running a party girl operation was too much like a square job, and it wasn't as lucrative in these dark days of the Depression, when free-spending sugar daddies evaporated along with the economic boom.

So Vivian turned to the faster and lusher art of blackmail, employing young girls as bait for balding, well-heeled suckers. She and Legs Diamond went into business together, shaking down shady stockbrokers whom she harvested from nightclubs. The "beauty and the blackjack" could be spotted together most evenings haunting the corner table of the notorious Club Abbey in the Harding Hotel. "Vivian and Jack had been taking the boys right and left," one of Gordon's friends told the *Daily News*. "They were the envy of every racket mob on Broadway."

Like Legs, Vivian was reckless and greedy. She was a heavy user of cocaine and sleeping aids like Veronal and Alinol and was an exceedingly belligerent drunk. If she suspected that one of her feminine accomplices was keeping more than her share of the loot, Vivian would set her up to be arrested by one of her pals on the vice squad.

As a shakedown artist, Gordon "found the Adler connection highly valuable," reported Grace Robinson. "Polly Adler's male acquaintances occasionally became Vivian's victims." Polly was no saint, but she wanted nothing to do with these dangerous badger games. This led to a number of heated arguments between the two women.

"The dead gal and Polly had a helluva quarrel shortly before the Seabury probe soft-pedaled Polly's racket," Robinson reported, right around the time of Judge Crater's disappearance. "Their fight was over some middle-aged heavy spender whom the Gordon gal brought to Polly's. Polly ordered her from the place in this guy's presence one night, and told other girls who were friends of hers: 'She'll never come in my house again!'"

Indeed, it soon came out that the garroted temptress and the missing judge had been seeing each other regularly in the months before he disappeared. They usually met up at the notorious Club Abbey, next to Polly's place, where she knew him merely as "Joe Crane." Vivian swore she had no idea what a "big shot" he was until the magistrates scandal broke. "If I'd dreamed he was Judge Crater, I'd have used different tactics," she told a colleague angrily. She may well have been one of the women who threatened to blackmail the judge just before he vanished. On August 7, 1930, the day after Joseph Crater was last seen, Vivian was arrested on charges of extortion that were later dropped.

Besides Vivian Gordon, there was one more tenuous connection between Polly and the lascivious justice. Three decades after Crater disappeared, Allen Churchill, a respected journalist and historian, described an early draft of Polly's autobiography, one of several that were widely circulated in publishing circles in the late 1940s and early 1950s. This manuscript claimed that the judge spent the final evening of his life in one of Polly's apartments and that "Crater suffered a fatal heart attack at the moment of peak enjoyment while indulging in the unique pleasures of the establishment." When Polly realized her predicament, she called a friend who spirited the corpse away and dumped it in the Hudson River. At this late date it is impossible to guess which, if any, portion of this story might be true. Still, it would have been no surprise to Broadway insiders if it were.

If there were any links between Vivian Gordon, Joe Crater, and Polly Adler, no one in City Hall or the Governor's Mansion was eager to expose them. Despite the salacious press coverage, the authorities continued to dismiss the Polly Adler angle. When pressed by reporters, the authorities offered a half dozen or more theories of the murder, encompassing every explanation except the obvious one: that Detective Andrew McLaughlin had arranged for his accuser to be permanently silenced before she squealed to Judge Seabury.

While the police dithered and dissembled, the story began to recede from the headlines. Then on March 3 it returned to the front pages with a bang. Vivian's sixteen-year-old daughter, humiliated by the very public discovery of her mother's secret life, killed herself with carbon monoxide. The innocent girl's "shame suicide," as the papers labeled it, turned Gordon's murder from a local scandal into a national sensation that threatened to blow the New York Police Department and Jimmy Walker's administration sky-high.

Suddenly everyone wanted to talk to the mysterious missing madam. "Polly could tell those New York cops plenty about Vivian Gordon and their party girl racket," jeered one of Vivian's girlfriends to reporters. "Why didn't they ask her about Vivian?"

Now the search was on for "New York's Empress of Crime." In a widely reprinted story, the *New York World-Telegram* reported that the police were now looking for an unnamed "Female Al Capone" who possessed "an encyclopedic knowledge of New York's night life."

> Were this woman to appear and tell all she knows, she would wreck the homes and lives of numberless men in the judicial, political and business world of this and other cities. She knows them all intimately. . . . Her empire reached into night clubs and speakeasies, into the precincts of the police, into the theaters and wandering gambling dens. Her obedient subjects were wantons of the chorus, "ponies" of the nightclubs, or girls in apartments whose sole business it was to await telephone calls and "take orders." Often she was arrested, but her slippery nature, smoothed and oiled and greased with cash, was demonstrated in the fact that she has never been convicted of any crime.

Up in Albany, Governor Roosevelt had been watching the appalling revelations of the Seabury Investigation with a perfect poker face, keeping his own counsel until he was forced to act. His cool demeanor slipped for the first time when the Gordon girl's suicide transformed this local imbroglio into a national soap opera.

Suddenly reporters noted a new air of anxiety in the Governor's Mansion, especially after Judge Seabury paid a "mysterious visit" to brief FDR in private. "So startling were the revelations made yesterday, that Governor Roosevelt speeded his plans to take a personal hand in probing the mystery," reported Grace Robinson in the *Daily News*. "A large package of documents, believed to contain the diary itself, went to Albany last night for the executive's inspection." Now Roosevelt seemed genuinely alarmed.

The governor's concern seemed to focus on Gordon's diaries and correspondence, which were rumored to include two to three hundred names of prominent men-about-town. Eminent businessmen and pillars of the community were besieging the district attorney and the governor's office with panicked calls. They became nearly hysterical after a bellhop at Manhattan's Vanderbilt Hotel, a well-known stopping place for high-profile politicians, told investigators that Gordon had blackmailed many of the naïve federal officials who came up from Washington, D.C., for "week-end parties."

Meanwhile District Attorney McLaughlin and Commissioner Mulrooney were panicking and turning against each other. As Roosevelt was combing through Gordon's diaries, the two lawmen had a "loud and stormy" shouting match in the prosecutor's office that lasted three hours, with a cluster of reporters listening at the door. The next day Roosevelt "assumed direct jurisdiction over the investigation," demanding the DA and the police commissioner answer directly to him and send him detailed daily updates on the progress of the case.

Thus far, Polly had played a colorful but minor role in the Seabury scandals. Now she took center stage. After conferring with Governor Roosevelt, the district attorney revealed that he was hiring the famous Pinkerton National Detective Agency—"the shrewdest manhunters in the country"—to search for Polly in Miami, Palm Beach, and Havana.

Even in the face of this direct insult to New York's Finest, the police stuck with the party line. "We know where Polly is," one high police official informed reporters, "but we don't want her. She was eliminated long ago." But when the top brass realized that it would be better for them to find her first—and that the Pinkertons had a head start on them—they sent a search party down south, headed by Joe Daley of the Broadway squad. By no coincidence, Daley was the plainclothesman who had shooed away Ruth Keyes the night Rothstein was murdered.

By March 8 newspapers from Maine to California were reporting that rival teams of policemen, Pinkerton detectives, and Seabury's process servers were all hunting for the notorious Polly Adler.

€

Meanwhile, the toll of mercenary magistrates, vice cops, and political appointees swept up in Seabury's net was mounting fast. "With bewildering speed the rumors of murky corruption, the stories of graft and the direct charges of misfeasance of office that have been rife in New York for several years seem to be coming to a head," observed Raymond Moley in *The New York Times*.

Mayor Walker, unaccustomed to being bombarded by the usually sympathetic press, decided he needed a last-minute vacation, six weeks in far-off Palm Springs, California. "With the police department up to its ears in troubles of its own; with the public at large muttering 'collusion' under its breath; with magistrates implicated in nearly every sort of scandal; with night club shootings, gang feuds, innocent girls being framed to fatten the purses of the gentry," sniped the Broadway columnist Rian James, naturally it was a perfect time for a jaunt to the Coast.

Jimmy slipped out just in time. On March 9, under fierce pressure from the newspapers and public advocates, Governor Roosevelt appointed Judge Seabury to lead a second panel to examine the dismal conviction record and professional incompetence of Manhattan's feeble district attorney, Thomas Crain.

On March 13 Georgia Gray, a star witness in the vice squad inquiry who was being held in protective custody, fell mysteriously ill just before she was scheduled to testify against Officer Daniel Sullivan. She was rushed to Bellevue Hospital, but the next evening the ill-fated showgirl was found lifeless on the floor next to her hospital bed. "Natural causes," proclaimed the Tammany-appointed city medical examiner.

"Another indication of the strange spell that seems to be invoked against persons who know anything about the outrageous framing of innocent women by vice cops with unexplained bank accounts," countered the *Daily News*.

With the death of yet another comely witness, public anger against the police reached a furious crescendo. Adding to the uproar, lewd rumors about Mayor Walker and his showgirl mistress were becoming so loud that the newspapers could no longer ignore them. On March 18 a coalition of good government organizations called on Roosevelt to demand Walker's removal from office.

Finally the governor could no longer temporize. But however he responded, aye or nay, he might jeopardize his path to the presidential nomination. At the very last moment, the Republicans of the state legislature rescued him: on March 24, they pushed through a sweeping investigation of Mayor Walker and his administration, chaired by Republican state senator Samuel Hofstadter and spearheaded, once again, by the redoubtable Judge Samuel Seabury. Seabury was now leading three separate investigations into every corner of the Tammany machine.

"The curtain rises," declared the *Daily News*, "on what promises to be one of the most tremendous dramas in the political history of New York City."

☾

Seabury wasted no time. In late April 1931, he presented the governor with formal charges against Mayor Walker covering an array of financial improprieties and no less than a million dollars in unexplained funds. Albany buzzed with suspense, but downstate Democrats were surprisingly untroubled. "It is an open secret that Tammany expects the Governor to dismiss the charges at an early date," reported the *Herald Tribune*, "in fact, they have scarcely discussed any other possibility."

Their confidence was well founded. On April 28 Roosevelt rendered his decision in one terse sentence: "I do not find sufficient evidence in these documents to remove the mayor or to proceed further."

The blowback was instant and even more intense than the governor had feared. The national press howled in condemnation of Roosevelt's apparent cowardice in the face of Tammany's threats, insisting that he had struck a suicidal blow to his presidential prospects. Nor did FDR's mealymouthed exoneration please Mayor Walker and his allies.

But it was just the answer Polly was hoping for: "I reasoned that with this shift in the spotlight the heat would be off me." There were other good omens. The talkative Georgia Gray was no longer a threat to anyone. The various proceedings against the vice squad were winding down, and the public's attention was moving on to other municipal outrages. The vice ring had been brought to heel. Commissioner Mulrooney tightened the rules of evidence in prostitution arrests and demoted three hundred plainclothesmen, including Irwin O'Leary, who was now walking a beat in outer Queens. (Nonetheless, department insiders considered it a victory that only a handful of officers were fired or held criminally liable.)

Perhaps most important, in early April a small-time thief named Harry Stein was arrested for Vivian Gordon's murder. The case was nothing more than a robbery gone awry, the police insisted. To Tammany watchers and Sucker Street cynics, Harry Stein had all the marks of a fall guy, paid to take the rap and put an end to the case. But the authorities were jubilant.

With the vice squad muzzled and the grafters lying low, the town was essentially wide open. It was driving Polly nuts that Sadie the Chink, Jenny the Factory, Peggy Wild, and the other madams who'd managed to stay out of Seabury's sight were making money hand over fist while she was out of the game.

And so, remembered Polly, "I began to think of going home. I needed money, I was bored with Miami, and I was tired of living the life of a lamster. So conning myself into thinking Judge Seabury had lost interest in me, I took the train north."

To celebrate her homecoming, she decided to throw a deluxe party in the private apartment she kept as a hideaway, at 201 West 77th Street and Amsterdam Avenue. She restocked the bar, called her best-looking girls, printed up cards to alert her trusted customers that she was back in business, and sent personal invitations to her most affluent clientele to join her on May 5.

The intrepid legmen of the *New York Daily Mirror*, who'd been working in tandem with Seabury's process servers to keep an around-the-clock watch on Polly's regular haunts, were the first to catch sight of her. Getting wind of the festivities, they put a twenty-four-hour guard on the building, planning to jump the moment she appeared on the street.

Sometime after midnight, when the party was at full roar, her private telephone rang. She picked up the receiver and heard the voice of a reporter at the end of the line telling her the jig was up, she was cornered.

Polly exploded, cursing the caller in her booming baritone. When the reporter informed her that the building was surrounded by process servers and newsmen who wouldn't leave until she surrendered, she shouted, "Go to the devil!" and smashed down the phone.

That was the end of the revels. By dawn, the only guest left was the stalwart Irwin O'Leary. Suddenly there was a pounding at the front door. If Irwin were found here, that would finish his career, so Polly barred the door while he made a getaway out the window and down the fire escape.

For four long hours, Polly stalled the process servers out in the hallway as they pleaded with her to accept the summons, while a lawyer from Judge Seabury's office peppered her with phone calls trying to convince her that she was not being arrested. It was only when the lunch hour rolled around, and peering out her third-floor window, she saw the first shift of process servers being replaced by a fresh team that she finally conceded she was beaten.

Down on Centre Street, Seabury's staff was ecstatic. Harland B. Tibbets, Seabury's chief counsel in the magistrates' investigation, was so excited that he "could not restrain himself and in his eagerness to tell the waiting world that Polly Adler had at last been caught," he called an on-the-spot press conference, reported Arthur Mefford, the *Mirror's* crack crime expert.

When she finally arrived at the courthouse, "dressed fashionably and well-tanned," noted the *New York Sun*, she was greeted cordially and ushered into a private room. For two hours, Harland Tibbets painstakingly went through the Women's Court docket books with her, trying to get her to identify the dates of her arrests and her various aliases. Although he laid on the charm, as Milton MacKaye of the *New York Evening Post* put it, Polly "proved a difficult person to deal with."

"I have nothing to say," she muttered testily to the reporters who followed her as she left the building, clutching a subpoena for further questioning.

Her next interrogator was the wily Irving Ben Cooper, an English-born crusader with a fiery temper, a nose for publicity, and a fierce grudge against Tammany Hall. Cooper had no use for Tibbets's courtesies and began hurling questions at Polly as soon as she sat down. He threw out name after incriminating name, but she denied all but the most innocuous associations.

She quickly realized that Seabury's men didn't care about her personally—they wanted to use her to get to the higher-ups. But that only heightened the danger from all sides. "I was impersonating a clam so successfully that Irving Ben Cooper was tearing his hair," Polly remembered with some satisfaction. He responded in kind, letting her sweat in the stiflingly hot waiting room and doing nothing to curb the packs of reporters who dogged her ankles. "It was just a part of the game of cops-and-robbers we were playing," said Polly.

She wasn't so sanguine when he began to delve into her financial records, combing through her bank and brokerage accounts, examining every deposit, canceled check and stock transaction, searching for payoffs to public officials and police. Polly played dumb, but too many witnesses had already said too much, allowing her inquisitors to lay traps for her. "Again and again, confronted with stories already told," observed the reporters eavesdropping outside the door, "she has exploded into indignant outbursts of Yiddish before grudgingly admitting the truth."

Although she was under oath, she was not allowed to have a lawyer present, so each session was a one-on-one duel of wits. Forbidden to take notes, every evening she dashed home to write up everything they'd discussed, then called her contact in the vice ring to relay the information. So far she'd been lucky. The interrogations had been behind closed doors, and while she remained a steady presence in the tabloids, none of them had published her real name or a photo of her face. But rumors were swirling that Irving Ben Cooper was planning to feature her as the star witness in a high-profile public hearing very soon.

Polly's "friends" in Tammany Hall weren't much help since Seabury had banned committee observers from the most sensitive interrogation sessions. She had a direct back channel to State Senator John J. McNaboe, the more belligerent of the two Tammany bulldogs assigned to the inquiry, but he didn't completely trust her accounts. When Senator McNaboe couldn't get his hands on the secret, heavily guarded transcripts of her sessions, he pressed her to get an attorney, offering the services of one of his associates, free of charge, who could keep a discreet eye on her. She declined his offer, but he convinced her she needed some sort of fixer. So she agreed to hire Jacob A. Segal, an old-school Tammany hack from the Lower East Side.

Segal was an odd choice. Clearly he had pull, Polly recalled, but "I did not trust him, and in the beginning played it very close to the belt. Even after he said he knew I was scraping the bottom of the barrel and was willing to act as my advisor for the small fee of two hundred and fifty dollars, still there was something about him I did not like and I continued to hedge."

Finally one evening, scared and overwrought after a long day under the spotlight, she let down her guard with Segal, spilling out her story in all its dangerous details. On her next visit, his fee leaped from $250 to $2,500, and it rose from there. In a rare moment of weakness, she'd handed "that prick" the tools to blackmail her, she recalled indignantly. "And he did—for years."

Left to their own devices, the newspapers speculated wildly about "Madame Adler," fueling the nasty rumors running through racketland. Some claimed she was an international trafficker in women and drugs, pointing to her purported travels to Havana and South America. That was probably half right, given her aggressive recruiting of new talent and her well-known hatred of drugs. Reporters spun stories of the "orgies staged at Polly Adler's parties," where magistrates, vice cops, and stool pigeons frolicked. One account described an epic night of debauchery, where guests included "a world famous, rotund orchestra leader directing a Dance of Nymphs, minus veils, while 4/9th of a big league ball team clapped hands. . . . Whoopie!—and a friendly vice cop, who lost his teeth, served the drinks." Honoring the masculine code of silence, the only men named in these accounts were the already-unmasked vice cops.

But it was the whispers of blackmail that she feared most. Doris Fleeson of the *Daily News* hit the extortion angle hardest.

> Her Park Ave. and Broadway clients—among them scions of some of the wealthiest Knickerbocker families—had begun to suspect in the interim that the costly "shakes" put on them by girls they first met at Polly's had been negotiated by Madame Adler herself. Many of her girls, some of them stage beauties, had also turned against her. The girls who kept their profitable love trysts in her luxurious dens had begun to suspect in Polly's absence that she had double-crossed them too—that she turned them in to the vice cops for split of the profits of their shakedowns.

"At first I laughed at some of the 'revelations' I was supposed to have made," Polly remembered, "but then I began to get worried. What if some of the people I was protecting started to think these reports were the McCoy?"

The papers reported that Judge Seabury had assigned her a twenty-four-hour-a-day bodyguard, to ensure she didn't go the way of Vivian, Georgia, and the hatcheck girl at the Hotsy Totsy. "What a joke! Aside from reporters, no one in New York came near me," scoffed Polly. She was so hot that even hardened hoodlums were avoiding her on the street.

With the disgraced vice squad temporarily out of commission, her rival madams were running at full capacity, while she was sitting on the sidelines, watching her savings dwindle. But with all the unwelcome publicity, she couldn't risk reopening. Besides, it wasn't as if her old customers were clamoring to spend an evening with "New York's Empress of Crime."

She was broke, depressed, and wallowing in self-pity when Arthur Flegenheimer came to her rescue.

☾

Dutch Schultz had made a lot of enemies as he rose through the ranks of the bootleg aristocracy, especially among the trigger-happy Irish hotheads, who resented the rising influence of the Jews and Italians. On one flank, Schultz was battling his old foe, Legs Diamond. On his other flank, he was at war with his disgruntled former employee, the deadly Vincent Coll, a creamy-skinned, blue-eyed mick by way of Hell's Kitchen.

In late May 1931, a couple weeks after falling into Seabury's clutches, Polly ran into Dutch at a cocktail party thrown by mutual friends from the theater. "I've been reading about you, Polly," he said approvingly. "You're aces in my book." By the end of the evening, they'd struck a deal. Polly needed cash to get back on her feet, and Dutch wanted a secure, full-service hideaway where he and his gang could lie low as they plotted their next moves, out of sight of his myriad rivals.

Around midnight that same evening, Polly was alone in her private apartment when the Dutchman arrived, accompanied by Lulu Rosenkrantz, a rugged, taciturn fellow who was Dutch's chief bodyguard and triggerman. "Lulu was a quiet guy," Polly remembered, "but oh boy, he must have been plenty loud with a gun in his hand."

"From now on, don't answer the phone or the doorbell," Dutch told Polly, then turned to Lulu, who was standing guard in the foyer. "I'm okay here. Call for me about ten in the morning."

Dutch made himself at home, slipping off his shoes and settling into the sofa in the living room, facing the door, while she poured them both a stiff drink. Arthur, as he preferred to be called in polite company, was full of questions, quizzing her about the Seabury Investigation, her political connections, and her customers. With all due deference, she declined to name her clientele.

"I like a dame that keeps her mouth shut. You got a lot of moxie, Poll," Dutch said approvingly. "You know, at this moment Vince Coll would part with fifty grand if he could lay hands on me."

"What good would fifty thousand do me if I'm sitting on the bottom of the East River in a hunk of cement?" she replied weakly.

"I'm not worried about you, Polly," he said with a slight smile. He stretched and yawned. "From now on you'll be seeing a lot of me."

In that case, she responded, she'd need cash up front. "Here's a start," he said, taking out a fat wad of bills and peeling off a thousand dollars. "If you run into any trouble getting an apartment, let me know. I got plenty of connections with apartment-house owners."

It was a long, tense night as Arthur jumped at every noise. Finally around dawn he ambled off to the only bedroom, without a word of thanks. Exhausted, Polly lay down on the couch but was too wound up to sleep. "I found myself listening to every little noise, listening for Mad Dog Coll who would pay fifty thousand dollars to kill the man in my bedroom," Polly remembered.

The next morning she arranged to rent a large apartment on West 83rd Street. That evening Dutch returned, bringing with him his two closest lieutenants, Bo Weinberg and Martin Krompier. Bo was a tall, hulking fellow, about ten years older than Polly, who enjoyed a reputation as one of the town's most accomplished assassins. "He was the brains of the outfit," remembered Polly. "It was my belief that Dutch feared him, maybe it was respect." Bo cut a sharp contrast to the diminutive Krompier, "a nice guy," in Polly's opinion, whose chatty, genial manner made him less intimidating company than Bo and Lulu.

When she described their new quarters, he seemed pleased. "I think we ought to have a little celebration," Dutch declared. "Polly, you're supposed to be the Ziegfeld of your profession—show us what you can do."

As she scurried off to phone some of her girls, he warned her that nobody else was to know he and the gang were there, and that she should call him "Pop" if anyone else was in the house.

The apartment on West 83rd became one of the gang's primary hideaways. No one was allowed in unless they were okayed by Lulu

Rosenkrantz, his main bodyguard, or a trusted associate. "It was like Grand Central Station, with mobsters coming and going at all hours," complained Polly.

She became rather fond of Bo Weinberg. "Bo had committed more murders than any other man I ever knew, but even when he was drunk there never seemed to be an ounce of malice in him," Schultz's lawyer, Dixie Davis, remembered with affection. Another favorite was Otto Berman, a round, bald, jolly little gambler whom all the boys at Lindy's called Abadaba. Abadaba was a brilliant accountant—he preferred the term *numerologist*—who helped Schultz manipulate the odds in his vast numbers operation. He was also the gang's court jester, who lightened some of Dutch's more murderous moods.

When Schultz was in residence, he usually stationed himself in the bedroom, propped up on Polly's ornate canopy bed, half dressed, smoking cigarettes and tossing the butts onto the floor. Most evenings he and any guests ate dinner around midnight, to the annoyance of the peckish girls and maids. He was the rare racketeer who liked to read and would often stay up into the early morning smoking and brooding over a book. "He seemed to fear the darkness," remembered Polly. Every day at seven p.m. he took a hot bath and, rather eccentrically, insisted that Polly be in the bathroom to scrub his back. "That was an excuse," she said, "he feared being left alone."

The boys weren't exactly gracious guests. When killing time, they devoured the daily papers, looking for their names and keeping abreast of underworld gossip, strewing the crumpled pages around the apartment, along with their cigarette butts and cigar ashes. They favored the sex-and-crime tabloids like the *Daily News* and the *Mirror*. As Charlie Lucky put it, "I didn't know enough words to read the *New York Times*." Like Polly, some of them even kept scrapbooks of their press appearances and griped when they didn't get the coverage they thought they deserved.

That summer of 1931 Dutch's feud with Legs Diamond was on the back burner. Legs was tucked away in upstate New York with his showgirl sweetheart, recovering from the most recent attempt on his life and fending off federal bootlegging charges. Along Broadway, there was heavy wagering on who would be slain first, Legs or Dutch. The smart money was on the Irishman.

At the moment, Dutch was focused on warding off the depredations of Vince Coll, whose psychopathic temper and crack marksmanship made him one of the Big Apple's most ferocious gunsels. Earlier in the year, fed up with taking orders, Coll had demanded that Dutch make him a full partner. When Dutch refused, Coll broke away and started his own gang, vowing to take down his former boss.

All that spring of 1931 he'd been hijacking Dutch's trucks, roughing up his customers, and assassinating his employees. Their low-simmering war reached a boil on May 30, two weeks after Dutch commandeered Polly's apartment, when Dutch's gunmen murdered Vince's older brother, Pete, on a Harlem street corner. Coll responded by destroying a fleet of trucks and slot machines and killing one of Dutch's men. Now all bets were off.

"By taking Dutch's money I was on the way out of my financial hole," she remembered, "but in return I had to put myself in bondage—from now on my life would be ruled by fear."

❨

Between her jousts with Seabury's probers, her regular appearances in the daily papers, the demands of her double-crossing lawyer, and the constant strain of the Schultz gang hanging around the house, Polly was stretched to the breaking point. As if things couldn't get worse, a half-dressed party girl from Polly's circuit, with the tabloid-ready name of Starr Faithfull, washed up dead on a Long Island beach, opening a Pandora's box of X-rated scandals, including mobsters, incest, and blackmail.

Next to her terror of stray bullets, it was the suggestion of blackmail that seemed to weigh heaviest on her mind. That week she made her debut in the most popular syndicated column in the country, O. O. McIntyre's "New York Day by Day." She could be sure that no fewer than 7 million readers read this blind item:

> Polly Adler, New York's vice queen was willing to plead guilty to being a procuress but would not consent to a confession of "shake downs." She explained: "A known blackmailer is shunned by society more than a leper. I do not want to go through the rest of my life with that horrible taint."

Perhaps the item was a coincidence, or maybe she planted it as a sotto voce signal to her former customers, a theatrical gesture of martyrdom to prove her innocence. Perhaps it was merely another blow to her already tattered ego.

Some of Polly's customers had begun to return. A few, like Bob Benchley and the bluff, burly actor Wallace Beery, proved to be genuine friends, offering aid, comfort, and money. Her comrade-at-arms, Showboat, had remained loyal when Seabury's interrogators tried to break her, even offering Polly a loan from her own savings. Polly had proudly declined. But most of her so-called friends were steering clear of her until this unfortunate outbreak of morality died down.

"As of June fifteenth, I was certainly moody," she remembered. That week was the annual convention of the Advertising Federation of America, some of her wettest and wildest johns—three thousand lusty admen, wielding fat expense accounts—and here she was, out of commission. More pressing still, the trial of the small-time gonif Harry Stein for the murder of Vivian Gordon was about to begin jury selection, carrying the prospect that she might be dragged into the case.

The Schultz gang was in residence on Tuesday morning as Polly was preparing to face another grueling afternoon with Seabury's lawyers. Suddenly the doorbell rang, followed by insistent knocking. Lulu admitted a small, dark-haired man in an expensive suit and led him to the bedroom where Dutch was lounging. All morning long, grim-looking goons bustled in and out of the apartment.

Finally Dutch summoned Polly to his bedside. "Polly, this is Dixie Davis, my mouthpiece, and from now on he's to be yours," he said, gesturing to the young stranger who'd arrived that morning. "He's on his way to the big time, and I trust him." Dixie Davis was a fast-talking, dough-faced young criminal attorney—"the kid mouthpiece," they called him—who served as a go-between and bagman for Dutch Schultz and Jimmy Hines as they took control of the numbers games in Harlem.

Well, Polly thought with resignation, at least he couldn't be worse than Jacob Segal.

"Dixie will be back this evening with six friends," Dutch continued, "and I'm letting you know in plenty of time to prepare a very special dinner with all the trimmings. Caviar and champagne and girls, all the best, get it?"

After Dixie left, Dutch called her back into his bedroom, where he was pacing the floor, nervous and intense. He told her the news that was already racing up and down the Avenue: early that morning Vince Coll had kidnapped Big Frenchy DeMange, Owney Madden's business partner, outside Texas Guinan's Club Argonaut, right across the street from Polly's 54th Street brothel. Coll was demanding that Madden and Big Bill Dwyer kick up $100,000 as ransom—no small sum even for them—and warning that if they didn't pay within forty-eight hours, Frenchy would be dead.

"There'll be no safety for any of us while that crazy mick is around," Dutch snarled. His eyes narrowed, and he growled confidentially: Did Polly have entrée to a speakeasy called the Film Club, a very tough closed-door joint over on Seventh Avenue?

Of course she did. She was welcome in all the Times Square niteries, high and low.

"Good," he replied. "That's where Coll's been hanging out and I want you to go here and take some of the boys with you. I'll let you know when."

"It was as if he'd told me he would let me know what day I'd die," Polly recalled with a shudder. Memories of the Hotsy Totsy massacre and the Club Abbey brawl ricocheted through her head. "Even if I survived the gunplay there, I would be rubbed out later the way the witnesses always were."

But saying no to the despotic Dutchman was out of the question, so she held her tongue and prayed he'd change his mind. When Polly arrived at Centre Street, her anxiety was visible to the reporters clustered in Seabury's outer office, who described her the next day as "a smartly dressed but very unhappy looking woman in her late thirties," looking nearly a decade older than her age.

All afternoon Seabury and Cooper hammered her about her relationship with the magistrates and police department, with a special emphasis on Detective Dennis Mahoney, the powerful president of the Detectives Endowment Association, who was the chief event planner for police stag parties and association dinners, and the former bodyguard for U.S. senator Royal Copeland. They quizzed her about phone calls from high-end hotels, about "furnishing feminine entertainers for conventions held here and elsewhere," and about the wide-open conditions in Harlem, demanding that she name the higher-ups who had protected her and used her services. Reporters eavesdropping outside the door described Polly sobbing as she denied it all. It was a rare crack in her battle-hardened facade.

She had little time to gather herself when she got home. Promptly at seven p.m. her new lawyer, Dixie Davis, arrived with six other heavy hitters, including Dutch's sometime ally, Ciro Terranova, the powerful East Harlem Italian gang leader and the patron of the much-maligned former magistrate Albert Vitale. They were all drinking heavily, including Dutch. When Dixie and his companions finally left at five a.m., Dutch ordered more champagne sent to his room and pulled in a girl named Ruth to keep him company.

At sunrise, Polly was sitting in the kitchen sipping coffee with Bo Weinberg and Marty Krompier. Suddenly bloodcurdling screams erupted from the bedroom. The boys tried to keep Polly from going in, saying Arthur was in a dangerous mood, but she shook them off and burst through the door. Dutch was perched on the side of the bed, fending off an enraged Ruth as she attempted to smash his skull with a half-empty champagne bottle.

Polly grabbed her and shoved her out of the room. Dutch looked like a madman only moments away from committing murder, she remembered. "I tried to calm him down with flattery, telling him he was too important a man to let himself get upset by a stupid little tart." But Dutch just kept repeating, "That dirty bitch! That dirty bitch!" He stormed out of the bedroom and began ransacking the apartment looking for Ruth. She was hiding in the maid's bedroom, but Bo insisted she'd left.

Dutch turned his frustration on her boss. "Polly, see to it that that dirty bastard doesn't make a quarter with you or with anyone else in this town!" he shouted.

Polly, too, must have felt the effects of the champagne because her reply was uncharacteristically impolitic. She wasn't anyone's keeper, she shot back defiantly.

Dutch promptly slugged her in the face, adding a few expletives for good measure.

"I held back the tears and stood still, just looking at him," she recalled, until finally he slammed out of the room and locked himself in the bedroom.

Polly retrieved Ruth from the maid's room and asked her what happened. The girl explained, still sputtering with anger, that she'd refused to hand Dutch a glass of champagne that was sitting closer to him than to her. The louse kicked her in the stomach, so she hurled the glass at him and was about to bean him with the bottle when Polly stepped in.

Much as Polly regretted it, she could do nothing but hand Ruth a roll of cash and tell her to leave immediately. Normally, she'd have taken the girl's side and tossed the obnoxious john out on his ear. But no one could be permitted to know the real identity of her ill-tempered bedmate.

The next day Arthur offered an apology, but as she noted, "It didn't cure my black eye."

By the time the boys shook off their hangovers the next day, Vince Coll had received his ransom money—at the steeply discounted rate of $25,000—and unceremoniously dumped Big Frenchy on the sidewalk outside the Club Argonaut. It was one thing to snatch show folk, saloon keepers, and bookies, but now the cocky kid had gone too far.

In all the hubbub, Dutch forgot about his request that Polly smuggle his crew of assassins into the Film Club. "To the best of my knowledge he only mentioned it once and warned me not to tell Bo about it," she told a friend later. "My feelings in the matter then is no different as I feel now. The Dutch bastard was offering my scalp to save his neck."

Relief came later that day, when Dutch went off in search of the baby-faced kidnapper. But her respite was short-lived.

Two days later, on June 18, the *Daily News* brought another shock. Lined up across the front page were the mug shots of six of her best customers. The U.S. attorney general had officially declared them the top "Public Enemies" in New York. Public Enemy No. 1 was Waxey Gordon, followed by "Broadway's Chairman," Owney Madden, then Larry Fay, "handy in any racket," with Bill Duffy and Ciro Terranova bringing up the rear. Public Enemy No. 4 was her new star boarder, the "Bronx Beer Baron" Dutch Schultz. Anyone who'd been around her house in the past few weeks would recognize the faces.

Two weeks later she discovered one of the maids at the kitchen table, looking at a photo of "Pop" Schultz in *Time* magazine. When the maid got up to put some champagne on ice, Polly ripped out the page and flushed it down the toilet. One of the gang later mentioned that Dutch had read the story in *Time* and noticed that the editors had misspelled "Flegenheimer," his real last name.

"But I don't think he ever wrote a letter to the editor about it," Polly noted wryly.

☾

On July 1 Polly made an improbable debut in the legendary *Ziegfeld Follies*, 1931 edition. As the economic depression dug in its heels, the Great Ziegfeld fell into such deep financial straits that racketeers were now his primary investors. Waxey Gordon and Dutch Schultz were backing Ziggy's two big shows this year, including his famous *Follies*.

Polly's friend Mark Hellinger, eager to branch out from newspaper work, composed a comic skit for the show satirizing *Grand Hotel*, the best-selling-novel-turned-hit-play and forthcoming film. He spoofed all the current hot topics on the Rialto, the Seabury Investigation, the inexorable rise of Hollywood, Al Capone's trial for federal tax evasion, and to her delight, Polly's newfound celebrity. The skit featured, in *Time* magazine's phrase, the "sputteringly Semitic" Jack Pearl as Cecil B. Goldwarner of Hollywood; her old friend, the nightclub phenom Harry Richman, as the hero "Baron Al Capone"; and speakeasy chanteuse Helen Morgan in the role that would be Greta Garbo's in the 1932 film, the glamorous, melancholy Russian ballerina "Mademoiselle Polly Adlervitch."

Ever the gentleman, Hellinger asked Polly if she minded the play on her name. "I said, to the contrary that was the kind of publicity I liked, and had kiddingly suggested that he ask Flo Ziegfeld to put my phone number in the program too." Polly went to see the show, and proudly saved the program in her trunk of keepsakes, along with her bulging scrapbooks.

But others were not so easygoing. Several days after the opening Hellinger got a mixed review from one of the Broadway mob, who suggested he might reconsider the name "Baron Al." There were "kids who saw the sketch and didn't quite get the drift of it," the mobster explained earnestly. "Suppose they took it into their heads that Al was being hurt by that sketch—and tossed a bomb into the theater some night to get even? . . . Now, Mark, you understand. I don't want you to change a single line. But—"

The muses had spoken: from then on the character was called "Little Caesar."

This would be Ziegfeld's final *Follies*. The heyday of the frothy musical revue had died along with that frothy decade. The Great Glorifier, now bankrupt, would follow it to the grave in 1932. Robert Benchley, reviewing the show for *The New Yorker*, called it "far from bad and not so far from good," observing with approval that at least it delivered on the promise of toothsome young girls, but he made no mention of Polly or her alter ego. More gratifying was the review in *Time*, which closed with an innuendo-laden compliment to the "deep curved Helen Morgan as Polly Adlervitch, the Russian danseuse who visits all their rooms in a business-like way, leaving green carnations as receipts."

☾

But Polly had little time to enjoy her turn in the footlights that summer. Day after day, Irving Ben Cooper continued his efforts to wear her down and trip her up. After she skipped out on her subpoenas a couple times, he started keeping her waiting in the stifling-hot outer office, for five, six hours at a time, before sending her home with orders to return the next day. He was a dogged and well-armed enemy, wielding reams of bank statements, canceled checks, and stock trading records.

At one point he became so frustrated with her obfuscations that he threw down his pencil in a fury. "How much schooling did you have?" Cooper shouted. "Your mentality is low!"

Now he'd hit her not-so-secret sore spot. Polly lashed back in fury. "If my mentality is so low, a smart educated fellow like you should have found out all you wanted to know from me a month ago!"

Then he turned to threats, raising his voice ominously. "If you don't cooperate, I'm going to call your parents down here."

"Go ahead. Call them. They're old and they know nothing about my affairs and it would probably kill them to be dragged down here. But if that's the way you do business—"

"Why don't you tell the truth?" he asked in exasperation.

"I am telling the truth," she insisted sullenly.

"I think we'd better let you have a talk with Mr. Samuel Seabury," he said with a sigh of resignation.

In contrast to his pugnacious assistant, Judge Seabury had a courtly, dignified air and treated Polly with scrupulous courtesy. He made no mention of the vice ring or the Women's Court, instead concentrating his questions on the Tammany bigwigs who'd patronized her parties, with a special focus on the mayor.

She responded with her usual routine of amnesia and denial.

Abruptly, he changed course. "Is this your check?" he asked politely.

When she saw it was a check from Irwin O'Leary, the blood drained from her face.

"It's a policeman's paycheck, is it not, Miss Adler? And you will notice that it is endorsed with a capital P." He pushed the check in front of her, holding it so that his finger covered the rest of the signature.

"It's not my handwriting," she said weakly.

"Think it over, Miss Adler. Refresh your memory, and give me your answer tomorrow."

She needed no reminders. Irwin had asked her to endorse it for one of their schemes, but just as she'd put pen to paper, she'd thought of how fishy it would look if anyone saw her signature on a policeman's paycheck, so she'd stopped, leaving only the *P* as evidence. It was the first crack in her formidable defenses.

Her next potential trap was the upcoming hearings to disbar the unscrupulous attorneys of Lawyers' Row who'd masterminded the vice ring along with the bail bondsmen. When the former Women's Court prosecutor John C. Weston returned to the stand as the lead witness, other judges in the courthouse paused their proceedings so they could join the spectators in the sweltering courtroom. Visibly nervous, Weston tried to recant on a few matters. The attorneys hadn't given him bribes, he insisted, but rather "tips" like a waiter might receive.

But on the question of the "notorious Polly Adler," he doubled down, describing his fear of her "influence."

"Influence with the police?" the referee asked.

"With everybody."

"Do you mean you were afraid you would be removed as prosecutor in the court?"

"More than that," Weston responded darkly.

Weston's rumblings about Polly's sinister powers thrust her once again into the headlines. But her story line was soon swallowed up by the relentless bloodshed of the gang wars and by Seabury's probe into City Hall.

"But then, just as I was beginning to sit back and relax, Irwin [O'Leary] stuck his neck in the noose," seethed Polly.

Thus far, Irwin had avoided the negative publicity awarded to his more egregious colleagues. He and Polly had coordinated their stories and stuck to them through the long, withering interrogations. Although he'd been accused of framing one Lillian Grenier, a fifty-one-year-old grandmother with a venomous grudge, and had been demoted along with the rest of the vice squad, he hadn't been indicted for any crimes and still held his job. By this point, observed *The New Yorker*, "the newspapers were thoroughly bored" with the vice ring scandals, so there was no reason for him to make headlines.

Chalk it up to the hubris, then, that when Mrs. Grenier dared to repeat her unflattering accusations during the hearing to disbar the lawyer who'd fixed her case, O'Leary indignantly volunteered to testify as a character witness for the disgraced mouthpiece. "I almost blew my top," Polly remembered with fresh outrage.

On July 22 Irwin arrived at the courthouse and was sworn in. He was on the stand for less than an hour, tendering the usual combination of self-righteous bluster and barefaced lies. The examination seemed to be winding down.

Suddenly Irving Ben Cooper, who had been sitting unnoticed in the back, stood up and asked permission to cross-examine the witness. The courtroom erupted with surprise as he strode to the bench.

Cooper pulled out a briefcase full of documents and photostatted copies of checks, letters, and accounts and laid them out in front of the befuddled cop. Then he leaned forward and asked: "When did you first meet Polly Adler?"

Irwin began to perspire and squirm in the witness chair.

Cooper seized the advantage, shoving document after document at him, plying him with questions, until Irwin's defenses began to crumble. In the space of an hour, Irwin admitted that he did indeed know her, but as Pearl Adler, claiming they'd met in a cabaret introduced by a forgotten friend. He described how they became such good friends that he'd picked up the habit of dropping by one of her Upper West Side apartments at least once a week, "taking her to dances, cashing checks for her and she for him, and giving her money to buy fifteen shares of Anaconda Copper stock."

"Didn't you know that she had a reputation of fourteen arrests?"

O'Leary shifted uncomfortably and wiped his brow. "No," he murmured unconvincingly.

When pressed on their shared investment accounts, Irwin explained he gave her the money to buy the stocks, and she gave him the stock to put into his safe deposit box. "I believe she had several brokerage accounts in my name," he explained. "She just used my name to trade on."

Then why, Cooper asked, when he opened the accounts, did he list his occupation as "florist" and give Polly's address, 110 West 69th Street, apartment 8C, when he lived with his wife and four children in Brooklyn?

"I don't know," O'Leary replied weakly.

His testimony lasted only ninety minutes, but the damage was irreparable. Officer O'Leary was "limp and shaken" as he left the courtroom with reporters swarming around him.

On August 5, Irwin was called to defend himself at a police department hearing. Again he insisted that he'd had no idea Pearl was a madam, and—now jettisoning his alias as a florist—he explained that she'd thought he was a Fuller Brush salesman. He admitted opening multiple stock brokerage accounts under the names of Irwin O'Leary, Pearl Adler, and Morris Adler, and he confirmed canceled checks that showed Polly frequently deposited from $100 to $500 to his credit in his bank accounts. He even confessed to signing the lease on her apartment on West 69th Street.

Yet like all the boys in blue, he remained defiant till the end. "You've got nothing on me," he declared as he stomped off the witness stand. "My relations with Pearl Adler were purely business and above board."

It was "the most colorful day of more than two weeks of testimony," *The New York Times* reported approvingly.

Polly maintained that it was her unwavering denials that kept him out of jail, even as he dragged her name through yet more mud. But she couldn't prevent him from losing his job in the depths of the Depression or from the humiliation of facing his wife and children.

☾

All that summer of 1931, the Schultz gang was in and out of the apartment as they hunted Vince Coll. "Although Dutch never again brought up the subject of my fingering Coll for him," remembered Polly, "I lived in terror that he would do so, and my heart would nearly stop every time Coll's name came into the conversation."

Even the best-connected crime reporters had trouble keeping track of the slaughter that season. One journalist estimated that it averaged out to a killing a day. "I could almost sense when a murder was to take place," remembered Polly. The key men, the big shots of the outfit, would hang around the apartment, the air thick with tension and cigarette smoke, waiting to hear that their gunmen had finished the job.

The turning point in the gang war came on the sultry evening of July 28, when a green sedan full of triggermen wielding sawed-off shotguns and a machine gun opened fire on a group of men standing outside an Italian social club in East Harlem. Five children playing on a nearby stoop were shot, and a five-year-old boy was killed.

The "Harlem baby killing," as the newspapers called it, galvanized the city. For years, New Yorkers had treated mob battles as if they were mere tabloid entertainment, reciting the myth that gangsters killed only each other. But the cold-blooded slaughter of innocent children finally aroused the citizenry from their complacency. In response, Commissioner Mulrooney rounded up all the usual suspects and issued "shoot to kill" orders. Even Jimmy Walker paused in his domestic dramas to express disapproval.

Witnesses were, predictably, silent. But now the gangsters, in a rare moment of self-serving good citizenship, decided it was time to put the finger on Vince Coll. "Coll was bad for business, hitherto closed-mouthed hoods said, excusing their violation of the underworld code of silence," remembered reporter Quentin Reynolds. "You never knew whom Coll would turn on next. The sooner he was out of circulation the better." The word went out to their friends in the press and their police connections: Coll was the "baby killer."

While Polly was regularly trooping down to the courthouse for yet more questioning, the carnage was mounting, in Damon Runyon's phrase, "until finally the only people making any dough in the town are the undertakers." Almost every day the newspapers brought tidings of yet another corpse to add to the ledger of revenge. The tabloids covered the war between the Dutchman and the Mad Dog as if it were a sports rivalry, tallying casualties, coining catchy nicknames, promoting personalities, and handicapping the teams.

One Saturday, several weeks after the *Ziegfeld Follies* premiere, the newsboys began flooding the sidewalks shouting "Extra! Extra! Slaying in the Bronx!" Polly hurried out to buy a paper, then sat down with a tumbler of scotch to read the headlines: "4 SLAIN, 12 WOUNDED IN BANDIT CHASE." It was a reprise of the Harlem baby killing, a high-speed chase spraying "a hail of lead and terror from the south Bronx to Inwood," killing two policemen, three gunmen, and a four-year-old girl, and leaving a trail of wounded bystanders.

This would surely bring down the wrath of both the underworld and the law. "The Coll men would be on the warpath," Polly realized, "and it was quite in the cards that my apartment would become the scene of just such a slaughter as had occurred in the Bronx."

Indeed, at that very moment, New York's top gang leaders, spearheaded by Dutch, were gathering for a secret meeting to hash out a solution to all this bad publicity. After much debate, they agreed to offer a $50,000 reward for Vince Coll's scalp. "This is a cold business proposition," a spokesman for Schultz told the *Daily News*. "We've got to get rid of these 10-cent creeps and wrong guys if we want to live."

Later that same night, the columnist Mark Hellinger stopped by Polly's house with terrifying news: word on the street was that Dutch and his gang were hiding out in one of her apartments. Nobody kept a closer ear to the ground than Mark. If he said it, it had to be true.

"Believe me, Mark," she replied, stifling her panic, "I realize the danger I'm in—but I don't know how to keep these people out. I read the papers tonight—who knows what's coming—but what can I do?" She forced a tense smile. "Who knows? Maybe tomorrow there'll be headlines about me pushing up daisies."

"Don't talk that way," the columnist snapped. "Don't you think that if this certain person knew it was pretty common knowledge he was hanging out at your place, he might consider it advisable to go elsewhere? Particularly now?"

Hellinger was right. If his safe house was no longer safe, then Dutch had no reason to stick around. Now she just had to work up the guts to suggest to "His Lordship" that he ought to move along. To calm her nerves and, as she joked, acquire a little "Dutch courage," she went out for a drink, then another and another, making the rounds until last call.

When she stumbled back to the apartment, she was too plastered to fit her key into the front door keyhole. She gave the safety signal, knocking lightly three times, and the door opened so fast that she nearly fell on her knees.

Dutch loomed over her, enraged, with Bo Weinberg just behind him. Dutch pulled her into the kitchen. "Where you been?"

She glared at him defiantly. "Out."

"Out where?"

"Just out."

"I thought I told you not to drink," Dutch barked. "Well, answer me! Didn't I?"

Suddenly her liquid courage evaporated.

"Well, maybe this'll teach you a lesson, you so-and-so!" His fist came down so hard on her head, she fell backward onto the floor. He made a move to kick her, but Bo seized him and pulled him into the living room.

Showboat helped Polly into a chair, and they huddled together in the maid's room until the men stomped out. As Showboat settled Polly into bed, her head throbbing with pain, humiliation, and fear, Polly started to sob. "Did you see tonight's papers?" she bawled.

"No, Miss Polly. They kept me on the jump," replied Showboat, before offering one consolation: "They ran up a real big bill. They seemed in quite a gay spending mood."

Of course they were, Polly replied. They were celebrating the bloody massacre of Coll's forces in the Bronx.

Finally, Showboat persuaded her to try to sleep. "But when she turned out the light and left me," remembered Polly, "I rose up and looked out the window, wondering if Coll's mob already was staked out around the apartment building."

☾

Then, for the first time in a long time, Polly caught a break. On October 4, 1931, police picked up Vince Coll in a hotel on West 23rd Street. His blond locks dyed black, sporting a mustache and horn-rimmed glasses as a disguise, he had been hiding out with two pretty young women and a bodyguard.

"I've been under a heavy strain and I'm sort of glad to get it over," Coll confessed to the detectives as he waited to be questioned at headquarters. As he was led to his cell, the Mad Dog broke into a hearty laugh. "Boy! I'll bet Dutch Schultz will go out and get drunk tonight!" he said, still chuckling. "He'll feel safe now with me in the can."

With the wind of public opinion at their back, and Franklin Roosevelt's political future on the line, the police began a high-profile crackdown on the Bronx mobsters, raiding every known beer drop, headquarters, and hideaway. Finally, the Dutchman decided that New York was a little too warm for comfort and betook himself to the neighboring town of Yonkers, where a man of his stature might be appreciated.

After a couple weeks without seeing either Dutch or his crew, Polly closed up the apartment at West 83rd. She reopened a full-service brothel in her old building on West 54th next to the Harding Hotel and began entertaining trusted customers who were willing to risk getting caught in her spotlight.

Perversely, Irwin O'Leary's downfall was Polly's gain, demonstrating to suspicious colleagues and customers that she was a vault of secrecy. All this high-profile publicity served to remind her more "sophisticated" clients of her charms.

As proof of her new celebrity, Walter Winchell's successor at the *Evening Graphic*, the lovable syndicated columnist Louis Sobol, included Polly in his salute to the remarkable women of Broadway, "the women whose chief asset is a set of smoothly working brains plus aggressiveness plus personality plus anything or everything that enables them to snatch a living out of this tough town." He classed "Polly Adler and her wares" next to Texas Guinan, Peggy Hopkins Joyce, Helen Morgan, and the cosmetics mogul Eve Arden. (For later editions, Sobol substituted a more opaque tribute: "I pass by Polly Adler, who made good in her own way.")

Irving Ben Cooper was still pestering her, but public attention had shifted to the melodrama playing out in City Hall. The newspapers barely noticed when that "old familiar of the vice inquiry," in the *Daily News's* phrase, showed up yet again to fulfill her final subpoena. November 6, 1931, her last day in the hot seat, passed without a whisper.

Now all guns were trained on the big prize: Mayor Jimmy Walker.

☾

Polly was starting to feel like her old self again as the Christmas holidays approached. Business was getting back to normal. The vice squads, now filled with rookie cops, were in retreat. And she'd finally paid off her heavy debt to her shyster attorney, Jacob A. Segal. Segal was still shaking her down for occasional "loans" that he had no intention of paying back, but that wasn't life-threatening. Vince Coll was currently standing trial for the Harlem baby shootings, and Legs Diamond was in another courtroom up in Albany facing charges of kidnapping. For the moment peace reigned on the street.

She'd survived the Seabury Inquisition without starring in a single public hearing, even as her name became a household word. She'd shielded her customers from embarrassment and her friends from prosecution. "No one—I repeat *no one*—went to jail because of anything I said during the Seabury investigation," Polly insisted. In truth, shockingly few of Seabury's grafters landed behind bars, and only one of the scurrilous attorneys of Lawyers' Row was disbarred. So perhaps that wasn't the triumph of underworld ethics she claimed.

It was early in the morning on December 18, and "I was finally beginning to regain a little peace of mind," she remembered, when the elevator operator called up to say that a gentleman giving his name as "Pop Brown" wanted to come up. She opened the door to find Dutch and six henchmen.

Dutch didn't say a word about her move. Instead he offered her a racketeer's apology, pulling her aside and handing her five hundred dollars in cash. "Next week is Christmas," he said, "buy yourself a gift. I may not see you until after New Year's." Then he added, "You better get some more of your kids in tonight, Polly. I've got some friends coming down in a while."

That night she hosted a full roster of the Harlem mob, thirsty, lusty, and in high spirits but remarkably well behaved. By morning the news was everywhere: Legs Diamond—the "human ammunition dump for the underworld," in *The New York Times*'s indecorous phrase—had been killed in a cheap rooming house in Albany, stinking drunk after a rendezvous with his mistress, a former Ziegfeld girl named Kiki Roberts.

One gunman had held him down while another pulled the trigger precisely three times, once in the front of his head, once in the back, and once from the side. All the wise guys on the Rialto agreed: craftsmanship like that could only be the work of Bo Weinberg.

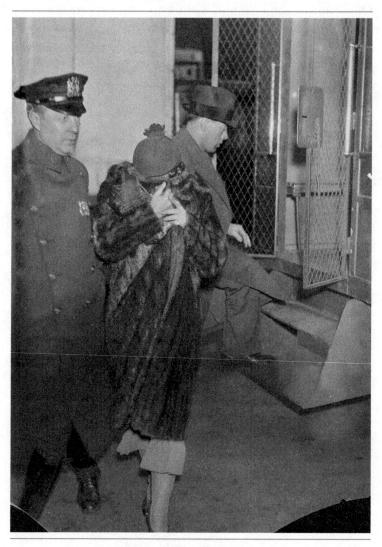

Polly exiting the patrol wagon and cursing the photographers
at the Yorkville Court, March 5, 1935

12

Café Society

As 1932 opened, New York settled into the third year of what would become known as the Great Depression. Half-finished skyscrapers loomed over the city, abandoned by their bankrupt owners, and the sidewalks were lined with empty storefronts. The breadlines stretched for blocks, and there were men in business suits peddling apples for a nickel on every street corner in midtown Manhattan.

Broadway was especially hard hit. Half of all legitimate theaters were dark, vaudeville was taking its last gasp, radio was killing the demand for live musicians, and even the movie palaces were finally feeling the blow of the lousy economy. Times Square had become a cut-rate Coney Island, overrun with souvenir shops, hot dog stands, orange juice kiosks, chop suey restaurants, and arcades.

As devastating as the last two years had been to the country—not to mention Polly's mental health—she would later count this moment as the beginning of her best years. "The Seabury investigation had sure as hell made my life easier," she recalled with relish. "The police no longer were a headache; there was no more kowtowing to double-crossing Vice Squad men, no more hundred-dollar handshakes, no more phony raids to up the month's quota."

The deepening economic depression and the uncharacteristic reticence of the police had created ripe conditions for her business. The national publicity, painful as it was, had made Polly a magnet for women on the make. With over a quarter of the population out of work, female talent was plentiful, and she was now turning away thirty or forty new girls for every one she hired.

Plenty of Polly's old customers were still doing just fine despite the Depression. Showfolk were setting aside their snobbery and moving into the booming field of radio, providing free entertainment to a broke nation. Madison Avenue, too, continued to pour money into her coffers, as ad agencies worked overtime to keep their clients spending.

The closing of so many late-night joints and high-end watering holes made her lush all-night hideaway more valuable to the lucky class who still had money to blow. The appetite for the darker, dangerous corners of the city ebbed as the economy contracted. The trust fund playboys who had retained their fortunes—perennial names like Astor, Vanderbilt, Whitney, Rockefeller, and Harriman—exhibited a new reticence about partying in public as kidnapping, blackmail, and badger games were on the rise. Polly's place was safer, more refined, with far better food and liquor, while still offering that thrilling hint of the forbidden.

To her astonishment, Polly's starring role in the Seabury scandals had spread her reputation to the hinterlands while burnishing her cachet among the swells. She had become the darling of "Café Society," as the syndicated columnists dubbed it. The term had been kicking around since the Armistice, coined by the society chatterbox Cholly Knickerbocker, to describe the mix of Social Registerites, European exiles, showbiz celebrities, literary lions, sports world luminaries, and ballyhooed beauties who frequented Manhattan's plush cafés, restaurants, and publicity parties, and fueled the Broadway columns.

Robert Benchley and Jock Whitney were the reigning kings of Café Society, although they had plenty of competition in their public pursuit of pleasure. The queen of the high-wattage nighthawks was Tallulah Bankhead, "theaters' saltiest sophisticate," who enjoyed long, lively affairs with both Bob and Jock. Tallulah asked Bob to introduce her to Polly when she returned to Broadway from London in 1931. "Perhaps not surprisingly, they talked about abortions, Tallulah suggesting that Polly must know one or two good abortionists to turn to when one of her girls got knocked up," as Bankhead's onetime assistant told it. Given her appetites, one never knew when that sort of information would come in handy.

Polly's former employee, the sultry torch singer Libby Holman, represented the surreal side of the smart set. She was regularly spotted helling around Harlem with a pack of A-list lesbians, including the omnisexual Tallulah, before marrying an heir to the Reynolds Tobacco fortune in November 1931. Eight months after their wedding, Libby was accused of fatally shooting her new husband through the head while pregnant with his child. Just another Cinderella story with a Broadway twist.

There were genuine debutantes, young daughters of the rich who were formally presented to society. But most of the women of Café Society enjoyed less substantial status. Exhibit A was Leonore Lemmon, the camellia-complexioned daughter of a Broadway ticket broker. Infamous for her tart tongue and fondness for bar brawls, Leonore spent many a late hour as a customer at Polly's. "She was a nifty lady, a good friend," remembered Leonore.

In those years Polly's neighborhood in the Fifties became notorious for its part-time prostitutes, "young women with cultivated accents, the residue of wardrobes of excellent tailoring and bitter smiles of contemptuous resignation," remembered that keen-eyed cosmopolitan Ernest Cuneo. The "debutramps," Walter Winchell dubbed them. Polly was a friend of last resort to many Café Society debs who'd been dispossessed by the Depression and were now scrapping for jobs as showgirls, saloon singers, and secretaries, only to discover they'd make a better living—and perhaps meet a better class of man—at Polly's.

Usually she arranged for them to live at the Barbizon Hotel for Women on East 63rd Street. When they were available to work, the women would leave a message on her professional answering service, addressed to Mrs. Polly Martin (or her current alias), with the phone number of where they could be reached that evening. For security, Polly always kept her own phone number unlisted.

Her operation was so discreet and her training so thorough, only insiders could tell which girls in the nightclubs were being paid for their company and which were legitimate glamour girls. "Let me tell you something," Leonore Lemmon emphasized, "many of the ladies in this town, right now, were groomed by what we used to call, 'God save us from Pearl Davis'"—yet another of her many aliases—"That was her Sunday name."

This was the prayer of the down-on-her-luck party girl: "God save us from Pearl Davis."

Guests now came to the house not only for her blue-ribbon lineup but for a chance to chat with the infamous Madam Adler. "Polly Adler had become a kind of freak celebrity," explained the talent agent and CBS publicity man Jap Gude, "and it became fashionable to drop in at her establishment . . . have a drink or two with one of the girls, or with Polly herself, and see and be seen. It was strictly a snob thing, like being at opening night of the opera season even though you loathed opera. It was also something to drop casually at '21' the next day: 'You'll never guess who I saw at Polly's last night.'"

She'd become part of popular culture. She appeared regularly in the syndicated columns of the Bistro Beat. Polly Adler references cropped up in suggestive songs and stag party skits, and were staples of the "lavender masters of ceremonies" and campy cross-dressing comedians currently in vogue in the nightclubs. Dining out on stories of Polly's exclusive bagnio became a subtle status symbol.

Not all the tales were true, she noted, and some of them weren't as dignified as she liked. "I naturally resented some of the stories which made me sound like an illiterate or a degenerate, or both," she said later. But they kept her name at the tip of the tongue in a way no Broadway publicist or Madison Avenue guru ever could.

☾

Now that Polly was back in the swing of things, she would have been glad to see less of Dutch Schultz and his desperados. But that wasn't in the cards. Schultz's reprieve from Vince Coll's assaults was short-lived. Coll was acquitted of the Harlem baby killing three days after Christmas, another notch on the district attorney's abysmal conviction record. With the Mad Dog back on the street, everyone was once again on nerves' edge.

Walter Winchell was now the reigning god of Broadway and the living symbol of Manhattan to newspaper readers and radio listeners across the country. As his star rose, he acquired nearly as many enemies—and toadies—as fans. He'd been barred from a half-dozen theaters, and most of the gilded nightclubs, and it was whispered that more than one young chorus girl had committed suicide after an unflattering appearance in his column.

Nonetheless, Polly welcomed him heartily. In return, Winchell was not exactly discreet about his friendly relations with the "Queen of Hookaville," as he dubbed her. Many of Winchell's "personal friends were whores or pimps," sneered one critic. "It has been said around Broadway that Winchell felt at home among whores because they, like Winchell, were selling themselves for so much a night."

Winchell often stopped by Polly's in the company of his old pal from vaudeville days, the dialect comedian Lou Holtz, who was pulling in some $6,000 a week in musical revues, nightclubs, and radio, and could afford Polly's steep prices. Oscar Levant, celebrity pianist and professional wisecracker, was astonished the first time Lou Holtz brought him to Polly's. "The tariff was $20 a head, so I had one turn," Levant remembered. "Holtz was all over the place and at the end of the evening screamed to Polly in a shrill voice, 'Pray, madam, tell me what is my fucking bill?'"

Winchell liked to brag that he knew every important gangster in New York except Dutch Schultz. Until one evening when Walter and Lou stopped by Polly's, glanced into one of the bedrooms, and recognized Schultz's unmistakable figure. Never as brave as he was brazen, Winchell yelped, "Let's get the hell out of here," and made a beeline for the door. Polly upbraided him the next time she saw the columnist; Dutch had recognized Winchell and Holtz in the hall, and it had hurt his feelings that they didn't want to join him for a cocktail.

One night toward the end of January, when Dutch and the gang were hanging around the house, the doorman called up to say that a "Mr. Abe" and three gentlemen whose names she didn't recognize were in the lobby. Sensing trouble, she went downstairs, where she found four hard-looking men with fedoras pulled low over their eyes waiting by the elevator. "A child could have spotted them as mobsters," she scoffed.

The apparent leader asked if they could come up.

"I don't receive strangers," she replied.

"We are very good friends of Peggy Wild's."

"Good, go there," Polly said tersely.

Upstairs, Bo Weinberg and the boys were waiting anxiously. As soon as she described the visitors, they grimly clapped on their hats and coats and headed out the door. "They didn't even say goodbye."

About one week later, on February 8, Walter Winchell printed a tip from Texas Guinan that assassins were arriving from Chicago to rub out

Vince Coll. "Local banditti have made one hotel a virtual arsenal and several hot-spots are ditto because Master Coll is giving them a headache," he added, surely giving Polly a headache of her own. Six hours after his column hit the newsstands, Coll was mowed down by machine guns in a drugstore phone booth by a crew of killers directed by Bo Weinberg. That was the end of the Mad Dog.

It was almost the end of Walter Winchell, as well. The irritated hit men, acting out the fantasy of every victim burned by Winchell's wicked tongue, put out a contract on the columnist's life. The terrified newspaperman was said to have paid Owney Madden $90,000 in exchange for cooling the ire of the murderous midwesterners. Texas Guinan decided that now would be an opportune time to take her chorus of cuties on an international tour. When Winchell received a subpoena a few weeks later from the grand jury investigating the slaying, he, too, fled three thousand miles to California, suffering what the newspapers called, with evident satisfaction, a nervous breakdown. He returned six weeks later, reported *Time* magazine, "with a new enthusiasm for law, G-men, Uncle Sam, [and] Old Glory."

☾

That spring of 1932 the hot glare of the press finally shifted to the duel between Mayor Jimmy Walker and Governor Franklin Delano Roosevelt.

Judge Seabury had been slowly building the case against "The Unholy Alliance" among gamblers, criminals, and Tammany, as the *Herald-Tribune* dubbed it. Now he was bringing the pressure to a climax. He was timing it to coincide with the Democratic presidential nominating convention in Chicago at the end of June, where the judge was hoping to advance his own presidential aspirations at the governor's expense.

Thousands of New Yorkers jammed the sidewalks outside the county courthouse on May 25, when the two adversaries finally squared off. Clad in a sharply tailored blue suit and low-slung fedora, Mayor Walker jigged his way through the crowd, clasping his hands over his head like a prizefighter entering the ring. But Walker's wisecracks were no match for Seabury's towering stack of bankbooks, receipts, letters of credit, and ledgers, documenting no less than a million dollars in unexplained accounts, lavish gifts, and luxury vacations paid for by "friends." It was a battle worthy of Madison Square Garden, complete with a hissing, cat-calling pack of courtroom spectators. Walker was bruised but unbowed as he left the courthouse, buffeted by shouts of "Atta boy, Jimmy!" and "Go get 'em, Jimmy!"

One week before the Democratic convention, Seabury sent his find-ings to Governor Roosevelt, calling for the removal of the mayor from office. FDR made no reply, throwing even his closest allies into a state of high suspense. Adding to the tension, Al Smith was coming out of retire-ment. Still nursing bitter disappointment over his own blighted presi-dential ambitions—and increasingly convinced that Roosevelt would be a fatal casualty in the war between Tammany and Seabury—Smith decided to make one last play for the White House.

Meanwhile Roosevelt was working his own charm offensive among the Broadway–Madison Square Garden kingmakers. A few weeks before the convention, Jim Farley, the powerful chairman of the New York State Athletic Commission, brought the governor to Billy LaHiff's Tav-ern, where the city's most influential newspapermen and entertainers mingled with the sporting fraternity and their political backers. Roo-sevelt made a big impression on the Broadwayfarers, while subtly giving the needle to Mayor Walker.

One of Roosevelt's emissaries also approached Frank Costello and Lucky Luciano, according to Lucky's later telling. Luciano and Costello had two main requests for the governor: force the New York State Parole Board to stop hounding Owney Madden, and get Samuel Seabury out of the picture before he did more damage.

"The only guy who could control Seabury was Roosevelt, and we figured that's where we had our ace," remembered Lucky. "We had most of the city's delegates to the convention in our pocket, so we could stop the Governor from winnin' the state of New York; maybe that'd cost him the nomination—if a guy couldn't carry his own state, he looked like a bum." If Roosevelt would muzzle Seabury, they'd throw all their muscle behind him at the Democratic convention.

On June 21, six days before the opening of the convention, Roosevelt sent Seabury's charges of financial impropriety and influence peddling to Mayor Walker and requested a formal reply. Walker brushed him off, informing the governor that he'd have to wait until Walker returned from Chicago. The blithe mayor seemed unable to read the seriousness of the situation, so accustomed was he to living without consequences.

That night out on Long Island, Jack Sharkey, the boxing mob's favorite patsy, was challenging the German fighter, Max Schmeling, for the heavyweight championship. A major title fight was always a good night for Polly. All the big shots were in attendance, including Waxey Gordon—who now preferred the more dignified name of Irving Wexler—and his crew from New Jersey. But Waxey was in a fury when he arrived. A new brewery he'd just opened in Brooklyn had been knocked off by local cops even though he'd paid a $50,000 bribe directly to City Hall to buy protection from raids. Waxey tried calling the gangland go-between, Dixie Davis, to find out what happened to his fix but couldn't get ahold of the lawyer.

Gordon was still seething as they made their way ringside, where the mayor happened to be seated right in front of him. Schmeling and Sharkey were pounding away at each other, with Walker shouting encouragement, when a man strode up to Waxey and handed him a note.

"That son-of-a-bitch got the dough, all right, but he never put the fix in!" Waxey snarled as he read it. He leaned forward, tapped the mayor on the shoulder, and rasped something into his ear.

Walker turned in his seat, white as a sheet. "Jesus Christ, Irving," he exclaimed. "I forgot about it completely."

Waxey grabbed Jimmy by the throat and began choking him, with a crazy grin on his face, until his thumbnails drew blood. His companions pried Waxey loose and hustled him out before he committed murder. It was one thing to be called a thief by a stiff like Seabury, but anyone stupid enough to steal from Waxey Gordon was no longer fit for office.

☾

The 1932 Democratic convention in Chicago "was filled with intrigue involving New Yorkers," as the reporter Morris Markey observed. Al Smith, Samuel Seabury, and Jimmy Walker all arrived in the Windy City determined to thwart Franklin Roosevelt.

The New York City delegation, with the exception of the Bronx, was backing Al Smith's last-minute drive for the nomination. But Roosevelt also had a formidable team of New Yorkers in his corner. His nominating campaign was being led by Bronx boss Ed Flynn and his right-hand man, Teddy Hayes, who were headquartered at Chicago's Congress Hotel, while the czar of the boxing world, Jim Farley, was corralling delegates on the floor of the convention.

New York's savvy racketeers were also out in full force. Over at the Drake Hotel, Lucky Luciano and Al Marinelli, Little Italy's Tammany representative, shared a six-room suite while Jimmy Hines and Frank Costello shared a suite in another wing, each well stocked with booze, cigars, and other welcome respites for the weary delegates. "We had Roosevelt and Smith guys comin' out our ears," remembered Lucky. "They all knew we controlled most of the city's delegates." The racketeers planned to hold back their support until the last minute, to maximize their influence.

For the first three rounds of balloting, the New York delegation split in Smith's favor. At that point, Frank Costello held a critical meeting with Roosevelt's advisers. "When Frank got the word that Roosevelt would live up to his promise to kill the Seabury investigation—I mean, like tapering off so he could save face—it was in the bag for him," as Lucky told it later. The gangster coalition gave the sign to their delegates to switch their support to FDR.

It was Lucky who broke the news to the old lion. In disbelief, Smith pressed for a reason. "Al," Lucky explained, "Roosevelt's promised he's gonna close his eyes to Seabury and keep 'em closed." To his astonishment, the mighty Smith began to bawl.

"Then he said somethin' that really made my blood run cold. He looked me square in the face and shook his head real sad. 'Charlie,' he said, 'Frank Roosevelt'll break his word to you. This is the biggest mistake you ever made in your entire life, by trustin' him. He'll kill you,'" Lucky remembered. "My bones told me that we'd walked into a trap—that Smith was right."

On the fourth ballot, Roosevelt won the Democratic nomination. The mob gave themselves plenty of credit for shifting the momentum of the urban political machines to him. At a minimum, as one New Yorker noted, they kept the key leaders of the Stop Roosevelt faction so drunk that they could hardly hold a conversation, let alone cast a vote.

The Broadway mobsters could also point proudly to their glowing new relationship with Senator Huey Long of Louisiana. Years later, Ed Flynn and Teddy Hayes insisted that the charismatic demagogue from

Louisiana was the man who cemented Roosevelt's final winning coalition, by holding in line those Southern delegates who had been tempted to bolt when told to turn their votes over to the patrician with the Republican name. "There is little question in my mind, all these years later, that without Huey Long's work Roosevelt would never have been nominated," insisted Hayes.

Senator Long, "a loudmouth who liked to drink," in Lucky's description, availed himself freely of the mobsters' hospitality, meeting with Luciano, Costello, Meyer Lansky, and Lansky's partner from Detroit's Purple Gang, Moe Dalitz, several times over the course of the convention. It was no coincidence that during those boozy conversations in the Drake Hotel, Long and Costello also worked out a deal to bring the mob's slot machines to Louisiana, with a thick cut of the illicit profits going into Long's pocket.

As happened so often when the criminal and political worlds tangled, Polly pops up again in the historical record. Besides being a heavy drinker with a rowdy, impulsive temper, Long was "an insatiable womanizer." Once he was in Washington he began regularly heading up to New York for "rest and relaxation," where, inevitably, he crossed paths with Polly's girls. As one reporter put it, "Huey P. Long, was no stranger to Polly's 'li'l drinkie' soirees."

The mob began cultivating Huey not long after he took his seat in the U.S. Senate in January 1932. Costello and Lansky saw a ripe target in the boisterous senator. New Orleans was an ideal spot to expand their gambling operations, and Huey Long, as corrupt as he was ambitious, was the man to make it happen. There were several competing versions of how Frank Costello gained his leverage with Long, none of them flattering to the Kingfish.

The story that made the papers and went down in mob lore was that in the summer of 1933, Costello saved Long from a severe beating at a party in Sands Point, Long Island, after the drunken senator peed on the shoes of the burly man next to him at the urinal. However, this version doesn't square with other details of their relationship.

Underworld rumor offered two alternative explanations, and both happened to fall right in Polly's bailiwick. One version, related by the mobster Joseph Valachi, claimed that on one of his trips to Manhattan, Senator Long impregnated a local teenager. When the girl's mother threatened to reveal the story to the press, Costello persuaded the girl to get an abortion and forget all about it.

But perhaps the most convincing explanation was offered by one of Frank Costello's most reliable biographers. As he told it, their bond was cemented when Long "became involved with a prostitute who was tied in with mobsters, and she arranged for a few candid photographs to be snapped while they were in bed. Blackmail ensued. Long then went to see Costello who was able to have the photos destroyed. A grateful Long then invited him to install his slot machines in New Orleans."

Of course, Polly insisted that she never dealt in extortion; this sort of scheme was closer to the handiwork of the late Vivian Gordon and Legs Diamond. But, as "the first lady of the underworld," in the *Daily Mirror*'s phrase—and a well-known hostess of the imprudent Senator Long—she undoubtedly did her bit to cultivate a warm relationship between the bootlegger and the senator.

After Chicago, the mobsters doubled down on their bet, providing the funds and manpower to help turn out a record number of voters in November. "I don't say we elected Roosevelt," said Charlie Lucky modestly, "but we gave him a pretty good push."

Nonetheless, Al Smith was right. Twenty-four hours after Roosevelt won the Democratic nomination, a warrant was issued for Owney Madden's arrest for violating parole. Within a year, Owney was once again sitting in a cell in Sing Sing. And Seabury wasn't going anywhere.

☾

With the White House in his sights and the full attention of the nation on him, Governor Roosevelt was now ready to decide Jimmy Walker's fate.

That summer, as FDR and his campaign advisers hashed out the Walker conundrum and the challenge of breaking Tammany's grip over the voters, those summer strategy sessions were a critical inspiration for the federal safety net system that would become known as Social Security. "Roosevelt ventured that just possibly Tammany could be undercut by taking from it the responsibility for the unemployed," recalled the economist Rexford Tugwell. "Tammany might be ruined if relief was really organized."

"The bosses did not know that their power was in jeopardy," Tugwell concluded, "but it was."

On August 11, 1932, Roosevelt reluctantly summoned Jimmy Walker to Albany for a public hearing where the mayor would finally respond to Seabury's accusations. For fourteen full days, Seabury and Walker dueled, with FDR serving as judge and jury. The sprightly mayor seemed to wither when he realized he had no leverage with the governor, and that the once-indulgent press had turned on him. It was Al Smith who struck the final blow in a private meeting at the Plaza Hotel. "Jim," he said bluntly, "you're through."

The marvelous Jimmy Walker threw in the towel on September 1, with one terse sentence: "I hereby resign as mayor of the City of New York, said resignation to take effect immediately."

On November 8, 1932, Franklin Delano Roosevelt was elected president of the United States by an overwhelming margin of victory. Two days later Jimmy Walker and his mistress sailed into exile in Europe. For all his sins, his constituents were sorry to see "our Jimmy" exit the stage.

"Whatever his critics may say about him, the glib, wise-cracking and debonair Jimmy made himself a national institution," the *Daily News* concluded. "The Walker administration will go down in the annals as a good-time-Charlie, whoop-do-do, never-to-be-forgotten three ring circus that may or may not have maltreated the taxpayers as Samuel Seabury contends, but it showed them a swell time for their pains."

As for Polly, she had outlasted and, arguably, outmaneuvered both Judge Seabury and the Committee of Fourteen. After Walker's resignation, the fervor that had fueled Seabury's crusade died down as quickly as it had arisen. Seabury had struck a victory for clean government, but he never attained the heroic stature or presidential momentum he longed for. "Everybody remembers Polly Adler, but nobody remembers who made her famous," complained one of Seabury's deputies; "but only how she beat the rap five times out of five, and we never found out."

A few weeks after the election, Polly could claim victory over another old nemesis when the Committee of Fourteen announced that it was permanently disbanding. The once-mighty moral uplifters fell victim to the cratered economy, changing sexual mores, and in a much-noted irony, the humiliating revelations of the Seabury Investigation.

☾

Franklin Delano Roosevelt was sworn in as the thirty-third president on March 4, 1933, at the nadir of the Great Depression. As soon as he entered office, President Roosevelt began working on an ambitious slate of programs to provide relief to the unemployed and spur economic recovery, what came to be known as the New Deal.

For the first time in years, a rustle of excitement and hope cut through the gloom that had enveloped the city since the Crash. All the shop windows that summer of 1933 were placarded with blue eagles, the emblem of the National Recovery Act, above the motto "We Do Our Part." Polly declined to post a blue eagle in her window, but she was certainly doing her part to support the New Deal.

Whatever Polly's relationship was with the new president, it was common knowledge that "Washington men" were now some of her most illustrious clients. In those early years, the Roosevelt administration was very much a New York City affair, drawing together Columbia University professors, Wall Street money men, social reformers nurtured by Al Smith, and select representatives from the Tammany machine. There was a constant flow back and forth between Manhattan and the nation's capital.

The NYC-DC coalition included social welfare advocates like Harry Hopkins, big-city political bosses like Jimmy Hines and Mayor Frank Hague of New Jersey, and wealthy "traitors to their class" like Averell Harriman, James Forrestal, and Robert Lovett, as well as the president's own hard-partying sons, Jimmy, Elliott, and Franklin Jr. A besotted Walter Winchell became FDR's chief mouthpiece, cheerleader, and sounding board in the press.

"The Hemingway syndrome was strong in the upper ranks of the New Deal in those years," remembered John Kenneth Galbraith, then a young government staffer. "It befitted a man to drink heavily, speak always with unvarnished directness, be unadornedly profane, play poker, enjoy the races, frequent the sporting restaurants and bars and, with exceptions, be dominant and successful with women."

On weekends, when they took a break from fighting to save America, they could be spotted in all the glossy watering holes of Café Society—"21," the Stork Club, El Morocco, Toots Shor's, Reuben's, and not infrequently, Polly Adler's. "They were all hotbeds of New Dealism for a long time when the bleeding hearts were helling-around the fleshpots and eating high on the hog," remembered the sports-reporter-turned-political-columnist Westbrook Pegler. "Leon Henderson, Frank Murphy of the Supreme Court, Jim Farley, Ed Flynn and Teddy Hayes and John Edgar [Hoover], the Eye That Never Sleeps, were painted on the walls of the [Stork Club's] Cub Room."

As charter members of what they jovially called the FRBC club—"For Roosevelt Before Chicago"—Jimmy Hines and Ed Flynn had become exponentially more powerful. In his efforts to defang Tammany, Roosevelt stripped the Hall of its traditional control over Manhattan's civil service spoils system, turning the distribution of federal funds and jobs over to Hines and Flynn. Jimmy Hines was, as one reporter scoffed, "the white-haired boy of the New Deal's patronage system." Although he was closer to the more educated and refined Ed Flynn, FDR spent many a lively social hour with Hines in those years. "They have talked over many things together," *The New Yorker* noted slyly, "—the President of the United States and the man who used to go to the fights with Dutch Schultz."

For the first time in American history, the luminaries of politics, finance, and show business were mingling as equals, often as guests at Polly's parties. "Polly Adler's was the meetinghouse for all Broadway in those days," remembered Oscar Levant fondly.

This was epitomized by the delicious rumor that Polly had been raided while entertaining Dutch Schultz in the company of "a drama critic; one of America's top humorists; and a man who bears one of America's greatest names in society and finance." All four of them escaped via the apartment's dumbwaiter, reported the columnist Leonard Lyons, but "the madam of the house gave priority to Schultz, because he was a fugitive."

Robert Benchley was a steady presence that winter of 1933–34, bringing the crème of Café Society. Tallulah Bankhead was in town with a new show, tearing through Harlem and screwing around with the well-married Jock Whitney and anyone else who caught her fancy. Benchley had a new mistress, Louise Macy, a charismatic twenty-one-year-old, who would go on to marry Harry Hopkins and become a favorite of President Roosevelt. Benchley, Louise, and, in the custom of the day, a "beard"—usually James Forrestal, soon to be secretary of the navy—

often spent the evening drinking at "21" until closing time, then headed to Polly's for a nightcap. "Louise called it slumming," remembered a friend. Of course, wherever Benchley went, the rest of *The New Yorker* clique followed. Polly was especially proud to count as a regular James Thurber, the irascible humorist and cartoonist who had supplanted Peter Arno as the magazine's iconic illustrator.

The randy boys of the Friars Club and Tin Pan Alley remained some of Polly's most loyal customers. Paul Whiteman still held the house record, hosting a five-day blowout for his chums that cost $50,000. Writing in her datebook that summer, Dana Suesse, the precocious young composer known as the "Girl Gershwin," succinctly summed up the in-crowd's ideal evening on the town: "Dinner—Lou Holtz, Oscar Levant, Irving Berlin; Polly Adler's." The guests at Polly's soirees included people "from all walks of life," remembered Suesse. "There were theater folk, literary giants, movie stars, and mobsters. Casting no aspersions on any-one, they simply were wonderful affairs."

The songwriter Alec Wilder recounted an epic night at Polly's with a half dozen or so friends, including Oscar Levant, Milton Berle, and the comedian Frank Fay, who was in the midst of a rancorous divorce from the actress Barbara Stanwyck. When Levant suggested they pay a late-night visit to Polly's, Berle endorsed this heartily, claiming Polly hired only "high class broads." The composer agreed, confessing to Fay that he had not been having success with women because, in Wilder's own words, "they tell me my penis is too small." The comedian assured him that Polly had trained her girls to be nothing but complimentary. "My problem is just the reverse," Berle chimed in. "When I leave a woman's bed, she always complains that she feels like she's just given birth to a baby."

The crew arrived in high spirits, treating the neighbors to a rollick-ing chorus of "Waltzing Matilda" as they knocked on her door. Polly shushed them and poured a round of drinks. Frank Fay began badgering Polly, trying to get her to admit that his soon-to-be-ex-wife had turned tricks for her in the mid-1920s. That was before she was Barbara Stan-wyck, when she was an ambitious teenage hoofer named Ruby Stevens, dancing at the El Fey Club. Naturally, Polly denied it, and naturally, Frank scoffed at her denial.

The boys called the evening a success, although the young women were not as enthusiastic, according to Wilder. Bearing out Berle's claims, one of the girls complained that she might have to go to the hospital after bedding him. Another was outraged that Oscar Levant "insisted on smoking a cigarette right in her face while having intercourse with her." Frank Fay presented Polly with a fat tip of a fifty-dollar bill. Later he confided to Alec that he'd asked Polly to recommend "the best male whorehouse in Manhattan." He had plenty to choose from, she said, as she wrote out the names and numbers.

Alec Wilder was delighted with the evening and returned many times. "The only complaint I had about Polly's place was you never knew where it was from day to day," he recalled. "She seemed to be moving all over the town, no doubt with the police hot on her trail."

Frank Fay might have been wrong about his ex-wife, but he had reason enough to be suspicious. Plenty of legitimate dames accepted discreet dates arranged by Polly, even with the risk of being recognized. Milton Berle loved to tell the story of hanging out with his pal, the young actor John Garfield, né Julius Garfinkle, in the mid-1930s. He was performing at the Paradise Club, a popular mob playground at the time, and dating a woman named Carole. The two men decided to stop by Polly's for dinner. "Sure, the world knew Polly as a madam," said Berle with rare sincerity, "but her friends knew her as an intelligent woman, fun to be with, and a good cook."

After eating, Polly excused herself to go back to the ever-demanding telephone, marshaling girls for her clients. "I don't know about you, Julie (his real name was Jules), but I feel sort of horny," Berle said to Garfield. Garfield, as it happened, felt much the same. So she offered to send two of her $100 girls—"Polly handled only the best"—to meet them wherever they preferred. "John and I went our separate ways to await our deliveries. When the doorbell rang at my place, there was Carole!"

This danger of exposure was magnified when the wise guys were involved. No one was more attentive to the female caste system than a racket man. If he discovered that "his girl" was secretly turning tricks, that unlucky lady risked a beating or a splash of acid across the eyes. Dorothy Lamour, a dusky young beauty queen from New Orleans who'd hustled a job crooning at the Stork Club, went on dates for Polly before hitting it big in Hollywood as the sexy sidekick in Bob Hope's and Bing Crosby's classic *Road to . . .* comedies.

Polly, reminiscing with her friend Virginia Faulkner, recalled the risk Lamour had taken when one of Dutch's henchmen, Rocco Delarmi, paid the rent on one of Polly's private apartments for six months.

"No, Ginny, he was not boffing me," she joked. "For all I know it could have been Dorothy Lamour, or some married woman. I recall the Dutchman warning me not to mention that Dot belonged to Polly's stable because one of his cuties was smitten with Dorothy, it appears to me that Rocky was the cutie. One thing in the Dutchman's favor he was trying to protect a female."

As if Polly could ever forget, these perils were brought home to her in the spring of 1933, during a small dinner party at her private apartment. Her guests included Becky Mae Shomberg, a former model who was now married to Louis Shomberg, a respected elder of the bootlegging syndicate better known as Dutch Goldberg. The other was Betty Buchalter, a former hostess at the Kentucky Club and the wife of Lepke Buchalter, the fearsome boss of the trade union rackets in New York.

The women were finishing dinner when there was a knock at the door. Polly opened it to find Frankie Carbo, a leading assassin for Murder, Inc., along with a handful of heavily muscled thugs. They pushed their way in and began busting up the apartment and roughing up the women.

Who would be bold enough to manhandle the wives of two of the syndicate's most powerful leaders? After a little investigation, Dutch Schultz provided the explanation. Louis Shomberg—"a loudmouth who likes to throw his weight around," in Polly's opinion—had been enraged that his wife dared socialize with a madam, with all that implied. The message was meant to ring clear: even among professional executioners, a prostitute was a pariah.

It was, undoubtedly, cold consolation to pick up the paper and find that she'd made Walter Winchell's column, with what might be read as an inside reference to her injuries from Carbo's visit: "Polly Adler is sick at the Poly-clinic. Polly want a wisecracker?"

☾

Polly never discussed her family's response to the Seabury Investigation except to allude to her mother's anger and her brother Sol's disapproval. Gittel had good reason to be unhappy. *Di Goldine Medina* had made her oldest son into a *gonif*, her brilliant Pearl a *kurva*, and her sweet middle son Irving into a *shikker*, a drunk. Polly tried desperately to please her mother, visiting whenever she could, and when there, remembered one cousin, she would "take off her nice clothes and wash the floors." But nothing could wash away the fact that she ran a whorehouse.

It was a relief when her parents and two youngest brothers decided to join other members of the family who had immigrated to what was formally known as the British Mandate for Palestine, or as the Zionist Jews called it Eretz Yisrael, the Land of Israel. "For once I was grateful for my father's restlessness," Polly confessed. "I don't think my mother really wanted to make her home there, but she wasn't going to be left behind anymore."

(☾

With the election of Franklin Roosevelt, the Prohibition era began drawing to a close. In anticipation of the repeal of the Eighteenth Amendment, Polly's bootlegging pals started moving into other sectors of the criminal economy. Some, like Frank Costello and Meyer Lansky, focused on the relatively respectable gambling rackets, expanding their operations in New Jersey, Miami, New Orleans, and Havana. Others, like Lepke Buchalter, doubled down on less savory enterprises like shaking down legitimate business, infiltrating labor unions, and dealing narcotics.

As for Dutch Schultz, he was flush from his multimillion-dollar numbers operation up in Harlem. But the orgy of press coverage over the last couple years had drawn the attention of the authorities. Inspired by the successful prosecution of Al Capone on federal tax evasion charges in 1931, the feds now turned these tactics on New York's Public Enemies, indicting Dutch Schultz in January 1933 and Waxey Gordon three months later.

With Waxey and Dutch lying low, and Owney Madden in Sing Sing for violating parole, Lucky Luciano stepped into the limelight. Charlie Lucky was now head of the Unione Siciliana, the city's Italian criminal network, and was leading the formation of what became known as the National Crime Syndicate, a cartel of major regional gang leaders formed to quell the bloodshed and bad publicity of the recent gang wars.

As Luciano moved up in the world, he began relying more on Polly for his sexual needs. "She was the only madam in the whole city I could trust," he claimed. "If you told her or one of her girls somethin', you knew it wouldn't go no further."

He had simple tastes. "I didn't go in for none of that leather and whip crap," Lucky later told a reporter. "I liked good-looking girls who could screw good and that's what Polly always sent me." He was a good customer but hardly a big spender by Broadway standards. If he was especially appreciative, he'd shove a five-dollar bill into the girl's bra as she dressed. "I didn't want to do nothin' different," he explained. "What do you think I was gonna do—spoil it for everybody?"

One unwelcome newcomer to Polly's house was Louis Pretty Amberg, a Brownsville boy who'd made a name for himself as an inspired sadist. "I heard of him for years but never had a desire to meet him," Polly remembered. "I wonder why he was nicknamed Pretty Amberg, there was nothing pretty about him, nor his character."

Pretty was the middle brother in a family of extortionists, drug dealers, shylocks, and unusually gruesome killers who dominated the Brownsville rackets. He took special pleasure in lighting people on fire, but his great claim to fame was his invention of the so-called sack murder, in which the victim was pinned in a heavy bag with his arms and legs tied in such a way that his struggling would progressively tighten a wire noose around his neck.

Over the last decade, Polly had hosted more murderers than she could count, but this one she could not stomach. Duke Ellington remembered her antipathy vividly. "Polly Adler would call Sonny and me once in a while after our gig in the Cotton Club to come downtown and entertain some of her more illustrious clients," Duke recalled of those years; "she got along great with all the mob guys except one dude called Pretty Boy Amberg (who got his nickname the same way a bald man is called Curly), who used to get his lunatic kicks by hanging the naked girls out of the window, swaying them back and forth by their ankles before he pulled them back in." (John O'Hara, an ambitious young writer for *The New Yorker*, used Amberg's habit of hanging naked party girls out of skyscraper windows as fodder for *BUtterfield 8*, his novel based on the unfortunate Starr Faithfull.)

Pretty was drawn to the bright lights of Broadway and basked in the company of entertainers, musicians, columnists, and showgirls.

He tipped heavily but took insult easily. He once punched his favorite bandleader, Louis Prima, in the face when he didn't play a requested tune. When Milton Berle made the mistake of heckling Pretty during his nightclub act, Amberg leaped up and began choking the comedian with his own tie and was stabbing him in the face with a fork until Marty Krompier stepped in.

Hostesses and chorus girls who spurned Pretty's advances found themselves nursing a bruised jaw, a black eye, or worse. He could often be found ringside at the Hollywood Club, on upper Broadway, where both Walter Winchell and Oscar Levant recalled seeing him order a tumbler of whiskey, then take out his set of false teeth and drop them in the glass—along with a Mickey Finn—commanding some terrified young cutie: "Now drink it!"

Whorehouses brought out the worst in Pretty and his gang. Polly heard horrific tales of how they had destroyed the houses of Jenny the Factory and Sadie the Chink, abusing the girls, ripping up the furniture, breaking windows, and setting the beds on fire.

The first time Pretty came to her house, Polly was in Hot Springs. When she called to check in, Showboat informed her that Amberg had been there the night before, along with some pals. "It seems as he was leaving in an ungentlemanly fashion," she recalled, "he threw a twenty-dollar bill at the girl he slept with. The girl, not knowing who Pretty was, insulted at being paid off like at a cigar counter, tore the bill in half and threw it at his majesty. Pretty picked up the pieces, put a match to it, and cagedly [sic] watched the girl's expression and walked out the door without as much as saying 'drop dead.'"

The next night Polly was invited to a dinner hosted by Joe Adonis, the most powerful of the Brooklyn bosses, who was also on holiday in Hot Springs. When she confessed her worries about Amberg, Joey A. just smiled and said, "Don't worry, Polly, he won't visit you anymore."

"I was told that word was sent to Pretty to keep away from me and my house. Pretty must have taken the order seriously and did keep away," she remembered with gratitude. At least for a while.

When Polly finally did, in her words, "meet the bastard" in person, it was back in New York at the King Terrace Club, on West 52nd Street, a well-known gangster hangout.

I was there with a crowd, quite a few of my girls were present. I almost died when Lou Schwartz, the owner, brought him over to the table and said, "Polly meet Pretty Amberg." I must have shit in my pants, I smelled something, maybe it was Pretty. I gave the girls the high-sign to sit tight on their charm, that this is one customer we can do without. I bawled the hell out of Lou for bringing Pretty over to my table, perhaps I shouldn't have, because Lou knew the meaning of disobeying the rulers of that period.

After that Pretty would call occasionally, asking her to send a dame to wherever he was staying. "When I heard his voice I always slipped the phone to Showboat, she knew how to handle the bum, he would pay the girl and send a bottle of scotch for Showboat." Occasionally, he came to the house with Dutch and his crew. When Polly complained, Dutch promised her that Pretty wouldn't visit without him. But even that was too often for her taste.

When Dutch reappeared on the scene in the summer of 1933, he was notably calmer, drank more sparingly, and had spiffed up his wardrobe. Although still keeping a low profile, he could be found most days up in Jimmy Hines's Monongahela Club and most evenings at Polly's joint on West 54th or just down the block at Dutch's nightclub, the Chateau Madrid, often in the company of Hines and Dixie Davis. He used Polly's house for private conferences, warning her in advance so she could make sure that outsiders were barred.

Politics was Dutch's new passion. In the upcoming mayoral race, Jimmy Walker's old foe, the Republican reformer Fiorello La Guardia, had a strong advantage given the deepening Depression and anti-Tammany mood. But it was the district attorney who mattered most in Dutch's line of work. Jimmy Hines was backing a loyal Tammany warhorse named William Copeland Dodge. Dodge was the ideal candidate, as Hines explained, because he was, "stupid, respectable and my man." Delighted at the prospect of owning his own DA, Schultz provided tens of thousands of dollars to Hines's campaign fund and a small army of hooligans to help out on election day.

The Associated Press declared the municipal election of 1933 the most violent, chaotic, and corrupt in a generation, marked by the "liberal use of blackjacks, brass knuckles, lead pipe, bricks, knives and hob-nailed boots." Such threats couldn't sink the redoubtable Fiorello La Guardia, but they were more than enough to sweep the stupid and respectable William Copeland Dodge into the district attorney's office.

⸙

On December 5, 1933, the Twenty-First Amendment to the Constitution was ratified, repealing the Eighteenth Amendment and bringing an end to the Noble Experiment. It was a rare moment of joy in a bleak winter.

Still, many were sorry to see the bad old days depart. "No matter what anyone says, the Prohibition era was fun, a real gasser," one madam remembered wistfully. "With repeal came the type of letdown one feels after a big screwing party is over."

The new era would be led by the bustling, squeaky-clean new mayor, Fiorello La Guardia, and the big thinkers of President Roosevelt's New Deal. La Guardia was sworn into office by Judge Seabury at exactly midnight on New Year's Eve 1933. He took his first official act as mayor a few minutes later, ordering the arrest of Lucky Luciano. In the coming weeks, he declared war on Frank Costello's slot-machine empire, proclaiming, "I'm going to grab every tinhorn gambler in the city of New York by the scruff of the neck and throw him over into New Jersey!"

If Polly feared that the return of legal drinking would dampen business, she worried in vain. The death of the intimate speakeasies only added to her appeal among the hard-drinking nighthawks who missed the furtive pleasure of the secret hideaways and the anything-goes camaraderie of the illicit nightclubs. She was in full swing that year, entertaining constantly, popping up in the Broadway columns, and appearing regularly in the chic hotspots and sporting venues, usually with a flock of beauties in tow.

Then a new menace arose on the horizon, an unintended side effect of the Seabury Investigation and the end of Prohibition. Seabury's breakup of the Women's Court vice ring created a vacuum in the bail bonding business. In their absence, Polly's old colleague Nick Montana, along with a number of smaller operators, set up a reasonably fair system to provide bonding insurance for prostitutes and madams. Ten dollars a week per girl and fifteen per madam ensured that in case of arrest, they'd be bailed out and provided with a lawyer to fix the case.

At the same time, with liquor now legal, the swollen population of former bootleggers were casting about for new sources of illegal income. A crew of hard guys from Little Italy, known loosely as "the Mott Street mob," decided to muscle in on Nick Montana and his compatriots. Polly knew some of them—they'd been Charlie Lucky's low-life men-of-all-work for years—and she harbored a deep antipathy for one of the leaders, Tommy "the Bull" Pennochio, who had personally addicted one of her girls to heroin.

Tommy the Bull and his mob began hammering Montana, arranging for him to be busted by the cops and sent to prison for a spell. Then they began shaking down the madams, using the threat of violence to persuade them to start paying a weekly bonding fee. Madams who resisted were badly beaten and their houses ravaged.

At first Polly avoided the attention of the Mott Street goons, but she was too rich a target to escape for long. One night they turned up on West 54th Street when Polly had two customers in the house. They steamrollered into the apartment, roughed up one of the johns, stole some cash, and threatened the rest of them.

"Let this be a lesson, you highfalutin bitch," the head hoodlum snarled as they left. "We've heard your crack that you won't cater to racketeers, but you'll be seein' *us* around whenever we feel like it."

They came back the next night. While the maid held them off at the door, Polly fled out the window and down the fire escape to her neighbor's apartment, where she hid out until the ruckus upstairs died down. When she returned, the apartment was in shambles, the floor littered with smashed-up lamps and dishes, the furniture tossed helter-skelter, and the upholstery slashed.

She'd have to close up the apartment for a while, but that would only delay their return. Without a word, Showboat took out a bottle of brandy and handed Polly a glass. "It was a time not for action but for anesthesia," Polly remembered, "and I drank myself into oblivion."

When she awoke at noon the next day, she found Bo Weinberg surveying the damage.

"I've just sent for Dutch," he told Polly. "You explain everything to him."

Dutch was furious when she told him of the shakedown. "Why in hell didn't you mention my name?" he demanded. "All this could have been avoided."

The following week, as she was cleaning up the house and replacing the furniture, she arrived home and discovered Dutch lounging in the kitchen, feet up on the windowsill, reading *Al Capone: The Biography of a Self-Made Man*, by the *Daily News*'s ace crime reporter, Fred Pasley.

"Where the hell you been all day?" Dutch barked.

"In Brooklyn. Did you hear from Bo?"

"Yeah," he said. The Mott Street thugs were coming by that night to apologize.

Suddenly, Polly burst into tears. "I'm going to quit this damn business," she sobbed. "I work like a slave twenty-four hours a day, and all I get out of it is a living and a headache. What money I do save goes into pay-offs when I'm pinched, or to fix up the place after it's been sabotaged by those strongarms. To hell with it! I'm quitting."

"Poll, you're not thinking straight," said Dutch. "You aren't gonna quit business because you can't. All this notoriety you've had—it's been great for bringing in customers, but it's gonna trip you up if you try to set up as a legitimate operator. Face up to it, kid; you're tagged as a madam and a madam is what you're gonna stay."

The bums showed up that night, as promised, looking chastened and almost apologetic. They even paid for their own drinks, she noted dryly, before taking their leave. They never darkened her doorstep again.

☾

Back in the city for the fall theatrical season, Bob Benchley asked Polly to arrange a private party for a group of six, including a U.S. senator, "who was much in the news just then, a famous woman writer, a movie idol, a prominent and lovely member of the fast fox-huntin' set," and Bob's current mistress, Louise Macy.

Polly arranged top-notch bohemian entertainment for the party, including a trio of glittering drag performers and the bawdy songstress Gladys Bentley, who reigned as New York's most famous lesbian. Bentley, a Black cabaret performer, was the darling of the sophisticated set who flocked to Harlem for taboo pleasures and a close friend of Polly and Tallulah Bankhead.

To protect the privacy of his VIP guests, Bob asked her to close the house to other customers, excluding even her working girls. But when she explained that there was a big college football game that weekend and she couldn't disappoint her Ivy League clientele, he relented. Bench claimed one wing of the apartment, and the boys got the rest.

But it wasn't the rowdy college boys who caused the trouble that night, for a change. It was Polly's girls, who were insulted at being banned from the A-list party across the hall.

One of the girls, a lush named Ellie, who'd been tippling with the college boys all afternoon, was especially annoyed at being left out of the private dinner. Ellie tried to slip into the private party by attaching herself to the movie idol on his way back from the bathroom, but Polly quickly hustled her out.

Both parties were soon at full roar. The evening-gowned drag queen act was such a success that the senator refused to believe the performers were actually men. But Gladys Bentley, in her signature white tux and tails, was the big hit of the evening with her ribald songs and innuendo-laden patter.

All evening Polly shuttled back and forth between the two gatherings, but was so busy she didn't notice that Louise Macy had made an incognito visit to check out the post-football festivities, pretending to be one of Polly's girls. About half an hour later Louise ran back into Bob's party, sobbing hysterically. "Oh, my God! Ellie fell out the window!" she cried. "I tried to hold her, but she fell."

The joint descended into pandemonium as Polly dashed through the house shouting orders to the maids and pounding on bedroom doors to rouse the guests before the law showed up. The college boys were enjoying the chaos and wanted to stick around, Polly remembered: "I nearly lost my mind before I could get rid of them."

They found Ellie on the sidewalk near the Harding Hotel, still alive, and carried her into the super's apartment. "I was pushed," she kept murmuring weakly. "She pushed me." Polly was certain Ellie was lying—Louise Macy "was not the sort of woman who went around pushing people out of windows"—but even so, she had to get Benchley and the rest of his party out of there before they were drawn into some sort of scandal.

But sweet old Bob Benchley insisted on sticking around. He even helped convince a pair of doctors to come to the house in exchange for a $150 "fee" for their silence, and they arranged for her to be examined at a private sanitarium nearby. Ellie suffered only a few broken ribs, as it turned out. Drunk and jealous, she had told Louise she was going to jump out the window to commit suicide. When Louise tried to grab her, her dress tore, and the girl tumbled off the windowsill, but landed onto the fire escape a few feet below. While Louise ran for help, Ellie sneaked down five flights and dropped from the first-floor fire escape to the sidewalk, where they discovered her.

When Polly returned to the house in the morning, she found Bob and his friends still there, waiting for news. "They were people who had everything to lose by becoming involved in a scandal," remembered Polly gratefully, and yet they stayed to help. "For my dough, when people behave as these did, that's class."

☾

For almost a decade, Polly had kept her headquarters on West 54th next to the Harding Hotel even as she'd hopscotched around the city. But the neighborhood had declined as Times Square grew seedier and high-dollar nightlife drifted east of Fifth Avenue. As the columnist O. O. McIntyre put it, "Broadway is in the wrong part of town these days."

Many of her customers, Jock Whitney most vocally, had been urging her to move for some time. The Harding Hotel, in particular, was a nest of potential kidnappers, and he was the ripest of targets. Jock even offered to make up any increase in rent if she'd shift her operations to the East Side. Now he made it an ultimatum: move or lose him as a customer.

After the run-in with the Mott Street mob, the brouhaha when Ellie fell out of the window, and Jock's ultimatum, a change of scenery seemed prudent. So armed with stellar references from her carriage trade johns, she rented a twelve-room apartment on the corner of 55th and Madison, above a row of small shops.

Styles had changed over her fifteen years in business. Older high-end bagnios leaned heavily on gilt, red velvet, and campy, exotic themes. Now, as one young cop remembered, "the better whore houses in town were furnished to look like a millionaire's apartment." She hired an interior decorator who did up bedrooms in shades of peach and apple green, to set off her collection of rose quartz and jade lamps. "Peach is a color that brightened the wan faces of the worn out whores (including myself) after a night's work," explained Polly.

The new flat boasted a satin-bedecked dining room that could seat fifty and a paneled library lined with books selected by Benchley and Dorothy Parker, many of them written by or about her guests and personally autographed. The bar area was done up in patriotic red, white, and blue, and there was a room for card games and screening spicy films. "Men often remarked that my apartment was done in excellent taste," Polly remembered proudly.

She had four girls living in and hired a second maid to help Showboat along with two top-notch cooks, so customers could drop by for a drink and a nosh anytime, night or day. After the bars closed at four a.m., her place became an after-hours supper club, serving eggs, hotcakes, and sausages gratis, an expense that she more than made up in liquor sales.

This would be her most famous house. The place had all the charm of the best speakeasies, the delicious sense of secrecy, intimacy, and spontaneity. The scene was *Gemütlich*, as the writer Sam Kashner put it, "a gang of swells, actors, and politicians milling around, talking, laughing, reading the newspapers, grabbing a bite and listening to the fights on the radio." Polly became a master at backgammon, the hot new gambling fad of the early 1930s, and many customers stopped by solely to play a few rounds with the madam over cocktails. She won a nice chunk of change that way and did the same when gin rummy came into vogue.

The novelist and travel writer Alec Waugh, scion of the illustrious English literary clan, remembered Polly's house in those years as louche, luxurious, and homey. Waugh was friendly with some of her regulars, the new crop of star writers at *The New Yorker*—Wolcott Gibbs, James Thurber, St. Clair McKelway, and John McNulty. But it was his married lover, "Mary G.," he called her, who introduced him to Polly.

Mary G. was cast in the mold of Tallulah Bankhead and Libby Holman—promiscuous, fond of recreational drugs, with a habit of making "unexpected passes" at both men and women. Separated from her husband, Mary was working for Polly at the time. "She was not short of money and whenever she had made some at Polly's she would take a couple of the girls up to Harlem and spend it on them," Waugh recalled.

"I couldn't keep her on," Polly told Alec later, "she was disrupting my entire business."

"It really was a club," remembered the writer fondly.

There was no solicitation. You sat around; you danced; you ordered drinks; no pressure was put upon you if you did not want to play. You took leave of your hostess just as you would at a cocktail party, and at the door a tall handsome dark girl would hand you a bill. It was usually less than you expected. Finance was never mentioned. Single drinks were a dollar a piece. I once asked Polly if she had any champagne. She shook her head. "No, Alec, there's no need for you to start ordering champagne here." If she knew the ship that you were sailing by, there would be an "au-revoir" cable signed by her and the particular girl whom you had cherished. Every year there was a Christmas card, with a parrot perched upon a ring. During the war, in far-off Baghdad it was nostalgic but reassuring to get that card each January.

Of course, running a twenty-four-hour full-service salon and harem was not easy. And it was frustrating to watch former bootleggers and ex-cons like Jack and Charlie Kerns at "21" or Sherman Billingsley of the Stork Club become legitimate businessmen and social arbiters while she had to stay in the shadows.

It was especially galling when they did it at her expense, like the nightclub proprietor who threatened to fire the club's doorman after he let Polly in. Worse yet was the humiliating night that Sherman Billingsley ordered her to leave the Stork Club in front of a roomful of diners. When she refused, he instructed the waiters to remove her table until finally she fled. But Polly was too powerful to blackball, so Billingsley regularly sent cases of champagne to her house as a bribe to keep her from returning.

Despite it all, she would look back on these as her golden years.

☾

As usual, trouble was stirring behind this glittering facade. In 1933 the idealistic young U.S. attorney Thomas E. Dewey put the invincible Waxey Gordon behind bars on tax charges. Now he was gunning for the Dutchman. At the end of November 1934, after dodging the U.S. Treasury Department for almost two years, Dutch Schultz surrendered to the authorities in Albany, to stand trial on tax evasion. Meanwhile, back in Manhattan, questions were growing about how Schultz's multimillion-dollar numbers racket could have flourished so freely unless the NYPD was protecting him.

Unlike a murder rap, federal tax charges were considered serious. But it was the local investigation that concerned Polly. Anyone examining Arthur Flegenheimer's whereabouts over the last two years would quickly find themselves at her doorstep.

In December she started to hear rumbles of trouble firsthand, when Inspector Charles L. Neidig, the new officer in charge of the silk-stocking East Side, dropped by to warn her that she was becoming a hot topic at police headquarters.

She had no pull with Mayor La Guardia's new police commissioner, Lewis J. Valentine, a straight-arrow, former shoofly with whom she'd first tangled years earlier. So Polly decided that this was, once again, an excellent time to take a long foreign vacation. Leaving the operation in the capable hands of Showboat, she bought a ticket for a six-week cruise through the West Indies, with an educational stop in Panama's famous red-light district.

One night about a week before she was to leave, four cops came by the house. By good fortune, her harem was spending the evening at the Waldorf Astoria, where the first annual meeting of major league baseball managers and club owners was being held. But the bulls weren't looking for girls—they were looking for a roulette wheel, or so they said. The building's doorman, suspicious that so many well-dressed couples were coming in and out of her apartment, had told the superintendent that she must be running a gambling operation, and he complained to the local precinct.

After a few drinks and some of Polly's patented persuasion, the sergeant suggested that she lie low, and he'd be in touch. Two days later he called to say she was in the clear. In gratitude, she asked the cops to dinner, then invited them to the cocktail party she threw the afternoon she sailed, three days before Christmas.

"I was both surprised and touched when I got to my cabin and found a huge basket of flowers inscribed, 'Bon Voyage from your four friends,'" she recalled.

☾

When Polly returned six weeks later, pressure was building on all sides in the long-stalled investigation into Dutch Schultz and Jimmy Hines. With few other viable leads, Polly looked like the best bet to crack open the case.

This time the police laid their trap with unusual care. They recruited the elevator operator to log all her visitors. They replaced the service elevator operator with an undercover officer who spent his shifts counting the number of sheets she sent to the laundry and the cases of champagne she emptied.

On March 4, 1935, Jimmy Hines's handpicked district attorney, William Dodge, was finally forced to convene a grand jury to investigate Schultz. The next day Police Commissioner Lewis Valentine ordered Inspector Charles Neidig to raid Polly's place on the double. They tapped her phone wires and stationed two men in the basement of her building to monitor her calls. They didn't have long to wait.

Polly had four girls living in, but only three were on duty that night. Yvonne Moore was a blond cabaret singer at the Kings Terrace. Eva Acosta was Cuban, with an hourglass figure and almond-shaped eyes, recently arrived from the red-light district of Panama.

They were joined by a petite twenty-one-year-old brunette from Kentucky, working under the name Dorothy Walker. Polly had employed her two older sisters before the Crash and had warned them against bringing their kid sister to join them in New York. Nonetheless, Dorothy had entered the family trade, and by her late teens she was earning top dollar "in the art of providing unconventional entertainment for men-about-town," as the *Daily News* described it. She'd recently graced the tabloids while testifying in court that she'd been paid $100 to be tied to a chair and whipped by another girl for the amusement of Robert Barbour, the wealthy brother of Senator W. Warren Barbour of New Jersey. Dorothy also developed a serious heroin habit. After she jumped bail on a narcotics charge earlier that year, Dorothy's sister begged Polly to hire her, knowing that she would help Dorothy kick the habit. And she did.

But lately Polly had begun to suspect the girl was using again. That evening she confronted her. Dorothy denied it angrily and stomped out, but a little later she returned, shamefaced, and silently handed Polly a hypodermic needle and two packages of heroin, which Polly hid in the pocket of one of her own suits.

Polly then went out for a bite to eat. When she returned, she had a message to call a number she didn't recognize, but when she did, it turned out to be a police station: "Figuring it was somebody's idea of a gag, I hung up." Also waiting for her was a telegram from a cop pal in Florida, hitting her up for train fare back to New York after going bust at the racetrack. She obligingly wired him the money and tucked the telegram in her jewelry box.

It was a Tuesday, a slow night, so it wasn't until nearly midnight that the boys in the basement got their lead. One of her Madison Avenue johns, a vice president of Batten, Barton, Durstine & Osborn (better known as BBDO) named Alexander "Lex" Duncan Chiquoine, called from the Waldorf Astoria, looking for a little fun for himself and a client. They arrived ten minutes later in evening clothes and fine humor. Polly didn't care much for the cocky Chiquoine, but she took a shine to his more refined friend, John C. Sterling, a vice president at the McCall Company, publisher of ultra-respectable women's magazines, and a big wheel in the advertising industry.

After a few drinks with the girls, the men called for Polly to pull out her film projector and screen some "home movies" from her recent vacation, which just happened to be in the same box as some very dirty and very illegal stag films. Down in the basement with their wiretaps, the cops were taking it all in.

A little before four a.m., the doorman called up to announce that a Mr. Fitzgerald was there to see her. At that time of day, it could only be a cop, Polly figured, stopping by for a freebie or to tip her off to an upcoming raid. But when she opened the door, a swarm of bulls led by Inspector Neidig plunged past her. Polly shouted curses as they tore their way through the house.

"One guy was keeping warm between the girls' legs when the cops broke in," Polly remembered. They discovered Alexander Chiquoine in bed with Dorothy and Eva Acosta, naked and scrambling for their clothes. The other bedroom was locked. When the cops finally found Yvonne and John Sterling, the couple were standing in the barroom fully dressed in evening clothes. "He was telling me his troubles and I was telling mine," the girl explained innocently. "I'm a good listener."

Meanwhile Polly was desperately trying to distract the patrolman guarding the exit, hoping to keep the others from finding the heroin and the incriminating telegram as they ripped the place apart looking for the blue movies. When he pressed her about the nude threesome in the bedroom, she replied hotly, "Why, that's nothing. These people are my guests. This is my home. They can do as they please."

"What are they doing in this joint?" he barked.

Now she lost her temper. "Joint! You call this a joint. You have some nerve. This is an A-number-1 house of assignation. The girls are first class."

As he flipped open his notepad, it hit her that she'd just confessed. Adding to her consternation, when the cops questioned the frightened johns, they admitted everything. Cornered, Polly finally relinquished the film canisters and the johns were allowed to leave, then she threw on her mink coat and climbed into the patrol wagon with the other girls for a miserable night in jail.

By the time she arrived at the courthouse the next morning word of the raid had spread. Photographers lined the sidewalks and staircases determined to finally get a decent picture of the elusive madam. "Short, stocky, with heavily rouged lips and cheeks and brightly tinted fingernails, she buried her head in the collar of her coat and kicked and shouted torrid words at the photographers who tried to take her picture as she was led into court," reported *The New York Times*.

Inside, she faced Magistrate Anna Kross, who had replaced the disgraced Magistrate Jean Norris as the token woman on the bench. Like Polly, Kross had immigrated in her youth from the Pale of Russia and was genuinely sympathetic to New York's working girls.

Be that as it may, when Polly refused to answer to any name other than her current alias, Joan Martin, Kross's "voice fairly dripped acid as she set my bail at two thousand five hundred dollars instead of the customary five hundred," remembered Polly (nearly $50,000 today). Polly faced two charges: running a disorderly house and possession of lewd films. That meant the bluecoats hadn't found Dorothy's dope or the incriminating telegram. "My relief was so great that I practically skipped all the way to the patrol wagon," she remembered.

After posting bail, she returned home to find a twenty-four-hour police guard stationed outside the building, putting an end to any further business in her grand apartment. There was nothing to do but place her furniture in storage and move to a hotel.

Commissioner Valentine declared himself "elated" over Madam Adler's arrest. "She is one woman I wanted to see brought in," he boasted to the assembled reporters. The newspapers also "greeted my return to the spotlight with whoops of joy," she recalled. No more ominous talk of a "Female Al Capone"—now "I was treated more as a 'character' than a public enemy." All the same, her pride must have been hurt by the derisive comments about her looks that peppered their stories. Although she was only in her mid-thirties, fifteen years of late nights, constant stress, and professional drinking had taken their toll.

Her parents were in Palestine, but she could be sure her Brooklyn cousins heard the news, after she was declared "The Queen of Night Life in New York" on the front page of America's leading Yiddish newspaper, the *Jewish Daily Forward*. Even more upsetting, while she was being booked, some rascal from the *Daily News* sneaked into her apartment and stole several personal photos, including one taken with her teenage brother, Sol, who was mortified when his friends saw it in the papers.

But Sol's feelings were nothing compared to the alarm rolling through the masculine quarters of the city when Magistrate Kross, an ardent feminist and vocal critic of the double standard in prostitution cases, announced that she planned to call the alleged customers to testify. If necessary, she would summon supporting witnesses from Polly's customer account book that had been seized during the raid.

When word of Polly's "little black book" book hit the papers, the district attorney was deluged by powerful men in various stages of hysteria. "The office of District Attorney Dodge has been cluttered up with a motley assemblage of unhappy politicians, panic-stricken Fifth and Park Avenue husbands and trifling wives of some of the husbands who had been in the habit of whiling away a few more or less idle hours in Polly's deluxe establishment," reported the *Mirror*.

Dodge assured everyone that he would not name any men publicly. "We all make mistakes, and it does not behoove anyone of us to tell the other how to live," he explained primly. Commissioner Valentine insisted that the book would be destroyed. But the prosecuting attorney for the case, assistant district attorney Maurice G. Wahl, agreed with Magistrate Kross, telling reporters that, if necessary, he would call the twenty men listed as having outstanding debts to Polly: "I don't care who they are. I'll call them in."

As for Alexander Chiquoine and John Sterling, both were married and both were horrified by this rare breach of tradition. In desperation, they arranged a secret meeting with Polly in a private suite at the Waldorf Astoria. When she arrived, Chiquoine got right to the point. "Why don't you plead guilty and get it over with?" he demanded.

"When I need advice," she shot back, "I ask a lawyer."

John Sterling appealed to sentiment, begging Polly to "think of their families."

"Were you thinking of them when you were with the girls?" she sneered.

They offered her ten thousand dollars to plead guilty, thus making a public trial unnecessary. She angrily spurned their bribe, preferring to take her chances alone. According to the *Mirror*, Polly was now threatening to "'tell a story that will stand the town on its ear if they indict me.'"

Ultimately, the outcry was loud enough to get a new magistrate assigned to the case. Her replacement, the eminent Jewish reformer Jonah Goldstein, was savvier politically than the fiery Kross. "I agreed with Anna Kross that it was all wrong to charge one without charging both, but we weren't making the law," Goldstein said later. "The influence reached right into the White House, and they got hold of the chief sitting magistrate and Mayor Walker, and they came to the conclusion that I would be the one who would know how to handle that situation, knowing my point of view."

Polly also acquired a new attorney, Samuel J. Siegel, Esq., a slick-looking shyster straight out of Central Casting, with narrow eyes and a pencil-thin mustache. Siegel specialized in cases where sex, money, and reputation collided, featuring lurid details and vulgar publicity. He defended demimondaines who put wealthy men in compromising situations, and wealthy men who liked to rough up young girls, society wives

who shoplifted or passed bad checks, disgruntled spouses seeking generous divorce settlements, and blackmailers posing as despoiled virgins in
breach of promise suits.

Over the next few days, Polly was in and out of court as her lawyer
wrangled with the magistrates, the prosecutor, and the district attorney over the charges and whether Polly would testify before the grand
jury investigating Schultz's Harlem numbers game and the vice rackets. When Polly refused to speak to the grand jury unless they offered
her immunity from prosecution, District Attorney Dodge promptly
came to her rescue. If she refused to waive her right not to incriminate
herself, then he would dispense with her as a grand jury witness, he
explained, since any claim of immunity would torpedo the criminal
case against her.

☾

The main event was scheduled for March 14, when the blue films were
to be shown and the sensational details would be laid out in Women's
Court. Public anticipation was so high that when Polly arrived, a cor-
don of policemen had to hold back the straining crowd. Upstairs the
courtroom was standing room only, crammed with spectators, press, and
underworld spies sent to study the faces of the undercover cops. Necks
craned and heads bobbed as Polly found a seat in front, joined by her
three stylishly dressed co-defendants. A Salvation Army officer threaded
her way through the courtroom passing out religious pamphlets that the
girls quickly tossed aside. Polly twisted in her seat, trying to shield her
face from the phalanx of photographers as she waited for the judge to
appear. "I've been the goat in these racket investigations for a long time,"
she growled at reporters. "I'm getting damned tired of it."

Finally, the trial was called to order. But just as the first police officer took the stand, Polly's lawyer requested a postponement, which
Magistrate Goldstein granted. The disappointed "thrill seers sighed in
audible dismay" when they realized there would be no screening of the
lurid "French films," in the *Daily News*'s phrase. "But there was general rejoicing and a renewed rush for special passes when it was learned
that the premiere would be transferred from the cramped quarters of
the woman's court to more spacious quarters in the Criminal Courts
Building."

In the absence of real news, the newspapers printed the rumors that had been percolating since the morning of her arrest: That Polly was being made a scapegoat for the current cleanup campaign. That she was being punished for not joining the Mott Street mob's bonding combination. That she was paying the price for having framed women who worked for her or for antagonizing her fellow madams. That both Dixie Davis and Polly would soon be telling all before the grand jury. And the most worrying rumor, that "Polly herself, is threating to 'blow the works'—that is, name many socially prominent persons, high state and city officials and men of distinction in all walks of life, unless she is given what she calls a 'square deal.'"

Walter Winchell's column caught the air of anxiety on the Rialto: "Bad business in the theaters and clubs last week but managers undecided whether it was due to the first week of Lent or the threat by the District Att'y to publish Polly Adler's chump list."

Through some last-minute maneuvering, Polly's employees went to trial without her on March 18. Yvonne Moore, the aspiring singer, was the only one of the women to testify for the defense, claiming that the night of the arrest, they had been "listening to the radio, playing cards and having a few cocktails with the men." Polly's lawyer and prosecutor Wahl had agreed that Alexander Chiquoine and John Sterling would not be called to testify. To his credit, Magistrate Goldstein objected to this brazen hypocrisy and insisted on making their names public, although only the proper New York Times dared print them.

In the end, the three women were found guilty of "loitering and prostitution." Eva Acosta was deported back to Cuba, Dorothy Walker was hospitalized for her heroin addiction, and Yvonne Moore, the only one who passed her Wassermann test, was given a suspended sentence.

Week after week, Polly's case was postponed as the lawyers sparred over whether one guilty plea would cover both charges, which court they would appear in, and what sort of deal might satisfy the judges, the defendant, the unhappy district attorney, and his outraged critics.

Finally, Polly took matters into her own hands. A few days before she was to be sentenced, she went to see Lucky Luciano. After conferring privately with him, she pleaded guilty to the charge of keeping a disorderly house on May 7.

"If I stood trial the lice caught in the raid would have been exposed, not that I particularly had love for them, but I felt in the eyes of the public and the judges, they would have called me a craven whore for exposing respectable married citizens!" Polly later told her friend Virginia Faulkner. "I also felt even if I had beat the charge of running a house, I sure would have gotten the limit on the dirty picture charge; that is why I pleaded guilty, and in doing so I gained more confidence from the customers, with the feeling that Polly would rather go to jail than expose us."

On May 10 Polly was sentenced to thirty days in women's prison and fined $500. The lewd-picture charge was dropped when the police couldn't prove from their wiretaps whether the defendants had been viewing pornography or Polly's home movies. Despite the rumors that she was being made the scapegoat for some mysterious cabal, she insisted later that "there was no under-world pressure to plead guilty. On the contrary it was Charlie Lucky that made it possible for me to get 30 days, $500 fine instead of the three years, (probably)."

"I felt that I had come out of it rather well," she recalled with justifiable pride.

☾

Polly spent the next twenty-five days in the women's prison in Greenwich Village, cutting five days off her sentence for good behavior. Of all the episodes in her long career, her stint in prison was the one she wrote about with the most freedom and detail, as well as with surprising warmth. Perhaps there was simply no point dissembling or rationalizing now that the world knew what she was.

That first night in prison was, as she wrote in her memoir, her "first peaceful night's sleep in three months" and arguably her first real rest since she entered this perilous life. She spent her sentence doing chores, making friends among the inmates and the staff, brooding over the past, and smarting at the snide commentary about her in the newspapers.

On June 2, the last day of her sentence—minus five days for good behavior—reporters and photographers clustered around the jail, hoping to catch her as she returned to freedom. But with the help of some of the prison workers who'd taken a shine to her, she sneaked out the side door before her official release time, where a cabbie friend was waiting to serve as her getaway car.

"Polly was a model prisoner," the prison's chief matron told the frustrated reporters. "She worked eight hours a day sewing towels and did good work. All the other women liked her, and she made friends quickly."

By this point, the grand jury investigation and the citywide vice cleanup had fizzled. Polly was their only trophy, a point made by Walter Winchell in his column the following week: "The policy inquiry was supposed to clean the town of numbers players, but all it did was to put Polly Adler to weaving rugs in the hoosegow." Just another long-shot Broadway bet that didn't pay off, he cackled.

☾

After getting out of the jug, Polly was worse than broke. This time she didn't have Dutch to help her get back on her feet, so she wired her brother Benny for some cash. Ben was in Chicago with a pretty, young wife, working his chosen profession as a second-story man.

At six p.m. Polly drove up to the Western Union telegraph office at Broadway and 65th, strolled in, identified herself as "Joan Martin," and inquired about a money order under that name. Out of nowhere, two detectives appeared, arrested her, and hauled her to the West 68th Street station, where she was booked as a fugitive from justice in Chicago.

"What's it all about?" shouted one of the police reporters as she climbed into the patrol wagon, covering her face from the photographers.

"I wish I knew what it was all about," she muttered.

The newspapers found out before she did. "Detectives had been tipped off by Chicago police that the money was Polly's share of the loot in a burglary for which a man and his wife are held in Chicago," reported the *Daily News*. Ben and his wife had been arrested the day before, under the aliases Joseph and Jean Rosen, as the masterminds behind a daring string of apartment robberies. They might have gotten away with their crime spree had Jean not left a fatal clue in each apartment: cigarette stubs stained with lipstick. The "Lipstick Burglars," the *Chicago Tribune* dubbed them.

The next morning Polly was back in court, but before any action was taken, the chief of detectives in the Chicago Police Department telegraphed to say they had no interest in her and she could be released. Her brother was not so lucky. He and his wife were tried, found guilty, and given long prison sentences. Benny was sent to the federal prison in Joliet, Illinois, where he spent much of the next few decades behind bars.

When Polly went to the police headquarters to claim the $1,250 the officers had seized from her and the 1934 Buick sedan they'd impounded, she was shocked to discover that the feds had appropriated the money as a down payment on the $16,181.41 they claimed she owed in taxes for 1927 to 1930. A wedge of seven husky cops surrounded her as she exited the headquarters and hailed a taxi. "But it doesn't matter," she insisted airily to the police reporter for the *Daily News*. "I'd just go on a champagne binge with it. In case you don't know, I'm going to marry a millionaire." She didn't disclose the name of the millionaire.

Polly put on a bold face and reopened her business as an out-call service. But the close call fueled her growing paranoia. She began avoiding old friends and rarely left the new hideaway she'd rented at 125 East 54th Street. Then, six weeks after leaving prison, the police dropped by to inform her that they had been tapping her phone wires ever since she moved in and suggested she move along to another neighborhood.

When she furiously protested that she wasn't breaking any laws, the lieutenant explained that the police department was getting heat from a prominent nightclub owner whom Polly knew from political circles. "He thinks you're living too close to his club, and you might hurt his business," said the lieutenant. "I know he'll resort to anything to get you moved," he added, hinting that the club owner would even plant drugs or a gun on her if necessary. He left with a warning: "Get smart and get out."

So she did, moving farther east, to 361 East 50th Street. But a few weeks later, Inspector Charles Neidig knocked on the door. She hadn't seen him since the trial.

"Polly," he said brusquely, "why don't you get wise? Why don't you quit before the Feds take you in tow?" The FBI had just arrested one of Manhattan's top madams, Mae Scheible, the former vice queen of Pittsburgh. "This is off the record, but they're on your tail too." He didn't care where she went, as long as it wasn't in his district.

So once again she packed up and moved temporarily into the Monticello Hotel, a fleabag on West 65th Street notorious as the site of one of Legs Diamond's many assassination attempts. At least here she would receive a warm welcome.

☾

Polly hadn't seen much of Dutch Schultz after he went on the lam in a doomed effort to avoid federal tax evasion charges. But he'd been a constant presence in the headlines since he turned himself in at the end of 1934. Federal prosecutors brought him to trial in July 1935, with high hopes. On August 2 the jury delivered a shocking verdict of not guilty.

The Dutchman's victory over the tax men made him both more paranoid and more arrogant. "Any guy who can lick the government can lick anybody," he boasted to Dixie Davis. Now he was talking openly about killing the mob's nemesis, Thomas Dewey, the aggressive U.S. attorney of the Southern District of New York.

On September 9, 1935, Bo Weinberg left a midtown Manhattan nightclub and was never seen again. Some blamed Pretty Amberg, who resented Bo's efforts to muscle in on his money-lending racket. Others whispered that Bo, expecting Dutch to follow Waxey and Capone to the federal penitentiary, had secretly been working on a plan to merge the Schultz operations with Charlie Lucky's organization. It was assumed that Dutch had gotten wind of this betrayal and sent his old pal to the bottom of the East River in a cement overcoat.

On the evening of October 23, Dutch was in the Palace Chop House in Newark, New Jersey, meeting with Lulu Rosenkrantz, Abadaba, and his chief enforcer, Abe Landau. At ten-thirty p.m., two men strode into the restaurant and emptied sixteen bullets into Polly's devoted customers, courtesy of Murder, Inc.

For nearly twenty-four hours, Dutch lay in a Newark hospital, delirious and rambling incoherently while a police stenographer recorded every word. He expired at eight-thirty p.m. on October 24, the victim, as Fred Pasley wrote in the *Daily News*, of a single slug from a semiautomatic pistol and too much newspaper publicity.

Across the river in Manhattan that same day, Dutch's lieutenant Marty Krompier narrowly escaped death in a Times Square barbershop. In Brooklyn, Pretty Amberg's body was found in a burning car, naked with his hands bound and a sack over his head. Two weeks later Chink Sherman's mutilated body was discovered in upstate New York.

Although Polly would miss Bo Weinberg and Chink Sherman, it was gratifying to see Pretty meet a fitting end. But Dutch was a genuine loss. It was Dutch who'd held marauders at bay, who'd thrust her deeper into political circles, and who'd kept her afloat when she was broke.

"I have often thought that he lived a lonely life," Polly said later. "I have heard that for several years before his death, Dutch had wanted to retire, but his fellow gangsters wouldn't let him. If this is true, then he must have been speaking from bitter personal experience when he told me that breaking away from a racket can't be done."

A few weeks before he was killed, Dutch Schultz was asked, "If you had your life to live over again what would you do?"

"I'd never take the name of Schultz," he replied firmly. "It's short, swell for headlines. You couldn't get Flegenheimer in a headline. If I'd stuck to it, I'd never been in trouble. Nobody'd ever heard of me."

It was his only known regret.

52nd Street—Swing Street—the last glorious outpost of the Jazz Age, 1948

13

The Big Shot

A s 1935 drew to an end, Polly began rebuilding her business after her sabbatical behind bars. She assembled a new crop of girls and paraded them through the nightclubs and Madison Square Garden, even making a surprise appearance at the opening game of the New York Giants' football season. The newspapermen and gossip columnists were delighted to have her back, and so were her customers.

But she'd lost her old zest for work. Money was flowing, and her clients were as starry as ever, but she took little pleasure in their patronage. "When possible, I'd encourage backgammon instead of conversation," she recalled. "It meant far less talking and, since it left a hand free to hold a glass, just as much drinking."

On the positive side of the ledger, the mortality rate in Polly's set declined precipitously after Dutch Schultz's demise. Word on the street was that it had been Lucky Luciano, in his capacity as chairman of the National Crime Syndicate, who'd okayed the hit against Dutch. With the Dutchman dead, Charlie Lucky was now declared Public Enemy No. 1 by the press, the police, and his fellow wrongdoers. The law hadn't been able to catch the wily Sicilian despite his myriad arrests for gambling, drug dealing, murder, and robbery. But the scourge of the underworld, Manhattan's recently appointed special prosecutor Thomas E. Dewey, was determined to change that.

In December word leaked to the press that Dewey was investigating a prostitution bonding ring and arrests were imminent. Polly wasn't especially worried. So it was an unpleasant surprise, in the first week of January 1936, when her old colleague Nick Montana was convicted of "compulsory prostitution" and led away to Sing Sing, sobbing inconsolably, to serve a twenty-five-year sentence.

Then on January 31, Polly received an anonymous phone call, tipping her off that there would be a citywide raid on disorderly houses the next day. She went into hiding and spent an anxious night checking in with Showboat, but when morning came with no unwelcome guests, she figured it had been a false alarm.

That is, until she picked up the morning papers. Forty-one houses had been hit that night, netting more than one hundred arrests. The victims included old friends and rivals like Jenny the Factory, Sadie the Chink, Peggy Wild, and a score of lesser madams with equally colorful monikers: Frisco Jean, Nigger Ruth, Gashouse Lil, Hungarian Helen, Silver-tongue Elsie, and Cokey Flo. The cops also swept up eleven "overlords of vice," the leaders of "a highly organized white slavery combination" known on the street as "the Mott Street mob." Bedlam engulfed the Centre Street courthouse the next morning as police processed the fractious prisoners. Each and every one of them was given an insurmountable bail of over $10,000, ensuring they'd all remain under lock and key.

Not to be outdone by the brash young special prosecutor, down in Washington, D.C., the publicity-loving director of the FBI, J. Edgar Hoover, announced his own nationwide campaign against "white slavery." On February 4, 1936, Mae Scheible, a top-dollar madam recently transplanted from Pittsburgh, was arrested by the FBI on charges of violating the Mann Act, forbidding the transportation of women across state lines for immoral purposes. Federal agents picked up June Reed, another high-end rival, a few days later.

Still, Polly insisted she had nothing to worry about. Dutch had kept her from the clutches of the Mott Street mob, and she was scrupulous about not violating the Mann Act. But her spies in the police department were ominously mum. So she boarded an express train to the West Coast, where she had a standing invitation to visit some old friends.

☾

California's City of Angels was littered with friends and clients who'd gone west to make their fortune in the movie studios. So Polly was looking forward to a warm welcome once she settled into her temporary digs, a house lent to her by a friend who was on the road.

As she often did when visiting a new city, she paid a courtesy call to the town's top madam. In Los Angeles that honor fell to Lee Francis. Madam Francis's house on Sunset Boulevard was a Hollywood institution that counted directors, producers, and top stars as regular customers. The stout, primly dressed madam invited Polly to lunch at the Brown Derby in Beverly Hills, where they cheerfully talked shop.

Over coffee, Polly's eye was caught by a good-looking young fellow with strawberry-blond hair at another booth. Back in Manhattan, he'd been the lover of Lucille Malin, a West Side madam and the recent widow of Gene Malin, a well-known female impersonator.

As she was trying to think of the young man's name, the waitress handed her a note with a phone number, asking her to call him later. Sonny Tufts, that was his name, a recent Yale graduate from an old New England family who'd studied opera and sung in nightclubs before heading to Hollywood. Polly phoned him that evening, listening patiently as he boasted of his recent show business successes, until she finally urged him to get to the point.

"You know, Polly, there were many of your friends at the Derby this noon who would have come over to say hello to you, but they didn't dare on account of the person you were with," he said righteously. "She's the most notorious woman in Hollywood."

"So am I a rabbi's daughter?" Polly erupted. "You have a very short memory, bub!" Sonny hadn't been too proud to take Lucille's money, to guzzle her booze or wear the monogrammed shirts and silk dressing gowns she'd given to him, and hadn't hesitated to spend her money on a plane ticket and rent while he established a foothold in the movies. "But now a madam was dirt beneath his feet," she remembered indignantly. (In an ironic twist, Sonny Tufts's B-movie career and drunken antics would later make his name a notorious punch line in showbiz circles, long after Lucille was forgotten.)

It was the same nearly everywhere she went. She hadn't counted on the hypocrisy of Hollywood, an empire built by cads, tarts, and libertines but obsessed with the facade of respectability. So-called friends from New York were afraid to be seen with her here, where the film studios kept an iron grip on public morality. "I had hoped for anonymity in Hollywood," she lamented, "but what I got was isolation."

Lonely as she was, New York was still too hot for her to return. She could see from the papers, this was not a typical vice crusade. All the madams arrested on the night of the raid remained in custody, as Dewey built his case against the Mott Street mob. When her former bondsman, Abe Karp, was arrested on February 16, Dewey was coming perilously close to Polly. So when her masseuse in Los Angeles suggested that she might find the far-off island of Hawaii more congenial, she leaped on the idea. Polly sailed on February 21, traveling first class on the SS *Malolo*, the most opulent ocean liner in America.

Her Hawaiian holiday was the first time she'd truly relaxed in many months. But having time and space to reflect also let loose a flood of regret and anger. She decided to process her feelings with paper and pen. "I sat down and scrawled 28 pages of pure bitterness and stored up anger at the raids by crooked cops, the years of insults and the intimidation and beatings by gangsters, who moved in on me in the 30s."

When Judge Seabury was first on the scene, Abe Lastfogel, the boy genius of the legendary William Morris Agency, had urged her to write a memoir. Literary pals like Bob Benchley had seconded the suggestion. At the time, nothing could've been less appetizing. The tabloids would've paid a pretty penny for it, but that would've just about covered the cost of her funeral. Now, as she contemplated a future beyond the skin trade, the idea of writing an autobiography was more tempting. After that first burst of enthusiasm, the impulse waned, but she tucked the pages away for safekeeping.

Polly had been in Honolulu over a month when incredible news arrived on April Fool's Day of 1936: Charlie Lucky had been arrested in Hot Springs, charged with being "the secret boss of New York's multi-million-dollar prostitution racket." Thomas Dewey claimed that Luciano was the head of a combination that controlled some three thousand prostitutes and two hundred brothels, earning an annual income of $12 million.

The underworld appeared genuinely shocked by this turn of events. Charlie Lucky was guilty of many things, but no one believed he was New York's "super-pimp," in Mayor La Guardia's florid phrase.

New York's "Public Enemies" list included some of Polly's best customers—
Waxey Gordon, Owney Madden, Larry Fay, Dutch Schultz, Billy Duffy,
and Ciro Terranova, June 18, 1931

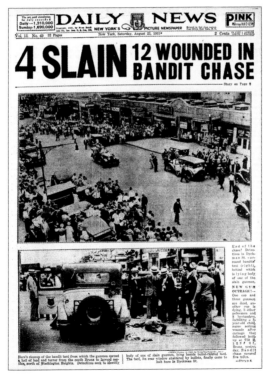

Polly panicked after seeing this headline
in the *Daily News*, August 22, 1931

Mayor Jimmy Walker entering the county courthouse for his showdown
with Judge Seabury, May 26, 1932

LExington 2-1144   New York City

Polly's business card in the Café Society years

Actress Dorothy Lamour—the "Sarong Girl"—moonlighted for Polly in the 1930s before achieving stardom with Bob Hope and Bing Crosby in the *Road to . . .* movies

The bawdy, cross-dressing cabaret singer Gladys Bentley was a favorite of Polly's patrons

Polly leaving court after pleading guilty to possessing indecent films, April 15, 1935

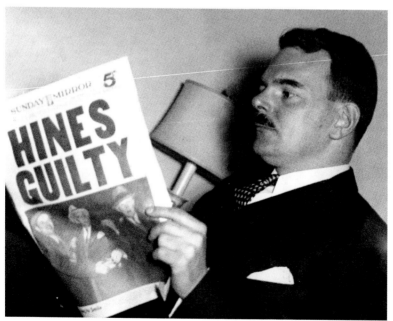

Gang-busting district attorney Thomas E. Dewey after convicting Harlem's Jimmy Hines on charges of corruption, February 1938

"Polly—I adore you—Francis":
inscription from the singer
Frank Sinatra

Polly with bandleader Charlie Barnet, comedienne Martha Raye,
her attorney Gertrude Gottlieb, and Gertrude's husband, Benjamin

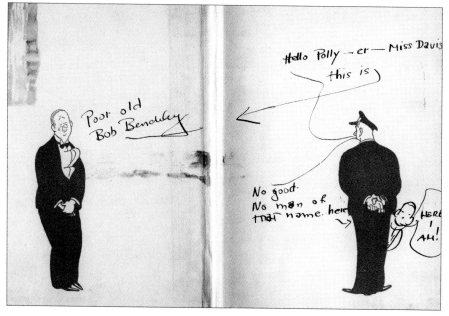

Robert Benchley's inscription to "Pearl Davis" in his book *Inside Benchley*,
illustrated by Gluyas Williams, 1942

Polly with her ghostwriter,
Virginia Faulkner, the
composer Dana Suesse,
and an unnamed man,
while working on her
memoir, August 1945

Polly in front of the famous Pickwick Bookshop on
Hollywood Boulevard in Los Angeles, 1953

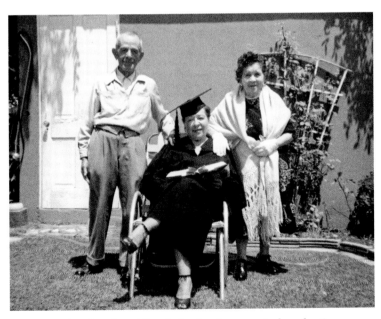

Moshe, Gittel, and Pearl after her long-awaited graduation
from Los Angeles City College, June 1958

Shelley Winters starring as Polly in the film version
of *A House Is Not a Home*, 1964

Like most people on the street, Polly insisted it was impossible that Lucky had anything to do with this scheme. "For one thing," she later wrote, "I used to supply the girls when Charlie Lucky entertained in his plushy hotel suites, and it hardly seems logical that if he had the alleged tie-ups, he would patronize a madam outside the combine."

But Lucky explained this discrepancy easily enough: the Mott Street mob dealt in cut-rate whorehouses, where the quality and hygiene were an affront to a fastidious man like himself. "I wouldn't let none of them come within ten feet of me as far as goin' to bed was concerned," he insisted—bearing out her point if not its spirit. "My girls come from Polly Adler or they was girls I knew from shows or from society. Period."

"Of course it was no secret that Charlie Lucky was mixed up in all sorts of rackets," Polly conceded. As the *Daily News* pointed out, everyone in the twilight world knew that Lucky was "the guy to see if you wanted to run a shady business without interference." Criminal plotters were happy to kick up a portion of their profits in exchange for Luciano's protection.

Still, she swore she'd never heard even the slightest whisper that he was the higher-up behind these lice. But Luciano himself seemed to contradict that claim, later telling columnist Leonard Lyons, "I once stopped some guys from breakin' up her place," referring to the Mott Street mob's attack on Polly's house in 1934.

It is true that, as in the tax evasion cases, the charge of compulsory prostitution was a slender reed compared to the many gruesome crimes that could reliably be attributed to Lucky. And not even Tom Dewey ever suggested that the boss was personally hammering madams with lead pipes or roughing up soiled doves.

But those who would clutch their pearls at the thought of a big shot taking a percentage of the profits from a well-run prostitution racket are naïve. Like gambling or bootleg whiskey, prostitution was a service that legitimate society was eager to buy and happy to rationalize. The much ballyhooed taboo against taking money from women was merely another example of the universal masculine code of silence that allowed almost any sort of sexual exploitation to take place as long as it wasn't acknowledged openly.

In point of fact, pimping and shaking down pimps and whorehouses were standard practice among young hoodlums-in-training. And it was an open secret that many convicts expected their wives and girlfriends to "go out on the turf," as one longtime Broadway detective observed, to earn money to make their stretch behind bars more bearable. "There is only one don't, one nice point of etiquette. The girl mustn't live with any other gangster or sell herself to any person in the underworld."

Eminent citizens like Waxey Gordon and Joe Adonis had long derived a good chunk of their income from whorehouses. And everyone knew that Al Capone and his mentor Johnny Torrio had built their early empires on the backs of prostitutes. Lucky later insisted that he and his fellow gunsels had always looked down their noses at Capone and Torrio. Maybe so. But it would be foolish to believe that such latter-day niceties were reason enough to turn down a steady stream of income from a common vice. As Lucky himself put it, when protesting the injustice of Dewey's charges, "Why should I want to take dough from the whores when my men were already taking it away from the pimps?"

On April 17, 1936, Luciano was extradited from Hot Springs to New York City and his trial date set. Only then did Polly book her return trip from Hawaii. "If it had not been for the bills piling up," she recalled ruefully, "I could never have pried myself away from those friendly islands."

☾

Lucky Luciano's trial opened on May 11, 1936. Charlie had plenty of reason for optimism. He and the other National Crime Syndicate leaders had become much more careful about insulating themselves from the rank-and-file criminals who put a percentage of every illicit dollar into their pockets.

But Lucky underestimated the vengeance that wrathful madams and drug-addicted hustlers could wreak. The bulk of Dewey's case centered on three prostitutes who were the only women who could directly connect Luciano to the leaders of the Mott Street combination. All three were heroin addicts who, after two drug-free months in police custody, had become much more amenable to breaking the underworld code of silence.

Several days after the trial began, Polly received a phone call from a big racket man whom she knew only by reputation, telling her to meet him in ten minutes outside her building. The man pulled up in "a battleship-size sedan," and without a word, she slid into the back seat next to another fellow she didn't recognize. The car was flanked in front and back by large black automobiles, as they drove a circuitous route through the darkened city streets. She had no clue where they were heading. "I knew that he was a friend of Lucky's," remembered Polly. "But if I hadn't known this, I would have sworn I was being taken for a ride."

The cars crossed under the Hudson River through the Holland Tunnel to New Jersey. They emerged in what seemed to be the tunnel's emergency garage, where she was led upstairs to a spacious conference room in the tunnel's administrative offices.

"I caught my breath! Gathered there were men from all the biggest rackets in New York," remembered Polly. It was a full quorum of the New York delegation to the National Crime Syndicate, attended by one of New York's most prominent lawyers. The attorney thanked her for coming, then plunged into the matter at hand. He handed her a list of the women being held as material witnesses in Lucky's trial and asked if she knew anything that might discredit them. Much as she would've liked to help Charlie Lucky, she explained, no doubt sincerely, none of them had worked for her, so she could add little to their efforts.

Nonetheless, Polly knew plenty of the players in the wider drama, including one of the star witnesses. Mildred Balitzer was a hard-bitten blond hustler who, in Polly's words, "testified that Charlie Lucky spat in her face when she appealed to him to allow Pete, her husband, to quit his racket of booking girls into houses." Mildred was told that Pete Balitzer, a degenerate gambler, was going nowhere till he worked off his considerable debts. Polly insisted that it was preposterous that a gentleman like Lucky would behave so badly. That is, she conceded, unless Mildred had somehow insulted Lucky by implying that he was a "prostitution man," and then, of course, he'd have cause to be so angry. Polly's former lawyer, the sleazy Samuel J. Siegel, also made a cameo appearance as both defense lawyer and witness.

The climax of the trial came on June 3, when Luciano insisted on taking the stand in his own defense. It didn't go well. When his own lawyer asked him, "Did you ever receive the earnings of a prostitute?" Lucky's failed attempt at Broadway wit—"I gave it to 'em, I never took"—left him with literal flop sweat. "Sweat beaded his swarthy brow," wrote Russ Symontowne of the *Daily News*. "He cringed at each new edged ques-

tion and hid beneath half audible 'I don't knows' and 'I can't recalls.'"
With each lie, Dewey wound the rope tighter, until Lucky admitted that
he'd been a dope peddler, bootlegger, bookmaker, tax cheat, and illegal
gun owner. But taking money from women, there he drew the line.

"A straw poll of newsmen who'd covered the trial came out 13 to 1
for acquittal. The jury, however, felt otherwise." On June 7, 1936, Lucky
Luciano was found guilty on sixty-two counts of compulsory prostitution, and subsequently sentenced to thirty to fifty years in prison.

"I was stunned," said gang leader Joe Valachi, summing up the official response of the underworld. "Charlie Lucky wasn't no pimp. He was
a boss." Perhaps the biggest shock to the racket boys was not that Lucky
fell but that it was a handful of two-bit hussies who took him down.

Looking back at this debacle years later, Lucky found himself echoing the Dutchman's regret. "It was my publicity that really cost me the
best ten years of my life," he told a reporter. "All the smart ones stayed
out of the papers."

◖

Polly escaped miraculously unscathed. But it was a hollow victory. After
Dewey's arrival on the scene, she would never again work with the same
ease. On her return from Hawaii, she reestablished herself in a six-room
apartment at 65 Central Park West, but with a more modest operation.
She could no longer afford the risks of a high-profile parlor house.

The dust from Dewey's campaign was just settling down when the
anonymous letters began arriving. The first one was delivered to police
headquarters on June 10, 1936. Ten days later a second, slightly more
elaborate version of the letter arrived at the Manhattan field office of the
Federal Bureau of Investigation:

Department of Justice, NYC

To Whom it May Concern,

　　If you are interested in cleaning up the greatest source of white
slavery, Polly Adler, operating at 65 Central Park West, #6C (name
Miller), Phone Endicott 2-9495, Endicott 2-9695, brings girls from
Penn. and Ills. [sic] She brot [sic] Bee bak [sic] with her on the
train from Chicago and she is still there. I wouldn't give her away

but she makes us girls stay with all the tough guys and the cops and never pays us for it. Sometimes we get black eyes too.

She is the big shot since you sent May Schieble away. And we get tired of buying her old clothes. The superintendent of the building he's her pal and there is an inside stairway so you will have a hard time to catch her. She lived at 77 Park Ave., name Arnold Ca 5-3484. She brought back that girl they deported when she was pinched last year from Cuba Eva Del Rio.

Well the cops go there and so only you can do something.

I guess she's got too many connections get closed up.

Just one of the Girls

When the FBI agents conferred with Inspector Louis Rosenfeld, who led the Third Division vice squad, they were surprised at how eager Rosenfeld was to collaborate on the case. His enthusiasm cut such a contrast to the usual attitude of resentment among the local cops that the feds were immediately suspicious.

Their doubts were confirmed when the FBI requested copies of Polly's fingerprints, mug shots, and criminal records, and the NYPD's Bureau of Identification informed them that Miss Adler had arranged to have all her criminal records expunged. Their disapproving conclusion was penciled into the margin of the FBI's internal memo: *"Partners in crime."*

Nonetheless, if someone were going to nab the "czarina of the bordello business," the NYPD insisted on doing the honors. On July 10, 1936, the same day the FBI request arrived, the police set up a wiretap on Polly's apartment at 65 Central Park West. By one-thirty the next morning, they had her in custody, along with the maid, a pretty blond dancer named Billie Tinsley, and two frightened, talkative johns. It was especially galling, Polly remembered, because "the leader of the arresting flatfect had fallen out of one of my beds the very morning of the pinch."

But she received a hearty welcome at the West 68th Street precinct, where she was treated with unusual gallantry. The lieutenant on desk duty shook her hand warmly and shooed away the reporters and photographers crammed into the waiting room, so she could make her exit without being caught on camera. He even waved to her as the patrol wagon rolled off to Jefferson Market.

Commissioner Valentine was visibly enraged when the aggrieved newspapermen pressed him to explain the chivalry of the officers who "played Sir Walter Raleigh to Polly Adler's Queen Elizabeth—bowing and scraping in the beaming presence of Manhattan's Madam No. 1," jeered the *Daily News*.

At the Women's Court, the magistrate assigned a heavy bail of $1,000 for her and $500 for Billie Tinsley. Polly's voice sank to a whisper as she entered her plea of not guilty. "Judge, I wish you'd reduce that bail," she rasped. "I'm broke. I owe so much now I won't be able to raise it. There'll be no question about my appearing on Monday."

In a sign of how tough times were, Polly scraped up enough money for her own bail bond, but the unlucky blonde spent a week in jail. Adding insult to injury, when Polly entered the courtroom for her hearing, she was handed a summons from the New York State Banking Department for a delinquent tax bill of $3,750.

This time she had no hesitation about calling the two johns who had been caught on the wiretap to testify. One of the men was married with two young children—that was her ace. When both men testified that they'd merely been enjoying an innocent cocktail, the case evaporated.

The FBI did not consider this the end of the matter, however. J. Edgar Hoover was now personally following Polly's case, and he pressed the special agent in charge of the New York field office to keep a close eye on her.

Enough was enough. "I was fed up with the wire-tapping and police double-crossings," she declared. "I was getting out."

She announced to her public that she was now looking for legitimate business opportunities. "I'm through having fights with the law, and I'm going to see if I can't open a nightclub," she told the Broadway columnist Justin Gilbert when she ran into him in Dave's Blue Room the next week. If Texas Guinan or Helen Morgan or Sherman Billingsley could do it, why not Polly? Walter Winchell repeated the bad news in his column, punctuating it with a regretful cluck of the tongue: "Tch!"

It wasn't a bad idea. The nightclub business remained fully mobbed up, with every aspect controlled by former bootleggers, from the linen service to the waiters' union. She tried to buy into a hatcheck concession—a common setup in which she'd pay club owners for the privilege of supplying pretty teenage girls to run their cloakrooms. Flirting and pouting for tips, hatcheck girls could pull in a nice chunk of change, with all the profits going to Polly. It was a surprisingly lucrative racket in those days of fur coats and fedoras.

But the atmosphere in City Hall had chilled since the freewheeling days of Prohibition. Mayor La Guardia had instituted regulations requiring every nightclub worker, from the bandleader to the washroom attendant, to be fingerprinted and registered with the city. She searched for other legitimate partnerships and less high-profile investment opportunities, but every time a potential partner found out who she was, the deal fell apart.

At a dead end, Polly decided, with typical hubris, that she would go right to the top, to speak with Commissioner Valentine himself about finding a way to go legit. The police reporters hanging around Centre Street were as astonished as the bluecoats when Polly "strolled casually into the Commissioner's anteroom and asked for an audience," wrote the *Brooklyn Eagle*.

When the secretary "gave her the old 'The Commissioner is very busy right now' line," Polly declined to wait, or give her name, or speak with any of his flunkies. She shrugged and said she'd write him a letter, then left as casually as she'd come.

"Dutch had been right; once you're tagged as a madam it's for keeps," remembered Polly with resignation. "I was a madam—or would be as soon as I'd plunked down a month's rent and opened my little black book. I couldn't live my reputation down—all right then, I'd live up to it."

☾

If she couldn't change her career, at least she could change her scenery. She decided to try her luck in Chicago, where hookshops were still a booming industry and she had some family. So that fall of 1936, she and her trusty assistant Showboat lit out for the Windy City.

First thing upon arriving, Polly called on the district's established madams, to make sure that she wasn't stepping on anyone's toes. They gave her a friendly welcome, so she set up in an apartment and called some old customers. "But my opening laid a terrific egg," she recalled. "The very same men who spent generously when they patronized me in New York were tighter than the bark on a tree in their own backyard."

Nor did she succeed in shaking off the FBI, who paid a "confidential informant" to keep tabs on her. The ham-fisted informant heard that Polly was "cheating," that is, she wasn't paying off the police or the local crime bosses, and was "running very much under cover." So undercover was she that he couldn't actually locate her, despite J. Edgar Hoover's demand for an "immediate and vigorous investigation."

Her new enterprise was a bust, but she wasn't yet ready to risk returning to the Big Apple. She was still in Chicago when that rotten year of 1936 ended. "I had no real friends there and nothing to do, and I was homesick and morose," so she decided to cheer herself up by throwing an extravagant New Year's Eve bash. She invited some local madams and any of their girls who were at loose ends, about thirty women in all. It turned into a rare "rip-roaring" hen party, fueled by case after case of champagne.

"Finally, just as at an office party, the girls overcame their awe of the madams and began to say what was really on their minds. One little creature announced between hiccups that she wouldn't be a madam for anything. "I'd rather be a prostitute," she said. "Madams don't have the fun we girls do. We're the ones that get to sleep with the men!" remembered Polly with a chuckle. "Nymphomaniacs are rare among prostitutes, and the others soon shouted her down with remarks impossible to quote here." In fact, she noted, quite a few of her giggly guests mentioned how much more fun it was to let loose without men around to dampen the mood.

The FBI was still pursuing Polly, although without much vigor, when the press once again blew her cover. On February 27, 1937, *Billboard* magazine, a major trade paper for the showbiz crowd, reported in its "Chicago Chats" column that "New York's Polly Adler is being seen around the local bright spots." After that, there wasn't much point in sticking around.

❦

On returning from Chicago, Polly rented a handful of well-appointed apartments, using friends and false names as a front, and reassembled her talent roster. From this point on, she ran primarily as an out-call business, which was about as glamorous as being a taxi dispatcher. Trusted customers and old friends still dropped in for a drink or a roll in the hay, and she still threw plenty of her famously eclectic private parties, but it wasn't like the high-flying days of yore.

Manhattan's West Side had lost much of its cachet in the lean years of the Depression. All the flashy watering holes were on the East Side now, although old stalwarts like Lindy's still drew the showbiz elite. Harlem's run as the slummers' playground ended with the infamous Harlem riot in the spring of 1935, a revolt against police abuses and a violent rebuke of the corrupt reign of Jimmy Hines. As the white tourist trade retreated, the big mob-owned cabarets decamped for midtown, although Harlem's intimate dives and jazz halls still attracted broad-minded ofays.

White folk looking for hot music and earthier pleasures now headed to Swing Street—the blocks of West 52nd Street between Fifth and Seventh avenues—lovingly dubbed "The American Montmartre" by *Variety*'s Abel Green. On Swing Street, the clubs were classic joints, carved out of two rows of crumbling brownstones bedecked with gaudy canopies and neon lights. The air was thick with cigarette smoke and music, tiny tables pressed up to the makeshift bandstands, with people and music spilling out onto the bustling sidewalk.

Polly was a familiar face in all the legendary Swing Street joints: Helbocks, Onyx, the Famous Door, Three Deuces, Kelly's Stable, Leon & Eddies, the Club Napoleon, and Club 18, the first insult-comic venue. "Every last one of them was owned, directly or indirectly, by the Mob," remembered the talent agent Swifty Lazar. She was a regular at the wide circular bar of the Hickory House, where Duke Ellington passed mellow afternoons and the first jam sessions were broadcast over the airwaves.

Duke Ellington had deposed Paul Whiteman as the reigning king of jazz, as the torrid sounds of Harlem moved front and center. Gone was the ricky-ticky, on-the-beat bounce of the foxtrot era. It was replaced by the propulsive rhythm, rollicking melodies, and dynamic shifts in meter that became known as "swing music." Swing music moved the hips rather than the ankles; where once the angular Charleston reigned, now the loose-limbed jitterbug was king.

The freewheeling music scene was always where Polly was most at home. She counted among her closest friends popular cabaret singers like Gladys Bentley, who headlined the Ubangi Club, and Spivvy, the bulldog-shaped, "foghorn voiced" house pianist at Tony's. She was particularly fond of Billy Daniels, a young velvet-voiced pimp-turned-nightclub-singer, who made "That Old Black Magic" a jazz standard. A mob favorite, he sometimes appeared in as many as three 52nd Street clubs in one night.

One of her dearest friends was Martha Raye, who became the most famous of the brassy "girl singers" of the swing era. She could blow the roof off any joint with her big voice and hammy personality. Born to vaudeville troupers, with no formal education, Martha was a hungry teenager hustling for work in nightclubs and radio when she first met Polly. In her later years, she'd be remembered for her big-mouth comic television persona, but back then she was a wide-eyed beauty, with long, slim legs, a capacious bosom, and a devilish grin. If, in the lean years of the early 1930s, she went on a few dates for Polly, few would've been surprised.

The bandleaders of the swing era put their predecessors in the shade, both in musicianship and in what one wag dubbed "bandleaderitis," the oversexed, over-the-top, high-living lifestyle of musical idols of any era.

Polly became especially close to the young saxophonist Charlie Barnet, when his hard-charging orchestra was booked into the Cocoanut Grove nightclub atop the Park Central Hotel. "We would come across madams and prostitutes every day or every week," remembered Barnet's young clarinetist, Buddy DeFranco, but when Polly was there, Charlie always provided her with a ringside table. The Cocoanut Grove was packed on the night of their premiere, DeFranco remembered. "'This is the most successful night of my career,'" Charlie crowed. "'Every hooker in town is here, including Polly Adler.' Polly gave him a big beautiful watch for the opening, and he was very proud."

Barnet modeled himself on his idol, Duke Ellington, in more ways than one. "His sexual escapades were legend," remembered critic Gene Lees. Barnet was married no fewer than eleven times, as best he could count, although his wives had to compete with the groupies and working girls who flocked to his boisterous shows.

"Charlie had all the girls he wanted—for free—he didn't need to go to Polly's," said the composer Alec Wilder. He was there like so many musicians were; because it was the coolest after-hours joint in the city. The girls were just a bonus.

"Charlie did not go in for 'used goods' too much. He preferred to be the one who 'broke in' a girl for Polly," as Wilder remembered it, and would dutifully report his findings to Polly after each bedside "audition."

One particular groupie at the Cocoanut Grove intrigued him. "She was tall, well-formed, and just reeked of sex," as Barnet described her in his autobiography. Loretta Dial, as she was known, was "wild and uninhibited, but friendly and without a mean bone in her body. We became lovers and it was not until sometime later that I found out she was one of Polly Adler's girls and was passing."

"Loretta was the most popular girl in her establishment in the late 1930s and early '40s," remembered a friend of Alec Wilder's. "Some of Polly's girls, apparently, lay prone in the missionary position until a customer had done the dirty deed. Not Loretta. Charlie told Alec she was the most uninhibited of all the girls. 'She would do anything,' Charlie said, 'but not at Polly's apartment.'"

Barnet's kindred spirit, the impish songwriter Jimmy Van Heusen, was introduced to Polly around the same time by her old Tin Pan Alley ally Jack Robbins. "I used to hang around Polly's a lot. I'd go and have a drink or play backgammon with her. I didn't pay to jump on any of her broads," Van Heusen remembered with pleasure. "I had a great time, drinking and playing with Polly and trying to nail all the girls in sight."

Van Heusen was an amateur pilot who encouraged Polly to get her own pilot's license, which she did under the coaching of her old chum Wally Beery. Like his pal Charlie, Jimmy had a long after-hours romance with one of Polly's girls, by the name of Gail. "Gail used to come out to the field with me when I was flying around," Van Heusen said. "Then she started to take lessons on her own. I saw her learner's permit one day and noticed her age—she was 14. She was like me. She started her business early."

Van Heusen and Frank Sinatra, an ambitious young crooner from Hoboken, New Jersey, began working together in 1940, when Frank was singing with the red-hot Tommy Dorsey band. After that, remembered a friend, Van Heusen's interests were "broads, booze, songs and Sinatra." Van Heusen was "the whoremaster," as one of Sinatra's girlfriends said disapprovingly, the guy who could always get a hooker at a moment's notice for the singer and his cronies.

At that time, Polly's legend far outshadowed the young vocalist's, although that would soon change. The first time they met, he signed her autograph book with the elaborate formality of a Damon Runyon character: "To Polly—a person I've heard of for some time—and whom I've finally met—a very charming person—my pleasure. Sincerely Frank Sinatra." A few years later, she got a far warmer inscription from the crooner: "Polly—I adore you—Francis."

The boxing crowd continued to make up a lively portion of her clientele. Polly was a ringside regular at Madison Square Garden, usually accompanied by a parade of her prettiest employees, mingling with the "political and underworld elite," as the *Daily News* put it. She was chummy with all the pugs owned by Owney Madden's old combination, led by Bill Duffy after Owney retired to Hot Springs.

She hosted Primo Carnera, the six-foot-seven "Tall Tower of Gorgonzola" imported from Italy, who'd won the heavyweight championship through a series of carefully orchestrated fixed fights. She was pals with the pugilist who snatched the crown from Carnera, "Madcap Maxie" Baer, who was notorious for killing a man in the ring. She took particular delight in "Slapsie" Maxie Rosenbloom, so named for his habit of slapping his opponents with his open glove. The two Maxies were renowned for their matinee-idol looks and their skirt-chasing shenanigans. Both Baer and Rosenbloom were such enthusiastic habitués of Polly's that they earned a public razzing from Paul Gallico, the *Daily News*'s premier sportswriter, just as Mickey Walker had years before.

Mickey Walker was, himself, still kicking around. He retired in 1935, dead broke from years of chasing along with the profligate Doc Kearns. In the spring of 1936, Mickey opened the Toy Bulldog Tavern across from the Garden with Bill Duffy's backing, only a few steps from where Jack Dempsey held court in his own bustling bar and grill. Walker's joint quickly became a Cauliflower Row hotspot.

One night at the bar, Mickey overheard his politically connected uncle mention that Mayor La Guardia was on the warpath against Polly and was planning to chase her out of town. "I figured I had to warn her that a raid was planned," Mickey said. He ducked out of the bar and grabbed a cab to her bagnio on Central Park South. Polly immediately began working the phones, calling her connections.

Since he was already there, Mickey decided to stick around awhile. "It was a quiet night, with only a few customers, and I had the place pretty much to myself," he remembered.

After a couple of hours, I knew I was in no condition to return to my saloon, so I decided to spend the night at Polly's place. The last thing I remember that night was Polly leading me into her private quarters and putting me to bed. When I woke up the next morning, Polly was gone. So were the girls. In fact, the joint was empty, save for the maid. I dressed and automatically reached into my pocket to feel my money. It was gone. I was cleaned out! Didn't have a dime. I had to borrow five bucks from the maid for carfare back to my saloon. I just couldn't believe that Polly had rolled me. That night, she came into my joint.

"Hey, Polly," Mickey whispered. "I had three hundred dollars in my pocket when I fell asleep. You were the only one in the room besides me."

Polly didn't deny it for a moment. "What the hell do you think I'm running, a free lunch counter?" she demanded.

"But I was there to do you a good turn," Mickey protested. "I'm your friend."

"What's friendship got to do with business?" she deadpanned.

"I had to laugh," said Mickey ruefully. "What could I do? That was Polly."

☾

In November 1937, Fiorello La Guardia was reelected mayor, and Thomas E. Dewey swept into the district attorney's office in a landslide victory, heralding a dangerous new era for Polly and her cronies.

Now Dewey set his sights on the ultimate "higher up"—Harlem's Jimmy Hines. Dewey made his move in February 1938, arresting the late Bo Weinberg's brainy brother, George, and Polly's former attorney, Dixie Davis. Bail was set at the eye-popping sum of $300,000, to pressure them to turn state's evidence. Hines played right into the prosecution's hand when he declined to bail out Dixie Davis. He'd broken a cardinal rule of the corrupt: never double-cross your bagman, especially when he is also your lawyer.

Polly's name wasn't coming up publicly, but she was getting static from the cops, forcing her to move again. It hardly seemed like a coincidence when the IRS filed a judgment against her claiming that she had vastly underpaid her taxes from 1927 to 1930, placing a lien against her of $12,425 (over $200,000 in today's money). After her long, dry interlude in Chicago, she didn't have enough cash on hand to pay off Uncle Sam, so she kept a low profile and stayed away from her usual haunts, hoping the feds might forget her.

The Treasury Department's patience ran out in February 1939, when they put the word out that "if she didn't come in for a tête-à-tête," federal agents would raid every one of her likely hideaways. When she emerged, she professed surprise. "You say I owe taxes," she told the fellows from the IRS. "I didn't know they had a right to collect taxes on such an income as that." Polly turned to her old friend Frank Costello, who had succeeded Charlie Lucky as leader of the National Crime Syndicate. Costello arranged to put up some $50,000 in U.S. government bonds to secure her time to pay the bill.

But her troubles were nothing compared to those of Jimmy Hines. On May 25, 1938, Hines was arrested and "charged with being a member of the Arthur (Dutch Schultz) Flegenheimer gang," as *The New York Times* put it.

All that summer, as the lawyers jousted, there were signs of fatal unease among the boys in blue. Hines was the chief "rabbi" of the NYPD, and his arrest created havoc in unexpected quarters.

Polly's sometime protector and occasional tormentor, Inspector Charles Neidig, was an early casualty. On July 4 Neidig was stripped of his command and transferred to the wilds of Ozone Park after it was discovered that he and two dozen of his men were heavily involved in professional gambling. The next day, Neidig "blew his brains out" with his service revolver, in Polly's words, afraid that Commissioner Valentine had discovered that "he was a partner in a gambling joint in Yorkville."

Three weeks later, another of Polly's inside men, Inspector Louis Rosenfeld, did the same, shooting himself in the head and leaving behind no fewer than eleven bank accounts. One month later Sergeant Christopher W. Confrey, who'd spent countless well-oiled hours in Polly's house, added to the growing tally of high-ranking suicides.

When Jimmy Hines came to trial in August, both George Weinberg and Dixie Davis testified at great length in damning detail. But Hines still had a trick or two up his sleeve. On September 12, 1938, the judge declared a mistrial on a technicality.

But Hines's reprieve was short-lived. When his new trial began the following February, even the sudden suicide of the prosecution's star witness, George Weinberg, wasn't enough to save him. On February 25, 1939, the indomitable Jimmy Hines was convicted. He would soon head upriver to join his crooked co-conspirators in Sing Sing.

☽

But local politics paled in the shadow of the horrific headlines coming out of Europe. Adolf Hitler's rise to power in Germany was being closely watched by both Polly's government customers and Broadway's Jewish community. By 1937 European émigrés were pouring into the city, fleeing Hitler's tightening grip. Dispossessed nobility, wealthy exiles, and confidence artists with aristocratic pretensions treated Polly's house as a private retreat from the flashbulbs and professional eavesdroppers of the Stork Club and El Morocco.

Polly's parents were among the arrivals. It didn't take long for Moshe Adler to tire of life as a Zionist pioneer in the land of Israel. In the fall of 1936, just after the outbreak of the Great Arab Revolt, as it became known, Moshe and his nineteen-year-old son Bernard—formerly Baruch, soon to be Bob—returned to Brooklyn. Gittel joined them two years later, just as the trickle of Jewish refugees from the Nazi regime was becoming a flood.

Along with the exiles came a swarm of international visitors in anticipation of the 1939 World's Fair. Democratic boss Ed Flynn, with the aid of Polly's old pal Teddy Hayes, was overseeing the planning and construction of the fair pavilions just over the East River in Flushing, Queens. With sixty nations and dozens of corporations planning exhibits, Polly's house was bustling with international visitors and corporate bigwigs. "Whenever it was a question of providing a visiting V.I.P. with the more informal type of female companionship I was usually appointed chairman of the subrosa entertainment committee," she bragged, "and, as a result, could boast a clientele culled not only from Who's Who and the Social Register, but from Burke's Peerage and the Almanach de Gotha."

"Looking back, I suppose I had now arrived at the climax of my career as a madam," she remembered with some ambivalence. There was one evening that she would always remember as a sort of symbolic summit in her search for *yiches*. She was laid up in bed with the rheumy eyes and runny nose of a terrible cold. The visitors who dropped in to cheer her up included "a famous composer, two well-known authors, a magazine editor, a top-flight interior decorator, two members of the Russian nobility who were now U.S. citizens, and a prince of a reigning royal house, his equerry and his American host."

(Her friend Virginia Faulkner, who heard the story the next day, recalled that one of them was Serge Obolensky, a deposed Russian prince and onetime brother-in-law of Vincent Astor, and maybe "that Danish prince, Agaard—but it may have been one of the Swedish boys.")

Over cocktails, one of the Russians posed a polite version of the perennial question: What's a nice girl like you doing in a place like this?

"Look at me, and then look around you—see the people who are here," replied Polly, with feeling. "I'm not beautiful, I'm not educated, I'm the daughter of a poor Jewish tailor from a little town in Russia. Ask yourself what I have in common with people like you—except being alive, except being human. It isn't my brains or my birth that entitle me to your company and God knows it isn't my looks—so what ground is there left to meet on? If I weren't a madam would you and he"—she nodded at her royal guest—"be sitting on my bed?"

"But, Polly, we don't come to see you because you're a madam," protested the editor. "If it was only that, well, then, why would we be in here with you? Why, as you say, would we be sitting on your bed, instead of a bed containing one of your girls?"

Polly began to cry. (It was a family trait, one relative recalled; the Adlers were prone to sentimental tears when in their cups.) "Don't get me wrong. Your being here, how can I tell you what it means to me?" she sobbed. "Who am I, Mrs. Vanderbilt, that I've got princes and famous celebrities sitting around watching me blow my nose on a piece of Kleenex?"

It was almost too good a story to be true: the girl from the shtetl attended by Russian noblemen. But Virginia Faulkner attested that it "did really and truly happen; and her speech about why she was a madam and how she felt about their being there is almost word-for-word as uttered. I have heard this story from others than Polly—as a matter of fact I was at her apartment the next night and got a playback on it."

The new clientele brought new challenges. "Toward the end of the Thirties, an increasing number of my clientele seemed sexually maladjusted. As the tension in Europe grew, and war became ever more imminent, people's peculiarities were intensified," remembered Polly. "Whorehouses always draw twisted people who are unable to satisfy their desires normally, but now it got so that I began to think of a patron who wanted the simple, old-fashioned methods as a 'truck driver.'"

Polly encouraged a reputation for running a "straight" house, but as more than one observer noted, for the right amount of money and a vow of discretion, she would do her best to fulfill almost any request. Married couples came seeking adventure or rejuvenation, and fetishists came in search of improbably specific scenarios. She entertained one elderly man who asked to "have one of the girls link her thumbs together and walk about the room as he called out 'Pretty Peacock,'" remembered one friend, the musical conductor Lyn Murray, with amusement.

"Polly told about flagellators and masochists she helped, although she claims it made her blush at times," recalled Murray. "The girls who got whipped were paid $100. Ben Marden, the nightclub operator, was a steady customer. Once he came in drunk and wanted to give the four girls he had ordered $500 each. Polly wouldn't let him. She took his money away from him to hold—$10,000. The girls told her later he had given them each a fifty-dollar bill he had secreted in his shoes."

She occasionally accommodated requests from men with an interest in other men. Not as a procurer, perhaps, but as a provider of a safe hideaway or an opportunity for bisexual experimentation. "As an increasing number of my clientele became indecisive in their sexual desires, I was forced to permit double features," quipped Polly.

Whether she was a lesbian herself was a matter of speculation among those who didn't know her well. She certainly had many friends in the lesbian and gay community and made no effort to conceal it. She was regularly spotted in the "pansy clubs" and was reported attending the famous Hamilton Lodge Ball, an annual drag ball that had become a major event with thousands of spectators. She'd been invited by one of the organizers, Phil Black, a popular female impersonator and community leader in Harlem. "Polly reportedly showed up dressed in a male tux, à la Marlene Dietrich, along with about six of her girls who were similarly dressed. Polly and her girls participated in the climactic 'Dance of the Fairies,' before an audience of thousands."

For many years, one of her closest friends among the customers was Jimmy Woolworth Donahue, the debauched heir to the Woolworth dime-store fortune. (Polly dubbed him "Mr. Chain-Store" in later tellings.) Woolworth was gay and made little secret of it. Nonetheless, he enjoyed the louche brothel atmosphere and sympathetic ear of high-end madams like Polly and Lucille Malin. Jimmy Donahue was a curious "mixture of promiscuity, exhibitionism, sadism," as one biographer described him. "Dorian Donahue," insiders called him, in tribute to his boyish looks and depraved habits. He enjoyed shocking his fellow Social Registerites and often employed prostitutes, both male and female, to stage elaborate practical jokes so perverse, they'd have landed him behind bars had his name not been Woolworth.

But Donahue was usually well behaved at Polly's. "Sometimes it got tiresome listening to him bellyaching about nothing, but he had a good sense of humor and was generous," she recalled. "If one of my girls strolled into the room on the chance that he might want to engage her, he would always rise, bow courteously, and present her with a hundred-dollar bill."

☾

New Year's Eve 1938–39 was "the biggest, wettest, craziest and merriest New Year's Eve since the caviar days of 1929," in the words of the *New York Journal American*. The economic recovery was gaining momentum, fueled by the rumors of war speeding across the ocean from Germany, Spain, Italy, and the Soviet Union. New York's Jews, who had been anxiously following the rise of Adolf Hitler in Germany long before the rest of America, felt a growing conviction that Europe would soon see mass bloodshed.

Business was brisk as money and men poured into the city and military-related industries ramped up production. "They were giddy days of high living and full wallets," remembered the debutante-turned-actress Diana Barrymore. "The depression was over and forgotten," at least in midtown Manhattan. "Money was plentiful, people were happy-go-lucky, out for a good time."

That spring the long-awaited World's Fair opened to great fanfare and bustling crowds. Diplomatically, the fair was a bust. By opening day, two of the sixty participating nations, Austria and Czechoslovakia, had been annexed by Hitler's armies. Bombarded by local critics like Walter Winchell and Fiorello La Guardia—who suggested the Nazis' exhibit ought to be a "Chamber of Horrors"—Germany withdrew from the fair entirely.

From Polly's perspective, however, it was a smashing success. "I received the ultimate, untoppable tribute to my business career. I entered the Valhalla of the American executive," she remembered with pride. "I, Polly Adler, was written about in *Fortune Magazine!*"

She was included in *Fortune*'s irreverent, in-depth guide for visitors to New York City, ranging from the highbrow to the low, with Polly representing a bit of both. The anonymous author knew what he was talking about, describing her operation in surprising detail, even mentioning her current rendezvous, "with two or three girls in an apartment, not far from Central Park West, in the Sixties."

Unfortunately, Polly had no time to savor her new status. As soon as the issue hit Mayor La Guardia's desk, she was on the move again. La Guardia was infuriated by the article, complaining that it was "humiliating to me" that *Fortune* knew the infamous madam's whereabouts when he, the mayor, did not. "Personally I think the article was lousy," he griped to the magazine's publisher, Henry Luce. "I think the writers were all right but someone got in the dirty work which proves my contention that the oldest profession in the world is not limited to one sex."

On September 1, 1939, Germany invaded Poland. Two days later Britain and France declared war on Germany. Within weeks Poland surrendered, and Germany and the Soviet Union divided the country between themselves. Under the new German-Soviet Nonaggression Pact, the designated border between Germany and the Soviet Union ran down the River Bug, just west of Polly's birthplace.

Once again little Yanow was on the front lines of a colossal war. On September 17 the Soviet Red Army began streaming into Poland from the east, conquering Pinsk and reaching Yanow on Yom Kippur. The

Soviets commandeered the property of the townspeople, Jew and gentile alike. Life was far worse on the other side of the border, where the Germans were systematically rounding up and slaughtering Jews. Yanow was teeming with Jewish refugees fleeing the Nazis.

By this point, most of Polly's family had long ago left for Eretz Israel or the United States. But that hardly eased the anxiety and grief that she and her landsmen felt as they scanned the papers for news and clustered around their radios listening for any hint of hope.

❦

Polly was now firmly established as part of the common cultural vocabulary, invoked for titillation, comic relief, or a touch of earthy realism. She popped up regularly in the syndicated gossip columns, and a spate of Pollyanna–Polly Adler mix-up jokes even landed her in the *New Yorker's* Talk of the Town. George S. Kaufman dropped her name into his 1939 hit play *The Man Who Came to Dinner*, although it was removed for the 1942 film version. She appeared as the character "Molly Levine," in a scathing roman à clef about the public relations industry by Rion Bercovici.

In 1940, when the twenty-five-year-old boy genius Orson Welles decided that his magnum-opus-in-progress, *Citizen Kane*, should feature a brothel scene, he secretly flew one of his actresses from Los Angeles to New York to meet Polly and soak up atmosphere. That too was cut by the Hollywood censors, but Orson Welles left his mark in her autograph book: "For Polly—A philosopher, an impresario, a lady of many parts, from her admirer Orson Welles." The compliment was rivaled only by Burt Lancaster's heartfelt inscription: "To Polly, who speaks facetiously of death, but who has more life than any ten people combined that I know of."

In 1939, Polly became a regular at a racy new Latin-flavored nightclub called La Conga, where she befriended Desi Arnaz, the club's young Cuban bandleader. Long before he found television fame with Lucille Ball, he was lighting a fire under Café Society with his infectious Latin rhythms and sexy showmanship.

Polly started dropping into La Conga nearly every night with three or four pretty girls in tow and occupying a prime table. One night Desi spotted a well-endowed redhead at Polly's table and asked the manager to bring him over for an introduction. He happily accepted Polly's invitation to join them for breakfast when he finished the last show. When he arrived at Polly's apartment, he was surprised to discover, as he was tucking into an elegant layout of caviar, scrambled eggs, and champagne, that his hostess was a madam and her beautiful companions could be hired by the hour. Watching him gloomily calculate the price of his desires, Polly laughed and said, "That's all right, sonny. This one's on the house."

"I've had my share of delicious sex in my life but that red head was something else," Arnaz recounted with satisfaction. "If there was anything I had not learned already, she taught it to me then. She was insatiable."

The "Latin heartbreaker," as the columnist Dorothy Kilgallen dubbed him, was a hit among the socialites of Café Society. "I was 21 years old, a good looking kid, and my two best women friends were from the top and bottom socially—Brenda Frazier, the debutante of the year, and Polly Adler," remembered Arnaz with pleasure. Desi was such a devoted customer that Polly instructed her girls to steer their dates to La Conga whenever they could. Plenty of nights the audience was split between Brenda Frazier's clique and Polly's posse, and it wasn't easy to tell the difference.

Arnaz liked to recount the story of the night he made his Broadway stage debut in *Too Many Girls*, a musical comedy written by Richard Rodgers and Lorenz Hart. After opening night on October 14, 1939, the show's creators all headed to La Conga to await the early reviews. The place was packed after the last floor show ended at four a.m. and Arnaz was sitting at a table loaded with top-notchers and society swells waiting for the morning papers to arrive. Suddenly Polly appeared out of the crowd and came barreling over to his table with a stack of newspapers over her arm.

"Cuban, you are the biggest fucking hit in town!" she hollered in her booming baritone as she slammed the papers down on the table and gave the bandleader a big kiss. "We're going to celebrate, so if you have any plans for later on, cancel them. Polly's place will be closed to everybody else until tomorrow night. My staff will feed and divert you until you drop. Then you'll know what it's really like to have *too many girls!*"

"She shook up that table pretty good, including me and I don't 'shook up' too easy," Desi chuckled. After Polly wandered off, Dick Rodgers's wife Dorothy asked who the tiny, loud lady was. Peter Arno, who knew all too well, explained; although as one historian noted, it was surprising that Larry Hart didn't pipe up, given the long-standing rumor that the lyricist's father had backed one of Polly's first Upper West Side brothels. Desi wasn't too "shook up" to accept Polly's invitation, although he was by the time he showed up at the theater the next day, late and hungover, where he got an earful from his director.

Polly and her girls were also honored guests at the Copacabana, Frank Costello's new supper club on East 60th, that topped the glitzy nightspots when it opened in the fall of 1940. She had an excellent relationship with another gold star entry in the Café Society rolls, Toots Shor's joint. Bernard "Toots" Shor had been a popular bouncer in Owney Madden's speakeasies before Repeal, then opened his own restaurant with Frank Costello's imprimatur. His swanky new saloon on West 51st Street next to Rockefeller Center was primarily a stag joint, where the main topics of conversation were baseball, boxing, and broads, although he grudgingly welcomed wives if necessary. Perhaps for that reason, his fellow barkeep Jack Dempsey noted, he "seemed to know every dishy babe in New York."

Toots catered to the sporting and showbiz crowds, to journalists, New Dealers, and Madison Avenue expense accounters—the hard-drinking men in gray flannel suits who pined for the old days of hip flasks and youthful hedonism. Many a good old boy capped off a long, boozy lunch at Toots's with a postprandial visit to Polly's. It was, most likely, Toots who introduced Polly to Joe DiMaggio, the New York Yankees' star slugger, when Joltin' Joe first arrived on the scene. In keeping with her customer-is-always-right philosophy, when DiMaggio complained that his knees kept slipping on her slick satin sheets, Polly gladly sent out for plain cotton ones to please her celebrity guest.

As the war in Europe commandeered the headlines, Toots's joint was abuzz with aging male egos, longing to be in action. Where the newspaperman's ideal was once the hell-raising, merrily nihilistic city reporter in the mode of *The Front Page*, the younger generation was enthralled by the high-minded machismo of Ernest Hemingway. All the ink-stained copy boys aspired to become foreign correspondents like John Gunther, "perhaps the world's foremost journalist," in *The New Yorker*'s estimation. His travelogues sold over a million copies and were translated into sixteen languages, winning him entrée to the smart set, a fat job in Hollywood, and the cover of *Time*.

They also earned Gunther a hearty welcome in Polly's parlor, where he and the madam passed many an hour playing chess. He liked to brag that he'd introduced Polly Adler to an "unsuspecting Eleanor Roosevelt," remembered the journalist Vincent Sheean—"they were on the same plane and John, typically, was acquainted with them both."

(

On December 7, 1941, the Japanese bombed Pearl Harbor, Hawaii, and the United States officially entered the Second World War. That winter the metropolis swirled with fearful rumors of imminent air attacks and Nazi spies. German submarines roamed freely up and down the East Coast and by March 1942 had sunk fifty-four U.S. ships.

In April 1942 Mayor La Guardia ordered a citywide "dim-out" of lights after sunset to throw off German bombers. For the first time in its existence, Times Square was dark. "I have never forgotten one morning when we met at Reuben's during the war years and you reprimanded me for wearing my jewelry," Polly reminisced with Walter Winchell years later. "You reminded me that we were at war and having blackouts, and that it was bad taste wearing klieg lights."

"The Second World War meant boom times again on Broadway and saw the appearance of a new crop of fat-cat spenders—the under-the-table traders known as black marketeers," remembered Polly. In response to a steep hike in corporate income taxes to pay for the war effort, companies began investing significant portions of their profits into advertising and public relations as a way to avoid paying taxes. This boon to the admen and publicists was passed directly on to Polly, who proudly counted the public relations guru Ben Sonnenberg and Madison Avenue's premier ad agency, BBDO, among her most important corporate clients.

Manhattan's streets were swarming with soldiers and sailors shipping off to battle, European refugees from battle zones, and khaki-mad victory girls. Food rationing was killing the restaurants, but theaters and hotels were overflowing. With the hotel room shortage, there were plenty of customers who seemed more interested in getting a roof over their heads than company in their bed. She found herself hosting parties for men who'd typically rent hotel suites, so she was making a killing on booze (also in short supply due to sugar rationing).

Despite regulations intended to muzzle opportunities for soldiers to buy sex, the flesh trade was booming. "The more desperate the times, the more men seek the great escape of sex," Polly observed. Among her customers she noticed a desperate, "devil may care attitude" that she'd never seen before, "even in a whore-house."

She remained blissfully unmolested by the bulls for the first year or so of the war. The only contact she had with the authorities was a warning not to allow enlisted men in the house. Officers were, apparently, welcome to whatever pleasure they could afford. "I resented the police warning and ignored it," she sniffed. After all, some of her young customers and even her own brothers were now grunts. The youngest—now known as Bob—was the first to enlist, five months before Pearl Harbor. By the end of 1942, her three brothers had joined him in the military, leaving only Benny, who still wore the uniform of the federal prison system.

The difference now was that plenty of her johns were young enough to be her sons. Some of them even called her "Mom."

☾

From February 1937 until early 1942 the FBI left Polly alone. But that changed in February 1942, when she was taking the waters in Hot Springs. A miscreant named Bob Shubert recognized Polly over the course of an evening drinking with her and several female friends, and decided to cook up a scheme to shake her down.

First, Shubert sent a letter to the special agent in charge of the FBI's Little Rock office, calling the bureau's attention to the fact that the notorious Polly Adler was in Hot Springs, associating with a prostitute from New York. He pointed out that if the two women had traveled together to Manhattan, this would be a possible violation of the Mann Act. Then, after having sex with one of Polly's call girls at the Arlington Hotel, Shubert approached one of the FBI agents in person, asking for his help in a scheme to blackmail Polly for $5,000. Even if the FBI didn't have a case against her, he figured Polly would gladly pay to prevent him from exposing her to the press.

Nothing came of Shubert's scheme, but now the FBI was back in the game. They put a "mail cover" on her apartment to track her correspondence and obtained her phone records for the last two years. By April they were calling this "the most important white slave case in the NYC Field Division," and the investigation was garnering interest from J. Edgar Hoover himself.

That fall they turned up the heat. There was some nasty publicity in the papers in September, when she was mentioned during the trial of a pimp out in Ohio. Hoover pressed the agents to double down in their efforts, certain that if they just looked hard enough, they'd find a federal violation.

On October 6, 1942, the SAC of the New York field office summoned Polly to the FBI headquarters in Foley Square to answer their questions. The SAC's description of the encounter was blunt: "Adler advised that she was a very good friend of former New York Mayor Jimmy Walker, Walter Winchell and many of the leading New York police officials." She was emphatic that "she did not intend to commit any Federal violations as she was well aware that the FBI was desirous of sending her away." While she was willing to occasionally cooperate as a confidential informant, as she sometimes did for the NYPD, she would not volunteer information. Encouraged by this report, Hoover pushed the agents personally, writing with irritation when he hadn't heard more news and instructing them to give him updates every two weeks.

They were sure they'd found a lead in her phone records, when they discovered several phone calls that seemed to have come from Winthrop Rockefeller, the youngest of the Rockefeller brothers and the black sheep of the family. A longtime luminary of Café Society, Winthrop was now a captain in the U.S. Army, stationed in Fort Gordon, Georgia.

But despite their considerable efforts, the FBI agents could not find a single prostitute, pimp, or madam who believed that Polly would ever violate the Mann Act. She was so famous that she didn't have to recruit, they insisted. Everyone wanted to work for her.

(

Life was changing for Polly's oldest and staunchest customers as they entered the 1940s. Many of them had fallen out of fashion. Others were simply worn out after a lifetime of cigarettes, copious booze, late nights, and the occasional dose of the clap. Some married much younger women—often decades younger—as a way to hold on to their youth. But more often they found themselves beset by jealousy and angst, incapable of sexually fulfilling their young wives in this era before erectile dysfunction drugs, and eaten up by fear that they were cheating with younger men (as often they were), feeling old, foolish, and washed up.

The cult of the party and the lionization of youth had curdled the great emblems of the speakeasy generation. The improvident newshounds and Round Table cynics of her youth were turning out pap for Hollywood and calling themselves artistic prostitutes for selling out their talents as they cashed their paychecks. The daring Dadaists of Broadway, Jimmy Durante and the Marx Brothers, were now considered nostalgia acts. Paul Whiteman had been passé for years; he was drinking heavily and suffered a series of nervous breakdowns, forcing him to break up his legendary orchestra. Gene Fowler would be diagnosed with prostate cancer; between the cancer and the operation to cure it, the old satyr was left impotent. In sympathy, remembered Gene's son, Polly "fired off a cable to Fowler, declaring that the President should proclaim all of southern California a disaster area, and order flags flown at half-mast from coast to coast."

They clung to the practical jokes and ribaldry of their early days, but now their hijinks struck a pathetic note. In the fall of 1942, Polly was living in a modest apartment at 150 East 52nd Street where she kept a couple of girls handy and welcomed old customers while she served drinks, worked the phones, and collected payment from the women returning from their dates. On Halloween Polly's good friend, the publicist Dick Condon, introduced her to his younger brother, Robert Condon, a twenty-two-year-old aspiring humor writer.

Excited to be meeting the legendary Polly Adler, Bob Condon was even more thrilled to find one of his idols, Robert Benchley, lounging in her living room. "Meeting Benchley was, to me, as though Polly had given me a gift certificate good for 100 bangs," he wrote later.

Bob Benchley, once the symbol of metropolitan wit and avant taste, now made his living in Hollywood playing bumbling, henpecked suburban duffers and comical drunks and lechers. His weight had ballooned to more than two hundred pounds and his convivial drinking had settled into intractable alcoholism. By this point, observed Condon, Benchley "visited solely for amusement and his fondness for Polly. If he took up a girl's time talking at some length he would always 'tip' her, but he had never tried the pleasures of the huge swan bed that was said to have belonged to John Gilbert."

Several men were there along with Bench, including the actor Charles Butterworth, a favorite drinking companion. They were chatting amiably with two young ladies, who were giggly from sneaking puffs of marijuana in the bathroom while Polly was occupied on the phone. "Benchley took the girls aside to explain what Halloween in the city was like," Condon wrote. "He gave them money and escorted them out the service door in the kitchen. Polly was busy on the phones, disbursing the troops, and the merry men in the parlor were swilling booze and waiting to see who would make the first move."

When the girls returned, Benchley took them into the bedroom and the girls reappeared a few moments later wearing papier-mâché pirate costumes, "and nothing else," that he'd sent them to buy at Woolworth's. Bench handed each girl a box of colored chalk and sent them down to the street. "Uncle Bob, as the girls called him, had instructed these simple country lasses that Halloween in New York consisted of hilariously chalking the smiling men who passed them and shouting 'Halloween!'" So they did, chalking up the paint on some automobiles for good measure.

In about fifteen minutes the doorbell rang. Polly opened the door to find the two girls and a uniformed policeman. "Why, my nieces!" she exclaimed with forced sweetness. "What has happened?"

Ever the gentleman, Benchley shouldered her aside and said, "Step in, officer, step in. We have nosy neighbors." He hustled the cop into the kitchen and offered him a hefty glass of rye.

While Bob was distracting the patrolman, Polly furiously tried to collar the girls. But they escaped her grasp, jumping into the elevator while the elevator boy was in the hall, then closing the heavy doors and refusing to open them. While they rode up and down, waiting out Polly's wrath, residents on other floors grew increasingly irate as they waited in vain for the elevator to stop. The superintendent was almost as livid as Polly was by this point.

As the minutes stretched on, Benchley suggested that perhaps the young mischief-makers were afraid of Aunt Polly's temper, so he volunteered to wash the cars himself. Bob Condon, watching the scene with amusement, offered to join him, and even the policeman lent a hand. While the boys were down scrubbing the cars—"with Benchley gallantly tipping his derby and offering rates to curious onlookers"—the super turned off the power to the elevator and laboriously hand cranked it down to the basement, where Polly finally cajoled the girls into opening the doors.

Back in the apartment, Benchley assured the still-fuming madam that the fault was his. Finally she relented, and the girls emerged from their hiding place in the bathroom while Benchley sent the nice policeman off with the rest of the bottle of rye. The jovial flatfoot had enjoyed the afternoon so much that he promised to drop by again soon. Benchley hastily explained that he was a traveling salesman, often on the road, so it was best to check with the doorman before calling. His wife, Pearl, didn't approve of drinking.

☾

That winter of 1942–43 was bleak in every way. The FBI was still breathing down her neck and in November, Thomas Dewey was elected governor, which did nothing for Polly's peace of mind. Germany's advances in Europe and a string of bloody defeats in the Pacific cast a pall over the holiday season. This would be the first New Year's Eve in years with no glowing ball in Times Square.

Around Christmas, Polly, stressed and exhausted, fell ill with pleurisy, an inflammation of the lungs accompanied by a high fever and intense, stabbing pain every time she took a breath. On the night of January 13, she was in bed at 51 West 74th Street, being nursed by her friend, Dora Maugham, a nightclub comedian known for her risqué monologues. Three of her girls and her new maid, Laura Smith, also happened to be in the house when, once again, the police arrived.

Why now wasn't clear. Polly insisted that it was a frame-up, that she'd been too sedated by medication to keep her house open. Maybe so. Whatever the reason, the cops had instructions from the top to haul her in.

It was the same old story with a slight twist. They bundled the girls and the maid into the patrol wagon, leaving Dora behind; she was too well known to arrest. Polly was sick enough that the next morning they took her by ambulance to Bellevue, Manhattan's public hospital. The only space they had was in the psychopathic ward. "At this point I didn't care," remembered Polly. "All I wanted was a place to lie down."

The difference this time was she finally had a first-rate lawyer, not a courthouse fixer or bar-licensed blackmailer. Her new attorney Gertrude Gottlieb would become famous for her civil rights work, but at that stage of her career she specialized in sex-related cases, female thieves and murderers, prostitutes and gay men who'd been arrested for soliciting cops. ("Dirty Gertie," the boys called her affectionately.) "I respected Mrs. Gottlieb as I have respected few people in life," Polly averred. "She stood for all the things and had all the qualities I most admired."

The trial on January 26 was anticlimactic. Only one of the police officers testified, claiming that one of the women had confessed. The judge was dubious, and when no other evidence was presented, he dismissed the case. "Mayor La Guardia asked to see the minutes of the case because the charge was so flimsy," remembered Polly with some satisfaction.

Polly wasn't going to wait to end up like Mae Scheible or June Reed. On February 6, 1943, she called the FBI's field office and asked for an appointment. She got right to the point: she'd heard that the FBI was on a cleanup campaign in New York, and she wanted to know if they were looking for her. If they were, she declared, she intended to quit and go legit. She was considering some business opportunities in Mexico.

She seemed on the level. In March she traveled to Mexico for the opening of a new racetrack, Hipódromo de las Américas, along with scores of Hollywood *machers*, members of the international set, high-rolling gamblers, and speculators looking to cash in on Mexico City's new cachet. She looked into investing in a resort hotel but balked at the high price.

So she moved on to California. Plenty of her old customers there still lived in fear of the town's professional rumormongers, but she got a heartwarming reception from the devil-may-care Wally Beery, who proudly squired her around to the town's fanciest nightclubs.

And, of course, there was sweet old Bob. When Polly first sat down in Chasen's restaurant, L.A.'s version of "21," a hangout for the Broadway-to-Hollywood crowd, she got the frost from every corner. That is, until she caught sight of Benchley waving at her from across the room to come join him. As they were happily catching up, the same prigs who'd been cold-shouldering her now swarmed the table, suddenly eager to say hello. When she whispered to Bob that they'd all been snubbing her only moments before, "Bench responded by giving them the full treatment—a brush-off that sent them scattering in all directions like a busted strand of dime-store pearls."

"Robert Benchley was the kindest, warmest-hearted man in the world, and ordinarily he would have cut off his right arm rather than do or say anything to make another person uncomfortable," remembered Polly. "But such petty gratuitous meanness always infuriated him, and he despised snobs and hypocrites."

When she returned to New York in April, the FBI summoned her once again, demanding a progress report on her foray to Mexico and California. She told them frankly that she was still operating a call flat, but that business was slow since the law had been causing so much trouble. After reading their report, Hoover told the agents to let him know immediately if she did move to Mexico City and to keep him updated. And he did not forget her, personally checking in long after the New York agents seemed to lose interest.

The women who knew her—and Polly herself—claimed that she escaped federal charges because she was scrupulous about never sending her girls across state lines to meet a customer, both to stay in compliance with federal law and to prevent her less high-minded employees from working badger games on foolish customers.

A more jaundiced eye, reading the historical record, might suggest that Polly's invincibility was due to her close working relationship with the National Crime Syndicate. For decades, criminologists, historians, and the underworld rumor mill have speculated about J. Edgar Hoover's well-documented indifference to organized crime and, in particular, to the New York branch of the Syndicate. By way of explanation, they point to the director's warm acquaintance with Frank Costello, his regular patronage of mob-backed niteries like the Stork Club, his passion for horse-track betting, and most salaciously, the oft-repeated rumor that someone in the Syndicate, most likely Meyer Lansky, possessed irrefutable evidence that Hoover was gay.

Unfortunately, Polly's story sheds no light on this question. But it is notable that on the few occasions when agents connected her to well-known criminals—in contrast to the usual penny-ante prostitutes and pimps—orders came down from FBI headquarters to drop that line of investigation immediately, with no further explanation.

☾

More and more, Polly dreamed of getting out of the business. The reasons to retire were easy to count.

She was painfully aware that times had changed and old comrades had moved on while she was stuck on the same treadmill. After years of pressure by La Guardia and Dewey, the heavy action among her mob pals had migrated to New Jersey, Los Angeles, and Miami. Many of her old showbiz contacts had become permanent citizens of sunny California or had decamped to the suburbs.

Like a film noir antihero, she was plagued by perfectly reasonable paranoia. The FBI was always lurking in the background. In the fall of 1943 agents finally succeed in interviewing their big fish, Captain Winthrop Rockefeller, who admitted to calling Polly twice from Fort Benning, Georgia. But nothing came of it. They caught her on a wiretap at Frank Costello's Copacabana, but that too was a dead end.

Nonetheless, she could never entirely shake the feeling that she was being bugged or followed, or that people were sneering behind her back. She was acutely aware that at any moment she could become a cause célèbre for some publicity-seeking lawman or reformer. Her nerves were raw, and she jumped every time the phone rang. Most nights, she found herself crying into her pillow, longing to shout, "Leave me alone!"

And, frankly, the skin trade wasn't as lucrative as it used to be.

Still, she kept at it, perhaps, as she suggested, because she had no idea who she'd be if she weren't the notorious Madam Polly Adler.

In the summer of 1943, Polly decided to take an indefinite sabbatical on Fire Island, a summer hideaway on a narrow spit of sand jutting off Long Island into the Atlantic ocean. Accessible only by ferry, the island had no electricity or automobiles and only three telephones. This rare isolation made it a popular getaway for New York bohemians. The village of Cherry Grove, in particular, attracted, in Dorothy Kilgallen's words, "the fugitives from Broadway, the television studios, Tin Pan Alley, Hollywood and the Greenwich Village bars." Fire Island was, as one writer put it, "the summer capital of homosexual America." If any place offered respite from the judgments of conventional society, this was it.

Polly rented a room under the name Pearl Davis in one of the island's many boardinghouses. She had no plans beyond enjoying the sunshine and the bar at Duffy's Hotel, the local gathering spot. On weekends, Duffy's "became a sort of Stork Club with Greenwich Village overtones," as Polly put it, swarming with "the long-haired boys and the short-haired girls."

One Friday, Polly was sipping a cocktail at Duffy's with two friends from New York when she spotted her longtime patron, *The New Yorker*'s Wolcott Gibbs. Gibbs was seated nearby with a large group, and they invited the ladies to join them for what turned into a long, lovely evening. Unfortunately, being seen with such high-profile companions blew Polly's anonymity.

The next morning she and her chums were back at Duffy's for breakfast, when another weekend visitor joined them, lamenting that she'd missed out on all the fun the night before.

"I hear there was a terrific party—and but swarming with intelligentsia—and, of all people, Polly Adler!" she exclaimed. "Well, as you can imagine, everyone's absolutely up in arms and appalled and horrified that this Adler creature's roaming around loose on the island, and *they say* on a talent hunt."

Polly was deeply wounded, although she put up a brave front as she lashed out at the woman. "Who are you to call me disgraceful?" she snapped. "I'm Polly Adler."

The busybody quickly excused herself, but there was no way to undo the damage.

On Monday, Polly had a date for lunch with the widow who ran the island's brown-shingled Western Union office, but when she arrived at her cottage, the widow proved to be no lady. "How dare you come here?" she demanded. "You've got a nerve, sneaking around pretending to be respectable, forcing yourself on—"

"I didn't force myself on you," Polly protested hotly. "It was your idea that we be friends. And I wasn't pretending to be anything."

"Humph! I notice you didn't say what business you're in."

"Because it doesn't concern you," Polly shot back.

"Doesn't concern me? *Doesn't concern me!* When I have two daughters? And to think I introduced them to you!" the widow squealed. "Now get off my porch!"

Years later Polly still fantasized about what she wished she'd said to that "dirty bitch." "It makes me feel like a big shit for not spitting in her face," she wrote later. She hesitated even to repeat the story, for fear that people, "may get the idea that I let people piss on me and took it, which is not true."

That was the end of her sun-soaked idyll. But she suffered one last insult as she ate dinner alone at Duffy's that last night. She suddenly realized that the pale, nebbishy man whom she'd been seeing over her shoulder for the last few weeks was an undercover cop. She stormed out of the restaurant in tears.

It was a crowning blow to her battered self-esteem. It was also the height of hypocrisy, given the sexual shenanigans that went on every night in Cherry Grove. "Midtown is still buzzing over the orgy on Labor Day weekend at Fire Island involving several well knowns," as Walter Winchell leered in his column only a few weeks later.

Polly returned to Manhattan feeling depressed and adrift. When she resisted the idea of talking over her troubles with a psychiatrist, her attorney Gertrude Gottlieb urged her to take stock of her life with pen and paper. Perhaps by putting her experience down in writing, she could untangle forty years of accumulated memories and traumas, and find a new pattern for the future.

With Gert Gottlieb's pep talk ringing in her ears as she left the office, Polly stopped at a stationery store and bought a thick pad of paper and a big bottle of ink. But the prospect of excavating her long-buried feelings was so overwhelming that she soon abandoned the project.

☾

The year 1944 was consumed by the war. In July, the Russians drove the Nazis out of Polly's hometown of Yanow. The town was in ruins and not one Jew was left alive. The only townsfolk to survive were those who fled to the forests and joined the tough Jews of the underground resistance movement.

In the fall of 1944, as an ailing President Roosevelt was elected to his fourth and final term, Polly decided to check out opportunities in the fast-growing desert town of Las Vegas. Gambling was legal in Nevada, and many of her old friends in the mob were pouring money into casinos and hotels there.

George Raft, whom she'd known since the days when he'd danced for foot money at the Club Durant and El Fey, had a business proposition for her. With the backing of the mob, they could open an exclusive, top-dollar bagnio in Las Vegas, where all the girls would be groomed to look like famous movie stars. The place would be fully protected from the law so she wouldn't have the headaches of Manhattan. As Raft told it later, "Polly was very interested in the proposal and was pleased with the terms, which included a rent-free apartment, a full time maid, and a chauffeur-driven car whenever she wanted it."

The gossip columnists described Polly's departure as a sure thing. "Pearl Davis, better known as Polly Adler, has retired to Nevada with a fortune of around a quarter of a million, which she'll invest in a gaming salon," announced the columnist Danton Walker. "Before Polly Adler left town, she tossed a big party for—of all people—local cops, including some who had arrested her," Dorothy Kilgallen reported. But something soured her prospects in Sin City, and soon enough she was back in New York.

On April 12, 1945, Franklin Delano Roosevelt died of a brain hemorrhage, plunging the city into mourning. But the gloom lifted on May 8, with the glorious news that Germany had surrendered to the Allies. The war in Europe was over! The city went mad with joy and relief. It was a great day to be in the business of selling champagne and sex.

It was also a moment for new beginnings. Polly had been rolling along well enough, fueled by the wartime economy, but that would be drawing down now. She was forty-five years old, too old to be staying up all night waiting by the telephone. Many of her longtime customers had abandoned the city for the suburbs or California. The harassment by the law, while in abeyance for the moment, showed no signs of ever really ending.

Polly had played it smart financially. She held a portfolio of blue-chip stocks and some real estate and had stashed away plenty of cash. She was finally ready to pursue her long-cherished plan to write her memoir. Dozens of mugs no smarter than she was—former police reporters, cheap-jack publicists, and smooth-talking grifters—had turned stories of gangsters and gold diggers into best-selling books and hit movies. Why couldn't she?

She launched "Operation: Autobiography" on June 17, 1945, at the

Englewood Cliffs Milk Farm, a "fat farm," in the parlance of the day, in New Jersey, not far from Ben Marden's famous Riviera nightclub. Here she poured out her story in longhand. But her momentum stalled after Anna Cohen, the owner of the milk farm, read the draft and offered the well-meaning suggestion that she write more about her childhood in Yanow and about herself—no easy task after twenty years of secrecy and self-protection.

She summoned her courage to start again, this time on holiday in Virginia Beach. Within a month, she had one hundred pages—"one hundred pages which seemed to me a waste of paper and a waste of time." In desperation she telephoned her friend Virginia Faulkner and Faulkner's lover, the composer Dana Suesse. The couple invited Polly to visit them in Connecticut, where they were collaborating on a musical comedy. Virginia typed up the manuscript and offered encouraging advice about "the writing racket." "But I found it painful to relive my life and decided to leave well enough alone," remembered Polly.

On August 15, 1945, Imperial Japan surrendered to the Allies, ending the war in the Pacific. By V-J Day, Polly had decided that the real obstacle holding her back was her "lack of know-how." And in that case the solution was "breathtakingly simple." "All my life I'd been yearning for an education—well, what was stopping me from getting one?"

Polly Adler was going back to high school.

Now that she had a plan, she was eager to get underway. One evening in late August, she stopped backstage at the Strand Theater to see Charlie Barnet, where his band was slaying audiences nightly with his pulse-pounding hit, "Skyliner." She was heading West, she told him excitedly. All she needed now was someplace to settle.

"Poll, I've just the place for you," he exclaimed. "I'm going on the road for four months and you can use my house in Los Angeles. It has a swimming pool, and I'll throw in the use of my Cadillac."

"You just sold me, Charlie," Polly shot back. "Next week I'll be leaning out your bedroom window, plucking the makings of my breakfast orange juice."

Her young friend Bob Condon helped her pack up the house, and a few days later she was ready to leave. All that was left of her life in New York was contained in a stack of battered trunks.

One of them, tagged "Memory Trunk," held the souvenirs and mementos of my thirty-two years in "Goldine Madina." There was a pile of old address books, a card file of girls who had worked for me, ledgers marked "Profits and Payoffs," and enough "stiffs" (bad checks) to paper the mansions of some of the men who had issued them. There were newspaper clippings and a stack of magazines containing articles about me, letters from friends, theater programs, banquet menus, Christmas and birthday cards. And at the very bottom of the trunk, almost buried under layers of mothballs, were the bird of paradise [Garnet] had given me, a pair of green sequin dancing shoes with high heels (the first I ever owned), my grade school diploma, and a torn shawl and a little girl's under shirt—all that remained of the "traveling outfit" in which I had set out, so eager for adventure, from Yanow. I gazed at the trunk with stinging tears—and then I had to laugh. Although the little girl had headed west to America instead of east to Pinsk, she was still on her way to Gymnazia.

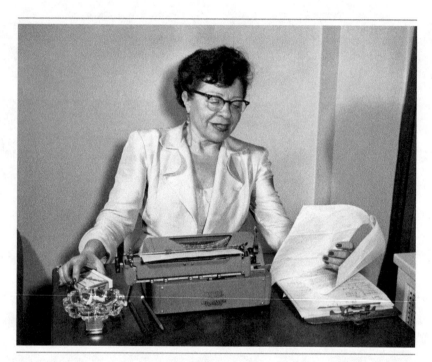

The aspiring author

14

Madam Emeritus

Polly arrived in Los Angeles in early September 1945. It was an ideal time and place for a fresh start. In those years of postwar prosperity, California was the land of reinvention, filled with souls from somewhere else seeking a place in the sun.

She was part of a general western migration of the Broadway demimonde in the 1940s. The epicenter of show business was shifting to Hollywood, Las Vegas was about to blossom as the vice capital of America, Palm Springs was now a private hideaway for gangsters, gay folk, and press-shy entertainers, and Burbank was fast becoming the new North Jersey, a wide-open harbor for gambling joints, bookmakers, and their henchmen. With more than half a million Jewish residents, L.A. was now the second-largest Jewish city in the world after New York.

In contrast to the cold shoulder she'd received on past visits to the city, this time Polly was welcomed with open arms, quite literally, when she made her debut that September at Slapsie Maxie's, a nightclub on Wilshire Boulevard run by her old friend, the boxer Slapsie Maxie Rosenbloom. "The ex-champ himself met her at the door, grabbed Polly and hoisted her off the floor," according to one account. "I'm hoited right in d'heart, Polly," Maxie pouted. "You didn't even let me know you wuz in town." The club was full of faces from the good old days, and her table was soon besieged by well-wishers, including former customer and A-list movie star John Garfield.

She could find plenty of old pals among the neon lights of Sunset

Boulevard, just outside the L.A. city limits. After World War II, the Sunset Strip was one of the country's leading adult entertainment districts, lined with cocktail bars, all-night delis, false-fronted gambling houses, massage parlors, steam baths, bordellos, gay bars, drag shows, and burlesque houses. Here were Hollywood's most glamorous nightclubs—Ciro's, the Mocambo, and the Trocadero—and the notorious Clover Club, an exclusive illegal casino—all run by refugees from the Broadway speakeasies.

Everyone was older, of course, and the ranks were thinning due to alcoholism, syphilis, heart disease, and the occasional bullet, but the same old crowd could be spotted in the more raffish parties, at the Santa Ana racetrack, or basking in the desert heat of Palm Springs.

One important face was missing. Two months after Polly arrived in California, Robert Benchley died a sudden, painful death from a cerebral hemorrhage attributed to cirrhosis of the liver, likely exacerbated by long-dormant syphilis. For his myriad friends—but especially those who had known him as the Pied Piper of the "Era of Wonderful Nonsense"—his passing was a symbolic blow. "When Robert Benchley died, the party was over," declared the writer John O'Hara.

For the Sunday school moralists, Benchley's life could be read as a cautionary tale. He "had a theory that everyone tends to become the type of person he hates most," observed his son, and what he'd become was a hopeless alcoholic, broken in health, no longer able to pursue the writing that made him proud, and getting less and less of the well-paying acting work he despised. In those final years, "Bob really hated himself," remembered one friend. "He was very bitter and would tell you openly that he didn't want to live any longer."

But for those who knew him as Polly did, he remained a beacon of the Jazz Age virtues of candor, tolerance, and existential playfulness. Benchley had a gift for bringing out the best in people—making them feel wittier, kinder, and more brilliant than they might have been—and persuading others to see what he saw. No one felt that more than Polly. Benchley gave the world a fuller and more nuanced appreciation of a woman most "respectable" people scorned. His unreserved friendship and proud patronage gave her the confidence and stature to take her place in the cultural firmament.

She returned the favor after his death by helping Bob's oldest son,

Nathaniel, when he was working on a biography of his father. For all Bob's failings in domestic life, the elder Benchley had passed along his fearlessness and generosity to his son. It was a compliment to all three of them that Polly played a critical role in removing the whitewash from Bench's legend, helping reveal the complex reality of a man of conscience bedeviled by his desires. As Nathaniel Benchley put it, without Polly's "patient and untiring help this book would have taken an entirely different twist."

☾

Polly's first stopping place was the Los Angeles neighborhood of Sherman Oaks, where Charlie Barnet was lending her the use of his house and car while he and his band were on tour. His neighbors were accustomed to hearing music blare and seeing pretty girls wandering around at all hours, but Polly was something new.

"The neighbors never knew who the eccentric old lady was at the Barnet residence," the bandleader remembered. That is, until the unfortunate incident when she forgot to use the parking brake on his car, and it rolled down the driveway and smashed into a telephone pole. The police filed an accident report that made the local papers, blowing Polly's cover. When the neighbors began whispering that the notorious Manhattan madam was planning to open a brothel in Sherman Oaks, it was time to move along.

Her friend Martha Raye invited her to stay in her house in Toluca Lake while she looked for a home of her own. In the spring of 1946, Polly purchased a tidy two-bedroom bungalow in the booming Los Angeles suburb of Burbank, home to aircraft makers, defense industry factories, and the film studios of Walt Disney and Warner Bros. It was also, according to the 1952 California Crime Commission, a "bedroom for hoodlums" who'd migrated from back east and discovered that the lawmen in Burbank were easier to bribe than those in L.A. proper. Mickey Cohen, L.A.'s leading crime boss, second only to fellow transplant Bugsy Siegel, was headquartered not far from Polly's cottage on Victory Boulevard.

She settled into suburban life surprisingly easily. "I love it there because I'm just a Russian peasant and I like to run around in my bare feet," she told a reporter. She drove a station wagon, planted a flower garden filled with roses and petunias, and adopted two standard poodles whom she doted on as if they were her own children. She enrolled in evening classes and finished her high school degree in nine months.

The only sign of anything unusual in her past was her vaguely erotic interior decor, left over from her bordello years—the tasteful nude prints on the walls, the jade lamps that provided a flattering twilight glow, her collection of crystal perfume bottles and art deco knickknacks, and "over the sofa a lurid picture of two women kissing," remembered one guest. Her bookcases bulged with autographed editions from literary friends and thick scrapbooks documenting her life in New York.

In a test of just how much she had changed, when Fiorello La Guardia stepped down as mayor of New York City in January 1946, "a friend called me long distance to ask if I'd be interested in re-opening my business in the East," she remembered. "I knew then I was cured—I had no wish to return, ever."

She'd accumulated a generous nest egg, with investments in real estate and a portfolio of blue-chip stocks that paid regular dividends. But she was too young to retire entirely. Hoping to cash in on California's postwar building boom, she took classes in real estate. "Polly Adler is now a prosperous real estate operator in California," reported Dorothy Kilgallen in her Broadway gossip column. But that was an exaggeration.

"Polly Adler is opening a Hollywood restaurant," announced Kilgallen's rival, Danton Walker. But that didn't pan out either. "I've thought of opening up a nightclub or a café, but then they are escapist industries too—my house, minus the girls," Polly said later. "No more of that for me."

She kept busy with old friends and night school and occasional holidays in Palm Springs and Las Vegas, but a lifetime of accumulated tensions and traumas didn't just fade away in the sunshine. Without the distractions of running a house, they only loomed larger. "I was living with a stranger," Polly remembered feeling, "a woman whose sudden crying spells bewildered me, whose bitterness unnerved me."

Much as she longed for a different sort of life, her insecurities made it hard to meet new people. "Sometimes I would cut loose and kid about my former profession, make jokes about myself, get in the cracks before anybody else could. But more often I would sit self-conscious and tongue-tied, afraid that if I joined in the conversation I would make some grammatical blunder or reveal my ignorance of the topic under discussion," she wrote. "When I was a madam, it wouldn't have mattered, but now it was different."

☾

All the while Polly kept pecking away at her memoir. "I'd type a page here and there whenever I felt miserable," she remembered. It was "a therapy which, along with school, kept me from going off my rocker."

Writing for therapy was one thing, but composing a publishable manuscript was a more daunting challenge. The more effort she put into it, the more discouraged she became. "Often, as I sat there at my desk, I'd think nostalgically of the good old days when I was wrestling with cops and drunks instead of nouns and verbs," she remembered.

But if she was tempted to give up on the project, she was loath to forfeit the attention that it brought her. Even as "madam-emeritus," as she dubbed herself, the Broadway chroniclers considered her doings valuable grist for their columns, printing regular updates on her new life out west and the progress of her much-touted book. In June 1946 she appeared, thinly disguised, in a short story by Wolcott Gibbs, published in *The New Yorker* and later incorporated into his novel *A Season in the Sun*. It was a deft retelling of her humiliation on Fire Island in 1943, through the eyes of the summer inhabitants who discovered she was a madam. Whether the prestige of appearing in *The New Yorker* outweighed the indignity of the incident was an open question.

When Polly visited Manhattan the following year, the Broadway columnists and hard-drinking habitués of Toots Shor's, "21," and the Stork Club buzzed with interest and some trepidation as she talked up her book project, currently titled "Ex-Madame X." Earl Wilson reported that the editor of the *Police Gazette*, Nat Perlow, was planning a biography of Polly Adler. But still there was no finished manuscript and no publisher.

Energized by the fact that so many newspapers "had reported that I was at work on my memoirs," Polly returned to her typewriter with renewed determination. "Every night I would vow that first thing in the morning I'd get to the desk, and every morning I'd trump up excuses to keep away from it." She rented a Dictaphone and recorded many hours of reminiscences with cigarette and scotch in hand. But turning her anecdotes into a life story was much harder.

In January 1948 Dr. Alfred Kinsey published *Sexual Behavior in the Human Male*, known colloquially as the Kinsey Report. Based on thousands of in-depth interviews and statistical surveys, Dr. Kinsey laid out conclusive evidence that male sexual behavior was far more varied and less bound to conventional morality than anyone but a madam might have imagined. The book was a cultural sensation, selling hundreds of thousands of copies, dominating the best-seller lists for months, and vaulting its author to international celebrity.

Inspired by his blockbuster success, she recast herself as a sex researcher, even referring to her former employees as "patients." Always a canny promoter, in August 1948 Polly wrote to Dr. Kinsey to see if he might consider writing a foreword to her book. She introduced herself with the awkward formality of someone whose skills were not quite up to her aspirations:

> Perhaps you are even aware that I am in the throes of writing the "great American novel," namely my life story. It is not as most people would assume an expose on the sex life of the American male. It is rather an expose on the causes of juvenile delinquency in our country as well as the rest of the world. But, a great part of it will also uncover the political corruption which contributes to the unsavory side of life of which I know a great deal.

Dr. Kinsey declined her invitation, Polly told a reporter, "but what a gentleman. In my letter I misspelled foreword 'forward,' and in his letter he misspelled it the same way." The two experts in their field struck up a friendship. He and two of his researchers came to lunch at her house several times. "We had so much in common to discuss," she confided to the columnist Irving Wallace. "But you know, I found him surprisingly prim and puritanical."

Inspired by Kinsey's warm response, she threw herself back into her writing. By September she had a first draft. "However, my first feelings of elation were rapidly followed by a terrible attack of cold feet," she remembered. Polly turned to her extensive network of literary friends for feedback, but their conflicting advice only muddied the manuscript further. "Too many cooks, spoil the brothel," she joked glumly.

She reworked the manuscript all winter, finishing a revised draft in the spring of 1949. But she was unsure about the title. "Ex-Madam X" didn't seem so dignified now that she was nearly an author.

One afternoon in Polly's backyard in Burbank, her old friend Dora Maugham was lounging in the sun watching Polly spray her rose trellis. "I wonder what the cops would think if they saw you, Polly Adler, so domesticated?" Dora mused.

"No doubt, they would be disappointed that my home is not a house," said Polly.

"Stop," screamed Dora. Polly was so startled she tripped, taking the trellis down with her. "You have just given the title of your book, 'A House is Not a Home.'" The new title lifted her confidence, as did the regular updates on the book's progress in the gossip columns.

Once she had a real draft in hand, however, it was clear that something was missing. She had no idea what. Until now, Polly had firmly resisted the idea of working with a ghostwriter. "Too much pride of authorship," as one friend put it. Finally she gave in and asked a new friend, the aspiring writer Eileen Bassing, to secretly revise her manuscript. By the fall of 1949, she was ready to send it out to publishers.

Polly's contacts in the world of publishing were formidable, but she was getting no bites on her own hook. Her friend Hastings Harcourt, the excitable son of the founder of the publishing firm Harcourt Brace, suggested she find a literary agent to represent her. Polly's first try was Helen Strauss, the head of the William Morris Agency's new book division. "She complained bitterly to Abe Lastfogel when I declined to represent her," remembered Strauss, adding snidely that she preferred to represent "books that could be written sitting up."

But things began looking up when Hastings Harcourt recommended she speak to Ann Watkins. Ann Watkins was the founder of her own eponymous literary agency, which represented high-prestige authors like Edith Wharton, Kay Boyle, Carson McCullers, Roald Dahl, Peter DeVries, and Dorothy Sayers. In 1947 she turned the agency over to her son Armitage Watkins but still kept a hand in the business.

Ann Watkins could see Polly's potential. Tastes had become more daring. The hard-boiled years of the Great Depression and the Second World War had eroded the genteel prejudices of readers and publishers. Wartime encounters between American soldiers and prostitutes, both domestic and foreign, softened some of the taboos around the topic of prostitution. And the Kinsey Report had made sexuality a subject suitable for women's magazines and the Sunday papers.

The Watkins firm agreed to take her on as a client. They assigned her to a farsighted young agent named Jean Parker Waterbury—whose clients included the African American novelist Zora Neale Hurston—to whip the book into shape for sale.

Throughout the spring and summer of 1950, her agent sent the manuscript to over a dozen publishers and magazines but got no takers. Some of the editors were wary of the rough state of the manuscript, and all were stymied by the challenge of how to frame the book to appeal to a prurient-minded yet easily outraged reading public. This wasn't 1913—it couldn't be a Sunday school tale of a white slave held against her will, or a fallen woman renouncing her sins. Yet not one of them could imagine how to tell a realistic story while making Polly a sympathetic heroine.

"The writing is bad, the angle is all wrong and the whole thing sounds phony," wrote a regretful Lee Barker of Doubleday. But even if they solved those issues, the real problem was that it was simply "impossible to justify Polly's profession." "Perhaps," mused Putnam's Ted Purdy in his rejection letter, "it's because she seems in the end to achieve an almost complete reversal of moral values, which might be disconcerting to some people." Several publishers admitted that they were scared off by the mere name "Polly Adler." It was hardly the first time her name recognition was used against her, yet it hurt all the same.

But for the moment, Polly was blissfully unaware of this caustic commentary. So she was over the moon when she picked up Walter Winchell's column in August and read that the distinguished firm of Harper & Brothers would be publishing her book, a claim repeated in *Variety*. Immediately she shot off a note to Ann Watkins to find out if it was true. It would have been less embarrassing if she'd just waited for Jack Lait's "Broadway and Elsewhere" column a week later: "Harper & Brothers turned down the manuscript of 'A House is Not a Home,' submitted by Polly Adler, the onetime Manhattan madame. The dignified house was horrified at the suggestion."

❦

Polly soldiered on. In the fall of 1950, she enrolled at Los Angeles City College, to the astonishment and amusement of many of her old friends.

She turned her fish-out-of-water adventures as a freshman coed into charmingly self-deprecating stories to be told over cocktails. But she kept her identity strictly hidden from anyone on campus. "My inferiority complex does not permit me to lift my hand to ask a question or volunteer an answer," she told her friend Virginia. "But in spite of the kidding I get, I am determined to continue."

Polly wasn't giving up on the book either. She suggested to her agents that they call on some of her own longtime friends and clients for aid. The soon-to-be-best-selling novelist Dick Condon promised to help in any way he could, and her former customer Philip Wylie offered to look at the manuscript.

Wylie had been a frequent visitor at Polly's in the 1930s, after he left *The New Yorker* for a prolific career as a freelancer. He'd had a major bestseller in 1943 with *Generation of Vipers*, a misogynist screed written from the unspoken perspective of a compulsive john, and he had recently published a novel entitled *Opus 21*, featuring the character of a high-end madam based on Polly. So he fancied himself something of an expert.

At the end of September 1950, Philip Wylie sent a scathing reaction to the manuscript to Polly's agent Jean Waterbury:

> The troubles here are various. One is Polly's personal angle. She seems to feel that everything she did happened to an innocent, naïve and unfortunate victim of very hard luck. Maybe so. But that was not the face she showed to the world; it therefore strikes a wrong and slightly incredible note in the book. Another is dullness. That is the moralistically, "I-never-did-anything-but-good" angle is wearisome in such an account.

From his perspective, the manuscript contained too much railing against vice cops and hoodlums and not nearly enough spicy stories of bad girls and high times in the house. Perhaps American men really were fated by their Puritan inheritance to behave badly, making her trade "as sordid and as monotonous as it sounds here. But I suspect otherwise," Wylie concluded. "What is lacking, I think, is any sense of how her customers felt."

This was rich irony from a man who insisted to his psychiatrist that he'd always made sure that the "lovely tarts" at Polly's bagnio enjoyed the sex as much as he did. "If she's a lesbian tart I let her be loved by her girlfriend or some girl she wants while I love her and am loved, to put it coldly," Wylie boasted. "That willingness by me was to them proof of caring for them."

As Polly well knew, for most "lovely tarts"—lesbian or not—whether the john "cared for them" was irrelevant. The only thing that mattered in "an a-trois situation" was whether they were paid extra for their trouble.

When her agent shared a discreetly edited version of Wylie's letter with Polly, she winced more than once. But she was defiant and distinctly unimpressed by his naïveté, especially his "criticism, and I quote, 'The face you show to the world is very different from the portrait you show as a victim of very hard luck.'"

"In my house I portrayed the part of an actress," she replied hotly. "My audience was not concerned with my feelings, nor did I care to divulge them. They came to unburden themselves and I was the jolly good fellow." She readily conceded that for her customers it was indeed a "house of joy." "But as for the girls—sex in a house was a one-sided enjoyment, mainly for the paying client. Sex beautiful was reserved by the girls for the lover or pimp."

☾

Polly was low in both spirit and flesh that fall of 1950. Years of hard living were catching up with her, and her mind was dwelling on the past and on her legacy. She was stung by Philip Wylie's response and by the rejections from publishers, and she spent many hours brooding over the injustices of the legitimate world.

Polly's relationship with her family also remained complicated. She suffered from the classic Yiddish curse, given a new twist by the Hollywood director Ernst Lubitsch: "You should have a lot of money, but you should be the only one in your family with it." Her parents had followed her to Los Angeles along with her brothers Sam and Bob. Polly supported them all on the dividends of her stock portfolio, invested under various family members' names, assets she controlled with an accountant's rigor. Yet even now her mother made no secret of her deep disapproval of her past. Nor did her prickly brother Sam, who was openly embarrassed by her notoriety even as he benefited from her largesse.

Of her family in California, only her beloved baby brother Bob seemed unconcerned.

It was in this mood of disillusionment and regret that Polly confessed her secret relationship with President Franklin Delano Roosevelt to her young friend Max Gershunoff.

As Max Gershunoff explained years later, Polly had become a familiar figure in Hollywood's flourishing gay underground. She was a particular favorite of the television producer Hunt Stromberg, Jr., whom she knew from New York. Stromberg was openly gay, a major taboo in the film industry, so like many of his compatriots, he found his niche in the newer, less prestigious field of television. (He would go on to produce lowbrow classics like *Green Acres*, *Lost in Space*, and *The Beverly Hillbillies*.) Stromberg was famous for throwing wild pool parties, well stocked with handsome male hustlers—just the sort of events where the presence of a madam was more titillating than shocking. It was at one of these parties that Polly befriended Max Gershunoff, a young musician who worked for the renowned concert promoter Sol Hurok.

Polly took a liking to Max—an artistic, ambitious young Jew from New York—and they began to spend time together, talking on the phone and going to parties together. "She was very direct, and of course with that voice, well, it could be fun but commanding," Gershunoff remembered. "You had to listen. She was very funny."

In their circles, he remembered, Polly was treated with respect. "Some would whisper about her but I never saw her snubbed." Then again, it was an outrageously campy community. Once after they spent an afternoon chatting at a pool party, she suggested that Max follow her into the women's dressing room to help her dry off. "One day you'll be able to say you dried Polly Adler," she joked. So he did. "She referred to her privates as the Russian General," he remembered with amusement. "She was very proud of her Russian general."

"She was usually very upbeat," said Max. "Her manner was that she'd been kicked around a lot, but had moved on." Nonetheless, the tidal wave of rejection from the publishers had hit her hard, and she often seemed to be brooding over the respect she craved but had always been denied, even by her own family. "She spoke much about the hypocrisy of society," he said, a sore subject in their set, but a particular hobbyhorse of hers.

One afternoon, they were driving together in his car when Polly piped up, out of the blue, "I would like to meet your mother. Do you think she'd want to meet me?"

"Well, why not?" asked Max.

"Because of everything," she replied morosely, then elaborated. "Her parents would not accept her at the dinner table for Passover or High Holy Days," remembered Gershunoff. "She was not religiously observant, but it hurt her."

"It's interesting that at a religious holiday I can't be with them at the same table, but they'll take my money," she said dolefully.

As they drove along, Polly continued to brood aloud. Then the conversation took another unexpected turn. Suddenly she mentioned that she had known the late Franklin Delano Roosevelt. To Max's astonishment, she explained that "she had something to do with the opposition to Roosevelt when he was governor of New York, running for President." Not just that, "she said that FDR was one of her clients and that she was being taken care of for the rest of her life by the contributions of Democrats."

Her tone was serious and matter-of-fact, neither boastful nor resentful. She was vague on the details, but it was Max's impression that she was confessing that she had remained silent under questioning in return for a substantial and steady payoff. "She had to suppress a lot politically because they would cut her off," as Max recalled.

The subject never came up again, but the conversation stuck in his memory. "I admired her," said Gershunoff years later. "I think she was one of the most important people in history."

€

Polly finally tasted victory in January 1951, when Theodore Amussen, the executive editor of Henry Holt & Co., called to offer an option on *A House Is Not a Home*. Polly had a lot of people pulling for her at Henry Holt, her agent observed, most notably Polly's former client Ben Sonnenberg, the powerful public relations consultant who served on Holt's board of directors.

Polly was ecstatic. "I acted like I had been on a drunk for weeks," she chuckled. The good news traveled quickly, and her phone rang constantly with congratulations.

"And then came the blow." The contract was in the mail, awaiting her signature, when suddenly Holt got cold feet. Ted Amussen explained that the objections had come from their lucrative school textbook division, for the old familiar reason. "I don't care if she wrote *Hamlet*," exclaimed the head of the division. If her name was Polly Adler it was no deal. Another unspoken influence might have been Holt's secret ties to FBI director J. Edgar Hoover. The firm's founder, Henry Holt, maintained a direct subterranean pipeline to Hoover, seeking his approval on all manuscripts, proposals, and contracts that might tread on the Bureau's interests. It would hardly be surprising if this one didn't pass his review.

After "the Polly Adler debacle," as Armitage Watkins called it, Polly considered giving up. But years of priming the rumor mill had created so much interest that she couldn't bear to admit defeat. So many friends, acquaintances, and newspaper scribes were asking about the book that finally, said Polly, "the old Adler fight returned."

That winter the agency sent the manuscript out to half a dozen more major publishing houses and tried to get it serialized in dozens of mainstream magazines. "Every morning I would fall over the postman in reaching out for my mail in hopes that my book was accepted," she wrote. "But it was the same old story." The editors were sure someone would make a fortune on the book, but they weren't willing to risk their own reputation.

When school let out for the summer, Polly set off for Manhattan "to do a little hustling on my own. By hook or crook I was going to find a publisher to take my book." Her arrival in the Big Apple was heralded by all the Broadway columnists, including Walter Winchell, who reported, erroneously, that she was "studying Greek and Latin!"

Now Ann Watkins herself, mostly retired from day-to-day affairs at the agency, decided to weigh in personally on the manuscript. She spoke firmly and candidly with Polly about how the book could be improved to "quicken its pace and reduce its length." She wrote up her suggestions for trimming it and making the story more sympathetic. But it was abundantly clear that Polly didn't have the skill or emotional perspective to manage the revisions herself.

In the end, Watkins convinced her that she should accept the help of a professional ghostwriter. Whenever pride was set against ambition,

Polly's choice was always ambition. Once she was reconciled to the idea of sharing authorship, even secretly, she knew just who she wanted: Virginia Faulkner.

Ginny Faulkner was a midwestern sophisticate who had thrown over Lincoln, Nebraska, for Manhattan and Hollywood. She had been a minor player in the Café Society scene of the 1930s. She ran with the prosperous lesbian crowd that flourished in the Broadway and Harlem *boîtes*, not exactly out but not exactly in the closet either. She had published several novels and written a musical comedy, and after a brief stint as a screenwriter, she now freelanced for *The Saturday Evening Post*, *Town & Country*, and other glossy magazines. She possessed a wicked sense of humor, an endearing hint of a lisp, and impeccable literary instincts. Most important, Polly trusted her.

Virginia agreed to help and launched immediately into an initial revision of the manuscript. Meanwhile Polly continued her nostalgia tour of her old stomping grounds. She was spotted in the audience at the Blue Angel, lunching at Delmonico's, cocktailing at Sardi's, and enjoying a late nosh at Reuben's Deli after taking in the smash hit musical *Guys and Dolls*, a rollicking homage to the gamblers and gold diggers of her youth, adapted from Damon Runyon's stories and directed by her old customer George S. Kaufman. She saw herself portrayed as "Molly Burden" in the stage version of Wolcott Gibbs's novel *Season in the Sun*—the cast went into "an amused tizzy" when they learned the real Polly Adler was in the audience. "I do wish Mr. Gibbs had come to see me," she told Robert Sylvester of the *Daily News*. "For technical advice only, of course."

She followed this with a triumphant return to Fire Island, the scene of her humiliation in 1943. Now the Broadway bohemians and her hard-partying gay friends welcomed her as a returning hero. "The social lioness of the Fire Island season so far turned out to be Polly Adler," crowed Dorothy Kilgallen. "At least six parties in her honor were held there over the week-end, a fact which should constitute a short but revealing commentary on the state of civilization in these parts."

Polly was still kicking up her heels in New York, when the long-awaited good news finally arrived. On September 19, 1951, Rinehart Publishing Co. offered an option on the book. This time it stuck.

The offer came from Stanley Rinehart, head of a family firm founded by his mother, the best-selling mystery writer Mary Roberts Rinehart. He'd been hesitant about the project until he gave it to his mother, "a thorough woman of the world." She sat up until four a.m. reading the manuscript and called him immediately with two words: "Buy it." It needed work, she said, but it "was a cinch to be a best-seller."

It was no coincidence that Polly's book—so fascinating yet frightening to male editors—came to life only through the determined intervention of a handful of famously forceful females: the civil rights attorney Gertrude Gottlieb, the powerful agent Ann Watkins, and the brand-name novelist Mary Roberts Rinehart—each at the head of her own eponymous firm—and Virginia Faulkner, a brilliant literary mind who would be largely responsible for restoring the novelist Willa Cather to the American canon.

Virginia, after working with Polly that summer, had had enough of her fussing over her precious manuscript. She typed it up in a memo: "Rinehart agrees to option, provided I write it. I say ok if (a) my name is not on it; (b) Polly goes back to California."

Polly was happy to oblige. For all the summer's fun, Manhattan was no longer her town. Like so many East Coast scoffers, she'd succumbed to the laid-back lure of Lotusland.

That fall Virginia and Polly worked together by phone and by letter, as Ginny pushed her for details and dates. The biggest challenge was Polly herself. She had an extraordinary memory, but it would mysteriously fail when pressed on certain subjects. She offered dodgy explanations that only muddled matters more, and when pinned down she sometimes became snappish.

"Killings were fast and furious those years, and could not keep up with dates on the latest slaughterings," she wrote uneasily to Virginia after one convoluted conversation; "if we keep on digging in the history of gangsterism of the Asperin [sic] Age, my book will read more like a biography of the gangsters and not my biography and whoredom."

Her "Must Not Mention" list included over a dozen of the Syndicate's most dangerous killers. Polly cut out Big Bill Dwyer and Nick Montana, who had introduced her to brothel keeping, and denied (unconvincingly) that Dutch Schultz socialized with Jimmy Hines at her house. References to the scandalous death of the party girl Starr Faithfull were cut entirely, as were her tangles with the IRS. The murder of Vivian

Gordon was included over Polly's protests, only after Virginia pointed out that her friendship with the strangled Broadway butterfly had been splashed across every newspaper in the country.

A friend at the *Daily Mirror* let Faulkner go through the paper's morgue, its vast files of past stories, which only added to the confusion. "She hasn't got a goddam thing straight," Virginia told Ann Watkins. "I have between twenty and thirty addresses of 'places of business' from Polly's notes and from the papers to try to match up with episodes. One newspaper story said that it is 'reported she moves her residence every 24 hours,' and it certainly seems that way to me."

Even the date of her birth was cloaked in mystery. "To my best recollection I said 1900 because it was a simple date to remember," Polly confessed. "Honestly darling I'm not trying to hide my age, I don't give a damn but I simply don't know."

Maddening as it was, Virginia wasn't unsympathetic. "I suppose she has a constitutional—or anyway vocational—horror of being pinned down," she wrote to Ann Watkins. "I don't know, every time I tell myself there must be some simpler way of making a living than writing, I think, well, look at the whorehouse business, you wind up writing anyway."

It was no easier for Polly. Virginia urged her to read various books about the Jazz Age to refresh her memories. Polly was especially infuriated by a cheap paperback biography of Frank Costello. "I know every character in the book, including the dead ones. They had a lot of nerve calling Lucky a supervisor of prostitution. He is one of the nicest gentlemen I have ever met, not barring the Vanderbilts and Whitneys," she fumed. "The so-called righteous public makes me sick. All my life I have been persecuted by the cops, judges and respectable people. Just who were those people to judge others. I didn't like the feeling of being spat on and I will not do the same to others just because I'm writing a book. So be at peace. We shall treat our Lucky as a human being."

By March 1952, they had a final draft, studded with highbrow epigraphs chosen by Virginia, from Shakespeare, Stendhal, Charles Dickens, Herbert Hoover, Ernest Hemingway, John Dos Passos, and John J. Raskob. "No other whore book has such dignity, thanks to you," Polly wrote with genuine pleasure.

Between Polly's self-protective instincts and the timidity of Rinehart's editor, John Selby, the plot had been thoroughly sanitized, leaving out "the unprintable and libelous parts" and the tales that were too unflattering or, frankly, too dangerous to share.

"In a few instances, anecdotes have been invented, but not out of the whole cloth—I think the words 'imaginative amplification' would be a truer description of the process," Virginia explained to Ann Watkins. "And so it is with 50% of the material in the book which, while not wholly unrelated to fact, either didn't happen when the book says it did, or didn't happen to 'real' (as opposed to composite) people; or else didn't happen at all, but was invented by me.

"My biggest failure has been in not even getting anywhere near suggesting the way Polly talks, which when you come down to it, is what makes so much of what she says funny," Virginia lamented. The Jewish dialect humorists "Milt Gross or Arthur Kober could do it: I can't."

Now began the arduous task of vetting the manuscript for legal snags and obtaining releases from the people she'd mentioned by name. Her lawyer for this task was Harriet Pilpel, a partner in the renowned law firm of Greenbaum, Wolff & Ernst, which specialized in First Amendment and sexual freedom issues.

Polly seemed genuinely surprised at how hard it was to persuade her so-called friends to sign releases. They seemed equally surprised to be asked. Walter Winchell begged off from being included. "I don't doubt that your 'A House is Not a Home' will enjoy popularity, since every house you ever had did," Walter wrote to her. Nonetheless, this was one of the rare times he declined the spotlight. "I don't want to embarrass the family," he explained sheepishly. "The decent thing about you, Polly, is that you never, to my knowledge, purposely did that to anyone—and that is why you have always found me on your team."

The ill-tempered humorist James Thurber was appalled when he received Polly's letter asking for permission to refer to him as "my old friend Jim Thurber" in a passing anecdote. "I always thought she was awful, but my lawyer, who is also the publisher's, says, 'It's a social document,'" he complained to New Yorker editor Hamilton Basso. But his delicate scruples didn't keep him from leering to Wolcott Gibbs about their fellow john and New Yorker scribe, St. Clair McKelway, "Maybe we should convince McKelway that he figures as No. 7 in her chapter called 'The Ten Best Swordsmen.'"

In earlier days, Dorothy Parker had offered to write a foreword to the memoir. But Polly abandoned that notion after concluding that Parker, a famous procrastinator, would "never get round to doing it." Perhaps she procrastinated in signing the release as well, since Dorothy was also cut from the final manuscript.

The biggest disappointment came from Polly's longtime housekeeper and second-in-command, Showboat, who was now working as the ladies' lounge attendant at the Hickory House on Swing Street. Showboat refused to grant permission for use of her character without a substantial payoff of several thousand dollars. On top of that, the novelist Edna Ferber—who shared a lawyer with Polly in Harriet Pilpel—objected to Showboat's nickname, since it was likely lifted from Ferber's epic-novel-turned-hit-musical of the same name. Polly—tight with a dime even in her flush days—was outraged and refused to pay her former comrade-at-arms.

"Anything nice or funny I could have said about the sun-burned race has left me, Showboat, the bastard made sure of that," she ranted to Virginia; "that black bitch saved every gift I ever gave her, every letter and I don't know to what length she will go to prove that she was the wheel that made Polly spin."

Showboat's absence was a material loss to the book and to the historical record, erasing just how much the glamorous faces of Café Society depended on a legion of Black women laboring behind the scenes. But it demonstrated once again that Showboat was her employer's equal in moxie and hard-nosed bargaining. "I would die if that skunk sued and won one cent in a lawsuit after all the grief she gave me," grumbled Polly.

☾

At the very end of 1952, Polly signed her final contract with Rinehart, receiving an advance of $7,500. There had been talk about Faulkner receiving a percentage of the royalties, but when Polly didn't repeat the offer in the final negotiation, Virginia let it go.

"To be frank—and off the record—it is just as well Polly has no financial claim on my services," Virginia wrote to Ann Watkins; "she has, as you know, a tendency to be interminable; and this past fall it has seemed to me she was unable to go to the bathroom without calling up Long Distance to consult about it. Also, it appeared to be her impression that as well as ghosting her book, I was to do the promotion, be available at all times for 'advice,' hold her up on any personal appearances connected with publicity, and for all I know—write her a sequel. As a free agent, I have been able to quash these notions; I doubt if it would have been possible, if I were on the pay roll."

Among Polly's family members, former associates, and customers, there was much suspense as rumors swirled about who might be named in the book. The *Jewish Daily Forward*, America's flagship Yiddish paper, contemplated buying the right to serialize the book but decided against it. As the *Forward*'s editor-in-chief explained to Polly's literary agent, "relatives of the book's author, longtime readers of our paper, have been in touch with me, pleading against any further exploitation of their family's shame. Their plea was so moving, and their anguish was so poignant, that I acceded to their request."

As they prepared for the book's release, Polly began ramping up her publicity campaign. In interviews she laid it on thick about how hard she'd worked to become a writer, bragging about her college grades, and telling reporters about her newfound love of dictionaries. She was shameless about claiming Virginia's work as her own. "I wrote my book all myself, most of it in longhand," she boasted to Aline Mosby of United Press International. "No one ever thought Polly Adler could write a book. But then, after all," she added, "I was creative in my own field."

Her long-awaited life story, clad in lurid scarlet with an old-fashioned candlestick telephone on the cover, appeared in stores on June 4, 1953.

A House Is Not a Home was an immediate sensation, receiving rave reviews in publications ranging from the *Police Gazette* to *Newsweek*. Old hands like Abel Green and Stanley Walker swore it was the "McCoy," as the old speakeasy crowd still liked to say, full of earthy truths and authentic portraits. High-toned rags like *The New Yorker* and the *Herald Tribune* marveled at the deft interweaving of fine writing and vibrant slang. The Yiddish papers gave it a surprisingly enthusiastic reception, with an unmistakable tone of pride in a tough Jewish girl who had beaten the odds. Critics were surprisingly few and were found in predictably conservative places.

A House Is Not a Home went into a third printing before the end of its first week on bookstore shelves. It held the number-two slot on *The New York Times* nonfiction best-seller list for thirteen weeks (second only to Norman Vincent Peale's *The Power of Positive Thinking*). Six months later *Publishers Weekly* named it one of the ten bestselling nonfiction books of 1953. Foreign rights were being snapped up; it would eventually appear in nearly a dozen languages.

Some of the book's success came from pent-up interest fed by the gossip columnists. All the Broadway chroniclers covered its release with a healthy dollop of nostalgia for the bad old days. Walter Winchell came through with a catchy blurb that summed up the old glamour: "After the Follies it was Polly's. Remember?" Over the following months Winchell kept up a steady drumbeat for the book that was echoed by lesser columnists.

As always, Polly's timing was well aligned with historical forces. In 1953 the country was transfixed by the publication of the Kinsey Report on female sexuality; the scandalous revelations of the Kefauver Commission on organized crime (featuring many of her old mob associates); and the nostalgic hit musical *Guys and Dolls* (ditto). That same year Saul Bellow's boisterous classic, *The Adventures of Augie March* (whose hero bore some resemblance to Benny Adler), won the National Book Award and ushered in a new fascination with Jewish American stories.

A large portion of the credit goes to Virginia Faulkner's brilliant revision. Reviewers regularly remarked on the book's surprising combination of elegance, erudition, and authenticity, fueling spirited debates in literary circles about whether Polly had employed a ghostwriter and, if so, who it might be.

When asked, Polly stoutly insisted that it was all her, which was, of course, just as Ginny wanted it. All the same, Virginia had enough craftsman's pride to compose a sealed letter addressed to future readers, showing how she had deliberately laced the manuscript with allusions to *The Wasteland*, T. S. Eliot's modernist masterpiece, to prove she was the true author if someone else tried to claim credit. It was also, she added, "my private comment on the material in the book, and on the meaning of Polly's life."

(As it happened, Polly, the newly minted English major, didn't share Ginny's admiration for T. S. Eliot. "'Wasteland' is supposed to be his masterpiece—he can have it," she told a reporter for the *New York Post*.)

Ignoring the fearful entreaties of the Rinehart sons, who were dead set against her appearing in public, Polly headed to New York to celebrate the book's release. She planned to exploit every public relations and brand-building trick she had in her arsenal.

For weeks, Polly was feted at parties both high and low. The first and rowdiest was a raucous shindig on Fire Island that resulted in no fewer than three fistfights. This was followed by "a literary cocktail party of quiet dignity" at "21," one of the last glorious survivors of the Swing Street speakeasies.

"As the author of a highly successful new book, A House Is Not a Home, her status has changed," sniffed columnist Danton Walker as he glanced at the high-toned guest list. But as far as "21"'s owners and the boys at the bar were concerned, it was merely Polly's due. When the proprietor Jerry Berns was pressed on why he'd host a party for the notorious Polly Adler, his answer was quick. "Why not?" he shrugged. "Where else would Polly go?"

The New York Times had righteously refused to run Rinehart's ads for the memoir. But after three weeks of warm reviews and that splashy party at "21," it decided to reverse its ban—just about the time the book landed on the Times best-seller list.

"I still had some snubs too," Polly told a sympathetic reporter, "and they still have the ability to hurt me cruelly." A number of radio and television shows extended invitations, only to withdraw them under pressure—a fresh frustration for someone who had spent her career dodging cameras. At least one department store canceled her book signing for fear of offending "their family trade." But for the most part, the book's reception was her dream come true. Finally she had redeemed the *yiches*, the intellect and moral stature, she'd yearned for since she'd left Yanow.

After two months of nonstop social whirl, she headed back to California, exhausted and happy to be home. "New York is no longer a place for a tired old gal," she confessed to Ann Watkins.

☾

Four months later, while she was still basking in the glow of the book's release, Polly's joy was shot to hell by a knock on her door from an agent of the Immigration and Naturalization Service. The newspaper coverage of Polly's lush party at "21" had so outraged an unnamed top government official that he pressured the INS to open an investigation into whether she had perjured herself when she took the oath of citizenship in 1929. If so, she was eligible to be deported from the United States—like her old friends Lucky Luciano, Joe Adonis, Meyer Lansky, and Frank Costello.

Polly was genuinely terrified by this turn of events, although she was breezy when asked about it. "Worried? Of course, I'm worried," she told a reporter. "I've got two weeks homework during the Christmas vacation and it's tough trying to concentrate on my studies with this terrible thing hanging over my head. The homework is something fierce. I have to read Goethe's *Faust* along with Voltaire and Dostoevsky."

Polly squirmed and fudged her way through a sworn deposition with the government interrogator, falling back on forgetfulness, her bona fides as a member of the literati, and rank perjury. She claimed, her memoir notwithstanding, that her apartment was merely a hangout for friends who would stop by for dinner or a game of backgammon. "I would serve drinks and very often they would make me gifts for entertaining them," she explained nervously. "A lot of showgirls used to come by and they would make me a gift for sitting around having a drink."

"Well, I'll be letting you know where to send the cigarettes," she cracked to Virginia Faulkner after the interview. Ginny took that as a bad sign: "So I guess—unless she manages to get a fix in—she really realizes they've got her backed agin' the wall."

But Virginia underestimated Polly. When the FBI again began dredging through her past, she retained Edward Bennett Williams, a top-flight criminal lawyer from Washington, D.C., who counted Frank Costello and Jimmy Hoffa as clients. The case lingered on for several years, but in typical fashion it seemed to fizzle out whenever the FBI's New York field office became involved. Her last interview with INS inspectors came at the end of 1956, when she regaled them with the story of that nightmarish dinner party in 1933 when mafia heavyweight Frankie Carbo beat her up as a lesson to the wives of Dutch Goldberg and Lepke Buchalter.

With that her FBI file abruptly and mysteriously ended.

❦

At the beginning of 1954, A House Is Not a Home was still selling steadily and excerpts were appearing in all the racy men's magazines. In September an inexpensive paperback pocket edition was issued that would go on to sell some 2 million copies over the next few years. "Funny thing," remarked one department store clerk. "No one will admit buying it for themselves. It's always a friend who wants to read it, or something like that."

Polly continued to receive fan mail from both sexes. "My publishers said I didn't have to answer all the letters," she confided to Art Buchwald, "but I told them if Mrs. Roosevelt can answer all her fan mail, I can answer all of mine." She continued to promote the book vigorously. "If there's an unautographed copy of my book on the West Coast, it's a collector's item," she quipped. She toyed with the idea of writing a sequel about the many women who worked for her, and even set out to tape some interviews with former employees.

To her delight, she was warmly welcomed to belles lettres by respected writers like the novelist Vladimir Nabokov, whose parting inscription to Polly could hardly have been more flattering: "It seems to me the very most fortunate experience of a lucky life to be here this evening and please count me as a devoted admirer." His comment was rivaled in warmth only by that of the novelist Mary McCarthy, who wrote simply: "Polly dear—I love you—what else is there to say?" Polly took particular pride in her new friendship with Dr. Kinsey and his hearty appreciation of her homemade chopped chicken liver.

After years of listening enviously as her customers rhapsodized over their grand tours of Europe, in the fall of 1955 she embarked on her own extended European holiday. She planned to promote the French, German, and Italian editions of her book, visit some Continental bordellos, and, if one believed the gossip, undergo a surgical face-lift in Switzerland. She did return looking awfully refreshed.

On her way home she traveled to Israel, where her book had been published in Hebrew to much fanfare, and where she had many family members, some of whom she'd helped financially. Like so many of her family encounters, this visit was unsatisfying. According to family lore, her Israeli cousins were too embarrassed to even speak with her about the book, and she left feeling deeply insulted.

Ironically, winning the respectability that she had craved her whole life seemed to sap Polly of the earthy charm, winning self-deprecation, and keen humor that had made her the force she was. Now she was just a tiny older lady who wanted to talk about how well she was doing in her college classes, making up for all those years when she had felt left out of the conversation.

Frankly, the scandalous Polly Adler, renowned for her bawdy wit and titillating charisma, had become a square. Everyone she ran into on her European tour remarked upon it.

After lunching with her in Paris, Art Buchwald devoted his entire column in the *Herald Tribune* to her newfound earnestness. She boasted to Buchwald of her college grade point average, her book sales, her bushels of fan mail, and her new stature among the women of her former profession. "Recently they raided some houses in California and they found the book on the bedstands," she bragged. "It's kind of like a Gideon Bible to many of the girls."

She had heard some complaints, she admitted. Some of her "creative" friends were jealous of her success. And some of her public "complained that I take them to the bedroom door and then slam the door in their faces. But that's what I intended to do. This book has dignity and I didn't want to fill it with a lot of smut."

When her old customer Alec Waugh ran into her at the Madrid airport, he was shocked by her transformation from mistress of revels to dowdy matron. He was desperately jet-lagged, with an early plane to catch the next morning, but he couldn't pass up the opportunity for a catch-up over champagne and caviar. "What an opportunity," he thought. "A dinner *à deux* with Polly Adler.

> In the old days one of her great assets as a hostess was her capacity to keep the talk light and lecherous—no dirty stories, no four-letter words, but the creation of an atmosphere which would make you think of love-making as the most reasonable occupation for human beings—a Decameron atmosphere. But that kind of talk belonged to the past. She now wanted to tell me about her courses at the university. She told me about the books she was reading. She recited her marks and credits. She recounted her difficulties with a particular professor. I could not have been more bored.

Waugh fought to keep his eyes open as she droned on. "I told myself, this can't keep on forever. Sooner or later she must get back to the old days. Memories of Mr. Benchley, that was what I was waiting for." He waited in vain. "On and on she went. 'French is my weak subject,' she informed me. 'That must surprise you, surely.' I was past being surprised."

The hours ticked by until it was one o'clock, the restaurant was empty, and the tables laid for breakfast. "I suppose we shouldn't keep them up any longer," she concluded mercifully. It was the last time Alec saw her.

The actress Myrna Loy summed it up best, after being introduced to the new and improved Polly at a New Year's Eve party in Paris: "The infamous madam who wrote *A House Is Not a Home* struck me as a lonely woman with a touching yen for respectability—whatever that is."

☾

In June 1958, Pearl Adler became a proud graduate of the Los Angeles City College, with her parents in the audience as she received her diploma. The ceremony came none too soon. Earlier in the year she'd had to nix an invitation to speak at Yale University due to ill health. Walter Winchell reported that she'd had a stroke, which she denied. It was only a severe case of shingles, she insisted, but it left one side of her face paralyzed.

Yet even now Polly still held a reputation as a quick-witted problem solver, remembered Leonore Lemmon, the brunette beauty who'd once reigned as the belligerent bad girl of Café Society. She had known Polly well during the war years. It was long rumored that Lemmon had occasionally gone on paid dates for Polly as a cash-strapped, publicity-seeking party girl. Now, thirty-six years old and no longer such a hot ticket, she'd recently become engaged to the actor George Reeves, known to children everywhere as the star of the *Superman* television series. Now Leonore was living with Reeves in Los Angeles, where she'd renewed her friendship with Polly.

Like all Lemmon's romantic relationships, it was tempestuous. On May 4, 1959, Walter Winchell reported that Leonore claimed that one of Reeves's former girlfriends had "threatened her with a .45 in Beverly Hills." As usual, Winchell was on to something.

A little after midnight on June 16, George Reeves was killed by a single gunshot in his upstairs bedroom. Downstairs, Leonore had been drinking heavily with Polly's old friend Bob Condon (their houseguest at the time) and his current fling, Carol Van Ronkel. Carol was the wife of a B-movie actor and screenwriter named Alford "Rip" Van Ronkel (also a warm friend of Polly's).

How Reeves was shot and by whom would be a matter of heated dispute and frantic cover-up. The L.A. police declared it a suicide, as did Leonore, but some insiders claimed it was murder. Near the end of her life, Leonore told a young reporter a different version of the story than she told the cops, one that placed Polly at the center of the tumultuous night.

In this late-life tale, Lemmon confessed that she didn't call the police right away when they discovered Reeves's body. Instead, she went to rouse Bob Condon and Carol Von Ronkel from the guest bedroom, so that Carol wouldn't be caught in Bob's bed. But the wanton wife was too soused to move.

In a perverse testament to a lifetime of cool competence, a desperate Leonore called Polly for help. "You better get Bobby out of here, would you please?" she pleaded. "He's in bed with a friend of mine."

Even in ill health, Polly, "that tough old broad," hopped into her car and drove from Burbank to Reeves's home in Benedict Canyon. What exactly transpired when she got there was understandably garbled. By best account, Polly left Bob there, since he was their houseguest, but managed to wrap the negligee-clad Carol in a coat and spirit her out of the house (it was hardly her first time moving a dead-eyed drunk), leaving Leonore to face the police.

It was Polly's final recorded escapade in eluding the law. By Leonore's lights, she carried it off magnificently.

☾

At the end of 1961, after more than forty years with a cigarette in her mouth, Polly was diagnosed with lung cancer. This was "The Big C," as Winchell dubbed it—"The Big Casino" where the odds were always lousy.

She made her final appearance in Winchell's column in March 1962, when he reported that she was gravely ill. Befitting her celebrity status, she was treated at Cedars of Lebanon Hospital in Los Angeles, hospital to the stars. On March 1 she underwent an experimental operation, removing the lower portion of her lung. But "the medical handicappers," to borrow a phrase, were not optimistic.

The notorious Polly Adler passed away at the appropriately early hour of 4:25 on the morning of June 9, 1962.

☾

For a legendary *balaboosta,* it was a sadly sparse funeral. Hollywood was thick with men who'd enjoyed her hospitality, but even in death, hypocrisy ruled. Her true friends—like Robert Benchley, Mark Hellinger, and Wallace Beery, those "fine old realists," in Stanley Walker's phrase— had beaten her to the grave. But Sinatra's swinging songwriter Jimmy Van Heusen, who never gave a damn what anyone thought, came to the funeral, one of the few film industry people who dared show his face.

By the time of her death, Polly was a certified American legend. Long, respectful obituaries ran in scores of newspapers across the country. *The New Yorker,* with tongue in cheek, put her in the company of the great Russian authors. "One thinks of Gogol, Turgenev, and Tolstoy, and of how uneasily they must have shifted in their seats in Heaven, realizing that they must someday make room for Polly Adler." It surely would have tickled both her vanity and her self-deprecating humor to read *Time's* final pronouncement: "The old cat died a literary lion."

Polly left a substantial estate of $100,000 to her family. Just before she died, she finally sold the film rights to A *House Is Not a Home* for the tidy sum of $75,000. She did not live to enjoy the delicious irony of seeing Joan Crawford, Barbara Stanwyck, Ethel Merman, and her old pal Martha Raye all scrapping to play Manhattan's number one madam on the silver screen.

The idea of an illustrious actress portraying her was the apotheosis of her quest for fame. One reporter described, rather snidely, an evening spent with Polly at Sardi's, the famous after-theater watering hole, following the book's release. In the celebrity-filled dining room, Polly buttonholed no fewer than three eminent performers—Lady Beatrice Lillie Peel, Carol Channing, and Lucille Ball—chirping, "My dear, I want no one else to play me in the musical version of my book than you. You would be just perfect as me."

"Above all, it is to be a respectable show," she told Channing, just as the redheaded Ball caught her eye across the room. "You're the only one to play me. Wasn't that Lucille Ball? She's so respectable. But I'm going to wait for you."

In the end, the role went to Shelley Winters, a forty-something blond Oscar winner who had recently appeared as a madam in the film version of *The Balcony*, a play by the avant-garde playwright Jean Genet. Set in a brothel in the midst of a violent political uprising, it was a surrealistic depiction of johns acting out their twisted, totalitarian fantasies. Polly invested in the American premiere of the play at New York's Circle in the Square Theater. By chance, she sat next to Shelley Winters at the premiere. "She did not approve of *The Balcony*," laughed Winters. "She was incensed at it—at that crazy kind of bordello. She really felt a call girl should please a client, make him happy."

The movie version of *A House Is Not a Home* was universally panned, although it had a few points in its favor. The costume designer, Edith Head, was nominated for an Academy Award, the title song by Burt Bacharach became a top-100 hit, and the actress Raquel Welch debuted as one of Polly's Follies. But the movie was leaden and unrealistic, the reviewers wrote, a morass of sentimental moralism flecked with hints of raunch. "Hard as it may be to believe, the authors of the screenplay of *A House Is Not a Home* have turned Miss Adler's gold into dross," lamented *The New Yorker*.

☽

Polly was hailed as a symbol of a decadent, long-gone era. But she preferred to cast herself as a modern Horatio Alger heroine. "A cynical person might say my life had been a typical American success story," she wrote. "From the arrival at Ellis Island up the ladder rung by rung—five dollars a week, ten dollars a week, a hundred dollars a week, a mink coat, a better address—from neighborhood trade to an international clientele—from a nobody to a legend."

Yet even those who scoffed at this sunny picture conceded Polly's extraordinary cultural significance. Her career coincided with New York's flowering as the most vibrant and powerful city in the world, and many of the players who made it so met and mingled in her parlor. As the cognoscenti liked to say, "If a bomb exploded in Polly Adler's house, the political and cultural life of the city would be wiped out."

To her admirers, her brothel was an intoxicating playground for madcap Broadway modernists and cutting-edge capitalists in hot pursuit of new pleasures. It was a space where the imagination was allowed free play, unfettered by outside eyes and conventional rules. In turn, her customers and employees turned these experiences into grist for the songs, movies, books, plays, and daring new notions in morals and mores that would define twentieth-century popular culture.

To her foes, she exerted a sinister outsize influence with powerful men whose after-dark decision making affected millions of Americans. One critic summed up the charges succinctly: "She provided a liaison between the underworld, politics, the professions, big business, and desirable women. Judges' tips were bartered in her plush parlor. Racketeer Labor bosses formulated deals there. Police officers were broken or made, and candidates for public office gained or lost party support as a result of conferences held at Polly's place." If we believe her claim that she procured women for Franklin Delano Roosevelt—and that her silence was critical to Roosevelt's election to the presidency—then her significance was even greater than her critics feared.

Of course, publishing a bestselling book boosted her legacy. "If nothing else, writing a book helps jazz up or tone down your obituary. Take Polly Adler, the most beloved of all the whorehouse madams. I would hate to count the number of cops Polly corrupted with bribes, not to mention the number of girls Polly just generally corrupted," observed the editor Harry Golden. "When Polly cashed her chips not too long ago, what did the obituaries read? Of course. 'Author Dies.'"

By publishing *A House Is Not a Home*, she did more than redeem and reinvent herself. Her backstairs chronicle of the early sexual revolution, and the secret role that illicit sex played in business and politics, was an eye-opener for millions of readers. If the 1950s was the "age of conformity," Polly gave it a shocking jolt, on par with her fellow authors of 1953, Alfred Kinsey, Simone de Beauvoir, and Hugh Hefner. As it happens, she read and approved heartily of both *Sexual Behavior in the American Female* and *The Second Sex*; she left no comment on the newly founded *Playboy* magazine.

If Polly ever met F. Scott Fitzgerald or read *The Great Gatsby*, the Great American Novel of the Jazz Age, she left no record of it. So we do not know what she would have made of his mythical bootlegger and his magical parties.

Surely she would have found the romance angle hard to swallow; reverence toward women was not a trait possessed by the mobsters of her acquaintance. Undoubtedly, she'd have had questions about how Gatsby handled the mechanics of hosting a massive house party every weekend; so much soiled laundry, so many dirty dishes! But the longings and struggles of Jimmy Gatz as he transformed himself into Jay Gatsby—his "heightened sensitivity to the promises of life"—and the violent destruction not only of his illusions but of his life itself, would have been hauntingly familiar.

When Fitzgerald began his novel in 1923, he drew his inspiration from the lavish hosts of the Broadway mob and a chance meeting with Arnold Rothstein, whom he recast as Gatsby's mentor Meyer Wolfsheim. But it was Polly who made real Fitzgerald's fantasy of the never-ending bacchanal as a glorious vehicle for pursuing the American dream. (It is fitting that the first recorded use of the phrase "American dream" appears in a 1912 novel about an upwardly mobile prostitute.) Like Gatsby, she cannily turned the cult of the party into a ladder to climb out of the gutter and into the upper rungs of society.

But Polly's version of the story is shorn of *Gatsby*'s grandeur, exposing the harsh reality behind the gauzy dreams and shimmering parties. She captured the barbarism of the bootleg barons when they weren't posing as tuxedo-clad bon vivants and moon-eyed lovers. She revealed how often the freewheeling flappers and glamour girls were really sad young women being paid to provide other people's pleasure.

Yet despite her passionate pursuit of posterity it was not Polly, New York's "Empress of Vice," but her male criminal colleagues who became twentieth-century cultural icons. Prohibition's excesses enshrined the gangster as an American archetype, whose lordly ambitions and tragic flaws are considered essential to understanding our national character. But there is no corresponding myth of the female outlaw who uses sex as her weapon against the world.

Why not? It certainly isn't because the lives of distaff lawbreakers are unrecorded or uninteresting. Scholars estimate that well over a billion pages have been written about prostitutes, covering every possible perspective. Hundreds of madams have published gripping and provocative memoirs, with more appearing all the time. Nevertheless, "the Scarlet-Woman-as-Horatio-Alger tale" has never grabbed the American imagination the way the rumrunners and racketeers did.

The most obvious explanation is that this is simply an extension of the conspiracy of silence around sexual power that has "systematically trivialized female erotic capital to discourage women from capitalizing on it at men's expense," as the economist Catherine Hakim argues. Stigmatizing the sale of sexual services has not ended prostitution any more than Prohibition vanquished drinking. But it has driven down prices and vastly undermined the economic and cultural power of women who would make their living by leveraging their erotic assets.

There is something else, though. Sex workers in general—Polly, in particular—are dealers in illusion; the illusions of intimate connection between strangers, of desires without limits or consequences, of spontaneous ecstasy on command, and whatever else the human id can dream up and pay for. Polly's mastery of this mysterious art was the source of her significance and contributed in no small measure to the glorious legend of the Jazz Age.

But Americans have little appetite for examining the dreary mechanics behind the spectacle of our dreams. Polly, for all her longing to be known, hid far more of her story than she shared, even from herself. If she has not received her historical due it is, in part, because she is a symbol whose reality contradicts the very myths that make this era so captivating and charismatic. That, as she would be the first to admit, is a tough sell.

But don't count her out. "I have always been a fighter and hope to Christ I never stop till curtain time," as she put it. Perhaps Polly's story is better suited to this twenty-first century, when there is urgent interest in exposing the intersections of sex and power, and dismantling the conspiracies of silence that protect powerful people from bearing the full cost of their desires.

Acknowledgments

I swore I'd never write another biography, this most unwieldy of genres. But then one festive evening, when I was feeling a little vain, someone—perhaps my editor Gerry Howard, perhaps Bill Thomas, the man higher-up—casually threw out the suggestion that I try a book about the Roaring Twenties. "How about Calvin Coolidge?" my husband, Bruce, piped up, a notion that was immediately nixed. Something sexy and scandalous, that was the ticket, everyone at the table agreed.

In retrospect, the idea was silly. I'd spent the last two decades immersed in the nineteenth century, keeping company with Calvinist ministers. A wiser soul would have foreseen the challenges of switching eras and perspectives so radically. But then I stumbled on Polly Adler's 1953 memoir, *A House Is Not a Home*, in the stacks of the Yale library. And once again I found myself beguiled by an extraordinary character and an epic, if now forgotten, American story, luring me down the primrose path.

It would be no small task to trade saints for sinners and ministers for madams. Had I known it would take thirteen years, I'd never have tried. But from the outset, this project seemed anointed by the muses. The first fine omen was the discovery that my former classmate Rachel Rubin had edited a new edition of *A House Is Not a Home* for University of Massachusetts Press. Generously, Rachel handed me a stack of newspaper clippings on Polly (a very valuable gift in those early days of digitalization), which sealed my fate.

My run of uncanny good fortune was just beginning. By coincidence, that same year I was invited by Melissa Homestead to speak in Lincoln, Nebraska, the home of Virginia Faulkner, Polly's ghostwriter. In a miraculous twist, I stumbled on Faulkner's personal notebooks documenting the composition of Polly's memoir, including many of the names, dates, and incidents that had been changed or excised. I offer my deepest, most joyful gratitude to the anonymous collector who was savvy enough to save them from destruction.

It felt like another miracle when I found the Yizkor memorial book documenting the Jewish community in Polly's hometown of Janow al yad Pinsk, which was destroyed during the Holocaust. I owe immense thanks to Lawrence Ackerfield, Debra Wolraich, and Marcia Hirsch, affiliates of the Yizkor Book Translation Project of JewishGen, and to my translators Martin Jacob and David Goldman.

My good luck intensified when investigative attorney Charles Eric Gordon volunteered to help me locate Eleanor Vera, who cared for Polly's last surviving brother, Sam Adler. Embarrassed by his sister's notoriety, Sam tossed out most of Polly's scrapbooks, keepsakes, recorded reminiscences, and signed first editions after her death, but Ellie managed to save several boxes, including many of the images that appear in this book. Without the farsightedness and generosity of Eleanor Vera and our anonymous collector in Nebraska, this biography would have been a pale shadow of itself.

That same remarkable year, Polly's cousin, the magnificent Smadar Gilboa, found me. Over the course of our friendship Smadar became a master genealogist who spent hundreds of hours tracking clues and answering questions. She was a true partner in the creation of this book, and I am profoundly grateful for her friendship.

These new relationships culminated in a magical weekend in Los Angeles, where I met Smadar, Ellie Vera, and Polly's niece Robin Adler, daughter of her beloved brother Bob, and Robin's stepbrother Rick Josephs, who welcomed me with the warmth of long-lost cousins. With Smadar's help I was also able to speak with Polly's extended family who offered key insights, including Steve Olchek, David Krikun, Sarah Warren, Frances Friedman, Marcia Freeman, Carren Dorian, Randy Dorian, Tzvi Allen Fishman, Gail Bass, and Rebecca Entwisle. I am very grateful to all of you.

After this my debts mounted quickly. I was obsessed with the hunt for evidence, and I pursued every angle, from the antiquarian to the cutting-edge. For this I depended on the vast resources of the Yale University Library system. I am especially grateful to the Yale Divinity School Library, where they cheerfully checked out my sinful books, and Sterling Memorial Library's interlibrary loan, microform, and acquisitions librarians, who dug up the obscure and the obscene for me. I also spent hundreds of happy hours in the glorious New York Public Library on 42nd Street and the Billy Rose Theater Division at Lincoln Center. I'd be there still if I could.

Scores of archivists, librarians, genealogists, researchers, and collectors helped smooth my path. Standouts included David Smith, Ron Arons, Richard Tuske, Ken Cobb, Ellen Belcher, Patricia Shawker, Joy Kestenbaum, Jenny Schwartzberg, Maggie Humbertson, Besty Jean Pease, Rebecca Jewett, Lucille Hodes, David Gary, Gregory Eow, Erminio D'Onofrio, Bill Paxton, Stephen Lasker, Mark Berresford, Sabrina Sondhi, Kelly Shand, Virginia T. Seymour, and the staff of the NYPL archives.

Bonnie O'Leary, Peter Mintun, Ron Bowers, Burton Peretti, Lee Saylor, Darwin Porter, and Stephen Riegel all shared gems from their personal archives. Gary Berman of Creation Entertainment LLC gave me access to Polly's autograph albums. Sheryl Spigel found Polly's probate records in Los Angeles (thanks to Suzie Rosmarin Smith for connecting us).

An array of scholars generously shared material and fielded questions, including Burton Peretti, David Stowe, Michael Alexander, Beverly Gage, Christopher Bonanos, Michael Maslin, Truman Fredrick Keefer, David Stenn, Claire Culleton, Elizabeth Alice Clement, Benjamin Feldman, Terry Teachout, James Kaplan, Jessica Pliley, Donald Spoto, James R. Parish, Michael Feinstein, Herbert Mitgang, William Mann, Gary Mamorstein, Ralph Blumenthal, Kevin C. Kirkpatrick, Brad Bigelow, Christian Cippolini, David Amoruso, Paul Devlin, Tony Burton, Brook Babcock, and Lily Nathan. My colleagues from Biographers International Organization (BIO) provided the professional collegiality I'd sorely missed the first time around.

I benefited tremendously from interviews and correspondence with Nathaniel Benchley, Don Bachardy, Scotty Bowers, Lionel D. Friedberg, Buddy DeFranco, Melodye Condos, Max Gershunoff, Patricia Willard, Marie Thurman, Leo Maxwell, Howard Sann, Burton Bernstein, and Patrick D. Hazard. It was a special pleasure to speak with Virginia Faulkner's friends and family, including Alison Chapman, Ron Hull, Steve Cox, and Virginia Knoll. David Black, whose father had close ties to Polly, and his wife, Barbara Weisberg, became close friends and one of the great prizes of this book (thanks to Ariel Swartly for connecting us).

Ten years into this odyssey, in an effort to break the spell of research and turn my focus to composition, I spent the idyllic summer of 2017 in residency at McDowell, Yaddo, and the Saratoga Race Course. Upon my return, Sandra Luckow lent me a lucky gold ring to spur my pace—heaven knows how long this would've taken without it. Throughout all this—indeed, for the last three decades—I relied on the camaraderie and wisdom of my kitchen council, Pamela Haag, Christina Klein, Kathleen M. Newman, and Elizabeth McAlister. My wonderfully supportive father-in-law, Henry Tulgan, deserves extra credit for never asking me when this project would be done; one of my deepest disappointments is that my mother-in-law, Norma Tulgan, a truly passionate reader, did not live to see his unspoken question answered.

As I finally approached the finish line in 2020, Gabrielle Colangelo served as my amanuensis when the Yale libraries shut down due to COVID-19, checking every quotation and citation. Photographers Beth Dixson and Karissa Van Tassel took my author photos. The team at RainmakerThinking—Cheryl

Wolansky, Kimberly Math, and Liz Richards—helped at every turn. At Doubleday I owe special thanks to editorial assistant Nora Grubb, production editor Nora Reichard, cover designer John Fontana, and editor in chief Bill Thomas, among many others.

Susan Rabiner, my brilliant, indefatigable literary agent, was also at the table that fateful night. She could have—arguably should have—suggested a more sensible path. Instead she supported my choices at every turn, never once betraying impatience or skepticism, even when I clearly deserved it. Without her iron backing, I'd have crumbled more than once.

My editor Gerald Howard rivaled Susan in his endurance, enthusiasm, and faith. Gerry has been my unwavering advocate from the day I met him to the day he retired—one week after I turned in the final manuscript in December 2020—and I owe him more than I can ever repay. In another stroke of luck, Gerry's able successor at Doubleday, Thomas Gebremedhin, has graciously shepherded the book to its debut.

But the most glorious figure in this hall of heroes is my husband, Bruce Tulgan. Now, as I draw this odyssey to a close, I am struggling to find words extravagant enough to express my fathomless love and profound gratitude for him. Of all my good fortune, finding Bruce has been the greatest. Over the thirteen years I spent burrowed in the library, he exhibited superhuman grace and good humor, indulging my quixotic obsession even when it stretched beyond reason. To borrow a phrase from the Jews: *Dayanu*—if that were all he'd done, it would be more than enough to earn him pride of place. But for thirty-six years, Bruce has been the rock on which I've built my life, serving as inspiration, comfort, and conscience and as my tireless champion. You are the best, most lovable and loving person I've ever met, Bruce, and I am the luckiest person in the world.

This book is dedicated to Julie and Paul Applegate. An unlikely choice of subject to dedicate to my parents, one might observe, although perhaps not much better than the libidinous minister of my first book. But it isn't so improbable. My father was a devoted Hemingway buff while my mother quoted Dorothy Parker from memory, and I learned at their knees to love wisecracking bookishness and playful unconventionality. They modeled that all-too-rare combination of kindness, curiosity, and broadmindedness that F. Scott Fitzgerald captured in the opening lines of *The Great Gatsby*, and that has served as a beacon as I traipsed through the dark underbelly of human nature. Their unconditional love made me feel like the world was mine to have and hold, in all its pain and glory. I love you both beyond measure and will spend the rest of our lives repaying your great gifts to me.

Notes

List of Abbreviations

Com14   Committee of Fourteen Records, New York Public Library, Manuscripts and Archives

PA   Polly Adler

PA-FBI   FBI Files for Pearl "Polly" Adler file #31-64473 and #31-44249; "White Slave Traffic in the NYC," file #31-HQ-47863, National Archives and Records Administration

VF   Virginia Faulkner

VF-HNH   Virginia Faulkner's *House Is Not a Home* private archive

Watkins   Watkins Loomis Records, Columbia University Rare Books and Manuscripts Library

Yizkor   *Yanow Near Pinsk Memorial Book*

1. From Nobody to a Legend

2   "palaces of joy": *Morning Telegraph*, July 10, 1927.

3   "suicide, divorce": Dempsey, *Jack Dempsey*, 7.

3   "still don't": PA to VF, October 13, 1951, VF notebook, 14, VF-HNH.

3   "hate pimps": Adler, *House*, 139.

3   "Party Era": Sylvester, *No Cover Charge*, 168.

4   "live himself": Kahn, *Flame of Pure Fire*, 118.

4   "sugaring": Evensen, *When Dempsey Fought Tunney*, 49.

4   "movement money": Lardner, *White Hopes and Other Tigers*, 66.

4   "without exposure": Evensen, *When Dempsey Fought Tunney*, xiv.

4   "by a skirt": Page, *Behind the Curtains*, 143.

5   "a real champ": Walker and Reichler, *Mickey Walker*, 112.

5   "Queen Madam": Ibid.

5   "in the teeth": Adler, *House*, 31.

5 "decent man": Ibid., 67.
6 "called whorehouses": Walker, *Danton's Inferno*, 84–85.
6 "family-run delicatessen": Drutman, *Good Company*, 212.
6 "longshoreman": Levant, *Memoirs of Amnesiac*, 114.
6 "'calling me mister'": Robert de Roos, unpublished typescript biography of Jimmy Van Heusen, 21–22.
7 "Romanoff in drag": O'Hara, *Selected Letters*, 433.
7 "about it much": Robert de Roos, unpublished typescript biography of Jimmy Van Heusen, 21–22.
7 "Big Shots": Sylvester, *No Cover Charge*, 128.
7 "be a madam": Adler, *House*, 74.
7 "house of assignation": Ibid., 251.
7 "clean living!": Lerner, *Dry Manhattan*, 40.
8 "Gomorrah": *Current Opinion*, April 1920, 523–24.
8 "And the high": Adler, *House*, 5.
9 "it's for keeps": Ibid., 282.
9 "came to me": Ibid., 285.
10 "has ever seen": *Variety*, August 24, 1927, 2.
10 "wanted to spend": Ibid.
11 "King of the Bootleggers": *New York Times*, February 2, 1934, 9.
11 "business entertainment": Sylvester, *Notes of Guilty Bystander*, 256.
12 "her benefactor": "Special Adler Supplement," 4, VF-HNH.
12 "a little vacation": *New York Times*, December 11, 1946.
12 "Wise Men of Gotham": *New York Sun*, July 17, 1927.
13 "Rolls-Royce cars": Adams, *Great American Sports Stories*, 151.
14 "Quitter!": Rice, *Tumult and Shouting*, 133.
14 "ill-scented finish": *The Messenger* (Madisonville, KY), July 23, 1927, 2.
14 "Battle of the Strange Coincidences": *Baltimore Sun* (Maryland), July 23, 1927, 10.
14 "be a whore": *People Today*, November 5, 1952, 62.
14 "New Women": Nelson, *New Woman Reader*, xi.
15 "they did me?": *Cedar Rapids Gazette* (Iowa), September 7, 1964, 27.
15 "pleasure towels": PA to VF, January 25, 1952, VF notebook, 45, VF-HNH.
15 "Showboat": PA to VF, various dates, VF notebook, VF-HNH.
16 "spectacular figure": *Variety*, July 27, 1923.
17 "snatch racket": Sullivan, *Snatch Racket*.
17 "painted slut": PA to VF, December 10, 1951, VF notebook, 51, VF-HNH.
17 "in the bedroom": Adler, *House*, 117.
17 "used to tell it": Ibid., 101.
17 Christopher Confrey: Minutes of the Magistrate's Court, 9th District Manhattan, July 22, 1927, 31:15, Municipal Archives, City of New York.
18 "gorgeous color": Adler, *House*, 100.
18 "back to the house": Ibid., 101.
18 "District Attorney": Chin, *New York City Police Corruption Investigation Commissions*, 3:86.
18 "horse to lose": Moley, *Tribunes of the People*, 46.
19 "be your client": Adler, *House*, 101.

2. Man Plans, God Laughs

21 "own importance": Adler, *House*, 7.

21 "Wandering Jew": Ibid., 8.

22 "suffered from wanderlust": David Krikun, interview by author, June 6, 2012.

22 "authority on everything": Adler, *House*, 8.

22 "on my pop": Ibid., 9.

23 "bowled over": Ibid., 9.

23 "demonstrative and outgoing": Ibid., 15.

23 "what went on": Ibid., 10.

23 " 's *past nisht*": Katz, *Shtetl*, 293.

24 "useful": Freeze and Harris, *Everyday Jewish Life*, 1.

24 "yellow ticket": Nathans, *Beyond the Pale*, 91.

24 "on her back": Kumove, *Words Like Arrows*, 215.

24 "against us?": Baron, *Treasury of Jewish Quotations*, 209.

24 "Jew hatred": Chanes, *Antisemitism*, 150.

25 "specifically permitted": Samuel, *World of Sholom Aleichem*, 4–5.

26 "devastation": Dowty, *Arabs and Jews*, 64.

26 "legislative pogroms": Dubnow and Shapiro, *History of Jews*, 309.

27 "all Jewish town": Khlavna Katsikovitz, "My Home Town (Memories)," *Ivanovo*, Yizkor.

28 "*bim-bam*": Yona Kravetz, "Yanov and its Jews," *Ivanovo*, Yizkor.

28 "for a living": Tsemach Portnoy, "Jewish Life in Yanov Near Pinsk," *Ivanovo*, Yizkor.

28 "business among Goyim": Kumove, *Words Like Arrows*, 106.

28 "get along with": Mordechai Bezdesky, "My Memoirs," *Ivanovo*, Yizkor.

28 "contemptuous friendliness": Samuel, *World of Sholom Aleichem*, 136.

29 "wild singing": Pinchas Katzikovitz, "Memories," *Ivanovo*, Yizkor.

29 "from the homes": Ibid.

30 "lineage of learning": Kotik and Assaf, *Journey to Shtetl*, 400.

30 "out of thin air": Dimont, *Jews, God, and History*, 362.

30 "become a prostitute?": Glenn, *Daughters of the Shtetl*, 17.

30 "Jewish tongues": Kumove, *Words Like Arrows*, xix.

31 "public gatherings": Book of Sirach 42:9–11, https://biblia.com/books/nrsv/Sir42.9-11.

31 "a woman": *Tractate Berakoth*, 84.

31 "second best": Adler, *House*, 10.

31 "noble eagle": Smadar Gilboa, interviews by author, January 2012.

32 "turned upside down": Yona Kravetz, "Yanov and its Jews," *Ivanovo*, Yizkor.

32 "very outgoing": Julian Dorian, interview by author, May 10, 2012.

33 "boss of the house": Ibid.

33 "between them": Adler, *House*, 7.

33 "well off": Ibid., 8.

34 "get an education": Ibid., 10.

34 "stuffed with banknotes": Weinberg, *World of Our Mothers*, 5.

34 "well educated": Antin, *Promised Land*, 111.

34 "not earners": Weinberg, *World of Our Mothers*, 9.

35   "teaching her promiscuity": Talmud, Tractate, Sotah 21b, Parush, 62.
35   "than a pogrom": Vital, *A People Apart*, 530.
35   "cringing peddlers": *New York Times*, October 2, 1903, 5.
36   "Beat the Jews!": Ansky, *Enemy at His Pleasure*, 5.
38   "names of the seasons": Antin, *Promised Land*, 18, 26.
38   "public school": Khlavna Katsikovits, "My Home Town (Memories)," *Ivanovo*, Yizkor.
38   "hour a day": Sarah Mednick, "A Collection of Memories," *Ivanovo*, Yizkor, 88.
38   "lives settled": Khlavna Katsikovits, "My Home Town (Memories)," *Ivanovo*, Yizkor.
39   "Gymnazia at Pinsk": Adler, *House*, 10.
39   "the Rabbi": Ibid.
39   "plenty of children": Goldman, *Living My Life*, 1:12.
39   "lead to Pinsk": Adler, *House*, 10.
40   "in installments": Ibid., 10–11.
41   "ice with father": Ibid., 11.
41   "Jewish girls": Lederhendler, *Jewish Responses to Modernity*, 217–18.
41   "on my way": Adler, *House*, 11.
42   "out the window": Ibid.
43   "one only": Adler, *House*, 12.
44   "the saying goes—good": Ibid., 12–13.
44   "Golden Land": Ibid., 13.

3. The Jazz Baby

47   "do was cry": Adler, *House*, 14.
47   "was petrified": Ibid.
48   "Isle of Tears": Epstein, *At the Edge of a Dream*, 34.
48   "white slave traders": Sorin, *Time for Building*, 48.
49   "move a muscle": Adler, *House*, 13.
49   "waved good-bye": Ibid., 13–14.
49   "city of 100,000": Graves, *Progressive Springfield*, 30.
49   "percent pep": Lewis, *Babbitt*, 652.
50   "City of Progress": Graves, *Progressive Springfield*, 30, 5.
50   "in Springfield": *Jewish Advocate*, July 31, 1914, 1.
51   "within myself": Adler, *House*, 15.
51   "Illiterate Adults": *Springfield Annual School Statistics, 1913–1914*, Chestnut Street Evening School, October 6, 1913, to March 26, 1914 term, admitted December 15, 1913, Springfield History Library. *Municipal Register of the City of Springfield for 1917*, Springfield 1917, Springfield History Library.
52   "the saving one": Adler, *House*, 15.
52   "made fun of me": Ibid.
52   "he relented": Ibid.
54   "in the World": Barrett, *Irish Way*, 23.
54   "about those years": Adler, *House*, 16.
54   bloodsucking bribes: *Jewish Advocate*, June 24, 1914.
55   ARMAGEDDON HAS BEGUN: *Springfield Republican*, August 2, 1914.
55   "of a factory?": Adler, *House*, 16.

56 "Pass the mustard, Rivke": Adler, *House*, 16.
57 "cold fish": Ibid.
57 "a *balaboosta*": David Krikun, interview by author, June 6, 2012.
57 "cheapest ghetto": Kazin, *Walker in the City*, 12.
57 "Jerusalem of America": Landesman, *Brownsville*, 208.
58 "illiteracy and hoodlumism": *Commentary*, May 1950, 158.
58 "six an hour": Aaronson and Hirshberg, *High as My Heart*, 24.
58 "by mistake": Aaronson and Hirshberg, *High as My Heart*, 12.
58 "living in Brownsville": *Commentary*, May 1950, 158.
58 "place of God": Howe, *World of Our Fathers*, 181.
58 "since there was none": Golden, *The Right Time*, 22.
59 "more democratic": Peellaert and Herr, *The Big Room*, 12.
60 "sleep fully dressed": Ibid., 17–18.
60 "bit of a rounder": Ibid., 19.
60 "bowl of water": Ibid.
61 "in this country": Glenn, *Daughters of the Shtetl*, 157.
61 "nifty stepper": Adler, *House*, 19–20.
62 "amateur nights": Ibid., 21.
62 "Fifth Avenue combined": Lazar and Tapert, *Swifty*, 20.
62 "Poor Man's Eden": Fowler, *Schnozzola*, 16.
62 "get hugged": Peiss, *Cheap Amusements*, 134.
62 "Sodom by the Sea": Pilat and Ranson, *Sodom by the Sea*, 5.
63 "got in Dutch": Durante and Kofoed, *Night Clubs*, 48.
63 "away from it": Kazin, *Walker in the City*, 12.
63 "big leagues": Turkus and Feder, *Murder, Inc.*, 8.
64 "our own boss": Lazar and Tapert, *Swifty*, 23–25.
64 "equally respectable": Burns and Fisher, *All My Best Friends*, 20.
64 "get husbands": Nash and Frazier, *Private Side of American History*, v. 2, 125.
64 "string quartets": David Krikun, interview by author, October 24, 2012.
65 "wanted finery": Adler, *House*, 18.
65 "unpent myself": Ibid., 19.
65 "pair of drawers": Ibid.
66 "The Vamp": Golden, *Vamp*, 55.
66 "trifle plump": Sicherman and Green, *Notable American Women*, 51.
66 "flapper": Allen, *City in Slang*, 69.
66 "as I please": Woods and Kennedy, *Young Working Girls*, 37.
66 "treating": Parascandola and Parascandola, *Coney Island Reader*, 117.
67 "spent $2.55": Peiss, *Passion and Power*, 65.
67 "in the trolley": *Survey*, July 3, 1909, 487.
67 "we all gotta!": Laughlin, *Work-a-day Girl*, 50.
67 "charity girls": Clement, *Love for Sale*, xvii.
67 "that family!": *Commentary*, August 1949, 174.
68 "Little Berlin": Khlavna Katsikovits, "My Home Town (Memories)," *Ivanovo*, Yizkor.
68 "in my position": PA to VF, December 10, 1951, VF notebook, 5, VF-HNH.
69 "hours or minutes": Clement, *Love for Sale*, 144.
69 "something for us": Ibid., 151.
70 "nothing to chance": Adler, *House*, 21.

70 "dancing sinful": Ibid., 22.

70 "'the deal at once'": Ibid.

70 "attentions were honorable": Ibid.

71 "our poverty": Ibid., 22–23.

71 "Willie Bernstein": Ibid., 23.

71 "almost strangled": Ibid.

72 "of all time": Ibid., 24.

72 "We all did": Frances Friedman, interview by author, July 6, 2012.

73 "knocked me cold": Adler, *House*, 24–25.

73 "could handle it": Ibid., 25.

73 "of his office": Ibid.

74 perform the procedure: Kaplan and Moore, *Gender and Jewish History*, 253.

74 "had hope": Adler, *House*, 26.

75 "what ails you": Ibid.

76 "happens to me": Ibid., 27–28.

76 "fifteen cents": Ibid., 28.

77 "for years": Richman and Gehman, *Hell of a Life*, 26.

77 "the same age": Frances Friedman, interview by author, July 6, 2012.

77 "and went": Adler, *House*, 28–29.

77 "gotten was older": Ibid.

4. What's a Nice Girl Like You Doing in a Place Like This?

79 "in the sun": Adler, *House*, 23.

80 "rogues and panders": Mencken, *Mencken's America*, 107–8.

82 "Gashouse District": Marcuse, *This Was New York*, 50.

82 "and his family": Adler, *House*, 29.

83 "in which to reside": Adler, *House*, 30.

83 "fairies": Chauncey, *Gay New York*, 60.

83 "Jewish Rialto": Marcuse, *This Was New York*, 34.

83 "old Fourth Ward": Josephson, *Al Smith*, 57.

84 "Second Ave.": "Report on Street Conditions on Second Avenue from Houston to Fourteenth Street," May 13, 1920, Box 34, Folder 1920, Com14.

84 "*Second Avenue Man*": Fried, *Rise and Fall of Jewish Gangster*, 5.

84 "not to interfere": "Report on Second Avenue Between Houston and Fourteenth Street," May 12, 1920, Box 34, Folder 1920, Com14.

84 "sink so low": Adler, *House*, 30.

84 "three times a day": Gay, *Unfinished People*, 154.

84 "Trio Corset Company": Adler, *House*, 30.

85 "strikers in history": *New York Evening World*, August 12, 1919, 3.

86 "above water": Adler, *House*, 30–31.

86 "eye opener": Ibid., 32.

86 "Yinglish": Shepard and Levi, *Live and Be Well*, 12.

87 "Gilded Ghetto": Shoenfeld, *Joy Peddler*, 99.

87 "*good* about yourself": Adler, *House*, 33.

87 "by taking it": Ibid., 34.

87 "their damn business": Ibid., 103.

88 "their entertainment": [Blair], *Madeleine*, 71.

88 "to our guests": Kimball, *Her Life*, 60.
88 "a hustler": PA to VF, October 13, 1951, VF notebook, 4, VF-HNH.
88 "girl of nineteen": Adler, *House*, 31.
88 "more gracious life": *Pageant*, Nov. 1953, 51.
89 "to be prostitutes": Granlund, *Blondes, Brunettes*, 33.
89 "is a lay": "Speakeasy-Night Club Report on Figaro Club, Inc., 200 East 85th Street," January 10, 1931, Box 35, Folder 1931, Com14.
90 "cohabited with her": Keller, *Inns and Outs*, 91.
90 "professional seduction": Gilfoyle, *City of Eros*, 175.
90 "an underworld": Henry A. Whitmarsh, "The Doctor and Citizenship," *New England Medical Gazette* 49 (1914): 351.
90 "racket mentality": Heyl, *Madam as Entrepreneur*, 200.
90 "changing her mind": Okun, *Woman Abuse*, 133.
91 "much more?": Rosen, *Lost Sisterhood*, 148.
91 "turn out blues": Barbara Sherman Heyl, "The Madam as Teacher: The Training of House Prostitutes," *Social Problems* 24, no. 5 (June 1977): 552.
91 "lack of hope": Adler, *House*, 128.
92 "Riverside Drive": Ibid., 32.
92 "class of hoodlums": Sutton and Reynolds, *I, Willie Sutton*, 76, 78.
92 "unlawful purposes": *New York Times*, March 5, 1920, 17.
93 "72nd Street?": Kisseloff, *You Must Remember This*, 182.
94 "for it constantly": Adler, *House*, 34. Polly is probably referring to "In the Valley of the Moon," composed by Jeff Brannen, published in 1914.
95 Sucker Street: Lait and Mortimer, *New York: Confidential!*, 19–27.
95 "Sunday afternoon": Heimer, *Big Drag*, 145.
96 "control of Hebrews": *New Age Magazine*, May 1913, 434.
96 "Beauty Trust": Page, *Behind the Curtains*, 61.
97 "beautiful girls": Glenn, *Female Spectacle*, 157.
97 "sex and business": Hirsch, *Boys from Syracuse*, 100.
97 "made them happy": Ibid.
97 "guilty this way": Ibid., 156.
98 "don't you know?": Adler, *House*, 35.
98 "another gag": Ibid., 35.
98 "rich people": Courtwright, Joseph, and Des Jarlais, *Addicts Who Survived*, 95.
99 "awful male hands": Smith, *No Bed of Roses*, 211.
99 "have to stop": Adler, *House*, 35.
99 "a letdown": Ibid., 35–36.
100 "by the parties": Ibid., 36.
100 "Wall Street man": Ibid.
100 "be a stenographer": *Carlsbad Current Argus* (New Mexico), October 5, 1979, 11.
100 "Riverside Drive": Loos, *Talmadge Girls*, 39.
100 "big time": Sutton and Reynolds, *I, Willie Sutton*, 83–84.
101 "votes Republican": Lippitt, *History of Class of 1909*, 3:262–63.
102 "in the world": Adler, *House*, 37.
103 "miss anything": Ibid., 36.
104 "years to come": Ibid., 37.
104 "me marrying": Ibid., 38.
104 "out of there": Ibid., 39.

5. Liquor and Lust

108 "the Rialto": Chauncey, *Gay New York*, 142.

108 "the Tenderloin": Gilbert, *Product of Our Souls*, 102.

108 "the brothel": Roe, *Great War on White Slavery*, 319.

109 "in New York": Ibid., 41.

109 "at leisure": Walker, *Night Club Era*, ix.

109 "Booze and Cunts": "Third One," January 3, 1920, Box 34, Folder 1920, Com14.

109 "a speakeasy": *New York Times*, April 5, 1929, 1.

110 "quick step": *Variety*, December 29, 1926, 35.

110 "army of vice": Woolston, *Prostitution in the United States*, 1:38.

110 "vice ring": *New York Times*, March 5, 1920, 17.

110 "disorderly women": *New York Times*, March 7, 1920, 15.

110 "woman racket": New York *Daily News*, December 7, 1930, 32.

111 "big-time pimp": Stern, *No Innocence Abroad*, 36–37.

111 fresh talent: Roe, *Great War on White Slavery*, 85.

111 "for his mistress": *Pageant*, November 1953, 51.

111 "his offer": Adler, *House*, 40.

112 "tempered with sadness": Ibid.

112 "Broadway than Cinderella": *New York Times*, May 25, 1920, 18.

113 "as a madam": Adler, *House*, 42.

113 "eyes wide open": *Pageant*, November 1953, 51.

113 "paid my rent": Ibid.

113 "decision for you": Adler, *House*, 40.

114 "running the country": Ibid., 48–49.

114 "single standard": Pliley, *Policing Sexuality*, 22.

114 "standard of drinking": Putnam, *Nonsenseorship*, 70.

115 "manifestation of 1921": *New York Times*, February 27, 1921, 15.

115 "sort of dancing?": *New York Times*, February 5, 1922, 25.

115 "suspicions it arouses": Cahalane, *The Policeman*, 273.

116 "legitimate enterprise": Adler, *House*, 44.

116 "back to Russia": Benjamin Adler, deportation hearing transcript, Dec. 19, 1919, RG 85, Records of the Immigration & Naturalization Service, Entry 9, File No. 54719/18, National Archives Building, Washington, D.C.

117 "corset factory": Adler, *House*, 43.

117 " '*Bliad!*' ": Ibid., 42–43.

118 "age of thirteen": Ibid., 53.

118 "costs no more": Ibid.

119 "*Morning Telegraph*": *Baltimore Sun*, March 3, 1921, 6.

119 "insinuating saxophones": Cromwell and Dougherty, *Dirty Helen*, 153.

119 "go-betweens": Committee of Fourteen, *Annual Report 1913*, 24.

119 "Astor corridors": *Broadway Brevities*, December 1, 1921, 14.

119 "ladies of leisure": Ibid.

119 "for a friend": Cooper, *Here's to Crime*, 178–79.

120 "tired businessmen": Cantu, *American Cinderellas*, 45.

120 "to the community": *New York Age*, July 7, 1923, 1.

121 "strong enough": McAllister and Miller, *The Kind of Guy I Am*, 87.

121 Polly's house: Adler, *House*, 45.

121 "flesh and blood": Ibid., 46.

122 "seemed so bad": Ibid.

122 "back to Ohio": Ibid., 46–47.

122 "bed with them": Ibid., 47.

123 "musical comedy": *Variety*, December 17, 1920, 12.

123 "man in the world": New York *Daily News*, March 18, 1927, 49.

123 "give her name": New York *Daily News*, August 28, 1925, 25.

123 "beautiful smile": Adler, *House*, 47.

123 "following week": Ibid., 47.

124 "when she died": Ibid.

124 "the prostitutes": Ibid., 43.

124 "Pearl Howard": Minutes of the Magistrate's Court, 9th District Manhattan, December 7, 1920, 27:145, Municipal Archives, City of New York.

125 "sentenced by a lady": Mitgang, *Man Who Rode the Tiger*, 192.

126 "Second Avenue?": Adler, *House*, 44.

126 "legitimate enterprise": Ibid.

127 "of the city": *New York Times*, January 1, 1921, 1.

127 "intense than before": Ibid.

127 "kind of celebration": Ibid.

127 "miniature Broadway": *New York Times*, January 9, 1921, 1.

128 "guess right": Ibid.

128 "act as bearers": *New York Times*, January 1, 1921, 1.

128 "special friend": *New York Herald Tribune*, March 14, 1931, 1.

129 "body snatchers": Van Raalte, *Vice Squad*, 53.

129 "Incorrigible Girls": Minutes of the Magistrate's Court, 9th District Manhattan, January 16, 1921, 27:166, Municipal Archives, City of New York.

129 "vice cop": Cooper, *Here's to Crime*, 242.

130 "The System": Hartshorn, *I Have Seen the Future*, 117.

130 "Siberia": Valentine, *Night Stick*, 18.

131 "Thou Shalt Not Squeal": *Collier's*, November 9, 1912, 10.

131 "beating you up": Ahearn, *How to Commit*, 17, 29.

132 "wise and cautious": Ibid., 60.

132 "and at play": McGowan, *Motor City Madam*, 63.

132 "Subway Circuit": Salwen, *Upper West Side*, 150.

133 "came in handy": *Pageant*, November 1953, 53.

133 "evening's pleasure": Adler, *House*, 44.

134 "house breakers": Carey and McLellan, *Memoirs of Murder Man*, 190.

134 "second-story man": *Real Estate Magazine*, July 1915, 83.

135 "a long time": *Brooklyn Daily Eagle*, July 9, 1921, 2.

135 "was going on": Ahearn, *How to Commit*, 63.

135 "legal books": McAllister and Miller, *Kind of Guy I Am*, 68.

135 "third degree": Thomas and Blanshard, *What's the Matter*, 130.

135 "press notices": Sutton and Linn, *Where the Money Was*, 52.

135 "where he is": *Daily Star* (Brooklyn), July 8, 1921.

135 "Pearl Koval": Benjamin Adler, July 12, 1921–January 17, 1925, Inmate admission register, *Sing Sing Prison, 1852–1938*, Box 31, Volume 73, New York State Archives.

136 "Old Sparky": Galvin, *Old Sparky*.

136   "boarding house": Goodnow, *Market for Souls*, 40.
136   "Sing Sing": McAllister and Miller, *Kind of Guy I Am*, 77.
136   "college for crooks": *Indiana Gazette*, June 30, 1926, 16.
137   "Pearl Davis": Magistrates' Court Docket Books, 9th District, Manhattan, July 19, 1921, 27:255, Municipal Archives, City of New York.
137   "from the Bronx": Dewey, *Later Works of Dewey*, 373.
137   "couple of judges": Mooney, *Crime Incorporated*, 4–5.
137   "Perjury Perch": Van Raalte, *Vice Squad*, 65.
137   "his own protection": *New York Times*, November 25, 1930, 23.
138   "businesslike way": Adler, *House*, 44.
139   "country-wide chain": Ibid., 51.
139   "lingerie shops": *New York Times*, December 4, 1921, 18.
140   "scanties": Doherty, *Pre-code Hollywood*, 111.
140   "hosiery shop": *Trow's General Directory*, 133:1421; *Women's Wear Daily*, June 28, 1922, 45.
140   "marked woman": Adler, *House*, 50.
140   Jean Norris: Minutes of the Magistrate's Court, 9th District Manhattan, July 22, 1922, 28:90, Municipal Archives, City of New York.
141   "Czar": *New York Times*, January 15, 1922, 1.
141   "rabid hatred": Walker, *Night Club Era*, 167.
141   "bends backward": *New York Times*, March 16, 1933, 3.
141   "rabbi": Valentine, *Night Stick*, 24.
141   "window display": Adler, *House*, 51.
141   "run my shop": PA to VF, October 9, 1951, VF notebook, 5, VF-HNH.
142   "largely of shoplifters": Adler, *House*, 51.
142   "police at night": Cromwell and Dougherty, *Dirty Helen*, 135.
143   "keep up expenses": PA to VF, October 13, 1951, VF notebook, 13, VF-HNH.
143   "they were friends": Adler, *House*, 54.
143   "poker games": Allen, *City in Slang*, 170.
144   "of the take": Adler, *House*, 54.
144   "called the hand": Ibid., 54.
144   "Playing the Tip": James, *It Was Never a Gamble*, 47.
145   "grift sense": Maurer, *The Big Con*, 142.
145   "villain's paradox": Gambetta, *Codes of Underworld*, 30.
145   "skin game": Katcher, *Big Bankroll*, 122.
145   "can be taken": Adler, *House*, 54–55.
145   "really heeled": Ibid., 55.

6. Thumbs Up with the Mob

147   "I'm busy": Carroll, *In Your Hat*, 19–20.
148   "saved for dinner": Ibid., 20–21.
148   "failure in life": Ibid., 22, 16.
148   "know well": Adler, *House*, 32.
149   "do not offend": Pietrusza, *Rothstein*, 3.
149   "the underworlds": Rothstein, *Now I'll Tell*, 42.
150   "money with interest": Ibid., 73.
150   "United States": Thompson and Raymond, *Gang Rule*, 55.

150 "to be whispered": Rothstein, *Now I'll Tell*, 208–9.

150 "breach of promise": McLaren, *Sexual Blackmail*, 95.

150 "fixer": U.S. Task Force on Assessment, *Task Force Report*, 100.

150 "air-brush of legality": Betts, *Across the Board*, 223.

150 "call flats": Ibid.

151 "every known racket": Reeve, *Golden Age of Crime*, 135.

151 "opium vampires": Mulhall, *Opium*, 56.

151 "rum or narcotics": Reeve, *Golden Age of Crime*, 131.

152 "good madam": Adler, *House*, 317.

152 "in all America": Ibid., 60.

152 "'get-rich-quick' kick": Ibid., 144.

152 "Baron of Yorkville": Shipton, *I Feel a Song*, 72.

152 "goulash houses": Betts, *Across the Board*, 101.

152 "in the world": Fried, *Rise and Fall of Jewish Gangster*, 4.

153 "religion—profit": Sifakis, *Mafia Encyclopedia*, 393.

153 "mercenary spirit": Ruth, *Inventing Public Enemy*, 55.

153 "major scale": Lacey, *Little Man*, 49.

153 "Manhattan's gangdom": [Recht], *Babylon on Hudson*, 156.

153 "hoodlum aristocracy": Cohn, *Joker Is Wild*, 113.

153 "of the day": Adler, *House*, 55.

154 "pick-pocket days": PA to VF, October 9, 1951, VF notebook, 11, VF-HNH.

154 "benefactor": "Special Adler Supplement," 4, VF-HNH.

154 "sense of humor": Katz, *Uncle Frank*, 63.

154 "named Daisy": *New York*, May 13, 1974, 47.

155 "other than gentlemanly": PA to VF, December 10, 1995, VF notebook, 7, VF-HNH.

155 "ready to croak!": Adler, *House*, 295.

156 "Notre Dame?": Gosch and Hammer, *Last Testament of Luciano*, 25.

156 "spotlight on him": PA to VF, December 15, 1951, VF notebook, 24, VF-HNH.

156 "very tough": Nown, *Arkansas Godfather*, 77.

157 "strike out": Heimer, *Big Drag*, 101.

157 "Smiling George": *Herald Tribune*, August 30, 1940, 32.

158 "slow pay": *New York Times*, October 14, 1975, 56.

158 "paid the bill": Adler, *House*, 56.

159 "piece of change": Ibid., 56.

159 "of the damned": *Herald and Review* (Decatur, Ill.), July 31, 1939, 4.

159 "on the chin": Adler, *House*, 60.

159 "with the mob": PA to VF, n.d., VF notebook, 27, VF-HNH.

160 "still alive": Adler, *House*, 55.

160 "on someone else": Ibid., 56.

160 "my expense": PA to VF, December 10, 1951, VF notebook, 13, VF-HNH.

160 "paper my garage": PA to VF, October 13, 1951, VF notebook, 17, VF-HNH.

160 "told to me": Ibid., 13.

160 "bake a cake": Adler, *House*, 56.

160 "gentleman when sober": PA to VF, December 10, 1951, VF notebook, 13, VF-HNH.

161 "brought them luck": Adler, *House*, Ibid.

161 "with relief": Ibid., 58.

162 "get even": Ibid., 56.

162 "lying to them": Ibid., 58–59.

163 "keep smiling": Ibid.

163 "New York": PA to VF, October 13, 1951, VF notebook, 17, VF-HNH.

163 "pushed around": Adler, *House*, 59.

164 "of All Nations": "Parlor House of Prostitution," April 1, 1932, Box 35, Folder 1932, Com14.

164 "torture chamber": Adler, *House*, 300.

164 "references were required": Weegee, "Sex with a Cover Charge," unpublished manuscript, Weegee Archive, International Center of Photography.

164 "awful looking creature": Bristow, *Prostitution and Prejudice*, 148–49.

164 "big mouth": Murtagh and Harris, *Cast the First Stone*, 299.

164 "known for it": Inspectors reports, December 19, 1930, Box 35, Folder 1931, 1932, Com14.

165 "for the body": Adler, *House*, 61.

165 "use the bathroom": PA to VF, October 13, 1951, VF notebook, 13, VF-HNH.

165 "like a flea": Adler, *House*, 61.

165 "Madam X": Ibid., 61–62.

165 "be let alone": Ibid., 63.

165 "type of businessman": Ibid., 59.

166 "to the top": Ibid., 60.

166 "bad habits in": Chandler, *The Big Sleep*, 33.

166 "sport and entertainment": Powell, *Ninety Times Guilty*, 122.

166 "Clean Burlesque": Shteir, *Striptease*, 72.

167 "king's mistress": Rose, *Wine, Women*, 40.

168 "welcome was Broadway": Ibid.

168 "nightclubs": Peretti, *Nightclub City*, 4.

168 "whisky barrel": Granlund, *Blondes, Brunettes*, 137–38.

168 "was a host": Rose, *Wine, Women*, 40.

168 "bumped off": Granlund, *Blondes, Brunettes*, 139.

169 "in the club": Rose, *Wine, Women*, 42.

169 "goes to money": Partridge, *Dictionary of Catch Phrases*, 146.

169 "cheap people": *Pageant*, November 1953, 51.

169 "fame and glory": Heimer, *Big Drag*, 143.

169 "indoor sport": Adler, *House*, 65.

169 "first-class": *Pageant*, November 1953, 51.

169 "the Ziegfeld": Ibid., 211.

169 "interior decorator": Adler, *House*, 63.

169 "for a house": Ibid., 63.

171 "sex plays": Houchin, *Censorship of the American Theatre*, 98.

171 "flashing her knish": Abbott, *American Rose*, 401.

172 "into the life": Adler, *House*, 138, 114.

172 "please everyone": *Suppressed*, January 1951, 36.

172 "discreet dame": Robert de Roos, unpublished typescript biography of Jimmy Van Heusen, chap. 3, 21–22.

172 "sought after": *Suppressed*, January 1951, 36.

173 "Polly's Follies": Signed photo from "Cora," Adler's photo album, Polly Adler Collection courtesy of Eleanor Vera.

173 "guttersnipe cadences": Weller, *Dancing at Ciro's*, 40.
173 "drinks and cocaine": Amherst, *Wandering*, 102.
173 "would seem jaded": Cohen, *New York Graphic*, 132.
173 "common prostitutes": *Times Record of Troy* (New York), April 17, 1968, 6.
174 "fine pitch": Adler, *House*, 60.
174 "has its drawbacks": Ibid., 61.
174 "at first glance": *New York Times*, May 11, 1924, 4.
175 "about a family": Maas, *Valachi Papers*, 65.
175 "go no further": Gosch and Hammer, *Last Testament of Luciano*, 151.

7. The Double Standard

177 "nonstop party": Adler, *House*, 105.
178 "gone through": Ibid., 105–6.
178 "Broadway appendicitis": Shoenfeld, *Joy Peddler*, 15.
179 "let down their hair": Adler, *House*, 113.
179 "metallic urgency": Fitzgerald, *Great Gatsby*, 19.
179 "kick up a fuss": *Suppressed*, January 1954, 37.
179 "just pretend": *New York Post*, June 9, 1953, Series III, Box 1, Adler Folder, Watkins.
180 "bad women": Bishop, *Hellinger*, 42.
180 "cannot love": Freud, *Sexuality and Psychology of Love*, 52.
180 "hook or crook": Ware, *Greenwich Village*, 111.
181 "look all right": *Esquire*, October 1974, 226–27.
181 "giving it away": *Vanity Fair*, September 2014, 312.
182 "Customers Amendment": Mackey, *Pursuing Johns*, 128.
183 "or their lawyers": Ibid., 145.
183 "legal phraseology": Ibid.
183 "we would go": Ibid., 120.
183 "in New York": Adler, *House*, 65.
183 "successful ones": Ibid., 60.
183 "for the girls": Ibid., 65.
184 "worth of champagne": Sylvester, *Notes of Guilty Bystander*, 10.
184 "upholstered sewer": Gavin, *Intimate Nights*, 50.
184 "damp cave": Fowler, *Schnozzola*, 48.
185 "feelings about it": Ibid., 60.
185 "cash from me": PA to VF, October 9, 1951, VF notebook, 11, VF-HNH.
185 "did they come!": Durante and Kofoed, *Night Clubs*, 123.
185 "of all time": Adler, *House*, 77.
185 "set to music": Chappell, *Restaurants of New York*, 117.
185 "popular they got": Burns and Fisher, *All My Best Friends*, 25–26.
185 "into de act!": Green, *The Great Clowns of Broadway*, 51.
186 "the same time": Cantor, Freedman, and Ardmore, *My Life*, 55–59
186 "bottom layers": Durante and Kofoed, *Night Clubs*, 123–24.
187 "what it meant": "The Wonderful World of Robert Benchley," *Biography in Sound*, May 8, 1956, NBC, https://bit.ly/3cyUEbX.
188 "career like mine": Adler, *House*, 73–74.
188 "deciding on pleasure": Fitzgerald, *My Lost City*, 132.

188   "Slumming": Heap, *Slumming*, 3.
188   "their spies": Stewart, *Stroke of Luck*, 107.
188   "vaudeville with Volstead": *Collier's*, February 6, 1926, 15.
189   "party, fun": McAllister and Miller, *The Kind of Guy I Am*, 97.
189   "American institutions": Cowley, *Exile's Return*, 75.
189   Algonquin Round Table: Fitzpatrick, *The Algonquin Round Table*.
189   "Cult of the Party": Seldes, *The Future of Drinking*, 115.
190   "socially pretentious": Frewin, *The Late Mrs. Dorothy Parker*, 45.
191   "charge account": Strode, *Eleventh House*, 126.
191   "male nymphomaniac": Meredith, *George Kaufman and His Friends*, 559.
191   "compulsive in both": Teichmann, *George S. Kaufman*, 158.
192   bootleg gin: Cerf, *At Random*, 34.
192   "hint of inebriation": Kriendler and Jeffers, *"21,"* 17.
192   "sophisticated nonsense": Baral, *Revue*, 156.
192   "'come in?'": Jenkins, *The Twenties*, 131.
192   "to do that": Sullivan, *Well There's No Harm in Laughing*, 115.
193   "anyone else": Rosmond, *Robert Benchley*, 118.
193   "'toddling along'": Ibid., 117.
193   "comfortably wicked": Wakeman, *Hucksters*, 276.
193   "New Yorkese": Drutman, *Good Company*, 209.
193   "pleasure mit you!": Winchell, *Winchell Exclusive*, 116–17.
193   "whole nature": Adler, *House*, 98.
193   "to Pawly's": Rosmond, *Robert Benchley*, 119.
193   "Duck Lip": Gerald Weales, "Don Stewart's Luck," *Sewanee Review* 85, no. 2 (1977): liii–lvi.
193   "public holiday": Donaldson, *Fitzgerald and Hemingway*, 322.
194   "crazy humor": *New York Times*, December 20, 1925, BR9.
194   "in those days": Frewin, *The Late Mrs. Dorothy Parker*, 66.
194   "creative artists": Hahn, *Romantic Rebels*, 250.
194   "lucky girl": Frewin, *The Late Mrs. Dorothy Parker*, 91.
194   "at his disposal": *Tucson Citizen*, July 7, 1970, 22.
195   "his own business": Altman, *Laughter's Gentle Soul*, 219.
195   "eagerness to learn": Adler, *House*, 94.
196   "New Tammany": *American Mercury*, September 1928, 1–12.
197   "keep Al honest": Slayton, *Empire Statesman*, 205.
197   "has never lifted": Eisenstein and Rosenberg, *Stripe of Tammany's Tiger*, 43.
197   "political machine": Glaeser and Goldin, *Corruption and Reform*, 85.
198   "New Tammany": *American Mercury*, September 1928, 1–12.
198   "pure and simple": Eisenstein and Rosenberg, *Stripe of Tammany's Tiger*, 102.
198   "needed one": Betts, *Across the Board*, 233.
198   "city hearted": White, *Masks in Pageant*, 463.
199   "Tammany hospitality": *New York Times*, June 14, 1924, 1.
199   "convention barrooms": *Pittsburgh Daily Post*, June 14, 1924, 4.
199   "is wet": *Variety*, October 27, 1922, 10.
199   "under cover": *Variety*, October 6, 1922, 10.
199   "derby hat": Loos, *Kiss Hollywood Good-by*, 194.
200   "rolled into one": Granlund, *Blondes, Brunettes*, 127.
200   "hollered for more": Adler, *House*, 72.

201 "now and then": Ibid.
201 "prostipretties": Winchell, *Winchell Exclusive*, 116–17.
201 "up in lights": Adler, *House*, 72.
201 "They were lechers": Marx, *Growing Up with Chico*, 130.
201 "dressing rooms": Chandler, *Hello, I Must Be Going*, 66.
202 "slums of entertainment": Hecht, *Child of the Century*, 405.
202 "Smith glorification meeting": *New York Herald Tribune*, April 23, 1924, 7.
202 "talk intimately with": Caro, *Power Broker*, 285.
203 "off of you": Slayton, *Empire Statesmen*, 209.
203 "political battlefield": *New York Times*, June 27, 1924, 4.
203 "State delegation": Whipple, *Noble Experiment*, 58.
203 "landed in New York": Tucker, *High Tide of Conservatism*, 95.
204 "for their patronage": Adler, *House*, 87.
204 "city in America": *New York Times*, December 23, 1940, 22.
204 "win bets with": Lewin, *How to Win at the Races*, 12.
205 "losing money": Gallico, *Farewell to Sport*, 182–83.
205 "Bootleg Trail": *New York Times*, December 7, 1923, 15.
205 "we were seated": Adler, *House*, 87.
206 "name to cash": PA to VF, December 10, 1951, VF notebook, 13, VF-HNH.
206 "a little drive": Adler, *House*, 87.
206 "to the Jug": PA to VF, October 11, 1951, VF notebook, 12, VF-HNH.
206 "any friends": Ibid.
207 "on the square": Adler, *House*, 88.
207 "thought of being": New York *Daily News*, August 16, 1924, 27.
207 "jock-crazy": Adler, *House*, 87.
208 "into the night": Ibid., 89–90.
208 "in New York": Ibid., 90.
209 "at the house": Ibid., 65–66.
209 "for me there": Levitt and Lowry, *Joe Frisco*, 56.
209 "send-off feed": *Variety*, September 17, 1924, 9.
210 "country mile": Adler, *House*, 66.
210 "a decent man": Ibid., 66–67.

8. The Party Girl Racket

213 "in the trough": Adler, *House*, 69–70.
213 "honky-tonks": *Variety*, October 25, 1925, 40.
213 "angels": O'Connor, *Broadway Racketeers*, 72.
214 "always a crook": Hellinger, *Ten Million*, 221.
215 "goals of life": Adler, *House*, 74.
215 "favorite jockey": PA draft acknowledgments, July 29, 1952, Series II, Box II.7, Folder "Adler, Polly," Watkins.
216 "famous in the underworld": *New York Evening Graphic*, May 7, 1931, 4.
216 "party girl racket": *Variety*, January 15, 1930, 8.
216 "stud book": Berebitsky, *Sex and Office*, 79.
216 "some women?": Ibid., 78.
216 "stag racket": *Variety*, October 13, 1926, 27.
216 "of a woman": Berebitsky, *Sex and Office*, 167.

216   "shared transgression": Gambetta, *Codes of the Underworld*, 72.

216   "great friends": *New York Times*, September 20, 1997, D3.

217   "I hold": Berebitsky, *Sex and the Office*, 16.

217   "virtue reigns": Mooney, *Crime, Incorporated*, 134.

218   "show broads!": Feder and Joesten, *Luciano Story*, 118.

218   "than in bed?": Ibid.

219   "of our anatomy": Miller, *Esquire's Jazz Book*, 8.

219   "a little jazzing": Murtagh and Harris, *Cast First Stone*, 205.

219   "do you?": Investigators reports, Box 36, Folder 49 Street—57th Street, and Box 35, Folder 1930, Com14.

220   "woman shy": Paul Whiteman, unpublished autobiography typescript, 26, Stephen Longstreet Collection, Howard Gottlieb Archival Research Center, Boston University.

220   "in those days": Ibid., 46.

220   "businessman's bounce": Berton, *Remembering Bix*, 364.

220   "out of jazz": Osgood, *So This Is Jazz*, 131.

220   "new dress": Pollack, *George Gershwin*, 296.

220   "boisterous ringmaster": De Long, *Pops*, 328.

220   "get fucked": Ibid., 281.

220   "King of America": *Brooklyn Standard Union*, August 14, 1923, 23.

220   "symphonic syncopation": *Variety*, January 10, 1968, 2.

220   "concert stage?": Paul Whiteman, unpublished autobiography typescript, 153, Stephen Longstreet Collection, Howard Gottlieb Archival Research Center, Boston University.

220   "jazz concerto": Phillips, *Shaping Jazz*, 68.

221   "metropolitan madness": Pollack, *George Gershwin*, 297.

221   "musically elect": Gross, *I Looked and I Listened*, 142.

221   "capital A": Gracyk and Hoffman, *Popular American Recording Pioneers*, 370.

221   "for parties": *New Yorker*, November 27, 1926, 26.

221   "payola": Segrave, *Payola in the Music Industry*.

221   "most performances": Meyer, *The Gold in Tin Pan Alley*, 157.

222   "came to town": *Variety*, March 1, 1972, 57.

222   "fancy house": Ibid.

222   "Hot jazz": Phillips, *Shaping Jazz*, 79.

223   "there tonight": Hasse, *Beyond Category*, 79.

223   "into a church": Balliett, *American Musicians*, 55.

223   "night with pleasure": Ulanov, *Duke Ellington*, 39.

223   "Duke's amazing music": Peress, *Dvořák to Duke Ellington*, 85.

223   "not enemies": Ulanov, *Duke Ellington*, 39.

223   "mixed there": Dance, *The World of Duke Ellington*, 64.

223   "Adler came in": Tucker and Ellington, *The Duke Ellington Reader*, 487.

223   "playing or dancing": Sylvester, *No Cover Charge*, 50.

224   "mob guys": George, *Sweet Man*, 47.

224   "in tips": Lawrence, *Duke Ellington and His World*, 72.

224   "on the side": Ibid.

224   "'Negro music'": Tucker and Ellington, *The Duke Ellington Reader*, 363.

224   "Colored Orchestras": Berrett, *Louis Armstrong and Paul Whiteman*, 150.

224   "interests them": Adler, *House*, 85.

224 "on the gold": Inabinett, *Grantland Rice and His Heroes,* 35.
225 "full of people": Adler, *House,* 85.
225 "H2 to O": Monin, *From Poverty Bay to Broadway,* 158.
226 "getting a slice": New York *Daily News,* March 9, 1925, 22.
226 "fight fan": Adler, *House,* 102.
226 "news viewpoint": Thompson and Raymond, *Gang Rule,* 114.
226 "Sweet Science": Liebling, *The Sweet Science,* 8.
226 "larcenous leprechaun": Kearns and Fraley, *Million Dollar Gate,* xi.
226 "no apology": Hayes, *With the Gloves Off,* 22.
226 "manipulator": Kearns and Fraley, *Million Dollar Gate,* xi.
227 Teddy Hayes: Walker and Reichler, *Mickey Walker,* 91.
227 "New Year's Eve": Kelly, *Shelby's Folly,* 77.
227 "pay for them": Walker and Reichler, *Mickey Walker,* 111.
227 "You sleep with him": PA to VF, October 19, 1951, VF notebook, 12, VF-HNH.
227 "fond of him": Adler, *House,* 86.
227 "Queen Madam": Walker and Reichler, *Mickey Walker,* 112.
228 "noblest artist": Fair, *Give Him to the Angels,* 3.
228 "fresh stuff": Ibid.
229 "by a book": Mitgang, *Once Upon a Time in New York,* 70.
229 "political genius": Hayes, *With the Gloves Off,* 52.
229 "Beau James": Fowler, *Beau James.*
229 "slightly wicked": *American Mercury,* November 1926, 272.
229 "bottle man": Golden, *For Two Cents Plain,* 235.
229 "in Tammany Hall": Fowler, *Beau James,* 36.
229 "with Walker": *Bangor Daily News* (Maine), December 31, 1976, 19.
229 "vote for him": Winchell, *Winchell Exclusive,* 53.
230 "our Jimmy": *Variety,* June 9, 1926, 45.
230 "the nomination": Griffin, *Wise Guy,* 312.
230 "be different": Fowler, *Beau James,* 142.
231 "holiday abroad": Ibid., 142–43.
231 "grow up sometime": Ibid., 144.
231 "Whiteman's fair boy": PA to VF, October 25, 1951, VF notebook, 17, VF-HNH.
232 "out of killing": Reynolds, *Headquarters,* 80.
232 "Hotsy Totsy Club": PA to VF, October 25, 1951, VF notebook, 17, VF-HNH.
233 "quaffing couples": *Variety,* April 13, 1927, 29.
233 "committed matrimony": *Variety,* August 19, 1925, 38.
233 "loved Elenore": PA to VF, October 25, 1951, VF notebook, 17, VF-HNH.
233 "didn't last long": Ibid.
233 "in jail": *Variety,* April 7, 1926, 43.
233 "unauthorized male": *Variety,* April 13, 1927, 29.
233 "guy in bed": PA to VF, October 25, 1951, VF notebook, 17, VF-HNH.
233 "blood poisoning": Rayno, *Paul Whiteman,* 116.
234 "Boy Scouts": Miller, *Supreme City,* 86.
235 "gossamer thread": *Shamokin News Dispatch* (Pennsylvania), September 22, 1925, 7.
235 "string of fillies": *Sports Illustrated,* January 20, 1964, 52.
235 "*Not unusual*": PA to VF, October 19, 1951, VF notebook, 12, VF-HNH.
235 "loaded with dough": Ibid.

235 "remain a champion": New York *Daily News*, January 24, 1926, 2.
235 "almost anywhere": Walker and Reichler, *Mickey Walker*, 112–13.
236 "batting an eye": Ibid., 113.
236 "real dictator": *Buffalo Times* (New York), August 28, 1925, 3.
236 "Dutch": *New York Times*, September 13, 1925, 1.
236 "Our Jimmy": New York *Daily News*, August 31, 1925, 5.
236 "pugilism": *Hartford Courant*, December 17, 1925, 45.
237 "'wide-open' town": *New York Times*, December 17, 1925, 1.
237 "history of Prohibition": *New York Times*, December 4, 1925, 1.
237 "came up": *News Journal*, December 4, 1925, 12.
237 like confetti: Adler, *House*, 80.
238 "fell for one": Ibid., 74.
238 "ornamental females": Ibid., 75.
238 "Stem's establishments": *Bristol Herald Courier* (Tennessee), February 1, 1931, 12.
238 "dance floor": *Variety*, February 25, 1925, 33.
239 "Beauty Brigade": Ibid., 34.
239 "it in me": Adler, *House*, 75.
239 "angel's paradise": *Variety*, February 9, 1927, 49.
239 "Mademoiselle Fifi": Slide, *Vaudeville Criticism*, 74.
240 "at the joke": Adler, *House*, 76.
240 "live forever?": Ibid., 76.
240 "whore-house": Kofoed, *Leg Man in Seven-League Boots*, 35.
240 "without prejudice": Weld, *Fly Away Home*, 86.
241 "School of Reporting": Fuller, *Third Face*, 59–60.
241 "Denver underworld": Smith, *Life and Legend of Fowler*, 196.
241 "favor him": Gabler, *Winchell*, 91.
241 "tinsel aristocracy": Klurfeld, *Winchell*, 47.
241 "Jazz journalism": Gauvreau, *Hot News*, 201.
241 "metropolitan personalities": Kinney, *James Thurber*, 329.
242 "behind-the-scenes atmosphere": Lee, *Defining New Yorker Humor*, 110.
242 "lady in Dubuque": Yagoda, *About Town*, 39.
242 "just read them": Wolcott Gibbs to James Thurber, n.d., James Thurber Papers, Box 2, "Correspondence about Ross" series, Beinecke Library, Yale University.
242 "libel them": Muir, *Headline Happy*, 102–3.
242 "whore house madam": Stuart, *Secret Life of Walter Winchell*, 65.
242 "mob bosses": Klurfeld, *Winchell*, 39.
242 "female seasons": Klurfeld, *Winchell*, 118.
242 "can openers": Walker, *Night Club Era*, 148.
243 "symphonically syncopated": *Wireless Weekly*, October 25, 1929, 13.
244 "do him good": Adler, *House*, 76.
244 "call him": Adler, *House*, 76.
245 "be convicted": Mayer, *Emory Buckner*, 205.
245 "name evaporated": *Brooklyn Eagle*, August 22, 1926, 18A.
245 "caveman tactics": *Variety*, January 20, 1926, 13.
246 "Jew bastard?": Lou Clayton, interview by Gene Fowler, unpublished typescript, 108, Gene Fowler Papers, Special Collections and Archives, University of Colorado Boulder.

246 "laughed at me": Adler, *House*, 81–82.
247 "dead or alive": Ibid.
247 "laughing merrily": Ibid., 83–84.
248 "could retaliate": Ibid.
248 "Big Shots": Sylvester, *No Cover Charge*, 129.
249 "'spend some more'": Adler, *House*, 77.
249 "ugly one at that": Darwin Porter to author, April 15, 2009.
249 "it to me": Adler, *House*, 77.
249 "Broadway usurer": Ibid., 80.
249 "theatrical district": *Billboard*, September 11, 1926, 22.
250 "people would say": Adler, *House*, 77–78.
250 "enough for you": Ibid., 78.
251 "calling him": Ibid., 78–79.
251 "for you": "Charmaine," music by Ernö Rapée, lyrics by Lew Pollack, 1926.
251 "lovesick schoolgirl": Adler, *House*, 79.

9. The Underworld Complex

253 "was cheaper": Fitzgerald, *My Lost City*, 112.
253 "orgy begins": *Brooklyn Times Union*, March 5, 1927, 51.
253 "Jazz Mayor": *Burlington Free Press*, November 6, 1925, 3.
254 "the city loved him": MacKaye, *Tin Box Parade*, 3–4.
254 "care of myself": Moscow, *What Have You Done*, 24.
254 "too tight": *Brooklyn Times Union*, March 5, 1927, 4.
256 "thousand or more": Adler, *House*, 91.
256 "a letup": Ibid., 91.
256 "Showboat": PA to VF, n.d., VF notebook, 58, 58a, 59, VF-HNH.
256 "home with her": Adler, *House*, 65.
256 "serve him": VF to PA, December 10, 1951, VF notebook, 54, VF-HNH.
256 "like the sun!": Adler, *House*, 98.
256 "saw them": Ibid., 91.
257 "live it down!": Ibid., 92–93.
258 "Yale University!": Ibid., 325–26.
258 "any of my girls": Ibid., 93.
259 "as his son": *Suppressed*, January 1954, 37.
259 "theatrical worlds": Adler, *House*, 94.
259 "underworld complex": Runyon, *Bloodhounds of Broadway*, 63.
259 "unsnobbish person": Stewart, *By a Stroke of Luck*, 171.
259 "some prostitutes": Investigators reports, Box 37, Folder "Nightclubs and Speak-easies on Numbered Streets," Com14.
260 "cuff in New York": Sillman, *Here Lies Sillman*, 133.
260 "Polly's phone number": Gardner, *Champagne Before Breakfast*, 42.
261 "New Negro": *Survey-Graphic*, March 1, 1925.
261 "of the race": *New York Times*, March 1, 1925, 6.
261 "Black Way": *Press and Sun Bulletin*, September 29, 1926, 26.
261 "Negrophile": Gehring, "Mr. B.," 162.
261 "black-and-tans": Wintz and Finkelman, *Encyclopedia of the Harlem Renaissance*, 121–22.

261   "he needed it": Lawrence, *Duke Ellington and His World*, 103.

262   "agreeable face": Bel Geddes, *Miracle in the Evening*, 223.

262   "low-down time": Adler, *House*, 73.

262   "go anywhere": Ibid., 228.

262   "right here": Stoddart, *Lord Broadway*, 286.

263   "nurse's uniform?": Porter, *Katharine the Great*, 28–29.

263   "my career": New York *Daily News*, March 18, 1979, 8.

264   "Pearl has!": Frances Friedman, interview by author, July 6, 2012.

264   "rotten ripe": Bradshaw, *Dreams That Money Can Buy*, 77.

264   "Susceptible masculinity": New York *Daily News*, December 11, 1932, 5.

264   "always 'No'": Adler, *House*, 118–19.

264   "How's the schoolgirl?": Ibid., 118.

264   "swelegant syncopator": *Akron Beacon Journal* (Ohio), December 17, 1929, 25.

265   "half-singing": Adler, *House*, 72.

265   "misty-eyed myself": Ibid., 111.

265   "happy juice": Sann, *Lawless Decade*, 190.

265   "'everybody p-p-pays!'": Adler, *House*, 73.

266   "white slavery scare": Keire, *For Business and Pleasure*, 73.

266   "for years": "Kentucky Club, 203 West 49th Street, May 10, 1927," Box 36, Folder "49 St.—57th St.," Com14.

266   "Mademoiselle Fifi": Slide, *Selected Vaudeville Criticism*, 74.

266   "stages 'circuses'": Investigator reports, October 13, 1926, December 2, 1926, December 18, 1927, Box 35, Folder 1927–30, Com14.

267   "Adler Positively": "Tenement at 170 West 77th Street, second floor. Mlle. Fifi Seballe," December 17–18, 1927, Box 35, Folder 1927–30, Com14.

268   "anyone at all": Sutton and Reynolds, *I, Willie Sutton*, 103.

269   "Sidney called": PA to VF, October 13, 1951, VF notebook, 13, VF-HNH.

269   "will I collect?": Ibid.

270   "very pleasant": Adler, *House*, 102.

270   "murder trade": *New York Times*, July 8, 1928, 111.

270   "Murder, Inc.": Turkus and Feder, *Murder, Inc.*

270   "of the evening": Adler, *House*, 295.

270   "really something": PA to VF, October 13, 1941, VF notebook, 14, VF-HNH.

270   "smart money": Ibid.

271   "inside the ring": Dempsey, *Dempsey*, 136.

271   "Long Count": Heimer, *Long Count*.

271   "bet a million": PA to VF, October 13, 1941, VF notebook, 14, VF-HNH.

271   "grand host": Ibid.

272   "Cops": Adler, *House*, 152–53.

273   "out of here": Ibid., 154–55.

274   "Thanks, Polly": Ibid., 159.

274   "was a cop": Ibid., 160.

275   "he-madam": Van Raalte, *Vice Squad*, 137.

275   "in the middle": Adler, *House*, 144.

275   "daisy chain": Investigators reports, February 28, 1928, Box 36, Folder 63rd Street to 85th Street—57 West 75th Street, #92, Com14.

275   "out of his hand": Adler, *House*, 145.

276   "pay up": New York *Daily News*, February 17, 1931, 6.

276 "protection money": New York *Daily News*, September 2, 1931, 10.
276 "afraid of him": *World Telegram*, July 14, 1931, Seabury Investigation scrapbooks, v. 2, Library of the New York City Bar Association.
277 "at a promotion": Adler, *House*, 145–46.
278 "cover up": Ibid., 147–48.
278 "Golden Land?": Ibid., 148–49.
278 "word and thought": Ibid., 150–51.
279 "toes this week": *Morning Telegraph*, June 15, 1928, 1.
279 "here fast": Adler, *House*, 149.
279 "in our car?": Ibid., 149–50.
279 John Weston: Minutes of the Magistrate's Court, 9th District Manhattan, June 15, 1928, 31:296, Municipal Archives, City of New York.
279 "take it": Ibid., 150.
280 "attractive little tart": *New York Times*, January 14, 1982, 1.
280 "all doubts": *New Yorker*, April 9, 1927, 40.
280 "secret harems": Shaffer, *Executive Connection*, 56.
280 "favorite Protestant": Golway, *Frank and Al*, 185.
280 "personal and intimate": Flynn, *You're the Boss*, 67.
281 "pay a check": Lardner and Rapoport, *Lost Journalism of Lardner*, 482.
281 "were fixed": *Los Angeles Times*, June 13, 1983, 7.
281 "idiom of Broadway": Scully, *Cross My Heart*, 330.
282 "French way": Nissenson, *Lady Upstairs*, 44.
282 "Mecca of the Demimondaine": *Broadway Brevities*, December 1, 1921, 14.
282 "State Committee": *New Yorker*, January 23, 1932, 23.
283 "beer and dough": *Press and Sun Bulletin* (Binghamton, N.Y.), October 18, 1928, 8.
284 "terrible sickness": Betts, *Across the Board*, 233.
285 "presidential election": Eisenberg, Dan, and Landau, *Meyer Lansky*, 105.
285 "good loser": Pietrusza, *Rothstein*, 10.
286 "looking for me": Mitgang, *Once Upon a Time*, 18.
287 "here on in": Pietrusza, *Rothstein*, 14.
287 "in that election": Fox, *Blood and Power*, 159.
287 "life to pieces": Eisenberg, Dan, and Landau, *Meyer Lansky*, 106.

10. The Jewish Jezebel

289 "a calamity": Cuneo, *Life with Fiorello*, 138.
289 "city machine": Ibid., 141.
289 "bullet as ballast": Clarke, *In the Reign of Rothstein*, 294.
291 "crap game": *Variety*, November 7, 1928, 41.
291 "on edge": Ibid.
291 "freelance model": New York *Daily News*, November 20, 1928, 2.
291 "highly-lacquered": *Altoona Mirror* (Pennsylvania), November 19, 1929, 15
292 "my girlfriend?": *The News* (Paterson, N.J.), November 28, 1928, 13.
292 "were for me": Ibid.
292 "beat it": *Detroit Free Press*, November 20, 1928, 2.
293 "high places": Kessner, *Fiorello H. La Guardia*, 162.
293 "don't know": *New York Herald Tribune*, November 19, 1928, 4.

294 "those things": DeArment, *Gunfighter in Gotham*, 209.

294 "be a witness": Adler, *House*, 161.

294 "New York": *Brooklyn Daily Eagle*, December 2, 1928, A3.

294 "very important": *Daily News Tribune* (Greenville, Ohio), November 27, 1928, 3.

294 "mystery woman": *Charlotte Observer*, December 7, 1928, 13.

295 "on them": New York *Daily News*, November 30, 1928, 4.

295 "the affidavit": *Brooklyn Times Union*, November 30, 1928, 1.

295 "the shooting": *Brooklyn Standard Union*, December 1, 1928, 2.

296 "strewn everywhere": Fitzgerald, *My Lost City*, 112–13.

297 "leather skins or something?": Condon, *And Then We Moved to Rossenarra*, 16.

297 "nice person": Adler, *House*, 331.

298 "small annoyances": Ibid., 160.

298 "vice cops": New York *Daily News*, March 25, 1931, 3.

298 "in the pokey": Adler, *House*, 161.

298 "Unholy Alliance": *New York Herald Tribune*, September 26, 1931, 14.

298 "patronizing me": Fowler, *Beau James*, 262.

298 "Tammany Hall": Caro, *The Power Broker*, 321.

299 "heavy price": Katcher, *Big Bankroll*, 256, 248.

299 "'lil' drinkie'": *New York Daily Mirror*, May 5, 1931.

299 "of the Bronx": New York *Daily News*, May 31, 1931, 5.

300 Polly Adler: Minutes of the Magistrate's Court, 9th District Manhattan, April 28, 1929, 32:213, Municipal Archives, City of New York.

301 "then soon": Levine, *"Legs" Diamond*, 67–69.

301 "Dutch Schultz": Sutton and Reynolds, *I, Willie Sutton*, 103.

301 "sheer terror": Sutton and Linn, *Where the Money Was*, 100.

301 "pushover for blondes": Berger, *Eight Million*, 252.

301 "showed to Polly": "Confidential Love Secrets: Every Word the Truth," February 1956, 32–33, 69, 734, PA-FBI.

302 "anything again": Singer, *Black and Blue*, 217.

302 "I'm blue": "(What Did I Do to Be So) Black and Blue," music by Thomas Waller and Harry Brooks, lyrics by Andy Razaf, 1929.

302 "little bonus": Singer, *Black and Blue*, 222.

303 "way of all flesh": PA to VF, n.d., VF notebook, 26, VF-HNH.

303 "time of day": *New Yorker*, June 13, 1931, 24.

304 "Lord Mayor of Gotham": *Nation*, August 29, 1929, 216.

305 "believe my eyes": Adler, *House*, 164.

305 "care of": Ibid., 164.

307 "shot himself": Ibid., 165.

307 "are crooked": *Sheboygan Press* (Wisconsin), November 2, 1929, 15.

308 "playing the numbers": White, *Playing Numbers*, 20, 12.

309 "Square gamblers": New York *Daily News*, March 2, 1930, 6.

310 "criminal judgment": New York *Daily News*, July 8, 1930, 2.

312 "missing persons": Mitgang, *Once Upon a Time*, 24.

312 "through his death": Jonah J. Goldstein, oral history interview by Douglas Scott, 1966, Columbia University, Rare Books and Manuscripts Library.

313 "the lawbreakers": Adler, *House*, 169.

313 "in court": Ibid., 168.

314 "'call houses'": *Brooklyn Citizen*, October 22, 1930, 1.

314 "shake-down ring": New York *Daily News*, October 25, 1930, 3.

314 "out fast!": Adler, *House*, 168.

315 "Polly had departed": *Morning Call* (Allentown, Pa.), November 18, 1930, 9.

315 "be recognized": Adler, *House*, 170.

316 "for weeks": Limpus, *Honest Cop*, 143.

316 "Polly Adler": New York *Daily News*, November 27, 1930, 4.

317 "truckloads": *New York Herald Tribune*, December 5, 1930, 1.

317 "getting theirs": Adler, *House*, 166.

317 "steady jobs": Cohen, *New York Graphic*, 138.

318 "I was missing": Adler, *House*, 173.

318 "dirty prick": PA to VF, November 1952, VF notebook, 51, VF-HNH.

318 "bastards framed": Ibid.

318 "little tin boxes": *Brooklyn Eagle*, December 12, 1931, 1.

319 "favorite nephew": *Brooklyn Eagle*, January 25, 1931, 1.

319 "is high": *Brooklyn Eagle*, February 8, 1931, 17.

319 "quiz a horse": Ibid., 17.

319 "their dialogue": Adler, *House*, 179.

319 "same time": *Brooklyn Eagle*, February 8, 1931, 17.

319 "leaving town": New York *Daily News*, April 27, 2000, 39.

11. The Female Al Capone

321 "many acquaintances": *New York Times*, February 27, 1931, 14.

321 "this man's town": New York *Daily News*, March 5, 1931, 4.

322 "of the slightest": Adler, *House*, 174.

323 "Adler's 'call list'": New York *Daily News*, February 28, 1931, 38.

323 "in the city": Adler, *House*, 174.

324 "mind occupied": Grace Robinson, "Memo to NYDN Desk," Box 36, Folder 3, Grace Robinson Papers, University of Wyoming, American Heritage Center.

324 "an employee": Ibid.

324 "Adler organization": New York *Daily News*, February 28, 1931, 4.

325 "loves the flame": Ibid., 31.

325 "beauty and the blackjack": New York *Daily News*, March 8, 1931, 9.

325 "mob on Broadway": New York *Daily News*, March 5, 1931, 4.

325 "Vivian's victims": New York *Daily News*, February 28, 1931, 3.

325 "'house again!'": Grace Robinson, "Memo to NYDN Desk," Box 36, Folder 3, Grace Robinson Papers, University of Wyoming, American Heritage Center.

326 "different tactics": New York *Daily News*, May 12, 1931, 4.

326 "pleasures of the establishment": Churchill, *They Never Came Back*, 80.

326 "shame suicide": *Yonkers Statesman* (New York), March 4, 1931.

327 "about Vivian?": New York *Daily News*, March 4, 1931, 4.

327 "Empress of Crime": *Latrobe Bulletin* (Pennsylvania), March 6, 1931, 8.

327 "night life": *Daily Record* (Long Branch, N.J.), March 5, 1931, 1.

327 "any crime": *Latrobe Bulletin* (Pennsylvania), March 6, 1931, 8.

327 "mysterious visit": *Brooklyn Eagle*, March 6, 1931, 1.

327 "executive's inspection": New York *Daily News*, March 6, 1931, 3.

328 "week-end parties": *Times* (Muncie, Ind.), March 6, 1931, 13.

328 "loud and stormy": *Brooklyn Standard Union*, March 7, 1931, 2.

328 "over the investigations": *Cincinnati Enquirer*, March 5, 1931, 3.

328 "in the country": New York *Daily News*, March 8, 1931, 4.

328 "eliminated long ago": *Brooklyn Standard Union*, March 7, 1931, 2.

329 "to a head": *New York Times*, March 15, 1931, Section 10, 1.

329 "of the gentry": *Brooklyn Daily Eagle*, March 10, 1931, 23.

329 "Natural causes": *St. Louis Post Dispatch*, March 17, 1931, 3.

329 "bank accounts": New York *Daily News*, March 17, 1931, 6.

330 "New York City": New York *Daily News*, April 4, 1931, 18.

330 "other possibility": *New York Herald Tribune*, April 21, 1931, 1.

330 "proceed further": New York *Daily News*, April 30, 2000, 35.

330 "be off me": Adler, *House*, 181.

331 "train north": Ibid.

331 "to the devil!": *New York Daily Mirror*, May 7, 1931, 3.

332 "been caught": Ibid., 11.

332 "well-tanned": *New York Sun*, n.d., *Sun* newspaper morgue, New York Public Library.

332 "to deal with": *New York Evening Post*, May 7, 1931, 3.

332 "nothing to say": Ibid., 2.

332 "we were playing": Adler, *House*, 186, 189.

333 "admitting the truth": *New York Daily Mirror*, May 11, 1931.

333 "continued to hedge": Adler, *House*, 187.

334 "that prick": PA to VF, December 10, 1951, VF notebook, 41, VF-HNH.

334 "for years": Adler, *House*, 188.

334 "Madame Adler": New York *Daily News*, May 7, 1931, 8.

334 "served the drinks": *New York Daily Mirror*, May 11, 1931, VF-HNH.

334 "their shakedowns": New York *Daily News*, May 7, 1931, 2, 8.

334 "the McCoy?": Adler, *House*, 186.

335 "came near me": Ibid., 187.

335 "Empress of Crime": *Latrobe Bulletin* (Pennsylvania), March 6, 1931, 8.

335 "in my book": Adler, *House*, 205.

335 "in his hand": PA to VF, December 10, 1951, VF notebook, 34, VF-HNH.

335 "in the morning": Adler, *House*, 208.

336 "lot of me": Ibid., 208–9.

336 "in my bedroom": Ibid., 209–10.

336 "of the outfit": Ibid., 210.

336 "it was respect": PA to VF, December 10, 1951, VF notebook, 34, VF-IINH.

336 "nice guy:" Ibid.

336 "what you can do": Adler, *House*, 210–11.

337 "at all hours": Ibid., 211.

337 "malice in him": Morton, *Gangland*, 123.

337 "*numerologist*": Adler, *House*, 213.

337 "left alone": Ibid., 211.

337 "*New York Times*": Gosch and Hammer, *Last Testament of Luciano*, 83.

338 "ruled by fear": Adler, *House*, 210.

338 "'horrible taint'": *Miami News*, June 7, 1931, 5.

339 "certainly moody": Adler, *House*, 202.

339 "trust him": Ibid., 213.

339 "kid mouthpiece": New York *Daily News*, February 3, 1938, 22.

339 "get it?": Adler, *House*, 214.

340 "witnesses always were": Ibid., 214–15.

340 than her age: *New York Herald Tribune*, June 17, 1931, 3.

341 "higher-up": *New York Daily Mirror*, June 17, 1931.

341 "That dirty bitch!": Adler, *House*, 216.

342 "black eye": Ibid., 217.

342 "save his neck": PA to VF, January 14, 1952, VF notebook, 26, VF-HNH.

342 "Bronx Beer Baron": New York *Daily News*, June 18, 1931, 1.

343 "editor about it": Adler, *House*, 211.

343 "Polly Adlervitch": *Time*, July 13, 1931, 21.

343 "program too": Adler, *House*, 220.

344 "Little Caesar": Hellinger, *Ten Million*, 228.

344 "far from good": *New Yorker*, July 11, 1931, 28.

344 "carnations as receipts": *Time*, July 13, 1931, 21.

344 sigh of resignation: Adler, *House*, 190.

345 "answer tomorrow": Ibid., 191.

345 "More than that": *New York Journal American*, July 14, 1931, Seabury Investigation scrapbooks, v. 2, Library of the New York City Bar Association.

346 "in the noose": Adler, *House*, 196.

346 "thoroughly bored": *New Yorker*, December 19, 1931, 55.

346 "blew my top": Adler, *House*, 196.

346 "meet Polly Adler?": *New York Sun*, July 22, 1931, *Sun* newspaper morgue, New York Public Library.

347 "fourteen arrests?": *New York Times*, July 23, 1931, 4.

347 "limp and shaken": Ibid.

347 "above board": *New York Sun*, August 7, 1931, *Sun* newspaper morgue, New York Public Library.

347 "weeks of testimony": *New York Times*, July 23, 1931, 4.

348 "into the conversation": Adler, *House*, 217.

348 "to take place": Ibid., 218.

348 "baby killing": New York *Daily News*, August 11, 1931, 6.

348 "the better": Reynolds, *Headquarters*, 116.

348 "baby killer": *Tennessean* (Nashville, Tenn.), August 11, 1931, 1.

349 "the undertakers": Runyon, *Bloodhounds of Broadway*, 45.

349 "in the Bronx!": Adler, *House*, 219.

349 "Bronx to Inwood": New York *Daily News*, August 22, 1931, 1.

349 "in the Bronx": Adler, *House*, 219.

349 "want to live": New York *Daily News*, August 24, 1931, 4.

350 "Particularly now?": Adler, *House*, 220.

350 "you so-and-so!": Ibid., 221.

350 "apartment building": Ibid., 222.

351 "in the can": New York *Daily News*, October 5, 1931, 4.

351 "tough town": *Star Tribune* (Minneapolis, Minn.), November 10, 1931, 10.

351 "and her wares": Ibid., October 13, 1931, 8.

351 "her own way": Ibid., November 10, 1931, 10.

352 "vice inquiry": New York *Daily News*, October 24, 1931, 4.

352 "Seabury investigation": Adler, *House*, 197.

352 "peace of mind": Adler, *House*, 222.

352 "in a while": Ibid., 223–24.

353 "for the underworld": *New York Times*, December 19, 1931, 1.

12. Café Society

355 "month's quota": Adler, *House*, 199.

356 "Café Society": Young, *New York Café Society*.

356 "saltiest sophisticate": Bret, *Tallulah*, 113.

356 "knocked up": Darwin Porter to author, September 14, 2009.

357 "nifty lady": Lee Saylor to author, April 22, 2012.

357 "contemptuous resignation": Strausbaugh, *Victory City*, 14–15.

357 "debutramps": *Saturday Evening Post*, August 13, 1938, 44.

357 "Sunday name": Kashner and Schoenberger, *Hollywood Kryptonite*, 134.

358 "'last night'": Kinney, *James Thurber*, 522.

358 "masters of ceremonies": McCracken, *Real Men Don't Sing*, 180.

358 "degenerate, or both": Adler, *House*, 228.

359 "Queen of Hookaville": Winchell, *Winchell Exclusive*, 116.

359 "much a night": Stuart, *Secret Life of Winchell*, 229.

359 "'fucking bill?'": Levant, *Memoirs of an Amnesiac*, 115.

359 "out of here": Thomas, *Winchell*, 60.

359 "say goodbye": Adler, *House*, 225–26.

360 "a headache": Gabler, *Winchell*, 155.

360 "Old Glory": *Time*, September 26, 1940, 77.

360 "Unholy Alliance": *New York Herald Tribune*, September 26, 1931, 14.

361 "get 'em, Jimmy!": New York *Daily News*, May 26, 1932, 6.

361 "like a bum": Gosch and Hammer, *Last Testament of Luciano*, 160.

362 "it completely": Starr, *Purveyor*, 29.

362 "involving New Yorkers": Golway, *Frank and Al*, 185.

363 "city's delegates": Gosch and Hammer, *Last Testament of Luciano*, 164.

363 "Smith was right": Ibid., 165.

364 "have been nominated": Hayes, *With Gloves Off*, 127.

364 "liked to drink": Gosch and Hammer, *Last Testament of Luciano*, 164.

364 "insatiable womanizer": Katz, *Uncle Frank*, 98.

364 "'li'l drinkie' soirees": *Confidential*, January 1954, 13–15.

365 "New Orleans": Katz, *Uncle Frank*, 98.

365 "first lady of the underworld": *New York Daily Mirror*, March 13, 1935.

365 "good push": Gosch and Hammer, *Last Testament of Luciano*, 166.

365 "it was": Tugwell, *Brains Trust*, 368.

366 "you're through": Fowler, *Beau James*, 325.

366 "effect immediately": New York *Daily News*, September 2, 1932, 3.

366 "for their pains": New York *Daily News*, September 2, 1932, 3.

366 "found out": *Princeton Alumni Weekly*, v. 70 (1969): 28.

367 "Washington men": Adler, *House*, 288.

367 "with women": Galbraith, *Life in Our Times*, 106.

368 "Cub Room": *Pittsburgh* (Pa.) *Sun-Telegraph*, January 22, 1951, 24.

368 "Before Chicago": Odegard and Helms, *American Politics*, 458.

368 "patronage system": *New Yorker*, August 8, 1936, 23.

368 "Dutch Schultz": Ibid., 24.

368 "those days": Levant, *Memoirs of an Amnesiac*, 114–15.

368 "a fugitive": *Evening Standard* (Uniontown, Pa.), June 20, 1962, 9.

369 "called it slumming": Rosmond, *Robert Benchley*, 186.

369 "Girl Gershwin": *New Yorker*, December 16, 1933, 12.

369 "Polly Adler's": Dana Suesse datebook, August 15, 1934, Peter Mintun Collection.

369 "wonderful affairs": Whorf, *American Popular Song Composers*, 199.

369 "birth to a baby": Darwin Porter to author, Oct. 5, 2009.

370 "on her trail": Ibid.

370 "good cook": Berle and Frankel, *Autobiography*, 186.

370 "there was Carole!": Ibid.

371 "protect a female": PA to VF, January 14, 1952, VF notebook, 26, VF-HNH.

371 "his weight around": Aarons, *Jews of Sing Sing*, 247.

371 "a wisecracker?": *Courier News* (Camden, N.J.), March 18, 1933, 10.

372 "wash the floors": Frances Friedman, interview by author, July 6, 2012.

372 "behind anymore": Adler, *House*, 236.

373 "go no further": Gosch and Hammer, *Last Testament of Luciano*, 151.

373 "for everybody?": Ibid., 152.

373 "his character": PA to VF, n.d., VF notebook, 27, VF-HNH.

373 "them back in": George, *Sweet Man*, 47.

374 "drink it!": *Kingsport News*, July 25, 1953, 4.

374 "'drop dead'": PA to VF, n.d., VF notebook, 27, VF-HNH.

374 "did keep away": Ibid.

375 "of that period": Ibid.

375 "Scotch for Showboat": Ibid.

375 "my man": White, *Playing the Numbers*, 183.

376 "hob-nailed boots": Moses, *Unlikely Union*, 235.

376 "party is over": Cromwell and Dougherty, *Dirty Helen*, 239.

376 "into New Jersey!": Stolberg, *Fighting Organized Crime*, 47.

377 "Mott Street mob": *Journal and Courier* (Lafayette, Ind.), February 5, 1936, 1.

377 "feel like it": Adler, *House*, 234.

378 "have been avoided": Ibid., 235–36.

378 "gonna stay": Ibid., 236–37.

378 "fox-huntin' set": Ibid., 229–30.

380 "out of windows": Ibid., 231–32.

380 "that's class": Ibid., 233.

380 "town these days": *Austin American* (Texas), August 28, 1932, Aug. 28, 1932, 4.

381 "millionaire's apartment": McAllister and Miller, *Kind of Guy I Am*, 100.

381 "a night's work": PA to VF, January 25, 1952, VF notebook, 36, VF-HNH.

381 "excellent taste": Ibid.

381 "on the radio": Kashner and Schoenberger, *Talent for Genius*, 147.

382 "entire business": Waugh, *Year to Remember*, 136.

382 "each January": Ibid., 137.

384 "'your four friends'": Adler, *House*, 246.

384 "of my list": Ibid., 242.

384 "men-about-town": New York *Daily News*, March 26, 1935, 16.

385 "I hung up": Adler, *House*, 248.
385 "cops broke in": PA to VF, December 10, 1951, VF notebook, 41, VF-HNH.
386 "good listener": *New York Herald Tribune*, March 20, 1935, 5.
386 "as they please": Ibid.
386 "in this joint?": *New York Times Book Review*, June 14, 1953, 18.
386 "first class": *New York Herald Tribune*, March 20, 1935, 5.
386 "led into court": *New York Times*, March 6, 1935, 1.
387 "patrol wagon": Adler, *House*, 253–54.
387 "brought in": *New York Sun*, March 6, 1935, *Sun* newspaper morgue, New York Public Library.
387 "public enemy": Adler, *House*, 254.
387 "New York": *Jewish Daily Forward*, March 6, 1935, 1.
387 in the papers: New York *Daily News*, March 6, 1935, 3.
387 "deluxe establishment": *New York Daily Mirror*, March 13, 1935.
388 "how to live": *New York Herald Tribune*, March 13, 1935, 5.
388 "call them in": *New York Times*, March 10, 1935, 28.
388 "with the girls?": Adler, *House*, 256.
388 "point of view": *New York Daily Mirror*, March 13, 1935.
388 "names were entered": Jonah J. Goldstein, oral history interview by Douglas Scott, 1966, Columbia University, Rare Books and Manuscripts Library.
389 "tired of it": New York *Daily News*, March 15, 1935, 4.
389 "Courts Building": Ibid., 3.
390 "'square deal'": New York *Daily News*, March 12, 1935, 6.
390 "chump list": *Reading Times* (Pennsylvania), March 19, 1935, 4.
390 "loitering and prostitution": *Jewish Daily Forward*, March 21, 1935, 1.
391 "expose us": PA to VF, December 10, 1951, VF notebook, 41, VF-HNH.
391 "three years, (probably)": Ibid.
391 "rather well": Adler, *House*, 260.
391 "in three months": Ibid., 262.
392 "made friends quickly": New York *Daily News*, June 3, 1935, 3.
392 "in the hoosegow": *Honolulu Advertiser*, June 10, 1935, 6.
392 "was all about": New York *Daily News*, July 12, 1935, 9.
392 "held in Chicago": Ibid., 4.
392 "Lipstick Burglars": *Chicago Tribune*, July 12, 1935, 2.
393 "marry a millionaire": New York *Daily News*, July 13, 1935, 6.
393 "get out": Adler, *House*, 280.
393 "your tail too": Ibid., 288.
394 "can lick anybody": Cockayne, *Hidden Power*, 138.
395 "can't be done": Adler, *House*, 238.
395 "heard of me": Cohn, *Joker Is Wild*, 113.

13. The Big Shot

397 "as much drinking": Adler, *House*, 287.
398 "compulsory prostitution": Stern, *White Ticket*, 210.
398 "Mott Street mob": *Journal and Courier* (Lafayette, Ind.), February 5, 1936, 1.
398 "white slavery": Langum, *Crossing Over the Line*, 33.

399   "in Hollywood": Adler, *House*, 291.

399   "beneath his feet": Ibid., 292.

400   "was isolation": Ibid.

400   "in the 30s": *Pageant*, November 1953, 52.

400   "prostitution racket": New York *Daily News*, April 2, 1936, 3.

400   "super-pimp": Donati, *Lucky Luciano*, 202.

401   "outside the combine": Adler, *House*, 294.

401   "society. Period": Gosch and Hammer, *Last Testament of Luciano*, 215.

401   "sorts of rackets": Adler, *House*, 294.

401   "without interference": New York *Daily News*, April 19, 1936, 2.

401   "up her place": *Morning Call* (Allentown, Pa.), August 6, 1955, 12.

402   "in the underworld": Willemse, *Behind Green Lights*, 309.

402   "from the pimps?": Stern, *No Innocence Abroad*, 39.

402   "friendly islands": Adler, *House*, 293.

403   "New York": Ibid., 295–96.

403   "prostitution man": Ibid., 225.

404   "'can't recalls'": New York *Daily News*, June 4, 1936, 6.

404   "felt otherwise": C. Joseph Greaves, "How Prosecutors Brought Down Lucky Luciano," ABA *Journal*, November 1, 2015, tinyurl.com/1dhgdhjn.

404   "was a boss": Maas, *Valachi Papers*, 146.

404   "years of my life": Gosch and Hammer, *Last Testament of Luciano*, 173.

404   "out of the papers": Newark, *Lucky Luciano*, 30.

405   "of the Girls": Rhea Whitley to J. Edgar Hoover, July 9, 1936, case file 31-44249, reel 195-A, near end of reel, PA-FBI.

405   *"Partners in crime"*: F. M. Headley, Report of SAC NYC, July 28, 1936, ibid.

405   "bordello business": New York *Daily News*, March 14, 1935, 2.

405   "of the pinch": Adler, *House*, 299.

406   "Madam No. 1": New York *Daily News*, July 11, 1936, 6.

406   "appearing on Monday": *New York Sun*, July 10, 1936, *Sun* newspaper morgue, New York Public Library.

406   "getting out": Adler, *House*, 299.

406   "open a nightclub": *Record* (Hackensack, N.J.), July 27, 1936, 14.

406   "Tch!": *Advance News* (Ogdensburg, N.Y.), August 8, 1936, 4.

407   "asked for an audience": *Brooklyn Eagle*, August 13, 1936, 1.

407   "'right now' line": New York *Daily News*, August 14, 1936, 49.

407   "up to it": Adler, *House*, 282–83.

407   "own backyard": Ibid., 310.

408   "under cover": R. Whitley, SAC NYC, to D. M. Ladd, SAC Chicago, October 26, 1936, case file 31-44249, reel #195-A, near end of reel, PA-FBI.

408   "vigorous investigation": D. M. Ladd, SAC Chicago, to J. Edgar Hoover, "Personal and Confidential," November 7, 1936, ibid.

408   "to quote here": Ibid., 126–27.

408   "bright spots": *Billboard*, February 27, 1937, 22.

409   "American Montmartre": *Cosmopolitan*, February 1937, 68.

409   "by the Mob": Lazar and Tapert, *Swifty*, 46.

409   "swing music": Schuller, *Swing Era*, 20.

409   "foghorn voiced": Gavin, *Intimate Nights*, 7.

410 "girl singers": Pitrone, *Take It from the Big Mouth*, 12.

410 "bandleaderitis": Levinson, *Trumpet Blues*, 113.

410 "very proud": Buddy De Franco, interview by author, January 5, 2011.

410 "were legend": Lees, *Arranging the Score*, 226.

410 "go to Polly's": Darwin Porter to author, November 30, 2009.

411 "audition": Ibid.

411 "was passing": Barnet, *Those Swinging Years*, 58.

411 "Polly's apartment": Darwin Porter to author, November 30, 2009.

411 "girls in sight": Robert de Roos, unpublished typescript biography of Jimmy Van Heusen, 21–22.

411 "business early": Ibid.

411 "songs and Sinatra": Sheed, *House That George Built*, 226.

411 "the whoremaster": *Vanity Fair-Movies Rock* special supplement, Fall 2007, 140.

412 "Frank Sinatra": Frank Sinatra to Adler, PA autograph albums, Heritage Auctions.

412 "you—Francis": Autographed Sinatra print, c. 1940s, Polly Adler Collection courtesy of Eleanor Vera.

412 "underworld elite": New York *Daily News*, April 3, 1935, 53.

412 "Tower of Gorgonzola": *Lincoln Star* (Nebraska), April 6, 1930, 16.

412 "Madcap Maxie": *Cincinnati Enquirer*, March 13, 1939, 14.

412 "raid was planned": Walker and Reichler, *Mickey Walker*, 113–14.

413 "That was Polly": Ibid.

414 "income as that": *New York Herald Tribune*, February 25, 1939, 3.

414 "Flegenheimer gang": *New York Times*, May 26, 1938.

414 "joint in Yorkville": PA to VF, n.d., VF notebook, 60, VF-HNH.

415 "de Gotha": Adler, *House*, 328.

416 "American host": Ibid.

416 "Swedish boys": VF to Ann Watkins, March 29, 1952, Series III, Box 1, Adler Folder, Watkins.

416 "of your girls?": Adler, *House*, 328–29.

416 "piece of Kleenex?": Ibid., 329.

417 "playback on it": VF to Ann Watkins, March 29, 1952, Series III, Box 1, Adler Folder, Watkins.

417 "'truck driver'": Adler, *House*, 337–38.

417 "'Pretty Peacock'": Murray, *Musician*, 111.

417 "in his shoes": Ibid.

417 "double features": "Gentlewomen Prefer Bonds," 6, VF-HNH.

418 "audience of thousands": Darwin Porter to author, October 26, 2009.

418 "exhibitionism, sadism": Wilson, *Dancing with Devil*, 88.

418 "Dorian Donahue": VF to PA, July 10, 1953, VF notebook, VF-HNH.

418 "hundred-dollar bill": Adler, *House*, 97.

418 "days of 1929": Barrymore and Frank, *Too Much, Too Soon*, 101.

419 "good time": Ibid.

419 "Chamber of Horrors": *Sacramento Bee*, May 4, 1937, 21.

419 "*Fortune Magazine!*": Adler, *House*, 333.

419 "in the Sixties": *Fortune*, July 1939, 48.

419 "humiliating to me": Butler, *Political Leadership*, 109.

419 "limited to one sex": Ibid.

420 "Molly Levine": Bercovici, *For Immediate Release*, 43.

420 "Orson Welles": Orson Welles to PA, PA autograph albums, n.d., Heritage Auctions.

420 "I know of": Burt Lancaster to PA, PA autograph albums, September 2, 1946, Heritage Auctions.

421 "on the house": Kanfer, *Ball of Fire*, 69.

421 "was insatiable": Arnaz, *A Book*, 76.

421 "Latin heartbreaker": *Miami News*, September 26, 1939, 9.

421 "and Polly Adler": *Vanity Fair*, April 2016, 151.

422 "too easy": Arnaz, *A Book*, 94–95.

422 "in New York": Dempsey, *Dempsey*, 236.

422 "foremost journalist": *New Yorker*, August 23, 1947, 30.

423 "unsuspecting Eleanor Roosevelt": Vincent Sheean, Diary 1946–1947, December 19, 1946, Vincent Sheean Papers, Box 1, Folder 39, Wisconsin Historical Society.

423 "klieg lights": PA to Walter Winchell, April 15, 1950, VF notebook, 73, VF-HNH.

423 "black marketeers": Adler, *House*, 341.

424 "escape of sex": Ibid.

424 "in a whore-house": PA to VF, October 9, 1951, VF notebook, 11, VF-HNH.

424 "ignored it": Adler, *House*, 341–43.

425 "Field Division": Report on Charles Lawrence, April 7, 1942, case file 31-64473, reel 314-A, end of reel, PA-FBI.

425 "sending her away": A. Rosen to J. Edgar Hoover, November 10, 1942, ibid.

426 "coast to coast": Smith, *Life and Legend of Gene Fowler*, 251.

426 "100 bangs": *Scanlan's Monthly*, June 1970, 75–77.

427 "nosy neighbors": Ibid.

428 "curious onlookers": Ibid.

429 "lie down": Adler, *House*, 345.

429 "Dirty Gertie": Duberman, *Stonewall*, 143.

429 "most admired": Adler, *House*, 349.

429 "so flimsy": Ibid., 348.

430 "snobs and hypocrites": Ibid., 292–93.

431 "Leave me alone!": Ibid., 351.

431 "Village bars": *Mercury* (Pottstown, Pa.), July 13, 1953, 4.

431 "homosexual America": Koppelman and Forman, *Fire Island National Seashore*, 12.

432 "short-haired girls": Adler, *House*, 350.

432 "introduced them to you!": Ibid., 351–52.

432 "off my porch!": PA to VF, November 1952, VF notebook, 51, VF-HNH.

433 "not true": Ibid.

433 "well knowns": *Gazette* (Cedar Rapids, Ia.), September 15, 1943, 11.

434 "she wanted it": Darwin Porter to author, December 17, 2009.

434 "gaming salon": New York *Daily News*, November 7, 1944, 30.

434 "arrested her": *Pittsburgh Post-Gazette* (Pennsylvania), November 20, 1944, 22.

434 "Operation: Autobiography": Adler, *House*, 361.

435 "well enough alone": Ibid.

435 "orange juice": Adler, *House*, 361–62.

436 "to Gymnazia": Ibid., 362.

14. Madam Emeritus

439 "wuz in town": *Confidential*, January 1954, 13–15.

440 "Era of Wonderful Nonsense": *Esquire*, September 1, 1934, 23.

440 "was over": MacShane, *Life of O'Hara*, 128.

440 "hates most": Benchley, *Robert Benchley*, 249.

440 "any longer": Meryman, *Mank*, 317.

441 "different twist": Nathaniel Benchley, *Robert Benchley*, inscription to PA, February 21, 1956, Polly Adler Collection courtesy of Eleanor Vera.

441 "Barnet residence": Barnet, *Those Swinging Years*, 158.

441 "bedroom for hoodlums": *Coronet*, May 1956, 59.

441 "my bare feet": Gentry, *Madams of San Francisco*, 303–4.

442 "women kissing": Murray, *Musician*, 112.

442 "return, ever": *Pageant*, November 1953, 52.

442 "in California": *Evening Herald* (Pottsville, Pa.), January 11, 1947, 2.

442 "Hollywood restaurant": New York *Daily News*, March 21, 1946, 31.

442 "that for me": *Pageant*, November 1953, 52.

442 "unnerved me": Adler, *House*, 363.

443 "was different": Ibid.

443 "my rocker": *Pageant*, November 1953, 52.

443 "nouns and verbs": Adler, *House*, 367.

443 "madam-emeritus": *People Today*, November 5, 1952, 59.

443 "Ex-Madame X": New York *Daily News*, May 8, 1947, 32.

443 "away from it": PA draft acknowledgments, July 29, 1952, Series II, Box II.7, Folder "Adler, Polly," Watkins.

444 "patients": Gentry, *Madams of San Francisco*, 303–4.

444 "great deal": PA to Alfred Kinsey, August 19, 1948, Kinsey Institute Collections, Indiana University.

444 "same way": *San Francisco Examiner*, November 26, 2002, 3.

444 "prim and puritanical": Wallace, *Sunday Gentleman*, 65.

444 "cold feet": PA draft acknowledgments, July 29, 1952, Series II, Box II.7, Folder "Adler, Polly," Watkins.

444 "spoil the brothel": Adler, *House*, 373.

445 "'Not a Home'": PA draft acknowledgments, July 29, 1952, Series II, Box II.7, Folder "Adler, Polly," Watkins.

445 "pride of authorship": Jean Parker Waterbury notes, March 16, 1951, Series I, Box 1.1, Watkins.

445 "sitting up": Strauss, *Talent for Luck*, 89.

446 "Polly's profession": Lee Barker to Jean Waterbury, March 20, 1951, Series I, Box 1.1, Watkins.

446 "some people": Ted Purdy to Jean Waterbury, 2, 1951, Series I, Box 1.1, Watkins.

446 "the suggestion": *Nevada State Journal*, September 16, 1950, 4.

447 "determined to continue": PA to VF, July 25, 1950, VF notebook, 84–85, VF-HNH.

447 "customers felt": Philip Wylie to Jean Waterbury, September 26, 1950, Series I, Box 1.6, Watkins.

448 "caring for them": Barshay, *Philip Wylie*, 10–11.

448 "lover or pimp": PA draft acknowledgments, July 29, 1952, Series II, Box II.7, Folder "Adler, Polly," Watkins.

448 "family with it": Dauber, *Jewish Comedy*, 166.

449 "very funny": Max Gershunoff, interview by author, October 5–6, 2010.

449 "Russian general": Ibid.

450 "take my money": Ibid.

450 "people in history": Ibid.

451 "came the blow": PA draft acknowledgments, July 29, 1952, Series II, Box II.7, Folder "Adler, Polly," Watkins.

451 "wrote *Hamlet*": Ibid.

451 "Adler debacle": William E. Buckley to Armitage Watkins, January 25, 1951, Series I, Box 1.1, Watkins.

451 "old story": PA draft acknowledgments, July 29, 1952, Series II, Box II.7, Folder "Adler, Polly," Watkins.

451 "Greek and Latin!": *Philadelphia Inquirer*, June 25, 1951, 15.

451 "reduce its length": Sheila Saint Lawrence to Elliot Schryver, July 18, 1951, Series III, Box 1, Adler Folder 1, Watkins.

452 "amused tizzy": *Oneonta Star* (New York), July 16, 1951, 13.

452 "of course": New York *Daily News*, July 17, 1951, 15C.

452 "these parts": *The Mercury* (Pottstown, Pa.), August 1, 1951, 4.

453 "Buy it": *Miami Herald*, August 9, 1953, 7F.

453 "best-seller": *Confidential*, January 1954, 13–15, 50–51.

453 "back to California": VF, HNH memo, n.d., Virginia Faulkner, Editor Papers, University of Nebraska Archives and Special Collections.

453 "biography and whoredom": PA to VF, December 10, 1951, VF notebook, 35, VF-HNH.

453 "Must Not Mention": VF notebook, cover page, VF-HNH.

454 "way to me": VF to Ann Watkins, October 15, 1951, Series III, Box 1, Adler Folder, Watkins.

454 "don't know": PA to VF, October 10, 1951, VF notebook, 4, VF-HNH.

454 "writing anyway": VF to Ann Watkins, October 15, 1951, Series III, Box 1, Adler Folder, Watkins.

454 "human being": PA to VF, October 10, 1951, VF notebook, 7, VF-HNH.

454 "thanks to you": PA to VF, n.d., VF notebook, 60, VF-HNH.

455 "libelous parts": Wallace, *Sunday Gentleman*, 64–66.

455 "I can't": VF to Ann Watkins, March 25, 1952, Series III, Box 1, Adler Folder, Watkins.

455 "on your team": Walter Winchell to PA, April 13, 1950, VF notebook, 73, VF-HNH.

455 "'social document'": Kinney, *Thurber Letters*, 566.

455 "'Best Swordsmen'": Ibid., 564.

456 "doing it": PA, queries to VF, May 30, 1952, VF-HNH.

456 "Polly spin": PA to VF, November 1, 1952, VF notebook, 58, 58a, 59, VF-HNH.

456 "she gave me": Ibid.

457 "pay roll": VF to Ann Watkins, Jan. 4, 1953, Series III, Box 1, Adler Folder, Watkins.

457 "to their request": W. Rogoff to Sheila Saint Lawrence, May 12, 1953, Series III, Box 1, Adler Folder, Watkins.

457   "my own field": *Baytown Sun*, September 16, 1952, 3.

457   "McCoy": *Variety*, June 10, 1953, 31.

458   "Polly's. Remember?": *Washington Post*, June 4, 1953, 53.

458   "Polly's life": VF to future readers, May 27, 1953, VF-HNH.

458   "can have it": *New York Post*, June 9, 1952, Series II, Box 1, Adler Folder, Watkins.

459   "quiet dignity": *Panama City News*, June 27, 1953, 9.

459   "would Polly go?": Kriendler and Jeffers, "21," 185.

459   "hurt me cruelly": *Pageant*, November 1953, 53.

459   "tired old gal": PA to Ann Watkins, August 29, 1953, Series III, Box 1, Adler Folder, Watkins.

460   "Voltaire and Dostoevsky": *Stars and Stripes*, December 28, 1953, PA-FBI.

460   "having a drink": Pearl Adler, record of sworn statement, December 25, 1953, INS investigation, PA-FBI.

460   "agin' the wall": "Highly Classified Special Adler Supplement," 3, VF-HNH.

461   "something like that": *Miami Herald*, August 9, 1953, 7F.

461   "all of mine": *New York Herald Tribune*, November 1, 1955, 25.

461   "collector's item": *Tucson Daily Citizen* (Arizona), July 4, 1953, 28.

461   "devoted admirer": Vladimir Nabokov to PA, n.d., PA autograph albums, Heritage Auctions.

461   "there to say?": Mary McCarthy to PA, August 22, 1953, PA autograph albums, Heritage Auctions.

462   "a lot of smut": *New York Herald Tribune*, November 1, 1955, 25.

462   "been more bored": Waugh, *Year to Remember*, 138–39.

463   "any longer": Ibid.

463   "whatever that is": Leider, *Myrna Loy*, 273.

463   "Beverly Hills": *Miami Herald*, May 7, 1959, 21.

464   "friend of mine": Leonore Lemmon, interview by Lee Saylor, May 1989.

464   "tough old broad": Kashner and Schoenberger, *Hollywood Kryptonite*, 255.

464   "The Big C": Winchell, *Winchell Exclusive*, 117.

465   "medical handicappers": Betts, *Across the Board*, 15.

465   "old realists": *New York Herald Tribune*, June 7, 1953, E4.

465   "literary lion": *Time*, September 4, 1964, 102.

466   "wait for you": *Washington Post*, October 13, 1964, C5.

466   "The Balcony": *Anderson Daily Bulletin* (Indiana), April 10, 1964, 4.

466   "make him happy": *New York Times*, August 30, 1964, X9.

466   "gold into dross": *New Yorker*, September 5, 1964, 106–7.

466   "nobody to a legend": Adler, *House*, 355.

467   "wiped out": Kashner and Schoenberger, *Talent for Genius*, 147.

467   "Polly's place": *The Leaf-Chronicle* (Clarkson, Tenn.), June 4, 1964, 10.

467   "'Author Dies'": Golden, *So Long As You're Healthy*, 312.

467   "age of conformity": *Partisan Review*, January–February 1954, 8–13, 15, 25, 29, 33.

468   "promises of life": Fitzgerald, *Great Gatsby*, 8.

468   "American dream": Phillips, *Susan Lenox*, I:411.

468   "Empress of Vice": New York *Daily News*, July 13, 1935, 6.

469   "Scarlet-Woman-as-Horatio-Alger-tale": Hapke, *Labor's Text*, 161.

469   "men's expense": Hakim, *Erotic Capital*, 6.

469   "till curtain time": PA to VF, November 1952, VF notebook, 46, VF-HNH.

Bibliography

A Word About Sources

For reasons of space, I have regretfully limited citations to direct quotations. Because Polly's world was uniquely riddled with myth-making and lie-spinning, I have tried whenever possible to refer to original sources and to thoroughly cross-check and contextualize them.

I was aided by two extraordinary private collections. The first is a cache of papers from Polly's ghostwriter, Virginia Faulkner, that list many of the real people and events that were cut or altered in *A House Is Not a Home*. The second is the remains of Polly's keepsakes, letters, photos, and inscribed books. Polly accumulated several trunks of memorabilia, including scrapbooks, reel-to-reel tapes, and transcripts of her reminiscences, a seven-hundred-page first draft of her memoir, and books signed by fellow authors. Unfortunately, when she died her last surviving brother, ashamed of his sister's profession, threw most of it away. I am very grateful to Eleanor Vera and a collector who wishes to remain anonymous for saving what was left of these treasures from destruction.

For those who wish to delve more deeply into this subject, a full list of the publications I consulted resides on the Zotero.org website. The New York Public Library houses key primary sources including undigitized newspapers and the Committee of Fourteen Records. The New York Municipal Archives owns the records of the Women's Court during Polly's early career, and her FBI file covers some of her later years. The Yizkor memorial book for Polly's native shtetl, Janow al yad Pinsk, was a miraculous online resource. Ancestry.com provided critical documentation, and Newspapers.com turned up hundreds of Polly's press appearances. I particularly recommend *Variety*, *Collier's*, *The New Yorker*, *The New York Times*, the New York *Daily News*, the *Brooklyn Eagle*, and the Hearst Sunday supplements. Urban reporters, frustrated by their inability to print all they knew, turned out dozens of barely fictionalized accounts of Polly's milieu, many of them made into Hollywood films, that provide vivid images and insights that can't be found elsewhere. My working notes will be on file in the Amherst College Archives, in hope of furthering future scholarship and debate.

Archives

Ancestry.com
Boston University, Howard Gottlieb Archival Research Center
Center for Jewish History, New York
Columbia University, Rare Books and Manuscripts Library
Heritage Auctions
John Jay College of Criminal Justice/CUNY, Special Collections
Kinsey Institute Collections, Indiana University
Los Angeles Public Library, History and Genealogy Department
National Archives and Records Administration
New York City Bar Association Library
New York City Municipal Archives
New York State Archives
New York Public Library, Archives and Billy Rose Theater Division
Newspapers.com
Ohio State University, Thompson Library Special Collections
Peter Mintun Collection
Polly Adler Collection courtesy of Eleanor Vera
Springfield History Library and Archives, Massachusetts
University of Colorado Boulder, Special Collections and Archives
University of Wyoming, Heritage Center
University of Nebraska, Archives and Special Collections
Virginia Faulkner's *House Is Not a Home* private archive
Yale University, Beinecke Rare Book and Manuscript Library

Books

Aarons, Ron. *The Jews of Sing Sing: Gotham, Gangsters, and Gonuvim*. Barricade Books, 2008.
Aaronson, Sammy, and Al Hirshberg. *As High as My Heart: The Sammy Aaronson Story*. Coward-McCann, 1957.
Abbott, Karen. *American Rose: A Nation Laid Bare: The Life and Times of Gypsy Rose Lee*. Random House, 2010.
Adams, Caswell, ed. *Great American Sports Stories*. Stamford House, 1947.
Adler, Polly. *A House Is Not a Home*. Rinehart, 1953.
Ahearn, Danny. *How to Commit a Murder*. Ives Washburn, 1930.
Allen, Irving L. *The City in Slang: New York Life and Popular Speech*. Oxford University Press, 1993.
Altman, Billy. *Laughter's Gentle Soul: The Life of Robert Benchley*. W. W. Norton, 1997.
Amherst, Jeffery. *Wandering Abroad: The Autobiography of Jeffery Amherst*. Secker & Warburg, 1976.
Ansky, S. *The Enemy at His Pleasure: A Journey Through the Jewish Pale of Settlement during World War I*. Metropolitan Books, 2002.
Antin, Mary. *The Promised Land*. Houghton Mifflin, 1928.

Arnaz, Desi. *A Book*. William Morrow, 1976.

Balliett, Whitney. *American Musicians II: Seventy-Two Portraits in Jazz*. Oxford University Press, 1998.

Baral, Robert. *Revue: A Nostalgic Reprise of the Great Broadway Period*. Fleet, 1962.

Barber, James David, ed. *Political Leadership in American Government*. Little, Brown, 1964.

Barnet, Charlie. *Those Swinging Years: The Autobiography of Charlie Barnet*. Louisiana State University Press, 1984.

Baron, Joseph L. *A Treasury of Jewish Quotations*. Jason Aronson, 1996.

Barrett, James R. *The Irish Way: Becoming American in the Multiethnic City*. Penguin Press, 2012.

Barrymore, Diana, and Gerold Frank. *Too Much, Too Soon*. Holt, 1957.

Barshay, Robert Howard. *Philip Wylie: The Man and His Work*. University Press of America, 1979.

Bel Geddes, Norman. *Miracle in the Evening: An Autobiography*. Pickle Partners Publishing, 2018.

Benchley, Nathaniel. *Robert Benchley: A Biography*. McGraw-Hill, 1955.

Bercovici, Rion. *For Immediate Release: A Novel*. Sheridan House, 1937.

Berebitsky, Julie. *Sex and the Office: A History of Gender, Power, and Desire*. Yale University Press, 2012.

Berger, Meyer. *The Eight Million: Journal of a New York Correspondent*. Simon & Schuster, 1942.

Berle, Milton, and Haskel Frankel. *An Autobiography*. Delacorte Press, 1974.

Bernstein, Burton. *Thurber: A Biography*. 1976; reprint William Morrow, 1996.

Berrett, Joshua. *Louis Armstrong and Paul Whiteman: Two Kings of Jazz*. Yale University Press, 2008.

Berton, Ralph. *Remembering Bix: A Memoir of the Jazz Age*. Harper & Row, 1974.

Betts, Toney [Anthony Zito, pseud.]. *Across the Board*. Citadel Press, 1956.

[Blair, Madeleine.] *Madeleine: An Autobiography*. Harper & Brothers, 1919.

Bishop, Jim. *The Mark Hellinger Story: A Biography of Broadway and Hollywood*. Appleton-Century-Crofts, 1952.

Bowker, Lee H., ed. *Women and Crime in America*. Collier Macmillan, 1981.

Bradshaw, Jon. *Dreams Money Can Buy: The Tragic Life of Libby Holman*. William Morrow, 1985.

Bret, David. *Tallulah Bankhead: A Scandalous Life*. Robson Books, 1998.

Bristow, Edward J. *Prostitution and Prejudice: The Jewish Fight Against White Slavery, 1870–1939*. Schocken Books, 1983.

Burns, George, and David Fisher. *All My Best Friends*. Putnam, 1989.

Cahalane, Cornelius F. *The Policeman*. Arno Press, 1970.

Cantor, Eddie, David Freedman, and Jane Kesher Ardmore. *My Life Is in Your Hands & Take My Life: The Autobiographies of Eddie Cantor*. Cooper Square Press, 2000.

Cantu, Maya. *American Cinderellas on the Broadway Musical Stage: Imagining the Working Girl from Irene to Gypsy*. Palgrave Macmillan, 2015.

Carey, Arthur A., and Howard McLellan. *Memoirs of a Murder Man*. Literary Licensing, 2011.

Caro, Robert A. *The Power Broker: Robert Moses and the Fall of New York*. Vintage Books, 1975.

Carroll, Renee. *In Your Hat*. Macaulay, 1933.

Cerf, Bennett. *At Random: The Reminiscences of Bennett Cerf*. Random House, 1977.

Chandler, Charlotte. *Hello, I Must Be Going: Groucho and His Friends*. Doubleday, 1978.

Chandler, Raymond. *The Big Sleep*. World, 1946.

Chanes, Jerome A. *Antisemitism: A Reference Handbook*. ABC-CLIO, 2004.

Chappell, George Shepard. *The Restaurants of New York*. Greenberg, 1925.

Chauncey, George. *Gay New York: Urban Culture and the Making of a Gay Male World, 1890–1940*. Yale University Press, 1989.

Chin, Gabriel Jackson. *New York City Police Corruption Investigation Commissions, 1894–1994*. W. S. Hein, 1997.

Churchill, Allen. *They Never Came Back*. Doubleday, 1960.

Clarke, Donald Henderson. *In the Reign of Rothstein*. Vanguard Press, 1929.

Clement, Elizabeth Alice. *Love for Sale: Courting, Treating, and Prostitution in New York City, 1900–1945*. University of North Carolina Press, 2006.

Cockayne, James. *Hidden Power: The Strategic Logic of Organized Crime*. C. Hurst & Co., 2016.

Cohen, Lester. *The New York Graphic: The World's Zaniest Newspaper*. Chilton Books, 1964.

Cohn, Art. *The Joker Is Wild: The Story of Joe E. Lewis*. Bantam Books, 1957.

Committee of Fourteen in New York City. *Annual Report, 1913*. New York, 1914.

Condon, Richard. *And Then We Moved to Rossenarra: Or, The Art of Emigrating*. Dial Press, 1973.

Conyes, Alfred. *Fifty Years in Sing Sing: A Personal Account, 1879–1929*. State University of New York Press, 2014.

Cooper, Courtney Ryley. *Here's to Crime*. Little, Brown, 1937.

Courtwright, David T., Herman Joseph, and Don Des Jarlais. *Addicts Who Survived: An Oral History of Narcotic Use in America Before 1965*. University of Tennessee Press, 1989.

Cowley, Malcolm. *Exile's Return: A Literary Odyssey of the 1920s*. Penguin Books, 1976.

Cromwell, Helen Worley, and Robert Dougherty. *Dirty Helen: An Autobiography*. Sherbourne Press, 1966.

Cuneo, Ernest. *Life with Fiorello: A Memoir*. New York: Macmillan, 1955.

Dance, Stanley. *The World of Duke Ellington*. C. Scribner's Sons, 1970.

Dauber, Jeremy. *Jewish Comedy: A Serious History*. W. W. Norton, 2017.

DeArment, Robert K. *Gunfighter in Gotham: Bat Masterson's New York City Years*. University of Oklahoma Press, 2013.

DeLong, Thomas A. *Pops: Paul Whiteman, King of Jazz*. New Century, 1983.

Dempsey, Jack, et al. *Dempsey*. Avon, 1959.

———. *Massacre in the Sun*. World, 1963.

Dewey, John. *The Later Works of John Dewey, 1925–1953*. Edited by Jo Ann Boydston. Southern Illinois University Press, 2008.

Dimont, Max I. *Jews, God, and History*. Simon & Schuster, 1962.

Doherty, Thomas Patrick. *Pre-Code Hollywood: Sex, Immorality, and Insurrection in American Cinema, 1930–1934*. Columbia University Press, 1999.

Donaldson, Scott. *Fitzgerald and Hemingway: Works and Days*. Columbia University Press, 2009.

Donati, William. *Lucky Luciano: The Rise and Fall of a Mob Boss*. McFarland, 2010.

Dowty, Alan. *Arabs and Jews in Ottoman Palestine: Two Worlds Collide*. Indiana University Press, 2019.

Drutman, Irving. *Good Company: A Memoir, Mostly Theatrical*. Little, Brown, 1976.

Duberman, Martin. *Stonewall: The Definitive Story of the LGBT Rights Uprising That Changed America*. Penguin, 2019.

Dubnow, Simon, and Leon Shapiro. *History of the Jews in Russia and Poland: From the Earliest Times until the Present Day*. Ktav, 1975.

Durante, Jimmy, and Jack Kofoed. *Night Clubs*. Alfred A. Knopf, 1931.

Eisenberg, Dennis, Uri Dan, and Eli Landau. *Meyer Lansky: Mogul of the Mob*. Paddington Press, 1979.

Eisenstein, Louis, and Elliot Rosenberg. *A Stripe of Tammany's Tiger*. Fall Creek Books, 2013.

Ellington, Duke. *The Duke Ellington Reader*. Oxford University Press, 1995.

Epstein, Lawrence J. *At the Edge of a Dream: The Story of Jewish Immigrants on New York's Lower East Side, 1880–1920*. John Wiley & Sons, 2007.

Evensen, Bruce J. *When Dempsey Fought Tunney: Heroes, Hokum, and Storytelling in the Jazz Age*. University of Tennessee Press, 1996.

Fair, James R. *Give Him to the Angels: The Story of Harry Greb*. Smith & Durrell, 1946.

Feder, Sid, and Joachim Joesten. *The Luciano Story*. David McKay, 1954.

Fitzgerald, F. Scott. *The Great Gatsby*. Charles Scribner's Sons, 1953.

———. *My Lost City: Personal Essays, 1920–1940*. Edited by James L. West III. Cambridge University Press, 2005.

Fitzpatrick, Kevin C. *The Algonquin Round Table New York: A Historical Guide*. Lyons Press, 2015.

Flynn, Edward J. *You're the Boss*. Viking Press, 1947.

Folsom, Robert G. *The Money Trail: How Elmer Irey and His T-Men Brought Down America's Criminal Elite*. Potomac Books, 2010.

Fowler, Gene. *Beau James: The Life and Times of Jimmy Walker*. Viking Press, 1949.

———. *Schnozzola: The Story of Jimmy Durante*. Viking Press, 1951.

Fox, Stephen R. *Blood and Power: Organized Crime in Twentieth-Century America*. William Morrow, 1989.

Freeze, ChaeRan Y., and Jay M. Harris. *Everyday Jewish Life in Imperial Russia: Select Documents, 1772–1914*. Brandeis University Press, 2013.

Freud, Sigmund. *Sexuality and the Psychology of Love*. Simon & Schuster, 1997.

Frewin, Leslie. *The Late Mrs. Dorothy Parker*. Macmillan, 1986.

Fried, Albert. *The Rise and Fall of the Jewish Gangster in America*. Holt, Rinehart, & Winston, 1980.

Fuller, Samuel, et al. *A Third Face: My Tale of Writing, Fighting and Filmmaking*. Alfred A. Knopf, 2002.

Gabler, Neal. *Winchell: Gossip, Power, and the Culture of Celebrity*. Vintage, 1995.

Galbraith, John Kenneth. *A Life in Our Times*. Plunkett Lake Press, 2019.

Gallico, Paul. *Farewell to Sport*. Alfred A. Knopf, 1938.

Galvin, Anthony. *Old Sparky: The Electric Chair and the History of the Death Penalty*. Skyhorse, 2016.

Gambetta, Diego. *Codes of the Underworld: How Criminals Communicate*. Princeton University Press, 2009.

Gardner, Hy. *Champagne Before Breakfast*. Henry Holt, 1954.

Gauvreau, Emile. *Hot News*. Macaulay, 1931.

Gavin, James. *Intimate Nights: The Golden Age of New York Cabaret*. Grove Weidenfeld, 1991.

Gay, Ruth. *Unfinished People: Eastern European Jews Encounter America*. W. W. Norton, 1996.

Gehring, Wes D. *"Mr. B," or, Comforting Thoughts about the Bison: A Critical Biography of Robert Benchley*. Greenwood Press, 1992.

Gentry, Curt. *The Madams of San Francisco: An Irreverent History of the City by the Golden Gate*. Doubleday, 1964.

George, Don. *Sweet Man: The Real Duke Ellington*. Putnam, 1981.

Gilbert, David W. *The Product of Our Souls: Ragtime, Race, and the Birth of the Manhattan Musical Marketplace*. University of North Carolina Press, 2015.

Gilfoyle, Timothy J. *City of Eros: New York City, Prostitution, and the Commercialization of Sex, 1790–1920*. W. W. Norton, 1992.

Glaeser, Edward L., and Claudia Goldin, eds. *Corruption and Reform: Lessons from America's Economic History*. University of Chicago Press, 2007.

Glenn, Susan Anita. *Daughters of the Shtetl: Life and Labor in the Immigrant Generation*. Cornell University Press, 1990.

———. *Female Spectacle: The Theatrical Roots of Modern Feminism*. Harvard University Press, 2000.

Golden, Eve. *Vamp: The Rise and Fall of Theda Bara*. Vestal Press, 1998.

Golden, Harry. *For Two Cents Plain*. Amereon, 1976.

———. *The Right Time: An Autobiography*. Putnam, 1969.

———. *So Long as You're Healthy*. Putnam, 1970.

Goldman, Emma. *Living My Life*. Alfred A. Knopf, 1931.

Golway, Terry. *Frank and Al: FDR, Al Smith, and the Unlikely Alliance That Created the Modern Democratic Party*. St. Martin's, 2018.

Goodnow, Elizabeth. *The Market for Souls*. Mitchell Kennerley, 1910.

Gosch, Martin A., and Richard Hammer. *The Last Testament of Lucky Luciano*. Little, Brown, 1975.

Gracyk, Tim, and Frank W. Hoffmann. *Popular American Recording Pioneers, 1895–1925*. Haworth Press, 2000.

Granlund, N. T. *Blondes, Brunettes, and Bullets*. David McKay, 1957.

Graves, George S. *Progressive Springfield, Massachusetts*. G. S. Graves, 1913.

Green, Stanley. *The Great Clowns of Broadway*. Oxford University Press, 1984.

Griffin, Marcus. *Wise Guy: James J. Johnston: A Rhapsody in Fistics*. Vanguard Press, 1933.

Gross, Ben. *I Looked and I Listened: Informal Recollections of Radio and TV*. Random House, 1954.

Gurock, Jeffrey S. *East European Jews in America, 1880–1920: Immigration and Adaptation: American Jewish History*. Routledge, 1998.

Hahn, Emily. *Romantic Rebels: An Informal History of Bohemianism in America*. Houghton Mifflin, 1967.

Hakim, Catherine. *Erotic Capital: The Power of Attraction in the Boardroom and the Bedroom*. Basic Books, 2011.

Hapke, Laura. *Labor's Text: The Worker in American Fiction*. Rutgers University Press, 2001.

Hartshorn, Peter. *I Have Seen the Future: A Life of Lincoln Steffens*. Counterpoint, 2011.

Hasse, John Edward. *Beyond Category: The Life and Genius of Duke Ellington*. Simon & Schuster, 1993.

Hayes, Teddy. *With the Gloves Off: My Life in the Boxing and Political Arenas*. Lancha Books, 1977.

Heap, Chad C. *Slumming: Sexual and Racial Encounters in American Nightlife, 1885–1940*. University of Chicago Press, 2009.

Hecht, Ben. *A Child of the Century*. Primus, 1985.

Heimer, Mel. *The Big Drag*. Whittlesey House, 1947.

———. *The Long Count*. Atheneum, 1969.

Hellinger, Mark. *The Ten Million*. Farrar & Rinehart, 1934.

Heyl, Barbara Sherman. *The Madam as Entrepreneur: Career Management in House Prostitution*. Transaction Books, 1979.

Hirsch, Foster. *The Boys from Syracuse: The Shuberts' Theatrical Empire*. Southern Illinois University Press, 1998.

Hoffman, Lawrence A., ed. *My People's Prayer Book: Traditional Prayers, Modern Commentaries*. Jewish Lights Publishing, 1997.

Houchin, John H. *Censorship of the American Theatre in the Twentieth Century*. Cambridge University Press, 2009.

Howe, Irving. *World of Our Fathers: The Journey of the East European Jews to America and the Life They Found and Made*. Open Road Media, 2017.

Inabinett, Mark. *Grantland Rice and His Heroes: The Sportswriter as Mythmaker in the 1920s*. University of Tennessee Press, 1994.

James, Conrad W., Jr. *It Was Never a Gamble: The Life and Times of an Early 1900's Hustler*. iUniverse, 2000.

Jarrett, John. *Toy Bulldog: The Fighting Life and Times of Mickey Walker*. McFarland, 2013.

Jenkins, Alan. *The Twenties*. Universe Books, 1974.

Josephson, Matthew. *Al Smith: Hero of the Cities: A Political Portrait Drawing on the Papers of Frances Perkins*. Houghton Mifflin, 1969.

Kahn, Roger. *A Flame of Pure Fire: Jack Dempsey and the Roaring '20s*. Harcourt Brace, 1999.

Kanfer, Stefan. *Ball of Fire: The Tumultuous Life and Comic Art of Lucille Ball*. Alfred A. Knopf, 2003.

Kaplan, Marion A., and Deborah Dash Moore, eds. *Gender and Jewish History*. Indiana University Press, 2010.

Kashner, Sam, and Nancy Schoenberger. *Hollywood Kryptonite*. St. Martin's Press, 1997.

———. *A Talent for Genius: The Life and Times of Oscar Levant*. Villard Books, 1994.

Katcher, Leo. *The Big Bankroll: The Life and Times of Arnold Rothstein*. Arlington House, 1959.

Katz, Leonard. *Uncle Frank: The Biography of Frank Costello*. Drake, 1973.

Katz, Steven T. *The Shtetl: New Evaluations*. NYU Press, 2009.

Kazin, Alfred. *A Walker in the City*. Harcourt, Brace, 1951.

Kearns, Jack, and Oscar Fraley. *The Million Dollar Gate*. Macmillan, 1966.

Keire, Mara Laura. *For Business and Pleasure: Red-Light Districts and the Regulation of Vice in the United States, 1890–1933*. JHU Press, 2010.

Keller, Julius. *Inns and Outs.* G. P. Putnam's Sons, 1939.

Kelly, Jason. *Shelby's Folly: Jack Dempsey, Doc Kearns, and the Shakedown of a Montana Boomtown.* University of Nebraska Press, 2010.

Kessner, Thomas. *Fiorello H. La Guardia and the Making of Modern New York.* Penguin Books, 1991.

Kimball, Nell. *Her Life as an American Madam.* Edited by Stephen Longstreet. Macmillan, 1970.

Kinney, Harrison. *James Thurber: His Life and Times.* Henry Holt, 1995.

Kinney, Harrison, ed. *The Thurber Letters: The Wit, Wisdom, and Surprising Life of James Thurber.* Simon & Schuster, 2003.

Kisseloff, Jeff. *You Must Remember This: An Oral History of Manhattan from the 1890s to World War II.* Harcourt Brace Jovanovich, 1989.

Klurfeld, Herman. *Winchell, His Life and Times.* Praeger, 1976.

Kofoed, John Christian. *Leg Man in Seven-League Boots.* Glade House, 1946.

Koppelman, Lee E., and Seth Forman. *The Fire Island National Seashore: A History.* State University of New York Press, 2008.

Kotik, Yekhezkel, and David Assaf. *A Journey to a Nineteenth-Century Shtetl: The Memoirs of Yekhezkel Kotik.* Wayne State University Press and Diaspora Research Institute, Tel Aviv University, 2002.

Kriendler, H. Peter, and Harry Paul Jeffers. *"21": Every Day Was New Year's Eve: Memoirs of a Saloon Keeper.* Rowman & Littlefield, 1999.

Kumove, Shirley, ed. *Words Like Arrows: A Collection of Yiddish Folk Sayings.* University of Toronto Press, 1984.

Lacey, Robert. *Little Man: Meyer Lansky and the Gangster Life.* Century, 1991.

Lait, Jack, and Lee Mortimer. *New York: Confidential!* Ziff-Davis, 1948.

Landesman, Alter F. *Brownsville: The Birth, Development and Passing of a Jewish Community in New York.* Bloch, 1969.

Langum, David J. *Crossing Over the Line: Legislating Morality and the Mann Act.* University of Chicago Press, 1994.

Lardner, John. *White Hopes and Other Tigers.* Lippincott, 1951.

Lardner, Ring, and Ron Rapoport. *The Lost Journalism of Ring Lardner.* University of Nebraska Press, 2017.

Laughlin, Clara Elizabeth. *The Work-a-Day Girl: A Study of Some Present-Day Conditions.* Fleming H. Revell, 1913.

Lawrence, A. H. *Duke Ellington and His World.* Routledge, 2004.

Lazar, Irving, and Annette Tapert. *Swifty: My Life and Good Times.* Simon & Schuster, 1995.

Lederhendler, Eli. *Jewish Responses to Modernity: New Voices in America and Eastern Europe.* NYU Press, 1997.

Lee, Judith Yaross. *Defining New Yorker Humor.* University Press of Mississippi, 2000.

Lees, Gene. *Arranging the Score: Portraits of the Great Arrangers.* Cassell, 2002.

Leider, Emily W. *Myrna Loy: The Only Good Girl in Hollywood.* University of California Press, 2011.

Lerner, Michael A. *Dry Manhattan: Prohibition in New York City.* Harvard University Press, 2007.

Levant, Oscar. *The Memoirs of an Amnesiac.* G. P. Putnam's Sons, 1965.

Levine, Gary. *Jack "Legs" Diamond: Anatomy of a Gangster.* Purple Mountain Press, 1995.

Levinson, Peter J. *Trumpet Blues: The Life of Harry James*. Oxford University Press, 1999.

Levitt, Paul M., and Ed Lowry. *Joe Frisco: Comic, Jazz Dancer, and Railbird*. Southern Illinois University Press, 1999.

Lewin, Sam. *How to Win at the Races: Education of a Horseplayer*. Wilshire, 1970.

Lewis, Sinclair. *Babbitt*. The Library of America, 1992.

Liebling, A. J. *The Sweet Science*. Farrar, Straus and Giroux, 2014.

Limpus, Lowell M. *Honest Cop, Lewis J. Valentine: Being a Chronicle of the Commissioner's Thirty-Six Years in the New York Police Department*. E. P. Dutton, 1939.

Lippitt, Henry. *History of the Class of 1909, Yale University*. Class Officers Bureau, 1928.

Loesser, Frank, Jo Swerling, and Abe Burrows. *Guys & Dolls: A Musical Fable of Broadway*. Frank Music, 1953.

Loos, Anita. *Kiss Hollywood Good-By*. Viking Press, 1974.

———. *The Talmadge Girls: A Memoir*. Viking Press, 1978.

Maas, Peter. *The Valachi Papers*. Putnam, 1968.

MacKaye, Milton. *The Tin Box Parade: A Handbook for Larceny*. Laugh Club, 1934.

Mackey, Thomas C. *Pursuing Johns: Criminal Law Reform, Defending Character, and New York City's Committee of Fourteen, 1920–1930*. Ohio State University Press, 2005.

MacShane, Frank. *The Life of John O'Hara*. E. P. Dutton, 1980.

Marcuse, Maxwell F. *This Was New York: A Nostalgic Picture of Gotham in the Gaslight Era*. LIM Press, 1969.

Marx, Maxine. *Growing up with Chico*. Prentice-Hall, 1980.

Maurer, David W. *The Big Con: The Story of the Confidence Man and the Confidence Game*. Bobbs-Merrill, 1940.

Mayer, Martin. *Emory Buckner: A Biography*. Harper & Row, 1968.

McAllister, Robert, and Floyd Miller. *The Kind of Guy I Am*. McGraw-Hill, 1957.

McCracken, Allison. *Real Men Don't Sing: Crooning in American Culture*. Duke University Press, 2015.

McGowan, Helen. *Motor City Madam*. Pageant Press, 1964.

McLaren, Angus. *Sexual Blackmail: A Modern History*. Harvard University Press, 2002.

Mencken, H. L. *Mencken's America*. Edited by S. T. Joshi. Ohio University Press, 2004.

Meredith, Scott. *George S. Kaufman and His Friends*. Doubleday, 1974.

Meryman, Richard. *Mank: The Wit, World, and Life of Herman Mankiewicz*. William Morrow, 1978.

Meyer, Hazel. *The Gold in Tin Pan Alley*. Greenwood Press, 1977.

Miller, Donald L. *Supreme City: How Jazz Age Manhattan Gave Birth to Modern America*. Simon & Schuster, 2015.

Miller, Paul Edward. *Esquire's Jazz Book*. Smith & Durrell, 1944.

Mitgang, Herbert. *The Man Who Rode the Tiger: The Life and Times of Judge Samuel Seabury*. Lippincott, 1963.

———. *Once upon a Time in New York: Jimmy Walker, Franklin Roosevelt, and the Last Great Battle of the Jazz Age*. Free Press, 2000.

Moley, Raymond. *Tribunes of the People: The Past and Future of the New York Magistrates' Courts*. Yale University Press. 1932.

Monin, Lydia. *From Poverty Bay to Broadway: The Story of Tom Heeney*. Hodder Moa Beckett, 2008.

Mooney, Martin. *Crime, Incorporated*. Whittlesey House, 1935.

Morton, James. *Gangland: The Lawyers*. Virgin, 2001.

Moscow, Warren. *What Have You Done for Me Lately? The Ins and Outs of New York City Politics*. Prentice-Hall, 1967.

Moses, Paul. *An Unlikely Union: The Love-Hate Story of New York's Irish and Italians*. NYU Press, 2015.

Muir, Florabel. *Headline Happy*. Henry Holt, 1950.

Mulhall, Sara Graham. *Opium: The Demon Flower*. H. Vinal, 1926.

Murray, Lyn. *Musician: A Hollywood Journal: Of Wives, Women, Writers, Lawyers, Directors, Producers, and Music*. L. Stuart, 1987.

Murtagh, John M., and Sara Harris. *Cast the First Stone*. McGraw-Hill, 1957.

Nash, Gary B., and Thomas R. Frazier, eds. *The Private Side of American History: Readings in Everyday Life*. Harcourt Brace Jovanovich, 1975.

Nathans, Benjamin. *Beyond the Pale: The Jewish Encounter with Late Imperial Russia*. University of California Press, 2002.

Nelson, Carolyn Christensen. *A New Woman Reader: Fiction, Articles and Drama of the 1890s*. Broadview Press, 2000.

Newark, Tim. *Lucky Luciano: The Real and the Fake Gangster*. Thomas Dunne Books, 2010.

Nissenson, Marilyn. *The Lady Upstairs: Dorothy Schiff and the New York Post*. St. Martin's, 2013.

Nolan, Frederick. *Lorenz Hart: A Poet on Broadway*. Oxford University Press, 1995.

Nown, Graham. *Arkansas Godfather: The Story of Owney Madden and How He Hijacked Middle America*. University of Arkansas Press, 2013.

O'Connor, John James. *Broadway Racketeers*. Horace Liveright, 1928.

O'Hara, John. *The Selected Letters of John O'Hara*. Edited by Matthew J. Bruccoli. Random House, 1978.

Odegard, Peter H., and E. Allen Helms. *American Politics: A Study in Political Dynamics*. Harper & Bros., 1938.

Okun, Lewis. *Woman Abuse: Facts Replacing Myths*. State University of New York Press, 1986.

Osgood, Henry Osborne. *So This Is Jazz*. Little, Brown, 1926.

Page, William Adino. *Behind the Curtains of the Broadway Beauty Trust*. Edward A. Miller, 1927.

Parascandola, Louis J., and John Parascandola, eds. *A Coney Island Reader: Through Dizzy Gates of Illusion*. Columbia University Press, 2014.

Partridge, Eric. *A Dictionary of Catch Phrases*. Routledge, 2003.

Peellaert, Guy, and Michael Herr. *The Big Room*. Summit Books, 1986.

Peiss, Kathy Lee. *Cheap Amusements: Working Women and Leisure in Turn-of-the-Century New York*. Temple University Press, 1986.

——. *Passion and Power: Sexuality in History*. Temple University Press, 1989.

Peress, Maurice. *Dvořák to Duke Ellington: A Conductor Explores America's Music and Its African American Roots*. Oxford University Press, 2004.

Peretti, Burton. *Nightclub City: Politics and Amusement in Manhattan*. University of Pennsylvania Press, 2007.

Phillips, Damon J. *Shaping Jazz: Cities, Labels, and the Global Emergence of an Art Form*. Princeton University Press, 2013.

Phillips, David Graham. *Susan Lenox: Her Fall and Rise*. D. Appleton, 1922.

Pietrusza, David. *Rothstein: The Life, Times, and Murder of the Criminal Genius Who Fixed the 1919 World Series*. Carroll & Graf, 2003.

Pilat, Oliver, and Jo Ranson. *Sodom by the Sea: An Affectionate History of Coney Island*. Doubleday, Doran, 1941.

Pitrone, Jean Maddern. *Take It from the Big Mouth: The Life of Martha Raye*. University Press of Kentucky, 2014.

Pliley, Jessica R. *Policing Sexuality: The Mann Act and the Making of the FBI*. Harvard University Press, 2014.

Pollack, Howard. *George Gershwin: His Life and Work*. University of California Press, 2007.

Porter, Darwin. *Katharine the Great: Secrets of a Lifetime . . . Revealed*. Blood Moon Productions, 2004.

Powell, Hickman. *Ninety Times Guilty*. Harcourt, Brace, 1939.

Putnam, George P., ed. *Nonsenseorship*. G. G. Putnam, 1922.

Rayno, Don. *Paul Whiteman: Pioneer in American Music*. Scarecrow Press, 2003.

[Recht, Charles.] *Babylon on Hudson*. Harper & Brothers, 1932.

Reeve, Arthur B. *The Golden Age of Crime*. Mohawk Press, 1931.

Reynolds, Quentin James. *Headquarters*. Harper, 1955.

Rice, Grantland. *The Tumult and the Shouting: My Life in Sport*. A. S. Barnes, 1954.

Richman, Harry, and Richard Gehman. *A Hell of a Life*. Duell, Sloan & Pearce, 1966.

Roe, Clifford Griffith. *The Great War on White Slavery, Or, Fighting for the Protection of Our Girls*. P. W. Ziegler, 1911.

Rose, Billy. *Wine, Women and Words*. Simon & Schuster, 1948.

Rosen, Ruth. *The Lost Sisterhood: Prostitution in America, 1900–1918*. Johns Hopkins University Press, 1982.

Rosmond, Babette. *Robert Benchley: His Life and Good Times*. Doubleday, 1970.

Rothstein, Carolyn Green. *Now I'll Tell*. Vanguard Press, 1934.

Runyon, Damon. *The Bloodhounds of Broadway and Other Stories*. William Morrow, 1981.

Ruth, David E. *Inventing the Public Enemy: The Gangster in American Culture, 1918–1934*. University of Chicago Press, 1996.

Salwen, Peter. *Upper West Side Story: A History and Guide*. Abbeville Press, 1989.

Samuel, Maurice. *The World of Sholom Aleichem*. Alfred A. Knopf, 1943.

Sann, Paul. *Kill the Dutchman! The Story of Dutch Schultz*. Da Capo Press, 1991.

———. *The Lawless Decade: A Pictorial History of a Great American Transition: From the World War I Armistice and Prohibition to Repeal and the New Deal*. Crown, 1960.

Schuller, Gunther. *The Swing Era: The Development of Jazz, 1930–1945*. Oxford University Press, 1989.

Scully, Frank. *Cross My Heart*. Greenberg, 1955.

Segrave, Kerry. *Payola in the Music Industry: A History, 1880–1991*. McFarland, 1994.

Seldes, Gilbert. *The Future of Drinking*. Little, Brown, 1930.

Shaffer, Caroline. *The Executive Connection*. Xlibris, 2010.

Shaw, Arnold. *Let's Dance: Popular Music in the 1930s*. Oxford University Press, 1998.

Sheed, Wilfrid. *The House That George Built: With a Little Help from Irving, Cole, and a Crew of About Fifty*. Random House, 2008.

Shepard, Richard F., and Vicki Gold Levi. *Live and Be Well: A Celebration of Yiddish Culture in America from the First Immigrants to the Second World War*. Rutgers University Press, 2000.

Shipton, Alyn. *I Feel a Song Coming On: The Life of Jimmy McHugh*. University of Illinois Press, 2009.

Shoenfeld, A. H. *The Joy Peddler*. Penuel Press, 1927.

Shteir, Rachel. *Striptease: The Untold History of the Girlie Show*. Oxford University Press, 2004.

Sicherman, Barbara, and Carol Hurd Green, eds. *Notable American Women: The Modern Period: A Biographical Dictionary*. Harvard University Press, 1980.

Sifakis, Carl. *The Mafia Encyclopedia*, 2nd ed. Facts on File, 1999.

Sillman, Leonard. *Here Lies Leonard Sillman: Straightened Out at Last*. Citadel Press, 1959.

Singer, Barry. *Black and Blue: The Life and Lyrics of Andy Razaf*. Schirmer Books, 1992.

Slayton, Robert A. *Empire Statesman: The Rise and Redemption of Al Smith*. Free Press, 2001.

Slide, Anthony, ed. *Selected Vaudeville Criticism*. Scarecrow Press, 1988.

Smith, H. Allen. *The Life and Legend of Gene Fowler*. William Morrow, 1977.

Smith, Marjorie Erskine. *No Bed of Roses: The Diary of a Lost Soul*. Sheridan House, 1941.

Sorin, Gerald. *A Time for Building: The Third Migration, 1880–1920*. Johns Hopkins University Press, 1992.

Starr, John. *The Purveyor: The Shocking Story of Today's Illicit Liquor Empire*. Holt, Rinehart & Winston, 1961.

Stern, Michael. *No Innocence Abroad*. Random House, 1953.

———. *The White Ticket: Commercialized Vice in the Machine Age, from the Official Records at the New York District Attorney's Office*. National Library Press, c. 1936.

Stewart, Donald Ogden. *By a Stroke of Luck! An Autobiography*. Paddington Press, 1975.

Stoddart, Dayton. *Lord Broadway, Variety's Sime*. W. Funk, 1941.

Stolberg, Mary M. *Fighting Organized Crime: Politics, Justice and the Legacy of Thomas E. Dewey*. UPNE, 1995.

Strausbaugh, John. *Victory City: A History of New York and New Yorkers During World War II*. Twelve, 2018.

Strauss, Helen Marion. *A Talent for Luck: An Autobiography*. Random House, 1979.

Strode, Hudson. *The Eleventh House: Memoirs*. Harcourt Brace Jovanovich, 1975.

Stuart, Lyle. *The Secret Life of Walter Winchell*. Boar's Head Books, 1953.

Sullivan, Edward Dean. *The Snatch Racket*. Vanguard Press, 1932.

Sullivan, Frank. *Well, There's No Harm in Laughing*. Edited by George Oppenheimer. Doubleday, 1972.

Sutton, Willie, and Edward Linn. *Where the Money Was*. Viking Press, 1976.

Sutton, Willie, and Quentin James Reynolds. *I, Willie Sutton*. Farrar, Straus & Young, 1953.

Sylvester, Robert. *No Cover Charge: A Backward Look at the Night Clubs*. Dial Press, 1956.

———. *Notes of a Guilty Bystander*. Prentice-Hall, 1970.

Teichmann, Howard. *George S. Kaufman: An Intimate Portrait*. Atheneum, 1972.

Thomas, Bob. *Winchell*. Garden City, 1971.

Thomas, Norman, and Paul Blanshard. *What's the Matter with New York: A National Problem*. Macmillan, 1932.

Thompson, Craig, and Allen Raymond. *Gang Rule in New York: The Story of a Lawless Era*. Dial Press, 1940.

Thurber, James, et al. *The Thurber Letters: The Wit, Wisdom, and Surprising Life of James Thurber*. Simon & Schuster, 2003.

Tractate Berakoth (Benedictions) Mishna and Tosephta. Macmillan, 1921.

Trow's General Directory of the Boroughs of Manhattan and Bronx, City of NY, 1922–1923. R.L. Polk & Co. Pub., 1932.

Tucker, Garland. *High Tide of American Conservatism: Davis, Coolidge, and the 1924 Election*. Greenleaf Book Group, 2012.

Tugwell, Rexford G. *The Brains Trust*. Viking Press, 1968.

Turkus, Burton B., and Sid Feder. *Murder, Inc.: The Story of "the Syndicate."* Farrar, Straus & Young, 1951.

Ulanov, Barry. *Duke Ellington*. Da Capo Press, 1975.

U.S. Task Force on Assessment of Crime. *Task Force Report: Crime and Its Impact—an Assessment*. President's Commission on Law Enforcement and Administration of Justice, 1967.

Valentine, Lewis Joseph. *Night Stick: The Autobiography of Lewis J. Valentine*. Dial Press, 1947.

Van Raalte, Joseph. *The Vice Squad*. Vanguard Press, 1931.

Vital, David. *A People Apart: The Jews in Europe, 1789–1939*. Oxford University Press, 1999.

Wakeman, Frederic. *The Hucksters*. Rinehart, 1946.

Walker, Danton. *Danton's Inferno: The Story of a Columnist and How He Grew*. Hastings House, 1955.

Walker, Mickey, and Joseph L. Reichler. *Mickey Walker: The Toy Bulldog and His Times*. Random House, 1961.

Walker, Stanley. *The Night Club Era*. Johns Hopkins University Press, 1999.

Wallace, Irving. *The Sunday Gentleman*. Bantam Books, 1976.

Ware, Caroline F. *Greenwich Village, 1920–1930: A Comment on American Civilization in the Post-War Years*. Houghton Mifflin, 1935.

Waugh, Alec. *A Year to Remember: A Reminiscence of 1931*. Bloomsbury Reader, 2012.

Weinberg, Sydney Stahl. *The World of Our Mothers: The Lives of Jewish Immigrant Women*. Schocken Books, 1988.

Weld, John. *Fly Away Home*. Mission, 1991.

Weller, Sheila. *Dancing at Ciro's: A Family's Love, Loss, and Scandal on the Sunset Strip*. St. Martin's Press, 2003.

Whipple, Sidney Beaumont. *Noble Experiment: A Portrait of America Under Prohibition*. Methuen, 1934.

White, Shane. *Playing the Numbers: Gambling in Harlem Between the Wars*. Harvard University Press, 2010.

White, William Allen. *Masks in a Pageant*. Macmillan, 1930.

Willemse, Cornelius William. *Behind the Green Lights*. Alfred A. Knopf, 1931.

Wilson, Christopher. *Dancing with the Devil: The Windsors and Jimmy Donahue*. St. Martin's Press, 2014.

Winchell, Walter. *Winchell Exclusive*. Prentice-Hall, 1975.

Wintz, Cary D., and Paul Finkelman. *Encyclopedia of the Harlem Renaissance: A-J*. Taylor & Francis, 2004.

Wolf, George, and Joseph DiMona. *Frank Costello: Prime Minister of the Underworld*. William Morrow, 1974.

Woods, Robert Archey, and Albert J. Kennedy. *Young Working Girls: A Summary of Evidence from Two Thousand Social Workers*. Houghton Mifflin, 1913.

Woolston, Howard Brown. *Prostitution in the United States*. Patterson Smith, 1969.

Whorf, Michael. *American Popular Song Composers: Oral Histories, 1920s–1950s*. McFarland, 2014.

Yagoda, Ben. *About Town: The New Yorker and the World It Made*. Scribner, 2000.

Young, Anthony. *New York Café Society: The Elite Meet to See and Be Seen, 1920s–1940s*. McFarland, 2015.

Yanow Near Pinsk Memorial Book (Ivanava, Belarus). Edited by Mordechai Nadav and Nachman Blumenthal. Association of Former Residents of Janow near Pinsk in Israel, 1969. https://www.jewishgen.org/yizkor/ivanovo/ivanovo.html.

Index

Page numbers in *italics* refer to illustrations.

Illustration Credits

Interior images

Polly Adler exiting paddy wagon, 1936 (page xvi), from Getty Images; Yanow marketplace (page 20) from *Yanow near Pinsk Memorial Book*; Polly Adler exiting patrol wagon, 1935 (page 354), from NYDailyNewsPix; Swing Street (page 396), from the Library of Congress. All other interior images are public domain, from the author's personal collection, or are provided by the Polly Adler Collection, courtesy of Eleanor Vera.

Insert images

Lindy's delicatessen (insert 1, page 5) and the Harding Hotel (insert 1, page 6), from the Museum of the City of New York; Connie's *Hot Chocolates* (insert 2, page 6), from the New York Public Library; Dorothy Lamour (insert 3, page 3) and Dutch Schultz wanted poster (insert 2, page 8), from Alamy; Arnold Rothstein (insert 1, page 4), Jefferson Market Women's Court (insert 1, page 4), Vivian Gordon (insert 2, page 8), and the gangster lineup (insert 1, page 7), from the Library of Congress; James J. Quinlivan (insert 2, page 5) and the *New York Daily News* clippings (insert 1, page 3 and insert 3, page 1), from NYDailyNewsPix; Jimmy Durante, Eddie Jackson, and Lou Clayton (insert 1, page 8), Libby Holman (insert 2, page 2), Gladys Bentley (insert 3, page 3) courtesy of the J. D. Doyle Collection; *Broadway Brevities* cartoon (insert 2, page 6) courtesy of Elizabeth Alice Clement; Gittel Adler and sons (insert 1, page 2) courtesy of Robin Adler; Duke Ellington and the Washingtonians (insert 2, page 1) courtesy of Steven Lasker; Irwin O'Leary (insert 2, page 5) courtesy of Bonnie O'Leary; Yanow street scene (insert 1, page 1) from the National Library of Israel, courtesy of the Ephemera Collection. All other insert images are public domain, from the author's personal collection, or are provided by the Polly Adler Collection, courtesy of Eleanor Vera.

ABOUT THE AUTHOR

DEBBY APPLEGATE is a historian based in New Haven, Connecticut. Her first book, *The Most Famous Man in America: The Biography of Henry Ward Beecher*, won the 2007 Pulitzer Prize for biography and was a finalist for the Los Angeles Times Book Prize and the National Book Critics Circle Award. She is a graduate of Amherst College and holds a Ph.D. from Yale University.

Living God's Politics

Living
God's Politics

A Guide to Putting
Your Faith into Action

Jim Wallis

with Chuck Gutenson
and the editors of *Sojourners*

HarperSanFrancisco
A Division of HarperCollinsPublishers

FIRST EDITION
Designed by Sharon VanLoozenoord

Library of Congress Cataloging-in-Publication Data

Wallis, Jim.
    Living God's politics : a guide to putting your faith into action / Jim Wallis ; with the editors of Sojourners magazine.—1st ed.
    p. cm.
    ISBN-10: 0–06–111841–9
    ISBN-13: 978–0–06–111841–8
    1. Christianity and politics—United States. 2. Christians—Political activity. I. Wallis, Jim. God's politics. II. Title.

BR526.W2655 2005
261.70973—dc22   2006043524

06 07 08 09 10 RRD(H) 10 9 8 7 6 5 4 3 2 1

Contents

Getting the Most from
Living God's Politics

WE ARE DELIGHTED that you are taking this opportunity to study *God's Politics* by Jim Wallis and to use this workbook as a way to more fully equip yourself to understand and live its message. *Living God's Politics* is not only a commentary on *God's Politics* (though it is that). Rather, *Living God's Politics* is intended to build upon the commitments presented in the book in three ways.

First, we provide resources and information aimed to help you probe more deeply into the major themes covered in *God's Politics (GP)*. Second, while it is important to understand the content of *GP*, it is more important to begin to live out its challenges in our daily lives. To that end, we have provided specific suggestions on a number of different activities that might enable you to act on the message of *GP*. At the end of the day, both *God's Politics* and *Living God's Politics (LGP)* are intended to help you think through what your faith means and to learn how that faith can be expressed in public life. *LGP* has been structured specifically for these purposes.

The material is arranged so that you might work through *LGP* and *GP* together over a period of eight weeks. Each week covers one theme from *GP*, and each day of a given week focuses on a particular aspect of that week's theme. In order to get the most from this study, we recommend that you gather together with others and undertake your reflections in a group setting. You could form a group from your congregation, school, organization, or other association. Either small groups or more formal Sunday school classes would provide excellent opportunities for community, fellowship, and study. In many cases, members of your group may choose to work together as you seek to study and act on your insights.

Second, we at Sojourners/Call to Renewal are constantly developing new resources and planning various ways to express a healthy and vibrant vision of faith in public life. We invite you to visit our Web sites (www.sojo.net and www.calltorenewal. org) to see the latest developments. In fact, when you visit our site, be sure to sign up for SojoMail, our weekly e-zine. (You can find it by going to www.sojo.net and clicking on SojoMail.) SojoMail is free, provides access to a wealth of resources and action ideas, and gives an entry into the Sojourners/Call to Renewal community.

Third, you can build on the material we present by making a firm commitment to each other for regular study and prayer as you work through *LGP* and *GP*.

It is our hope that the experience will be life-transforming for you and your study partners. However, for it to be so, you will need a core of firmly committed people who are passionate about hearing the full breadth of the biblical call to social justice and are willing to experiment with what they have heard. We encourage you and your group to consider establishing a covenant to read and be prepared for each week's study. Please go to the Sojourners Web site and use the "meet up" feature to locate other folks in your area who are interested in studying together. Let us know how your study is going.

Now let's take a look at the eight-week format. As noted, the study consists of weekly sessions built around the central themes addressed in *God's Politics*. Those themes and the order in which they will be covered are as follows:

Week One: Faith and Politics

Week Two: War and Peace

Week Three: Economic Justice

Week Four: Poverty

Week Five: A Consistent Ethic of Life

Week Six: Racism

Week Seven: Strengthening Family and Community Values

Week Eight: Hope for the Future

Each week is prefaced with the connection between *GP* and *LGP*. In particular, we will indicate the appropriate chapters from *GP* to read in conjunction with that week's theme. We will not repeat the content from those chapters, though we will provide a brief summary of each. Some chapters are used in more than one week. These introductions serve as the bridge between the workbook and the book. During the course of each week, specific aspects of the theme will be examined by means of a focused reading for each day of the week. The subtopics remain the same from week to week, as follows:

Day 1: Introducing the Topic

Day 2: Considering the Evidence

Day 3: Reading the Bible

Day 4: The Christian Tradition

Day 5: Living Examples in the Contemporary Church

Day 6: Putting Faith into Action

Day 7: Group Meeting and Reflection

Each week you and your group will consider one theme from *God's Politics* from a number of different perspectives. Some are aimed at providing a better grasp of the issue (Days 1 and 2); some at how Christians have thought about this issue (Days 3, 4, and 5), and one day each for considering specific ways that you might live out concern for that issue (Day 6) and for personal and group reflection (Day 7).

You can organize and schedule your group in any of a number of ways. However, we suggest that Day 7 would be the best day to meet as a group. By then you will have processed the week's material as individuals. Your group meeting will allow you to consider the issue together using the suggested questions and discuss each other's personal reflections. It is important that your discussion explicitly consider the focus of Day 6. Of course, you should feel free to creatively move beyond the suggestions that we have included. Look for opportunities to select actions that meet the needs of your particular community. Don't feel discouraged if you are unable to plan an action item with regard to each and every theme. However, strategically choosing ways you will act on what you are learning is critical to the study. So even if you cannot engage in some activity from Day 6 each week, consider selecting a subset of the themes on which to undertake particular actions.

The appendix to this book provides a number of ideas on how to engage in different kinds of social action, from letter-writing campaigns to educational events to community organizing to demonstrations to nonviolent civil disobedience. Some forms of social action fit better than others with particular themes we will study together. In our material for Day 6 of each week, we have listed brief examples of the kinds of social action we see as best fitting each theme. To avoid repetition, however, we have provided the details in the appendix. As noted above, please feel free to step outside the box and come up with your own creative ways to act on *God's Politics*.

Once again, welcome to this study! It is our prayer that God's Spirit will be active in your life as you seek to live out the biblical call to justice and love.

Before You Start

As YOU PREPARE to work through *God's Politics* with *Living God's Politics* as a guide, take a few minutes to prepare yourself by recording your current thoughts on several questions. Reflect, either individually or with your study group, on the following:

1. Before you begin to read through *God's Politics* and *Living God's Politics*, consider what you think of the relation between faith and politics—particularly how faith should inform and guide us on political issues. Does God have a "politics"? Why do you say this?

2. Construct a list of factors that you think must be taken into consideration when developing commitments that adequately reflect God's intentions for our public life together. In other words, how would a society that lives according to God's intention that we work for the common good be organized and structured? What kinds of public and social institutions would it have? What would its priorities be?

3. What point is *God's Politics* trying to make with the subtitle "Why the Right Gets It Wrong and the Left Doesn't Get It"? As you read through the book, develop a list of things you would say to the Right and then to the Left if you were given an opportunity to address them. Be sure to defend your list from a faith perspective.

Take notes on your reflections so you will have them available after the study in order to assess whether and how your thinking has changed. At the end, we will return to a similar set of questions. Enjoy your study! Now on to Week 1.

Living
God's Politics

Week One

Faith and Politics

THE **TOPIC FOR** this first section is the relationship between faith and politics. This theme relates particularly to the introduction of *God's Politics* as well as to chapters 1 to 3, 5, and 6. Chapter 4 is related as well, and it will also be associated later (along with chapter 6) with the concluding theme of hope. Be sure to review chapters 1 to 3, 5, and 6 during the course of working through this first section of *Living God's Politics*. The following paragraphs provide a brief overview of each of those chapters.

Introduction: Since politics is ultimately about ordering our communal life together, it is far too important an aspect of human life to be considered outside of God's care and attention. God has a "political perspective," one might say, rooted in God's identity as Creator and expressed in the Bible. However, God's politics always challenges our politics. We too easily pursue ideological agendas that serve our own interest. God's politics is never ideological, but always intends to benefit human well-being. In particular, God reminds us of our obligations to the persons we often neglect—the poor, the vulnerable, and those otherwise on the margins. God's politics challenges both the political Left and the political Right to offer a new vision of faith and politics, a vision more in line with God's intentions and the common good.

Chapter 1: Many people feel that there is no political option that does justice to their understanding of the Christian faith. They feel that Christian language has been co-opted by the Right and used to accomplish ends that are not consistent with a full expression of the faith they hold. Likewise, they feel that the Left has tended to treat them as if their faith were irrelevant for political life. These folks long for a return to a genuine faith that transcends these options. They embrace a faith that unapologetically engages the public political discourse while insisting upon a moral vision consistent with that taught and lived by Jesus and the biblical prophets.

Chapter 2: "Without vision the people perish" (Proverbs 29:18). This ancient biblical proverb actually makes one point, but it implies an equally important second point. On the first, it is clear from history that where ambiguity and confusion are evident and there is an absence of vision, the people suffer. Without vision, there is no "road map" to a better tomorrow. On the second point, the people also suffer where there is wrong or misguided vision. When you are going in the wrong direction, "making progress" is not a virtue. Now is the time to develop an alternative vision for the intersection of religious and public life and to call public institutions to accountability for how well they serve the common good, rather than the good of special interest groups.

Chapter 3: To suggest that God is concerned only with our private lives implies a "household god"—a god who watches over our private piety but cares little about public life. Such a god is not the God of the Judeo-Christian heritage. God is deeply personal and is clearly concerned about our personal morality. However, even a quick read through the Bible reveals a God who is also very interested in the shape of our social values and public life. In particular, God is concerned that public institutions prevent the exploitation of society's most marginalized persons. God gives commands aimed at preventing such exploitation, and those passages dealing with divine judgment make it clear that God takes very seriously the extent to which our public life includes those concerns for justice.

Chapter 5: At its worst, religious fundamentalism seeks political power to impose a theocracy; secular fundamentalism, on the other hand, attempts to confine religious faith only to private expression or houses of worship. The real question is not whether religious faith should influence a society and its politics, but rather how: What form of influence would be most consistent with our faith and provide the best opportunity to positively impact our culture? For example, the religious Right that emerged in the 1980s preferred a more partisan approach, seeking to gain control of the levers of power in order to enact change. The civil rights movement, on the other hand, was more morally based and politically independent, seeking to motivate change from the outside.

Chapter 6: There are three dominant political options in America. One is conservative on everything—from cultural and family concerns to economic and foreign policy issues. The second is liberal on everything across the same spectrum. The third is libertarian—liberal on cultural/family issues and conservative on fiscal/economic policy. A fourth option, one that is largely missing within the current American political scene, is traditional or conservative on issues of family values and sexual integrity, for example, while progressive or populist on issues of economic justice and peacemaking. Some are beginning to see the false dichotomy embodied by viewing everything as either liberal or conservative, and Christians have an opportunity to lead a significant change in the political landscape of this country.

DAY 1 Introducing the Topic

Early on, *God's Politics* makes the claim that "God is personal, but never private." In fact, *God's Politics* emphasizes that point by making it the subtitle to the third chapter. It is a point that is far more important than is often realized. While on the one hand God cannot somehow be relegated merely to the nonpublic areas of our lives, on the other hand God must be understood as also concerned with the personal aspects of our lives.

Central to the Christian faith is the idea that God is not a remote, uncaring, impersonal God, but rather is fully engaged and interactive with creation. But what does it mean to affirm that God is personal? Well, first and foremost, to be a person is to be in relation with others. In other words, the basic idea behind the term "person" is not that of a lone individual, but rather of an individual who stands among and in relation to others. Obviously, we do not cease being persons when we are alone; however, who we are as persons is built from our relationships with one another. We are who we are precisely as a consequence of the various relations we have had with other persons over time. If those relationships had been different, we would, in a very real sense, be different people. To be a person is to be in relation with others, and for the Christian, those others include God and the rest of creation.

Christian ethicist Stanley Hauerwas once said that the Bible is not so much a book about what we ought to do as it is a book about who God is, and what we ought to do flows from that knowledge. We have been created so that relationships, both with God and with the rest of creation, are a major factor in forming us as specific persons. All of us bear the marks of our various relationships, and this is a powerful reminder of how much God intends us to impact each other for the better.

To claim that God is always personal, then, is important at several different levels. First, it affirms the reality that God is not distant and uncaring. Rather, God desires a deeply personal relationship with each and every one of us. Second, it affirms the deeply community-oriented "way of being" that God intends for us and that we embody when we enter into loving relationships with those around us. In short, we realize our personhood as God intended it to be when we love God with our whole hearts and our neighbors as ourselves. Robert Mulholland, professor of New Testament at Asbury Seminary, emphasizes the close connection between these two great commands by translating them (roughly): Love the Lord your God with all your heart, mind, soul, and strength, and *another way of saying the same thing,* love your neighbor as yourself. When we combine these two points, we see that God is intensely concerned about our personal moral and spiritual growth. What we must not miss is that, because of the way that God has created us to be persons in relationship, God is equally concerned about how we organize ourselves into communities and the social structures and rules that organize our common life.

The second part of the claim from *God's Politics* is that "God is never private." For Christians, there is a sense in which everything changed with the life of Jesus. With his exemplary life, death, and resurrection, a new order has been ushered into existence. The essential affirmation of the post-Easter period is that "Jesus is Lord." Unfortunately, in our contemporary setting, this affirmation has lost some of its force. It is often reduced to little more than a statement about personal piety; that is, we live as if the affirmation were "Jesus is Lord of my private life." This is true enough, but to limit Jesus's primacy to our private lives is to miss the biblical claim that Jesus is now Lord over all creation, personal and communal, private and public. If we claim the primacy of Jesus as Christ, then we cannot worship idols or allow any other political or religious leaders to make claims on our faith—a faith that belongs to God alone. Christians need to recapture the boldness of the biblical vision for our communities and public institutions that flows from a fuller realization of the vision of Jesus.

If we fail to see God's personal nature, we will miss the importance God places upon our development into the persons we ought to be. We will also miss the extent to which God intends our character to be worked out within community. In turn, this will lead us to miss the extent to which God cares about the manner in which we organize our social life and communities and structure them so as to allow for the flourishing of all God's children. As *God's Politics* points out, the Hebrew prophets did not miss either of these points in their critiques. It is worth reflecting on how the prophets Amos or Isaiah might speak God's truth to power structures in our contemporary setting. Without an adequate sense of the implications of the relationship between God and creation, we miss the fact that God cares about the nature of the institutions we establish in our communal (that is, public) everyday lives. A great danger is the tendency to conceive of God and God's concerns as merely private matters.

All of this means, then, that Christians must prayerfully examine the Bible and the history of the church to be certain that the social life we establish adequately addresses the issues that God expresses most concern about. These issues include personal morality (sexual integrity, for example) as well as public morality (the community's obligation to care for "the least of these," for example). Neither alone is adequate.

We often hear those on the political Right argue that concern for the poor is valid but that such concerns are to be addressed on the personal level, either by persons or by churches, but not by governments. This is a much too anemic view of God's concerns. Public policies, priorities, and programs are all part of the system established to organize our shared lives. For Christians, this means arguing for policies, priorities, and programs that defend and protect "the least of these." An attitude of "each one on his or her own" will not pass biblical muster.

The implications this has for Christian life are remarkable. For example, conventional wisdom has it that two subjects forbidden from polite conversation are religion and politics. Yet it is hard to imagine two subjects of more consequence for day-to-day human life. Perhaps we need to learn a new sort of civility that will allow us vigorously to engage each other, seeking to come to a better consensus about realizing God's intentions in our public life.

In conclusion, let us remember that God is always personal and never private, which means that God is interested in human life and in moral choices at all levels, from the personal to the church to the local community to the nation and, finally, to the entire world.

DAY 2

Considering the Evidence

Imagine you are a person deeply mired in catastrophic poverty, a member of an ethnic minority concerned about workplace protections, or a person with an illness for which treatment would be long and expensive. Or imagine you are a member of the solid middle class worried about the demise of the middle class. Or that you are reasonably well off and hoping to … well, stay well off. In each of these cases, you are imagining yourself as a person with deep and serious concerns related to your well-being and that of the society in which you live. Now imagine that someone said to you that you should not bring these concerns with you as you participate in public political dialogue. Would that make sense?

In a similar fashion, many persons of deep religious faith find it hard to imagine why the factor that most constitutes who they are and guides their political and economic choices—their faith in God—should be set aside from public discussion. For many, the separation of faith and society (as distinct from the separation of church and state) is not simply mistaken, it is impossible. If one takes following Jesus to be the very core of Christian faith, then one cannot leave that behind when dealing with public policies and institutions.

Now, it is important to clarify that engaging politics from the perspective of faith does not mean violating the separation of church and state. In fact, quite the opposite. Even a quick review of the history of the church shows that persons of faith are pretty much as likely as other groups to exploit political power when they hold it. For example, when religious groups move from one region to avoid religious persecution, they often end up persecuting the nonreligious in their new region once they gain power. So the separation of church and state, which ensures that no one particular religion becomes the official state religion, is critical to a healthy democracy. While few religious groups claim openly that they want to form a state church, as we see in history these things have a way of "just happening."

There is no reason, however, that affirming the basic rightness of church-state separation has to mean excluding persons of faith from the public debate over social policy and the direction of public institutions. Nor must persons of faith feel it inappropriate to utilize the insights they gain from their religious traditions in forming their moral compass on policy matters. However, it would not be appropriate for people of religious faith to argue for nondemocratic policies or for exclusion or inclusion of others on the basis of religion. As long as individuals remain free to use their faith in their decision making, a healthy sense of a separation of the state from favoring any particular church or religious movement is not at all inconsistent with bringing one's faith to bear on social and political matters.

The next question one must consider is the form that participation should take. Perhaps one of the greatest temptations for those who participate in the political process is the ease with which one gets drawn into the "power game." After all, if one has strong commitments, then there is a great temptation to see one's political connections as a means to grasp the reins of control in order to bring into reality the perceived better way of being that arises from one's faith commitments. This is what German philosopher Friedrich Nietzsche called the "will to power"—the deep-seated need to exert our will over others. When we find ourselves in positions of power and authority, it is easy for the pursuit of power to be self-confirming in our own minds. Why would God have allowed us to take power if we were not fully equipped to use it? This can be a slippery, arrogant, and terribly dangerous slope.

Another role that people of faith have sometimes been drawn into is that of chaplain to the state, a sort of religious courtesan. The courts of power do not like to be challenged, and remaining close to them often means giving up the ability to be prophetic and to speak truth to power. People thus co-opted are sometimes reduced to keeping the peace between the exploiters and the exploited, instead of standing up for those victimized by the powerful.

How does a person maintain a prophetic stance that "speaks truth to power"? The prophetic task involves both *modeling* what God intends and *speaking out* for policies and institutions that support the biblical mandates for peace with justice. People of faith, and the church as a whole, have made important political and social contributions in the United States.

The abolition of slavery, the fight for women's suffrage, the passage of child labor laws, and the advocacy for civil rights are a few of the movements driven by people of faith because of their religious convictions. The method used by Martin Luther King Jr.—engaging the powers without becoming one of them—is an example of how the church should challenge and engage unjust political institutions. King wrote that the church is to be neither master nor servant of the state, but rather its conscience—that is, to be prophetic.

DAY 3 — Reading the Bible

There is little debate among Christians today over the claim that God has specific expectations for the moral conduct of our personal lives. What is sometimes missed is that there are serious implications for our public life together that flow directly from our faith in Christ. Today, we examine the Bible to explore how

God's moral expectations of us as persons in relation with God and with the rest of creation inform both our individual conduct as well as our public conduct.

That God has expectations for us is immediately clear from the creation accounts themselves. There we are told that God entrusts Adam and Eve with care for the Garden of Eden, and ultimately, for the earth. By the time we get to the story of Noah, we find that humanity has become so evil that God destroys the earth and starts again. Later, we come to the explicit statement of the kinds of expectations God has with the instruction to the people at Mt. Sinai—the Ten Commandments. The commandments divide into two sets: (1) those dealing with the relationship between God and humanity and (2) those dealing with the relationship between and among humans. In essence, we are to honor God and our fellow creatures. The commandments take specific form in declaring idolatry and the misuse of God's name as immoral, and they also identify the immorality of stealing, adultery, lying, and longing for the possessions of others. Despite broad consensus among Christians and much of the larger population over these personal edicts, the public side of what it means to be a person in relation with God and the rest of creation is often more disputed.

We frequently hear it claimed that Jesus was not interested in politics. Perhaps this error arises from too narrow a description of the term "politics." The term comes from the Greek word "polis," which simply means "city." So, the term "politics" in its most general sense is not about the endless debates between political parties, but rather about the manner in which human societies are to be organized. To think that Jesus had no interest in this sense of politics makes a division between private and public that is a contemporary invention, one that is justified by neither the Bible nor church history.

For example, in Luke 4:18, when Jesus stands in the synagogue and announces his ministry—"The Spirit of the Lord is upon me, because he has anointed me to bring good news to the poor"—his language is from the Hebrew prophets who proclaimed God's intentions regarding the sorts of characteristics our shared lives should exhibit. All of life is to reflect the divine intent: to care for the marginalized and the sick and to welcome the stranger. It would be strange indeed for Jesus to consistently teach and live these themes in the scriptures but somehow intend them for only the private realm. If anything, Jesus expands and deepens our obligations, both individually and corporately.

Perhaps one of the most powerful summaries of the reality of God's intentions across all levels of human life is expressed in Paul's letter to the Colossians. Here we are told that "in him [Jesus] all things were created, in heaven and on earth, visible and invisible, whether thrones or dominions or principalities or authorities— all things were created through him and for him" (Colossians 1:16). In other words, there is no power of government or public institutions that is beyond Christ's authority. Public institutions, whatever form they take, are subject to the ethics of peace, justice, and care for the least of these that God mandates. The values—implicit and explicit—in Jesus's teachings should be central to our understanding of their right role in ordering our lives together.

Romans 13 is sometimes cited in discussions about the role of public institutions, but too often it is separated from the teachings in Romans 12. In Romans 12, Paul lays out what our life together should look like. Then, in Romans 13, he presents an affirmation of public institutions that realize the sorts of common, public life that would follow from the exhortations of Romans 12. To read chapter 13 as some sort of carte blanche for public officials would be to forget the preceding chapter. More obviously, it would overlook the fact that Paul was, himself, later executed by the state.

The point is straightforward. God cares about the nature and characteristics of our lives—both our personal lives and our public institutions. We are called to do what we can to shape public institutions and what they do. We should strive for public institutions that reflect God's intentions.

DAY 4 — The Christian Tradition

The early Christians did not openly participate in the mechanisms of the state. In the first three centuries, church leaders were overwhelmingly opposed to participation in the military. In fact, the early church often found itself on the receiving end of abuse from the Roman Empire. Christians were sacrificed in the "gladiator sport," fed to lions for the sick amusement of others. When the Roman Empire collapsed, some blamed the early Christians, who were charged with an atheism characterized not by the rejection of any concept of God, but rather by the rejection of the pagan "gods" of Rome—a charge that prompted Augustine to write in defense of Christianity. Given that milieu, the reticence of early Christians toward political entities is certainly understandable.

Due to these hostilities, there was little opportunity for direct involvement by early Christians in the formal political process. This, however, did not preclude Christians from offering a critique from outside the corridors of power—indeed, they frequently had comments to make about the political situation. In the heyday of the Roman Empire, the emperor was understood to be divine, and citizens of the empire were expected to affirm that Caesar was lord. This presented a problem, because of course the early church was centered on its affirmation that Jesus was Lord. The direct implication of affirming the lordship of Jesus was the denial of the lordship of Caesar. There was a direct correspondence between the life of faith and political life. In fact, the two were so intertwined that Caesar could not allow his authority to be challenged by those placing the authority of Jesus over his own. Those who openly claimed Jesus as Lord were often killed. A merely "private" faith, on the other hand, would not have been perceived as a threat by Rome.

When Emperor Constantine legalized Christianity in the empire, much of this tension changed. In what many view as a compromise with the empire, Christians were now viewed more favorably. Christian thinkers began to address openly the vexing questions of how the life of faith and the political life are related. Augustine formulated a position that made explicit the distinction between church and state by writing about two "cities": the city of God (characterizing the life of faith and its end in heaven) and the city of "man" (characterizing human life and its management).

From these early writings developed the doctrine of the "two kingdoms," which Martin Luther later expounded upon. The first was described as the earthly kingdom presided over by the relevant political powers. The second was the heavenly kingdom, or the kingdom of faith, ultimately presided over by God but watched over on earth by the church. Augustine had a significant impact on the way the church tended to think of the intersection of faith and politics.

This dichotomy led some to understand that faith is to be lived out only in private and that the public management of human societies is to be undertaken by secular authorities. The work of Augustine, however, did not intend this conclusion. When the Roman Empire collapsed, the church quite willingly moved in and assumed "secular" authority.

Through history Christianity has had various relationships with the state: it has been persecuted by the state; it has operated as the primary power over government when there has been a state religion; and it has acted as a prophetic corrective to the state, while maintaining a separation that allows for religious diversity. In a participatory democracy, the best interest of the country is served when religion appeals to the common good from consistent moral grounds. It was from those grounds that Martin Luther King Jr. and the civil rights movement changed America.

DAY 5   Living Examples in the Contemporary Church

When we think of the engagement of faith and politics, the temptation is to think of something big, something of international significance. Most of what we hear on the evening news relates to matters that capture national attention. However, if we dismiss local concerns, then many of us would rarely find opportunities to live our faith in political action. What are the opportunities for living our faith on the local level?

A Lexington, Kentucky, group known as Communality, part of the burgeoning house church movement, helps show us the way. Communality meets in small groups in homes; members enjoy a meal together, then engage in worship and discussion.

They invite any and all comers to share dinner and time together with them. They describe themselves as a group of Christians putting "skin on the missional church." They host presentations on various social justice topics and are always on the lookout for ways to live out their faith by caring for "the least of these."

I'VE SEEN THE MOUNTAINTOP . . . REMOVED

Sometime back in 2004, a Christian group called Communality became aware of an issue known as "mountaintop removal." This procedure was begun by the coal companies as a less expensive way to remove coal from deep within the mountains of West Virginia, as well as in the states where rich coal reserves are hidden inside ancient formations.

Mountaintop removal is just as it sounds—the coal company quite literally blows the top off of a mountain. As you can imagine, this creates massive problems for the area's residents. One West Virginian described living near the mountains as feeling like he was "in the middle of a war zone." To achieve the necessary removal of the top of a mountain, hundreds of thousands of tons of dynamite are used. But worse than the sound is the sediment. What can be done with thousands of tons of rock? The coal companies dump it into the valleys below. This, plus the loss of ground cover, often leads to massive flooding in the valleys below the coal operations.

There are many other issues involved. The huge trucks carrying the coal create ruts so deep that cars can no longer go down certain roads. And one mother described the anguish she felt from the fact that the water had turned so brown due to runoff that she could no longer bathe her daughter.

Still, all of this occurs hundreds of miles away from Lexington. Why should a group of Christians living in the city care about the mountains? As Communality became aware of the issue, they started asking the same question. But one of the deep values of the community is the interconnected nature of life. They believe that what happens in the hills of West Virginia has significant impact on the lives of people living in cities far away. Matters of injustice in one place have a way of spreading injustice all around. People were suffering from this problem while city folks enjoyed the benefits of cheaper energy that results from this procedure. Communality members felt compelled to action.

Not many U.S. Christians have paid much attention to this issue. Allen Johnson and Christians for the Mountains (www.christiansforthemountains.org) have been among the few voices within the church seeking justice in this area. So as they got involved, many of the relationships they began to develop were outside of the faith community. Some environmental groups were decidedly anti-faith.

Communality offered one of the best resources they had available to the environmentalists—space. They had a community house in the city, and a number of groups had banded together to seek to raise awareness on the issue. This gave Communality a point of interaction. They fed the activists. They housed them. Relationships developed that would never have existed otherwise.

Communality has been involved in other ways, including helping to promote an educational campaign and going to the mountains to observe the suffering firsthand. But perhaps their greatest contribution is relationship. By being willing to enter into friendship with those who are active in key issues, they are living out the Christian story.

WILL SAMSON*

Where will the efforts of Communality lead them? No one knows, of course, but in their effort to speak for those residents of communities threatened by the practice of mountaintop removal, they made new friends. In addition to those they sought to defend, some of the environmental groups were able to see Christian faith in a new light. Rather than being offended at what Samson calls an "anti-faith" position, the members of Communality looked past this bias in search of dialogue. Their efforts were rewarded. They gained colleagues with whom to work for social justice in the area of mining and corporate accountability.

What are the parallel concerns in your area, and how might you forge alliances to combat the injustices?

DAY 6   Putting Faith into Action

As noted earlier, many have observed that religion and politics seem to be the two subjects that are not to be engaged in public conversation. Why is this? It is hard to imagine two things more important than these in determining the shape and form of our communities and our shared lives. Persons of faith are formed by their religious beliefs, and religious belief deals intimately with how we live together in community. An important two-part question, then, is, What kind of community does our faith call us to, and how should our social and political institutions be structured to make that a reality?

Perhaps the most important thing that we can do to integrate our faith and our politics is to change the perception that faith and politics should not be discussed in polite company. This means seeking to engage our fellow believers on political matters, not just for the sake of debate, but rather to see how our faith informs our political commitments. If we carry on this discussion politely, but passionately, we should be able to succeed in demonstrating that this important dialogue can be undertaken both amicably and seriously.

From the list of potential activities in the appendix, there are several that could be used to explore this issue. We suspect that the sort of movement we have suggested begins with education. Some excellent starting points would include preparing a course of study or outlining a series of sermons for your local church. Provide both

---

* *Will Samson is a student at Asbury Theological Seminary in Wilmore, Kentucky.*

a biblical and a theological basis for teaching people how to connect their faith commitments and particular political visions with action. Primarily, your goal is to create an environment that is conducive to dialogue on faith and politics. This environment should not only tolerate but actually welcome varying opinions and points of view.

Also, look for opportunities to broaden the public discourse. Write letters to the editor of local newspapers. Offer opinion pieces. Call in to radio talk shows. Get involved in key local, national, and global issues. Every other year is an election year in the United States. Use this rhythm to create a calendar for your teaching series. In the off-years, offer general studies about the relation between faith and politics and studies on the biblical role of government. In election years, assuming this background has been provided, focus on electoral issues and ballot initiatives. (Of course, if you do so on behalf of a church or other nonprofit group, make sure to do it in a nonpartisan manner.)

There are two very specific ways to influence positively the relationship between politics and religion. First, *God's Politics* argues that we must not allow ourselves to be forced to narrow our conception of biblical morality. It is common in our contemporary situation for politicians to employ "divide and conquer" strategies when it comes to influencing religious voters. To avoid this, we need a broader vision of biblical morality that moves beyond so-called wedge issues to insist that the Bible requires us to address a whole range of issues.

Second, we must be attentive to opportunities to work together on areas of common concern. While people on the extremes of the political spectrum might have a hard time finding agreement on issues, most people are in the broad political middle and can find common ground on many individual issues. Often we are divided by our methods more than by our goals. We can agree that poverty should be alleviated or abortions reduced, so how might we work on these issues together? When religious folks on both sides of the political spectrum stand up to speak with a unified voice to the corridors of power, political leaders begin to listen. *God's Politics* makes this point nicely: "Couldn't both pro-life and pro-choice political leaders agree to common ground actions that would actually reduce the abortion rate, rather than continue to use abortion mostly as a political symbol?"

DAY 7

Group Meeting and Reflection

1. Discuss the extent to which religion and politics are intimately related. What evidence from the Bible or Christian tradition would you cite to support the relationship between the two?

2. Is it appropriate to think that God has a perspective on politics? To adequately reflect on this question, define the term "politics" from what you see

as a Christian perspective, show where that definition connects with Christian faith, and then discuss what it might mean to think of God as having a political perspective.

3. What are the implications of the title of *God's Politics*? What would it mean to affirm that God holds "political" commitments? As you read through the book, keep paper and pencil handy and try to outline the set of commitments God might have if this presentation is correct.

4. What is meant by the affirmation that God is personal, but never private? What implications would this have for how we think of political responsibilities?

5. On pages xxii through xxiv of *God's Politics,* the content of the "God Is Not a Republican ... or a Democrat" ad is presented. Review it and discuss your agreement or disagreement. Be sure to provide a basis for your rationale, preferably from within the religious tradition. Would this list make a useful guide for evaluating different political candidates? Why or why not?

6. Not many politicians would suggest that their faith leads them to be "pro-war," "pro-rich," and only "pro-American." Why would *God's Politics* suggest that, in practice, many U.S. politicians are asserting exactly that? How would you assess their claim?

7. *God's Politics* notes that "religious action is rooted in a much deeper place than 'rights'—that place being the image of God in every human being" (page 5). Reflect upon and discuss how this impacts our political commitments.

8. Assume you have a five-minute audience with the leadership of the current administration. What would you say in those five minutes to present a serious Christian political and moral agenda?

9. For a political vision to be moral and Christian, what are the elements that it must include? (Don't look for specific policy content here. Rather, think about what principles would guide the selection of policy content.)

10. Make a list of the ten political issues you would consider most relevant for persons of faith. How would you prioritize them based upon your faith? Why?

War and Peace

AS WE MOVE to Week 2, our topic changes from the relation between faith and politics in general to Christian attitudes toward war. This topic is covered in chapters 7 through 12 of *God's Politics*. In Days 1 and 2 of this week, we will focus on the war in Iraq, about which we know more now than when *God's Politics* was written. Be sure to review chapters 7 through 12 in *God's Politics* in preparation for this week's study.

The following is a summary of those chapters.

Chapter 7: Bad decisions too frequently arise out of fear—fear for our families, for ourselves, for our property. When we are fearful, we are ripe for manipulation by those who promise that, if only we will trust them, they will keep us safe. The terrorist attacks of September 11, 2001, changed our lives. As is often the case, the fear created by these attacks led us to accept policies that offered to reverse our newfound vulnerability. It is essential, however, that as Christians we take a step back from our fear, remembering who it is we ultimately trust, and ask the harder questions aimed at getting to the roots of terrorism. That will help us offer a better response than those that spring only from fear.

Chapter 8: Today, the primary positions that Christians hold with regard to war include the "just war" theory, active nonviolence, and pacifism. (The latter two are often lumped together.) In Iraq, it was clear that Saddam Hussein was a terrible dictator, and removing him from power was a desirable goal. But was that enough to justify the U.S. invasion of Iraq? In fact, no form of the just war theory allows for "preemptive" war-making such as the U.S. attack against Iraq. We have learned in the past few years that virtually all the intelligence used in the run up to the war was at best mistaken or at worst manipulated. Ironically, the nature of the war and how it was sold to the American public has actually weakened our ability to combat genuine threats of terrorism.

Chapter 9: History teaches us that few things are more dangerous than the potent combination of religious fervor and nationalistic zeal. The temptation to appeal to God to further our own interest is a blatant misuse of religion. Yet such appeals are too often made from all sides of the political spectrum. Our fears cloud our judgment, and we become ensnared in the civil religion that arises from the marriage of God with national interests and agendas. We are vulnerable to embracing actions and policies that we normally would never consider. As British historian Lord Acton observed, "Power tends to corrupt; absolute power corrupts absolutely." That observation seems to hold true for countries as well as individuals. Being the world's only "superpower" seems to have had a negative effect on the United States' ability to conduct foreign policy in an ethical manner consistent with international law.

The word "empire" has been used by senior Bush advisers[1] (and others) to describe American power in the world, and the concept is often defended by the president, even using religious language. But in biblical terms, religious nationalism is a form of idolatry, and as such it must be resisted by people of faith.

Chapter 10: Unfortunately, it is too often the case that people don't begin to ask questions about peacemaking until a crisis point is reached—or worse, until after hostilities have begun. Genuine peacemaking, however, recognizes that conflict can occur any time there is a human encounter, and it seeks proactively to sow the seeds of peace prior to crisis.

The realities of war justify the claim that "war is hell." It is important to keep these realities in mind as we seek to find creative ways to resolve conflict and reduce violence. An important part of peacemaking is the willingness to look below the surface, to locate the presence of injustices that have the potential to foster hostility. By addressing and defusing the underlying causes, peacemakers can actually work against war before it starts. Even when a crisis is upon us, however, we must first look for nonviolent ways to respond.

Chapter 11: A resolution to the conflict between the Israelis and the Palestinians would be a huge step toward regional and even global peace. At the same time, the long history of animosity between the two sides makes people wonder whether a lasting peace with justice can ever be found. Any step forward, however, must begin with truth-telling. For example, while U.S. media have paid significant attention to Palestinian violence against Israelis, much less notice has been given to Israeli violence against Palestinians. Once the truth is told with impartiality, the international community will need to adopt an evenhanded strategy toward the legitimate rights and aspirations of both groups for security and self-determination.

Chapter Twelve: Genuine, lasting peace can only be based upon a real sense of security, which includes aspects that are personal, national, and global. Real security means, among other things, the assurance that all people have access to the essentials of life—such as adequate food, water, and housing. The prophet Micah offers a vision of the world where swords are beaten into plowshares and where nations do not make war against other nations. He goes on to envision everyone having their own "vine and fig tree," living free and unafraid. In short, a secure future will require dealing with causes and not merely symptoms.

DAY 1 | Introducing the Topic

The Christian church historically has held three positions regarding war. For the first 300 years of the church, most Christians rejected war—and participation in Caesar's armies—as inconsistent with Christian faith. The majority of Christians in the early church took quite seriously Jesus's imperative to "love your enemies" and "resist not evil with evil." Some even accepted martyrdom rather than kill others in war. Beginning in the fourth and fifth centuries, primarily through the writing of Augustine, the church began to develop what became known as the "just war" theory, which claims that under certain conditions Christians can participate in warfare. During the Middle Ages, the church actually encouraged warring for certain "holy causes," and the result was the notion of war as crusade, a position that is now almost universally rejected.

Christian rejection of war, such as that practiced since the earliest days of the church, is often given the label of "pacifism," and many times the position is mischaracterized as Christian "passivism"—implying that the tactic is withdrawal and nonengagement. Christian peacemakers do not and cannot argue for "doing nothing." Instead, they argue that Christians are called to reject the use of lethal force, in war or elsewhere.

But the positive, peacemaking actions proposed and carried out by those rooted in the church's peace tradition are often ignored, belittled as unrealistic, or overlooked. This often results in peacemakers being asked at the last minute, when hostilities are imminent, "So, what do we do now? Nothing?" When this happens, the Christian peacemaking position is distorted into a purely reactive one, where the concern for peace is raised only at the verge of war. Instead, Christian peacemakers argue that one must engage in serious peacemaking activities long before the outbreak of war. Peacemaking requires vision, persistence, and a proactive engagement with the root causes of war and injustice. Ronald J. Sider's *Non-Violence: The Invincible Weapon?* and Peter Ackerman and Jack DuVall's *A Force More Powerful* (both the book and film) are excellent resources that outline successful cases of the use of nonviolent resistance in the face of aggression. There are many successful examples of nonviolence in action, including conflict resolution, and the church should work to teach each generation how to build on these successes and reclaim the tradition of Christian peacemaking to deal with conflict, oppression, and violence.

Despite Christianity's early understanding of the biblical call to peacemaking, by the fourth century the church's position began to change. In 312, the Roman general Constantine became emperor. During his reign Christian persecution was suspended and Christian worship was allowed by law. In what many consider a great compromise, there developed an accord, rather than an antagonistic relationship, between the Christian church and the imperial government. This led to the development of the just war theory.

This theory is based on a set of criteria used to determine if the use of force is justified. It was established in order to limit war and decrease violence: the idea was to make war the rare exception. Augustine's criteria said that the decision to go to war must be based on proving just cause, right intention, and legitimate authority. According to Augustine, merely the protection of private property or even self-defense of persons would not constitute a just reason for going to war. The criteria have become more nuanced over time, but just war criteria are still largely based on these three pillars, and they represent the majority view in most churches today.

In today's world, where there are civil wars, terrorist networks, nuclear weapons, and rogue states, the doctrine of just war is severely challenged. Many churches today claim that they support wars based on whether or not those wars meet the just war criteria. But how many people actually know what the criteria are?

Just war criteria are divided generally into two categories, designated by a pair of Latin phrases. The first, *jus ad bellum,* identifies the criteria that must be rigorously applied *before* going to war. The second, *jus in bello,* identifies the criteria for conducting oneself in the battlefield once one is already *in* a war.

The first set of criteria, applied before going to war, generally include the following:

1. *Just cause.* A just cause exists when war is necessary to protect innocents, to protect human rights, or to preserve conditions appropriate for human existence, but not for a narrowly defined national self-interest.
2. *Right intention.* Augustine argued that our love both for those attacked and for the attackers must be our driving motivation and that the only just goal is the restoration or establishment of a just peace.
3. *Legitimate authority.* Only recognized nations have the authority to declare and conduct wars. Under certain modern international agreements, even nation-states may not constitute legitimate authority.
4. *Reasonable likelihood of success.* Even if one is certain to "win the battle," one must be able to prove that there is a reasonable chance that use of force in the end will make the situation demonstrably better.
5. *Last resort.* Before military force is used, every other effort to resolve the injustice—including diplomacy and other nonviolent measures (such as third-party treaty inspections, embargoes or sanctions, and other forms of nonmilitary international pressure)—must be tried and given a reasonable chance of success.
6. *Comparative justice.* In just war criteria, the aggrieved party must have suffered an injustice substantially and measurably greater that what the other side has suffered.

According to just war theory, all of these criteria must be satisfied before one can allow for the use of military force, a quite rigorous test. The purpose is to steer legitimate authorities away from the use of force. Today, most (some would say all) contemporary wars fail to meet all the criteria.

Even in the waging of a war, it is not allowable for an authority to do "whatever it takes." Just war theory also maintains that a war must be *conducted* in a just fashion, using the following criteria:

1. *Discrimination.* The waging of war must discriminate between military and civilian targets, with no "intentional" targeting of the latter. For example, if you know that 15 percent of your "smart bombs" are going to miss their targets and if those targets are close to civilian facilities, can you really say the civilian deaths were "unintentional"?

2. *Proportionality.* The use of force must be proportional to the injustice that occurred, and the destruction and loss of life that will result from the use of force must be less than the anticipated good to be gained. Many, if not most, just war theorists would argue that this completely rules out the use—or threatened use—of nuclear, chemical, and biological weapons of any kind.

3. *Noncombatant immunity.* No one may intentionally attack those not directly engaged in the conflict—that is, civilians are immune. Some argue that any war that results in the loss of noncombatant lives is inherently unjust.

4. *Respect for the dignity of the enemy as a bearer of God's image.* It is wrong to demonize the enemy, especially as a method for garnering support for war. All combatants and prisoners should be treated with the dignity they deserve as human beings.

5. *Right intention.* The restoration of a just peace must be the primary focus in order to avoid the use of indiscriminate means and engaging in acts of revenge.

In the next section, we will consider the "war on terrorism," in general, and the war in Iraq, in particular. We will attempt to apply the just war criteria to each situation. In preparation, consider these questions:

1. The dictionary defines war as: (1) a state of usually open and declared armed hostile conflict between states or nations; (2) a period of such armed conflict; (3) a state of hostility, conflict, or antagonism; (4) a struggle or competition between opposing forces or for a particular end, such as a class war or a war against disease.[2] Under what definition would the "war on terrorism" come? Is the term applied metaphorically? Can you think of a better way to frame the issue?

2. Does the notion of a "preemptive" war fit the just war criteria? Why or why not?

3. Considering what you know about the war in Iraq, how does it conform to the criteria for a just war? In what ways does it not comply?

Considering the Evidence

DAY 2

Let's consider various aspects of the Iraq war in light of the just war criteria. First, review the criteria for going to war. These include just cause, right intention, legitimate authority, reasonable likelihood of success, last resort, and comparative justice.

Perhaps the easiest to consider is the criterion of *legitimate authority*. According to just war principles, as a nation-state the United States constitutes a legitimate authority. However, to the extent that the case for war was based on U.N. resolutions, the United States would not constitute a legitimate authority without U.N. approval. Furthermore, signatories to the U.N. Charter are not permitted to pursue war with other signatories unless they have U.N. approval. In the case of war against Iraq, under these conditions the United States is not the proper legitimate authority for pursuing war because (1) both the United States and Iraq are members of the United Nations, and (2) part of the case for war was based on U.N. resolutions. Therefore the United Nations would be the legitimate authority.

Did a *just cause* exist for the invasion of Iraq? The Bush administration's rationale for the war has varied over time, but the primary reasons cited have been these: (1) Iraq was allegedly involved with the terrorist attacks of September 11, 2001; (2) Iraq supposedly had weapons of mass destruction that threatened the United States; (3) Iraq stood in violation of U.N. resolutions; (4) Saddam Hussein was an evil leader who needed to be replaced.

The first two assertions, time has shown, were not true. The United States has not provided grounds for linking Iraq with the attacks of September 11. In fact, evidence shows that al Qaeda viewed Iraq as a secular Islamic state and therefore an enemy. Additionally, much of the "evidence" offered that Iraq had weapons of mass destruction was very thin and was contradicted by reports from inspection teams. In December 2005, President Bush finally admitted that, regarding Iraq's possession of weapons of mass destruction, "much of the intelligence turned out to be wrong."[3]

The third assertion, that Iraq was in violation of one or more U.N. resolutions, is indisputably true. But many observers believed the U.N. weapons inspections were successfully "containing" Iraq. In addition, other nations also stand in violation of U.N. resolutions. For example, Israel and Turkey have numerous violations, yet war has not been engaged against them. More important, however, is that the United Nations itself did not support war against Iraq as the best response to that country's clear violations.

Finally, Saddam Hussein was indeed a terrible dictator, but sadly there are many terrible dictators around the world. Military invasion and occupation of each of their countries is obviously not feasible, and such military intervention to effect "regime change"—which of course would violate international law—is not a just cause for war. Removing Saddam would be a just cause, but not by going to war with such costs and consequences.

Now let us examine the criterion of *right intention.* This is notoriously difficult to determine; most folks have enough trouble discerning their own motives. Right intention is to be judged on the basis of how a proposed war minimizes the "just cause"— the conditions that have led to a disturbance of the peace—and therefore restores peace. If there was no just cause for waging war on Iraq, then it is difficult to determine how one might assess right intention.

Was there a reasonable *likelihood of success* in launching war on Iraq? In other words, is it likely that the situation in Iraq will have improved after the war dramatically enough to outweigh the death and destruction resulting from the war? Notice that the standard is "likelihood," not "possibility." The history of Iraq, with its long-standing civil tensions, has to be taken into account. Border and boundary issues, along with deep ethnic divisions—which have not been resolved since Iraq was carved out of the Ottoman Empire by the French and British in 1920—must also factor into the "likelihood of success." U.S. military dominance was not in question as we contemplated war in Iraq. But was there reasonable likelihood that the United States could "win the peace"? The tragic events of the past three years have revealed major miscalculations.

Now, let's examine whether all other reasonable alternatives to war were tried before going to war. A very important issue is whether or not the sanctions and inspections imposed on Iraq were working. If inspections were working, then *last resort* had not been reached. As *God's Politics* notes, there was wide agreement among diverse Christian groups—and also among members of the United Nations—that the war was not necessary and that Iraq was being adequately "contained" by other means. The countries in the region surrounding Iraq did not agree that Saddam Hussein was an immediate threat. Finally, the evidence presented by the United States of Iraq's "imminent threat" in the run-up to the war was met with widespread skepticism. These skeptics have been proven right. By the criteria established, this was not a war of last resort.

To make the case for *comparative justice,* one would have to demonstrate that Hussein's rule in Iraq constituted a grave injustice against the United States— that the United States had suffered an injustice substantially and measurably greater than that suffered by the Iraqi people. An attempt to satisfy this criterion may have prompted the administration to try to link Iraq with the September 11 attacks, an allegation of connection that turned out to be false.

The overarching question we faced three years ago was, According to the six criteria, were the conditions surrounding the invasion of Iraq adequate for Christians to support the war as a just war? Most Christian bodies around the world concluded no.

Let's also consider the just war criteria that apply to how a war is conducted once it has begun. Since the war in Iraq is still under way, we do not have all the evidence, but we can examine these criteria based on what we currently know. The criteria include discrimination, proportionality, noncombatant immunity, right intention, and respect for the image of God in all humans.

U.S. forces use so-called smart munitions for "precision strikes" against urban populations in Iraq, targets that previously would have been off-limits because of the likelihood of civilian casualties. From 2003 to 2005, 53 percent of civilian deaths in Iraq involved explosive devices, with children disproportionately affected. "It appears that whatever their military advantages and benefit to soldiers," a dossier on Iraq war casualties states, "'stand-off' weapons which put a substantial distance between soldiers and their intended targets are the most likely to cause unintended harm to bystanders."[4] This alone is enough to challenge the criterion of *discrimination*.

The initial war strategy presented to the American public was a campaign of "shock and awe," a method of warfare intended to destroy the enemy's will to fight through an initial display of overwhelmingly destructive force. How should this be assessed in light of the criterion of *proportionality*?

Reports on civilian casualties during the war range from as low as 25,000 to more than 125,000. It appears that a significant percentage of those killed were noncombatants, mostly the elderly, women, and children. Given that, can we say that the United States has conducted this war in a fashion that satisfies the criterion of *noncombatant immunity*?

The criterion of *right intention* requires using only the force needed for the restoration of a just peace. Along with other aspects of the war, the cases of U.S. military personnel abusing and torturing prisoners—or allowing the conditions that led to the abuses—at Abu Ghraib and other detention centers constitute a failure to meet the requirements of right intention, as well as a violation of the final criterion, *respect for the dignity of the enemy* as a person bearing God's image. Wars are almost always characterized by the demonization of the other side, and we now have to factor in detainee abuse and prisoner torture as well.

So what is *your* assessment? From the perspective of just war criteria, is the U.S. war against Iraq just? Was it just to launch the war? Has it been conducted according to just war principles? And have these issues been adequately debated in the public discourse about the war?

Finally, can we apply the just war criteria to the so-called war on terrorism? To evaluate the conflict in light of the just war criteria, we would need to be able to talk about a war on specific terrorists, terrorist groups, and their supporters. From there, one could evaluate just cause, legitimate authority, right intention, last resort, etc.

Christians must engage critically with policies that are used to fight the war on terrorism. Even though terrorists always engage in activities that fail to meet the just war criteria (for example, targeting noncombatants), that does not guarantee that those fighting the terrorists are always acting justly. In other words, there may be injustice on both sides, and Christians ought to lead efforts aimed at redressing injustices that serve as a root cause of violence and that help to fuel terrorism.[5]

After September 11, most Americans wanted a strong response, and there were two paths that could have been taken. One spoke the language and spirit of justice and invoked the rule of law in promising to bring the perpetrators of terrorist violence to accountability. Those who so violated the standards of civilized life, and the human values we hold most dear, should never be allowed to escape judgment and punishment—and the danger of even more terror must be urgently prevented.

The other path used the language of war and invoked a spirit of retribution and even vengeance, emotions we can all understand. A "war on terrorism" summons up the strength and resolve to stop these horrific acts and prevent their cancerous spread. But the war language fails to provide moral and practical boundaries for that response. It often leads to indiscriminate retaliation and the "collateral damage" of even more loss of innocent life, as we have now seen in Iraq.

In the final analysis, a theory that simply analyzes whether a war is "just" is not enough—and throughout history, the just war theory has been used much more to justify war than to prevent it. Christians are called to go much deeper even than the prevention of war, to engage in pursuits that actively further the cause of peace.

Glen Stassen, a Christian ethicist at Fuller Theological Seminary in Pasadena, California, has identified ten practices involved in what he calls "just peacemaking." They include the following:

1. Support nonviolent direct action.
2. Take independent initiatives to reduce threat.
3. Use cooperative conflict resolution.
4. Acknowledge responsibility for conflict and injustice and seek repentance and forgiveness.
5. Advance democracy, human rights, and religious liberty.
6. Foster just and sustainable economic development.
7. Work with emerging cooperative forces in the international system.
8. Strengthen the United Nations and international efforts for cooperation and human rights.
9. Reduce offensive weapons and weapons trade.
10. Encourage grassroots peacemaking groups and voluntary associations.[6]

These practices could reduce both war and terrorism.

Perhaps one of the greatest challenges for Christians in the twenty-first century will be the development and strengthening of efforts like these, so that we can truly be about the things that make for peace.

DAY 3   Reading the Bible

Perhaps one of the most unfortunate aspects of much contemporary Bible reading is a tendency to see the Bible as a disparate collection of narratives and sayings, rather than a total work that must be taken in context. The Bible is a single story that moves from somewhere to somewhere. As the biblical literature unfolds, deeper movements become evident.

Let's examine several biblical passages relating to war, peace, and the use of violence. When those who support a given war are asked to provide a biblical basis, there is often an immediate appeal to the Hebrew scriptures (that is, the Old Testament). A person might say, "Well, God told Joshua to go to war against the inhabitants of the land. Therefore, God allows war." Passages such as the Joshua story in the Hebrew scriptures—texts that show God allowing war or explicitly commanding it—demonstrate, so the argument goes, God's toleration of war. Is this argument biblically sound? Or is this a proof-texting approach that ignores a larger movement within the Bible?

Vernard Eller, in *War and Peace: From Genesis to Revelation,* shows how the Bible's treatment of issues relating to the use of violence develops over time. Eller explains that, as the biblical story unfolds, God engages in acts and gives instruction to wean humans away from violence. Eller draws attention to the violence inherent in early societies. He points out how God's directions to people, though appearing harsh to us, were actually moves toward violence *reduction.* For example, the injunction to repay "an eye for an eye" was a move toward proportionality and away from clan wars that started as a result of a single death. To move humans away from violence, God calls a particular people who are to live in ways consistent with God's intentions.

In Deuteronomy 17, for example, God gives instructions that are aimed at keeping Israel reliant on God alone and—even when Israel has a king—forbidding them from putting their trust in military strength.

In the book of Isaiah, a major transition occurs in the biblical story arc as the image of the Suffering Servant is introduced. The new message from God is that redemptive violence is not the way to resist evil. Instead, redemptive suffering is the path God intends. In Isaiah 53, the Suffering Servant overcomes evil by taking on suffering rather than engaging in violent conflict. For Christians, the Suffering Servant foreshadows Jesus, but that imagery also stands as an indication of the norm God intends for human behavior.

By New Testament times—say, between the years 170 BCE and 140 CE—there was a belief within Judaism that the messiah would be a military leader who would reestablish a free homeland. It is noteworthy that Jesus never succumbed to pressure to join with the militant insurgent groups—called the Zealots—in an effort to oust the Romans from Jerusalem.

If we look directly into Jesus's own actions and teachings, we will find a clear portrayal of the nonviolent teacher of peace. For example, the Sermon on the Mount instructs us to be "peacemakers," to "turn the other cheek," and to "not resist evil with evil." Suffering and patience are indicated as praiseworthy. When Jesus is taken by the authorities and a disciple draws his sword in defense, Jesus instructs him to put the sword away. "All who take the sword," says Jesus, "will perish by the sword"

(Matthew 26:52). This warning against the use of violence is consistent with Jesus's teachings and actions throughout the gospels.

There are a few New Testament texts that are sometimes cited to claim that Jesus did not reject the use of violence. One is the "cleansing of the temple" (Matthew 21:12–13 and parallels). Some argue that Jesus used a whip to run the money-changers out of the temple. However, far from single-handedly overpowering the temple guard, it is more likely that Jesus used the whip to run the animals out of the temple. The fact that the whip used was one normally used to herd cattle only makes this a more likely reading. Another text cited is: "And let him who has no sword sell his mantle and buy one" (Luke 22:35–38). Why would Jesus tell someone to buy a sword, say those using this text in defense of violence, if he didn't intend for that person to use it? And yet we know that Jesus's intention was not to have weapons used to protect or defend him, because a few verses later he rebukes Peter for using the sword. In Luke 22:38, when Jesus is heading off to the Garden of Gethsemane, he indicates that they are going into a hostile situation. The disciples say that they have two swords, and Jesus responds, "It is enough." However, what he actually says is, "Enough!" Jesus is not affirming that they should bring along their swords. Rather, realizing that they have completely misunderstood his comment, he intends to cut off further discussion. "Stop, enough already!" is the intended message.

When these texts and images are taken together, one gets a powerful picture of God moving through time and teaching us that nonviolent suffering and even non-violent resistance have primary place in the "battle" between good and evil. Jesus models this for us in his life and cross, and our call to be imitators of Christ means we must face this issue seriously. Can a person be both a Christian and a supporter of just war theory that allows the use of violence in extreme cases? Many have thought so—Augustine in the fourth century, Aquinas in the thirteenth, and others. In fact, today just war theory is more widely accepted than Christian pacifism.

So where do we go from there? Surely, there seems a strong preference for nonviolent resistance from the scriptural references we have seen. If we decide that this evidence can be overcome in a way that allows for just war, then we as Christians must certainly favor interpreting the criteria strictly.

DAY 4 — The Christian Tradition

Many Christians are surprised to learn that the early church overwhelmingly believed that to follow Jesus meant to reject the way of violence. Prior to 200 CE, most Christian voices argued against the participation of believers in war. From 200 CE to the Edict of Milan in 313 CE—when Constantine legalized Christianity—the vast majority of Christian teachers still taught and defended nonviolence as the only legitimate Christian option.

Consider the words, for example, of an early Christian theologian, Justin Martyr: "We who formerly murdered one another now refrain from making war even upon our enemies."[7] And, from Irenaeus, another early church leader, we hear similarly:

> The new covenant that brings back peace and the law that gives life have gone forth over the whole earth, as the prophets said: "For out of Zion will go forth the law, and the word of the Lord from Jerusalem; and the Lord will rebuke many people; and they will break down their swords into plowshares, and their spears into pruning hooks, and they will no longer learn to fight." ... These people [i.e., Christians] formed their swords and war-lances into plowshares ... that is, into instruments used for peaceful purposes. So now, they are unaccustomed to fighting. When they are struck, they offer also the other cheek.[8]

In both cases, the early church took Jesus's command to turn the other cheek and to pray for enemies as equivalent to commanding nonparticipation in war.

In several different places, Egyptian church teacher Clement of Alexandria also denied Christians the use of violence. Here are a couple of examples: "It is not in war, but in peace, that we are trained"; and "Christians are not allowed to use violence to correct the delinquencies of sins."[9]

Early Christian apologist Tertullian was even more direct, taking on the question of participation in war directly:

> "Nation will not take up sword against nation, and they will no more learn to fight." Who else, therefore, does this prophecy apply to, other than us? For we are fully taught by the new law, and therefore observe these practices.... The practice of the old law was to avenge itself by the vengeance of the sword. It was to pluck out "eye for eye," and to inflict retaliatory revenge for injury. However, the teaching of the new law points to clemency. It changes the primitive ferocity of swords and lances to tranquility. It remodels the primitive execution of war upon the rivals and enemies of the Law into the peaceful actions of plowing and cultivating the land.[10]

And again Tertullian wrote:

> A man cannot give his allegiance to two masters—God and Caesar.... How will a Christian man participate in war? In fact, how will he serve even in peace without a sword? For the Lord has taken the sword away. It is also true that soldiers came to John [the Baptist] and received the instructions for their conduct. It is true also that a centurion believed. Nevertheless, the Lord afterward, in disarming Peter, disarmed every soldier.[11]

Regarding someone who was already in the military when he become a Christian, Tertullian wrote, "[W]hen a man has become a believer and faith has been sealed, there must be either an immediate abandonment of the military office, which has been the course of many—or else all sorts of quibbling will have to be resorted to in order to avoid offending God."[12]

Roman church leader Hippolytus made a similar claim, writing: "A soldier of the civil authority must be taught not to kill men and to refuse to do so if he is commanded, and to refuse to take an oath. If he is unwilling to comply, he must be rejected for baptism.... If an applicant or a believer seeks to become a soldier, he must be rejected, for he has despised God."[13] During this period, there was little distinction between soldiers and the equivalent of police—the same force often served both functions. Some felt that Christians could participate in normal order-keeping exercises that police undertook. The problem came when the police officer was required to be a warrior and engage in killing.

Origen, another leader of the early church, wrote: "We have converted into pruning hooks the spears that were formerly used in war. For we no longer take up 'sword against nation,' nor do we 'learn war any more.' That is because we have become children of peace for the sake of Jesus, who is our Leader."[14]

The Christian position on war began to change when Constantine legalized Christianity with the Edict of Milan. The defense of the empire became increasingly intertwined with the protection of the church. By the time of Augustine (354–430 CE), the situation was ripe for his articulation of a Christian interpretation of the just war theory. Thus in a further compromise of its earlier view, the church moved from a position that completely rejected Christian participation in war to one that saw the use of force in the defense of the empire to be "wholly just." Since Augustine, the just war theory has undergone further refinement, as noted earlier, but most contemporary advocates of the just war theory appeal to his work.

The other main Christian position regarding war—pacifism or nonviolence—reemerged in the sixteenth-century Reformation with the Anabaptist tradition, and later in the Society of Friends. While a minority, these Christian traditions seek to be faithful to their understanding of the teachings of Jesus and the early church.

DAY 5 — Living Examples in the Contemporary Church

We often hear inspirational stories of great things done by individual persons. Often these stories do not tell us about the support community that was there to form, train, advise, and support those "individuals" who engage in heroic acts. Notice, in what follows, all the players involved in the formation of a young man named Shane. When he engaged in his acts for peace, he carried with him all those who had helped prepare him to act when the time came. The silent majority in the background is a powerful metaphor for the church.

LIVING FOR PEACE

Shane Claiborne was the popular kid in his high school. He was the prom king and part of the "in" crowd. He was planning on making it big, making lots of money, and living out his perception of the American dream. Shane also had a very typical faith experience for a kid in America. He made a faith decision at a Christian festival. He attended church. He became a part of a youth group—several of them, actually, attending whichever group had the most exciting offering at the time. So how, from this very traditional upbringing, did he end up in Iraq, at a time of war, promoting peace?

Well, there were a few steps in between.

Shane began to ask questions about why so many people who were following Jesus acted nothing like that man from Galilee. How did disciples become so unlike the One they claimed to be modeling their life after? Further, the life Christians were being called to lead seemed to have little to do with the great sacrifice that accompanied Jesus's life. Shane began to ask why "preachers were telling me to lay my life at the foot of the cross and weren't giving me anything to pick up."

Seeking to truly imitate Christ can have big consequences for an individual. Shane attended a Christian college (Eastern University), got involved with the poor and homeless in Philadelphia, and started a community of faith in the inner city in a place that had been abandoned by many within the church. Following Jesus can take you to crazy places. In Shane's case, it also ended up taking him to Iraq.

After the September 11 terrorist attacks, the whole nation wondered how to react. Nowhere was this discussion more active than in the U.S. churches. The world turned to America asking, "What would Jesus do?"

The initial response of the nation was patriotic. In the year following the attacks, the United States imported $51.7 million worth of American flags, most of which, ironically, were made in China. There was a great sense that the nation was united, and favorability ratings for public officials reached all-time highs.

In the two years after the attacks, the United States invaded Afghanistan, seeking the terrorists responsible for the September 11 attacks. By March 2003, sights were set on Iraq. Shane Claiborne saw the country as blindly rushing into an invasion for which we had no justification. Rather than simply joining the ranks of those content to complain about the illegal war on Iraq, Shane chose to act.

In the six months leading up to the invasion of Iraq, Shane fasted and prayed. He sought the direction of his Christian community. In the end, he knew that he was being called to Iraq to speak of God's peace. He joined the Iraq Peace Team, which consisted of priests and other clergy, veterans, doctors, journalists, and students. In the war zone, he hoped to offer the peaceful message of Jesus. (His war journals can be read online at www.thesimpleway.org/macro/shane_iraq.html.)

Shane went over to show others the love of Jesus and was amazed to find radical followers of Jesus already there. He went over to help transform the situation and was transformed himself. The popular kid, the prom king, was now the peace activist.

Shane's actions had an impact on people beyond those he met in Iraq. His war journals have been a great inspiration to others, as news of his actions spread virally on the Internet, and he has been invited to speak in significant places.

Inspired by stories like Shane's, a group of students at Asbury Seminary in Kentucky began gathering every Monday evening to pray for reconciliation in the world and to ask how it might begin in their own personal relationships. They are not ready to go to a foreign land and put themselves in the line of fire, but they are asking what part they could play in bringing peace to the world.

Shane would not consider what he has done exceptional. He would tell you that he was just following Jesus.

WILL SAMSON*

DAY 6 — Putting Faith into Action

The appropriate ways to live out "God's politics" with regard to war and peace will depend upon the contemporary situation in which we find ourselves. Do we live in a time or culture of peace? Are we merely "between wars"? Are we in the prewar buildup stage? Or the postwar cleanup? Or is our nation currently at war?

Let us consider the different phases along with the sorts of actions that might be appropriate to each. Of course, any of these actions can be undertaken during any of the phases.

During a period of relative peace, there are two important activities that need engagement. Begin by supporting organizations, causes, movements, or projects that are aimed at sowing the seeds of peace.[15] These might include victim-offender reconciliation projects, conflict resolution efforts in countries with a history of strife, racial and economic justice programs, or similar projects that dig deeply into bringing people together who are divided by difference or history and giving them the necessary tools to build a better future together. Choose one or two that you can actually participate in within your own community.

Many Christians are not knowledgeable enough about how the church has viewed war and peace. Classes can be organized to address the subject, and materials can be prepared that help deepen people's understanding of the issue. Bring in practitioners as well as educators so that the information is linked to real people living these issues today. Once the group has learned and discussed these traditions, consider bringing in representatives from other faith traditions (such as Judaism, Islam, and Hinduism) to discuss their faith's tradition regarding war and peace.

---

* *Will Samson is a student at Asbury Theological Seminary in Wilmore, Kentucky.*

When a nation is preparing for war, an adequate understanding of faith-based views on war becomes critical for persons to have rational, accurate, and critical participation in the public discourse. It is important for churches to help their members gather accurate information about the conflict, as well as to help them present a perspective rooted in the church's commitment to peacemaking. Then awareness can be translated into participation in the public discourse. Churches should be places of moral and ethical leadership for the whole community. This means providing the guiding principles of our Christian tradition and helping people apply them to the current situation. Letters to the editor, opinion pieces, letters to Congress and the administration, Web sites, and open forums should aim to instruct, educate, and give witness to our beliefs—not berate. Christians should state clearly and succinctly our position on the war and the theological or ethical principles that led us to that conclusion. It might be appropriate to undertake public demonstrations, prayer vigils, or other nonviolent actions to demonstrate the urgency of the situation. In all these actions, it is important to come to collective discernment and understanding within a spiritual community or community of faith.

If war breaks out, then many of the steps indicated in the preceding paragraph may still be in order, though now it becomes critical to intensify those activities. At some point, acts of civil disobedience might also be appropriate. This is a serious step that should be undertaken only by those who have been through nonviolence training, and only at the end of an extended period of negotiation with those in positions of power who are making the decisions about war. Once war breaks out, lives will be lost on both sides. Unfortunately, noncombatants will likely suffer most. This realization only makes more evident the critical nature of our participation. Review in some detail the activities proposed in the appendix, and look for more creative ways to reduce violence and teach people how to resist the temptation to use violence to resolve conflicts.

DAY 7 — Group Meeting and Reflection

1. An alternative response to the terrorist attacks on September 11 is outlined on page 91 of *God's Politics*. Assume a major newspaper came to you and asked that you provide a plan that offered an appropriate religious response to September 11. What would your points be? Why did you choose them?

2. Serious attempts to undermine terrorism must include a willingness on the part of the powerful to examine their own past mistakes and genuinely attempt to rectify them. Research what some of those mistakes might be. What things come to mind?

3. Discuss "Ten Lessons to Defeat Terrorism" (*God's Politics,* page 105). Identify strengths and weaknesses. What would you add?

4. Discuss and assess "Lessons of War" (*God's Politics,* page 120).

5. Reflect upon "Putting Down the Mighty from Their Thrones" (*God's Politics,* page 129). How would you characterize the reversal of power relations described there? To what extent do the gospels, in fact, reverse these relations? What does it mean to live out this reversal in our everyday lives?

6. *God's Politics* quotes columnist George Will's comments on domination (page 146). Discuss the quote and assess it from a theological perspective.

7. Discuss preemptive peacemaking strategies—that is, methods and engagements that might be undertaken prior to the outbreak of war that would advance a just peace. You might begin by identifying issues that would constitute an injustice that could lead to war.

8. *God's Politics* cites Gerald Schlabach's work (page 165), drawing attention to the differences between how police forces operate and how militaries operate. How might these concepts be brought to bear at an international level to avoid war?

9. To what extent do you think the Israeli-Palestinian conflict drives international terrorism? What steps would you support to bring about a just peace in the Middle East?

10. Chapter 12 of *God's Politics* has the subtitle "Cure Causes, Not Just Symptoms." What are some of the underlying causes of global insecurity? What contribution do we make to those causes? How might we contribute instead to global security—both in our personal lives and choices and in our participation as citizens who influence national policies?

Economic Justice

GOD'S POLITICS asks what it means for an economy to be structured in a way that constitutes justice for all of its members. There are implicit advantages and disadvantages for different participants in free economies. We have to consider what factors, from a Christian perspective, must guide our arguments for reforming economic practices and institutions. This theme relates particularly to chapters 12, 13, 16, and 17 in *God's Politics*. Read or review those chapters. Below is a brief recap.

Chapter 12: The chapter begins by recognizing the role fear plays in how we respond to threats and the extent to which we feel vulnerable. It ends with the recognition that lasting peace must be based on a sense of security that includes personal, national, and global levels. Real security means, among other things, the assurance that all people have access to the essentials of life—such as adequate food, water, and housing. The prophet Micah offers a vision of the world where swords are beaten into plowshares and where nations do not make war against other nations. He goes on to envision everyone having their own "vine and fig tree," living free and unafraid. Bringing about a secure future and making that vision a reality will require dealing with causes and not merely symptoms.

Chapter 13: Thousands of Bible verses affirm our obligation to care for the poor. Despite this clear and abundant teaching, some people try to argue that when Jesus said, "The poor you will have always with you" (Matthew 26:11), it somehow provided justification for doing little or nothing about poverty—as if Jesus had said there would always be poor people among us, so why do anything about it? However, this misreads both the immediate and the broader contexts of his words. First, this verse comes after Jesus's anointing by the woman at Bethany, prior to his death on the cross—Jesus will not be among the disciples for much longer: "You will not always have me." Second, Jesus is making a judgment about the social location of his followers—that to follow Jesus means we will always have the opportunity, and the gift, of working on behalf of those he called "the least of these."

Chapter 16: Former Treasury Secretary Paul O'Neill said, "Part of the genius of capitalism [is that] people get to make good decisions or bad decisions. And they get to pay the consequences or enjoy the fruits of their decisions."[1] Yet corporate traders and executives who make really bad decisions rarely "pay the consequences."

More often it is the workers and consumers who suffer the results. When self-interest and profit are placed ahead of the common good, those most vulnerable suffer the most. In the longer term, we all suffer the subsequent breakdown in society. The Bible includes specific commands intended to prevent the accumulation of extreme wealth, because this is directly tied to abuse of the poor.

Chapter 17: There seems to be a new level of interest in addressing global poverty. At the same time, however, the global community has fallen behind in its efforts to meet the U.N.'s Millennium Development Goals (which we'll look at on Day 2) in the crucial areas of education, health, and targeted poverty reduction. For the first time in history, we have the information, knowledge, technology, and resources to bring the worst of global poverty to an end. What we seem to be lacking is the moral and political will to do so. Taking advantage of poor countries is too easy for developed nations and multinational corporations that are eager to increase profits. People of faith need to lead the way in generating new moral energy for addressing global poverty.

DAY 1 — Introducing the Topic

Before we can begin a discussion of economic justice, we must spend some time working through definitions of the term—what exactly is *economic justice*? Obviously, to use the term "economic" is to speak of buying, selling, and trading various goods and services, but what would make one way of "doing economy" more or less "just" than another? This requires a definition of justice, and for followers of Jesus it must be one that is consistent with the Bible and Christian teaching.

Plato and Aristotle defined justice as giving to a person what that person deserves. Unfortunately, this led Plato to distinguish between persons based upon their "quality" or "virtue." Thus a person wasn't measured by individual acts or choices, but by his or her place in society as ruler, soldier, or "other." This led to certain rules of justice being seen as appropriate for certain kinds of people: certain laws applied to the ruling class, while another set of rules applied to laborers or slaves. Justice did not mean that all received equal opportunity.

Justice more consistent with Christian teaching reflects the very character and intentions of God. And since all human beings possess the equality of being created in God's image, it means equal opportunities, regardless of race, class, gender, or other discriminatory factors. It necessarily includes aspects of divine mercy, since God's actions are both just and merciful. We cannot drive a wedge between the notions of justice and mercy. This invites us, as Christians, to see God's own actions as embodying perfect justice, while also embodying mercy.

Similarly, while we must affirm "equality" in some sense in our affirmation of justice, we do not have to conceive of justice as dictating "equality" of outcomes.

In other words, a just economic playing field does not require that all persons have the exact same income, live in the same size house, etc. In fact, rewards for various types of work may vary, as long as the variations are not disproportionate to the quality and quantity of work. However, this is no carte blanche to make the moral standard "what the market will bear," because history frequently shows that the market operates unjustly.

The American Friends Service Committee summarizes principles that promote a just economic playing field as follows:

> Economic justice means building a fair economy that works for everyone. It means fair trade policies that protect workers' rights to organize and to receive a living wage for their work at home and abroad. It includes budget and tax policies in which corporations and wealthy individuals pay their fair share, and which support good schools and childcare, affordable healthcare and housing, retirement security, and a safety net for those in need. It promotes the common good by funding public services. It means calling for new national priorities that reduce wasteful military spending and redirect tax dollars to helping our children, elders, and communities meet their needs. It includes notions of a social contract in which society and individuals fulfill their mutual responsibilities to each other.[2]

The National Association of Evangelicals puts it this way:

> Economic justice includes both the mitigation of suffering and also the restoration of wholeness. Wholeness includes full participation in the life of the community. Health care, nutrition, and education are important ingredients in helping people transcend the stigma and agony of poverty and re-enter community. Since healthy family systems are important for nurturing healthy individuals and overcoming poverty, public policy should encourage marriage and sexual abstinence outside marriage, while discouraging early onset of sexual activity, out-of-wedlock births, and easy divorce. Government should also hold fathers and mothers responsible for the maintenance of their families, enforcing where necessary the collection of child-support payments. Restoring people to wholeness means that governmental social welfare must aim to provide opportunity and restore people to self-sufficiency. While basic standards of support must be put in place to provide for those who cannot care for their families and themselves, incentives and training in marketable skills must be part of any well-rounded program. We urge Christians who work in the political realm to shape wise laws pertaining to the creation of wealth, wages, education, taxation, immigration, health care, and social welfare that will protect those trapped in poverty and empower the poor to improve their circumstances.[3]

These summaries begin to get at the issues that connect the terms "justice" and "economy." For a deeper and more thorough examination, we could hardly do better than to cite the ten principles drawn from the U.S. Catholic bishops' 1986 pastoral letter on Catholic social teaching and the U.S. economy, titled *Economic Justice for All*. The ten principles are listed below.

1. The economy exists for the person, not the person for the economy.
2. All economic life should be shaped by moral principles. Economic choices and institutions must be judged by how they protect or undermine the life and dignity of the human person, support the family, and serve the common good.
3. A fundamental moral measure of any economy is how the poor and vulnerable are faring.
4. All people have a right to life and to secure the basic necessities of life (e.g., food, clothing, shelter, education, health care, safe environment, economic security).
5. All people have the right to economic initiative, to productive work, to just wages and benefits, to decent working conditions, as well as to organize and join unions and other associations.
6. All people, to the extent they are able, have a corresponding duty to work, a responsibility to provide for the needs of their families, and an obligation to contribute to the broader society.
7. In economic life, free markets have both clear advantages and limits; government has essential responsibilities and limits; voluntary groups have irreplaceable roles, but cannot substitute for the proper working of the market and the just policies of the state.
8. Society has a moral obligation, including governmental action where necessary, to assure opportunity, meet basic human needs, and pursue justice in economic life.
9. Workers, owners, managers, stockholders, and consumers are moral agents in economic life. By our choices, initiative, creativity, and investment, we enhance or diminish economic opportunity, community life, and social justice.
10. The global economy has moral dimensions and human consequences. Decisions on investment, trade, aid, and development should protect human life and promote human rights, especially for those most in need wherever they might live on this globe.

In addition, in his 1991 encyclical *Centesimus Annus*, Pope John Paul II noted that Christian faith envisions a "society of work, enterprise, and participation" that "is not directed against the market, but demands that the market be appropriately controlled by the forces of society and by the state to assure that the basic needs of the whole society are satisfied."[4] In the midst of our responsibilities, we must hear the call to devote particular attention to those on the margins of society, who are particularly exposed to life's uncertainties.

Economic justice, then, is not merely about equality, nor is it something that one can easily profile on a chart, reduce to numbers, or bring about via hard and fast rules. Rather, to engage in the struggle for economic justice is to recognize that we must learn to understand circumstances through an integration of God's justice, mercy, grace, and love. Our first engagement must be driven by the call to love God by loving our neighbors as ourselves.

Two things, then, are at the center of economic justice: (1) recognition that God expects each of us to engage in acts of mercy and justice aimed at creating a fair and just economic playing field, and (2) recognition that God intends that public institutions have their own role to play in establishing just economies. Pope John Paul II summarized these factors in noting that Christians are not opposed to the free market but demand that it be policed in order to serve the common good.[5]

Considering the Evidence

Given this understanding of economic justice, particularly as summarized in the ten principles named by the Catholic bishops, it is pretty clear that both domestically and internationally the United States faces a number of challenges. In what ways can we work to develop economic systems that better embody those principles? Again, from the American Friends Service Committee:

> In today's global economy, many people are experiencing hunger, hardship, and the impact of a growing inequality of wealth, power, and access to basic resources. Around the world, 1.2 billion people live in "extreme" poverty. Here at home, 45 million Americans lack health insurance, and 1 in 3 cannot afford decent housing. Meanwhile, more than 60 percent of U.S. corporations paid no federal taxes for 1996 through 2000. The total net worth of America's 3,000 wealthiest individuals reached $955 billion while the median weekly wage for an American worker was $625.[6]

How can we accept that some live in extreme poverty and lack access to basic health care while some live with extreme wealth and the most profitable corporations go tax-free? Many of those who live in extreme poverty try to survive on the equivalent of $1 per day while the richest 3,000 persons hold wealth of nearly $1 trillion. Can we consider any economic system just that creates and allows such inequities to exist? Unfortunately, the story gets worse.

As chapter 17 of *God's Politics* notes, in September 2000 the United Nations established an agenda for overcoming fundamental economic injustices on a global level. The development targets were called the Millennium Development

Goals (MDGs). They outlined poverty reduction goals to be accomplished by the year 2015. Eight goals covered the eradication of extreme poverty, primary school education for all children, gender equality, reduction of infant mortality rates, improved health care for mothers, environmental care, and international cooperation for global development. In September 2005, the U.N.'s annual Human Development Report concluded that little progress had been made on these goals and that fifty countries had actually lost ground on at least one of them. The report noted growing disparities of wealth and poverty both within and between countries as well as disparate access to resources and distribution of power. Let's look at some specifics.

- According to current trends, 827 million people will live in extreme poverty in 2015.
- Fifty countries are currently falling behind target on at least one Millennium Development Goal.
- A further sixty-five countries risk failing to reach at least one of the goals by the year 2040.
- In eighteen countries, the current Human Development Index (HDI: a measure of poverty, literacy, education, and life expectancy for countries worldwide) is lower than it was in 1990, when the index was first produced. Twelve of these countries are in Africa, and the other six are former Soviet republics.
- The twenty-four countries with the lowest HDI rating are all in Africa, with Niger at the very bottom of the list.
- The fifty persons in the world with the most personal wealth have combined income that exceeds that of the poorest 416 million.
- There are 2.5 billion people (40 percent of the world's population) currently living on less than $2 per day.
- These 2.5 billion are the recipients of only 5 percent of the world's income, while the richest 10 percent receive 54 percent of the global income.
- The gap between the richest and poorest is growing in 80 percent of these countries while it is declining in only 4 percent.[7]

These facts paint a picture of global inequity and a corresponding increase in those suffering at the lowest end of the income strata. The U.N.'s 2005 Human Development Report notes that while "some important human development advances have been registered ... the overall report card on progress makes for depressing reading." The report goes on to identify the implementation of policies aimed to reduce income and wealth distribution inequities as the highest priority.

Many rightly put attention on trade issues as central to establishing a just global economy. As the U.N. report notes, "Trade policies of rich countries generally greatly disadvantage developing countries." For example, since rich countries have disproportionate representation in trade-negotiating processes, they are able to further slant the playing field in their favor, and generally do so.

The International Monetary Fund (IMF) is an international organization created by the United Nations in 1946 as part of a financial reconstruction effort in the wake of World War II. It was created to oversee the global finance system by monitoring exchange rates and balance of payments as well as providing loans to countries and monitoring repayments. The IMF regularly requires countries borrowing from the fund to accept certain "conditionals" before they can receive funds. These conditionals require the borrower to privatize public institutions and to open their markets to free trade, with little concern for the damage done to low-income people.

Further, while rich countries typically require that developing countries open their own markets to free trade, those rich countries often continue protectionist policies for their own markets, such as farm subsidies to protect their farmers against lower-cost producers in other countries. The United Nations estimates that this practice alone costs developing economies $72 billion per year. Given that the United Nations has estimated that the entire world's hungry could be fed for $40 billion per year, these agricultural subsidies are literally starving people in developing countries.

If we turn our attention back to the United States, we will also find some very disturbing numbers. In order to get a glimpse into the seriousness of the gap between the rich and the poor, we have to look at both the wealth gap and the income gap. In 2001, it was estimated that the total net worth of Americans was $42.4 trillion. The "wealth" pie was divided up as follows:

- The richest 1 percent held 32.7 percent of all wealth.
- The richest 5 percent held 57.7 percent of all wealth.
- The richest 10 percent held 69.7 percent of all wealth.
- The richest 50 percent held 97.2 percent of all wealth.
- The poorest 50 percent held 2.8 percent of all wealth.[8]

The wealth gap has been growing for some time. For example, from 1983 to 1998, the richest 1 percent of Americans saw their share of wealth increase by 42.2 percent while the poorest 40 percent saw their share of wealth decline by more than 76 percent.

Income distribution in 2001 was not quite as severely skewed as wealth distribution, but it was still quite one-sided. Here's a look at the "income" pie:

- The top 5 percent had 21 percent of all income.
- The top 20 percent had 47.7 percent of all income.
- The top 40 percent had 70.6 percent of all income.
- The top 60 percent had 86 percent of all income.
- The lowest 20 percent only had 4.2 percent of all income.
- The lowest 40 percent only had 14 percent of all income.[9]

Of course, it is understandable that wealth distribution would diverge even more than income distribution. Those on the low end of the income scale are expending most or all of their income to purchase life's necessities, while those on the high end are investing most of theirs and thus increasing their wealth. Over time, this accumulation of wealth in the hands of a few also gathers political and market power in their hands. This slants the playing field ever steeper to the advantage of the rich.

DAY 3   Reading the Bible

What does the Bible have to say about economic justice, which is closely related to the concept of mutual responsibility? According to scripture, does God intend for us primarily to "watch out for number one," or are we called to give ourselves for each other in relationships of deep interdependence?

Many passages throughout the Bible are best understood within this context, and several early ones are of particular importance. The early chapters of Genesis give an accounting of God's creation of the world, the subsequent disobedience of humans, and the various consequences that led to a world spiraling ever deeper into chaos. In Genesis 12, we find the beginning of God's plan to set things right with the call of Abraham. Notice in particular that, in verse 3, Abraham is being called not just to be blessed *but in order that he might be a blessing to all*. Similar language is picked up when Abraham is told that he will be a blessing to the other nations. Already we see an important aspect of the deeply interdependent nature of the lives that God intends for us.

Then we come to the fifteenth chapter of Deuteronomy. The idea of being called to serve God for the sake of others is expressed in several ways in this chapter. First, God indicates that there will be no one in need because God will provide adequately. But God also gives instructions on how to structure a "Sabbath economy" based on certain social disciplines. These included gleaning laws (that is, laws requiring that some fruit be left in the fields for the poor) and clearing the slate for those in debt bondage every seventh year. "Such legislated social disciplines of wealth restructuring in Israel were intended as a hedge against the tendency of human societies to concentrate power and wealth in the hands of the few, creating hierarchical classes with the poor at the bottom," writes theologian Ched Myers. "The vision was that if 'Sabbath economics' was practiced," Myers continues, "then 'There will be no one in need among you' (Deuteronomy 15:4). But the practical Deuteronomist, anticipating rightly that the people would forever be hedging on the demands of social justice, adds that compassion is the plumb line of the law: 'For there will never cease to be needy ones in your land, I command you: Open your hand to the poor' (Deuteronomy 15:11)."[10]

In this brief picture of an economy consistent with God's intentions, God gives primary attention to mechanisms intended to prevent the rise of a class of permanently dispossessed people and a class of those with extreme wealth. Sounds a lot like a system built on the concern for economic justice, doesn't it?

Leviticus 25 also addresses a periodic leveling of the economic playing field through "years of jubilee." Every fiftieth year, all lands were to be returned to their ancestral owners—again, a specific means to prevent vast accumulations of wealth in the hands of a few. This likewise would keep people from hedging on the social justice that God requires.

Another example of God's concern for the poor and desire for a just economic system is expressed in the laws about collateral. "If ever you take your neighbor's garment in pledge, you shall restore it to him before the sun goes down; for that is his only covering and it is his mantle for his body; in what else shall he sleep?" (Exodus 22:26–27, RSV). God's sense of economic justice is precisely the reverse of our own economic practices. When a poor, "higher-risk" person wants to borrow from a bank, higher fees and interest are demanded, or loans are simply denied. God, however, is more interested in the care of the poor.

The prophet Amos also reveals the intensity of God's concern for basic economic justice:

> Thus says the Lord: For three transgressions of Israel, and for four, I will not revoke the punishment; because they sell the righteous for silver, and the needy for a pair of sandals—they who trample the head of the poor into the dust of the earth, and push the afflicted out of the way; father and son go in to the same girl, so that my holy name is profaned; they lay themselves down beside every altar on garments taken in pledge; and in the house of their God they drink wine bought with fines they imposed. (Amos 2:6–9)

Here God pronounces judgment on the nation of Israel because of its failures to act with economic justice. First, Israel has become a nation that sells the poor so that those in power may accumulate more wealth. Second, the failure to observe God's commands to care for the poor and marginalized has led other nations to blaspheme God's name. How so? When by not living up to God's intentions we call into question both God's goodness and God's very existence, our sin leads others to make faulty judgments about God. Third, the reference to "garments taken in pledge" announces perverse disobedience of God's command that those garments are to be returned by sunset. Not only are they kept, but now the holders are using them for their own luxury before the very altar of God!

Since God has given these instructions as part of the laws of Israel, it is impossible to claim that God intends care for the poor to occur only in the "private sphere." In these and other passages, God gives commands to the people corporately and punishes them corporately for their failure to obey.

Since public institutions play a major role in the shape of our shared lives, it would not be possible to order our lives in a way that is consistent with God's intentions without involving these public institutions. Any serious attempt to live in a way that is consistent with God's expectations cannot exclude a role for governments and other social institutions.

This point is amplified in Ezekiel 16. God is again about to pronounce judgment on Israel. This time God compares the Israelites' sins to the sins of the citizens of Sodom. According to Ezekiel 16: "This was the guilt of your sister Sodom: She and her daughters had pride, excess of food, and prosperous ease, but did not aid the poor and needy. They were haughty, and did abominable things before me; therefore I removed them when I saw it" (verses 49–50). Tony Campolo, emeritus professor at Eastern University, once noted that if the sins of Sodom constituted "sodomy," then sodomy includes pride, luxury, and the failure to hear the cry of the needy. Again, economic justice is front and center.

Next let's consider Jesus's own teachings. His warnings about economic justice show up regularly. Unfortunately, perhaps because many read them from a social position of affluence, these passages are often muted in interpretation or preaching. For example, how often do we think deeply about God's judgment on the man whose crops were so plentiful that he planned to tear down his barns and build bigger ones? What's wrong with that? He earned it all through hard work—why not retire early? However, when this man took the bounty of God as his own personal property, God called him a fool. Of course, this does not come as a surprise once we reflect upon the intimate connections between Jesus's mission statement in Luke 4 and the issues we've already examined from the Hebrew scriptures. Consider Luke 4:18–19:

> The Spirit of the Lord is upon me, because he has anointed me to bring good news to the poor. He has sent me to proclaim release to the captives and recovery of sight to the blind, to let the oppressed go free, to proclaim the year of the Lord's favor.

The immediate context advises us that Jesus is quoting from the prophet Isaiah, and many have pointed out the "Jubilee-like" language repeated here. While Jesus is not limiting his ministry to what we would call economic or social justice issues, he clearly adopts them as a central part of his ministry and mission in the world. For example, in the account of the final judgment in Matthew 25, care for "the least of these" moves front and center and becomes the basis by which to identify those who are or are not Jesus's followers.

Consider the story of the rich man and Lazarus in Luke 16:19–31. Lazarus, as far as we know, is not a relative of the rich man, nor does Lazarus have any claim on the rich man other than being a fellow human in need. We know that the rich man "dressed in purple and the finest linen and feasted in great magnificence every day" (verse 19). Lazarus is "full of sores, and desiring to be fed with the crumbs which fell from the rich man's table" (20). Note the extreme wealth gap. God takes very seriously that the rich man does not expend any of his great wealth to ease Lazarus's suffering. The rich man's neglect to care for Lazarus is the most significant factor in determining the rich man's fate—namely, that he goes to hell!

Concern for the poor and others on the margins of society also appears in the epistles of the early church. For example, the letter of James covers the threat of greed and materialism from a number of perspectives. The writer reminds us that riches and material goods are transitory, hardly worth as much energy as we normally invest in them (see James 1:9–11). If we are to imitate Jesus, we can't treat other people differently according to their wealth status. God is not a respecter of wealth, nor should we be (see James 2:1–13). Finally, the writer strongly admonishes that wealth obliges us not only to pray for the poor, but also to assist them (James 2:14–17).

Paul, in 2 Corinthians 8:15, describes the economy of the first Christians by drawing on the book of Exodus when he writes that "the one who had much did not have too much, and the one who had little did not have too little." Here, Paul suggests that we should be aware of the needs around us and use any extra we might have to help meet them. This challenges the contemporary tendency to allow ourselves to be driven only by self-interest.

We could easily extend our study into many, many other places within scripture, but we will leave that as an exercise to the reader. What is clear is that God takes economic justice seriously, at the level of the individual person, at the level of the church, and at the level of public institutions.[11]

DAY 4 — The Christian Tradition

The biblical test of any economic structure is whether we count the interests of others as being as important as our own, and how well we protect the poor. Did the early church pick up on these concerns from scripture? Yes, they did.

In the twenty-first century, there has been a strong tendency to view economics from a mostly capitalist, free-market perspective. Because of this, some of the early church's teachings may sound strange to us.

The early church had mixed feelings with regard to private property. Generally it was affirmed, but with the recognition that all that one "owns" is really held under stewardship from God. Given that, the church emphasized the obligation to steward one's resources in a way that aimed to meet the needs of others. Jesuit writer William Ryan notes that "in the 17th century we find Bossuet, the renowned preacher at Notre Dame Cathedral in Paris, telling the rich that they must care for the poor, for it is only they [the poor] who can open the gates of heaven for the rich."[12]

The question of what constituted a fair profit was another subject that both the early church leaders and later Christians addressed. The concern for justice was always at the forefront. Justice was understood not as "what the market would bear," but rather as what served human need and community. For example, Thomas Aquinas, writing in the thirteenth century, argued: "To keep back what is due another"—such as a fair wage—"inflicts the same kind of injury as taking a thing unjustly."[13]

On the communal nature of the world's resources and our obligation to use them to benefit the common good, hear Ambrose of Milan, a fourth-century bishop:

> Why do the injuries of nature delight you? The world has been created for all, while you rich are trying to keep it for yourselves. Not merely the possession of the earth, but the very sky, air and the sea are claimed for the use of the rich few.... Not from your own do you bestow on the poor man, but you make return from what is his. For what has been given as common for the use of all, you appropriate for yourself alone. The earth belongs to all, not to the rich.[14]

Again, in our contemporary setting, ownership and utilization of the earth's resources are often seen very differently than they were by the Christians who lived closest to the time of Jesus. For example, how many of these warnings offered by Ambrose could be connected directly to legislation passed within the last few years that radically individualizes the ownership of natural resources, cutting the connection to a broader community?

We've already mentioned the story of Lazarus and the rich man from the second half of Luke 16, but how many have ever heard it preached like this?

> Indeed Lazarus suffered no injustice from the rich man; for the rich man did not take Lazarus' money, but failed to share his own. If he is accused by the man he failed to pity because he did not share his own wealth, what pardon will the man receive who has stolen others' goods, when he is surrounded by those whom he has wronged? I shall bring you testimony from divine Scripture, saying that not only the theft of others' goods but also the failure to share one's own goods with others is theft and swindle and defraudation.
>
> ... [Y]ou have stolen the goods of the poor. [The] rich hold the goods of the poor even if they have inherited them from their fathers or no matter how they have gathered their wealth. Deprive not the poor of his living. To deprive is to take what belongs to another; for it is called deprivation when we take and keep what belongs to others. By this we are taught that when we do not show mercy, we shall be punished just like those who steal. For money is the Lord's, however we may have gathered it.[15]

St. John Chrysostom, who wrote the above, might not last long in today's churches if he so boldly charged the rich with their obligations to the poor!

The wealth that comes our way comes with obligations and accountabilities, as do all things that one holds in trust. Our economic life must be driven by a love and concern for the poor among us and around the world. The idea that economic justice could bear any resemblance to social Darwinism ("survival of the most economically fit") would have been foreign, even repugnant, to the early church.

DAY 5 — Living Examples in the Contemporary Church

Advocacy for greater economic justice often seems futile. What can one person or a small group of people really do? The following story about how two women in a local church affected the views of their member of Congress on debt relief suggests that one person *can* make a difference.

JUBILEE BEGINS WITH ME

Pat Pelham lives in Birmingham, Alabama. About four years ago, she felt called to help people in need. Her pastor at Independent Presbyterian Church suggested she get their church involved in Bread for the World.

Pat and her friend Elaine Van Cleave came to hear me talk about Bread for the World at Our Lady of Sorrows Catholic Church. After that event, Pat and Elaine started to organize. They got their church's hunger committee involved in Bread for the World.

Three years ago, they invited their member of Congress, Rep. Spencer Bachus, to a Bread for the World dinner at Independent Presbyterian. I sat on his left, and the Presbyterian Hunger Action Enabler for Birmingham—a Republican Party activist—sat on his right. We urged Bachus to cosponsor the anti-hunger legislation that Bread for the World was pushing that year. Rep. Bachus had never before sponsored such legislation. But he called Pat the next evening and said, "I doubt that this will win me many votes, but I don't want to be responsible for even one child going hungry."

At the beginning of 1999, the Jubilee 2000 network was getting organized. Rep. Bachus had become chair of the international committee of the House Banking Committee, where any congressional action on debt relief would have to start. Pat, Elaine, and two friends from Independent Presbyterian flew up to Washington, D.C., at their own expense to take Bachus a debt-relief petition with 400 signatures.

"I don't know much about economics or international finance," Elaine explained. "But I do know that about 30,000 children die every day from hunger and other preventable causes, and, as a mother, that really bothers me. . . . [I]t would help a lot if you would sponsor this Jubilee legislation."

"What's the connection between so many children dying of hunger and debt relief?" Bachus asked. "All I know," Elaine said, "is that if I had to choose between paying a debt that I had inherited from my parents and buying food for my children, the choice would be clear." Bachus agreed to be an original sponsor of our bill and became its most passionate advocate.

Treasury Secretary Lawrence Summers told me that testifying before Bachus's sub-committee convinced him to change U.S. policy toward poor-country debt. If this conservative Republican urged cancellation of debts for the poorest countries, it was time for a change.

Spencer Bachus, a Southern Baptist, is a straightforward Christian. When the Banking Committee held its hearing on poor-country debt, Bachus said, "If we don't write off some of this debt, poor people in these countries will be suffering for the rest of their lives. And we'll be suffering a lot longer than that."

He held up a statement from Pope John Paul II and said, "I haven't read much by Catholics before, but I don't know how any Christian could read what the pope is saying here and not agree that we need to do something about the debt of these countries."

Bachus lobbied his conservative colleagues, including the Republican leadership of the House, for U.S. participation in international debt relief. Bachus says that he had come to see the world differently because of the church people back home who had approached him about Jubilee.

"I really hadn't thought much about places like Africa before," Bachus said. "Now, when Congress debates whether U.S. health care is too expensive at $2,200 per capita per year, I'm struck that a country like Ethiopia spends $10 on health care per capita per year."

Pat Pelham didn't do this by herself, of course, even in Birmingham. Across the country, several thousand people have been just as active as Pat on the Jubilee legislation. But there is a very clear line of causation between the grassroots activism of Pat and her friends in Birmingham and a significant breakthrough for justice in the world.

DAVID BECKMANN*

Ultimately, churches must get involved in building a more just economy at a variety of levels, all the way from encouraging individual giving to advocacy for appropriate public policies. Our witness is always stronger when we endeavor to put into practice in our local communities what we are defending more broadly. It is encouraging to find followers of Jesus who are putting into action the call to care for people living in poverty. Undoubtedly, there are many, many churches across our country that are seeking creatively to live out the divine call in our lives. We often hear a great deal about what is discouraging about the church today. Keep on the lookout, though, for these pearls of the kingdom of God.

DAY 6 — Putting Faith into Action

An important first step for engaging in activities intended to enhance economic justice is education. It is important to open a conversation that reveals the

* David Beckmann is president of Bread for the World. This text appeared in Sojourners, July/Aug. 2000, vol. 29, no. 4, p. 47.

basic inequities that exist. For example, why do some of the hardest workers end up with the lowest wages? Is it just for someone to work full-time and yet not make enough to care for her family? Is health care a luxury or a basic human right? What are the federal poverty guidelines for this year? How do these poverty markers compare to what it actually takes to live in the different parts of the country? What is the living wage movement all about, and how should Christians be involved with it?

There are two factors to keep in mind when working on education about economics. First, some of our most deeply seated presuppositions are held with regard to what constitutes economic fairness. It is important to include material from a range of sources in any educational program. This gives those from varying backgrounds and experiences several windows into the conversation. We need to give much attention to the biblical and theological justifications for economic justice concerns and how to address them. Second, this is an area that calls for creativity, such as dramatic or visual presentations of economic disparities that allow participants to see the consequences of economic injustice firsthand.

Once the education phase is completed, there are numerous ways to become involved in the ongoing debate. Write letters to the editor and opinion pieces tied to specific initiatives in your local area that are impacted by questions of social justice. Does your community have a living wage campaign? Consider joining with an organization in your area that engages in justice-oriented activities in order to amplify your efforts and build community.

Consider starting an economic accountability prayer group. There are a number of these small groups in the United States and beyond who come together around the "Household Sabbath Economics Covenant."[16] They inventory their own household economies, learn about more just ways of structuring their economics, and help support one another as they implement changes or face setbacks.

Go back once again and review the actions of the early church that are reported above. Virtually every congregation in the United States is near or in a community that has economic needs. A great deal of work is yet to be done before "justice rolls down like the waters," which means the opportunities are myriad. We have given only a couple examples of ways to get more actively involved with issues of economic justice. There are more in the appendix. Pick out one that holds personal interest and start there.

DAY 7

Group Meeting and Reflection

1. How does lack of access to adequate food, clean water, housing, health care, and other basic necessities of life contribute to conflict and violence? How might this be corrected?

2. What Bible passages do you remember about God's concern for those on the margins of our society? What do you think God's expectations for us are with regard to these concerns (both at the personal and public levels)? What steps would you suggest to begin to live into those expectations?

3. What do you think Jesus had in mind when he commented that we will always have the poor with us? Put the claim in its broader biblical context. (Deuteronomy 15, for example, observes that there should be "no poor among you.")

4. What are some popular caricatures of people who live in poverty—from politicians and in the culture? If you had a chance to speak to political leaders or the producers of TV shows, movies, or music that portrays poor people, what would you say to them?

5. *God's Politics* critiques a common perception of capitalism, as in the quote by former Treasury Secretary O'Neill, regarding the risk/consequence nature of the economic system (page 259). Discuss the critique; and if you find it correct, discuss ways to hold monied interests more accountable.

6. *God's Politics* notes that CEOs have an obligation "to the common good, not just to the bottom line" (page 264). From a Christian perspective, how might we define "common good"? On what, as Christians, would we base such a definition?

7. Assume you were going to make a presentation to a group of wealthy business-people on the notion of economic justice. What are the four or five primary points that you would make?

8. Review the Millennium Development Goals. What has your church done to elevate awareness of these goals? What could be done to increase Christian awareness and response to the Millennium Development Goals?

9. Where does your church invest its money? Does it invest in socially screened funds and community development banking institutions that serve the poor?[17]

10. Discuss the "Top Ten Facts" on international trade (*God's Politics*, page 279). How do trade agreements impact you? As people of faith, do we identify ourselves first with others of our faith across the world, or do we identify ourselves first as Americans? How might this impact how we view trade policies?

11. *God's Politics* says, "For the first time in history we have the information, knowledge, technology, and resources to bring the worst of global poverty to an end. What we don't have is the moral and political will to do so" (page 270). Do you agree? If so, what might we do to help create the moral and political will?

Week Four

Poverty

IN THE PREVIOUS CHAPTER, we covered economic justice, a broader topic than our current theme—poverty. The relationship between the two is obvious: when economic systems are not just, poverty is one of the most insidious results. Please be sure to review chapters 13 through 15 of *God's Politics* as you work through this material. The following paragraphs provide brief summaries of each chapter.

Chapter 13: Thousands of Bible verses affirm our obligation to care for the poor. Despite this clear and abundant teaching, some people try to argue that when Jesus said, "The poor you will have always with you" (Matthew 26:11), it somehow provided justification for doing little or nothing about poverty—as if Jesus had said there would always be poor people among us, so why do anything about it? However, this misreads both the immediate and the broader contexts of his words. First, this verse comes after Jesus's anointing by the woman at Bethany, prior to his death on the cross—Jesus will not be among the disciples for much longer: "You will not always have me." Second, Jesus is making a judgment about the social location of his followers—that to follow Jesus means we will always have the opportunity, and the gift, of working on behalf of those he called "the least of these."

Chapter 14: The sheer frequency of such verses makes it clear that poverty is a central moral concern for Christians. Thirty-seven million Americans live beneath the official poverty line, and even families that earn just above that level of income have trouble affording life's essentials. Neither of the two major political parties prioritizes the needs of the poor—indeed, the poor often seem little more than pawns in the partisan political debate. Given God's concern for those on the margins of society, we as Christians must ally ourselves with the voiceless millions.

Chapter 15: Jesus once commented that where our treasures are, there our hearts will be also. Similarly, the manner in which a family, church, city, or nation budgets its resources reveals its true priorities—what it loves and what sorts of things it values. When money goes for warfare or tax cuts at the expense of those on the margins, it reveals that our vision of the common good excludes others. The budgets we make and support have consequences—either by making the economic playing field more level and just or by making it less so. We cannot avoid the conclusion that budgets are moral documents and should be assessed by Christians on the basis of how they protect the interests of those most at risk.

DAY 1 Introducing the Topic

We are all familiar with the term "poverty," but how many of us have reflected on what the term really means—and, more important, on what living in poverty is like? Poverty means not having access to the basic essentials of life, including (among others) food, shelter, clothing, and health care.

Think about what this means. If you are living at or below the poverty level—where you do not have access to the bare essentials of life—you will not be making trade-offs between, say, eating at a fast-food place or a sit-down restaurant for dinner. Nor will you be deciding between that three-bedroom brick house with two and a half baths and an entertainment room or a four-bedroom house with a detached garage and three baths. No, the trade-offs you will be facing will be more like putting a roof over your family's head versus having health care. Or maybe you will be fortunate and have both today, but your spouse will have to quit taking medications for a few days. In other words, the trade-offs are about which life essentials you will give up. And if you happen to have a child with a chronic health problem, any chance of getting ahead is traded for the hope of just getting by.

A popular stereotype of the person living in poverty is someone who just doesn't want to work or who can't hold down a job. But such stereotypes miss the fact that children are among those most exposed to poverty. The stereotype is mistaken in another way, as it increasingly is the case that many of those who live below the poverty line are also employed.

It's difficult to find work that pays reasonably well and is also within walking distance of affordable housing. Thus in order to work, a person needs transportation. Of course, folks with few financial resources can rarely afford to own reliable transportation. Unless you live in an area with a good mass-transit system, you will have to come up with the money to buy a vehicle. Don't forget that you will also need to pay vehicle taxes and registration fees, maintain a fund for repairs, and acquire enough money for at least liability insurance—as well as gas. Mass transit, if available and close by, may be less expensive, but you will need to adjust your schedule to fit the transit schedule. And if you have children, to be able to hold a job you will need to make enough money—beyond food, shelter, and clothing—to cover child care.

It's common for single parents to leave home before sunrise and travel for more than an hour to a job where the level of pay provides little or no genuine opportunity to get ahead, or even to catch up. Repeating the long travel in the evening, those parents may face the dark before they return home. In the meantime, children have been left either on their own or with grandparents (if they are close by), or have been taken to child care. Many Christians have expressed concern about the breakdown of the family. Yet many of us remain too quiet when it comes to establishing social policies and public institutions to address poverty and to support the kinds of efforts that truly help families be strong.

The moral of the story is this: work is not working for many. It is not generating enough income for poor families to escape the circumstances that poverty creates and reinforces. To see why that might be the case, consider that the current poverty level for a family of four in the United States is $19,350. Any family with an income level below that amount is living in poverty. If one of the adults is working full-time at a minimum-wage job, and that person is the only wage earner, the family income will be $10,712, or just over 50 percent of the poverty level. If both parents work at that type job, the total income will be $21,424. However, given that both parents will be out of the house, some of that money—often a sizable chunk—will go toward child care. After these expenses, what will be the effective pay rate for the second working parent? Half of minimum wage?

The causes of poverty are much debated, and as *God's Politics* observes, sometimes the debate *about* poverty consumes so much energy that there seems to be little actual progress in alleviating it. Perhaps the two most debated questions are: (1) What are the causes of poverty? and (2) What course of action has the best chance of alleviating it? While it is relatively easy to identify correlations between poverty and particular public policies, establishing a causal link is more difficult. This leaves the poor suffering the agony of the trade-offs noted above, while the policymakers continue the debate. No doubt there is genuine concern on both sides of the political aisle, but it is time to move beyond debate to solutions. People are more important than theories. Rather than engaging the same old debates—such as whether poverty is related mainly to lifestyle or to lack of real economic opportunity and good domestic policies—we need to experiment with creative solutions. For example, we might consider solutions that put the poor and the wealthy in closer proximity, creating more mixed economic neighborhoods and business zones. We primarily need solutions that see the status quo as unacceptable.

We have the ability to end extreme poverty on a global level. The question is whether we have the will. The old "trickle-down" theories have been shown to be bankrupt when it comes to, well, "trickling down." What is most heartbreaking, from a Christian perspective, is how little the church has taken the lead on this issue— the most frequently addressed social issue in the Bible—although thankfully, that is changing.

Extreme poverty is far too common in the majority of the world. More than 1 billion people live on less than $1 per day. Droughts, partially resulting from climate changes brought on by pollution and nonsustainable agricultural practices, have destroyed crops and food supplies in many of the poorest countries. Farm subsidies have contributed to making agriculture unprofitable for poor farmers. International trade is governed by institutions that tilt the playing field in favor of the wealthiest countries. Trade negotiations are driven by those wealthy countries, which use their existing economic and military might to force unfavorable conditions on poorer countries. One cannot help but think of Isaiah 10:1–4, which castigates the lawmakers who prevent the poor and needy from gaining justice.[1] When we enjoy the low prices created by farm subsidies or the exploitation of foreign markets, to what extent do we participate in the poverty to which these policies contribute?

DAY 2 — Considering the Evidence

Before we turn our attention to current facts and statistics on poverty, let's look at the history of the last 100 years in the United States to see how the issue of poverty has changed. The pre–Civil War economy was based on the most dire system of oppression possible, of course: actual slavery. The late 1800s and early 1900s saw a laissez-faire American economic system: there was little government regulation, and there were virtually no trade unions. Business owners were allowed to do what they deemed appropriate in order to maximize profits. Abuse and exploitation of workers were common. The old Tennessee Ernie Ford song "Sixteen Tons" captured some of that reality:

> Sixteen tons, and what do you get?
> Another day older and deeper in debt
> St. Peter don't you call me, 'cause I can't go
> I owe my soul to the company store.

Company stores were able to price products so that miners never could quite get ahead. The basic essentials cost too much to purchase with their wages, so they borrowed from the store to survive. Unsafe working conditions, child labor, long work days and work weeks, and no time off were part and parcel of the working conditions of many.

This fostered a "trickle-up" economics that allowed ever-increasing accumulations of wealth for a few at the top. The gap that opened between the poorest Americans and the richest Americans, along with the economic instability these conditions invited, created a big problem. As we know, the bottom fell out of the U.S. economy in the late 1920s, and the country found itself in the midst of the Great Depression. It is estimated that the mid-1930s saw a poverty rate of nearly 50 percent in the United States: half of all Americans could not obtain the basic essentials of life. By 1940, an estimated one-third of Americans were in poverty.

With the election of Franklin Delano Roosevelt in 1932 and the institution of the New Deal, a serious attempt was made to use national and state institutions to solve the problem of poverty. At the time, one of the highest poverty rates was among the elderly. The introduction of Social Security began to reduce significantly the number of elderly living in poverty. Through the 1940s and 1950s, the poverty rate steadily declined, until by 1965 it was just over 15 percent. During this period, the gap between the poorest and the wealthiest grew very little, and the growing prosperity of the middle class became the country's economic driving force.

In 1965, Lyndon Johnson launched the "war on poverty," and the poverty rate continued to decline until it reached a low in 1973 of just over 11 percent. Since then the level of poverty assistance (adjusted for inflation) has declined, and the poverty rate has fluctuated; in late 2005 the rate was just under 13 percent. The lesson: poverty rates are impacted positively by public-sector intervention. And they are impacted negatively when the public sector fails to take appropriate steps to reduce wealth inequality and to protect those on the margins.

The United States' current poverty rate of 12.7 percent equals about 37 million Americans living below the poverty line. Thirteen million of those in poverty are children—in fact, 17.8 percent of all children live below the poverty line.[2] Children have always constituted a disproportionate share of those in poverty.

Access to health care is among the essentials most quickly lost by those living in poverty. Estimates indicate that 45 million Americans are without health insurance. Recently, Congress cut Medicaid and similar programs in order to fund tax cuts for the wealthiest and the war in Iraq, making it even more difficult for poor people to access adequate health care.

It is generally estimated that, in most areas of the country, an amount double the poverty rate is actually needed to live. Consider the following hypothetical budget for a family of four living at the poverty rate of $19,350:

Housing	$8,100/year ($675/month)
Utilities	$1,200/year ($100/month)
Food	$8,760/year ($2 per person per meal)
Transportation	$2,860/year ($55/week, public transit or low-cost car and insurance)
Clothing	$1,600/year ($400 per person per year, secondhand)
Social Security taxes	$ 1,480
Total expenses	$24,000

We are already more than $4,000 over budget! What are we going to cut to get to $19,350? You could avoid most transportation costs if you walked to work, except you would still need to get groceries and other items home. Besides, what are the chances of finding work close to home? The closer to town, the higher the rent. You could cut the whole $4,000 excess if you figured out how to cut the average meal to $1 per meal per person per day. If you rented housing on or near a farm, you might be able to raise some vegetables or fruits. For most people, however, the prospects aren't good. Ron Sider invites us to reflect on what is not included in this budget:

> No household appliances, no vacations, no toiletries, no birthday or Christmas gifts, no recreation, no visits to the dentist, no private health insurance, no donations for church, no child care, no movies, no travel outside the city, no private music lessons, no sports equipment for the children. Poor people, of course, do have some of these things. However unthinkable from a middle-class perspective, somehow they manage to spend less on some of the other items or receive help from family, friends, or church.[3]

Take a look at your own budget, compare the two, and then ask what you would have to give up to live at the poverty level.

Consider the following statistics[4] regarding the assets of the wealthiest Americans and ask yourself, "As a Christian, can I continue to support public policies that result in such inequality?" If your answer is no, how might those policies be corrected?

Distribution of Wealth Ownership, 2001

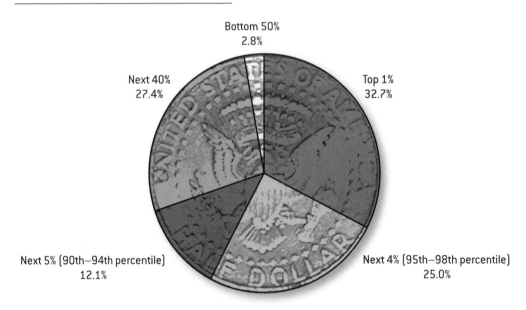

Bottom 50%
2.8%

Next 40%
27.4%

Top 1%
32.7%

Next 5% (90th–94th percentile)
12.1%

Next 4% (95th–98th percentile)
25.0%

DAY 3 — Reading the Bible

A seminary professor started a class on New Testament interpretation with the question, "What is the most disbelieved verse in the Bible?" Fearing a setup, students were slow to respond. The professor continued, "The passage in Mark 10, where Jesus says it is impossible for a rich man to enter the kingdom of heaven." Most of the students were taken by surprise, but the professor went on to explain: "Because we are so wealthy, we Americans have only two choices. We could give up our wealth for the poor. Or we could interpret this passage in a way that holds it at arm's length, making it about motivations or attitudes. It can be about anything except what we are obliged to do with our wealth."

God expresses genuine and consistent concern for the poorest in society— and that concern begins long before the teaching and preaching of Jesus. In *God's Politics,* we read that there are more than 2,000 verses in the Bible that deal with the poor and with God's commands regarding them.

For example, we find the following in Exodus: "If you lend money to my people, to the poor among you, you shall not deal with them as a creditor; you shall not exact interest from them" (22:25). God's concern for the precarious existence of the poor leads God to expect different treatment for the poor than for the non-poor. In the next few verses in Exodus, God makes it clear that we are not intended to act dishonestly to protect the poor, but we should make the protection of the poor an integral part of establishing just social institutions.

Of course, God fully realizes we have a tendency to be self-centered. This is explicit in the following earlier-quoted passage: "Since there will never cease to be some in need on the earth, I therefore command you, 'Open your hand to the poor and needy neighbor in your land'" (Deuteronomy 15:11).

Many suggest that we cannot do anything about the condition of the poor. In the above passage, however, God commands us to keep our hands open to provide for the poor. Deuteronomy 15 also includes the command to observe years of debt release every seven years, when all debts are to be forgiven.

These commands are not to be taken merely as guidelines for individuals, to be voluntarily obeyed by one person or another, but corporate commands. Consider, for example, that God frequently includes the warning of punishment for failure to obey:

> May the Lord defend the cause of the poor of the people, give deliverance to the needy, and crush the oppressor. (Psalm 72:4)

> Hear this, you that trample on the needy, and bring to ruin the poor of the land, saying, "When will the new moon be over so that we may sell grain; and the sabbath, so that we may offer wheat for sale? We will make the ephah small and the shekel great, and practice deceit with false balances, buying the poor for silver and the needy for a pair of sandals, and selling the sweepings of the wheat."
>
> The Lord has sworn by the pride of Jacob: Surely I will never forget any of their deeds. Shall not the land tremble on this account, and everyone mourn who lives in it. (Amos 8:4–8)

> Ah, you who make iniquitous decrees, who write oppressive statutes, to turn aside the needy from justice and to rob the poor of my people of their right, that widows may be your spoil, and that you may make the orphans your prey! What will you do on the day of punishment, in the calamity that will come from far away? To whom will you flee for help, and where will you leave your wealth ...? (Isaiah 10:1–3)

It is clear God is concerned about the exploitation of the poor. Virtually everyone would agree with this. But millions of people remain in poverty, and the poor continue to be exploited. Why?

Most of us likely do not see the effects our choices have on poor individuals or families or communities. We think that because we do not hold slaves or force workers to take low-wage jobs, we are not part of the problem. But is it so simple? If we buy products from companies known to run sweatshops, aren't we complicit with the executives that run them? Aren't we supporting and affirming their policies? When we support legislation, do we encourage our elected representatives to support poverty relief? Do we support living wage movements? Few of us openly exploit the poor. However, we must also consider the consequences of our choices—particularly their impact on the marginalized.

Just as the Bible warns us about exploiting and abusing the poor, so it encourages us to engage in actions that benefit the poor: "Those who despise their neighbors are sinners, but happy are those who are kind to the poor" (Proverbs 14:21). "Those who oppress the poor insult their Maker, but those who are kind to the needy honor God" (Proverbs 14:31). "Whoever is kind to the poor lends to the Lord, and will be repaid in full" (Proverbs 19:17). "Those who are generous are blessed, for they share their bread with the poor" (Proverbs 22:9). "If you wish to be perfect, go, sell your possessions, and give the money to the poor, and you will have treasure in heaven; then come, follow me" (Matthew 19:21). And from Isaiah:

> Is not this the fast that I choose: to loose the bonds of injustice, to undo the thongs of the yoke, to let the oppressed go free, and to break every yoke? Is it not to share your bread with the hungry, and bring the homeless poor into your house; when you see the naked, to cover them, and not to hide yourself from your own kin? (58:6–7)

In all these passages we see the extent to which God offers blessing to those who take up the cause of the poor. Why? Because being mindful of those in need is an expression of God's own nature.

In short, God intends that there be no poor, while God realizes that our self-centeredness will make it such that we will always have the poor among us. To be imitators of God, however, we must join God in coming to the defense of the poor. This must be true both in our personal acts of mercy and in our support of public institutions and policies that incorporate protections for the poor. The biblical call to live modestly and to understand our wealth as a gift from God (not a right or a prize for our righteous or smart actions) means that all must take seriously care for the poor.

A foundational biblical principle is that every single human life has a fundamental dignity, because we are all created in the image of God. This is largely connected to our human purpose of being made for relationships with God and with each other. Few things rob humans of their dignity more than poverty. We must engage with each other in ways that defend human dignity, an obligation that includes addressing the root causes and consequences of poverty.

We close with an admonition from Corinthians:

> I do not mean that there should be relief for others and pressure on you, but it is a question of a fair balance between your present abundance and their need, so that their abundance may be for your need, in order that there may be a fair balance. As it is written, "The one who had much did not have too much, and the one who had little did not have too little." (2 Corinthians 8:13–15)

DAY 4 — The Christian Tradition

It's not surprising that poverty is closely connected to issues relating to a just economy. It is most often injustices within economies that contribute to a breakdown in community, which results in some people being unable to obtain the bare essentials. In other words, if we take seriously the words of the previous biblical verses, we would restructure our economy to be more just for "the least of these." Of course, restructuring threatens to restrict the ability of those in power to accumulate without limit, so there would be resistance. Let's look at some teachings from the early church that relate to our concern for those in poverty.

Consider these words from a second-century Christian writing called the Didache:

> Do not be one who holds his hand out to take, but shuts it when it comes to giving. If your labor has brought you earnings, pay a ransom for your sins. Do not hesitate to give and do not give with a bad grace, for you will discover who [God] is that pays you back a reward with a good grace. Do not turn your back on the needy, but share everything with your brother [and sister] and call nothing your own. For if you have what is eternal in common, how much more should you have what is transient![5]

Notice again the connection between helping the needy and seeing them as part of your family. All are now united under God, and our obligations to the poor are analogous to family obligations.

Basil the Great, a theologian who lived and worked during the fourth century, was concerned for the poor and recognized the obligations the rich have toward them:

> "Whom do I injure," [the rich person] says, "when I retain and conserve my own?" ... Such are the rich. Because they were first to occupy common goods, they take these goods as their own. If each one would take that which is sufficient for one's needs, leaving what is in excess to those in distress, no one would be rich, no one poor.... Is God unjust to distribute the necessaries of life to us unequally? Why are you rich, why is that one poor? Is it not that you may receive the reward of beneficence and faithful distribution ...?[6]

In a classic sermon to the rich, St. Basil explained that when some have more than others, it is their obligation to use their wealth to help others:

> That bread which you keep, belongs to the hungry; that coat which you preserve in your wardrobe, to the naked; those shoes which are rotting in your possession, to the shoeless; that gold which you have hidden in the ground, to the needy. Wherefore, as often as you were able to help others, and refused, so often did you do them wrong.[7]

Could there be a clearer statement than this—that what we have in excess of our basic needs belongs to the poor and hungry? St. Basil doesn't even grant that the giving of excess is worthy of praise; if it is excess, *it already belongs to the poor.*

Finally, consider a piece from St. John Chrysostom. In it, he speculates on what could be done if we lived as we're called to in Acts 2:

> Let us imagine things as happening in this way: All give all that they have into a common fund. No one would have to concern himself about it, neither the rich nor the poor. How much money do you think would be collected? I infer—for it cannot be said with certainty—that if every individual contributed all his money, his lands, his estates, his houses ... then a million pounds of gold would be obtained, and most likely two or three times that amount.... And how many of the poor do we have? I doubt that there are more than 50,000. How much would be required to feed them daily? If they all ate at a common table, the cost could not be very great. What could we not undertake with our huge treasure! Do you believe it could ever be exhausted?
>
> And will not the blessing of God pour down on us a thousand-fold richer? Will we not make a heaven on earth? Would not the grace of God be indeed richly poured out?[8]

Here John not only depends on the beneficence of Constantinople's wealthy, but also suggests that God would richly bless those living out God's intentions.

As we can see, these early Christians did not defend the right of the rich to have all they could get. They were more interested in reminding the wealthy of the serious obligations their wealth carries.

DAY 5 — Living Examples in the Contemporary Church

Christian churches could make an immediate and drastic impact on resolving domestic and global poverty if they committed themselves to that task. Public and private sectors have a role to play in poverty relief, and it is good to see churches becoming increasingly active in charity (through soup kitchens and food pantries) and justice (in their attempts to influence public policy). In the following vignette, we see how the *personal* nature of faith finds *outward* expression in Chicago's New Community Covenant Church.

FAITH: NOT A PRIVATE PRACTICE

Pastor Peter Hong asserts that Chicago's New Community Covenant Church "exists to provide an alternative to those tired of religion." But the four-year-old, ethnically diverse congregation certainly embraces its identity as both spiritual and religious. "So much of what has gone wrong in the evangelical community is this notion that the Christian faith is a private faith," says Hong. "It may begin as a personal faith, but it was never meant to be a private faith."

This distinction describes well a church equally invested in the spiritual lives of individuals and in its religious role as a corporate and communal body. Community is an underlying value of all the congregation's ministries, from service- and fellowship-oriented small groups to lay-led prayer before Sunday worship. Hong notes the closeness of the words "community" and "communion," a theological connection echoed by fellowship team leader Olivia Littles: "We talk about how Christ's death and resurrection reconciled us not only to Christ but also to the world."

New Community does more than talk about such doctrines. It strives to respond to Christ's apostolic call to geographically concentric circles of ministry, from local to global, because, as Hong explains, "we believe that this is where the heart of God is." The congregation is involved in international missions; it also runs a warming center a few blocks from the church office. The latter began three winters ago as an outgrowth of ad hoc ministry to neighborhood homeless people. A homeless acquaintance asked church staff member Katie Sandford where the nearest warming center was; Sandford and other staff responded by creating one. The largely volunteer-run facility now serves more than thirty people daily, providing daytime access to material supplies, communications, and social services referrals. "Most important," says Sandford, "people are treated with dignity and respect."

These same values motivated the multiethnic and justice-seeking team of women and men that founded New Community. The church has since outgrown multiple worship spaces and added a second service, bearing witness to its identity as an alternative not to religion itself so much as to irrelevant or inadequate expressions of religion. Hong sees New Community as part of a broader trend toward a faith both personal and communal, of a "transition from the old paradigm to a new one."

STEVE THORNGATE*

There are other churches where sermons and Sunday school classes focus on ways to become directly involved in outreach to those on the margins. Some churches, for example, have a class that alternates Sundays between in-church Bible study and community-based relief efforts: one week they have a traditional Sunday school class focused thematically or on a specific book of the Bible; the next they travel to local community outreach centers, help organize food pantries, or participate in an inner-city church service. Participants have found that the practice of ministerial outreach complements and deepens the study experiences on alternate weekends. Virtually any church could imitate this model.

DAY 6   Putting Faith into Action

No area in the United States is beyond the reach of poverty. Hungry children are almost certainly within a short drive of your home. This means that opportunities to make a difference in the fight against poverty are also nearby. There are a variety of ways to engage peace and justice struggles—particularly those related to poverty—and many involve concrete opportunities for "hands-on" work.

Many churches and parachurch organizations maintain a variety of ministries for those who need help making ends meet. In addition, there are secular soup kitchens, food and clothing banks, and shelters that take in the homeless and provide meals and a place to sleep for the night. These facilities are constantly in need of help—from food servers and dishwashers to facility organizers and good repair people. You can also donate food, extra clothing, or cash. For Christians it is necessary to build relationships of love, care, and support with those who are struggling, not just give money from arm's length. You might also consider working with your church to develop its own outreach ministry for those in need in your community.

Many of the opportunities identified in the appendix are also applicable here. Few people realize the depths of poverty, either in the United States or internation-

---

* *Steve Thorngate is an editorial assistant at* Sojourners. *From* Sojourners, *December 2005, vol. 34, no. 11, p. 15.*

ally. Consequently, it is critical to develop and use good educational resources. For example, you might put together a series on "the face of poverty" and "the face of wealth." You could present key statistics on poverty and wealth so that members of your congregation might begin to see the demographics of economic disparity. In the course of any educational program, it will be important to show the biblical and theological connections. Conduct a "live in poverty" exercise where the group develops a budget based on what a family could afford to buy on a poverty-level budget. It would be worth discussing what is and is not included in the budget. What has been left out to make ends meet? Perhaps your group could agree to live by that budget for a week or a month. With an exercise like this, it is important to debrief afterward. Discuss what insights you have gained. Another exercise is inviting participants to write a "money journal" that details the messages they were given around money as a child and how that background impacts their view of money today.

There are many excellent conferences and events around the country that deal with different aspects of poverty and wealth. Consider attending one by yourself or with others from your church or community.

DAY 7 — Group Meeting and Reflection

1. What role might government play in securing justice for the poor? What role might the church play?

2. Develop a plan for improving the statistics shown on page 223 in *God's Politics* over the next five years.

3. Identify five facts related to poverty that you think most reflect the severity of the problem. Identify five facts related to wealth that you think most reflect the severity of the problem.

4. What are some of the underlying causes of extreme poverty and excessive wealth? How would you set about tackling some of those causes?

5. Does the biblical notion of "aliens" (Leviticus 19:33–34) and the commands God gave regarding them guide us in developing a Christian immigration policy? If so, what would that policy look like?

6. Discuss what *God's Politics* means in its claim that budgets are moral documents. How would you try to make this point to your friends?

7. Go to www.whitehouse.gov/omb/budget/fy2007/ and review the U.S. budget. Imagine you are asked to testify before Congress on the moral implications of the existing budget, but you have only ten minutes to make your presentation. What points would you try to make?

8. Do you agree with *God's Politics'* assessment that the biblical prophets would be very critical of the Bush administration's budget priorities? Why or why not?

9. Why has the repeal of the federal estate tax become such a hot-ticket item for many conservatives? Consider the intent behind the years of jubilee and years of debt release in Leviticus 25 and Deuteronomy 15. Comment on how these passages speak to a possible repeal of the estate tax.

10. Assess the validity of *Washington Post* columnist E. J. Dionne's concern (addressed in *God's Politics*, pages 251–252) about the Bush administration's faith-based initiatives.

11. What should twenty-first-century Christians do about the biblical notion of economic "leveling" that *God's Politics* talks about? What are ways the jubilee message could be brought into the twenty-first century?

Week Five

A Consistent Ethic of Life

IN WEEK 5, we turn our attention to discussing a consistently pro-life position. The term "pro-life" has been largely equated with the opposition to abortion. But *God's Politics* argues in chapter 18 that a consistent ethic in support of life cannot be focused on a single issue. Familiarize yourself with chapter 18, and read below the brief summary of the chapter's definition and defense of a consistent ethic of life.

Chapter 18: Catholic Cardinal Joseph Bernardin of Chicago coined the phrase "a seamless garment of life," linking a number of issues related to the defense of life—abortion, euthanasia, capital punishment, nuclear weapons, poverty, and racism.[1] A consistently pro-life position must bring each of these components into a holistic ethic of life. Too often, promoting a culture of life has focused only on banning abortion. On this issue, the Left tends to exclude those who are opposed to abortion, while the Right tends to narrow the pro-life discussion so that it includes almost nothing besides abortion.

DAY 1

Introducing the Topic

"Pro-life." "Pro-choice." These are two labels with which Americans are well acquainted. Unfortunately, both tend to be used more for their bumper-sticker value than to promote substantive dialogue or to convey a consistent and sophisticated position. We need to move beyond the false dichotomy set up by these two phrases and embrace instead a position more holistically grounded in unapologetic and unconditional support for human life and well-being.

Those on the political Right are correct in insisting that abortion is a moral issue and should not be considered just another form of birth control. At the same time, those on the Left are correct in defending the dignity of women and in saying that simply criminalizing abortion will not create a culture of life. Some have argued that abortion should be "safe, legal, and rare," but often little is done to realize the third leg of this proposed triangle. So where does this leave us? As people of God, what can we learn from our tradition as we embrace the goal of valuing each and every life?

When Cardinal Bernardin used the phrase "seamless garment of life," he intended an unconditional embrace of life across a whole range of issues, as noted above, including abortion, euthanasia, capital punishment, war, nuclear weapons, poverty, and racism. By this standard, to be pro-life only in the sense of being opposed to abortion is to be *conditionally* pro-life: if the life in question is that of an unborn child, then one is for defending that life. Bernardin suggests that we must not allow our defense of life to be so narrowly focused. Let's consider briefly some of the issues listed above.

For example, how do we understand capital punishment in terms of a consistent ethic of life? The number of executions in the United States has decreased in recent years, according to the Death Penalty Information Center, as has citizen support for capital punishment. One of the major reasons is the increasing concern that innocent people may be sentenced to death. Since 1973, 119 people in 25 states have been exonerated and released from death row because of evidence of their innocence. As these cases have received national exposure, more Americans have come to question the institution of capital punishment.[2]

"Honorable people have disagreed about the justice of executing the guilty," writes Catholic sister Helen Prejean in her book *The Death of Innocents: An Eyewitness Account of Wrongful Executions,* "but can anyone argue about the justice of executing the innocent?"

Of particular interest to Christians is Prejean's account of recent developments in the Catholic tradition's position on capital punishment. In his 1995 encyclical *Evangelium Vitae* (Gospel of Life), Pope John Paul II stated that even murderers possess human dignity and the practice of the death penalty should therefore be "rare, if not nonexistent" in modern societies. While some theologians argue that capital punishment is permitted in rare cases in defense of society against an imminent threat to citizens' lives, the Catholic Church now stands in principled opposition to the death penalty. "The entire argument for self-defense changes ... when violent offenders are incarcerated and thereby rendered defenseless," writes Prejean. "Where, then, is the threat of an immediate violent assault on citizens?"

Prejean also articulates the principled theological argument against the death penalty when she shows how Christian misunderstandings of atonement lead some to an inappropriate support of capital punishment. She believes that the traditional satisfaction theory of atonement contributes to Christians' support of the death penalty, and she calls this theology into question: "Is God vengeful, demanding a death for a death? Or is God compassionate, luring souls into love so great that no one can be considered 'enemy'?"

Ultimately, for Christians who believe that Jesus preached a way of nonviolence, the teachings of Karl Barth and John Howard Yoder are critical. Both argue that since Jesus was the victim of a state-sponsored execution, no Christian can support this mechanism as a just means of preserving social order for either the innocent or the guilty.

We have already discussed Christian responses to war and peace in Week 2. A consistently pro-life position would take a strong stance against war and work in whatever means possible to support nonviolent ways to resolve injustice and conflict internationally and within countries as well.

We must also consider the continuing destruction of our environment as part of a "life stance." There is widespread agreement that global warming is endangering our quality of life on the earth, that the rainforest is declining at an alarming rate, and that our dependence on fossil fuels is becoming an insupportable strain on the environment. A consistent and wide-ranging ethic of life must make care for the environment a central concern.

Poverty and racism are also concerns that fit into a consistent ethic of life. These are addressed in detail in Weeks 4 and 6. A consistently pro-life position must also include the goal of affordable health care for all people. Every day, individuals are forced to make trade-offs between food and life-saving medicines, between needed health procedures and housing. More than 45 million Americans have no health insurance, and a disproportionate number of these are children. Concern for these issues is essential to a broader pro-life position.

Additionally, a pro-life stance must examine nuclear weapons. The United States is the only country to have used nuclear weapons against a civilian population. When the U.S. dropped nuclear weapons on Japan in World War II, more than 300,000 Japanese died, and 95 percent of them were civilians. Nuclear weapons cause indiscriminate mass annihilation. They are tools of terror. By their very nature they violate the moral principles of justice, discrimination, and proportionality that are laid out in the just war principles we examined earlier. Nearly all major Christian churches, and many Jewish and Muslim bodies, have spoken out against nuclear weapons—encouraging support to freeze, lockdown, and eliminate nuclear weapons.

"So-called realists," writes David Cortright of the Fourth Freedom Forum, "claim that the advocates of nuclear abolition are utopians. On the contrary, the naive utopians are those who believe that governments can maintain nuclear weapons in perpetuity without their actual use, either by accident or design. As former Defense Secretary Robert McNamara has said, the indefinite combination of human fallibility and continued reliance on nuclear weapons will lead to catastrophe and the destruction of cities."[3]

Nuclear abolition is realistic. Treaties against biological and chemical weapons already exist, and it is past time for a similar ban on nuclear weapons. "Only God has the authority to end all life on the planet," writes William Sloane Coffin in opposing nuclear weapons. "All we have is the power." It is time to relinquish that power, to serve rather than usurp God by preserving life.

In the next section, we will take a look at some of the statistics related to these areas, in order to better grasp the serious nature of each. For now let's summarize the positions that might constitute a consistent ethic in support of life.

- Specific plans aimed at genuinely and significantly reducing the number of abortions should be put into place. These must include steps to promote availability of health care and nutrition for mothers and children, improve and streamline adoption processes, and reduce child poverty.

- A platform of restorative justice for those convicted of committing crimes should be developed. Such a platform must hold offenders accountable and demand reparation for victims while also seeking reconciliation with victims and the restoration of human dignity to everyone involved. The public must be educated on the ineffectiveness of capital punishment. It does not serve as a deterrent to capital crimes (even the U.S. Justice Department shows no correlation between executions and a reduction in violent offenses); it is more expensive than life in prison; and it is irreversible. This last point is especially important when we factor in the fallibility of the criminal justice system, the inherent racism in that system, and the unequal access to a credible defense because of income.

- The use of nuclear weapons—in any circumstance—must be taken off the table. The international community must conduct multilateral negotiations to reduce the number of nuclear devices in military stockpiles and develop a reliable means of policing. The United States will have to lead and be willing to expose itself to the same tests expected of other countries.

- We must aggressively pursue protection of the earth's resources and the care and well-being of humans as part of biosystems. We must consider the long-term effects of our energy choices, manufacturing policies, wasteful lifestyles, etc. It makes little sense to defend the unborn unless we also take care to ensure that they will have a healthy environment in which to flourish.

- Poverty and racism must be eliminated. Both exclude people from resources—social, psychological, and material—and a consistent ethic of life does not allow for such exclusion.

- Finally, because it values the sanctity of all lives, a consistently pro-life position works for a reduction in the use of violence to settle international disputes, leading to the abolition of all war, and in the meantime actively pursues the "things that make for peace" (Luke 19:42).

DAY 2

Considering the Evidence

A consistently pro-life position must fundamentally address the issue most often associated with the term: abortion. Such a position would include steps aimed at reducing the number of pregnancies terminated. According to the Alan Guttmacher Institute (the leading source of abortion statistics), the number of abortions per year in the United States reached a high in 1990 of more than 1.6 million.

The number then declined throughout the 1990s and dropped to just under 1.3 million by 2000. Since then, it has begun to rise slightly. The institute suggests that the biggest contributor to declining abortion rates has been increased education about and availability of contraceptives. Also, since abortion rates have increased significantly among poor women, focused efforts to improve economic conditions among the poor will likely further reduce abortions.

From 1972 to 2004, there were more than 40 million abortions in the United States. In a single year, 1995, there were approximately 26 million legal and 20 million illegal abortions worldwide, resulting in a worldwide abortion rate of 35 per 1,000 women aged 15 to 44. Among the subregions of the world, Eastern Europe had the highest abortion rate (90 per 1,000) and Western Europe the lowest rate (11 per 1,000). Among countries where abortion is legal without restriction, the highest abortion rate, 83 per 1,000, was reported for Vietnam and the lowest, 7 per 1,000, for Belgium and the Netherlands. Abortion rates are no lower overall in areas where abortion is generally restricted by law (and where many abortions are performed under unsafe conditions) than in areas where abortion is legally permitted.[4]

Who has abortions? Statistics show that the profile of a woman in the United States seeking an abortion is young (54 percent under age 24), never married (54 percent), poor or low-income (57 percent under 200 percent of the poverty line), and minority (52 percent African American or Latino).[5] The major reasons given by women seeking abortions are that they cannot afford a child and that they lack health care for themselves and their children. Thus some abortions could be prevented by making health care and other needed support more widely available to mothers and infants. A consistent ethic of life cannot reduce concern for the life of children after they are born.

A group of members of Congress, working with the Democrats for Life organization, are preparing a package of legislative proposals that would actually do something to address the conditions that lead to abortions. The package includes programs that address appropriate sex education for teenagers, pregnancy counseling, protection of women from domestic violence, and adoption reform; *and* increased funding for pre- and postnatal health care, for the Women, Infant, and Children nutrition program, and for other programs that support women and children. Supporters of this legislative package have named it "95-10," because of their goal of reducing the number of abortions by 95 percent in the next ten years. The legislation addresses both the causes of unwanted pregnancies and the need to support infants and their mothers after birth. It's a good example of a common ground initiative that could actually accomplish results rather than further intensifying rhetoric.

Capital punishment is another critical component of a consistently pro-life agenda. What do we need to take into consideration when constructing a consistently pro-life stance with regard to criminal justice? Data from the NAACP Legal Defense Fund's Death Row USA for the final quarter of 2005 indicated that the number of people sentenced to death in 2005 was 65 percent fewer than in 1998. The Death Penalty Information Center's analysis of death row population figures from the report showed that 106 people received a death sentence in 2005, down from 125 in 2004 and dramatically lower than the 300 per year recorded in the late 1990s.

Even as the use of the death penalty continued to decline in the United States, the number of murders and the national murder rate dropped in 2004. According to the recently released FBI Uniform Crime Report for 2004, the nation's murder rate fell by 3.3 percent, declining to 5.5 murders per 100,000 people in 2004. In 2004, the number of executions, the number of death sentences, and the size of the death row population all declined compared to 2003.

Additionally, many studies show that lifelong incarceration is less expensive than trying, sentencing, and executing a prisoner. "Every dollar we spend on a capital case is a dollar we can't spend anywhere else.... We have to let the public know what it costs [to pursue a capital case]," said John M. Bailey, Connecticut's chief state's attorney. The death penalty comes at a high price—morally and financially. In Texas, a death penalty case costs taxpayers an average of $2.3 million, about three times the cost of imprisoning someone in a single cell at the highest security level for forty years. In Florida, each execution costs the state $3.2 million. In financially strapped California, one report estimated that the state could save $90 million each year by abolishing capital punishment. The New York Department of Correctional Services estimated that implementing the death penalty would cost the state about $118 million annually.[6]

More important are serious questions about the fair application of the death penalty, as those who are poor and/or minorities are much more likely to be executed than are middle-class whites. According to Amnesty International, even though African Americans and whites are murder victims in nearly equal numbers of crimes in the U.S., 80 percent of people executed since the death penalty was reinstated in the United States have been executed for murders involving white victims. More than 20 percent of black defendants who have been executed were convicted by all-white juries. Biblical evidence leads us away from a "retributive" approach to justice and toward a "restorative" theory of justice. A consistent and unconditional ethic of life must reject capital punishment.

We turn our attention next to the biblical basis for arguing that a consistent ethic of life extends beyond only opposition to abortion to the seamless garment of life of which Cardinal Bernardin spoke.

DAY 3 — Reading the Bible

The Christian tradition affirms that the source of God's creative act is love and overflowing goodness. God creates to bring into existence a world in which

God can share that love with creation. So the creation is filled with living creatures, and it provides an environment for the development of loving relationships among creatures and between God and creatures. A consistent ethic of life is an affirmation of God's intentions for creation and for relationships. In what ways, then, can we affirm that God is "pro-life"?

At every stage of the creation narrative in Genesis, the Bible declares that "God saw it, and it was good." Do we sometimes skip past this too quickly? This simple affirmation is worth some consideration. What is being affirmed, and why is it good? God affirms many things as good: the creation of light, the separation of land from water, the creation of vegetation, the ordering of the world into seasons and into nights and days, the creation of animals—first in the sea, then on land. Finally, God affirms as good the creation of humans as bearers of the image of God. They are good because they conform to the divine intent to build an environment filled with creatures that can love and enjoy their Creator and be loved in return.

There is a special sense of satisfaction expressed on the sixth day. After creating all things, God declares them not just good but "very good." Historically, people have frequently misread passages that warn us not to cling to the world, as if these passages intended us to hate God's creation. A consistent ethic of life must find its starting place in an appropriate appreciation for the created world.

The contemporary "pro-life" movement often uses Deuteronomy 31:19 as its fundamental text: "I set before you today life and death. Choose life." But to use the text simply for that purpose is to miss the richness of what Moses is saying. The book of Deuteronomy is a single presentation of God's instructions, through Moses, to the Israelites. Throughout the Torah (the first five books of the Bible) and especially in Deuteronomy, Moses sets before the people an ethic of life, one characterized by obedience to all instructions given. At the end of the Torah, in the passage in question, Moses readily admits that the people might choose disobedience, which is to "choose death." Moses is pleading with the people, essentially saying, "I have given you God's instructions on how to live. To live in this way is to realize that God's instructions lead to life as God intended. To live contrary to God's intentions is to choose a way that leads to death. I implore you, choose the way of life." It is this "way of life" that undergirds a consistent ethic. Let's look at what the Bible says about some of the specific issues.

There are a number of biblical passages often used in the abortion discussion. "For it was you who formed my inward parts; you knit me together in my mother's womb. I praise you, for I am fearfully and wonderfully made" (Psalm 139:13–14). "Thus says the Lord, your Redeemer, who formed you in the womb: I am the Lord, who made all things" (Isaiah 44:24). And, to the prophet Jeremiah, God says: "Before I formed you in the womb I knew you, and before you were born I consecrated you; I appointed you a prophet to the nations" (Jeremiah 1:5). While these verses do not address abortion, they do articulate a view that life is present before birth.

In Week 2 we took up the question of war: How are we to consider Christian participation in war in light of the Bible's teachings? We cannot affirm war merely on the basis of God's having allowed it in the Old Testament. Instead, we must determine how passages involving God and war are to be read within the overall story of the Bible, with particular attention to the significance of the life and teachings of Jesus.

In Weeks 3 and 4, we examined the issues related to poverty and economic justice. Earlier in Deuteronomy and elsewhere in the Torah, God gives instructions regarding just economies. These include such features as years of release, years of jubilee, gleaning laws, and collateral laws, all aimed to protect the poor and marginalized. There are instructions regarding sanitary habits and crop rotation to protect the earth for future generations. While God affirms a distinction between the chosen people and the rest of the world, the point is the role of the chosen as mediators of God's grace, leaving no room for anything like contemporary racism. All this is included in the "life" that the Israelites must choose.

When it comes to capital punishment, we must consider several factors as we assess the biblical position. Throughout the Bible, God reveals a move away from violent to nonviolent responses to injustice. In some cases, God's seemingly harsh directives exist within an extremely strict honor-code society that used violence to maintain social order. The instruction on proportional punishment—to exact "an eye for an eye" (Exodus 21:24, Leviticus 24:20)—must be situated within the context of the day, which often included the practice of exacting *dis*proportionate revenge against offenders. For example, a group might exact revenge for murder by killing the murderer's entire family. Though "an eye for an eye" sounds to us like an expression of strict judgment, to those to whom it was given "an eye for an eye" was a movement toward reducing and limiting violence.

This movement continues throughout the Bible and reaches its high point in Jesus's teachings and actions. John's gospel (8:3–11) tells the story of a woman caught "in the very act of adultery" (though no mention is made of her equally adulterous partner). She is taken before Jesus by the religious leaders, the keepers of the law of Moses. There is no debate among them about what the law requires. She is to be stoned. Jesus, however, approaches the crisis from another angle. He does not go first to the most obvious and simplistic interpretation of the law of Moses. Instead, he responds in a way that reveals a deeper question about the nature of sin: "He that is without sin among you, let him first cast a stone at her" (John 8:7). Is Jesus setting aside God's clear commands? No. He is simply setting aside proof-texting legalisms and restoring the original heart of mercy to the law. He says in Matthew's gospel: "Think not that I have come to abolish the law, or the prophets: I have come not to abolish, but to fulfill them" (5:17, RSV). Can we see ending capital punishment as, in fact, fulfilling the heart of the biblical law, which is mercy?

We have argued that the progressive revelation of God's expectations is to move us away from seeing violence as a solution to our problems. We also observed that, by instructing people to observe "an eye for an eye," God was moving people in the direction of reducing violence and restoring right relationship. In fact, Jesus deals with the text directly when he says, "You have heard it said, 'An eye for an eye, and a tooth for a tooth': But I say to you, 'That you resist not evil: but whoever smites you on the right cheek, turn to him the other also" (Matthew 5:38–39).

In Romans 12, Paul instructs us to not exact retribution but rather leave this to God: "Beloved, never avenge yourselves, but leave room for the wrath of God; for it is written, 'Vengeance is mine, I will repay, says the Lord.'" A consistent ethic of life, then, cannot include capital punishment based on a retributive theory of justice. Instead, we deal directly with the social and personal crises that violently threaten the community and seek accountability and restoration whenever possible.

DAY 4 — The Christian Tradition

We have used the phrase "consistent ethic of life" to refer to a moral commitment to defend the sanctity of life in a holistic and unconditional fashion. Such a commitment affirms the sanctity of the life of not just the unborn but all people, even our enemies. Consequently, a consistent ethic of life must be concerned about war, poverty, abortion, euthanasia, capital punishment, and racism. Of course, in common usage, a person who claims to be "pro-life" frequently is implying only a position against abortion.

The term "pro-life" was coined in 1973 following the federal Supreme Court decision *Roe vs. Wade,* which overturned all state laws outlawing abortion. Ethics professor David Gushee expresses concern about the term "pro-life," claiming that its evangelical proponents "never have undertaken a full-blown intellectual analysis and exposition, from within our own tradition, of the concept of the sanctity of life."[7] It is toward such "full-blown intellectual analysis" that we point.

The early church took seriously Jesus's injunction to "love our enemies" (Matthew 5:44). Some early church thinkers (Clement of Rome and Justin Martyr, for example) not only opposed Christian participation in war but also denied that a Christian could serve as an executioner. Often they were not so much in debate with the empire about executing criminals as they were working out the implications of the radical change the world had undergone as a result of Jesus's life and teachings. Even if the pagans engaged in execution, those who named Jesus as Lord were not to participate in this practice.

It is clear that the church has had a strong tendency to draw a tight connection between the affirmation that humans are the bearers of God's image and respect for the dignity of life. For example, some expressions of the just war theory are explicit in defending the dignity of the person on the basis of bearing God's image. A detailed examination of the writings of the church would find frequent reference to the theme of honoring the image of God that each of us bears. It is perhaps for this reason that the early church was also opposed to suicide. The surrounding culture seemed to have little problem with suicide—indeed, in some circumstances, suicide was considered an honorable choice. This was not the case within Christianity, however. Oddly, though, there was, within the early church, a notable strand of those who expressed desire for martyrdom. They felt it an honor to suffer for their faith, and death was the ultimate suffering.

By the time we get to the Middle Ages, the church had pretty much universally taken the position that suicide was inconsistent with Christian faith. For example, Thomas Aquinas indicated that suicide was wrong because it violated our innate desire to live, because it harmed others whom we leave behind, and because God, as the giver of life, is the only one who can take life. So, admitting some development over time, it is fair to say that a study of the history of the church indicates that the sanctity of life should lead us to preclude suicide or euthanasia.

In Week 4, we went into some detail about the problem of poverty; in Week 6 we will do the same with racism. Because both of these issues relate to a person's access to life-giving and life-affirming resources, neither can be omitted from a discussion about a consistent ethic of life.

It is clear that the church has tended to draw a tight connection between the affirmation that humans are the bearers of God's image and respect for the dignity of life. For example, some expressions of just war theory explicitly defend the dignity of the individual on the basis of bearing God's image. The writings of the church include many calls to honor the image of God that each of us bears.

There is no doubt that the prevalent view in the history of the church is a condemnation of abortion. The church has tended to err on the side of protecting life and promoting sexual fidelity, rather than come down hard and fast on precisely when personhood begins or the soul enters the flesh. The church's voice has been relatively consistent in its opposition to abortion, although Christian views of how to handle exceptional cases has been a bit more diverse. It is worth noting that before the Enlightenment, the church saw abortion as more a communal sin than an individual one. The termination of a pregnancy signaled a failed marriage or partnership. It signaled that the community was not creating the proper environment where mothers and babies could thrive.

The church has opposed abortion, but it has also been forthright in reminding us of our obligations to the poor and others on the margins. It is hard to say that one has a consistently Christian position on the sanctity of life if one focuses solely on the unborn and leaves the born to fend for themselves. A consistently pro-life position seeks to make abortion rare, defends the human dignity of women, and favors a wide range of services for the care and protection of women, children, and families. A consistently pro-life position does not focus on symptoms without also paying attention to underlying causes. What are the conditions that create hopelessness, which in turn leads some to pursue abortion as a solution to problems? How does lack of adequate health care contribute to a sense of limited choices? How does the ethic of "individualism" lead us to value our own convenience over the life of a child? As we address this range of issues, we move ourselves toward an increasingly consistent ethic of life.

Finally, we should note that people within the church have often spoken of the desensitizing impact a failure to respect life in any of these areas can have on all the others. While some may find capital punishment acceptable because the criminal "deserves" it, state-sanctioned executions contribute to a "culture of death." In *Resident Aliens,* Stanley Hauerwas and Will Willimon ask why we are surprised that the culture that defended its use of atomic weapons against cities in Japan could now come to see abortion as acceptable.[8] War, abortion, capital punishment, poverty, euthanasia, and racism—a position that values the sanctity of human life must address these all.

Living Examples in the Contemporary Church

FINDING ANOTHER WAY:
Abortion Adversaries Seeking Real Solutions

A pro-choice activist describes what it's like when a major pro-life protest occurs in her city: "I'm the one who calls in the army [of volunteer clinic escorts].... It's like a war. I don't like it. I'm tired. I want to see if there's another way to deal with this issue."

So on a brilliant spring day she joined 100 other people in Madison, Wisconsin, in the first national conference of the Common Ground Network for Life and Choice. For four days pro-choice activists, clergy, doctors, and women's clinic directors could be found with pro-life activists, clergy, lawyers, and crisis pregnancy center volunteers in workshops, strategy sessions on teenage pregnancy and adoption, and—perhaps the biggest surprise—friendly conversation.

These people didn't ignore their very real differences on the core issue of abortion, but they also didn't allow those differences to distract them from seeking the "common ground" that exists even among adversaries.

The Common Ground Network came together in 1993 out of dialogue and joint action between pro-choice and pro-life supporters in Buffalo, St. Louis, and elsewhere. The network links such Common Ground groups around the country, providing resources, training, and facilitators.

Activists from both "sides" of the abortion issue sit down together for extended discussion under specified ground rules: respectful speech and behavior; a desire to understand; a pledge to refrain from attempts to convert and convince; and confidentiality.

Discussion moves from issues directly related to abortion (What's the life experience that's led you to the position that you've taken?) to related topics suggested by group members (What are your beliefs about birth control? How do we best teach our children about sexuality?). A goal is to identify areas of agreement and possible cooperative work. Examples have included promoting adoption and developing a mutual "code of conduct" for public hearings concerning abortion.

Participants are not expected to give up their pro-choice or pro-life activism. In between dialogues, they often continue to face each other as adversaries in the media, in city council chambers, or across demonstration lines.

"Common ground" does not mean compromise. While compromise has a rightful place in our society, groups affiliated with the network begin with an understanding that there are core principles on which neither side in the abortion issue conflict can compromise. This doesn't, however, preclude the possibility of civil dialogue and coming together on other principles.

In view of the verbal and physical violence that has characterized the abortion debate in the United States, for adversaries in that debate to meet with listening ears, handshakes, confessions of stereotyping, forgiveness, and statements of basic human respect for one another is not a trivial thing. These groups serve as a needed witness in a country at war with itself on many fronts.

Still, Common Ground groups are not only about people unexpectedly "getting along"—an oddity to be noted and then dismissed. Most participants have a commitment to their communities—a desire that they be safer, more caring places to live, where even sharp disagreements do not bring about violence and torn relationships. They want to see practical changes that increase the resources, justice, equality, *and* choices available to women and families—and many don't see other options.

"I don't think anything else is working, and [Common Ground] is our only chance," said Connie Cook, a pro-choice participant in Common Ground of the Quad Cities (Davenport, Iowa). At the conference one could sense a tangible desire that Common Ground efforts might be like yeast, eventually permeating and changing our country's public discourse on the abortion issue.

Could the Common Ground approach change the way we talk about other issues as well? The Buffalo Coalition for Common Ground has been testing this out, helping to organize, for example, a Common Ground dialogue day for the Presbytery of Western New York on the question of the ordination of gays and lesbians. The coalition is currently planning a day this fall on teen pregnancy, which will bring together people working on the issue, teenagers, and their parents for Common Ground–style conversation.

"This approach requires lots of preliminary work—collecting good data on the topic, making sure you get the right people," says Stan Bratton, one of the founders of the Buffalo Coalition. "Balance is the crucial thing"—without which one side or another may feel that the planners are promoting a certain position or agenda. For the teen-pregnancy forum, planners have brought in Planned Parenthood, pro-life adoption agencies, the city school board, the Catholic diocese, the Hispanic Coalition, a predominantly African American hospital, and the coordinator for youth services for the county, among many others.

> The Common Ground approach is not easy, and its impact and achievements may be modest. It is quiet and grassroots, not flashy and well known. But for the greater good to be true and lasting, it has to be built one brick at a time. Common Ground offers one concrete model for how we might begin building up, instead of tearing down.
>
> JULIE POLTER*

DAY 6 Putting Faith into Action

The set of issues that come under the broad topic of a "consistent ethic of life" are some of the most contentious in American public life today. In particular, the issue of abortion immediately evokes very strong responses. As writer Amy Sullivan reminds us, "For 30 years, abortion politics has required Americans to choose sides. You are either pro-choice or pro-life. If a politician supports a parental notification law, he or she is labeled pro-life by abortion rights supporters. But if the political leader also opposes a 'partial-birth abortion' ban, the anti-abortion side will tag him or her as unacceptably pro-choice. There is no word for a middle-ground position in American politics."[9] Given the great passion that attends these issues, it would be hard to overstress the importance of factual accuracy. We must educate and speak to the more than two-thirds of Americans who actually fall into the middle ground on this issue, "believing that abortion should be available in some," says Sullivan, "but not all, circumstances."[10] Educational activities are central to moving from slogans to serious solutions on how to reduce the rate of abortion.

Whether or not one agrees with court opinions on abortion, it is worthwhile to examine the factors considered by the courts. And since we have argued that a holistic and consistent ethic of life runs much deeper than simply the abortion issue, it is necessary to engage also in a broader educational exercise—one that covers U.S. and global abortion trends but also addresses poverty, infant and general health care, and the use of the death penalty and its disproportionate punishment of minorities and the poor.

While it is critical to structure educational efforts in a way that expands this discussion into all the areas we have discussed, it is also likely that individuals will choose to specialize in particular issues. A team approach is useful. The methods of activism mentioned in the appendix might be used in a way that allows individuals to focus their own attention while still participating in an overall voice for a broader and more holistic ethic of life. For instance, a letter or opinion piece might be written by an individual with a particular interest in a given topic but then be signed by all members of a group or by a group identity established for this purpose.

---

* *Julie Polter is an associate editor at* Sojourners. *This text appeared in* Sojourners, *Sept./Oct. 1996, vol. 25, no. 5, pp. 10–11.*

There are also many opportunities to participate in demonstrations and acts of nonviolent resistance that bear witness to individual components of a consistent ethic of life. See the appendix for ideas about such possibilities.

DAY 7 Group Meeting and Reflection

1. Develop a one-page statement outlining what you think would be a consistently pro-life political position. Imagine what critiques might be offered by others and integrate those critiques into your response. Keep in mind the various facts and statistics cited throughout this chapter.

2. Discuss the various points of the opinion written by Justice Blackmun in *Roe vs. Wade*.[11]

3. Read Cardinal Bernardin's 1983 speech "A Consistent Ethic of Life: An American-Catholic Dialogue."[12] How would you go about building a biblical case for a consistently pro-life position? What key themes would you integrate into your position?

4. Discuss the underlying causes that give rise to abortion. What sort of proposal to seriously reduce the number of abortions do you think would attract wide support?

5. What arguments would you use if asked to defend the death penalty? To argue for its abolishment? Discuss and critique both positions.

6. How would you characterize your denomination or group's response to the AIDS crisis? If you find it inadequate, what steps should be taken to begin to correct this?

7. Assess the following claim from *God's Politics*, page 79: "Couldn't both pro-life and pro-choice political leaders agree to common ground actions that would actually reduce the abortion rate, rather than continue to use abortion mostly as a political symbol?"

8. *God's Politics* cites Cardinal Bernardin's call for a "seamless garment of life." What does this mean? Would you defend the sort of position this suggests? Why or why not?

9. What other important "life" issues would you include in your "seamless garment"?

Racism

THE ISSUE OF RACISM is a persistent one in American culture. Slavery is no longer a legal economic practice, treaty rights with Native Americans are at least tacitly acknowledged, and equality has been written into our legal systems. But racism is persistent largely due to the fact that the correction of racial prejudice in the laws did not come with restorative justice, nor did it address "institutional racism" in various societal policies and structures or—perhaps most important—the deeply rooted sin of racism in the human heart. In this week's study, we will turn our attention to the issue of racism and its expression in contemporary society. *God's Politics* covers this issue in chapter 19. Read or review that chapter as you work through this section. The following paragraph provides an overview of the material.

Chapter 19: Telling the truth about race has always been difficult in the United States. We must start by acknowledging that, as I wrote in a *Sojourners* resource, "The United States of America was established as a white society, founded upon genocide of another race and then the enslavement of yet another."[1] I noted that, theologically speaking, racism is America's "original sin." Slavery and the subsequent discrimination against African Americans in the United States is a magnitude of injustice that requires national repentance. And that is also true, in different ways, regarding the multicultural mosaic that makes up twenty-first-century America. If Jesus has broken down every dividing wall between Christians, then Christians must have a united front in battling every kind of discrimination, bias, and racism.

DAY 1 — Introducing the Topic

What exactly is racism? Is there a common definition? And, most important, what are racism's underlying causes?

The above-mentioned article, titled "America's Original Sin," gets at the heart of the matter. Prejudice may be a universal human sin, but racism is more than an inevitable consequence of human nature or social accident. Rather, racism is a system of oppression for a social purpose—a purpose that is often economic in nature. The equation that results is "Racism equals prejudice plus power."

In the United States, the original purpose of racism was to justify slavery and its enormous economic benefit. The particular form of racism on this continent was inherited from the Spanish, who viewed the indigenous peoples of the Americas as "animals." The English justified their own slave trade with Africa by defining Africans not merely as unfortunate victims of bad circumstances, war, or social dislocation but rather as less than human, as objects, chattel, property to be bought and sold, used and abused.

The high standards set by the Declaration of Independence (all persons endowed by the Creator with inalienable rights, etc.) were not upheld in the early days of the United States. Native Americans were massacred and driven off their lands. Kidnapped Africans were not given any rights but rather were treated as subhuman property.

While slavery has been around for as long as recorded history, it has not always been racially motivated. Slavery has sometimes been the result of economic misfortune, war, or social dislocation. Plato even argued that certain people were fit to be slaves due to their inherent abilities.

Of course, given the economic benefit of free labor, there is never any shortage of people willing to make arguments justifying such racism. Yale Divinity School theologian Miroslav Volf notes that demonization is often used to justify the mistreatment of one group by another.[2] In order to justify unjust tactics pursued for economic reasons, people often make demonizing statements to create a critical moral distance between those in power and those without power. To the church's eternal embarrassment, Christians have too easily become the supporters and theological enablers of racist practices.

In the contemporary period, we dress up our racism in new justifications. Why do we continue to struggle with a racial divide in this country? The popular TV show *ER* once featured an interchange between an African American nurse and a white doctor. When a black gang member was brought into the emergency room with a gunshot wound, the doctor provided treatment, but the youth died. The brother of the dead gang member threatened to sue the doctor for not giving adequate treatment because of racial bias. The doctor then asked the nurse, his friend, "Do you think I gave this patient substandard treatment due to his race?" She responded, "To you folks, it's never about race; but to us, it always is."

Theologian James Perkinson put it this way: "'Race' as definitive of the central relationship organizing social wherewithal and political opportunity in the history of [the United States] yields a structure of white domination and non-white subordination in general, but also a particular paradox of empty passivity on one side of the color line and potent struggle on the other."[3]

Some people think that they have moved beyond racism because some of the most offensive and overt forms of racism are gone. Yet subtle forms continue to survive. The 2005 Academy Award–winning movie *Crash* explores some of the variations and subtleties of race and racism. This provocative film examines the complexities of racial conflict in America, in the context of post–September 11 Los Angeles. The multiethnic cast examines fear, bigotry, and racism from multiple perspectives as a number of lives intersect. Film reviewer Roger Ebert said, "One thing that happens, again and again [in *Crash*], is that people's assumptions prevent them from seeing the actual person standing before them." The dialogue in the film includes many different languages that are often not translated for the viewer into English subtitles on the screen. What feeling does this create in the viewer? How might it illuminate or critique nativist "English-only" movements in the United States? The director, Paul Haggis, makes sure that the film shows various racial and ethnic stereotypes that people hold. But the script plays with these stereotypes, twisting them to show how they are fundamentally false and yet have superficial elements of reality. Consider viewing this film with others and hosting a discussion.

Racism can be very deeply hidden, and it can show up in our interpersonal practices at unexpected times. If we are white, many of us, if candid, can think of times when we have consciously used white privilege to our own advantage. Our entire society is set up to allow our white skin to ease our way. If we are people of color, many of us, if candid, can think of times when we have allowed our bias against those with economic or social power over us to block us from having a more human interaction. Many aspects of our society are set up to put obstacles in the way of people of color. The frustration and bitterness that can build up in response to these obstacles have the potential to eat away at all our souls.

As we work through this week, let us be particularly attuned to our emotional responses, to honestly see where racism or bias is at work within us. It is not possible for whites in America to claim to be "beyond race." If we accept that fact, we can begin to heal and grow toward the person Christ calls us to be. On issues around race and racism—perhaps in even deeper ways than with the other themes we have been discussing—our first step forward is the recognition of our own need for repentance.

DAY 2 Considering the Evidence

In this section, we will consider several statistics about the ways that people of different races are able to access the resources available in our country today. The picture is not a pretty one. The sad but inescapable conclusion is that racism is alive and well in America, and that minorities are suffering the consequences in very concrete ways.

According to the 2000 census, the U.S. population in that year was roughly 75 percent white, 13 percent Latino ("Hispanic," in Census Bureau language), 12 percent African American, 4 percent Asian, and 1 percent Native American.[4] Even using these statistics it is important to remember that Census 2000 saw the first major overhaul of the census questionnaire in forty years. "The big issues for Census 2000 revolved around our social identity crisis—specifically how we define 'race,' 'ethnicity,' and 'culture,'" wrote Rose Marie Berger in her article "Knock, Knock. Who's There?" She noted that "since 1977, people have been required to identify themselves on census forms by choosing only one racial group—black, white, American Indian and Alaskan Native, Asian or Pacific Islander. In 1997, Congress decided *against* adding a single 'multiethnic' category to Census 2000, opting instead to allow multiple checks under 'race.' This increases the racial options from 15 to 32,000 possible combinations."[5]

The census notoriously undercounts minorities. In 1990, racial and ethnic groups, renters, and children were severely undercounted. Asian Pacific Americans were undercounted by 2.3 percent, compared to a 0.8 percent undercount of whites. The undercount rate for Latinos was 5 percent, the highest for any race or ethnic group except American Indians. This is important because census data are used to allocate more than $180 billion of federal funds, to redistrict local, state, and legislative boundaries, to reapportion congressional representatives, and to gather demographic data. The numbers matter.

Using census data, we can compare the median incomes of the major groups—namely, white, Latino, and African American—and see how the incomes have changed between 1972 and 2001.[6] The median income in white households increased from $36,510 in 1972 to $44,517 in 2001. For Latinos in the same time period, median income increased from $27,552 to $33,565. For African Americans, it increased from $21,311 to $29,470.

Note that "economic booms" disproportionately help white households and offer the least for African Americans. Also, while progress is slowly being made, by 2001 both Latinos and African Americans shown in this data fell behind the income levels of whites by as much as a third.

Areas that reveal the extent of racial disparity include poverty levels, incarceration rates, and access to health care. On poverty, we can summarize the data rather quickly. Shown below are poverty rates for 1959, 2000, and 2004. (*Note:* The Census Bureau omits some data—hence the gaps below.)

Poverty Rates

	1959	2000	2004
Blacks	55.1%	22.5%	24.7%
Whites	18.1%	9.5%	10.8%
Latinos	21.5%	21.9%	
Asian	9.8%		
Total	22.4%	11.3%	12.7%

The picture is even more discouraging when you consider the poverty rates among children. In 2004, the poverty rate for African Americans under age eighteen was 33.6 percent, for Latinos it was 28.9 percent, and for whites 14.8 percent.[7]

Incarceration rates are also higher for minorities, and many studies have provided evidence that racial bias is a large part of the reason. One example is the phenomenon commonly known as "DWB" (driving while black). An African American out for an evening drive is more likely to be pulled over by the police than a white driver—for no reason other than race. Likewise, members of minority groups commonly receive more severe prison sentences than white people when found guilty of the same crime. In post–September 11 America, this is especially true of Americans of Middle Eastern descent. According to news reports, in cases involving non-Muslim Americans and corporations charged with violating sanctions against Iraq, the government has asked for warnings or civil penalties, not jail. On the other hand, Americans of Middle Eastern origin convicted of the same charges have been given extremely long jail sentences and high fines.[8]

The incarceration rates for minorities, and for African Americans in particular, are significantly higher than they are for whites. In 2000, whites—who total 75 percent of the general population—made up 35 percent of the prison population. Latinos—who made up 13 percent of the general population—were 18 percent of the prison population. African Americans—who were 12 percent of the general population—made up 44 percent of those in prison. In 2000, the total prison population was comprised of almost two-thirds non-whites, while the general population was more than two-thirds white.[9] According to The Sentencing Project, a nonprofit organization nationally recognized as a source of criminal justice policy analysis, data, and program information: "As the national inmate population has increased in recent decades, the impact of these changes on minority communities has been particularly dramatic. Two-thirds of the people in prison are now racial and ethnic minorities, and for black males in their twenties, one in every eight is in prison or jail on any given day. Moreover, black males born today have a one in three chance of going to prison during their lifetime, compared to a one in seventeen chance for white males. These trends have been exacerbated by the impact of the 'war on drugs,' with three-fourths of all drug offenders being persons of color, far out of proportion to their share of drug users in society."[10] The most glaring example is the disparity between sentencing for possession of crack or powder cocaine. Possessing 5 grams of crack cocaine carries a mandatory minimum penalty of five years, the same as possessing 500 grams of powder cocaine. Approximately two-thirds of those who use crack are white, yet 85 percent of crack defendants are African American. Thirty percent of powder cocaine defendants are African American.[11] While looking at these facts and figures, keep in mind that each statistic represents a man or a woman with loved ones—with spouses, friends, parents, and often children.

What are the reasons for this disparity? Is it a discriminatory justice system? Does poverty create conditions that fuel crime among minorities? Do white privilege and power tilt the playing field against persons of color? Is it a combination of these and other factors? Why are Latinos and African Americans more prone to being charged with crimes, more prone to getting prosecuted—and more prone to having a poor defense?

Perhaps most disturbing of all are the racial disparities in the number of executions and death row inmates. "In 82 percent of the studies [reviewed]," a 1990 U.S. General Accounting Office report on death penalty sentencing revealed, "the race of the victim was found to influence the likelihood of being charged with capital murder or receiving the death penalty, i.e. those who murdered whites were found more likely to be sentenced to death than those who murdered blacks." From 1976 to the present, African Americans convicted of killing white people have been 17 times more likely to be executed than white people convicted of killing African Americans. In October 2005, death row across the country consisted of the following racial distribution: 45.5 percent white, 41.7 percent African American, 10.4 percent Latino, and 2.3 percent "other."[12]

Racial profiling, incarceration rates, and statistics on the death penalty and death row all reveal conclusively that African Americans are disproportionately on the receiving end of harsher treatment in the justice system, and Latinos aren't far behind. Again, why is this the case?

Are we ready to face the demon of racism that still hovers over life in America? Are we ready to put legs on the claim that all are endowed by our Creator with certain inalienable rights, and that equality and justice for all are at the very center of those rights? Until we do, we will not live up to the divine call for our lives.

DAY 3 — Reading the Bible

Any discussion of the Bible and racism should begin with the observation that all persons are created in the image of God and therefore stand before God as equals. The first eleven chapters of Genesis, which track the human decline into sin, remind us that we humans are far from God's intentions for us. God's call to Abraham and Sarah in Genesis 12 reveals the beginning of God's grand rescue mission. Perhaps the Hebrew Bible's greatest step forward in that plan is the Exodus from Egypt and the giving of the law at Sinai. God begins the process of restoration of the wayward creation. The law, then, is first and foremost about establishing who this God is who has taken Israel as a chosen people. God does not intend that the people be misled by the pagan cultures that surround Israel. Within this context, God's call for separation from the surrounding cultures is for purposes of education and binding God's people to the covenant. It is not separation based on race.

"In biblical terms, racism is a demon and an idol.... To be even more specific, it is the idolatry of whiteness, the assumption of white privilege and supremacy, that has yet to be spiritually confronted in America and, especially, in the churches.... We might even inquire into the ancient spiritual practices of exorcising demons when dealing with one so virulent as racism."[13]

Theologian Bill Wylie-Kellermann writes that idolatry might be the main spiritual mechanism by which the divinely created diversity of the human family becomes twisted into "a power of division, a device of injustice, a demonic servant of death."[14] To put it another way, racism is an issue of justification. How does one justify one's faith? In Christ or in worshipping one's power?

The teachings of Jesus—and later of Paul—make it clear that there is no basis for separation and exclusion based on race.

Let's examine the parable of the Good Samaritan in Luke 10:25–37. This parable is answering a question posed by a religious leader seeking to "justify himself" (verse 29). The question is this: Who is my neighbor? It is clear that this religious leader expects an answer that will reinforce his current behavior. What he gets, however, is rather different! Rather than affirm existing patterns, Jesus tells the story of a man who, while traveling between Jerusalem and Jericho, is robbed and left for dead by the side of the road. One by one, religious leaders—models of religious faith—"pass by on the other side," ignoring the man. But a Samaritan, a member of a group of people hated by the religious leaders, not only stops to help but makes longer-term provision for the injured victim as well. In other words, the hero of Jesus's story is a member of a group looked down upon by the people gathered around him. Jesus not only destroys any basis for exclusion, but also no doubt tweaks his hearers by making the one they respect least the hero.

In the New Testament Paul concludes that claims of justification, meaning, and self-worth located in any ideology or institution (indeed, in anything but God's grace alone) ultimately prove bondage to sin and death. Galatians 3:28 affirms that in Christ there is no longer a basis for racial, ethnic, class, or gender distinctions. The dividing wall has been broken down by Jesus. Among those who follow Jesus, there can no longer be such cultural, racial, ethnic, class, or gender divisions. One immediately wonders how the contemporary church is fairing, given the highly segregated nature of weekly worship in the United States. Wylie-Kellermann reminds us that "'whiteness' is itself an ersatz cultural reality, a social artifice without real substance, virtually a fabrication and a falsehood. That a lie should pre-empt and usurp the truth of God's grace is, well, the work of death's power in this world."[15]

To further see the extent to which racism is unacceptable in the life of Christian faith, consider the Acts 10 account of Peter and Cornelius. Cornelius, a Roman centurion, is recognized as a "devout man who fears God," though he is not a Jew. His desire to know God is reflected by his actions, and God honors Cornelius by sending Peter to him. But God also has to prepare Peter, who is still influenced by old ways of seeing non-Jews. When Peter goes to Cornelius, God has prepared the way. When Cornelius tells Peter of his experiences—he was told by an angel to summon Peter so that he could hear the Christian message—Peter is amazed and responds that God shows no partiality among persons. All are in need of restoration to God, all are acceptable who come, and distinctions based on race or anything else are ruled out. Cornelius, who was once outside the family of God, is now welcomed— even though he is not Jewish! As people called to live out God's intentions, we have no basis for excluding those different from us. We reject racism because of our desire to see people as God sees them, not as we might normally see them.

Paul picks up these themes when he discusses the "wall of hostility" identified in Ephesians (2:14). The hostility referred to there is not racism as such but the division between Jew and Gentile that the fledgling church had resolved to overcome in its life and community. The wall, in one sense, was quite literal. Wylie-Kellermann reminds us that there was in the temple a barrier defining and setting off the court of the Gentiles. Gentiles were forbidden on threat of death from entering the interior courts. Paul, as a matter of fact, was accused of transgressing that very wall with a friend (Acts 21:27–36). He was arrested and imprisoned for breaking the segregation laws.

Paul's letter to the Ephesians, written while Paul was in jail, argues that in Jesus's death and resurrection the dividing wall of hostility has been broken down and a new humanity has thereby been created in the One who is our peace. It continues:

> For this reason I, Paul, a prisoner for Christ Jesus on behalf of you Gentiles—assuming that you have heard of the stewardship of God's grace that was given to me for you, how the mystery was made known to me ... that is, how the Gentiles are fellow heirs, members of the same body, and partakers of the promise in Christ Jesus through the gospel.
>
> Of this gospel I was made a minister ... to preach to the Gentiles the unspeakable riches of Christ, and to make all men see what is the plan of the mystery hidden for ages in God who created all things; that through the church the manifold wisdom of God might now be made known to the principalities and powers in the heavenly places. (Ephesians 3:1–10)

Taking the liberating word of Jesus to the Gentiles requires addressing the powers directly and putting the "apartheid" wall on notice.

The gospel of Mark, as scripture scholar Ched Myers has shown, incorporates similar themes.[16] In Mark's gospel Jesus sends the disciples repeatedly over to "the other side" of the "sea." Mark is the first person to call that turbulent Galilean lake a "sea," thereby invoking not only the power of chaos but the whole history of crossing to liberation.

"What could be truer to our own experience of trying to build alliances or friendships or communities with sisters and brothers on the 'other side'?" writes

Wylie-Kellermann. "We hear an invisible whisper that says, 'Stay home,' striking fear in our hearts and prompting our despair. It may be a silent storm within, simply awkward and cool, or one raging with hostility. Once again, that storm, that blustering barrier, must be named and rebuked with authority. It's nothing short of a baptism to set off in faith into those troubled waters."[17]

Finally, perhaps one of the most powerful images relating to ethnic inclusion in all of scripture is Revelation 7:9: "After this I looked, and there was a great multitude that no one could count, from every nation, from all tribes and peoples and languages, standing before the throne and before the Lamb, robed in white, with palm branches in their hands."

What more powerful picture of radical inclusion than this? We should focus our attention on two important points. First, this vision does not include the dissolution of ethnic diversity. Notice that the writer has not lost his ability to distinguish between persons of different ethnic backgrounds. Indeed, he explicitly recognizes that there are persons present from all nations, tribes, and languages. Persons from any and all groups are welcome, and they are united in their adoration of the Lamb who was slain. Second, while those ethnic diversities remain (can we be so bold as to declare them celebrated?), they no longer create division or hostility. All people are now bound together under the aegis of the cross with a deeper bond than could be threatened by differing ethnic backgrounds.

DAY 4 — The Christian Tradition

> I still have a dream ... that one day this nation will rise up and live out the true meaning of its creed: "We hold these truths to be self-evident: that all men are created equal." I have a dream that one day on the red hills of Georgia, sons of former slaves and sons of former slave owners will be able to sit down together at the table of brotherhood. I have a dream that one day, even the state of Mississippi, a state, sweltering with the heat of injustice, sweltering with the heat of oppression, will be transformed into an oasis of freedom and justice. I have a dream my four little children will one day live in a nation where they will not be judged by the color of their skin but by the content of their character. I have a dream today.
>
> MARTIN LUTHER KING JR.[18]

The church has a checkered history when it comes to the issue of race relations. One of the low points for white Christianity in America came during the period prior to the Civil War. Much of the church not only turned a blind eye to slavery, a blight on the soul, but often provided biblical arguments in defense of the white majority holding black slaves. We will not repeat here those despicable arguments, but Christians—both white and black—must understand this part of our past if we are to move forward together.

While errors are always easier to see in hindsight, some Christians at the time had the gift of foresight and called the church to a better way. Lecturing on possible hindrances to revival, in 1834 Connecticut preacher Charles Grandison Finney had this to say:

> Revivals are hindered when ministers and churches take wrong ground in regard to any question involving human rights. Take the subject of slavery, for instance. The time was when this subject was not before the public mind. John Newton continued in the slave trade after his conversion. And so had his mind been perverted, and so completely was his conscience seared, in regard to this most nefarious traffic, that the sinfulness of it never occurred to his thoughts until some time after he became a child of God. Had light been poured upon his mind previously to his conversion, he never could have been converted without previously abandoning this sin. And after his conversion, when convinced of its iniquity, he could no longer enjoy the presence of God, without abandoning the sin for ever.[19]

While slavery in the United States has been abolished, can we say that the underlying seeds of racism and prejudice have been eliminated? Given some of the statistics cited above, it would be hard to conclude that as a nation we have outgrown racism. To work to overcome racism in our society, it is instructive to consider the methods used by those who opposed slavery. These methods can be expanded to expose less obvious forms of racism today.

One of the powerful voices against slavery during the late eighteenth and early nineteenth centuries was the English politician William Wilberforce. Interestingly, the last letter written by John Wesley was to Wilberforce. In it, Wesley wrote:

> But if God be for you, who can be against you? Are all of them together stronger than God? O be not weary of well doing! Go on, in the name of God and the power of his might, 'til even American slavery (the vilest that ever saw the sun) shall vanish away before it.
>
> Reading this morning a tract wrote by a poor African, I was particularly struck by that circumstance that a man who has a black skin, being wronged or outraged by a white man, can have no redress; it being a "law" in our colonies that the oath of a black against a white goes for nothing. What villainy is this?[20]

Wilberforce had been converted under Wesley's ministry, and it seems the two shared a great passion to see the injustices of slavery and any other form of prejudice undone. What strategies, then, did Wilberforce employ?[21]

Wilberforce lived from 1759 to 1833 and spent about forty years fighting against slavery in Great Britain. Slavery was deeply embedded in the culture and was viewed by many as an economic necessity—particularly by those who benefited most directly. David Gushee observes sadly that, while Wilberforce was able to change the culture of slavery in Great Britain using political tools, in the United States a civil war was required. A key driver of change was Wilberforce's ability to embed his call in the grid of "moral values." Gushee writes:

> One reason that the abolitionist struggle succeeded in Great Britain was the way that Wilberforce appealed to Christian moral values. He hammered away at the theme that slavery violated the law of God even if it was currently permitted by the law of [humanity]. He appealed to the conscience of a nation that was officially Christian and actually included quite a large number of devout Christians. Slavery, he argued, contradicted the moral values that the entire nation as a whole claimed to embrace. The rights and freedoms of the slave-owning class, he argued, needed to give way to the more fundamental and God-given right to liberty of those they enslaved. It took decades for this message to sink in, but it finally did.
>
> There are many lessons in the dramatic story of slavery's abolition in Great Britain, but here I want to reflect on the way in which religiously grounded moral values were employed in the debate. Wilberforce did not hesitate to make moral appeal based on explicit Christian convictions, both because that was his own passionately held worldview and also because it was the official worldview of the entire nation. Wilberforce, of all people, knew that Great Britain fell grievously short of its supposed beliefs every day, but he still found it quite effective to call the nation back to what it said it believed. When he did, no one could argue on principled grounds that slavery was a good and Christian practice. It was slave owner self-interest against the compelling moral values woven into the fabric of national life, and finally self-interest lost.[22]

Much of Western culture is rooted in the Judeo-Christian heritage. Wilberforce was able to tap into the basic moral and ethical commitments of that heritage and call for repentance from slavery on the basis of those commitments. Today, at a time when racism is not as overt as in slavery, yet still quite present, can we take a page from Wilberforce's playbook? Can we once again call our culture to accountability on the basis of Christian moral values? Or has our culture so lost touch with those values that we can no longer call people to better behavior on this basis?

Perhaps even more powerful than the white abolitionists were the black abolitionists and preachers who led the way out of slavery. In 1829, David Walker, the son of a slave father and a free black mother, also used Christian moral and religious language to make his point, concluding that as a result of the sin of slavery God would punish America:

What nation under heaven, will be able to do any thing with us, unless God gives us up into its hand? But Americans, I declare to you, while you keep us and our children in bondage, and treat us like brutes, to make us support you and your families, we cannot be your friends. You do not look for it do you? Treat us then like [humans], and we will be your friends. And there is not a doubt in my mind, but that the whole of the past will be sunk into oblivion, and we yet, under God, will become a united and happy people. The whites may say it is impossible, but remember that nothing is impossible with God.[23]

Henry Highland Garnet, who had escaped slavery in Maryland, was a Presbyterian minister in New York. In 1843 he delivered a powerful sermon to the National Negro Convention in Buffalo, New York.

The declaration [of independence] was a glorious document. Sages admired it, and the patriotic of every nation reverenced the God-like sentiments which it contained. When the power of government returned to their hands, did they emancipate the slaves? No; they rather added new links to our chains. Were they ignorant of the principles of liberty? Certainly they were not. The sentiments of their revolutionary orators fell in burning eloquence upon their hearts, and with one voice they cried, liberty or death. Oh what a sentence was that! It ran from soul to soul like electric fire, and nerved the arm of thousands to fight in the holy cause of freedom.[24]

In addition to the male abolitionists, we also recall the white female abolitionists like Lucy Stone, who taught fugitive slaves how to read and write; Sarah and Angelina Grimké, who spoke against slavery even though their father was a slave-holder; Abby Kelly, who joined Frederick Douglas on his first speaking tours, and others. And the incredibly courageous black women abolitionists: Maria Miller W. Stewart, who spoke publicly in 1832 on "the cause of God and the cause of freedom"; the Quaker leader Sarah Mapps Douglass; Margaretta Forten, founder of the Philadelphia Female Anti-Slavery Society; Sarah Parker Remond, who preached in the United States and Great Britain on the immorality of slavery; Harriet Tubman, who personally helped about 300 slaves escape to freedom on the Underground Railroad.

Finally, we must remember Sojourner Truth, born Isabella Baumfree into slavery in unspeakable conditions. As her hatred toward her white masters grew, she asked God to help her escape. In a spiritual vision God gave her an escape plan. She walked away from slavery, left her slave ways on the cellar floor, and stepped into freedom. Her new name marked her liberation. At the 1851 Ohio Women's Convention, Sojourner Truth hoisted the male preachers and abolitionists by their own petard.

And how came Jesus into the world? Through God who created him and woman who bore him. Man, where was your part? But the women are coming up, blessed be God, and a few of the men are coming up with them. But man is in a tight place, the poor slave is on him, woman is coming on him, and he is surely between a hawk and a buzzard.[25]

There are a number of ways in which one can build a case for rejecting racial prejudice, including the concept of the common good. As we saw in the previous section, there is no correct reading of the Bible that supports racial discrimination. From a Christian perspective, such discrimination is simply immoral. The abolitionists were right to appeal to Christian moral convictions in the fight against slavery, as was Martin Luther King Jr. in the fight for civil rights. We would do well to do likewise in our own time as we combat the remaining vestiges of racism in all their expressions.

DAY 5 — Living Examples in the Contemporary Church

In addition to the life of the church itself, there are a variety of parachurch ministries that engage in issues related to the themes of *God's Politics*. In the following account, John Potter relates to us the transformative power of his tour through key locales of racism and the civil rights struggle in the South. John's opportunity was facilitated by a ministry on the campus of Chicago's North Park University. As you read his account, from his initial struggle with deciding to participate through the misinformation he had to endure and finally to his return home, imagine the various ways that racism still distorts how we think about so many things.

🌿
LOOKING BACK TO MOVE FORWARD

"You won't actually go through with this," I silently told myself as I wrote the note. "This is one of those things you know you should do, but you won't." It was a Sunday night "College Life" worship service at North Park University in Chicago, and a speaker had asked those in attendance to commit to doing something that would be a challenge, then write that act down on a Post-it note. The idea was that whatever we wrote would be something that reflected our desire to live Christ-like lives: necessary, but difficult. It was one of the rare moments in which I can truly say that I felt God's call. I wrote down, "Apply to Sankofa."

The "Sankofa" journey is an annual four-day pilgrimage to the southern U.S. that focuses primarily on black and white relations and stresses personal transformation. As someone brokenhearted, frustrated, and angered by the sinful racial injustice of America's past and present social fabric, I'd been interested in the trip throughout my time in college. But as a shy and self-conscious person, and one for whom close relationships usually aren't formed quickly, I'd generally steered away from such hard-core endeavors, no matter how much I felt I *really should* go. I didn't realize that God would use that Post-it note challenge as a means to keep Sankofa in my mind and on my heart for many months.

What I was beginning to realize around the time that the application process for Sankofa began—and what I would understand much more deeply by the end of the trip—was that for me, a white male at a largely white school and in a society that was often geared toward my profile, whether or not I wanted to "deal" with racism and talk about it on a daily basis was a *choice*. For most minorities—including those at small, predominantly white Christian schools—it is not a choice. For those most affected by systemic, social, and personal racism, the reality of racial injustice is something that *must* be encountered every day.

I was sickened by the fact that I had gotten so used to being comfortable in a society that usually catered to me that I was unwilling to experience others' nearly constant discomfort. I submitted my application and prayed for better knowledge of God's vision for justice, and for Jesus to lead me toward reconciliation.

"Sankofa" is a Swahili word meaning to look back and reclaim the past in order to move forward toward understanding. Those accepted into the trip—about fifty students my year—began to prepare for the journey by participating in three weekly sessions led by Dr. Rupe Simms, North Park's professor of Africana Studies. We examined and discussed African history, African American history, and the civil rights movement—as well as racism and racial injustice in general—through lectures, dialogues, readings, and films. Students were each assigned a partner of the same gender but different ethnicity and encouraged to get to know one another outside of the preparatory classes before the trip. These preliminary classes were honest, difficult, and open to discussion and sharing—but they were nothing compared to actually getting on the bus.

Led by North Park campus ministries director Paul Johnson, we piled on the bus and began our excursion by driving through the night. Our group journeyed to Louisiana, Mississippi, and Tennessee. The core of the experience was communicating with and getting to know better one's partner, and dialogue topics were often given by a leader to discuss in twosomes. The microphone at the front of the bus was periodically opened up to the group at the end of a discussion or after one of the race-related films that the students watched on the bus.

It was at various times uncomfortable, frustrating, exciting, and emotionally trying to have the spirit of honest dialogue and truthful confrontation so nurtured and encouraged. Topics of discussion ranged from personal experiences of overt racism to thoughts on history, as well as systemic and social racial injustice. For those whose ideas of racism are limited to personal attitudes and grudges held against certain ethnicities or direct verbal expressions of racism, the stories of minority students and the facts on systemic racism presented were shocking.

In my experience, many of the white students were defensive and quick to dismiss others' stories of racism as either isolated incidents or coincidences. It can be difficult for white students to reconcile the vast differences between the reality they've experienced throughout life and that of minority students. It became clear to me that what was needed on the trip was for the white students to listen and for the nonwhite students to vent and to teach.

When we reached Louisiana, we paid a visit to Frogmore, a historic, preserved cotton plantation. It was alarming to see the ignorance of the site's tour guides, who spoke of the difference between "good slave masters and bad slave masters"—only the "bad ones" beat or raped their slaves. History was being rewritten and distorted to reflect a twisted "ideal" of the South that never was: slaves happily working away in the fields, singing and having a great time; spacious living quarters and an abundance of only the best food for the slaves; as well as top-notch doctors paying slaves a visit when they got sick. It was an in-your-face confrontation with the blatant racism still very much alive in the United States today.

In Mendenhall, Mississippi, we met with Pastor Timothy Keys, president of the Mendenhall Ministries, founded by well-known Christian activist John Perkins in the 1960s to provide services to and meet the physical and spiritual needs of Mississippians in poverty. Keys spoke openly with our group about issues that we presently face as college students in a city as diverse and segregated as Chicago. It was truly eye-opening to be immersed in the concerns and dialogue of black North Parkers, a group that I had known only on the periphery of my experience at school.

In Jackson, Mississippi, we visited Jackson State University to see an exhibit called *Without Sanctuary: Lynching Photography in America*. It was an extremely difficult point in our trip, one in which the inhuman and hateful history of America and of black and white relations—the history that is brushed over in most white students' education—was put in front of our eyes for us to try to understand.

Our final destination was Memphis for a tour of the Civil Rights Museum. For Americans to move forward in reconciliation it is vital for us to fill ourselves with knowledge of the struggles and victories of the past—especially given the fact that the civil rights movement is still the fairly recent past. What came to mind for me while seeing and hearing the many stories in the museum was that, as *God's Politics* emphasizes, *we* are the ones we've been waiting for. Our proper response to looking back at history and understanding it clearly and accurately is to identify the ways in which the struggles are still apparent today in our immediate surroundings, and to use the knowledge and experience we've gained to push things forward ourselves.

After the museum, we walked in small groups along Beale Street. What I still remember vividly from that relaxed last evening after a weekend of sometimes painful revelation was how strongly I felt a sense of grace—God's grace in redemption and resurrection, that past mistakes and sins can be wiped away with the hope of building the kingdom, but also the grace that my brothers and sisters of color extended to me. We had just spent a weekend focusing on the horrible things white people have done to people of color throughout history and still today, and I was accepted and treated as a friend with no questions asked. What a wonderful example of Jesus's grace toward humanity.

We spoke throughout the journey of an "aha" moment we might experience, in which the whole idea of Sankofa suddenly clicks and works for you—where you see history and its implications for today and suddenly "get" how it all works together and how you can respond. For me, the "aha" moment was realizing that the real journey starts when you get off the bus at the end of the trip. The Sankofa trip is an introduction to a life of seeking reconciliation and right relationships, of working to dismantle racism and injustice in all that one does.

It is a constant challenge to live up to what I took away from this transformative experience, now seeing for myself and understanding more deeply the reality of racism for people with whom I've formed relationships.

JOHN POTTER*

DAY 6 — Putting Faith into Action

Many of the themes that we discuss in this book can be most clearly understood through experiential educational events. This is especially true of racism. One of the great problems that still surrounds the issue of racism is the extent to which white Americans continue to believe that the problem has been solved. They tend to claim that the sorts of things that racial activists point to as evidence of lingering racism are misunderstood. This suggests that our culture at large will be quite resistant to the more common means of education. We may need to get more creative.

One potential tool that can help deepen understanding is drama. The Internet is a good place to find good dramatic pieces that help to focus attention on particular aspects of the problem of racism. If you are part of a larger support group working on race issues, you and your partners might create a dramatic presentation that draws attention to particular racial concerns in your area. As you select dramatic materials, you should consider just how ready your potential audience is to be confronted by these issues. The goal, of course, should be to draw your audience in so that they, too, feel the alienation and dissonance of racism.

Another resource is found in tests aimed at revealing the many privileges that the majority enjoys. An example is the remarkably powerful tool called the privilege test. Everyone lines up on the center line of a basketball court. Participants are told that there is an important prize at the front of the gymnasium and that they are to race for it. Before the race starts, however, there are certain restrictions. If you are a person of color, take one step back; if you were raised by a single parent, take one step back; if you had more than fifty books in your house as a child, take one step forward; if your parents read to you as a child, take one step forward; and so on. The list is quite long. It is also very moving. Participants are often embarrassed to realize how privileged they have been. Others are moved to see how far they have come even with unprivileged childhood experiences. Sometimes, participants are moved to express

---

John Potter is online giving development assistant at Sojourners/Call to Renewal.

appreciation to parents for the fine job they have done in difficult circumstances. The bottom line is this: all feel the force of the different ways that life experiences, many explicitly tied to racial prejudices, can affect our lives. When planning such an activity, be creative—but keep your focus on the experiential.

Be sure to consider ways in which you can employ many of the different ways of being socially active that are outlined in the appendix. Look for opportunities to engage in letter writing; antiracism and diversity training in church, community centers, and the workplace; or helping your pastor with sermon preparation and the celebration in church of significant dates in the history of racial justice and reconciliation.

DAY 7   Group Meeting and Reflection

1. Discuss the strengths and weaknesses, as well as the implications, of the definition of racism. What is your perception regarding the state of race relations in the U.S. today? What about in your church?

2. What do you make of the high incarceration rates of minorities?

3. The Sunday morning worship hour has been called the most segregated hour in the United States. Why is this so?

4. Do you agree that it is a fact that historical prejudices have created circumstances in which minority groups have less opportunity than the white majority? If so, is this a moral problem? What ought the church to do about it?

5. What are the connections between racism and poverty? What do you know about the history of reparations for slavery? What is the unfinished business of slavery in America?

6. Develop a four-point plan to alleviate the worst abuses of racism still present in the United States.

7. What are the worst expressions of racial prejudice in your neighborhood or city? Where have you gotten your information? What might be done to "lift the mask"?

8. What do you consider to be the primary causes of any racial prejudices you have encountered? To what extent have you encountered racial prejudice in the church or in Christian circles? What rationalizations that empower racist behavior and attitudes do you think people have come to accept?

9. What would it mean, and what would it take, for our society to move toward investing less in the idea of "whiteness" (as opposed to ethnic categories such as Irish or German)? In what ways could this be a genuine step toward racial justice, rather than just multicultural window dressing over continuing inequity? What would such a change mean in your daily life?

Strengthening Family and Community Values

YOU ARE NEARING the end of your study of *God's Politics.* In the next to last week, we turn our attention to the legitimate concerns that both the political Left and the political Right have regarding the family structure in the United States. Read chapter 20 in connection with this week's study. The following paragraph provides a very brief summary of the chapter's material.

Chapter 20: The concepts of family and community are complex and important ones for Christians. On the one hand, the extended family has been a hub of spiritual and other development back into ancient times. On the other, Jesus calls his followers to a broader sense of family than the narrowly defined, contemporary nuclear family. God calls us into existing communities that certainly include the nuclear family, but also include the extended family, the surrounding community, and the church family. The strength and health of the bonds between family and community are essential to the common good. An explicitly spiritual sense of community needs to be reestablished within our churches, our neighborhoods, and our national politics.

DAY 1 ## Introducing the Topic

The term "family" is often used as a code word, with too little concrete meaning; it is used to bring to mind a set of related ideas that are not necessarily connected to the idea of family. Instead, it is used to construct a particular way of seeing and connecting an array of issues. For example, when you hear someone speak of "family values," what does it evoke? This phrase has been carefully constructed and used to connote a position that opposes sex education, abortion, gay and lesbian rights, pornography, and "sleazy entertainment." In addition, it often expresses a position that focuses primary attention on the "nuclear family," conceives women first as homemakers, and favors a strongly patriarchal social order.

Now, before we proceed with our analysis, it's important to note that to offer critique of a position as too narrow is not to deny that it has some validity. Too often, critique is taken as wholesale rejection, and we must be more cautious on such serious matters as the health of our families and engage in building common ground wherever possible. This means affirming each side when we can. For example, we will argue that the vision of family values embraced by the political Right leaves out too much. While doing that, however, we can agree that pornography has inundated our society and has coarsened our judgment on sexual matters. We can agree, as *God's Politics* says, that "infidelity, betrayal, broken relationships, and casual sex are undermining the health and integrity of our society" (page 322).

While affirming these points, we must also notice what is missing. When you hear the term "family values," it is rarely connected to the idea of overcoming poverty, which as we have seen is a major threat to family life. It is rarely expressed in a way that makes clear the intimate connection that God intends to exist between families and communities. It particularly fails to recognize that our accountability for others extends well beyond our own immediate families. In fact, one could argue that the Right's version of "family values" encourages individualism. It tends to put forth a very narrow sense of family and community that fails to do justice to the rich sense God intends.

Unfortunately, the ambiguous manner in which the term is used obscures important facts and weakens the public debate. For example, the tendency to use the term "family" primarily in reference to the so-called nuclear family can be misleading. The idea of "family" as nuclear family is a fairly recent construct, only a couple of centuries old. This way of thinking of family makes the term individualistic and private, and it tends to miss the richer sense of family that has been in play through most of the rest of our history.

What does a more biblical concept of family look like? If we examine the Hebrew scriptures, we find the standard notion of family to be much more along the lines of what we call the extended family. There would be a head of the household and his wife, and the sons and their wives and children would live close by. In addition, some displaced persons might also be taken in and become part of the extended family. This provided a much broader, cross-generational concept of family than the contemporary nuclear family. The Bible speaks of extended families of more than a hundred members. We are explicitly told that Abraham's extended family included sixty-six people. While we need not import these details into the contemporary period, reflecting on such models helps us to see the inadequacy of the individualism that is part and parcel of the family values debate. We must begin to think in much broader and communal terms. Our discussion needs to extend beyond the boundaries of the typical "family values" debate if we are to reimagine a more Christian way of being.

To the question, Is the family under attack? we must answer with an emphatic yes. However, the attack is much deeper and more profound than is generally described. First, the family is under attack by discussions that define the term too narrowly. The paradox, of course, is that those doing most of the talking about family values often misdiagnose the problem, making matters worse. Second, the family is under attack on a broad range of fronts including poverty, domestic violence, divorce, missing male parental figures, health-care access, and a consumer-oriented approach to sexuality. The failures of both the political Right and Left are evident here, as *God's Politics* notes (page 326):

> [T]he answer to the "family values" crisis may not be a return to traditional roles for men and women and combating gay marriage, as the Right suggests, but rather in supporting the critical task of parenting—culturally, morally, and economically. Here again, both the Right and the Left are failing us. The Republican definition of family values, which properly stresses moral laxness but ignores the growing economic pressures on all families, simply doesn't go deep enough. Similarly, the Democrats are right when they focus on economic security for working families but wrong when they are reluctant to make moral judgments about the cultural trends and values that are undermining family life.

Both economic factors and broader cultural factors contribute to the dissolution of families. Where do we find hope? The short answer is in building communities that bear more resemblance to biblical notions of family. One good place to start should be the church.

DAY 2 — Considering the Evidence

As we have seen, "family values" have been discussed in the public sphere with a rather narrow sense of family. There are only a limited number of places where one might find communities that embody anything like a deeply biblical view of family.

Data from the 2000 census provide insight into the health of American households. Of the 281.4 million people who lived in the United States in 2000, 273.6 million of them lived in "households," broken down in this way:

Total households	105.5 million
Family households	71.8 million
Married couple heading household	54.5 million
Single mother heading household	12.9 million
Single father heading household	4.4 million
Non-family households	33.7 million
Single person	27.2 million
Multiple persons	6.5 million[1]

Family households are defined as a group where at least one person is related to the householder in some way, including blood relations and adoption relations. Given concerns over the prevalence of divorce, it is worth noting that about 75 percent of those living in households defined as "family households" live in families with married parents. Let's consider some of the other factors indicating the health of these families and see if our analysis can give us a better sense of the ways that the family may be in jeopardy.

Most have heard the claim that somewhere around half of marriages end in divorce. But, as is often the case, the answer you get depends on the question you ask. Perhaps it is more helpful to think about the numbers shown above regarding families that are headed by only one parent and then to consider the number of persons who have been divorced one or more times. Not all such families are headed by a single parent resulting from divorce (some are widows and widowers, for example). It is nevertheless the case that single-parent families, especially families headed by a single mother, are among those most likely to be in poverty or economically disadvantaged.

Let's look now at the percentage of people who have been married and then divorced, from data recently reported by Christian pollster George Barna.[2]

Denomination/Religious Group	Divorced
Nondenominational Protestant	34%
Jewish	30%
Baptist	29%
Born-again Christian	27%
Mainline Protestant	25%
Mormon	24%
Catholic	21%
Lutheran	21%
Atheist/Agnostic	21%

What is striking is the higher divorce rates among the more conservative Christian denominations. Space does not allow examination of the reasons why this might be true, but the issue is a very important one. One last detail on overall U.S. divorce rates: taking all people, religious and not, into account, the U.S. has the highest divorce rate of any country in the world. Again, it would be worth reflecting on why this is so. It adds credence to the following claim from *God's Politics* (page 331):

> To say gay and lesbian people are responsible for the breakdown of the heterosexual family is simply wrong. That breakdown is causing a great social crisis that affects us all, but it is hardly the fault of gays and lesbians. It has very little to do with them and honestly more to do with

heterosexual dysfunction and, yes, "sin." Gay civil and human rights must also be honored, respected, and defended for a society to be good and healthy. It is a question of both justice and compassion. To be both pro-family and pro–gay civil rights could open up some common ground that might take us forward.

Oversimplification of the cultural landscape does not help move us toward solutions, and the lack of stability in marriages, particularly among Christians, suggests that a "remove the log from our own eye first" strategy is appropriate.

The question that has to be addressed is whether poverty is a result or a cause of marital instability. As Christians, our concern for families in general and for the quality of life for children in particular requires us to deal with both alleviating poverty to strengthen families and strengthening families in order to alleviate poverty. In other words, we must take steps to make divorce more rare and two-parent households more common, while also working to overcome stagnant wages, the rising cost of housing and child care, and the negative consequences of "absent parents" in families where low wages require both parents to work.

While there is debate about what is cause and what is symptom, there is no question of a strong correlation between child poverty and the marital status of the household. It is not surprising that when people have jobs they are better able to function as parents—single or married. The highest child poverty rates are among family households with a single mother as the head of the household. In addition to income disparities, access to health care and other similar benefits are least available to children living with single mothers. Thus, *God's Politics* notes, "The legitimacy of the family values debate has been demonstrated in the clear links that have been made between the problem of family breakdown and the social ills of youth delinquency and crime, drug use, teenage pregnancy, welfare dependence, and the alarming disintegration of civic community, especially (but not exclusively) in poor neighborhoods" (page 325).

Most of the discussion here has focused on children in poverty, but our elders are also at risk. Social Security insurance addresses the economic plight that many people find themselves in when they are no longer able to work. To the detriment of the common good, the recent political discussion on Social Security has been almost exclusively focused on privatization. Fifty-seven percent of Americans now say that privatization is a "bad idea," and 71 percent of seniors are "hostile" to the idea.[3] Nevertheless, the only Social Security proposals addressed by Congress include private accounts; they also cut benefits and do not address the coming Social Security shortfall or include steps to extend the program's solvency. "Addressing Social Security requires a moral framework that helps shape prudential judgments about proposals and political leadership," writes Yonce Shelton, national coordinator and policy director of Call to Renewal. "If we want congressional leaders to listen to the people and broaden the debate, we must help them understand what is at stake for *all* Americans, including widows and orphans, the ill and disabled, low-income elderly, and children. We need to put the people—us—back in the conversation, help move the discussion to higher ground, and urge leaders to keep the promise for *all* God's people."4

The issue we must work on has to do with replacing our individualistic sense of family with a more communal—and more biblical—concept. We now turn our attention to the family as understood through the biblical lens.

DAY 3   Reading the Bible

Few things are exploited in contemporary politics more than the notion of family. Those on the Right have correctly drawn attention to the importance of the family in building a strong society. Unfortunately, they have so narrowed the concept that it hardly bears resemblance to that rich notion of family that has been in play for most of history. On the other hand, those on the Left have a broader sense of the societal obligations that attend supporting families. Unfortunately, they often miss the importance of the personal aspects emphasized by the Right.

In this chapter, we examine the debates about family that arise in the Bible itself. Earlier, we noted that it would be a mistake to think of the modern nuclear family as adequately representing the nature of family in the Bible. Rather, the biblical model is closer to our concept of an extended family, which might also include adoptees and workers.

In Luke 14, Jesus makes it clear that love of family cannot be the supreme value for his disciples. The allegiance to Jesus and to the kingdom must be so great that we "hate" our families by comparison. This is amplified in Matthew 19 when Jesus affirms that those who have given up the insular security of the family economic system to cast their lot with the poor and serve the kingdom are true disciples. In Mark 3, Jesus has just launched his public campaign and is in trouble not only with the religious leaders (who think he is demon-possessed), but also with his family (who have come to "seize him" because people are saying he's crazy). Jesus separates himself from his family, saying, "Who are my mother and my brothers?" (Mark 3:33) to demonstrate his larger point that "a house divided against itself cannot stand" (Mark 3:25). In other words, the revolution of values that Jesus is calling for will require even a reexamination of "blood ties." "Jesus is remembered by both friend and foe," writes S. Scott Bartchy, a professor of Christian origins and the history of religion at UCLA, "... to have redefined the basis and limits of family life, rejecting blood ties in favor of the faith-based sibling-like bond that he created among his followers. Persons who do God's will have become Jesus' siblings with God alone as their parent (see Mark 3:35, Matthew 12:50, and Luke 8:21)."5

There are also relevant examples in Acts and in Paul's letters. In Acts 16, for example, we are told that the entire household of the jailer of Paul and Silas was baptized. Several letters of Paul end with particular greetings to extended families in the area of the church being addressed.

Bartchy has this to say about Paul's interpretation of "family":

> A close reading of Paul's Greek in his letters reveals that he not only knew about Jesus' radical redefinition of "family," but also made it his core relational term to describe the converts in the faith-related, household-based congregations to whom he wrote. Paul profoundly affirmed and implemented Jesus's vision of a society based on the surrogate kinship of faith-related siblings. This shared vision ... favor[ed] relationships rooted in the individually chosen and deeply shared commitment to the will of God as revealed by this Jesus. Paul's basic model for his new communities was a family of such "brothers and sisters," without any person in the group, including himself, enjoying the traditional authority and privileges of an earthly parent.

God has created us all to flourish—to be fulfilled by living out the fullness of what God created us to be. Relationship is critical to our living out God's intentions for us. When we ask what form and what role the concept of family has in Christian faith, the short answer is that the family is to be an encouragement to living out the life that God intends. At the center, "family" must be more relational and communal, and less individualistic.

DAY 4 — The Christian Tradition

The early Christians offered a genuinely attractive and distinct alternative to the surrounding cultures. While not always realized in daily life, the early church called for a radical sense of family leadership not based on the Roman patriarchal model (which was itself in flux as women became property owners).

Marriage, as we understand it in the modern sense as "a monogamous, lifetime, romantic union between one man and one woman centered around producing and caring for children," says religious studies professor Ellen T. Armour, "would have been a foreign notion to pre-modern Christians."[6] As we said earlier, the typical Greco-Roman family consisted of a household with wife, husband, children, in-laws, and slaves. The male family head, says Armour, "held life or death power over every member of his household and had sexual access to his wife, his mistresses or lovers, and his slaves." This was the accepted model of most early Christian families and the model Paul is trying to influence.

As the Catholic tradition has emphasized, from the early period on, the importance of the household was so central to the life of the church that the family could be called the "domestic church." Consider, for example, this from Catholic family writers Marie and Brennan Hill:

> The early church began in house churches, where families were the heart of the communities and from which ministers were first called to use their personal gifts to serve the needs of the larger community. The family is the most intimate experience of church, the place where love, forgiveness, and trust should first be encountered. This is the family church, whose members are called to embody Christ in everyday life.[7]

Notice the importance of the concept of "house church." One can easily imagine the development of stronger ties within the local communities as worship happened not only in larger corporate gatherings, but also in the intimacy of each other's homes. We have here an excellent image of both the importance of the extended family unit and the new family of "brothers and sisters in Christ" gathering to worship.

David Balch, professor of New Testament at Texas Christian University, notes:

> For historical perspective it may be worth recalling that in the culture of the early Christians, as important as the family was, it was secondary because Christians' primary commitment was to Christ. This created tensions within the household. At least one effect of early Christianity was to foster a religious perspective that supported some plurality of family systems. For example, women functioned in new ways in early Christian communities—they took on more active, verbal roles. And slaves related to masters in a different way. There was also a reversal in the way that children were perceived: They were seen not just as potential members but as full members of the community—as is suggested by some passages in the gospels, especially in Mark. So there were more family options in a Christian setting than was the case in the broader culture.[8]

One could say that the early Christian movement contributed to the breakdown of the Roman patriarchal family unit. The emphasis of the first Christians was on mutuality in decision making and on empowering one another in ministry based on the gifts of the Holy Spirit. There was not a uniform experience, but the family and community values that Paul emphasizes are those of caring for the least, mutuality, forgiveness, economic sharing, welcoming the stranger, and creating living units that reflect solidarity with the marginalized.

"The definition of household in the early Christian community was in fact very complex," David Balch reminds us:

> You'd have poor people living on the top floor, the wealthy on the ground floor and those of medium income in the basement. In the same house you would have very different economic units. In that kind of structure,

the gospel's idea of the reversal of values has a concrete setting. There was not the kind of zoning we have in modern cities, in which you are able not even to see the poor; you lived in the same houses with them. How to relate to these various people in the household was a primary question for early Christians. There's a lot of literature—especially, for example, in Luke—about caring for the poor in relationship to the household.

At times the church, in its effort to strengthen families, has been unable to properly assess the engines driving damage to the family. The fathers of the early Christian church were ambivalent on a number of things—private property, free markets, charging interest on money. This ambivalence was because they realized in these things the potential for abuse.

"Capitalism undermines traditional social structures and values," writes conservative commentator George F. Will. "It is a relentless engine of change, a revolutionary inflamer of appetites, an enlarger of expectations, a diminisher of patience. It has taken its toll on those values and those institutions that conservatives hold most dear: family farms, local government, traditional craftsmanship, historic homes and buildings."[9]

Unrestrained capitalism appeals centrally to values at odds with the gospel. It is driven by self-interest, but Christians are called to put others' interest ahead of our own. It needs willing, mobile, and committed workers, but Christians have other allegiances and commitments that sometimes stand in the way. For example, children need parents who are present, but advanced capitalism needs workers willing to make the tough sacrifices of time and energy. Too easily, a robust sense of family is the first thing sacrificed on the altar of economic growth.

"It is ironic that the people who want to preserve family values are often the greatest defenders of capitalism," says Mary Stewart Van Leeuwen, a professor at Eastern College. "Now these people would obviously say, 'Oh, well, when we defend capitalism we aren't defending the peddling of pornography.' Well, why not? If you say that the market is to be left to a matter of rational choice among buyers and sellers, without government interference, then why would you make an exception for one kind of transaction?"

In the Christian tradition, the definition of family has changed significantly throughout history. We do well to remember, says Armour, that

> whether to accept divorce and endorse second marriages, for example, was a major issue for the church in the mid–20th century. Yet today, even many conservative protestant churches advertise divorce recovery workshops. Pews in many churches are filled by so-called "blended families." Divorce is no longer a bar to ministry in mainline denominations. Interracial marriages were also highly controversial on religious grounds, yet no major denomination considers race a bar to marriage today.[10]

There have been many forms of family in history. The most common, as we've noted above, is the extended family, where relationships across generations create strong social networks and living arrangements. These extended families and households provide security and stability for all the members, and multiple role models for children as they grow.

How can Christians explore models of family and community today that promote stability and protect the vulnerable?

DAY 5 — Living Examples in the Contemporary Church

There are numerous ways in which our social fabric can be structured to encourage and strengthen families. Living this out in light of God's intentions has implications for both public and private institutions. In what follows, Molly Marsh provides a summary of the family-affirming ministry of a church in downtown Washington, D.C. As we see here, for the church and Christians to argue for a new way of being, we must be willing also to embody it.

"REMEMBER WHOSE YOU ARE"

Shiloh Baptist Church sits squarely on the corner of 9th and P Streets in northwest Washington, D.C., a grand and dignified fixture in the city's Shaw neighborhood—a community that has seen its fair share of unemployment, drug abuse, and skyrocketing housing prices. On a fall Sunday morning, the church is bursting with electricity, its 1,300-seat sanctuary nearly full as several choirs lead the congregation in praise and "hallelujahs." In the sanctuary around them, stained-glass windows, based on tribal patterns of southern Africa, are among the reflections of the church's 142-year history and its beginnings as a congregation of free and enslaved African Americans.

The church, one of the oldest African American congregations in D.C., is biblical in its theology, with a strong sense of mission, hospitality, and service. Rev. Wallace Charles Smith, Shiloh's senior pastor (and a Sojourners board member), reminds worshippers during his sermon to remember whose they are. "Jesus's blood has signed my name," he says. "What is the inscription on your life?" "The Shiloh Spirit," the weekly bulletin supplement, announces the congregation's focus on spiritual disciplines; for the next several months members will read Richard Foster's *Celebration of Discipline* and talk about its themes of inward, outward, and corporate discipleship at the church's Thursday night Bible studies.

When the worship ends, parishioners stream into the Henry C. Gregory III Family Life Center, which sits right next door, for Bible study, meetings (the list printed in the bulletin for this day is two inches long), and after-church fellowship, or to play basketball in the gym upstairs or take a meal at The Tuning Fork, a small diner inside the center. During the week, the center also provides a day-care center, programs for teen mothers, computer and GED classes, and help with food, clothing, and transportation for those who need it. Grief support groups, AIDS programs, affordable meals for senior citizens—some of the church's 4,000 members volunteer with or staff these and many other activities.

The physical structures facilitate the church's three-fold mission, envisioned by Smith and his team of ministers as a "Ministry of Building by Caring"—caring for one's self; for family, friends, and members; and for the community around them. It's a vision that parishioners put flesh to, not just among each other, but throughout the Shaw neighborhood.

MOLLY MARSH*

We have often heard it said, "Give someone a fish and that person eats for a day. Teach someone to fish and that person eats for a lifetime." This is a good explanation as to why faith-based organizations are making a difference in the social service arena. The faith-based service organizations that are most effective are those that teach skills, along with meeting immediate needs.

Traditional methods of social service delivery have often resulted in one-time solutions to recurring problems. Faith-based organizations are often located in the communities they serve and are seen as stable entities by the generally underserved, often ignored populations surrounding them.

In the United States, faith was the motivating factor in the development of many social services. Orphanages, schools, hospitals, and private homes for seniors are just a few examples. This tradition continues today as programs and services to address issues of homelessness, poor or absent health care, educational gaps, hunger, and poverty are sponsored by and delivered through local community-based efforts.

Shiloh Baptist Church's Family Life Center Foundation in Washington, D.C., is an example of an effective organization that strengthens marriages and families and the local community through empowerment, skill development, and advocacy.

Following are eight programs that represent the foundation's work.

The Child Development Center. Established in 1958 as a low-cost day-care and educational development program for preschool children, this center provides academic preparation and instruction uniquely designed to meet the individual needs of each child for physical, social, emotional, and academic development.

The Senior Center for the Deaf and Hard-of-Hearing. This center had its inception in 1982 and offers daily health, educational, and wellness activities for deaf and hard-of-hearing participants. In providing case management,

---

* *Molly Marsh is an associate editor of* Sojourners. *This text appeared in* Sojourners, *Dec. 2005, vol. 34, no. 11, p. 19.*

counseling referrals, and transportation services, the senior center is a magnet for this "special" population.

The Male Youth Project. Since 1982, this program has been transforming the lives of many teenage boys. With a dedicated cadre of committed male mentors, it provides training in literacy, math, science, and computer skills. Through this project boys ages eight to eighteen receive character, ethical, and moral development as well as a strong academic enhancement foundation.

The Shiloh Debutante Program. This program differs from other debutante programs in D.C. because it provides a combination of character, academic, leadership, and spiritual development activities for high school girls. In helping each debutante identify and develop her respective gifts and talents, this program nurtures, inspires, encourages, and enhances academic growth. College scholarships are given annually to high school seniors in the nine-month program.

The Human Services Program. In fulfilling its commitment to assist families whose coping skills are diminishing faster than finite resources, this program provides counseling, emergency funds, transportation, clothing assistance, and referrals to needy adults facing serious crises in their survival endeavors.

The Community Computer Center. With the use of state-of-the-art computers, learners of all ages receive computer training to enhance employability or improve basic skills. Weekend and summer programs are also available.

Church/Community Partners Against HIV/AIDS. This one-of-a-kind program provides outreach, technical assistance, forums, discussion groups, seminars, and workshops to persons infected with or affected by HIV/AIDS as well as those capable of assisting the HIV/AIDS community—including faith-based organizations, beauty and barber shops, nail salons, and community groups.

Teen Mothers Take Charge. More than 200 teen mothers benefit annually from the counseling referrals, social services, and other benefits this holistic program provides. The needs of teen mothers are addressed as the program continues to have success in reducing incidences of pregnancy among unmarried teen girls.[11]

Through these programs, the foundation is able to provide after-school program services, academic enrichment, HIV/AIDS counseling and testing, financial assistance, preschool care, nutrition and health information, interpreting services, social and health-care referral services, and case management. In the end, all are tools for engaging and strengthening families.

DAY 6 — Putting Faith into Action

In a very real sense, many of the issues that we have discussed in earlier chapters also relate to strengthening families and communities. Becoming more politically active will give us an increased level of empowerment to take on the issues that threaten families and local communities. Preventing wars and supporting alternative ways to resolve conflict will contribute to stronger families and communities. In promoting economic justice and poverty reduction, we will defend families and help communities to become more stable and self-sufficient. The embrace of a consistent ethic of life will contribute to a greater sense of the sanctity of life and to the value of each and every person. And given the proportionate damage done to minority families, working to solve racism will help us fortify families and build strong, diverse communities. How could all these actions not help strengthen families?

A huge question in the matter of strengthening families is how we can go about including in our concept of family the biblical concept of extended families along with our nuclear families. This will require a strengthening of the commitment to both, and will require us to begin to see our church family and the broader community as also having a claim on us. This will not be an easy step, and a good deal of patience will be required. However, solid and persistent and repeated education through a variety of channels will begin to change things over time.

In addition to a deeper and richer sense of family, we need for persons on both sides of the political divide to wake up to the valid points being raised by the other side. We must move beyond false dichotomies and sound-bite rebuttals to serious dialogue on what are clear contributors to the many problems that families face. Both economic and sociocultural factors make a difference. We must look for ways to lift families out of poverty, but also look for ways to stem the high divorce rate in America. We must accept responsibility as a society to make sure that working families do not get trapped in poverty due to unjust wage or hiring practices, but we must also work to elevate our attention to the damage done by a society that uses sexual references to sell just about everything. We must realize the importance of good parenting skills, and take the steps necessary to make sure that adequate opportunities exist for all. In other words, we need to come together to put forward a *bipartisan* agenda that deals with *all* these problems.

Work with your local community and neighborhood to figure out ways to educate others and to elicit their perspectives. Build partnerships and use the tools in the appendix to raise awareness on these issues. Since the "family values" debate will be with us for some time, the opportunity will constantly be before you to take proactive steps to get the message out. Most of all, be sure to live that message out daily in your own neighborhoods and churches.

DAY 7   Group Meeting and Reflection

1. The "nuclear family" is a historically new concept found primarily in highly industrialized Western countries. What concepts of family are represented in the Bible?

2. What do you feel are the greatest pressures on families in the U.S. today? What evidence might you identify to make the point?

3. Why are "extended families" not still the norm in the United States? Are there particular forces that have broken down the extended family? What are they? What might be done about them?

4. What biblical principles do you use when examining the rights and privileges of Christians who are also sexual minorities? Where do you draw your biblical values when it comes to the rite of marriage in the church for same-sex and opposite-sex members? What do you know about the church's history of marriage and commitment between same-sex couples and opposite-sex couples?

5. *God's Politics* discusses the *Survivor* television series. What cultural trends are uncovered by this analysis? What impacts do you think series such as this have on the broader culture?

Hope for the Future

FOR THE LAST seven weeks, we have looked at issues that require the attention of persons of faith. We started with the question of the relationship between faith and politics. From there, we discussed six specific areas of concern—war/peace, economic justice, poverty, a consistent ethic of life, racism, and strengthening families. We hope that in each week's study you have discovered ways in which you, in your local community, can begin to embody that "better way of being" toward which God calls us.

We turn our attention now to the many grounds for hope that stand before us. With every challenge comes opportunity, and with opportunity comes God's empowerment for a better tomorrow. The task before us may not be easy, but radical change rarely comes easily. Join us as we forge ahead toward that better future!

For this week's study, please review chapters 4, 6, and 21 from *God's Politics*. A very brief summary of those chapters follows.

Chapter 4: Constructive criticism is a good thing, in politics as with all else. To be able to see clearly into the current situation and to offer critical analysis is a vital part of participation in the democratic process. However, this process should aim to be more than just a "politics of complaint" that identifies problems but offers no insights as to what might constitute a better way. Protest should point toward that better way through a vision that involves personal and social transformation and the presentation of solutions. Being "for" an alternative brings positive energy and opens new possibilities in the political debate that focusing only on criticism does not. In short, protest is a good and important thing, but the offering of alternatives is an even more powerful contribution to the political dialogue.

Chapter 6: There are three dominant political options in America. One is conservative on everything—from cultural and family concerns to economic and foreign policy issues. The second is liberal on everything across the same spectrum. The third is libertarian—liberal on cultural/family issues and conservative on fiscal/economic policy. A fourth option is profoundly needed on the American political scene—traditional or conservative on issues of family values and sexual integrity, for example, while progressive or populist on issues of economic justice and peacemaking. Now, as some people are beginning to recognize the false dichotomy in seeing everything as either liberal or conservative, Christians have an opportunity to lead a significant change in the political landscape of this country.

Chapter 21: Prophetic faith does not see the primary battle as the struggle between belief and secularism. The real struggle of our times is the fundamental choice between cynicism and hope. Will we be lost in a hopelessness engendered by the daily recounting of various failures? Or will we be empowered by a dream for a better tomorrow? The decision for hope is based upon what we believe at the deepest level of our being—what we hold as our most basic convictions regarding the world and our dreams for the future. In the midst of the failures, there are always little signs of a better tomorrow—a better tomorrow that should be embraced and encouraged by all who follow the Risen One.

DAY 1 — Introducing the Topic

What constitutes "hope for a better tomorrow"? The last chapter of *God's Politics* begins with two citations, one from Isaiah and one from Revelation:

> Do not remember the former things, or consider the things of old. I am about to do a new thing: now it springs forth, do you not perceive it? (Isaiah 43:18–19)

> And the one who was seated on the throne said, "See, I am making all things new." (Revelation 21:5)

These verses are pregnant with hope. *The Chronicles of Narnia* by C. S. Lewis frequently foreshadow a new and exciting turn of events by noting that "Aslan is on the move." In other words, the Christ figure in the novels is no longer in the background, but is moving out to take a place of action. In the above-quoted biblical passages and in the Lewis novels, we see a similar notion—God is on the move, already planting the seeds that will spring forth in something so fresh and good that, in each case, it can only be characterized as a "new thing" that God is moving us toward.

Frequently the writers of biblical narratives relate what seems like a hopeless situation, one that seems to provide no basis for expecting, or even grasping for, a new and better tomorrow. Yet time and time again, after the writers lay out for us the difficult circumstances, they continue the narrative with two hopeful words, "but God ..." Things might look really bad, there may seem to be little or no basis for hope, *but God* is on the move and about to do a "new thing." When the Israelites lived in Egypt, Pharaoh made slaves of them and worked them mercilessly. But in the midst of their anguish, God heard their cry and moved to deliver them by preparing, calling, and sending Moses to lead his people out of Egypt to a new and better place. Even earlier, when Abraham and Sarah grew too old, so they thought, to have children, Abraham began to make plans for an heir that was not his blood descendant. But God remembered his promise, and Sarah, though old, bore Isaac. Yes, sometimes hope seems almost extinguished—but God is not finished.

As noted in *God's Politics,* the most serious temptation that Christians face is the temptation to lose heart, to give up hope, and to surrender to the despair of the moment. When this happens, cynicism is often the result. Despair, cynicism, and then acquiescence and acceptance of the state of hopelessness as the status quo mark the descent into an inability to imagine a better future or to strive toward one. As Christians, we must never forget that the hour may be dark, *but God* is on the move already. Can we perceive it? (Before we proceed, go back to *God's Politics* and reread pages 347 to 351, and reflect on how the power of belief that a new future was possible enabled the overcoming of evil.)

Perhaps the first step toward a new tomorrow is the ability to name the present darkness. Often we find ourselves inundated with a sense of confusion, a vague awareness that something is not quite right, but without being able to name the source of these feelings. Right now, there are numerous reasons for discouragement. We are engaged in a disastrous war in Iraq that was not wisely undertaken; economically, the playing field has been shifted to favor those already well-to-do and to harm those already on the margins; political discourse is rancorous, and bipartisanship seems merely a vestige of the past; and, perhaps most sadly, we find that the loudest voices coming from the "church" often seem more opposed to than supportive of the gospel of Jesus. There are many reasons to be discouraged; there is much temptation to fall into despair and cynicism. Might it be the case that, even in the midst of all this, God is already on the move?

Those on both the Right and the Left who name current circumstances as fundamentally a spiritual failure are, we think, largely correct. Our culture, even the Christian aspects of our culture, has repeated an error often recorded in scripture—namely, becoming immersed in idolatry, an idolatry that makes our comfort more important than our obligations to care for those less fortunate. Israel often fell into the idolatry of nationalism, the tendency to see God's call as first and foremost about receiving a blessing, and failed to see that they were to be recipients of a blessing *in order to be a blessing to others.*

Once the first step toward unleashing "hope for a better tomorrow"—naming the problem—has been tackled, we then begin to envision the nature of that better tomorrow. Recall the passage from the Hebrew Bible, "Without vision the people perish."

A vision for a better future includes a realization that being created in the image of God means being created first and foremost for relationships of self-giving love. It means reaffirming the biblical call to self-denial for the sake of others and a willingness to fight both injustice and expressions of Christian faith that enable and empower the continuation of injustice. It involves repentance for past failures and a concrete and specific determination to embody, at every level, God's intentions for how our shared lives are to be structured. The Christian vision, in its most basic form, means learning to imitate Christ in his giving of himself for all those whose lives he touched.

When asked the greatest commandment, Jesus gave an answer that tied love of God and love of neighbor closely together. He said that we are to love God with every fiber of our being and that we are to love our neighbors as ourselves. In fact, the way the commandment is worded suggests that one simply cannot do one component without the other. This is the vision that drives hope for a better future: a hope that we can recover the communal orientation of the life that pleases God, in spite of the contemporary popularity of "independence" and "autonomy."

The basis for hope must rest, then, on our ability to name the problem, to envision or to imagine a better way, and then to embody that better way—each of us in our own little corner of the world. Take time to review the epilogue of *God's Politics,* "We Are the Ones We've Been Waiting For," and its appendix. We name there several individual instances of folks seemingly raised up by God to wage change in their spheres of influence. As the Sojourners/Call to Renewal team travels across the U.S. and in other countries, we are seeing a consistent and growing dissatisfaction with the current state of affairs—dissatisfaction bold enough to attract and to empower a whole new generation of persons passionate about living out Christian faith in every nook and cranny of human existence. From Maine to California, from Florida to Washington state, God is on the move, raising voices clamoring for change.

Will that movement achieve the critical mass necessary to formulate and bring into reality the Christian vision for a better, more just way of being? It will if and only if each of us decides that, as *God's Politics* puts it, we are going to bring about a change in the wind, a change in the popular expression of the will of the people. No politicians can resist such a wind change, no administration can overlook it, and we are the ones to bring it about. God is already on the move, bringing that "new thing" into being. The question is, as Archbishop Desmond Tutu once asked a group of seminarians about to be ordained: "Are you ready to join with God?" Are we ready, or will we succumb to our doubts, fears, and cynicism? We are betting the future on the belief that the former is the case. Let us together, hand in hand, become God's partners in realizing that new and better future!

DAY 2   Considering the Evidence

Once, not too long ago, a chapel service at a Christian college in the United States went on for more than a week, 24/7. The effects of this week of intense reflection, repentance, and renewal would spill out beyond that particular campus for weeks and months afterward. Some say the effects are still being felt in certain circles. Nothing in particular led anyone to think, in advance of the service, that all heaven was about to break loose. The chapel speaker for the day only gave a brief testimony and invited prayer and reflection—what followed was completely unexpected.

One of the leaders of this college was out of town and had to be advised of the "revival" by telephone. He confessed that his absence was a good thing, for if he had been in town he almost certainly would have stopped what was going on. Why? Not because he was opposed in any way whatsoever to spiritual renewal, but rather because he would have doubted that this particular form was a genuine spiritual awakening.

This is worth reflecting on at some length. Here a person in leadership of an explicitly Christian college readily admits he might have squelched a move of the Spirit on his campus if he had had the opportunity—a move of the Spirit that, in retrospect, has been judged quite significant. What do we learn from this story? Well, first and foremost, we learn that the Spirit of God is radically free to bring about renewal in many different forms—and not necessarily the form we expect. Consequently, we must exercise due caution in our evaluation of "movements of the Spirit," paying far less attention to particular forms than to the fruits of the movement. Who knows what God might do and how it might be done? As we pray and work for reawakening to the gospel in our day, let us also pray for eyes to see what God is doing.

Without becoming prescriptive about the form that a move of the Spirit might take, we can consider what elements might be present. How might one characterize a new awakening? What might fuel it? What might stand as obstacles?

The term "Great Awakening" is generally used to describe periods of intense religious fervor that have occurred two or three times in U.S. history. Four conditions of these "awakenings" can be identified:

1. During these periods of intense change, as in all times of change, tensions that existed between the "old" and "new" ways of being created a good deal of anxiety. Whether in the past or today, such tensions often invite reflection on deeper things, which find their root in spirituality. In other words, an uncertain social climate calls us back to our spiritual roots.
2. Prior to past awakenings in the United States, there was a breakdown of community. One of the early awakenings was preceded by the move from the more dense urban areas of Europe to the more widely spread frontier settlements of the "new" world. Community bonds were stretched and snapped, largely replaced with a frontier spirit characterized by radical individualism. This emphasis on individualism increased the stress faced by many on the frontier. Of course, the many inherent dangers of frontier life contributed, but the lack of the community relationships that God has intended for us was also a major factor.
3. This environment invited, or perhaps demanded, a high degree of autonomy and independence if one were to survive. Opportunities for engagement with others in developing lives of active discipleship became increasingly difficult,

and a corresponding loss of respect for authority followed. In particular, church authority waned, and by the third generation, many on the frontier were outside any meaningful interaction with the life of the church.

4. The relevant writings of the period expressed concern with what we would call a decline in piety. In short, neither the corporate nor the personal lives of most people at the time were perceived to be particularly well aligned with God's intent, and awareness of the breakdown was growing.

All four conditions set the stage for openness to spiritual renewal. Our contemporary circumstances are not identical, but we can ask ourselves what conditions we experience that might give rise to similar problems and relational breakdowns.

The first Great Awakening of spiritual renewal in the new world came in the early 1700s. The outcomes of this spiritual awakening included the following:

1. There was an obvious and significant elevation of the importance of the religious life for each and every person. Lives of personal piety once again flourished.

2. Renewed appreciation for the Christian faith resulted, but it was for a faith that tended to be somewhat less doctrinaire than previously. A common, overarching Christian faith developed that still left a good deal of room for disagreement.

3. There was an elevated concern for education. During this period, many great institutions of learning were established, and there was a commitment to make education widely available.

4. There was a move to a concept of salvation that involved not only God's saving action but also the human response, which raised awareness of our own responsibility for our relationship with God and with others.

5. There was a renewed vigor to deal with the social ills that faced everyone.

6. A tendency toward theocracy gave way to a more democratic understanding of human self-governance.[1]

Before we ask what we might do to foster such a new movement of the Spirit in our time, let's turn our attention to the biblical witness to see what insights we might gain there.

DAY 3 — Reading the Bible

As mentioned before, the last chapter in *God's Politics*, "The Critical Choice," opens with two Bible passages (Isaiah 43:18–19 and Revelation 21:5). Our hope, as Christians, lies in the "new thing" that those passages refer to—a new thing that God is doing. It is not just a new thing that we must wait until the end to see. Rather, the new thing we look forward to has already arrived in the life, death, and resurrection of Jesus. In that radical change lies our hope—a hope that has already entered the world, but that must be realized again in each and every generation. Hope can be ignored, but it is there to be tapped into whenever we are willing to be used by God to realize once again that "new thing" (or, to put it another way, whenever we allow "new creation" to break in).

"Hope" in scripture is usually connected in some way to God. "Our soul waits for the Lord; God is our help and shield" (Psalm 33:20) is but one example of how biblical writers assert that the trustworthy basis for hope is God. Many times, however, we allow ourselves to misplace our hope. We think that a better future lies in material success or in gaining power over our destiny in some way. Of course, the perception that we have power over our destiny is little more than an illusion, as the parable of the barns in Luke 12 reminds us. Here, the owner of a farm finds himself with more harvest than he can store. He decides to build bigger storehouses in order to guarantee his future security. However, he does not live out the night; his confidence in his ability to make himself secure was baseless.

Some have argued that human existence is a crushing reality without hope. When things are going well, we do not give much thought to the future. We rightly are taken up in the moment. Yet these experiences do not last forever, and we come to times when our own sinfulness or that of others comes crushing in upon us. Our desire is for escape. How can we bear up under the pressure of estrangement from each other and from God? To hope, then, is to look forward to a time when what seems like the impossibility of the present can be put behind us as we enter a new day. But how does the Bible characterize that "new day"?

The best context is the gospel of John's presentation of the morning of the resurrection. There are striking similarities between the language of John 20 and the language of Genesis 1. The morning of the resurrection is referred to as the morning of the first day of the week. The women come to a place characterized as a garden. They come expecting to find a death and the disordering of life that follows from death. Instead, when they get there they find that the light has overcome the darkness and that life has sprung forth from the midst of death. John tells us that new creation has broken out, and that this new creation surpasses the old. After all, the curse that had wrought havoc in the world has now been overcome in Jesus's giving of himself. The words of the One at the tomb are a powerful expression of hope: "Why do you look for the living among the dead?" There is no greater hope than to find life in the place where we expect to find death!

God bringing life from death is a common biblical theme. At the initial creation of the world, the Spirit of God moves over a lifeless and formless void. Yet, from this, God brings forth all manner of life, from the least creature to the ones who will bear God's own image in the world. God's plan to redeem the world and restore it to right relationship begins with the call of Abraham and God's promise to him that he will become the father of a great nation. As time passes, however, Abraham begins to wonder how God is going to pull this off. He and Sarah, his wife, are getting too old for children. Once again, though, God calls forth life from death—in this case, a child from a barren and "dead" womb.

When God calls the Hebrews as a chosen people, it is not because of their inherent goodness or greatness, but rather because of their "smallness." From "no people," God calls forth and creates a people. In both the Old Testament and the New, the lesson of God's calling life from death is occasionally brought home with the ultimate object lesson: the raising back to life of one who is dead. The resurrection was the supreme act whereby God called life from death. Peter, speaking of the church, uses similar language to describe the call of Israel. Peter says that we were not a people, but God has called us together and, as a consequence, we are now a people indeed.

In addition to God's calling life from death, we can also identify some of the expectations that attend new creation. The prophets tell us, for example, that God will pour out the Spirit on people so that they might bear witness to all that God is doing. In Deuteronomy, we are given a picture of life lived out in accord with God's purposes, characterized by freedom from oppression and the absence of poverty. When Jesus lays out his kingdom vision in Luke 4, it includes freedom from oppression, good news for the poor, and sight to the blind. In Acts 2, we are given a picture of life lived out in the reality of new creation and characterized by the complete and total sharing of goods and life among believers. New creation and good news are but two aspects of the same reality—new creation *is* good news, for it carries with it a hope for human flourishing that cannot exist apart from it.

Look around and reflect on the evil and wrongdoing you find in the world. Do you see oppression, hunger (both physical and spiritual), injustice, prejudice, hostility, and struggling families? If so, fear not, for the promise of new creation is already here. If we overlook this glorious reality, we empower the forces of darkness to limit the expressions of new creation.

Let us not be bound by imaginations that are unable to peer into the darkness and see buds of fresh life and possibility waiting to be summoned forth. Rather, let us be awakened and filled with the Spirit; let us put on the armor of God. New creation is here, and we are agents of that new creation. If we may stretch the metaphor, we are secret agents of new creation—agents sent out by God to sow the seeds that will burst forth in that better tomorrow for which we all long. Before going on to the next section, read again chapter 21 of *God's Politics* and let us covenant together: *We will, with God's help, be agents of new creation.*

DAY 4 · The Christian Tradition

In every generation, Christians have embodied hope for the future, though that hope has often taken very different forms. For many of us who grew up in conservative churches, the tendency was to see the world as "going badly." Our only hope was that the long-anticipated return of Christ was just around the corner. Even if things *appeared* to be going badly, the longer-term battle had been won by God in Christ. Whatever the current state of things, we could "grit our teeth" and hang on, since the return of Jesus was just around the bend.

One of the interesting things about church history is that in every generation some have had this same belief, and with great confidence. Each generation could point to evidence in contemporary situations that was believed to be fulfilling prophecy. As one might expect, given the Bible's use of phrasing involving the "millennium," perhaps in no period were people so sure of the impending end of the world as in the late 900s. Obviously these hopes for the immediate return of Christ have been wrong so far.

However, we ought to be careful not to draw improper conclusions from this. God is indeed leading creation somewhere. More specifically, God is leading creation toward a day when, at last, things will conform to the divine intent. Such a hope dominates Christian faith throughout the church's history. Without getting into the particular theories about the end of this age, perhaps the two most helpful passages (or sets of passages) are located in the New Testament. The first is from the fourteenth chapter of John's gospel. Here, Jesus speaks of the coming day when all his followers across time will live together in the presence of God—in God's "house." The second passage is from the latter part of the book of Revelation. Although interpretations of this book are disputed, we can agree that the image of the heavenly banquet draws our attention and our sense of hope. Whatever interpretation we have of all this, hope for the future has been a consistent part of Christian faith.

In addition to the sort of hope that comes from anticipation of the kingdom of God, different movements within the church have placed hope in human activism. In fact, the church has conceived of hope in two primary ways. One group has tended to favor quietism, withdrawing from engagement in social change and simply awaiting God's intervention. The other group has tended to favor activism, focusing its efforts on driving societies to change; this group has been more likely to think they were charged to lead creation to the kingdom. On one hand, one could see how both of these movements have been mistaken. But one could also see them as correct in other ways.

In reality, Christian faith calls us to a way of being that involves both approaches. It has been described as "praying as if all depends on God and acting as if all depends on us." A robust activism that arises out of a deep confidence in God's goodness, love, and faithfulness: these are essential elements of the hope we are to have. Faithful Christian activism is always rooted in the deep understanding that it is ultimately the outpouring of God's grace that brings salvation, and that our actions for justice and peace in this world grow out of that saving grace and are empowered by it, but do not replace it.

Wherever an overly pessimistic view of the future is present, hope suffers. Circumstances can become so overwhelming that we can no longer see a way forward. When this happens, it is easy either to surrender to hopelessness or to give up on our own ability to contribute to improving those circumstances. One has to wonder, though, what it is that causes us to give up our hope and to despair. We are all familiar with the biblical injunction not to fear, and we are reminded that as we love better, we will fear less. Is it not fear, of one thing or another, that squelches our hope? And, in the end, isn't fear mostly a loss of faith?

Our task, as followers of the One who was dead and is alive again, is to be agents of hope in all that we do. To get a glimpse of why hope ought to characterize the way we view the future, take a moment to review each week's Day 5 reflection from this study. Each case includes examples of hopeful disciples who realize that their hope is ultimately in God but simultaneously act as if God's hope is worked out through them. "Pray as if all depends on God; live and act as if all depends on you!"

DAY 5 Living Examples in the Contemporary Church

There is a very real sense in which the actions that we have listed in the contemporary church in each of the other Day 5 sections are examples of hope in the contemporary church. Weeks 1 and 2 outlined hope for a better way of understanding the relationship between faith and politics and hope for a future in which the church more effectively bears witness to the Prince of Peace. In Week 3, we looked at ways in which the contemporary church seeks to make a difference on matters of economic justice. Weeks 4, 5, 6, and 7 dealt with the church's attempt to create a better future in the areas of poverty, defense of life, racism, and strengthening families.

Take a few minutes to read again those earlier vignettes. This week, be prepared to discuss how each embodies hope and how churches in your local area might begin to effect change in these areas.

Let's return to chapter 21 of *God's Politics* and look for the vignettes embedded in that presentation. Prepare to discuss these as well. In particular, select at least one of them to focus on during your time of discussion for the week. If possible, let each member of the group have ten minutes or so to make a presentation on the one that each finds most significant. Some members of the group may have their own story to tell about how a church or parachurch group they've been involved with has attempted to live out a prophetic hope for a better day. Encourage them to share that story with the rest of the group.

After working through these discussions, talk about your own perception of churches in your area as beacons of hope for the future. A movement to actualize a better day will require a whole host of churches and persons. The challenge will be to create an environment of hope coupled with a sense of faithfulness to and dependence upon God's guidance for us. Balancing the two is not easy, but it is necessary. Also, reflect on the extent to which the old paradigms of "liberal on everything" or "conservative on everything" have broken down. Many who are progressive politically are conservative to middle-of-the-road on many theological issues. As *God's Politics* suggests, the development of a "fourth option" that draws from the prophetic religious tradition to combine the strengths of both sides could be a real source of hope.

This new politics is "traditional" or "conservative" on issues of family values, sexual integrity, and personal responsibility, while being very "progressive," "populist," or even "radical" on issues like poverty and racial justice. It affirms good stewardship of the earth and its resources, supports gender equality, and is more internationally minded than nationalist—looking first to peacemaking and conflict resolution when it comes to foreign policy questions. The people it appeals to (many religious, but others not) are very strong on issues like marriage, raising kids, and individual ethics, but without being "rightwing," reactionary, or mean-spirited, and without scapegoating any group of people, like homosexuals. These people can be pro-life, pro-family, and pro-feminist, all at the same time. They think issues of "moral character" are very important, both in a politician's personal life, and in his or her policy choices. Yet they are decidedly pro-poor and pro–racial reconciliation, they are critical of purely military solutions, and they are defenders of the environment.

Prophetic politics—the new politics toward which we're working—would not be an endless argument between personal and social responsibility, but a weaving of the two together in search of the common good. The current options are deadlocked. Prophetic politics wouldn't assign all the answers to the government, the market, or the churches and charities; rather, it would patiently and creatively forge new civic partnerships where all individuals do their share and everybody does what they do best. Prophetic politics wouldn't debate whether our strategies should be cultural, political, or economic, but would show how they must be all three, led by a moral compass. It is a vision that would find new agreements and new common ground solutions on the issues affecting our country.

You will notice that we've left the next two pages blank. Over the course of the next few months, engage in your own "ministry of hope." Then use these pages to customize your copy of *Living God's Politics* to include your story of how you are embodying hope for a deeper realization of the kingdom of God.

My "ministry of hope"

DAY 6 — Putting Faith into Action

Nothing is more powerful in social activism than embodying a confidence that the best is yet ahead of us. We have discussed many issues in the course of this book, and all can be seen in two ways: as threats and challenges or as exciting opportunities to help in creating that better tomorrow. By becoming socially active in the ways mentioned in previous Day 6 sections, you testify to all those around you, indeed to the entire world, that you have not lost hope and that while you might recognize the challenge and the impinging darkness, you have decided to be an agent of the light. Every time you engage in one of those activities that we have identified as "living God's politics," remind yourself that you have chosen to take the path of hope and be a part of the solution rather than a part of the problem.

What specific things can you do to integrate your activism into an overall message of hope? First, make sure that your educational events are aimed both to convict and to inspire. Don't pull any punches when it comes to identifying problems and their severity. But, at the same time, nurture a budding optimism that the light is dawning and that your audience can sign on to help bring the light to the rest of the world. Likewise, when you engage in a dramatic presentation, be sure that the identification of the problems is tempered with optimism and hope. Do not leave your audience broken and disenchanted with the future.

Second, in writing letters and opinion pieces, whenever possible offer a vision for the future. It is far too easy to become mired in the politics of complaint, and there is surely much to complain about. However, do not forego opportunities to offer better ideas for tomorrow. Be on the lookout for things to affirm, things that offer hope for tomorrow, and then use your letter- and opinion-writing skills to rally the hope of others.

Finally, surround yourself with friends, and be there for each other. Bear each other's disappointments and encourage each other. Rarely will everyone in a group be discouraged at the same time. This helps guarantee that even on the darkest days someone will be able to see the silver lining.

DAY 7 — Group Meeting and Reflection

1. "The biblical prophets were never just complaining; they were imagining a newer world." *God's Politics* (page 47) puts this in the context of offering proposals rather than simply raising objections. What steps would you take to prevent efforts to forge a better tomorrow from being hijacked by complaining?

2. Pick one of the books of the prophets (such as Amos, Joel, or Micah) and read through it quickly. How would you characterize the prophets' criticism as well as their constructive proposals?

3. Reflect on the notion of prophecy as "articulating moral truth." Does this concept offer guidance to how Christians might engage politics? What strengths and weaknesses might be inherent in this approach?

4. *God's Politics* outlines three major political options and argues for a fourth. These are: (1) conservative on everything, (2) liberal on everything, (3) libertarian, which is liberal on social issues and conservative on fiscal issues, and (4) conservative on most social issues and liberal on most fiscal/economic issues. Would this option provide a more consistent biblical position? Why or why not?

5. In a recent op-ed piece, one well-known writer objected to the hard "liberal" vs. "conservative" distinctions. This writer went on to observe that few folks are genuinely either conservative or liberal on all the issues. How might we begin to restore some dignity to the dialogue by moving away from these easy categories?

6. What do you make of the popular claim that "secular humanists" are the underlying threat to our culture? First, how would you identify "secular humanists"? Second, what positions would you expect them to hold? Finally, how would those positions threaten the culture in general and Christian faith in particular?

7. How would you characterize "hope," and how does this concept play a role in our daily lives and daily decision making?

8. Discuss the various examples of hope in this chapter. Which one(s) do you think best make the point? Why?

9. Review the predictions on pages 368 to 372 of *God's Politics*. What three would you choose to invest yourself in realizing? Why? What concrete steps would you take?

A Summary of Social Activism Techniques

JUST ADD CONSCIOUSNESS: A GUIDE TO SOCIAL ACTIVISM

By Liz Carty, Jane Fleming, and Stephanie Seidel

CONTENTS

This appendix[1] focuses on activism opportunities for students, but all of the ideas can be applied among a wide range of age groups, issues, and organizations. With a little tweaking, you can make any of the following suggestions succeed for *your* group!

CONDUCT A LETTER-WRITING CAMPAIGN

It takes only a piece of paper and a pen to be an effective advocate. People often ask, "Will my letter make a difference?" Yes, it will! Congressional staff members say all it takes is ten to twenty handwritten letters to draw their attention to an issue.

Since writing a letter takes only a few minutes and requires limited supplies, it is the perfect advocacy tool to take anywhere on campus or in your community. Write letters at a group meeting, after class, or at a related event. National, state, and local organizations that follow the issues you care about can provide helpful information, such as sample letters and fact sheets. Also, check out the Cyber-Activism section of this guide for information on how to effectively use email to communicate with legislators.

If you're an active young person, you can write to the representatives of your school's district and state, or of your hometown. Check out the Web sites listed in the reference section below to find your members of Congress by zip code. If you're hosting a campus-wide letter-writing table, don't worry about knowing the address of each member of Congress. Students can always write to the representative and senators from their school's district and state.

For more targeted letters, write to your representatives who are on key committees. Web sites—including the ones listed in the reference section below—and congressional guides in public libraries list the committees each member of Congress serves on and explain what the committees represent. Don't be tempted to write to a key representative to whom you have no connections. Many congressional offices disregard mail that is not from a student or constituent in the district or state.

Most congressional offices respond to handwritten letters with information about their positions on the issue. If your elected official is not supportive, find answers to his or her concerns. If your representative takes your recommended action, write a thank-you note. It shows you care enough to watch how your representative responds. Be sure to stay in touch with that person throughout the year, track the progress of your issue in Congress, and let your representative know you voted on election day!

Important contact information:

Representative _____
U.S. House of Representatives
Washington, D.C. 20515

Senator _____
U.S. Senate
Washington, D.C. 20510

Capitol Switchboard: (202) 224-3121

President _____
The White House
1600 Pennsylvania Avenue NW
Washington, D.C. 20500

White House Comment Line: (202) 456-1111

Sample Letter

The following sample shows the essential elements of a persuasive letter to an elected representative. (Note that the numbers shown in the letter correspond to the numbered tips that follow.)

The Honorable Robert Smith
U.S. House of Representatives
Washington, D.C. 20515

Dear Representative Smith (1):

Thank you for supporting the recent House legislation to increase the minimum wage by $1 over two years (2). As you know, the debate is not over yet (3). In this critical time, I urge you to continue to push for passage of an increase in the minimum wage of at least $1 over the next two years (4).

One in ten households in the U.S. cannot afford the food their families need. In my work at Shepherd's Table in southwest Houston, I have met many hard-working families whose full-time job does not make ends meet (5). A higher minimum wage would help these families make work pay and put food on their tables.

Your leadership on these issues is very important. I look forward to working with you to help end hunger in our world.

Sincerely,

Ann McCurry
123 Stella Link
Houston, TX 77012 (6)

Tips

1. Always start with the proper title: Honorable or Representative/Senator.
2. Be brief and courteous. Many effective letters are only four or five sentences long. If you can, begin your letter by thanking your representative for a recent vote or speech that you appreciated. Check out voting records to find out about votes you favor and how elected officials have voted.
3. Time your message to be most effective. The legislative process list on page 134 (under "Time Your Message") shows at what key times to write your letters to have the most impact.
4. Be specific. Identify the particular legislative proposal you are writing about, and briefly explain why you want your representative to support or oppose it.
5. Write your own letter and personally sign it. Think about what makes you change your mind on an issue. It is not always the fact-filled argument, but a concerned person who shares his or her own experiences and observations.
6. Put your return address on the letter as well as on the envelope. Most congressional offices respond to constituent mail with a letter. Your address shows your member of Congress that you are a constituent, as either a student or a registered voter in the congressional district or state.

References

www.vote-smart.org is a nonpartisan organization that tracks voting records and contact information.

thomas.loc.gov supplies research on specific legislation. It is a service of the Library of Congress.

www.networklobby.org includes tools for lobbying Congress and local elected officials, as well as the steps to a bill becoming a law.

www.bread.org is the Web site for Bread for the World, a grassroots advocacy organization that tracks hunger-related legislation and shows how members of Congress are voting on key issues.

www.sojo.net contains action alerts on critical issues of the day.

Advice from a Seasoned Letter-Writer

After educating ourselves as a group on the issue, we plan our letter-writing campaign about a month in advance. We set up our letter-writing table for three consecutive days, usually Monday, Tuesday, and Wednesday of the same week. We set the table outside, or just inside, a different building each day for about four hours during a popular time.

At the table, we are always sure to have plenty of paper, pens, envelopes, sample letters (which should be only a paragraph or two), clipboards, and several lists of representatives and senators by state. We make posters with facts and a sample letter around the table to attract attention to it. Making sure no one can pass the table without looking at it is key.

We always have two volunteers behind the table, coordinating and distributing the materials and answering questions. The volunteers behind the table make the letter-writing campaign run smoothly and without confusion.

We also have at least two to three volunteers in front of the table, with clipboards and paper in hand, actively approaching people. The volunteers in front of the table are crucial to getting a high number of letters. If people aren't asked to write, they most likely won't ask what's going on. An effective way to confront people is to approach confidently, with a friendly smile, explain the issue in one or two sentences, and then ask if they could take a minute to write a letter. We continuously emphasize to everyone that their letter can make a difference in the lives of hungry people. This is particularly important on campuses, since many young people don't vote because they feel that they can't make a difference.

One last piece of advice for your letter-writing campaign: Never sit! Those working the campaign are supposed to be the ones most committed to the campaign and most excited to be a part of it.

—TERRY MAMBU, VILLANOVA UNIVERSITY

MEET WITH YOUR MEMBER OF CONGRESS

Few actions can match the effectiveness of meeting with your member of Congress face to face, whether at his or her Washington office, a district office, or a community forum. Elected officials are strongly affected by the opinions of constituents who are committed enough to a specific concern to arrange a visit.

Tips

Call your representative's appointment secretary to schedule a meeting time. Tell the scheduler what topic(s) you want to cover, and be sure to mention how many people you'll have with you. Some congressional offices are small. If you're bringing a large group, the office staff may need to prepare an alternative meeting space. Small groups are okay; you don't need to promise a crowd.

If you're a student, organize a diverse group from your campus's congressional district to attend. Consider what may help persuade your representative. For example, if your member of Congress has a particular religious persuasion, invite prominent community leaders from that faith tradition to accompany you on the visit.

You don't have to be a policy expert, but you do have to be well prepared. You should be conversant with the main points of the legislation you're addressing without engaging congressional staff in a heated debate. Prepare main talking points that are key to your position.

Ask your member of Congress to take a specific action. As an active citizen, you may be tempted to bring many issues into your visit, but you will be more effective if you focus on one or two main issues in the short time you have.

You may be told, either before or at the meeting, that you will meet with a legislative aide instead of your representative. Don't be discouraged. Aides are usually well informed and offer critical advice that will help shape the representative's position on a range of issues.

You may have only a few minutes with the member of Congress or aide, so keep it short and stick to your talking points. If you have more time, you can discuss additional points about the issue and hear your host's views and opinions.

After your visit, stay in touch with the office by sending a thank-you note. This is your opportunity to build a relationship with your member of Congress. Follow up in a timely manner with any requested materials and information. If the member of Congress commits to take a specific action, keep an eye on it.

CARRY OUT A PHONE-CALLING CAMPAIGN

Sometimes legislation moves so quickly on Capitol Hill that there's no time to write letters or arrange a visit; in that case, telephone calls are a fast and personal way to express your concerns.

Tips

Call your member of Congress at his or her Washington, D.C., office. Call the Capitol switchboard at (202) 224-3121, and ask for your member.

Identify yourself and your affiliation (your school, your group, or your hometown).

Ask to speak with the member of Congress or the legislative aide handling the issue. If neither person is available, leave a message with your name, address, and phone number with the receptionist.

If you're generating numerous calls, ask callers to leave a message with the receptionist. Since you're trying to build a positive relationship with the staff, you don't want to overload the legislative aide with too many calls. A few callers can contact the aide to let him or her know that there are many messages with the receptionist about the issue.

Keep your message brief. As when writing an effective letter, be sure to make a specific request of your representative.

Be prepared to have background information on your issue available to send to the office if there are any questions. Contact organizations like Sojourners, Bread for the World, and Oxfam America that follow the issues you care about for helpful resources.

Setting Up a Phone Tree

To generate a persuasive number of calls, form a telephone-tree network of activists to pass a message along to your member of Congress at crucial times in the legislative process. Every person on the network delivers a suggested message to the congressional office. This flood of calls can sway an undecided vote or convince a legislator who wonders where the public stands on the issue.

- Choose a coordinator to maintain and activate the phone tree. This person will pass along the message to several key people, who will continue to pass the message on to other members.
- Make a list of the current phone numbers of your members.
- Select a few key people to be responsible for calling up to ten people.
- Give these key people the names and phone numbers of members to be called.
- Be sure to pass along a short and concise message. Since the message will go through the tree, it needs to be clear enough for everyone to write it down and repeat it to the congressional office.
- Keep your phone tree current and working. After the phone tree has been activated, the last person on the tree should call the coordinator to verify that the message made it through the network.

TIME YOUR MESSAGE

Whether you are conducting a letter-writing campaign, activating a phone tree, or visiting with your member of Congress, be sure to time your action to have the most impact. You can exert the most influence by taking action at these key points in the legislative process:

- Before a bill is introduced, you can help generate support for the legislation and urge your member of Congress to be a sponsor of the bill.
- When a bill is introduced, urge your representative to cosponsor it. As a cosponsor, your member of Congress can show his or her support for the bill before it comes up for a vote. A long list of both Republicans and Democrats shows broad and unified support for a bill.
- A key stage in the legislative process is when a committee or subcommittee is "marking up" the bill—that is, considering the individual provisions and making requested changes. If your member of Congress is on the committee or subcommittee, be sure to voice your opinion about provisions you would like to have removed or changed.
- When the bill goes to the House or Senate floor for a final vote, urge your members of Congress to support it or oppose it.
- For the status of the bill you are following, check out www.vote-smart.org, thomas .loc.gov, and organizational Web sites that track the issue you care about. (See "Getting Involved," the section immediately following this appendix, for a comprehensive listing of organizations.)

USE THE MEDIA

Tips

Develop and maintain a "press list" (which consists of the reporter's name, title, address, phone number, email address, fax number, and deadlines). Be sure to include wire services (Independent Media, Associated Press, Reuters), local and regional newspapers/magazines, local e-zines, local TV news and talk shows, local cable stations, and special interest publications (ethnic, college, high school, religious, punk, trade, professional).

Meet with reporters, DJs, talk-show hosts, and editors personally, to develop a relationship and establish rapport. See where their interests lie. Follow up with phone calls to give them story ideas or to give them an update on your program.

Read reporters' stories. Give them feedback—make them aware you are reading, watching, and listening to them. By reading their stories, you will know the best person to contact for your media outreach.

Be prepared to give reporters facts, accurate information, quotes, historical background information, and if possible an "exclusive," meaning they are the reporter breaking the news.

Return reporters' calls as soon as possible.

Use all the "free" resources the media offers, such as the calendar column, op-ed pieces, letters to the editor, press releases, and public service announcements.

Op-Ed Pieces

Op-ed pieces are a highly effective way of expressing your opinion in the newspaper. Op-eds are opinion pieces that appear opposite editorial pages. At their best, they are persuasive, well-thought-out, well-written, short in length (usually about 800 words) but longer than a letter to the editor, and authored by a high-profile person or someone who has experience with the issue. The op-ed should be timely and present a strong, well-informed position supported by facts.

Letters to the Editor

Letters to the editor represent your perspective in the local newspaper and can be a counter-argument for articles that you don't agree with. They also:

- Reach a large audience
- Are monitored by elected officials and other decision makers
- Create an impression of widespread support for or against an issue

The following guidelines will help you write an effective letter to the editor:

Be Direct

Make one point (or at most two) in your letter. Because letters are often edited, state the point clearly in the first paragraph. Start with a catchy opening, and use the active voice.

Be Timely

Address a specific issue of current importance, or take on an article, editorial, or letter that recently appeared in the paper you're writing to. If the latter, refer to the title, date, and author of the piece you're agreeing with or disputing.

Support Your Facts

If the topic you're addressing is controversial, consider sending documentation along with your letter—but don't overload the editors with too much information. Refute or support specific statements, address relevant facts that are ignored, and avoid attacking the reporter or the newspaper.

Find a Local Angle

Try to explain the issue's local or personal impact, to bring the issue home for readers. Look at the letters that appear in your local paper. If a certain type of letter is printed more often than others, try to follow that approach.

Know Your Audience

Familiarize yourself with the coverage and editorial position of the paper. Be professional: this is not a letter to a friend. Write for the community that reads the paper—for example, don't try to discuss technical terms if the audience won't know the technicalities of the issue.

Maximize Use of the Letter

Send the letter to neighborhood, alternative, high school, and college papers. The smaller the publication, the more likely it will get published. Get other people to write letters as well. If your letter doesn't get published, perhaps someone else's letter on the same topic will.

Pay Attention to Logistics

Check and adhere to the newspaper's letter specifications, especially regarding word limits. Write in short paragraphs (three sentences long), find out the editor's name, include your own contact information (name, address, phone number, email address), and type or email the letter.

Press Releases

A press release is a full and succinct account of your story/event, usually one or two pages, and should be written as a news article. Press releases help editors write an article. In fact, some small community newspapers will actually print your press release "as is."

- The first paragraph is the lead. In one to three sentences, it answers, "Who, what, when, where, why, and how?" The lead must grab the editor's attention.
- The second paragraph is the bridge. It names the source of the information and serves as a transition for the more detailed information.
- The third paragraph is the body. The information given in the lead is explained in detail in the body. This is the place to add quotations, facts not included in the lead, and general information on the organization.
- Finally, a photograph can be included to grab attention.

You may want to follow up any press release with a phone call and/or a personal visit. That additional contact may increase a reporter's or editor's interest in the story.

Logistics

Type the release, double-spaced, on letterhead with wide margins. At the top include the name and phone numbers for the contact person, the date and time for the story's release, and a short headline. When there is more than one page, type "–MORE–" at the bottom. The last page should conclude with "###" or "–END–." Fax the release to the newspaper's editor or to a reporter with whom you have a relationship.

Public Service Announcements

Public service announcements (PSAs) are short messages that radio and television stations air free of charge on behalf of community organizations. Contact your local public service director at the television and radio stations serving your area for the exact requirements for placing a PSA. That person may even be able to help you produce the PSA.

- Make the PSA personal and give it a sense of immediacy, remembering that PSAs are designed to be *heard*.
- Try to grab the interest and attention of the target audience.
- Use active voice and present tense when possible.
- Inform listeners/viewers how they can contact your organization—include your phone number and Web site. Be prepared for increased calls.
- Include accurate facts, dates, and names. Answer the questions, "Who, what, why, when, where, and how?"
- Read your PSA aloud. Does it read smoothly? Are the words too difficult to pronounce comfortably?

- Fit your message to the time slot: on average, 10 seconds = 25 words, 30 seconds = 75 words, 60 seconds = 150 words.
- Send a thank-you letter to the public service director and/or the DJ or TV host that airs the PSA, and ask your friends to do the same. Station personnel like positive feedback!
- If you're hoping that your PSA will engender television coverage, remember that TV stories are short and simple (usually only thirty to sixty seconds); the assignment editor often decides the day's coverage the day *before* and thus needs advance warning; and generally only events held before 3 P.M. can be covered on the day itself.

ORGANIZE A TEACH-IN

Visualize young people gathered in a church or a community center in the 1960s to listen to Howard Thurman and Martin Luther King Jr. teaching about how to organize and describing the underlying issues of racism. They were conducting what are often called "teach-ins"—probably the most successful teach-ins of the previous century. It's your turn now!

- Decide what you want to do. This will depend upon your audience and how ambitious you are. You can show a movie, invite a speaker, have a forum of students and professors, or do a workshop on a specific skill or topic. You can even do all of these things over a few days and call the result a conference. One model is to host a two-part series: at the first session you could show a video, for example, and at the second host an interactive workshop.
- Reserve a room, confirm the speakers (have a backup plan in case they don't show!), check to make sure you're not competing with a concert or other popular event, get any needed visual aids (video, flip charts, etc.), make (or order from a national organization) educational pamphlets, and get food and drinks.
- Get the word out! Why bother organizing a teach-in if no one comes? Set an attendance goal. Put up posters or write the information with chalk on sidewalks or chalkboards. Gather up your friends. Go to other meetings where people might be interested in the topic, and tell them about the teach-in. If you're on a campus, ask professors to give extra credit to students who attend the teach-in and write a paper for class.
- Create your agenda. Make your teach-in fun and interactive. Do an interesting icebreaker to get the teach-in started.
- Conduct the teach-in! Get participants' contact information to keep them informed on any next steps that develop. Offer at least one way they can immediately take action. For example, they might be able to send online faxes before they leave. (See also the earlier information about conducting a letter-writing campaign.)

Not all teach-ins go by that name. *Open mikes* and *speak-outs* are great ways to maximize young people's voices on controversial issues and to encourage them to exercise their rights to free speech. If you're a student, find out if your campus has a "free speech zone." Common areas like the cafeteria are the perfect setting. The downside to this activity is the lack of control. Having a clear message will help, but remember that you want people to express their views. Keep in mind the noise you will create, and make sure you're not disruptive to others.

Debates and *panel discussions* are a great way to get both sides of an issue aired, so make sure you truly have all points of view equally represented. In these forums, as in any type of teach-in, be respectful of opposing views.

SAMPLE
Agenda for an International Monetary Fund (IMF) Teach-In

Do introductions. Have all participants tell their first name and say one word that describes why they are at the teach-in. (10 minutes)

Check labels. Have people check the clothing label of their neighbor, looking for the country of origin. Have people describe the conditions under which they think the clothes were made. (10 minutes)

Educate. Show video introducing the IMF. Review your prepared notes on the flip chart about what "structural adjustment" is and how many countries are in debt. (20 minutes)

Break into small groups. Break into groups of four and discuss what you thought about the video and the role of the IMF. (10 minutes)

Brainstorm. Regroup and list action steps the group can take to combat the problems created by the IMF. (15 minutes)

Determine next steps. End the teach-in by having everyone write on a piece of paper one action step that he or she will take. Ask people to display their action steps at home to remind themselves of commitments made. (5 minutes)

COORDINATE A DEMONSTRATION

Young people often take an active role in planning and participating in large-scale demonstrations in Washington, D.C. Smaller demonstrations happen daily on campuses and in local communities. The book *The Future Is Ours* by John W. Bartlett suggests keeping the following in mind when deciding on what type of demonstration to hold: you *rally* for something you support, and you *protest* against something you oppose.

Consider the following types of demonstrations:

Vigil. Typically a quiet event at night with candles to honor and remember lost lives or victims. Example: Take Back the Night.

Sit-in. An event where people occupy a public or private space, typically a decision maker's office, and don't leave until a stated demand is met or negotiated. Example: a sit-in held at a university's president's office because of sweatshop labor being used to make the school's apparel (see below).

March. A group of people, holding signs and chanting, who walk from a designated point to a communal destination in order for a message to be conveyed to the public and to decision makers. Example: Million Man March.

Picket line. People, holding signs and chanting, who march outside a building or office. Example: union workers on strike.

SAMPLE
Protesting Sweatshop Labor

Putting pressure on the university administration to ban sweatshop labor from being used to produce campus products at Georgetown University in Washington, D.C., really gained momentum when a student from the university visited a factory in Latin America and saw a cap with the Georgetown logo. Student activist Michael Levinson said, "The sit-in at the president's office that we organized came after months of educating ourselves, the campus, and the administration about the issues. We won full public disclosure, meaning that we know the locations of the factories that are making Georgetown apparel. We also created a 'code of conduct' that all of our vendors must agree to follow." To date, more than eighty campuses have had similar success.

Civil Disobedience

The basic definition of civil disobedience is the refusal to obey civil laws regarded as unjust, usually by employing methods of passive resistance or by using nonviolent tactics to (indirectly) protest laws, actions, or policies—for example, by peacefully violating *other* laws. The ACLU describes civil disobedience as the vigorous public expression of controversial views. It is a cherished and vital part of American democracy, protected by the First Amendment to our Constitution. Nonviolent protest—even if unlawful—should always be met by a nonviolent response by police. For more information and ideas, check out the *Handbook for Nonviolence* by the War Resisters League.

It's important to remember that (1) all types of demonstrations require planning, and (2) a demonstration needs to be part of an overall strategy.

Tips

Core group of organizers. Assign specific roles to people, such as media representative, outreach director, permit coordinator, and publicity manager.

Turnout. Numbers are important, because the public and the media look to the number of people you can mobilize and equate that to the level of support you have for your issue. Develop a specific strategy, including a goal for the number of people you will recruit to attend the demonstration. Check out the "Get the Word Out" section (below) for ideas on recruiting people.

Permits and officials. Know your rights regarding use of space on campus or in the community. Gather all necessary permits so that the protest is not shut down for a logistical reason. Talk to the campus or community police about the demonstration. If you're planning to risk arrest, have trained legal observers at the event to take notes. The ACLU (www.aclu.org) is extremely helpful in clarifying your rights and responsibilities.

Equipment. Make sure you have everything you need (megaphones, poster board, first aid kit, tarps for rain, information flyers) and that the electrical and sound equipment works.

Press packets. Prepare folders for the press with detailed fact sheets, letters to the editor written by your group, press releases, and recommendations for a solution to the issue for which you're rallying. Make sure you include a one-pager with major points for those reporters who need a quick reference. See "Use the Media" (above) for more tips.

Slogans and chanting. Come up with catchy slogans the group can quickly learn. Get participants to chant loudly but not belligerently. Keep in mind that you want to educate, not alienate, the passersby.

Signs. Make signs that have bold letters and a clear message. Most passersby don't have the time or inclination to stop and chat with demonstrators, so it's important that your signs catch their attention and send a clear message. Once you catch someone's attention, that person is more likely to listen to the facts or hold a hand out to receive a fact sheet.

Puppets. Life-size puppets dramatize your issue and serve as a great visual for the media while the demonstration is happening.

Speakers. Gather a diverse group of people to speak, including those who are directly affected by the issue. Aim to involve young and old people, people of varying races and levels of education, and varying physical abilities (make sure they have accessibility). Give short time slots for each speaker—this is a demonstration, not a teach-in.

Timing. Hold your demonstration around a time when decision makers will be near you—for example, at a convention.

Weather. Consider a backup plan if your demonstration is scheduled to be outside. You might, for example, assign a rain date on all your flyers and promotional materials.

Visibility. Hold the demonstration where there's lots of traffic (cars or pedestrians).

Options. Consult www.interlog.com/~ksimons/198.htm for a comprehensive list of methods of nonviolent action. Give serious consideration to which method would achieve the best results for your particular issue.

TAKE CREATIVE ACTION

In today's busy world, how do you get people to stop and take notice? Creative action can be a great way to get attention and help to educate others about an issue.

Tips

Focus your creative action on a specific target and message.

Creative actions don't have to be theatrical; you can make a banner, billboard, or anything visual, for example.

Research history—the civil rights movement (Martin Luther King Jr.), nonviolent actions (Gandhi), apartheid (South Africa)—to learn more about direct action techniques already taken, including challenges and successes.

Here are some examples:

100 Chairs[2]

To demonstrate the growing wealth divide in the United States, line up 100 chairs in a high-traffic place on campus. Have 10 people spread out over 70 chairs (lying down, stretching out) while 90 people squeeze themselves onto the remaining 30 chairs. This shows that 10 percent have 70 percent of the wealth, while all the rest (90 percent) have only 30 percent of the wealth.

You can modify this exercise using 10 chairs and 10 people. You can also use this same concept to demonstrate other statistics, adjusting the number of chairs and people as needed.

Human Bar Graph[3]

Have 100 students line up to represent the president's salary, while a single person represents a janitor's salary. A sign or spokesperson explains what's represented by the human bar graph.

Interactive Theater

Create a controversial five-minute skit on some issue (for example, hunger, homelessness, racism, sexism). Act out the whole skit once for your audience. Then repeat the skit, allowing people in the audience to say "Stop" at any point. The person stopping the skit then replaces a character he or she chooses and changes the play. Hold a discussion at the end.

Guerrilla Theater

Create a dramatization that highlights your issue. For example, when Georgetown University students were protesting sweatshop labor in the production of campus wear, they staged a fashion show in a high-traffic area of campus. Students donned clothes with the university logo, and as they strutted down the walkway, the emcee talked about the substandard wages paid to workers who assembled the clothes. Guerrilla theater was often used in the 1980s to dramatize death-squad abductions in Central America: students would stage an "abduction" in the cafeteria. This creative action engaged many students in Central American solidarity work.

Invisible Theater

Create a situation that will draw onlookers into a discussion about an important issue. For example: two people go into a clothing store where sweatshop labor is being used to manufacture the clothes. The cell phone of one person rings. "Hello. Yeah, I'm here shopping at [Name of Store].... What? You're kidding! They use sweatshop labor to produce their clothes? Hey [to the second shopper, in a loud voice so that others can hear], did you know that [Name of Store] uses sweatshop labor to make their clothes?" Draw the other shoppers and staff people into a discussion of living wages as a human right.

Modeling

Make an issue real for people by modeling it in visible, physical form. For example, build shantytown housing on campus to demonstrate how people not earning a decent wage are forced to live in many countries. Sleep out in your quad to demonstrate homelessness in the United States.

References

www.sojo.net for information and alerts on budget and economic justice activities
www.faireconomy.org for information on a campus living wage campaign
www.globalexchange.org for updates on boycotts and demonstrations
www.coopamerica.org for listings of ethical companies and boycotts

INITIATE CYBER-ACTIVISM

Activists today have a tool that the previous generation didn't: the Internet. Savvy computer users can use the Internet to help them organize an event, disseminate information, and contact their representatives.

Rallying a Large Group of People for an Event (Virtual Organizing)

As the November 1999 Seattle WTO and the April 2000 IMF/World Bank protests showed, the Internet can be an extremely powerful organizing tool.

Tips

Create a Web page to go with your event. Make your emails short, and direct people to a hyperlink to the Web for more details. Make sure your page is always up-to-date.

Find a service provider that allows people to easily subscribe to your listserv (try groups .yahoo.com or groups.msn.com).

Creating a Listserv/Electronic Mailing List

A listserv is a single email address that actually contains your "list" of email addresses. Listservs are a way to discuss issues, organize, and share ideas and resources with a group of people. You can create your own (for your particular event/cause) and also join existing ones to keep up on the issues. Make sure to actively collect email addresses at all your events, and use your listserv to keep activists informed and connected.

Find out more by looking at these cyber-activist Web sites with resources for virtual organizing:

www.netaction.org/training/, which offers NetAction's virtual activist training reader

www.afj.org, Alliance for Justice, which offers e-advocacy for nonprofits

www.organizenow.net, which offers technology and training to advance and sustain social change

Creating connections among the local activists in your city/town can be an important way to sustain you in your work. Check out www.idealist.org to search for the activists near you. Get together and support each other in your work. This can be a great social network as well!

Lobbying Your Representative Online

Even though most representatives have email addresses and even Web pages, legislators usually respond better to the traditional lobbying tactics of visits, letters, phone calls, faxes, and postcards. It's best to experiment with a variety of tactics to see which works with your representative(s).

When you send an email to your representative, always include your mailing address in your email. Many emails will be taken seriously only if you include your physical address, because that's the only way a legislator knows you're in his or her district.

Take a look at "Conduct a Letter-Writing Campaign" (above). An effective email letter should follow the same guidelines as a snail-mail letter.

Use the following Web sites for information on how to contact your federal, state, and local representatives:

www.senate.gov to contact the U.S. Senate

www.house.gov to contact the U.S House of Representatives

thomas.loc.gov to contact the Library of Congress

www.vote-smart.org to access a nonpartisan organization that tracks voting records, campaign finance information, issue positions, performance evaluations, and contact information

FINANCE YOUR ACTIVIST PROJECTS

Money—we all need it for the activities we want to organize. Often activists are called the "out-of-pocket" sector because we use our own money to fund our projects. However, there are ways to fund activism without going broke!

Tips

Check with activist organizations in your community and with national and international nonprofits and businesses. Often they have funds to support a specific issue. They can at least send you free educational materials to distribute at your event.

Look up foundations on the Web. There are many that support young people and activists. For example, check out www.foundationcenter.org.

If you're a student, try to get funds from your campus—perhaps from the student activity center, student government, or the political science department (or other departments relevant to your issue). Make a pitch to the university committee that plans speakers and alumni events.

Hold a fundraiser. Make it fun. Have a theme party, cookout, house party, rave, talent show, or car wash. Check out www.alternativebreaks.com for other great ideas.

GET THE WORD OUT

Publicity is a key element in the success of any campaign. Build a movement by educating people about your issue and then mobilizing them to join your events. Be consistent, frequent, and creative with your marketing tactics.

Tips

Create a core concept that can be expressed in seven words and put it on everything you publish. For example, a group of young people working on body image and eating disorders came up with "Mobilizing young people to eliminate eating disorders."

Make up baseball cards with the "villains" or "heroes" of the movement, and include statistics, facts, and interesting information about the people on the cards.

Write personal letters to people inviting them to participate, telling them the specific skills they possess and how those skills could be used in the project.

Use chalk on sidewalks, streets, and chalkboards to advertise an event or message.

Run a classified advertisement with the heading, "Looking for Activists."

Create a controversial billboard ad.

Post your flyers on community billboards, corporate bulletin boards, and/or nonprofit bulletin boards.

If you're a student, ask professors and teachers if you can speak for two minutes before or after a class.

Get a magazine to run an ad for you. This requires relationship building.

Ask the campus and community radio and TV stations to run a PSA.

Run your campaign in waves. The first week you put up posters with one line or symbol. The next week you add on to that line or symbol. The next week you add on to the previous week. By the fourth week the flyer should convey a complete message.

Create a symbol that represents your movement; then make stickers incorporating that symbol, and post them everywhere.

Post your flyers in restaurants and bars, always asking permission first.

Make up buttons and bumper stickers, and hand them out.

Produce T-shirts with your message and Web address—make them funny or controversial.

Give away compact disks with a label that has your message and Web address.

Use the Internet—emails, banner ads, and pop-up messages.

Hand out flyers, T-shirts, bumper stickers, or posters—all with your message and Web site—at a concert.

Ask a store if you can use their window for a display on your issue and/or event.

You know those free postcard stands at restaurants and coffee shops? Get a postcard printed for your issue—it's not expensive.

For protests, get rain parkas made up with your message on the back.

Order fortune cookies that have your message or facts about your issue inside.

When ordering T-shirts, stickers, business cards, or any promotional material, consider having the articles union-made to ensure that they aren't made using sweatshop labor. Check out www.unitehere.org (click on "buy union") for a resource in your community.

Use Flyers

Flyers are expected and necessary tools of publicity. They can be used creatively, consistently, and frequently. In preparation for the Oxfam Hunger Banquet at one university, students hung colorful flyers with simple, catchy phrases that conveyed their most immediate message in order to gain the attention of lots of casual passersby. Doors and walls along stairwells are typically excellent spots because it's hard to dismiss flyers when they're hung at eye level. Students can also hang informative flyers in bathroom stalls, on bulletin boards, near drinking fountains, in the library lobby, and near tables at the student union. Consistency and use of your campus's unique resources will help ensure that you've reached many people.

Flyers are a great chance to inform and convince people of the importance of your issue with thoughtful and creative art and words. They might include pictures, tables, graphs, copied articles, and a collage of facts—anything with the potential to really move the reader.

Plan Ahead and Follow Through

Be sure to plan ahead and follow through. Three weeks before the Oxfam Hunger Banquet mentioned above, the sponsoring organization announced the date, time, and place of its upcoming event. They had a representative attend the student government's weekly meetings to publicize; and they advertised through the Residence Life Office, which may require student RAs and hall counselors to decorate bulletin boards or plan educational and service hall programs. Asking these students, and other organizations like fraternities, sororities, and health- and gender-related student groups, to post information or promote an event can really increase participation. Cosponsoring events and pooling funds with other student organizations to bring a high-profile guest speaker to the campus or community can also result in successful events and memorable experiences.

Be Creative

Effective publicity usually means attracting the optimal number of participants. To do this, creative advertising that draws a diverse and large crowd is recommended. As an example, to gain attention for an upcoming international festival on campus, the hosting organization obtained school permission to borrow golf carts and play music as organizers safely drove around campus passing out flyers between scheduled class times. This creative approach grabbed the attention of many.

Getting Involved

Now that you've read this book, we encourage you to become involved in your community. Here are some organizations that are active around the country and provide information on how you can become involved. They cover the political spectrum, and many of them address multiple issues discussed in this book.

> Sojourners/Call to Renewal
> 3333 14th Street NW, Suite 200
> Washington, DC 20010
> Phone: (202) 328-8842 or (800) 714-7474
> Fax: (202) 328-8757
> Web site: www.sojo.net and www.calltorenewal.org
> e-mail: sojourners@sojo.net and ctr@calltorenewal.org

For free regular updates, please sign up for the SojoMail e-zine at www.sojo.net.

Sojourners and Call to Renewal share an overarching statement of mission: to articulate the biblical call to social justice, inspiring hope and building a movement to transform individuals, communities, the church, and the world.

Sojourners, established in 1971, is a nonprofit organization whose mission is to offer a voice and vision for social change. Sojourners attracts a diverse group of evangelicals, Catholics, and Protestant Christians, as well as others who are united on issues of justice and peace.

Call to Renewal is a national network of churches, faith-based organizations, and individuals working to overcome poverty in America. Through local and national partnerships with groups from across the theological and political spectrum, Call to Renewal convenes the broadest table of Christians focused on antipoverty efforts.

The Covenant for a New America is a policy platform intended to move beyond the debate between Left and Right by seeking to create a common commitment to identify, pursue, and bring about real solutions to poverty. The covenant lifts up both personal and social responsibility with policies that address the individual decisions and social systems that trap people in poverty. It identifies policies that move beyond looking solely to charity or only to government. It acknowledges that budgets are moral documents and that budget priorities can help or hurt poor people—and that negative family and cultural values also impact low-income people.

A combination of policies in four major areas will allow the covenant's vision to engage concretely with the policymaking process. We seek changes that will promote (1) a living family income for all who work; (2) the rebuilding of neighborhoods and communities; (3) the strengthening of families and the renewing of culture; and (4) an end to extreme global poverty.

For more information, see www.covenantforanewamerica.org. Sojourners/Call to Renewal is launching a new congregational network aimed at empowering, resourcing, and connecting clergy and laity interested in issues of social justice, peace, and spiritual renewal. A variety of resources for preaching, teaching, and issue advocacy, as well as discounts on Sojourner's/Call to Renewal conferences and events, will be included in the network offering. We are excited to be able to provide these tools and would like to offer you the chance to get in on the ground floor. To find out more and to receive announcements about the rollout of the program, please indicate your interest by going to www.sojo.net/network and providing your contact information.

In addition, consider the following organizations, listed in alphabetical order:

Asset-Based Development Institute. Provides resources and tools for communities and governments involved in capacity-based development initiatives.
(847) 491-8711   http://www.northwestern.edu/ipr/abcd.html

Bread for the World. A nationwide Christian citizens' movement seeking justice for the world's hungry people by lobbying our nation's decision makers.
(202) 639-9400   www.bread.org

Catholic Charities USA. Works to reduce poverty, support families, and empower communities by providing for people in need and advocating for justice.
(703) 549-1390   www.catholiccharitiesusa.org

Center for Public Justice. An independent organization for policy research and civic education whose mission is to equip citizens, develop leaders, and shape policy.
(866) 275-8784   http://www.cpjustice.org

Children's Defense Fund. Works through education and advocacy to ensure every child a healthy, fair, safe, and moral start in life for successful passage to adulthood.
(202) 628-8787   www.childrensdefense.org

Christian Community Development Association. A nationwide network of grassroots community-based organizations working to provide social and spiritual service to those in poverty.
(773) 762-0994   www.ccda.org

Christian Peacemaker Teams. Promotes biblically based and spiritually centered peacemaking and emphasizes creative public witness, nonviolent direct action, and protection of human rights.
(773) 277-0253   www.cpt.org

Church World Service. The relief, development, and refugee assistance ministry of thirty-five Protestant, Orthodox, and Anglican denominations in the United States.
(800) 297-1516   www.churchworldservice.org

Direct Action and Research Training Center (DART). A national network of community-organizing efforts, many of which are congregation-based.
(305) 576-8020   www.thedartcenter.org

EMU Center for Justice and Peacebuilding. An organization founded to further the personal and professional development of individuals as peacebuilders.
(540) 432-4490   http://www.emu.edu/ctp

Equal Exchange. Offers fair-trade coffee, tea, and chocolate through partnerships with faith communities and congregations.
(774) 776-7400   www.equalexchange.com

Evangelical Environmental Network. An evangelical ministry whose purpose is to "declare the Lordship of Christ over all creation"; published the 1994 "Evangelical Declaration on the Care of Creation," a manifesto seeking to relate biblical faith to environmental problems.
(202) 554-1955   http://www.creationcare.org

Evangelicals for Social Action. Promotes a lifestyle marked by service to poor and powerless people, reverence for life, care for creation, and witness to Jesus Christ.
(610) 645-9390   www.esa-online.org

Families Against Violence Advocacy Network. A broad-based network of organizations, families, and individuals committed to promoting alternatives to violence.
(314) 918-2630   http://www.ipj-ppj.org

Gamaliel Foundation. A national network of community-organizing efforts, many of which are congregation-based.
(312) 357-2639   www.gamaliel.org

Habitat for Humanity. Brings families and communities in need together with volunteers and resources to build decent, affordable housing through a national network of affiliates.
(912) 924-6935   www.habitat.org

Industrial Areas Foundation. A national network of community-organizing efforts, many of which are congregation-based.
(312) 245-9211   http://www.industrialareasfoundation.org

Interfaith Center for Corporate Responsibility. Works through education, organizing, and stockholder resolutions to promote more socially responsible actions by corporations.
(212) 870-2295   www.iccr.org

Interfaith Worker Justice. Works to educate and organize the faith community in the United States on issues and campaigns to benefit workers.
(773) 728-8400   www.iwj.org

International Justice Mission. A human rights agency that rescues victims of violence, sexual exploitation, slavery, and oppression.
(703) 465-5495   http://www.ijm.org

Jesuit Volunteer Corps. A Catholic lay-volunteer program whose individuals work in grassroots organizations across the country to provide services to low-income people.
(202) 687-1132   www.jesuitvolunteers.org

Jubilee 2000 USA. Works as part of an international campaign to educate and advocate for debt cancellation for the world's poorest countries.
(202) 783-3566   www.jubileeusa.org

Lutheran Volunteer Corps. Provides one-year service terms in urban social-justice organizations and promotes simplicity and community living as part of that commitment.
(202) 387-3222   http://www.lutheranvolunteercorps.org

Mennonite Central Committee. A relief, service, development, and peace agency working in fifty-eight countries among people suffering from poverty, conflict, and natural disaster.
(717) 859-1151   www.mcc.org

Micah Challenge. A global Christian campaign working to deepen our engagement with the poor and to challenge leaders to achieve the Millennium Development Goals.
www.micahchallenge.org

Mission Year. Offers Christian young adults a one-year term of living and serving in a poor inner-city neighborhood alongside a solid local church.
(773) 847-8856   www.missionyear.org

National Association of Evangelicals. Works to extend the kingdom of God through a fellowship of member denominations, churches, organizations, and individuals; published the 2004 "For the Health of the Nation," an evangelical call to social responsibility.
(719) 268-8214   www.nae.net

National Coalition of Barrios Unidos. Works to prevent youth violence in urban neighborhoods and promotes "gang truces," community development, and employment.
(831) 457-8208   http://www.barriosunidos.net

National Conference of Catholic Bishops/United States Catholic Conference, Department of Social Development and World Peace. The national public policy agency of the Catholic bishops.
(202) 541-3000   www.usccb.org/sdwp

National Congress of Community Economic Development. A faith-based initiative that works to promote and facilitate faith-based community economic development.
(202) 289-9020   www.ncced.org

National Living Wage Resource Center (ACORN). Provides a clearinghouse of information and resources on living wage campaigns around the country.
(718) 246-7900, x230   www.livingwagecampaign.org

NetWork. A national Catholic social justice lobby that educates and organizes to influence the formation of federal legislation to promote economic and social justice.
(202) 347-9797   www.networklobby.org

Network 9:35. A collaborative fellowship working to nurture and strengthen congregations, pastors, and leaders who are committed to holistic ministry.
(610) 645-9390   http://www.network935.org

One Campaign. An effort by Americans to rally Americans—*one* by *one*—to fight the emergency of global AIDS and extreme poverty.
www.one.org

Pacific Institute for Community Organization (PICO). A national network of community-organizing efforts, many of which are congregation-based.
(510) 655-2801   http://www.piconetwork.org

Pax Christi USA. The national Catholic peace movement that strives to create a world that reflects the peace of Christ by exploring, articulating, and witnessing to the call of Christian non-violence.
(814) 453-4955   http://www.paxchristiusa.org

Prison Fellowship. Works to provide a biblical and comprehensive assault on crime through in-prison programs and programs with children of prisoners and victims of crime.
(800) 206-9764   www.pfm.org

Public Campaign. A nonpartisan organization dedicated to reform that aims to dramatically reduce the role of special interest money in America's elections.
(202) 293-0202   www.publicampaign.org

Pura Vida Coffee. Fair-trade coffee organization rooted in a desire to empower the poor in coffee-growing regions of the world.

(877) 469-1431   www.puravidacoffee.com

Salvation Army. Affiliates across the country providing a wide range of social, medical, educational, and other community services.

(703) 684-5500   www.salvationarmy.org

United for a Fair Economy. Works to educate and organize on the dangers of the growing income, wage, and wealth inequality in the United States.

(617) 423-2148   www.faireconomy.org

Volunteers of America. A national nonprofit, spiritually based organization providing local human service programs and opportunities for individual and community involvement.

(800) 899-0089   http://www.voa.org

World Relief. Equips churches and communities to help victims of war, poverty, disease, hunger, disasters, and persecution.

(443) 451-1900   www.wr.org

World Vision. An international partnership of Christians seeking to follow Jesus Christ through working in relief and development programs with the poor and oppressed.

(253) 815-1000   www.worldvision.org

Notes

Week Two: War and Peace

1. Ron Suskind, "Without a Doubt," *The New York Times,* Oct. 17, 2004, sec. 6, p. 44.
2. *Merriam-Webster* Online, www.m-w.com.
3. http://www.whitehouse.gov/news/releases/2005/12/20051214-1.html.
4. "Iraq Body Count: A Dossier of Civilian Casualties 2003–2005," http://reports.iraqbodycount .org/a_dossier_of_civilian_casualties_2003-2005.pdf.
5. See Lee Griffiths, *The War on Terrorism and the Terror of God* (Grand Rapids, MI: Eerdmans, 2002).
6. Adapted from Glen Stassen, ed., *Just Peacemaking: Ten Practices for Abolishing War,* 2nd ed. (Cleveland, OH: Pilgrim Press, 2004).
7. Ca. 160, Alexander Roberts and James Donaldson, *The Ante-Nicene Fathers (ANF)* 1.176 (Peabody, MA: Hendrickson, 1994). In several of our discussions for Day 4 of the different weeks, we will examine the writings of the early church. For the most part, these are writings on Christian faith from the first five or so centuries of the church. Because the Christian tradition has recognized the important contributions that this group of writings has made to the development of the church and its expression of its faith, the writers were identified as "fathers" of the church.
8. Ca. 180, *ANF* 1.512.
9. Ca. 195, *ANF* 2.234; ca. 195, *ANF* 2.581.
10. Ca. 197, *ANF* 3.154.
11. Ca. 200, *ANF* 3.73.
12. Ca. 211, *ANF* 3.100.
13. Ca. 200, *Apostolic Tradition* 16.17–19.
14. Ca. 248, *ANF* 4.558.
15. See Stassen, ed., *Just Peacemaking.*

Week Three: Economic Justice

1. "Transcript: O'Neill on Enron Mess," Fox News, January 13, 2002. http://www.foxnews .com/story/0,2933,42952,00.html.
2. From www.afsc.org/economic-justice/LearnAbout.htm.
3. "For the Health of the Nation," National Association of Evangelicals, 2005. http://www.nae .net/images/civic_responsibility2.pdf.
4. *Centesimus Annus,* no. 35.
5. *Centesimus Annus,* no. 35.
6. See www.afsc.org/economic-justice/LearnAbout.htm.

7. http://www.globalpolicy.org/socecon/inequal/2005/10compendium.pdf.
8. http://www.faireconomy.org/research/wealth_charts.html.
9. http://www.faculty.fairfield.edu/faculty/hodgson/Courses/so11/stratification/income&wealth.htm.
10. Ched Myers, "Behold, the Treasure of the Church," *Sojourners*, Sept./Oct. 1999, vol. 28, no. 5, p. 33.
11. For further reading, consider Ron Sider's *For They Shall Be Fed* (Dallas: Word, 1997).
12. http://www.coady.stfx.ca/resources/publications/publications_coadylectures_notes.html.
13. http://thewitness.org/agw/gillett.html.
14. *De Nabuthe Jezraelita* 3, 11, cited in http://thewitness.org/archive/may2000/may.reuther.html.
15. *Second Sermon*, St. John Chrysostom, "Seven Sermons on Wealth and Poverty," www.byzantines.net/byzcathculture/wealth.html.
16. Sabbath Economics Collaborative, http://www.sabbatheconomics.org.
17. The Bartimeus Covenant Investors Community (http://www.bcm-net.org/page4/covenant_investment.html) provides substantial information on investing for justice.

Week Four: Poverty

1. "Ah, you who make iniquitous decrees, who write oppressive statutes, to turn aside the needy from justice and to rob the poor of my people of their right, that widows may be your spoil, and that you may make the orphans your prey! What will you do on the day of punishment, in the calamity that will come from far away? To whom will you flee for help, and where will you leave your wealth, so as not to crouch among the prisoners or fall among the slain? For all this his anger has not turned away; his hand is stretched out still."
2. See http://www.nccp.org/pub_cpf04.html.
3. Ron Sider, *Just Generosity* (Grand Rapids, MI: Baker Books, 1999), p. 20.
4. United for a Fair Economy, http://www.faireconomy.org/research/wealth_charts.html.
5. www.ccel.org/ccel/richardson/fathers.viii.i.iii.html.
6. www.apuritansmind.com/Stewardship/EarlyChurchWealth.htm.
7. www.apuritansmind.com/Stewardship/EarlyChurchWealth.htm.
8. www.apuritansmind.com/Stewardship/EarlyChurchWealth.htm.

Week Five: A Consistent Ethic of Life

1. Joseph Cardinal Bernardin, "A Consistent Ethic of Life: An American-Catholic Dialogue" (Dec. 6, 1983), http://www.hnp.org/publications/hnpfocus/BConsistentEthic1983.pdf.
2. See Tobias Winright, "Executing the Innocent," *Sojourners*, Aug. 2005, vol. 34, no. 8, p. 42.
3. David Cortright, "Hiroshima, Nagasaki, and Nuclear Realism," SojoMail, Aug. 9, 2005.
4. Stanley K. Henshaw, Susheela Singh, and Taylor Haas, "The Incidence of Abortion Worldwide," *Family Perspectives*, vol. 25, supplement, January 1999.
5. www.guttmacher.org/presentations/abort_slides.ppt.
6. Richard C. Dieter, "Misspent Millions," http://www.deathpenaltyinfo.org/article.php?scid=45&did=385#sxn1.
7. See Dr. David P. Gushee, "The Sanctity of Life: An Evangelical Exploration," http://www.uu.edu/programs/pew/Pew%20Application%20Gushee%202005.pdf.
8. Stanley Hauerwas and William H. Willimon, *Resident Aliens* (Nashville, TN: Abingdon Press, 1989).
9. Amy Sullivan, "Abortion: A Way Forward," *Sojourners*, Apr. 2006, vol. 35. no. 4, p. 15.
10. Sullivan, "Abortion," p. 15.

11. See the Supreme Court's opinion at http://www.tourolaw.edu/patch/Roe/.

12. Bernardin, "A Consistent Ethic of Life."

Week Six: Racism

1. Jim Wallis, *America's Original Sin* (Washington, DC: Sojourners, 1992), p. 8.

2. See *Exclusion and Embrace: A Theological Exploration of Identity, Otherness, and Reconciliation* (Nashville, TN: Abingdon Press, 1996).

3. See *White Theology: Outing Supremacy in Modernity* (New York: Palgrave Macmillan, 2004).

4. The percentages add up to more than 100 percent due to some overlap. For example, the Census Bureau indicates that Hispanic or Latino respondents can be "of any race." The goal is to give a general idea of the disparities that exist in incarceration rates, for example, and the percentages that given groups constitute of the overall U.S. population. For more precise numbers, go to the Census Bureau Web site at http://www.census.gov/prod/cen2000/dp1/2kh00.pdf.

5. *Sojourners,* Mar./Apr. 2000, vol. 29, no. 2, p. 10.

6. The following data are a summary from the Census Bureau via http://www.infoplease.com/ipa/A0104552.html. For a more detailed breakdown, see http://www.census.gov/hhes/www/income/income.html.

7. Data taken from http://www.census.gov/hhes/www/poverty/histpov/hstpov2.html.

8. See James Ferguson, "Double Standard," *Sojourners,* Apr. 2006, vol. 35, no. 4, p. 10.

9. Data compiled by Human Rights Watch. For more details, visit www.hrw.org/backgrounder/usa/incarceration/.

10. http://www.sentencingproject.org/issues_07.cfm.

11. http://www.sentencingproject.org/pdfs/5077.pdf.

12. www.deathpenaltyinfo.org/article.php?scid=5&did=184.

13. Jim Wallis, "America's Original Sin," *Sojourners,* Mar./Apr. 1998, vol. 27, no. 2, p. 9.

14. Bill Wylie-Kellermann, "Exorcising an American Demon: Racism Is a Principality," *Sojourners,* Mar./Apr. 1998, vol. 27, no. 2, p. 17.

15. Wylie-Kellermann, "Exorcising an American Demon."

16. See, for example, Myers's books *Binding the Strong Man* (Maryknoll, NY: Orbis Books, 1988) and *Who Will Roll Away the Stone?* (Maryknoll, NY: Orbis Books, 1994).

17. Wylie-Kellermann, "Exorcising an American Demon."

18. Martin Luther King Jr., "I Have a Dream" (1963) from *A Testament of Hope* (New York: Harper & Row, 1986), p. 219.

19. http://whatsaiththescripture.com/Voice/Revival.Lectures.4.html#LECTURE%2015.

20. http://wesley.nnu.edu/john_wesley/evangelist/JWE-12.htm.

21. In the following, we are indebted to David Gushee.

22. See www.uu.edu/centers/christld/moralld/v1n3.htm.

23. *David Walker's Appeal, in Four Articles: Together with a Preamble to the Coloured Citizens of the World, but in Particular, and Very Expressly, to Those of the United States of America,* rev. ed., with introduction by Sean Wilentz (New York: Hill & Wang, 1995), http://www.pbs.org/wgbh/aia/part4/4h2931t.html.

24. Henry Highland Garnet, "Call to Rebellion," 1843, found at http://startribune.com/dynamic/story.php?template=print_a&story=646719.

25. Sojourner Truth, *"Ain't I a Woman"*; see www.sojournertruth.org/Library/Speeches/Default.htm.

Week Seven: Strengthening Family and Community Values

1. www.censusscope.org/us/chart_house.html.
2. The online Barna report is no longer posted, but a summary of statistics can be found at http://www.religioustolerance.org/chr_dira.htm; and commentary from *Christianity Today* can be found at http://www.christianitytoday.com/ct/2000/010/30.47.html. You will note that the *CT* article places the 1999 national divorce rate at around 25 percent, but these numbers are highly disputed and largely dependent upon definitions. Some estimate that divorce rates could be as high as 50 percent, for example. The Barna numbers are intended to remind us, as people of faith, that we have not done a good job of "practicing what we preach."
3. *Wall Street Journal,* July 14, 2005.
4. Yonce Shelton, "Budgets, Social Security, and the Common Good," http://www.sojo.net/index.cfm?action=sojomail.display&issue=050719#2.
5. S. Scott Bartchy, "Secret Siblings," *Sojourners,* Nov. 2004, vol. 33, no. 11, p. 32.
6. Ellen T. Armour, "Christian 'Family Values' Have Changed Throughout History," www.sojo.net/index.cfm?action=news.display_archives&mode=point_of_view&article=POV_050202_armour.
7. See http://www.americancatholic.org/Newsletters/VAT/aq1004.asp.
8. "Family Values, Christian Values," *Christian Century,* Jan. 31, 1996, cover story; http://www.findarticles.com/p/articles/mi_m1058/is_n4_v113/ai_17907603.
9. www.littlegeneva.com/?m=200210.
10. Armour, "Christian 'Family Values' Have Changed Throughout History."
11. http://shilohflc.org/programs.html.

Week Eight: Hope for the Future

1. www.wfu.edu/~matthetl/perspectives/four.html.

A Summary of Social Activism Techniques

1. Adapted from "Guide to Social Consciousness," Oxfam America. Used by permission.
2. United for a Fair Economy. www.faireconomy.org/activist/creative/popular_theater.html.
3. United for a Fair Economy. www.faireconomy.org/activist/creative/popular_theater.html.

Acknowledgments

When we began to see how many local churches and small book groups were studying the hardback version of *God's Politics*, we realized how many more might want to do the same when the paperback version came out. It was then that the idea of a companion volume emerged to help those small groups and provide more resources for study, reflection, and response.

I want to thank my publisher, Mark Tauber, and my editor, Eric Brandt, at HarperSanFrancisco for supporting and shaping the idea. But most of all, I want to thank Chuck Gutenson, an extraordinary Asbury Theological Seminary professor who spent a year with us at Sojourners to help shape our capacity to resource the churches. Chuck is a theologian, an educator, and a fine writer. After many conversations, he suggested a framework for *Living God's Politics* as a study guide and began the drafting. Then Duane Shank became involved, as he always does, and finally the *Sojourners* magazine editorial staff, especially Jim Rice and Rose Berger, did the final editing. With help like that it was easy for me to be involved all along the way. This was truly a team effort and we hope it aids your study, shapes your reflection, and guides your action.

Jim Wallis
July 2006

Notes

Notes

Notes

Notes